H. A. L. FISHER

A HISTORY OF EUROPE

VOL. II

*From the Beginning of the
18th Century to 1935*

Collins

THE FONTANA LIBRARY

First published by Eyre & Spottiswoode 1935
First issued in Fontana Library 1960
Eleventh Impression November 1970

PUBLISHER'S NOTE

The Author's Preface to the one volume edition of 1936
has been printed in the present edition
The bibliographies have been revised by Mr. Neil McKendrick
of Gonville and Caius College, Cambridge.

© H. A. L. FISHER, 1935
PRINTED IN GREAT BRITAIN
COLLINS CLEAR-TYPE PRESS: LONDON AND GLASGOW

A HISTORY OF EUROPE
VOL. II

Too many of the really important and enduring
books in the fields of history, literature, philosophy, science, archaeology and art are not
obtainable at prices which the reader can
easily afford. The aim of the Fontana Library
is to make available in a pleasing format at a
low price books which are both intelligible to
the layman and indispensable to the scholar.

PREFACE

I BEGIN this book with neolithic man and conclude with Stalin and Mustapha Kemal, Mussolini and Hitler. Between these rough and rugged frontiers there are to be found some prospects flattering to human pride which it is a pleasure to recall to memory, the life-giving inrush of the Aryan peoples, the flowering of Greek genius, the long Roman peace, the cleansing tide of Christian ethics, the slow reconquest of classical learning after the barbaric invasions, the discovery through oceanic travel of the new world, the rationalism of the eighteenth, and the philanthropy and science of the nineteenth centuries. One intellectual excitement has, however, been denied me. Men wiser and more learned than I have discerned in history a plot, a rhythm, a predetermined pattern. These harmonies are concealed from me. I can see only one emergency following upon another as wave follows upon wave, only one great fact with respect to which, since it is unique, there can be no generalizations, only one safe rule for the historian: that he should recognize in the development of human destinies the play of the contingent and the unforeseen. This is not a doctrine of cynicism and despair. The fact of progress is written plain and large on the page of history; but progress is not a law of nature. The ground gained by one generation may be lost by the next. The thoughts of men may flow into the channels which lead to disaster and barbarism.

My opening themes are Greece and Rome, barbarism and Christianity. The discovery and colonization of the new world, the rise of nation states and the full development of the capitalistic system, belong to a later but still, having regard to the six thousand years of civilized life upon the planet, relatively recent period. Steam and electricity are more recent still. It is possible that two thousand years hence these two scientific inventions may be regarded as constituting the "Great Divide" in human history.

Book III describes The Liberal Experiment, using the adjective Liberal in no narrow party sense, but as denoting the system of civil, political and religious freedom now firmly established in Britain and the Dominions as well as among the French, the Dutch, the Scandinavian and American peoples. And if I speak of Liberty in this wider sense as experimental, it is not because I wish to disparage Freedom (for I would as soon disparage Virtue herself), but merely to indicate that after gaining ground through the nineteenth century, the tides of liberty have now suddenly receded over wide tracts of Europe. Yet how can the spread of servitude, by whatever benefits it may have been accompanied, be a matter for congratulation? A healthy man needs no narcotics. Only when the moral spine of a people is broken may plaster of Paris become a necessary evil.

For extended bibliographies the reader is referred to the Cambridge Ancient, Mediaeval and Modern Histories, to the authorities cited in J. B. Bury's edition of Gibbon's *Decline and Fall of the Roman Empire*, Lavisse's *Histoire de France*, Stubbs' *Constitutional History of England*, and other standard histories. I have confined myself to drawing attention at the end of each chapter to a few illustrative books, choosing by preference those which are modern and accessible in the English or French languages.

I have to thank my wife, Mr. Leopold Wickham Legg and Mr. David Ogg for their great kindness in reading the proofs; Mr. D. A. Reilly, of All Souls College, for several useful suggestions with respect to the opening chapters; and, for much valuable counsel in the later part of the work, my old friend Sir Richard Lodge, who at eighty years retains unimpaired his remarkable gifts of historical judgment and information.

January, 1936   H. A. L. FISHER

CONTENTS

MAPS IN THE TEXT

LAETITIAE SACRUM

CHAPTER LVII

THE EIGHTEENTH CENTURY IN ENGLAND AND FRANCE

Prestige of England after 1714. *John Locke. Voltaire. Montesquieu. The character of French philosophy. The physiocrats. English government in the eighteenth century. The age of George II. The disorders of France. Obstacles to reform.*

THE ENGLISH revolution of 1688, followed and confirmed by the accession of the Hanoverian dynasty, exercised a great influence on European thought. The spectacle of a revolution accomplished without bloodshed and unattended by any of those evils which were thought to be essential to popular government since the unfortunate upheavals of 1648, of a revolution resulting in such palpable benefits as religious toleration, the freedom of the press and parliamentary government, created a very general feeling of surprise and admiration. England, despite her revolution, had emerged richer and stronger than ever. On land and sea she had been the dominating spirit of the great alliance which had given check to Louis XIV. She could wage war and make peace and carry through the delicate operations of a change of dynasty without inner convulsion. Moreover, she had immensely strengthened her domestic position by her union with Scotland in 1707.

If ever a philosophy had been vindicated by events it was the Whig philosophy which lay behind the English revolution. John Locke was its great oracle. All the quintessential thought of the age of enlightenment is to be found in the writings of this humane and sober Oxonian doctor, the theory that ideas are not innate but reflected from the report of the senses (*Essay on Human Understanding*, 1690), the theory that civil government is founded on the consent of the governed, the view that the right to private property is based on labour, the doctrine of religious toleration, and of a rational education of the young. From Locke and his great scientific contemporary Isaac Newton, as also in a lesser degree from Henry St. John, Lord Bolingbroke, a body of rationalizing thought passed into France, where it was taken up, commented on and developed until, in its light, most of the established institutions of the country appeared to be shabby, outworn, and indefensible.

The man who was principally responsible for popularizing the new English ideas in France was a writer, so active, brilliant, long-lived, and influential, that he made himself the first figure in Europe. Voltaire, smarting from the tyranny and inequality which prevailed in his own country, for he had been thrown into the Bastille without trial for challenging a nobleman, came to England in 1726, and lived there till 1729. Here he was confronted with the astounding sight of a free' animated, and cultured people. He was introduced to Pope' read Addison and Swift, Bacon and Locke, Newton and Shakespeare. In his *Lettres sur les Anglais*, published in 1733, he explained to his compatriots the lineaments of this happy and surprising society, where a man was free to say or publish what he liked, where there was no torture or arbitrary imprisonment, where religious sectaries of all kinds were permitted to flourish, and among them a religious sect called the Quakers, who were so courageous as to denounce war as unchristian. "An Englishman," he writes, "goes to heaven by the road he pleases. There are no arbitrary taxes. A nobleman or a priest is not exempt from paying certain taxes. The peasant eats white bread and is well clothed, and is not afraid of adding to his hoard for fear that the taxes may be raised next year." A little later (1729-31) another great Frenchman came to England to study these instructive islanders. Montesquieu's report was no less enthusiastic. "England," he writes in his *Travel Notes*, "is the freest country in the world. I make exception of no republic. And I call it free because the sovereign, whose person is controlled and limited, is unable to inflict any imaginable harm on anyone." In the *Esprit des Lois* (1748), a philosophy of history which achieved a vast popularity and exercised a profound influence, he laid down (erroneously) that the true secret of English liberty consisted in the separation of the judicial, executive and legislative powers.

A leading feature of the movement of thought so

inaugurated in France was its active concern for the re-generation of society. The niceties of metaphysical specula-tion did not appeal to the clear, practical mind of Voltaire, or, indeed, to any of the French thinkers of the Voltairian age. The metaphysic of Locke and of his French disciple Condillac was a sufficient instrument for their purpose, which was to apply the human reason, coolly and dispassionately, without theological predilections and restraints, to the removal of the intellectual detritus of the middle ages and to the amendment of man's estate. Accordingly there grew up in France a body of philosophical and humanitarian literature, of pamphlets and histories, philosophical and educational treatises, tragedies and comedies, culminating in a great encyclopedia in thirty-four volumes (1751-72) which rendered not only to France, but to all Europe, the incomparable service of attack-ing all that was cruel, all that was superstitious, all that was obsolete, unequal and unjust in the constitution of European society, and in the fabric of its religious and social beliefs. Some writers were frankly and blatantly irreligious. Voltaire and Rousseau, the most prominent of all, were anti-clerical deists.

This literature of opposition, passing into other countries through the medium of the French language, which had super-seded Latin as the *lingua franca* of intellectual Europe, exercised an effect not the less important by reason of the fact that no European country save England was then ripe for parliamentary institutions. The atmosphere of Voltaire was breathed in the autocratic courts of Berlin and Vienna, St. Petersburg and Madrid. It was the age of enlightened despots. In the eyes of Frederick II of Prussia, of Catherine II of Russia, and of Joseph II of Austria, all that was needful to the improvement and elevation of society could be achieved by the paternal conduct of an autocratic ruler.

It was not, then, the advocacy of democratic government which gave to the message of the French philosophers its wide and commanding appeal. Voltaire was no democrat. What mattered to him and others was not the control of the levers of government, but freedom in all its shapes, freedom to think, to speak, to write, to act. Liberty was the universal remedy, the necessary mainspring of all progress, for given liberty all else would follow, the triumph of reason, the end of persecution, the disappearance of the superstitions of rival churches which obscured the face of that common religion which was believed to be natural to mankind. The prescription was valid throughout the world. It was a principle widely, though not universally, accepted among French thinkers that human nature was all of a piece in every age and every clime. How different the past was from the present was not clearly perceived, despite the great historical monuments of Voltaire and Gibbon, until the Waverley Novels had given to a later generation an imaginative vision of societies very different from their own.

The general trend of the French intellect in the eighteenth century was abstract, logical, cosmopolitan, much influenced by the exciting novelties of science and by the thought of the large perspectives of happiness for man which were expected to follow from the unimpeded application of common sense.

The fierce anti-clericalism of the French philosophers of the eighteenth century, like the militant atheism of the Russian Bolsheviks, sprang from the conviction that a tyrannical and obscurantist hierarchy stood straight in the path of intellectual and social progress. There can be little doubt that Voltaire, by assailing its manifest defects, improved the quality of French Christianity; or that the critical work of the philosophers, though often open to the charge of shallowness and unfairness, was amply justified by the very serious depravation which had come over the French Church. But the great objects aimed at by the French philosophical school were not negative but positive. Of these, many are now so fully secured in the institutions of the more enlightened parts of Europe that books which first issued from the printing press with the force of a revelation appear to the modern reader to be full of theories which it is worth no one's while to discuss. But there is one quality in this great body of French literature which retains its peculiar freshness and charm, and helps us to understand the spell which it cast upon the more intelligent and public-spirited of our forefathers. The literature of the *Aufklärung*, as the Germans call it, is the literature of confidence and hope.

If the philosophers had lost their belief in the doctrine of the churches, they had acquired a faith in the dignity and perfectibility of man. A great surge of optimism sweeps through the French political literature of the eighteenth century. A large number of intelligent people in the most intelligent country of Europe believed that if only the rubbish of the Gothic ages could be swept away with a strong broom, man, whose nature was good and susceptible of infinite improvement, would march from strength to strength. "If laws are good," said Diderot, "morals are good." Nobody was disposed to place limits upon the power of legislation to improve human nature indefinitely. "It is the good legislator," says Helvetius, "who makes the good citizen."

Part of this sanguine literature was devoted to a criticism of those economic principles of state regulation which France had inherited from Colbert. The physiocrats were believers in the power of Nature, if left to herself, to bring men on to levels of prosperity not to be dreamed of under a régime of local or national restrictions. This doctrine, which had great influence, contained a profound fallacy and an important truth. The French economists held the theory that land was the sole source of wealth, and consequently that the needs of the state should be met by a single tax on agricultural values. That is a fallacy: for land is only one among many sources of wealth, and no one tax, however equitable, will meet the legitimate needs of a state. But they saw the important truth that all trade is an exchange of goods and services, and that the artificial obstructions placed by states upon the passage of wealth from one locality to another, or from one state to another, are injurious to prosperity. In their own country the doctrines of the physiocrats led during the revolution to the abolition of the internal customs duties in France, the ill effects of which were so graphically described by our observant English traveller Arthur Young. In Britain their teaching, coming from Quesnay, the physician of Louis XV, to Adam Smith, the famous Glasgow professor, led to results even more important and eventually to the adoption of that system of free trade, which during the century of our greatest prosperity and the years of our sternest trial was found to serve us well.

The literature which has so far been touched upon was marked by the qualities of optimism and rationality. But there was one powerful voice, more influential perhaps in the long run than any of that age, which sounded a different note. Jean

1712-Jacques Rousseau of Geneva was neither a philosopher nor a
78 materialist, but a visionary. Though his intellect was pellucid,
it was fed from the deep springs of his natural instincts and
romantic emotions. He did not believe in progress or in the
subdivision of labour or in any mechanical or material method
of improving the lot of man, but finding the world full of
cruelty, misery, and waste, and the vaunted civilization of
Europe a mass of corruption and tyranny, set himself to draw
the outline of a society in which a good man could live. That
is the purpose of the *Contrat Social* (1762), which struck
France with the force of a new gospel.

Rousseau's sovereign remedy for human ills is very simple.
It is the application of virtue. The good state is one in which
every member (duly educated for the civic life) contracts to
conform his will to the general good. Only a society of
virtuous citizens, each agreeing to do to others as he would be
done by and spontaneously consenting to general laws framed
not for the furtherance of particular interests but for the
common advantage, could be called good. Such is the essence
of Rousseau's political doctrine. The good state is based not
on force nor on greed, but on the virtuous will of all its
members.

The book worked like an enchantment. It was brief,
eloquent, telling. The opening sentence alone, "Man is born
free but is everywhere in chains," was a challenge to civilization. What again could be more seductive to the poor and the
downcast than the vision of a society founded on the general
will? Rivers of revolutionary sentiment were released by this
single phrase. Yet it was too often forgotten that in Rousseau's
mind the sovereignty of the general will was nothing else but
the rule of virtue herself.

It has been said of Rousseau by Mme. de Staël that "he
inflamed everything but discovered nothing." The phrase "he
inflamed everything" points to an important truth, for to an
astonishing degree he set France aglow with the ardour of his
sentiments and his dreams. But is it equally true that he discovered nothing? In the aristocratic society of the eighteenth
century he announced the virtues and believed in the
sufficiency of the common man.

The English constitution of the eighteenth century, though

far in advance of anything existing on the continent of Europe, was not the perfect model of enlightenment which the sanguine enthusiasm of the French philosophers imagined it to be. It had many grave defects. Its system of religious toleration, its system of parliamentary government, were both imperfect. The theory still prevailed that the state was a close Anglican preserve, permitting indeed the public profession of Protestant worship, but excluding the dissenter from any share of public power and responsibility and even from the enjoyment of the best educational opportunities. So tenacious were the Anglican squires and clergy of their ascendancy that Parliament was not open to Protestant dissenters till 1828, or the Universities of Oxford and Cambridge till 1871. The Tories of Queen Anne's reign wished to go further still. By the Occasional Conformity Act they would have deprived the dissenter of the privilege of sitting upon a town corporation, and by the Schism Act would have put down their schools and ruined their education. It is one of the blessings of the Hanoverian succession that the Whigs reversed this calamitous policy, that they repealed the Schism Act, and by the passage of the annual Indemnity Acts released dissenters from legal penalties which they would otherwise have incurred by taking municipal office.

Even thus limited, the blessings of toleration were not extended to Roman Catholics, who, in England, were forbidden till 1779 to practise their worship in public, while in Ireland, where they might brew political mischief, they were subjected to a system of special and cruel disabilities.

The government of England during the first two Hanoverian reigns was an aristocracy. The great Whig families controlled the House of Lords, and through their influence on the pocket boroughs, returned the majority of the House of Commons. The Tories, who were probably more numerous, though less wealthy, suffered for more than fifty years the penalties attaching to parliamentary opposition by reason of their compromising association with the Jacobite cause. But in the real government of the country, which was local and not parliamentary, in the Quarter Sessions and Petty Sessions of the Justices of the Peace, the Tory squire was allowed to exercise the full measure of his social and political weight. In the execution of the game laws, the trying of poachers, and the punishment of vagabonds, these unpaid amateurs discovered a means of satisfying their craving for public usefulness and importance, and were so kept quiet and contented, while Whig magnates stood at the wheel at St. Stephen's.

By an accident unforeseen in the days of William III and Anne the supreme executive came to be vested under the first two Hanoverian kings in a Cabinet composed of the members of a single party and responsible to Parliament. George I could speak no English, and after the experiment of conducting business in French with his ministers had broken down, absented himself from the meetings of the Cabinet. The long 1721- and wise administration of Sir Robert Walpole consolidated 42 the Whig party, confirmed the authority of the Cabinet, and established the position of the Prime Minister. After that momentous administration the true principle of responsible government, that is to say of government by a Cabinet responsible to a parliament which is in turn responsible to the electorate, was established.

The success which attended the establishment of Cabinet government may be ascribed to another historical accident. The natural preference both of William III and of Anne was for mixed non-party Cabinets. For the sovereign to draw advisers from each party to his Council advertised the impartiality and exalted the power of the crown: but this experiment of a coalition, only occasionally possible under these two reigns, broke down when George I ascended the throne and learnt from his Whig friends that the Tories were conspiring in the Jacobite interest to drive him out of the country. From that moment Whig Cabinets and Whig parliamentary majorities were the order of the day. The custom was established that Cabinets should be of one political complexion and that they should really govern the country. It was an accident and a happy accident. During the ten years of George III's personal rule, when Cabinet government was reduced to a shadow, England experienced the greatest political reverse in her history through the loss of the American colonies.

Being, however, controlled by a wealthy territorial class, the British parliaments of the Hanoverian age were not remarkable for the gift of social compassion. The penal laws which were allowed to remain on the British statute book until they were reformed away by the efforts of Romilly and his friends in the next century were a disgrace to a generally humane and good-natured people. Nothing was done by the state for popular education. Town government remained corrupt, mediaeval, and unpopular, until the great cleansing of the Municipal Corporations Act in 1835. The fact that the Glorious Revolution had been primarily made to protect the ancient customs and charters of the towns, as well as the prerogatives of Parliament, from the innovating and auto-cratic invasions of James II, was a force making for con-servatism. The Whigs, exulting in their Revolution Settlement, were too apt to think that it had settled everything. This was an error. Parliament, in particular, was far from perfect; but the Whigs who idealized Parliament were slow to see that a legislature elected by forty-shilling freeholders in the counties and by small oligarchies in the towns was no true and sufficient mirror of national interests and opinions. Even Burke, the most imaginative of all Whig writers, saw no necessity for parliamentary reform. He was in favour of reducing the power of the Crown over Parliament, but not of widening the area of parliamentary representation. The eighteenth century was content that the great bulk of the middle class as well as the poor should be excluded from the sacred circle of the parliamentary Constitution.

Parliamentary corruption was another evil unnoticed by the French admirers of English institutions, and tolerated, despite opposition protests, at Westminster and in the constituencies. Bribes were offered and accepted by voters and members. There is reason now to think that this evil may have been exaggerated by contemporary critics. That it existed is certain. The expectation that even a small number of posts and pensions will be available for those who vote straight exercises an influence reaching far beyond the circle of those who are thus rewarded. Despite these defects, the country prospered and was happy. The sleepy Anglican Church, the sleepy and unlearned universities, the rosy foxhunting squires, and the top-booted, hard-drinking legislators at Westminster were not ill adjusted to the slow pace of that old agricultural society. There was no deep chasm between the classes; there were no difficult economic questions to vex the brain of Parliament. The Industrial Revolution had not yet begun to create in northern England a new population of bitter factory outcasts in vast inorganic aggregations of insanitary houses. The towns were still small. The sports and amusements of the countryside were generally enjoyed. An air of comfort and stability, typified by the stout red brick houses of the Georgian age, pervaded the country. In some sense, but for the horrid intervention of a Highland raid in '45, which had it been successful would have thrown everything back into chaos, England under George II must have seemed to all who were above the level of poverty to have reached a position of assured and fortunate inner peace. It was a society singularly free from disquieting and torturing doubts. It was harassed by no social problems, it required of Parliament no vast programmes, but was content with a small annual output of petty local legislation. Romance had not yet dawned upon a rational society, content to ask of life only what life could give, a society so stable and harmonious, so little superstitious or emotional, so sure of itself and apparently so well protected from the ruinous follies of the zealot that its like had not been seen in Europe since the days of the Antonines.

The English political literature of the eighteenth century bears the imprint of this felicity. Though it is spirited and combative, it has no quarrel with the foundations. Neither Swift nor Defoe, neither Addison nor Steele, neither Bolingbroke nor Hanbury Williams encourage their countrymen to believe that they are living under a régime of intolerable indignity and injustice. The quarrels of England are parliamentary, the disputes of political côteries, of the ins and the outs. Not even Wilkes, the radical, who opened new ground in the first decade of George III's reign, disputed the beauty of the Glorious Revolution or the value of the principles on which it was based. It was otherwise in France, where the persecution of an intolerant Church, added to the capricious and secretive tyranny of the state, provoked a literature of violent derision and contempt.

The internal problems of France which first in the later years of Louis XIV had begun to attract the attention of philosophic thinkers were primarily financial. No French government had dared to impose upon the whole French people a uniform and equitable system of taxation. Every government in its effort to conciliate followers in this quarter and in that had granted exemption from certain taxes. The nobles, the clergy, a large section of the bourgeoisie were dispensed from the *taille*, or property tax. Similar exemptions were enjoyed by many important provinces, especially by those which had recently been united to the French crown. The principle of privilege in taxation had been carried so far, and was bound up with so many class prejudices and traditions of provincial pride and autonomy, that it was exceedingly difficult to uproot. Only a strong government supported by a powerful body of popular opinion could successfully overcome the vast number of vested interests which were concerned to oppose its abolition. The old French monarchy, despite its immense prestige, was unequal to the task.

There were two possible avenues of approach, the method of constitutional reform and the method of autocratic action. The first method was inapplicable. A legislative assembly responsible to a popular electorate was wholly alien to French tradition. No statesman proposed it. No king would have accepted it. No government could have brought it into being without a violent convulsion. It was the nemesis of the long autocracy of Louis XIV that the habit of effective thinking on constitutional problems had been suspended, so that when, during the sombre last days of that vainglorious reign, Fénelon and others began to question the value of autocracy, their thoughts ran backwards to the older aristocratic constitution of France. They dreamed of more nobles associated in the task of government and dallied with the idea of reviving the mediaeval States-General, which had not met since 1614. The memory of this cumbrous and anachronistic body, without organization, without executive authority, without social cohesion, and without experience of affairs, blocked every fruitful avenue to constitutional reform. Its meeting in 1789 was not the beginning of government in France, but the signal for chaos.

Autocracy, at least, was in the later tradition, but was allowed no free sphere of action. The Parliament of Paris, restored by Philip of Orleans to its old position of authority, and supported by the twelve Provincial Parliaments, strewed 1715 the path of fiscal reform with insuperable obstacles. These lawyers had a horror of new taxes and new ideas. They burned philosophical books and voted down reasonable proposals for obtaining money from the public. But though they stood for obscurantism in thought and privilege in finance, they enjoyed an extraordinary measure of popularity as the sole organ of opposition to a profligate and discredited court. It argued high courage on the part of Chancellor Maupeou to suppress them in 1771. But the prospect of radical administrative reform to be undertaken by the Crown was hardly opened ere it was again blotted out. In 1774 the Parliaments were restored by a new king anxious to gain the love of his subjects. The compliance of Louis XVI with popular sentiment, though intelligible, was disastrous, for to any comprehensive and rational reformation of the French state a privileged oligarchy of hereditary lawyers could be trusted to oppose a stout and obtuse resistance.

BOOKS WHICH MAY BE CONSULTED

Lecky: *History of England in the Eighteenth Century.* 1878.

G. M. Trevelyan: *History of England.* 1926.

J. Locke: *Essay on Human Understanding.* Ed. A. C. Fraser. 1894.

Churton Collins: *Bolingbroke, a historical study, and Voltaire in England.* 1886.

John Morley: *Voltaire.* 1921.

H. Higgs: *The Physiocrats.* 1897.

Leslie Stephen: *The History of English Thought in the Eighteenth Century.* 2 vols. 1902.

A. Sorel: *Montesquieu.* 1887.

A. De Tocqueville: *L'Ancien Régime et la révolution.* 1860.

H. Taine: *L'Ancien Régime.* 1876.

F. Rocquain: *L'Esprit révolutionnaire avant la Révolution.* 1878.

Aubertin: *L'Esprit public au Dix-huitième siècle.* 1889.

The Political Writings of J. J. Rousseau. Ed. C. E. Vaughan. 1915.

Voltaire: *Dictionnaire philosophique.* 1765.

Voltaire: *Lettres écrites de Londres sur les Anglais.* 1734.

Lavisse: *Histoire de France,* Vol. IX.

J. H. Plumb: *Sir Robert Walpole: the making of a statesman.* 1956.

J. H. Plumb: *England in the Eighteenth Century.* 1950.

CHAPTER LVIII

THE SWEDISH METEOR

The decade of Christina. The conquests of Charles X. The preservation of Poland and Denmark. The Northern War, 1700-21. Patkul and the anti-Swedish Coalition. Charles XII and Peter of Russia. Poltava. The downfall of Sweden.

THE TRIUMPHS of Gustavus and his marshals, which raised Sweden to a pinnacle of military renown, were followed by a decade of Swedish history less important, indeed, but hardly less arresting than the long story of marches and counter-marches, battles and sieges by which it was preceded. Christina, like her father Gustavus, was a creature of genius. For ten years (1644-54) this amazing and capricious young woman glittered in the eye of Europe, scattering her bounties with a prodigal hand, performing feats of physical endurance which the hardiest veteran of her father's army might admire, and charming by her brilliant and indefatigable curiosity the choice circle of philosophers and literati who had been enticed to Stockholm by the magnet of her sympathy, her favour, and her largesse. Then, out of feeling for the Roman Church, into which she was received, or from a sudden weariness and dislike for the routine of business, or desiring to create a spectacular effect, the "Pallas of the North" resigned her throne in favour of a cousin. Charles X was that dangerous thing a mere soldier. Campaigning was his master passion. To him is due the first of the two great northern wars which ultimately brought Sweden to the ground, raised Brandenburg to a position of predominance in northern Germany, and opened the gateway into western Europe for the portentous figure of the Russian Bear.

To this firebrand, questing for enemies, Poland and Denmark presented themselves as obvious targets for attack: the first a papistical country, ruled by that elder papistical branch of the Swedish house of Vasa, which had not yet given up its title to the Swedish throne; the second the old hereditary enemy, the kingdom which had once ruled all Scandinavia, which still held Norway and the three southern provinces of Sweden, and by its position north and south of the Sound could command the trade of the Baltic. Charles threw himself first on Poland, then on Denmark. He overran Poland, he overran Denmark. There was a point alike in the Polish and in the Danish campaign when the military success of the Swedish army seemed to be complete and unqualified. And yet it is instructive to notice that when peace was signed at Oliva and Copenhagen (1660), and Charles, dying premature-1672 ly, had ceased to trouble, Poland and Denmark were not left as dependencies of Sweden, and that the most substantial gains from the Polish fighting were reaped, not by Sweden, which put out great efforts, but by the Elector of Brandenburg, who without any troublesome exertion acquired the Duchy of Prussia in full sovereignty as the price of his promised support of the Poles.

If Charles had emancipated the Polish serfs, he might have counterbalanced the prejudice created in the minds of a pious Catholic population by the sacrilegious behaviour of his Lutheran troops. But he was not so intelligent as to anticipate Napoleon, and, having nothing to offer the Poles but blows, insults, and Protestantism, was turned out of the country by a national rising assisted by Austria. It is important to notice the action of Austria. That great Catholic monarchy could not afford to see Catholic Poland under the heel of the Lutheran Swedes.

Just as the survival of Poland was an Austrian interest, so the rescue of Denmark from the Swedish clutches was the concern of Holland, England, and France. A Dutch fleet saved Copenhagen. A composite army of Dutchmen and Danes, Poles and Austrians beat the Swedes at Fünen. When there seemed a chance of the old familiar landmark of the Danish kingdom being obliterated under the surge of Swedish militarism, a concert of maritime powers intervened to repel the flood. The trade of the Baltic was an international interest. While the maritime powers were well content that the Scanian Provinces (in south Sweden) and the island of Bornholm should go as a prize to the Swedes, the existence of an independent Denmark south of the Sound seemed to them to be an international necessity.

SWEDISH POSSESSIONS IN 1662

English Miles
0   50   100   150

▨ *Swedish Territory*

Fifty years divide the peace of Oliva from the outbreak of the second great northern war (1700-21), which was destined to seal the doom of Sweden as a great power. Russia was rising; the Hohenzollerns had schooled a redoubtable army in Brandenburg; but Sweden, sheltered by the powerful diplomatic support of France, maintained her ground. So strong was the prestige of the Vasa dynasty that after a minority of twelve years Charles XI, a silent, boorish king, without magnetism or charm, but brave and dutiful, and the hero of victories against the hereditary Danish foe, was able to break the power of his nobles and with the assent of burghers and peasants to establish an autocracy. Dying in 1697, this enigmatic but successful sovereign left behind him an army, a revenue, and an empire. The Swede ruled in Finland and stood sentinel round the gulf of Bothnia. His flag flew over the great ports of Reval and Riga. He denied western Pomerania to Brandenburg, Bremen and Verden to Hanover, the Scanian or southern provinces of Sweden to Denmark. He held the little island in the river Neva, upon

1703 which Peter the Great was soon to build with Swedish prison labour the Nevsky Prospect in his capital of St. Petersburg.

The prime mover in the undoing of Sweden was a member of that Baltic baronage which shares with the landowning class in Hungary the name of being the proudest and hardest aristocracy in Europe. Johan Reinhold Patkul was a Livonian who cherished a strong personal grudge against the Swedish Government. In common with others of his order, he had been attacked in his private fortune by a comprehensive measure for the resumption of alienated crown property, had offered a vigorous resistance, and had in absence been condemned to a traitor's death. From that moment the fierce Livonian made it his object to bring the Swedish Empire toppling to the ground. Passing from capital to capital, he wove the network of a war coalition, caught Augustus of Saxony, who had been elected King of Poland and coveted Livonia; caught Peter of Russia, who, finding no help in the west for his Turkish war, was turning his eyes to the Baltic littoral; and, easiest of all, caught Frederick of Denmark, who saw in a recent marriage of a Swedish princess to a Duke of Holstein Gottorp a stab at the fatty part of the Danish anatomy. The prudent Elector of Brandenburg refused to be caught, but the coalition was full powerful without him. In May, 1700, the Saxons invaded Livonia and started the long war which changed the weights and balances of the north.

The moment appeared to be propitious. Charles XII of Sweden in 1700 was an inexperienced boy of whom only it was known that he had claimed and been accorded the autocratic power of his father. That this tall, austere, intellectual lad would in the hour of his country's greatest peril reveal the qualities of a hero of Scandinavian saga, that he would prove to be an inspired and indomitable leader of men, that his decisions would be as swift as his will was imperious and his courage sublime, that he would think no enterprise too wild or too desperate and no labour too exacting, that he would throw himself successively at Denmark and Saxony and knock them out of the ring by a series of smashing blows and brilliant marches, and that his first encounter with the army of Peter the Great, waged in a November snowstorm before the walls of Narva, would be a victory so crushing that, even if it had not been won against an army four times the size of his own, it would be memorable in the annals of warfare; these were developments which routed every calculation and appeared to portend a transformation of Europe. With a speed which seemed miraculous the young Swede broke through the circle of his enemies and had them beaten on every front. Even Marlborough was prepared to salute him as a great master of war.

Unfortunately, he lacked sanity. While Marlborough was always as cool as ice, Charles was in a constant blaze of excitement and indignation. For a nature so fierce and temperamental the habits engendered by autocracy were not a blessing but a curse, for when his judgment went astray, no force could deflect it to the paths of common sense. Failures, hardships, defeats, humiliations had no effect upon his inhuman confidence or unending resource. A fatalism, born of early success, carried him buoyantly through every vicissitude, while Sweden, bled white through his obstinate ambition, descended swiftly in the scale of power until she forfeited for ever her place of command and usefulness in the affairs of Europe. His greatest mistake was to underrate the Russians. Having defeated 40,000 raw troops at Narva, Charles believed the Muscovites to be contemptible fighters of whom he could always dispose at his leisure. Accordingly, instead of stiffening the Swedish defences in the Baltic provinces, he devoted six critical years to the displacement and condign punishment of his enemy the Elector of Saxony and to the establishment of a nominee of his own on the Polish throne. What he achieved was remarkable, but while he was capturing Polish cities or carrying the war into Saxony, Peter of Russia, who had re-organized his armies and discovered in Sheremetieff a skilful general, secured the precious Baltic provinces (1701-4). Good judges have opined that if Charles had been willing to accept the Saxon offer of peace after his victory at Klissow in July, 1702, he would have saved, at least for the time being, this essential region of the Swedish empire.

However this may be, there can be no doubt that, having once lost the Baltic provinces, Charles took the wildest and least hopeful course for their recovery. After he had settled with Poland and Saxony and compelled Austria to give redress to her Silesian Protestants he marched off into the heart of Russia to dethrone the Tzar. Here in the vast roadless tracts of marsh and forest and in the pitiless cold of a Russian winter, his small army of superb veterans encountered an enemy far more formidable than the Russian Guard. Unprovided against frost, shrunk to half their original strength by disease and privation, and disappointed in their hopes of a great Cossack reinforcement in the south, the Swedes went into action against overwhelming odds at Poltava on June 28, 1709, and were annihilated. "Now by God's help," exclaimed the Tzar, as he saw the effects of his efficient French guns on the wasting ranks of the enemy, "are the foundations of St. Petersburg securely laid for all time."

The Tzar was right. He had secured on the field of Poltava Russia's window on the west. Charles, who had been disabled by a wound from directing the battle, escaped to Bender in Turkey, and had nine more years of romance before him. But though he stirred up the Turks to make war upon Russia (1711-13) and ultimately returned to his native country, reck-less and uncompromising as ever, he never succeeded in reversing the decision of Poltava. That battle rang down the curtain on the Swedish empire. Poland reverted to Augustus of Saxony. Brandenburg seized the greater part of Swedish Pomerania. Peter added Riga and Reval to his Baltic conquests. The army of a powerful coalition, including Hanover and Prussia, as well as Saxony, Russia, and Denmark, forced the capitulation of Stralsund (December 23, 1715), the last remaining Swedish stronghold on the German coast, after a long and brave defence. Even so, Charles, escaping to Sweden, dreamed of victory. In the hope of fresh conquests as bargaining counters with the enemy, he invaded Norway, and there, laying siege to an obscure fortress, the wild, bare-headed figure in top-boots, who had swept through Europe like a tornado, calling for sacrifice after sacrifice from his Swedes, but never losing their support and devotion, met a soldier's end. Three years later (Peace of Nystad, August 30, 1721) the Baltic provinces, the chief prize of the long contest, passed by consent from Sweden to Russia.

BOOKS WHICH MAY BE CONSULTED

R. Nisbet Bain: *Christina of Sweden.* 1890.

R. Nisbet Bain: *Charles XII and the Collapse of the Swedish Empire.* 1895.

Voltaire: *Histoire de Charles XII roi de Suède.* 1732. *Tr.* W. Todhunter. Everyman's Library. 1908.

Hallendorff and Schuck: *History of Sweden.* 1929.

D. Ogg: *Europe in the Seventeenth Century.* 1925.

M. Roberts: *Gustavus Adolphus: A History of Sweden.* 2 vols. 1953-8.

E. F. Hecksher: *An Economic History of Sweden. Tr.* G. Ohlin. 1954.

CHAPTER LIX

PETER OF RUSSIA

*Russia in the seventeenth century. Reverence for the hereditary
principle. The two dynasties. The rise of the house of Romanoff.
Rivalry with the Poles. Early western influence. Peter the
Great. Azoff. Peter turns westward. Foundations of St.
Petersburg. Peter's reforms. Russia takes part in western
politics.*

WHILE THE contemporaries of Louis XIV in Paris and London
were enjoying the delights of a refined sociability, the subjects
of the Tzar of Muscovy were sunk in oriental barbarism and
gloom. Save for a few monastic schools there was no education. The free life of the intellect was a thing unknown in a
country where illiteracy was general, and where a clergy
ignorant, slothful, and fanatical, instead of devoting any part
of its vast wealth to the advancement of knowledge, was
prompt only to suppress the first glimmering of intelligent
curiosity. There are certain primitive forms of entertainment
which belong to all Asiatic peoples. These the Russians
possessed. They delighted in ballads and hymns, in the song
of the blind minstrel or in the eloquence of the wandering
story-teller, in dancing and buffoonery, and in the epic poems
of their race; but they had another amusement to which the
real Orient was a stranger. Nowhere was bestial drunkenness
so widely and patently practised, by women as well as men,
by statesmen as well as peasants, by the monks and priests, no
less than by the laity. Since women were kept in strict seclusion, life save in the foreign quarter of Moscow was bare of
society. The humblest dairy maid in Brittany would have had
more to say for herself than the thickly painted spouse of a
rich boiar, her back flayed by the stripes which it was the
habit of the Russian husband complacently to administer,
and of the Russian wife submissively to accept.

The Tzar was the proprietor of his land and people. There
was no parliament, there were no free towns or corporations,

since the unfortunate extinction of republican liberty in Pskoff and Novgorod at the end of the fifteenth century, nor was there any organized social hierarchy. Justice was openly bought and sold. The cancer of corruption, which is historically traceable to the fact that the grand dukes of Muscovy chiefly rose to power not by force of arms but by their sucessful bribery of Tatar officials, had eaten so deep into the habits of the nation that no efforts were availing to excise it. Taxation was little better than state brigandage. So backward was the country in economic development that most of its industry and commerce was in the hands of the Tzar. Western travellers visiting Russia in the seventeenth century depict a violent, immoral, and shapeless society, jealously secluding itself from aliens, and held together only by a savage brutality. The Tzar flogged his boiars, the boiars and landlords flogged their domestic slaves and predial serfs, the bishop flogged his priests, the abbot his monks, the husband his wife, and the father his children. In every particular of dress, deportment, custom, and law, there seemed to be the sharpest distinction between Russia and the west. The Russian males wore long dresses and long beards. "To shave the beard," said Ivan the Terrible, "is a sin that the blood of all the martyrs cannot cleanse. Is it not to deface the image of God created by men?" The wildest cruelty and the most unspeakable forms of vice were here combined with the grossest superstition, and with a steady aversion, encouraged by the black monks and white priests, from every novelty, however harmless, imported from the west. It is an indication of the Russian mentality of this age that the one spiritual agitation which disturbed its frozen stillness was a manifestation not of progress but of blind obscurantism. The Raskoll (1668 *ff.*) was a widespread and passionate movement of dissent against some trifling, but reasonable, liturgical changes introduced by the Patriarch Nicon.

Russia, then, was the Orient. So little were the Russian people regarded as an integral part of the European community that among the proposals mooted at the court of Henry IV of France was a scheme for a great crusading movement of the west to expel the Muscovites and Turks from European soil. The judgment of Olearius, an intelligent German, who visited Moscow in 1636, is equally unfavour-

able. "If a man consider the natures and manner of life of
the Muscovites, he will be forced to allow there cannot anything be more barbarous than that people. . . . They never
learn any art or science or apply themselves to any kind of
study; on the contrary they are so ignorant as to think that
a man cannot make an almanack unless he be a sorcerer, not
foretell the revolution of the Moon and the Eclipses, unless
he have some communication with Devils."

This turbulent, but nevertheless conservative, people were
for a period of over a thousand years governed by two
dynasties, the house of Ruric, originally Swedish, and the
house of Romanoff, whose chief recommendation was
derived from a marriage connection with that older line. It
is a singular illustration of the habitual reverence of the
Russians for the hereditary principle that when Boris
1598 Godounof, a most capable usurper, secretly made away with
Dmitri, the second son of Ivan the Terrible, and the last off-
shoot of the family which had created the earliest Russian
state on the Dnieper, introduced Christianity from Byzantium, founded the grand duchy of Moscow, and delivered
Russia from the Tatar yoke, the people refused to believe
that Dmitri was dead. How could it be that a family which
had reigned since the ninth century should thus suddenly
disappear? False Dmitris, first a renegade monk who
became a Catholic and the husband of a Catholic, then a
robber, appeared in turn, captured the enthusiasm of the
peasants and Cossacks, and with help from Poland and
Sweden threatened to dissolve the state into its barbaric
elements.

But then in 1612, at the darkest hour, when Sigismund III
of Poland was in Smolensk, and the Swedes were in Novgorod, and Poles were in the Kremlin, there occurred an
event memorable in Russian history, and characteristic of
an emotional and religious people. The real question which
Russia had to decide was whether it would submit to a Polish
Tzar with such slender guarantees for the preservation of the
Orthodox Faith as that prospect held out. Letters went out
from the monastery of Troitza putting the issue before the
cities, and the nation rose with an emphatic reply. The
leaders of the great patriotic upheaval were a butcher and a
prince, the butcher Minine of Nischni-Novgorod and the

Prince Pozharski. It is their glory that they raised a national army and drove the Poles out of Moscow, and that as the result of their action, the assent of a national assembly was secured to the elevation of Michael Romanoff, son of the Patriarch Philaret, to the Imperial throne.

Michael was an insufficient lad of fifteen, but of a family **1613** near to the people, and strong in the benediction of the Church. Rather than have a Pretender brought in upon the backs of the Polish army, or see the Orthodox Church jeopardized by the accession of a Polish king, the boiars of Moscow resolved to support an inexperienced lad and the people to lay at his feet their childish and passionate loyalties. The admiration which had been paid to the house of Ruric was now transferred to the Romanoffs.[1] The Tzar was the elect of God, the little father of his people, the healer of the troubles. The dynasty took root and flourished. It produced Peter the Great and Alexander II, and other figures less stupendous, who shone in the forefront of world affairs, and then, after three hundred years of power, the Romanoffs perished suddenly, as they had suddenly emerged, among the storms of war and revolution. The blameless Nicholas, the kindest, the weakest, the most humane of the Tzars, the only perfect gentleman in a long list of Russian rulers stretching **1917** back to the ninth century, was forced off his throne and butchered in the bloodthirsty carnival of a Bolshevist triumph.

The new dynasty inherited a warfare with the Poles which had been chronic since the fifteenth century. To the Russian mind the peculiar malignity of the Pole lay in two circumstances, his Roman religion and his political union (solidified at Lublin in 1569) with the grand duchy of Lithuania, which, unlike the little Lithuanian republic of today, comprised vast tracts of territory, once Russian, and since they were inhabited by the White Russians and Little Russians of the Orthodox Church, likely to become Russian once more. The Pole, in a word, appeared to the Muscovite to be a very violent kind of heretic and a very dangerous breed of poacher. He was not only a Catholic but he was an aggressive Catholic. It was bad enough that he should have Lithuania; it was worse that Polish Jesuits should endeavour to seduce the Lithuanians by the modern compromise of a "Uniate"

[1] Genealogical Table A.

Church, Roman in allegiance, Slavonic in ritual, when they could not carry them bodily into the Roman fold. Moreover, there was no end to the airs and impudence of the Poles. When Russia was in trouble the Poles had not scrupled to take advantage of her distress. They had supported the Pretenders, made themselves masters of Moscow, burned 1610 down part of the city, and claimed the Russian crown. The Poles were cleverer and more intellectual than the Muscovites; it was easier for them to draw upon the military experts of the German wars; but the nobles were madcaps; and the country had been greatly weakened since the monarchy had been made elective in 1572 on the extinction of the male line of Jagello. There was a wild ferment in this nation of Hotspurs, as they pressed forward after objectives too variously contrasted to be successfully combined, an advance towards the Dnieper, an advance towards the Baltic, not to speak of a dashing thrust at the heart of Russia itself. One of the earliest services of the house of Romanoff was to curb this Polish-Lithuanian exuberance. In 1667, after a five years' war, Little Russia and the sacred city of Kieff returned to Muscovy.

The process by which the grand dukes of Moscow, who had first risen to power as the tax-collectors of the Tatars, gradually shook themselves free of their Asiatic masters, and working outwards from their forest capital, advanced to the Caspian, the Black Sea, and the Baltic, though little noticed in the west until the star of Peter the Great began to shine upon the horizon, was nevertheless always assisted by applications of western energy and science. Ivan the Great, 1462- who married Sophia Paleologus, niece of the last Greek 1505 Emperor, and doubled the extent of the grand principality of Moscow, attracted Greek and Italian architects and engineers to his court, and owes much of his success to Fioravanti degli Alberti, his Italian master of artillery. The historic victory of Kazan, which administered to the Tatars the greatest repulse of the century, and brought the territory of 1533- Ivan the Terrible (the first grand duke to call himself Tzar), 1584 to the brink of the Caspian, was clinched by the indispensable 1554 help of a German engineer. The opening of the White Sea trade route was the work of English adventurers. In genius and energy Peter the Great was the wonder of his age, yet without the experience of western ways, which he gained as a youth through mixing with his Swiss, Dutch, and Scottish friends in the foreign quarter of Moscow, he would never have conceived his great ambition; as later, he would have been powerless to carry that ambition into effect had it not been for the opportune aid of western experts and western guns. The vast native powers of the Russian people needed for their release and control a shock from the intellectual batteries of the west.

Peter grasped the helm in 1689, violently displacing his sister Sophia who held the regency. He was then seventeen years of age, a Titan in physical strength, and possessed of all the gifts, including a strong dash of intimidating and capricious ferocity, which were needed to force unwelcome novelties on the Russian people. His temperament, which was one of astounding power and exuberance, led him into every extreme of fantastic tomfoolery and sullen gloom. For the first six years of his reign he was content to leave the dull work of government to others, while he held carnival with his boon companions in the Sloboda or foreign quarter of Moscow, devising fireworks, singing in the streets, building boats, arranging sham fights, or playing practical jokes on his friends. Even when he began to take his work more seriously, it was never certain how serious he was. A wild, disconcerting vein of schoolboy irresponsibility, leading him, even as a man of fifty, to make an April fool of St. Petersburg, persisted to the end. His personal habits, save that his energy and curiosity were inexhaustible, were those of a drunken, dirty, Muscovite operative, happy in rough companionship and in the heaviest and even the most odious forms of toil, so that he performed, as occasion offered, and with abounding zest, the rôles of a bombardier, a pilot, a shipwright, and an executioner, not to speak of the more refined occupations of a dentist, an engraver, and an operating surgeon. No inhibition, moral, religious, or social, hampered his action. He immured his sister, discarded his first wife, exhumed and defiled the corpse of his uncle, and for fear that his westernizing policy might be reversed, murdered, after hideous tortures, his intelligent but reactionary son. Servile prostrations he abhorred and prohibited. He cared little for his own dignity, and whether out of an inverted pride or a hearty plebeian simplicity, thought no task or situation beneath him. It did not injure him with his people that his second wife was a common Livonian serving maid, that his profligacy was unabashed, or that for days together he would be incapacitated for business by drunkenness. He was the epitome of his country, with its inconsequence in action, its tumultuous moods, its passionate lusts, and generous fellow feeling. Yet when he died at fifty-three the sentiment of relief was universal. The mice, as a wit portrayed it, looked on gleefully at the funeral of the cat.

To a young ruler anxious for naval power and trade expansion no objective was more tempting than Azoff, the great Turkish fortress at the mouth of the Don, which could be reached by water from Moscow. Here, then, before the walls of Azoff, Peter gained his earliest experiences of war (1695), and here with the aid of a fleet, brilliantly improved after an initial failure, he reaped the reward of his patience, his energy, and his resource. The capture of Azoff (1696) was justly applauded as the first victory ever gained by the Russians over the Turks. But the young Tzar, who was a realist, kept his head.

A nearer view of the Black Sea problem disclosed formidable difficulties to be solved only with the help of a western ally. For such an ally Peter searched the west, and, returning empty-handed from his travels, preferred the Baltic to the Black Sea in the order of his military objectives. It was easier to found St. Petersburg than single-handed to wrest the Crimea from the Tatar and the Turk. Sharply deserting the distant scene of his boyish triumph, the Tzar exhibited in a momentous decision the correct judgment of a statesman.

From the first blow struck at Sweden until his death in 1725, Peter was almost continuously at war; and it is against this warlike background with its campaigns against the Swedes, the Turks, and the Persians that his domestic work must be viewed. To make an army as good as the Austrian, a navy as good as the Dutch, and a Civil Service as good as the Swedish, and to wring from the peasants, upon whom he imposed more widely than before the bonds of serfage, the supplies which were necessary for the conduct of his wars, these were the most constant preoccupations of his unstable mind. There was nothing in his policy calculated to alleviate the burden of the poor or to promote the ends of social justice. What he wanted for his people was the science, the power, and the material amenity of western life.

The great achievement of Peter is that, clearly apprehending the superiority of the west, he succeeded by the sustained effort of a lifetime, and in the teeth of violent prejudices, in lifting his country on to a palpably higher level of civilization. To Lefort of Geneva, the boon companion of his youth, whose house in the German quarter was the scene of many unedifying revels, he probably owed his initiation into western ways, and it was beyond doubt Lefort who suggested the western voyage (1697) which marks a dividing line in the history of Russia. Thereafter Peter was never likely to forget the lessons which Amsterdam or Deptford had to give to the sailor, or Vienna to the tyro in military science. The westerners had learnt the art of life and the secrets of power. They could make ships, guns, and tools, they understood money and comfort and rational amusement, they read and wrote, mingled freely with women, and in their paved and lighted cities had created for themselves an existence which was neither savage nor cloistered. What could be done in the west, Peter resolved could and should be done in Russia also.

First of his compatriots he saw the value of a capital on the Baltic. St Petersburg, the prize of a long war hastily undertaken, was a guarantee that the precious contact with the west would not be broken, and that Russian influence would make itself felt in western politics. It was more than a city, it was a flag. It stood for that stream of tendency in Russian life which welcomes and accepts the west, as against that other native philosophy, Slavophile in the nineteenth and Communist in the twentieth century, which, viewing the Russian as a civilization wholly divergent from the European, and not benefited by admixture with it, regards Moscow as the real heart of the Russian state and the proper centre for its government. To men of this type, Peter's city on the Neva appeared little better than a social centre for the Baltic barons and an outpost of Germany on Russian soil.

A mutinous movement of the Russian pretorian guard (Streltzy or musketeers), easily suppressed, but terribly punished, created the initial atmosphere of panic required in the 1698 country for a reforming Tzar. With true insight Peter struck hard at those elements in the social life of the Russians which were most deeply rooted in tradition, the beards and gowns of the men, the seclusion of the women, the wealth and independent ·authority of the monks and priests. He even abolished the Patriarchate of Moscow, and placed the 1721 Church under a Holy Synod in which priests were represented as well as bishops.

After changes so revolutionary, it was a comparatively light matter to create vocational schools, to reform the currency and the calendar, to deduct eight letters from the alphabet, to set up a senate and a system of public offices, and to build a navy. The deep-seated corruption of the official world, though he had the satisfaction of hanging a fraudulent Governor of Siberia, successfully defied his attack. His second wife, Catharine, the Livonian, was an unblushing blackmailer.

To civilize a nation so deeply sunk in corruption was a task exceeding the span of any one ruler. Peter had no money for "the social services." His educational schemes, so ambitious on paper, came to little in practice. There were neither the funds, nor the teaching staff, nor the widespread disposition to learn, without which a great educational advance cannot be achieved. Nations do not grow new tastes to order; and education, like the sea, was a taste which the Russians slow to acquire. Nor was Peter, who during a critical epoch of the Poltava campaign was blind to the world through liquor, the man to give to the Russian people a sense of administrative method. Could he have shared the sobriety of Charles XII or Napoleon, what feats might he not have accomplished! Yet it was a great achievement to have given to the Russians, as Peter undoubtedly did, the three primary constituents of a modern state, an army, a navy, and a civil service. Though there were western influences in the Muscovite court ever since Ivan III, it was he who first opened the western widow wide upon the Russian world; nor since his day has that window been closed. The first Russian newspaper, the first Russian hospital, the first Russian museum derive from him.

Though he had taken no steps to secure the future, his work survived the ebb and flow of prejudice and passion.

He was succeeded in turn by his widow, his grandson, his niece, and his daughter.[1]

Behind these figureheads stood capable Germans like Oster-mann, for seventeen years foreign minister, or Munnich, the Commander-in-Chief of the Russian army under Anne of Courland, or else Russians of the Petrine school like Bestu-chief, the principal adviser of Elizabeth. The old social and political isolation was broken down. A close alliance with Austria was, until the death of Elizabeth in 1762, the corner stone of Russian policy.

So by the enterprise of a barbaric technician of genius Russia was brought into the diplomatic system of Europe, where she occupied a position which was not wholly unlike that of England, being at once of the continent and yet attracted by distant interests in which the continent had no concern. Asia was at her back door. Only a low line of rolling pine-clad hills, first traversed by Yermack when Shakespeare was a youth, divided the Russians from the forests, the water-ways, and the prairies of Siberia, where, save that the rivers run south to north, Nature seems to repeat on Asiatic soil the experiment which gives to Canada its charm and its challenge. But just because the colonial empire of Russia had not to be sought across the seas, but was there for the taking, the Asiatic pull on Russian policy was not immediately evident, and only in the nineteenth century, when the Muscovite was brought face to face with Britain and Japan, a factor of paramount importance. In the eighteenth century it was not so much the East as the South and West that appealed to the framers of Russian policy. The West offered its technicians and its philosophy of enlightened despotism, the South a long succession of tempting conquests. There were the garden lowlands of the Caucasus, and the Crimea with its sunlit Riviera, and the Bosphorus, most enchanting of sea channels, which leads out of the grim Euxine to the warm water port of Constantinople and thence past the isles of Greece to the Holy Land. It is easy to understand the power which such prospects as these exercised over the Russian people. They wanted the warm water port and the access to the Aegean and the control of the old Greek city to which they believed them-selves entitled as heirs of the Byzantine Empire. They were

[1] Catharine I, Peter II, Anne of Courland, Elizabeth.

consequently compelled to regard the Turk as the power which stood between Russia and the sun and to adjust all their diplomatic relationships to that fact. The friends of the Turks were their enemies, the enemies of the Turks were their friends. Catharine II, the greatest of Peter's successors, understood this, though she was German by birth and French by education. For her too the Southern question dominated everything. It was in her reign that Poland was partitioned as a move in the game of Southern policy, the Crimea annexed (1783), and the Russian flag firmly planted on the shores of the Black Sea.

BOOKS WHICH MAY BE CONSULTED

Kluchevsky: *History of Russia. Tr.* C. J. Hogarth. 1911-31.
Rambaud: *Histoire de la Russie.* 1884.
A. Bruckner: *Peter der Grosse.* 1878.
A. Toynbee: *A Study of History,* Vol. III. 1934.
Macaulay: *History of England.* 1858-62.
R. Nisbet Bain: *Slavonic Europe.* 1908.
R. Nisbet Bain: *Pupils of Peter the Great.* 1895.
K. Waliszewski: *Pierre le Grand.* 1897.
B. H. Sumner: *Peter the Great and the Emergence of Russia.* 1951.

CHAPTER LX

THE TURK AND THE CHRISTIAN

Strength of the Turkish army. Suleyman the Magnificent. The age of Turkish expansion. The Treaty of Torok, 1606. Tyranny and indulgence of Turkish rule. Divisions of Christendom. Turkish decline and revival. Austria as a Christian bulwark. Poland, its inner weakness and internal foes. John Sobieski. French opposition. Christian victories, 1683-99. Venetian conquest of the Morea. Christian nationalism. The real enemy of the Turkish Empire. Austria's internal problem and services to Europe.

THE immediate successors of Mohammed the Conqueror were not likely to forget that by a sustained effort of persevering valour a small and rude oriental tribe had been brought from the heart of Asia to the command of an empire stretching from Bagdad to Morocco, and from the Persian Gulf to the Crimea and the Danube. Superiority in arms had given them an empire, and they were wise enough to see that only by superiority in arms would that empire be maintained. The army, then, was the first object of preoccupation, and since for many years the Sultans possessed the only regular standing army of importance in Europe, they were able to make themselves formidable to their subjects and their neighbours. In gunnery, engineering, and the commissariat arrangements the establishments of the Sultan were above the average of the age; nor could any western state oppose to the Spahis and Janissaries, who were recruited by a tribute of Christian children, troops comparable for the fanaticism of their spirit or the prolonged severity of their training. For more than a century the Sultans reaped the reward of their military zeal and solicitude. A passionate loyalty to the Commander of the Faithful reinforced a blind and fanatical adherence to the Faith.

With such leadership and profiting by the divisions of the Christian world, the Turkish Empire continued to grow.

Under the chivalrous and cultivated Suleyman the Magnificent, who reigned from 1520 to 1566, the Turks, as has been already noted, took Rhodes from the Knights Hospitallers, exacted a tribute from Transylvania and Moldavia, and robbed the Austrians of seven-tenths of Hungary. These victories on sea and land against the appointed warders of the Christian Faith sent a shudder of apprehension through Europe. Never again, though a century later Candia was wrested from the Venetians, and Kameniek, a key fortress, from the Poles, was the Ottoman Empire so powerful as under the reign of this exceptional Turk, who combined with the energy of a soldier the gift for civil organization and an unaffected sympathy for art and letters. Thereafter symptoms of incipient decline began to reveal themselves. A succession of weak and profligate Sultans produced the evil results which are inevitable in a state where everything depends on the character of an autocrat. Corruption invaded the government, indiscipline the army. The Janissaries and Spahis were permitted to marry, and the tribute of Christian children began to be remissly levied, and then in the seventeenth century ceased altogether. The Treaty of Torok, in 1606, relieving Austria from a humiliating tribute and fixing the boundary between Turkish and Austrian territory, marks the point of time at which the first momentum of Turkish conquest in Europe comes to a stay, and the Turks, in a bargain with the enemy, bring themselves to concede a point of vantage.

So miserable had been the state of the Byzantine empire before the Ottoman conquest that by a large number of the Christian subjects of the Porte the strong rule of the Turk must almost have been regarded as a boon. The Christians, indeed, were excluded from political power, made subject to a special tax, and were on more than one occasion exposed to the risk of systematic extermination. They possessed, however, in the defects and limitations of their conquerors, the indispensable guarantees for a not intolerable existence. The Turk was cruel but indolent, overbearing but stupid. Having no aptitude for industry or commerce, he was content to allow the Christian to carry on the occupations of the shopkeeper, the merchant, and the artisan; and since he had no culture of his own to impart to others, the Greeks, the Bulgars, and the Serbs lived under his loose and irregular rule, practising their religious rites, preserving their ancestral customs, and offering to the Koran under the aegis of their Patriarch a quiet but inflexible resistance.

Two things, then, specially distinguished the Turkish rule in Europe, its tyranny and its indulgence. For the quarrels of the Christian churches the Turks exhibited a profound and contemptuous indifference. As soon as they had renounced their intention of converting the world to Islam, they were content to leave the infidels to stew in the juice of their irreverent wickedness. No course could have been more consonant with Turkish interests. Many a Protestant in Transylvania and Hungary, rather than come under the ferule of the Jesuit, elected to live under the Crescent; and in the competition for Hungarian support, which characterized the Danubian wars in the later half of the seventeenth century, there was no factor which weighed more heavily in the balance for the Turks than their habit of religious toleration, or more adversely to the Austrians than the declared system of persecution which had already destroyed the Protestants of Bohemia and now menaced the lives and properties of their Magyar co-religionists.

The empire thus widely spread and strictly organized for the purpose of war had two main enemies, the Shiites of Persia, and the confused and tumultuous forces of European Christianity. During the whole course of their history the Turks have been concerned to provide for a defence on two widely separated fronts.

But for one circumstance their task would have been insuperable. The European world was incapable of a concerted effort. It was the division between the Greek and Latin churches which brought the Turks into Constantinople, it was the religious rift in Latin Christianity, coupled with the rivalry of Francis I and Charles V, which enabled them to consolidate and extend their conquests, and it was the feud between the rival houses of Habsburg and Bourbon, enlisting as it did conflicting loyalties and sympathies in every court in Europe, which opened out to them in the later half of the seventeenth century new prospects of successful encroachment on Christian territory.

Happily for Europe, the epoch of the Thirty Years' War,

when Protestants and Catholics were making a shambles of Germany, coincided with one of those spells of moral enervation which from time to time come over the Ottomans. In virile force and ruthless intelligence the house of Othman has been one of the great dynasties of the world; but there have been grave lapses from excellence, one of which covered the first half of the seventeenth century. The Turks, however, possess a fund of moral recuperation which again and again has confounded their antagonists. Half a century of corruption and disorder was followed by a sharp revival of tone and discipline. In the year 1656, during the long reign of the eccentric Mohammed IV, an elderly Albanian was summoned to take the post of Grand Vizier. Albania is a small country, but rich in characters as stern and dominating as its barren mountains. Scanderbeg was an Albanian; Mohammed Ali, the founder of modern Egypt, was an Albanian, and at this juncture, when the affairs of Turkey were in the gravest disorder, the empire was once more clamped together by the ferocious rigour of the Albanian Mohammed Kiuprili. For more than twenty years viziers drawn from the Kiuprili family enabled the Ottomans once again to play a vigorous and menacing rôle in south-eastern Europe, and to strain the defences of the western world.

The task of defending Europe from the Turks lay primarily with the Catholic house of Habsburg. The great rôle of Austria in European history, and one of the main justifications for the Austrian empire, lay just in the fact that it stood for centuries as the south-eastern support of Latin and Germanic civilization against Islam. But while the force of the Sultan was unified and compact, Leopold of Austria was not even master of his hereditary states. In particular his authority was contested in Hungary, where a powerful body of nobles, hating German troops, fearing the prospect of German taxation, and above all resenting the intolerance of the Roman Church, were in active correspondence with the enemies of the empire. Bohemia, indeed, was crushed beneath the Austrian heel: but if troops were to be obtained from Germany, it could be only by the consent of the Princes of the Diet, and in face of the hostile diplomacy of France. Yet, even in the middle of the seventeenth century, mediaeval sentiment counted for something. At a real crisis of the

1658-
1705

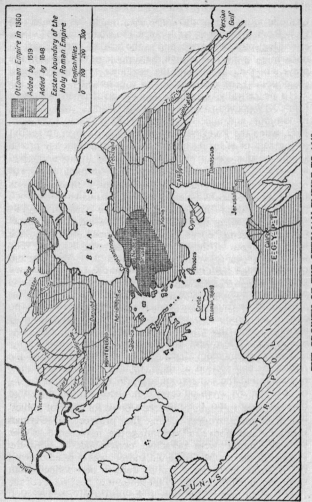

THE GROWTH OF THE OTTOMAN EMPIRE TO 1648

Catholic faith, the Archduke of Austria, in his capacity as Holy Roman Emperor, could appeal to what remained of the crusading spirit in Europe, and as the head of Latin Christendom, might expect to receive the support of the Vatican, the prayers of the Church, and the assistance of an army, small, cosmopolitan, miscellaneous, and improvised.

His nearest ally, assuming that the golden persuasions of Louis XIV proved to be ineffectual at Warsaw, was the vast, tumultuous, and uncertain republic of the Poles. Ever since 1572, when the Polish nobles, refusing any longer to submit to the rule of a strong government, insisted that the crown should be made elective, the condition of this country had been one of complete moral and political disintegration. The king was a cypher. He had no machinery for collecting taxes, no standing army, and since any member of the Polish Diet, on any pretext, however slight, might impose an absolute veto on its proceedings, no means of effecting constitutional changes, or of procuring for his country any ordinary legislative progress. The Diets were biennial, but since they were composed of armed nobles, some in receipt of Austrian, and others in receipt of French, pensions, who rarely separated without tumult or bloodshed, they had none of the attributes which should characterize a national parliament. There was no nobility in Europe of higher metal than the Polish, no cavalry who rode into battle so magnificently and absurdly accoutred, but though diamonds were plentiful, discipline was scarce. The extent and composition of a Polish army at any given moment depended on the willingness of the nobles, or any section of them, to take the field with their retainers, and the same voluntary principle broke the spring of its efficiency. Even on campaign, obedience was measured by inclination, and the most successful commander might find himself weakened by voluntary withdrawals proceeding from pique, fatigue, or political machinations. The Lithuanians were diametrically opposed to the Poles, and the Poles to one another. A peasantry of predial serfs and a Jewish middle-class stood outside the pale of the constitution, despised, unfriended, and oppressed.

Two great calamities befell this unfortunate people soon after they had imprudently abandoned their old hereditary kingship. By calling (1587) to the Polish crown Sigismund

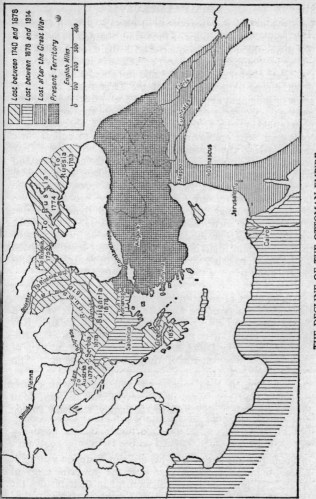

▨	Lost between 1740 and 1878
▧	Lost between 1878 and 1914
▤	Lost after the Great War
●	Present Territory

English Miles
0   100   200   300   400

THE DECLINE OF THE OTTOMAN EMPIRE

Vasa, who thereupon was received into the Roman Church, they incurred the hostility of Protestant Sweden. That was a formidable liability. The quarrel with the strongest military power in the north was almost sufficient in itself to exhaust the defences of the Poles; but it did not stand alone.

All through the first half of the seventeenth century a spirit of indignant apprehension had been growing in volume among the Cossacks of the Ukraine. Jesuit missionaries had been attacking the Orthodox Faith. Polish absentee landlords had been employing despicable Jews to collect their rents. In 1648 the Cossacks could stand it no longer. They rose in revolt under Bogdan Kelmnitzky, their Hetman, and with the aid of the Russians and Tatars and, by an accidental concurrence of circumstances, of the Swedes, shook the Polish State to the ground. By 1650 the problem of the survival of Poland had been raised and more than one scheme for its partition put out. But though the republic had many jealous neighbours, it was agreeable for the present to Christendom that it should survive, so long as it was weak enough to cause no embarrassment to Austria and sufficiently venal to serve the purposes of France.

A wide tract of country, known as Podolia, extends along the middle waters of the Dniester and the Bug, serving as a border territory between Wallachia and Polish Poland. It is through Podolia that a Polish army must march southeastward upon the Turks, and it is along the famous strip of dark black soil which runs through the vast Podolian plain that Tatars and Turks rode northward against the Poles. On this familiar fighting ground, still strewn with castles ruined in the Tatar Wars of the seventeenth century, John Sobieski, a Polish nobleman of old family, suddenly sprang into fame as a great commander.

Among the few entirely creditable incidents in Polish history is the choice in 1674 of that great soldier to be king of Poland on the strength of his brilliant Podolian victory at Khoczim in the previous year over the powerful army of Ahmed Kiuprili. At a critical moment in their history the Poles, shaking themselves free of French intrigues, picked out their best man to lead the state. It was a rare gleam of wisdom. Not until M. Paderewski was made Prime Minister of the revived Polish republic after the Great War was the performance repeated. Then, for the second time, the Poles invited their greatest and most accomplished man to guide the State.

Sobieski's record, though not altogether consistent—for as a youth he fought for the Swedes against his native country—is that of a Catholic and a patriot. Everything about him was on a big scale—the vast corpulence of his body, the range of his culture, his energy in action, his immunity from petty jealousy and intrigue, and the rich and abounding geniality of his temperament. He was one of the few leaders of his time who struck hard, struck often, and drove his victories home. Whenever the king of Poland appeared on the field he led his Poles to victory. By 1675 he had forced the Turks to cede all Podolia (save for the fortress of Kameniek) and two-thirds of the Ukraine to his country; but his object was far greater than a local or Podolian triumph. He dreamed of a crusade to drive the Turk from Europe. "To give the barbarian," he said, "conquest for conquest, to pursue him from victory to victory over the very frontiers that belched him forth upon Europe; in a word, not to conquer and curb the monster, but to hurl him back into the deserts, to exterminate him, to raise upon his ruins the Empire of Byzantium, this enterprise alone is chivalrous; this alone is noble, wise, decisive."

All Europe was not of that mind. While Sobieski was endeavouring to stir up opponents all over the world against the Turks, Louis XIV was employing every artifice to secure the neutrality of Poland in the struggle which everyone knew to be impending. In this enterprise he was unsuccessful; but the patent rivalry of Paris and Vienna was one of the circumstances which contributed to the launching of a vast Turkish enterprise aimed immediately at Vienna and ultimately at Rome.

The repulse of the incompetent Kara Mustapha from the walls of Vienna in 1683 marks the beginning of that long process of Turkish decline which was sealed by the Treaty of Lausanne in 1923. The initial blows of Sobieski opened the way to a war for the control of the middle Danube, which was illustrated by a series of Imperialist victories. It was then that the old Austrian empire, employing commanders drawn from Germany and Savoy, rolled the Turks back across the Danube. It was in these campaigns that the Prince Eugène, the ally of Marlborough, and the darling of Protestant England, first made his renown. His crowning victory of 1699 Zenta led to the Peace of Carlowitz, under which all Hungary and Transylvania were ceded to the Austrians and all Podolia and the Ukraine to the Poles.

One Christian conquest which is registered in this epoch-making treaty was premature. The Venetians, stimulated by 1686- the Pope and encouraged by the Turkish repulse, had em-94 barked on a campaign for the reconquest of Greece. With the aid of Hanoverian redcoats and other German mercenaries, they repossessed themselves of Dalmatia, drove the Turks from the Morea, and in a bombardment of the Athenian acropolis inflicted irreparable damage on the Parthenon. At the Peace of Carlowitz they were permitted to retain their spoils. But Greece was not destined to be a Venetian colony. 1699- After nineteen years of life under the Lion of St. Mark the 1718 Morea returned to its Turkish masters. The Venetians, who under Francesco Morosini were strong enough to conquer, were unable to retain their position. No Greek loves an Italian, nor any orthodox Greek a Roman Catholic; nor did the Aegean traders welcome the strict principles of Venetian monopoly. The mild rule of the republic perished without regret, having failed to excite enthusiasm in a population too deeply abased by centuries of oppression to respond to the spur of the Latin mind, and well content to regard the Sultan as its secular, and the Greek Patriarch of Constantinople as its religious, chief.

It was no call from the Vatican which rolled back the hosts of Islam in the eighteenth, nineteenth, and twentieth centuries. The last blast on the trumpet of Godfrey de Bouillon was blown by John Sobieski, while Catholic and Protestant factions were struggling for mastery in the court of Charles II, and Louis XIV was invading the Spanish Netherlands and subsidizing the Sultan. The real force which exploded the old Turkish Empire was not Roman, but Greek, not cosmopolitan, but nationalist. It was the determination of the depressed Christian peoples of the Balkan peninsula, of the Greeks, the Serbs, the Bulgars, the Roumans, to throw off the yoke of their Turkish oppressor and to enjoy an independent national life of their own. How this aspiration in the Balkan peoples slowly ripened, how it received steady encouragement from the Orthodox Church of Russia, from the Panslavists, and from the imperial ambitions of the Tzars, until finally Serbian nationalism, supported by Russia, and threatening to undermine the Austrian empire, led to the Great War of 1914, will be recounted later. Then also it will be noted how, when the Tzardom of the Romanoffs had fallen, and Russia was dissolved in revolution, France, reverting to her old diplomatic tradition, helped to preserve Constantinople for the Turk.

Meanwhile the victories of Prince Eugène, by hauling all Hungary back into Austria, left the Habsburg emperors with one of those desperate problems of internal government which, like the Anglo-Irish question, admit of no smooth and satisfying solution. The Archduke of Austria found in the elective kingdom of Hungary a proud Magyar nobility, exercising dominion over subject peoples of an alien race, speaking a language which few Germans knew, cherishing customs which no German shared, containing many families who were Protestant and many who for generations had sided with the Turk—a rude, semi-oriental aristocracy of land-owning warriors temperamentally more akin to the Pole than to the German, and having little affinity with the musical and artistic côteries of Vienna. How was the Emperor to handle this difficult, mettlesome, half-pagan people? How adjust his relations to the Teuton and the Slav? How make of this miscellany of incompatible races a stable Catholic and monarchical State? Was it possible to centralize and germanize the whole mass after the Bohemian model? Was it possible to construct a federation in which each race should have its appropriate share of power? Or was the most workable expedient one which placed sovereignty in the hands of the Germans and the Magyars as the most virile and military races, leaving each to manage his own barbarians?

The old Austrian empire, which attempted to solve these problems in the eighteenth and nineteenth centuries, and then, like the Ottoman empire, broke up after the Great War through the explosive force of nationalism within it, has many admirers and apologists among those who regard nationalism as the chief political curse of the human race.

For such this Catholic State, guided in its religious policy by the Jesuits, and carrying out among its subjects, many of whom at the beginning of the eighteenth century were half barbarian and half pagan, a mission of religion and civility, exercises a great attraction. They see in it an attempt to realize upon a small scale that ideal of a Christian society, embracing all races and tongues, which it has been the professed aim of the Church to realize on earth. In the Pax Austriaca, as in the Pax Britannica—though if they are Catholics they prefer the Austrian to the British peace—they descry a form of polity superior to the national state, because it appeals from nationalism to some higher and larger principle of human association. They recognize the difficulties under which the old Austrian empire laboured, the oppressions which it exercised, the unpopularities which it typified; but they deplore its disappearance. Cumbrous, tyrannical, unintelligent as the Austrian Government often seemed to be, it nevertheless continued to hold together, over a wide and difficult area of Europe, excitable and incompatible peoples and to give them some aspersion of the Latin and Teutonic culture of the west.

Had the Austrian empire, like the United States of America, been the product of the free association of self-governing states, it might safely have defied the storms of time. The indispensable basis of assent was wanting. The state was the chance result of dynastic marriages, connoting nothing higher than allegiance to a family, reposing on no basis of common custom, achieving its religious unity by a persecuting force. Jesuits, soldiers, and police held together a polity which, for lack of such mechanical bonds, would have dissolved into its elements. In the old Austrian empire life was lived merrily, happily, fruitfully. It was a Catholic state, monarchical in its forms, conventional in its beliefs, having that full and exquisite enjoyment of art and science which may most easily by found where Jews are numerous, but wanting only a political soul and the breath of freedom.

This is to anticipate. In the early half of the seventeenth century Austria was the spear-head of the Counter-Reformation and the oppressor of Bohemian liberty. Later she rendered two services to Europe, as welcome to the spirit which prevailed in England as these earlier achievements were abhorrent: the repulse of the Turks in the east, and in the west her indispensable and loyal support of the two Protestant and maritime powers in their stern struggle against Catholic France. So little may the policy of a state be deduced from the religious convictions of its citizens that the continued independence of the Dutch republic, the partition of the vast Spanish inheritance, and the successful establishment of the Protestant succession in England may, to no small degree, be ascribed to the spirited exertions of the old Jesuit-ridden 1919. Austrian state, which received its quietus by the Treaties of 20 St. Germain and Trianon.

BOOKS WHICH MAY BE CONSULTED

W. R. Morfill: *Poland*. 1893.
Dyboski: *Poland (Nations of the Modern World)*. 1933.
N. A. de Salvandy: *Histoire du roi Jean Sobieski*. 2 vols. 1876.
J. B. Morton: *Sobieski, King of Poland*. 1932.
W. Coxe: *House of Austria*. 1847.
G. Finlay: *History of Greece. Ed.* H. F. Tozer. 1877.
D. M. Vaughan: *Europe and the Turk*. 1350-1700. 1954.
B. H. Sumner: *Peter the Great and the Ottoman Empire*. 1949.
W. C. Reddaway: *The Cambridge History of Poland,* Vol. I.

CHAPTER LXI

PEACE AND PRUSSIA

The Age of Reason. Anglo-French amity. The Spanish menace. Charles VI and the Pragmatic Sanction. The Polish War of Succession. France wins Lorraine. Walpole and Fleury. Character of eighteenth-century wars. The rise of Prussia. Geographical disposition of the Prussian state. The Hohenzollern house. Character of the Prussian. Frederick William I.

THE War of the Spanish Succession was followed by a period
1713 of relative tranquillity rare in the history of Europe and precious for the advancement of its civilization. The Treaty of Utrecht, based on a wise series of compromises, left behind it no immediate occasion for rancorous dispute. Though Austria and Spain were disappointed, all the belligerents had, in effect, gained by the division of the Spanish inheritance. To the weak and ill-established governments of Philip of Orleans, Regent of France, and of George I, King of England, peace was an essential condition of security.

It is fitting that the Age of Reason should have been heralded by the unusual spectacle of a political alliance between England and France, the two nations whose intellectual co-operation was the most important single fact during the eighteenth century. The joint armies of Britain and France have rarely failed of success from the days of Julian the Apostate to the triumph of Haig and Foch. Their
1713- joint diplomacy was now triumphant. For twenty-five years
39 Europe was saved from a general conflagration. Wars, indeed, were not altogether avoided. There was conflict between Spain and Austria, between England and Spain, and finally, over the Polish succession, between France, with Spain and Savoy as auxiliaries, and the joint power of Austria and Russia. But it would seem as if the element of savage perseverance was wanting to these hostilities. To Fleury, who was a parsimonious bigot, as to Walpole, who was a robust economist, the lavish expenditure and waste of war

were abhorrent. If war they must have, and they could not altogether avoid it, they were determined that it should be waged with economy, limited in scope, and at the first possible opportunity brought to a conclusion.

To those who consider the many reasons tending to bring France and Spain together, their common inheritance of the Latin and Catholic tradition, their colonies exposed to the rivalries of the English and the Dutch, their common subjection to the Bourbon house, and the removal of the one apple of discord which had so long poisoned their relations through the transfer of the Netherlands from Spain to Austria by the Peace of Utrecht, it may seem strange that at any period after that date France should have preferred the English to the Spanish alliance. But the relations of States are often affected by personal accidents. Louis XIV was succeeded by a child so delicate that it was long uncertain 1715 whether he would live to man's estate; nor was it until a Dauphin was born to Louis XV in 1729 that the succession in the direct line seemed to be secure. In the interval it was apprehended that Philip V, the first Bourbon king of Spain, might, despite a formal renunciation, lay claim to the French Crown. Nobody in Paris wanted Philip; and the unwelcome contingency that he might exchange Madrid for Versailles was for many years sufficient to sow dissension between the two Bourbon powers and to give support to the precarious friendship between England and France.

The first danger to the public law of Europe came from the ambition of Elizabeth Farnese, the second wife of Philip V of Spain, who was prepared to set Europe in a blaze, if she could obtain in the duchies of Parma and Tuscany an adequate endowment for her sons. The violent will of this masterful woman was seconded by the brilliant resource of the son of an Italian vine dresser, whose energy and inspiration, despite a grotesque and ignoble appearance, were long remembered by the people of his adopted land. If the dreams of Cardinal Alberoni had been fully realized, the Austrians would have been driven from Italy, the Hanoverians from England, and the Regent from France, while all three countries would have passed under the influence and direction of a revivified Spain. These far-reaching plans were frustrated by the effective accord of the French and English governments. One 1718

Spanish fleet was destroyed off the Sicilian coast by the
English navy; another, carrying help to the Scottish Jacobites,
was dispersed by storms in the Bay of Biscay. The conspiracy to kidnap the Regent was unmasked in Paris. The
dashing Cardinal, who had not scrupled to attack the
Austrians while with the encouragement of the Holy See
they were engaged in a war with the Turks, was forced by the
joint pressure of England and France to withdraw from the
service of Spain. All his plans had miscarried, and with his
fall (1719) the first attempt drastically to revise the Utrecht
settlement broke down in failure.

Undaunted and incurable, Elizabeth Farnese persevered
in her maternal designs. The ends which Alberoni had hoped
to secure by a direct attack on Austria, the Dutchman
1725 Ripperda, yet another foreign minister in the Spanish service,
endeavoured to obtain through a close understanding with
the court of Vienna. Again Europe was brought to the brink
of a general war. Again the spectre of Austro-Spanish
hegemony raised for a time its minatory head, and again the
Hanoverian dynasty was threatened by a secret understanding between the Jacobite faction and the foreign enemies of
England. Yet once more a friendly undertaking between the
prudent rulers of France and England saved the peace of
Europe.

At this time Austria was ruled by the man whom England
at a great expenditure of blood and treasure had vainly tried
1711- to set upon the Spanish throne. Charles VI, unexpectedly
40 succeeding his brother Joseph in Vienna, was of the stiffest
Habsburg clay, at once ungrateful for past help and obstin-
ately tenacious of past pretensions. So stupid was he that,
but for one circumstance, he might have created as much
trouble in Europe as Elizabeth Farnese. Having no children
but a daughter, who under the Salic law was excluded from
the Austrian succession, he was compelled to solicit the assent
of the leading powers of Europe to a family statute known
as the Pragmatic Sanction, which, notwithstanding the legal
obstacle, provided for the accession of Maria Theresa to the
undivided inheritance of the Habsburg state. A sovereign
in quest of political favours from others is never in the best
position for pressing an advantage; and the astute diplomatists in London and Paris were not slow to appreciate the

bargaining counter which chance had placed in their hands. Their price was high. To Walpole Charles conceded the virtual suppression of the Ostend East India Company, which threatened English interests in the Indian Ocean. The French, holding their hand, were even more successful, for out of the Emperor's necessities Cardinal Fleury, their sagacious Prime Minister, wrung the reversion to the duchy of Lorraine.

The occasion for this last concession was provided by one of those brief and limited wars which are characteristic of this period of diplomatic sobriety and material progress. The Polish War of Succession arose from the fact that Louis XV, who had married Marie, daughter of Stanislaus Lesczinski, desired on political and family grounds to replace his father-in-law on the Polish throne. It was a foolish policy, as Fleury saw, for Russia stood behind Austria in backing Augustus, the Saxon candidate, and had an army at hand, while the French were leagues away from the Polish scene.

It was idle, then, to suppose that the war aims of France could be achieved by operations in the distant plains of Poland. The imperial possessions in Italy and on the Rhine offered a nearer and more practical objective, and Italy was accordingly the main theatre on which the brief war of the Polish Succession was waged. Here France, with the ill- 1733- compacted aid of Spain and Savoy, succeeded, despite 8 fluctuations of fortune, in delivering a sensible blow at her antagonist. A Spanish army under General Montemar drove the Austrians from Naples, and there established that ill-fated 1735 dynasty of Neapolitan Bourbons which for its tyranny attracted the scornful wrath of Gladstone and was at last sent about its business by Garibaldi's Red Shirts.

The conquest of the Neapolitan kingdom was the most important stroke in a war languidly conducted upon a limited and parsimonious scale and brought to a conclusion at an early opportunity. To the natural indignation of the Emperor, England and Holland refused to be drawn into the quarrel, and since imperial success in Poland was balanced by imperial failure in Italy, the court of Vienna listened to the overtures of Fleury. The treaty, known as the Third Treaty 1738 of Vienna, by which that aged ecclesiastic closed the Polish struggle, is justly regarded as a beautiful model of French diplomacy. Though he had spent little and ventured little, the cardinal was able to extract a brilliant advantage from an unreasonable and unpopular war. It was settled that Duke Francis of Lorraine should marry Maria Theresa, the heiress of the Austrian throne, and succeed to the reversion of Tuscany on the death of the last ruler of the house of Medici. In exchange for these shining prospects it was agreed that Francis should resign Lorraine to Stanislaus, and that after the death of the old Polish king the province should pass to France. French historians never cease to congratulate themselves on the skill by which, out of the bitter failure of French hopes in Poland, there emerged by a dazzling and unexpected feat of legerdemain the acquisition of Lorraine. But the miracle could never have been accomplished but for two things; Charles's need of the French assent to the Pragmatic Sanction, and the determination of Walpole to keep the peace. So the Polish War, which might easily have brought ruin upon Europe, passed away with little more than a few sieges and battles. Save that a Bourbon succeeded a Habsburg in Naples, and that the succession to Lorraine was secured for France, the political map of Europe was practically undisturbed. Diplomacy had been very busy for these twenty-five years. It was an era of congresses, of triple and quadruple alliances, of alarums of war, of conspiracies and intrigues of all kinds. Yet behind these endless agitations there was in Paris and London, by a rare stroke of good fortune, a steadfast will to peace guiding the actions of important persons. The Franco-British understanding, inaugurated by Stanhope, a gallant English gentleman, in conjunction with Dubois, a clever French rogue, was improved and consolidated by two far greater statesmen who continued their work. It would be difficult to conceive a sharper contrast than that between Cardinal Fleury, Prime Minister of France from his seventy-fourth to his ninetieth year, and Sir Robert Walpole, who for an even longer span dominated the political scene in England: the one an emaciated intellectual, wise, patient, serene, incomparable in diplomatic finesse, and raised above the passions and vices of the world; the other a coarse, pleasure-loving Norfolk squire, but the best financier and parliamentarian of his time. Yet so far as it might be given to two men to repress the combative instincts of

Europe, that privilege was vouchsafed to these strange allies, each of whom, in pursuit of his own clear conception of the national interest, was compelled to tread the same pathway of international peace.[1]

The wars of the eighteenth century were not the product of great popular or racial movements, sustained and promoted by a powerful press. In general the peoples were condemned to bear the cost of wars which they had no part in promoting and in which they were but faintly concerned. Not that the governments of the eighteenth century, in pursuit of aims which were prevailingly dynastic, were altogether impervious to outside opinion. The French king listened to his fiery nobles. The Spanish monarchy might always rely on the support of popular sentiment in an attempt to evict the English from Gibraltar. The great traditional hostilities, however unreasonable, however inopportune, such as the feud between France and Austria, or between England and France, were sunk far too deep in the national consciousness to be uprooted by a generation of original diplomacy. Walpole and Fleury between them had done their best to maintain the fabric of Europe as it had been settled by the peace treaties of Utrecht and Rastadt; but the lesson of European history is that Europe is never settled, but always restless and uneasy. In the declining years of Walpole and Fleury a new force of startling and unmeasured potency burst upon the scene and involved the continent in the havoc and carnage of a general war. That force was the Prussia of Frederick the Great.

England grew. Prussia was manufactured. Until the later half of the seventeenth century nothing in the political complexion of Germany announced the coming of this powerful state. Then the house of Hohenzollern, which had been ruling in Brandenburg since 1417, threw up for the first time a really remarkable man. Frederick William, known as the Great Elector, after his victory over the Swedes at Fehrbellin (1675), an affair slight in itself, but hailed as an augury of coming greatness, had conceived clearer notions of efficiency in government than were then commonly prevalent. Out of an

---

[1] This is consistent with the existence of a good deal of diplomatic friction between the two countries after 1731.

unpromising, dispeopled, and divided inheritance he fashioned by his systematic encouragement of immigration and by his administrative and military reforms (for he regarded his people as material to be shaped and handled at will) the embryo of a modern State. There was nothing amateurish or haphazard about Frederick William's method. An army, a navy, a Civil Service, an improved postal system, a graduated income-tax, even an African colony, announced the quality of his ambition. All could not be realized. The colony went down before the powerful rivalry of the Dutch. The navy had to wait for Tirpitz and Kaiser William II, but the note of high ambition had been struck.[1]

1685-
1713   The Electoral title was no longer sufficient for Frederick William's successor. In consideration of favours to come, Frederick I obtained from the Emperor the right to be crowned King of Prussia, and to the horror of clerical
1701   Europe imposed the crown upon his own head in the cathedral of Königsberg The alliance of the new Protestant kingdom was eagerly courted, and in the wars of Marlborough Prussian contingents played their part and watered the fields of Blenheim, Ramillies, and Oudenarde with their blood.

The weakness of the state lay in its geographical dispersion, for it was triply divided, with Brandenburg, Henry the Fowler's March against the Wends, at the centre, while away to the east across a block of territory once German, but between 1466 and 1660 subjected to Poland, lay ducal Prussia, and far westwards in the Rhineland the small duchies of Cleves, Mark and Ravensberg, over which since 1666 the Great Elector exercised full and acknowledged sovereignty. Between these divided members of an unpremeditated state there was no necessary or organic connection. Chance had brought them together under a common sovereign; chance might dissolve the partnership. The history of ducal or east Prussia had run one course, that of Brandenburg another. East Prussia had been part of a territory originally inhabited by a primitive, heathen, non-German people who, in the thirteenth century, had been driven into the Christian fold by the cold steel of the German Order of Knights, and by them governed for two hundred years, until the Order was shattered by the growing military power of Poland and East Prussia

[1] Genealogical Table **B.**

became a fief of the Polish crown. The early history of Brandenburg had been hardly less promising, for only with the coming of the Hohenzollerns did this region emerge from the humiliating vicissitudes of partition, repartition, and mortgage to which all German properties were exposed. The Hohenzollerns are among the able families of Europe. As Burgraves of Nuremberg they had lived in the sunshine of imperial favour and on the customs dues of a thriving city. In Brandenburg they had adopted artillery when it was novel, Lutheranism when it was assured, Calvinism in time to enable them to receive with open arms the industrious Huguenot refuges from France, and to compel their Lutheran subjects to a wise and profitable toleration of other forms of Protestantism than their own. One art, however, they did not possess. The Brandenburger could not win the good graces of East Prussia. It is noticeable that both in 1617, when John Casimir was admitted by the king of Poland to that Polish fief, and in 1660, when the Great Elector obtained the duchy in full sovereignty, the East Prussians manifested the keenest annoyance. Indeed, it was only by the use of force that the opposition of the East Prussian Diet was in that latter year overcome.

The Prussian is a distinctive European type. Goethe, who lived in Weimar and may be taken to represent the mid-German view of the Prussians, speaks of them as barbarians. There was an uncouth vigour and asperity about this remarkable people which jarred on the more refined susceptibilities of the Saxon, the Franconian, and the Rhinelander. To what causes the special characteristics of the Prussian race are to be attributed, whether to the Slavonic blood which flows through their veins, or to the harsh north German climate, or to the stern military tradition which nature imposes upon a state undefended by geographical frontiers or, if to all these causes, in what proportion: these are questions which admit of no precise answer. Let it suffice that before the eighteenth century had half run its course the world was aware that this vivid and masterful people, so sparingly furnished with the graces of life, presented by reason of their frugality, their discipline, their skill in arms, and heroic capacity for sacrifice a new and formidable problem for the statesmen of Europe.

In contradistinction to other Germans, the Prussians had a

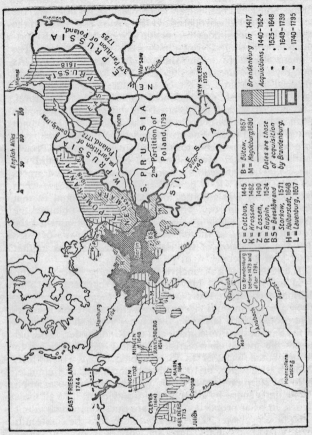

THE GROWTH OF BRANDENBURG PRUSSIA

Brandenburg in 1417
Acquisitions, 1440–1524
" 1525–1648
" 1649–1739
" 1740–1795

C = Cottbus, 1445
K = Krossen, 1482
Z = Zossen, 1490
R = Ruppin, 1524
BS = Beeskow and
       Storkow, 1571
H = Halberstadt, 1648
L = Lauenburg, 1657

B = Bütow, 1657
M = Magdeburg, 1680

Dates are those
of acquisition
by Brandenburg.

strict sense of service to the State. Their rulers could count, not upon their judgment, for the sturdy population of Prussia had no mind for politics, but upon a blind, ungrudging obedience to the word of command and upon a technical probity which ensured that every task would be faithfully discharged. It was a land of the Categorical Imperative, not only in the sense that Immanuel Kant, the apostle of the austere doctrine of Duty for Duty's sake, was Prussian to the marrow, but also because respect for duty was nowhere more savagely or successfully imposed. In this regard King Frederick William I, the·father of Frederick the Great, set a notable example. No country could wish for a more economical sovereign or one who in his simple, dutiful, puritanical life more aptly illustrated the best characteristics of his people.

Prussia owes much to the peaceful rule of this homely but eccentric monarch—a large, well-trained army, a centralized administration, a good system of popular schools, closer tax-collecting and budgeting, and a full treasury. Yet the man had the mind of a drill-sergeant, the manners of a boor, and the moods of a savage. His army of giants was collected by the methods of a slave-driver. A tempestuous violence, tinged with insanity, wrecked the happiness of his home. It is characteristic of the brutal strain which was combined with Frederick William's Old Testament morality that, having quarrelled with his gifted and uncomprehended son, he condemned him to witness, as one of many penalties, the decapitation of a cherished associate and friend.

In the evening of his life Frederick paid an historian's tribute to the father whose savage tyranny had wrecked the happiness of his youth. "Under Frederick the First," he writes, "Berlin had been the Athens of the North. Under Frederick William the First it became its Sparta. Its entire government was militarized. The capital became the stronghold of Mars. All the industries which serve the needs of armies prospered. In Berlin were established powder mills and cannon foundries, rifle factories, etc. Frederick William the First strove less to create new industries than to abolish useless expenditures. Formerly, mourning had been ruinously expensive. Funerals were accompanied by extremely costly festivities. These abuses were abolished. Horses and carriages were no longer allowed to be draped in black, nor were black liveries given to servants. Henceforth people died cheaply. The military character of the government affected both customs and fashions. Society took a military turn. No one used more than three ells of cloth for a coat. The age of gallantry passed away. Ladies fled the society of men and the latter compensated themselves with carousals, tobacco, and buffoonery."

BOOKS WHICH MAY BE CONSULTED

W. E. H. Lecky: *History of England in the Eighteenth Century*. 8 vols. 1878-90.

B. Williams : *Stanhope*. 1932.

John Morley: *Sir Robert Walpole*. 1921.

E. Armstrong: *Elizabeth Farnese*. 1892.

T. Carlyle: *Life of Frederick II of Prussia*. 6 vols. 1858-65.

E. Lavisse: *Histoire de France*, Vol. VIII.

F. S. Oliver: *The Endless Adventure*. 1930-1.

Œuvres historiques de Frédéric le Grand; Nouvelle édition, 1830; II, *Histoire de mon temps*.

A. Sorel: *L'Europe et la Révolution Française*. 1885-1903.

P. Vaucher: *Sir Robert Walpole et la politique de Fleury*. 1924.

R. Lodge: *Great Britain and Prussia in the Eighteenth Century*. 1923.

J. H. Plumb: *Sir Robert Walpole: the making of a statesman*. 1956.

P. Gaxotte: *Frederick the Great*. Tr. R. A. Bell. 1941.

CHAPTER LXII

EUROPE AT WAR, 1740-63

The Silesian duel. The marine and colonial rivalry of England and the Bourbon powers. Frederick II and Maria Theresa. The War of the Austrian Succession. The interference of England and the re-entry of Prussia. The '45. The Peace of Aix-la-Chapelle. The diplomatic revolution. The impolicy of France. The Seven Years' War. William Pitt. Frederick's Annus Mirabilis. Reasons for Prussia's survival. England's colonial gains. Canada. India. The genius of Clive. The Peace of Prussia. War results for England and Prussia compared.

THE middle years of the eighteenth century are marked by a gigantic struggle which alike in its earlier and later phase revolves round two main international rivalries, the one, that between Prussia and Austria, startling from the shock of its novelty, while the other was of all European quarrels the most familiar. The War of the Austrian Succession and the Seven Years' War sprang from a common source. In 1740 Frederick II of Prussia drew the sword because he was determined to make himself talked about by the conquest of Silesia. In 1756 he launched a second war for fear that Silesia might be wrested from him. For twenty-three years, Silesia with its rich linen industry, undeveloped iron ores, and fine mercantile waterway, threw Catholic Austria into one scale, and the rude upstart power of Protestant Prussia into the other. Once kindled, the fire spread widely. Every political appetite was aroused. The most stable political frontiers were challenged. Almost all the continent was embroiled in a quarrel carried on at a huge cost of blood and treasure, and with many sharp vicissitudes of fortune. At one moment it seemed that Austria would be brought to the ground, at another that France would be dismembered, at a third that Holland and the Netherlands would be annexed by the French, at a fourth that Prussia would be overwhelmed by the Russians and Austrians. Yet, in spite of these violent oscillations, little change was effected in the political map of Europe, by fifteen years of hard fighting, beyond the transference to the Prussian crown of Silesia, a prize seized at the outset of the first war by an act of the blackest treachery, but defended against a world of enemies by the genius and pertinacity of a great soldier.

Meanwhile a controversy, springing from a different root and fraught with a more important issue, was proceeding between England and her commercial and maritime rivals France and Spain. The war between England and Spain, which broke out over the Spanish right of search in 1739, and was soon merged in the more critical struggle between England and France, was not made by statesmen in London, Paris, or Madrid. Wherever an Englishman met a Spaniard or a Frenchman on the high seas he espied a rival and a foe. It was a struggle not of courts and cabinets, but of men on the spot, of sailors and merchants, smugglers and privateers, of lumbermen, settlers, and free traders, of rival mercantile companies, brawling and quarrelling either along the Spanish Main or in Acadia and Newfoundland, or along the banks of the Ohio or the St. Lawrence, or under a burning Indian sky among the rice fields of the Carnatic, or the canes and mango trees of Bengal. Inevitably the unregulated competition for trade, colonies and dominion in Asia and America provoked innumerable collisions between the Anglo-Saxons and their Latin rivals. Unauthorized quarrels swelled out into unauthorized war. It was in vain that Sir Robert Walpole endeavoured to avoid being drawn into hostilities over the Spanish right of search in 1739. Popular clamour, echoed and reinforced by an eloquent opposition in Parliament, forced him into war. It was sufficient that English vessels, trading in the Spanish Main, should have been roughly searched for contraband by Spanish guard ships, and that English sailors loaded with chains should have been consigned to filthy Spanish prisons. In England the complaints of sailors and merchants always find a ready hearing, and the story that a wicked Spaniard had lopped off Captain Jenkins' ear sent the country into convulsions of fury, which only a declaration of war, as impolitic as it was unjust, was able to assuage.

The marine and colonial contest, which was thus inaugurated against the judgment of England's wisest statesman, lasted with little intermission (for when formal hostilities ceased, informal and local fighting none the less continued) until the Peace of Paris in 1763. Then it was made manifest that the sceptre of colonial dominion had passed from France to Britain. In India and Canada, thanks to the victories of Clive and Wolfe, British influence was triumphant and unchallenged.

This change in the balance of colonial power which, little as its true significance was appreciated at the time, constitutes one of the great revolutions in human history, could hardly have been brought about save for the continental war. The English ships, both of the commercial and of the royal navy, were more numerous than the French and the Spanish, because with England, though not with George II, maritime and colonial interests always came first, whereas with France and Spain the sea was neglected for the land. There are few errors in French history more calamitous than the decision which was taken in 1740 to join Frederick of Prussia in his attack on Maria Theresa. By that decision France became involved in an exhausting continental war, offering her so many temptations, exposing her to so many risks, and calling for so many sacrifices, that she could take little thought for her scattered settlers over sea. The French navy was accordingly neglected, and the error was not repaired until Canada and India had passed into British hands. It is one of the ironies of history that the blunder which helped England to become mistress of the seas also contributed to secure the predominance of Prussia in Germany.

It was not only a blunder but a crime. France had solemnly accepted the Pragmatic Sanction, which guaranteed to Maria Theresa the succession to the Austrian throne, But the government of France was always liable to be swept into war by the headlong passions of a military aristocracy. The prudence of the king and Cardinal Fleury was overborne. To Marshal Belleisle and his following of titled firebrands the prospect of wiping out old scores against the ancient enemy at a time when she seemed to be helpless and unfriended overbore every scruple of conscience and foresight. "What," they asked, "is an obligation to an opportunity?"

Rarely has a sin against international good faith been in the end more amply punished.

No mist of ancient rivalries clouded the clear eye of Frederick II. That cool young realist, a bad German but a good Prussian, bore no grudge against Austria, nor were his passive and most unpolitical subjects lusting for conquests. But the field was clear for ambition. With a strong army, a full treasury, and an obedient people, the Hohenzollern was master of his fate. No loyalties restrained his freedom. He was prepared to throw his sword now in this scale, now in that, as Prussian interests seemed to demand. The manipulation of political forces, unhampered by religion or chivalry, by respect for engagements, or by any feeling for the German race, was the mark of his reign, and his equivocal contribution to the public life of Germany. That he saw himself and the world through plain glass, that he spurned delights and lived laborious days, viewing himself always as the first servant of the Prussian state, and that he possessed to an almost unequalled degree the gift of leadership in war and peace, are qualities which have compelled the admiration of the world. The German may find flaws in the sovereign who never affected to conceal his contempt for the language and literature of the Fatherland; but the Prussians are right in regarding the great Fritz as one of the master builders of their state. In the blaze of his transcendent service they readily condone the fact that he was an infidel in religion, a cynic in politics, and that in his intellectual outlook upon life he was a disciple of Voltaire. They see in him the sovereign who made the Prussian army feared through Europe, who founded the reputation of Prussia as a military state, and added new and important provinces to his Prussian inheritance. They honour him as a commander, generally victorious, but never greater or more resourceful than in the darkest hour of defeat, as a king who brought his country through great trials into peace and security, and raised it to a position of indisputable predominance in Germany. To the tender conscience shrinking from the long catalogue of dubious acts beginning with the perfidious seizure of Silesia, and ending with the first partition of Poland, by which Frederick attained his ends, they reply that such were the international morals of the age, and that the Hohenzollern was no worse than his contemporaries. The doctrine that the end justifies the means is a necessary part of the Prussian apology for Frederick II.

His ambition was high but not exorbitant. Asking much of his people, but always for a Prussian and a practical end, he was nevertheless not indifferent to the advantages of a balance of power. The Europe for which he fought was one in which Prussia strengthened by Silesia faced an Austria not otherwise aggrandized. Such a Europe was vouchsafed him by the Peace of Aix-la-Chapelle in 1748. By using the Prussian army as a diplomatic instrument, he had obtained his objective. Now it had been thrown into the fray, now suddenly withdrawn, now again launched against his old enemy. Alternately he had saved Austria from France by a treaty, and France from Austria by an attack. His interventions and withdrawals had been in each case decisive, so that of all the combatants in the eight years Frederick alone had reason to be satisfied. While everyone else went empty-handed, he had won Silesia. Yet there was a fly in the ointment, for another long war had yet to be fought before the proud spirit of Maria Theresa was brought to acquiesce in her loss.

In October, 1740, the Emperor Charles VI, dying without male issue, left to Europe an occasion for demonstrating that the principles of honour, chivalry, and good faith were not altogether banished from international relations. His daughter Maria Theresa was a young married woman, in-experienced in affairs. Her treasury was empty, her army weak. Her title to succeed to the undivided inheritance of the Austrian Habsburgs had been recognized by every important court in Europe (Bavaria excepted) and in most cases for value received. Yet neither her sex, nor her inexperience, nor the solemn guarantees which had been given to her father availed the Queen of Hungary. Within a year of her succession she was involved in a desperate struggle to save the inheritance of her ancestors from a rapacious coalition headed by the very powers who were specially pledged to respect it.

The first blow was struck by Frederick II, who, without a particle of provocation, swooped down upon Silesia, and on the field of Mollwitz, thanks to the steadiness of his Prussian infantry, advertised the weakness of Austria to the world. It was vain to suppose that after such an Austrian reverse the struggle could be localized. From every quarter of the sky the vultures came flocking to the prey. France wanted to rob Austria of the Netherlands and Luxemburg. Bavaria desired the Imperial Crown and an eastward extension of her boundary. The elector of Saxony, who was also king of Poland, was anxious to claim a share in an empire which was threatened with dissolution. In the anti-Austrian coalition, France, the old enemy of the Habsburgs, acted as the spearhead, believing that the moment had come, with the aid of this new and unexpected Prussian power, to establish once and for all her political predominance in Europe. For a time everything prospered with her designs. Her army penetrated into Bohemia and captured Prague, while the Bavarians threatened the safety of Vienna. It was arranged that the Imperial Crown, which for more than three hundred years had been accorded to the head of the Habsburg house, should be transferred to Charles Albert of Bavaria, who contested Maria Theresa's title and was resolved to assail her territories. At no time in her long and chequered history, until the last year of the great war, did the fortunes of Austria sink so low as in the early summer of 1741.

Then followed a remarkable reversal of fortune. In the hour of her tribulation Maria Theresa threw herself upon the loyalty of her Hungarian subjects, and found in that chivalrous and warlike aristocracy a fiery response. The Bavarians were driven out of Munich, the French out of Prague. By a singular irony of fortune Charles Albert, the new Emperor, was compelled to sign a treaty renouncing his pretensions to the Austrian succession, and ceding his hereditary dominions to the Queen of Hungary until the general peace. By the summer of 1742 the wheel had turned full circle. The aggressive policy of France had reacted upon her. The invader of Bohemia was now compelled to look to the defences of Alsace and Lorraine. England and Sardinia had thrown their weight into the Austrian scale, and a June, fortunate battle at Dettingen, the last in which an English 1743 king drew the sword, encouraged the idea that an invasion of France might now be successfully attempted by two armies advancing respectively from points situated upon the middle and the upper Rhine.

The main cause of this sudden revolution of fortune is to be found in the action of the King of Prussia. Frederick intended to keep Silesia, but was not prepared to squander an unnecessary Prussian thaler or Prussian life upon its acquisition. At any moment he was willing to treat with the Queen of Hungary, always provided that he was guaranteed his Silesian conquest. On that basis he went out of the war in October, 1741. On that basis again he went out of the war in July, 1742, this time taking Saxony with him from the ranks of Austria's opponents. Freed by the Peace of Berlin from her most formidable opponent, and exhilarated by a surprising succession of victories, Maria Theresa resolved to exploit her success to the full. The most dazzling possiblities appealed to her ardent imagination, the annexation of Bavaria, the conquest of Alsace and Lorraine, the recovery of Naples and Silesia. The war which opened with a plan for the ruin of Austria passed into a war for the dismemberment of France. In the heat of her indignation and the flush of her victories the Queen of Hungary scorned the notion of peace. *July, 1743*

In this implacable attitude England, deaf to the advice of its wisest statesman, ranged herself by the side of Maria Theresa. Walpole, who had been opposed to the war with Spain, was no less averse from inviting a rupture with France: for he foresaw that the first consequence of such an entanglement would be a Jacobite rising, which might shake the Hanoverian dynasty to the ground. But peace had become unfashionable, and Walpole was driven from power to make way for counsellors who would respond more nearly to the excitable mood of the country and the king. Carteret, the most accomplished, but not the most prudent, of men, sprang into the saddle, and with his master, who was above all things a Hanoverian, committed the country to a continental campaign. A treaty signed at Worms between England, Austria, and Sardinia, revived the scheme of a grand alliance, fortified by English subsidies, against the ambitions of France. *Feb., 1742* *Sept., 1743*

The allies had reckoned without Frederick. That astute sovereign had watched with growing anxiety the course of Austria's triumphs in the west. "It is a capital error in politics," he observed, "to trust a reconciled enemy," and

Frederick reposed no trust in Maria Theresa. So far from believing that she was truly reconciled at the Peace of Berlin, he was convinced that the queen studied revenge. Accordingly, while an Imperial army under Prince Charles of Lorraine was occupied in Alsace, Frederick, throwing principle to the winds, broke the peace, invaded Bohemia, and seized Prague (September 16, 1744). At once the whole complexion of the war was altered. The re-entry of Frederick placed Austria again upon her defence, and liberated France from a grave peril. A series of most glittering prizes offered themselves invitingly to the government of Louis XV, the conquest of Belgium, the dethronement of King George, the establishment of a Catholic dynasty on the English throne. A French army under the skilful leadership of Prince Maurice de Saxe entered the Austrian Netherlands, and twice (Fontenoy, May 11, 1745, and Lauffeld, July 2, 1746) compelled an English commander to accept defeat.

That the great French plan miscarried was at bottom due to the preponderance of English power at sea and to the continuing affection of the English people for the Protestant cause. Channel storms dispersed an invading fleet. English privateers ruined French commerce; and it was given to Charles Edward, who raised the Stuart banner in the Highlands in 1745, to experience the bitter truth that an unpopular Hanoverian king could yet command the passive support of a lethargic but very Protestant population. The Jacobite cause, which enlisted so many romantic hopes and loyalties, foundered on the field of Culloden (April 16, 1746), but was in ruins from the moment that it became evident that Englishmen were not prepared to rally to Prince Charlie as he made his southward progress from Carlisle to Derby. Scanty as were the claims of George II upon the affections of his subjects, his throne was too firmly established to be upset by a small army of wild Gaelic swordsmen from the Highlands of Scotland. The reckless adventure, which has been glorified by the genius of Sir Walter Scott, served to consolidate the Protestant monarchy, and to spread its power through many a wild and lonely glen to the northern tip of Caithness. The subjugation of the Highlands was the solid and enduring result of the '45. Marshal Wade's roads and Pitt's Highland regiments completed the Act of Union and opened out to the Catholic inhabitants of northern Scotland the lavish resources and manifold opportunities of a great empire.

In the eastern theatre of the war neither party gained a decisive advantage. If Frederick was compelled to relax his hold on Bohemia, he was still in a position to inflict such defeats upon his adversary at Hohenfriedberg and Sohr, that on the strength of these personal triumphs, and with the help of a useful victory won by his Saxon allies, he brought the Austrians to sign a peace at Dresden, which guaranteed him Dec., Silesia and Glatz.   1745

Equally fierce, equally indecisive was the bloody struggle for supremacy which proceeded south of the Alps. Here Austria and Savoy were pitted against the two Bourbon kingdoms. And here, as in Germany, the Austrians were in the end compelled to cede a point to the adversary. The Peace of Aix-la- 1748 Chapelle, which closed the war, allotted the duchy of Parma to Don Philip of Spain.

To this war of sharp vicissitudes, in which no nation had won victories which were not offset by grave losses, there was finally an end, induced rather by fatigue than by satisfaction. Nothing was really settled by the Peace of Aix-la-Chapelle, neither the naval and commercial duel between England and the Bourbon kingdoms, nor the Silesian duel between Austria and Prussia, nor the struggle for hegemony in Italy, nor the fate of the Netherlands, perforce retroceded at the peace to Austria, but destined to be recaptured by revolutionary France. In India England had suffered reverses ere long to be brilliantly retrieved; in the gateway to Canada she had captured the strong fortified port of Louisburg, a base in Cape Breton Island, which pointed to ulterior designs.

Englishmen had never greatly liked this War of the Austrian Succession. The opposition, led by William Pitt, a fiery young orator, who was to become a great war minister, thundered against the subsidies to Hanoverian and Hessian troops, and alleged, not without cause, that the ship of British policy was steered by a Hanoverian rudder. The money power of England seemed to be ill employed in nourishing a continental war, the main purpose of which was suspected to be the protection of Hanover, and the main result of which was that the Netherlands were overrun by the French, and that England was invaded by the Highlanders. Neither was it agreeable to France to contemplate the ruin of her foreign trade, through the depredations of English corsairs, the reverses of her navy, the miscarriage of her Jacobite enterprise, or the long purse of the islanders, who, when their armies had twice been defeated on the plains of Flanders, were ready to hire a Russian army to redress the balance. Rather than face these thirty thousand Russians, the government of France was disposed to peace, and in exchange for the return of Louisburg, to withdraw her troops from Holland and the Netherlands.

Of all the practical arts diplomacy is the most conservative. In the War of the Austrian Succession fidelity to an old tradition had made England the friend and France the enemy of Austria. As it had been in the past, so it was assumed that it must always be. The memories of ancient quarrels, as when Turenne and Condé measured swords with the Imperialists or Marlborough and Eugène confronted the marshals of Louis XIV. coloured the imaginations of men and shaped their policies. But when it was found that a long and costly war waged upon this diplomatic pattern led to no decisive result, the question naturally arose whether the diplomatic pattern was not an anachronism. What had Austria got out of the English alliance? What reason had France to acclaim the aggrandizement of Prussia? Which of the two powers, Catholic Austria or Protestant Prussia under its soldier king, would be most helpful to England in her impending and inevitable struggle for colonial empire with France? From these doubts and discontents there emerged a diplomatic revolution. As early as 1751, letters were going from Maria Theresa to "Madame my very dear sister," the reigning mistress of the French king.

In diplomacy personality is always a factor. Frederick was a misogynist who found in the three dominant women of his day a perpetual invitation to scurrilous and well advertised wit. Maria Theresa, the devout, unforgiving Empress, Madame de Pompadour, the all-powerful mistress of Louis XV, Elizabeth, the licentious, vodka-drinking Tzarina of Russia, gave occasion to gibes which went the rounds of Europe, and lashed the courts of Vienna, Versailles, and St. Petersburg to a fury of indignation. If the reckless insults which Frederick hurled at "the Apostolic Hag" and "Mlle. Poisson" (for the Pompadour was said to be the daughter of a fish wife) did not make the diplomatic revolution, at least they helped it on its way. The Tzarina was tough. Yet even Elizabeth, in her intervals of sobriety, must have been roused by a nickname which consigned her to the worst depths of animalism, infamy, and vice.

The Austrian alliance, so violently opposed to the diplomatic traditions of France, was unpopular from the first, and since it led to disorders, helped to widen the gulf between the monarchy and the nation. Yet there is no reason to think that the French treaties with Austria were the result of the wounded vanity of a beautiful woman. The grounds for a Franco-Austrian alliance were sound enough, since it was reasonable to surmise that a German state so strong as the Prussia of Frederick had already shown itself to be was likely to be too strong for the comfort of France.

What, however, is open to criticism is not the original Franco-Austrian Treaty, which was defensive only, but the **Aug** subsequent instrument which pledged France to an offensive **1756** and defensive alliance with Maria Theresa. The interests of France at this juncture of history were singularly ill served by another continental war. Her nationals were already struggling with the ancient enemy in the backwoods of America and in the plains of the Carnatic, and she would have been better advised to concentrate her efforts on the defence of her overseas possessions, which were already menaced by the formidable activity of their English rivals. It is, however, a remarkable fact how little public opinion in France was alive to the true character of the war into which her statesmen were leading her. So far from being concerned with India or Canada or the West Indies, the small section of France which was politically minded was passionately absorbed by the quarrel between the Crown and the Parliaments, between the liberalism of the Jansenists and the deists, and the persecuting Catholicism of the Jesuit Order, and with a wide range of constitutional problems suggested by the inevitable comparison between the free institutions of England and the secretive autocracy of France. So unpopular was the crown, so detested were the priests, and so violent was the spirit of criticism and revolt, that good judges, like the Marquis d'Argenson and the Earl of Chesterfield, writing in the middle of the century, discerned the signs of impending revolution. The vigorous and intelligent direction of a great war could hardly be expected in such an atmosphere. While the literary class was engaged in fighting the battle of tolera- tion and freedom, the lawyers in the Paris Parliament offered a vigorous resistance to any attempt to enlarge the con- tracted basis of taxation. An imaginative grasp of war aims, a readiness to bear war burdens, a capacity to give to the people of France the unity of direction which is required by any great war effort, were wholly wanting to the quick- witted but short-sighted corporations of lawyers, whose busy and acrimonious contentions obscured the larger issues of the time.

The Prussian advance into Saxony (September, 1756) which launched the Seven Years' War has been compared to the invasion of Belgium, which lit the flames of a yet greater conflict. And if the parallel is not exact, for Saxony, though outwardly innocent, cannot be acquitted of meditating mis- chief, it is nevertheless true that Frederick's action in suddenly rushing troops into a peaceful neighbour state, in seizing its capital and treasure, and in incorporating its army forcibly with his own, appeared to contemporaries to be a flagrant violation of international law. The proofs of an anti-Prussian coalition discovered in Dresden did not weigh against the patent fact that the King of Prussia was the first to wreck the peace. The Aulic Council at Vienna deprived him of his dominions and titles and called upon the German Diet to send an army of execution against the criminal.

The dangers and difficulties which now confronted Frederick were enormous. A ring of powerful enemies menaced him on every side: in the south the Austrians, in the east the Russians, in the west the French and Imperialists, in the north the Swedes. Against such a combination, draw- ing as it did from almost limitless resources of man-power, and at once able to put into the field armies twice as numerous as his own, Frederick was at a serious disadvantage. Whereas the Russians and Austrians could replace an army which had been shattered in battle, Prussian casualties could not be made good.

Amidst a world of enemies Frederick found an ally in

England. "The King of Prussia," observed George II, "is a mischievous rascal, a bad friend, a bad ally, a bad relation, and a bad neighbour, in fact, the most dangerous and ill-disposed prince in Europe." But the policy of England was now directed not by George II, but by William Pitt, in whose fiery imagination the Prussian king was magically transformed into the champion of the liberties of Europe and the pillar of the Protestant faith. Pitt did not send an English army into the eastern theatre of war; but English subsidies nourished the continental war, while English raids on the French coast, and English and Hanoverian support for Prince Ferdinand of Brunswick, who upheld Frederick's cause in western Germany, sensibly relieved the pressure which France might otherwise have exerted on his western flank.

Yet it is Frederick and Frederick alone who saved Prussia from obliteration. The Prussian army, though largely recruited from aliens, had been fashioned by its infidel commander into a unit religiously schooled to every sacrifice. As it marched into action, nerved by the inspired eloquence of its artist king, and warmed by the stirring music of a Lutheran chorale, it was persuaded that the Protestant God was fighting on its side. The most terrible losses, since they did not weaken the iron purpose of the leader, failed to demoralize the brave men who had fallen under his spell. Reduced to a third of its original strength after the fierce fighting of the opening year, the army of Frederick continued to defend against overwhelming odds the right of the Prussian nation to exist. It was of little moment that Berlin was plundered by an enemy raid in 1757, or that for many months in succeeding years a Russian army practised its notorious barbarities on Prussian soil. The soul of Prussia was not in a place but in a man, who beneath all his superficial gifts, graces, and accomplishments, his fugues and sonatas, his French verses and philosophic speculations concealed the ancient granite of his warrior race.

Never was his resistance more brilliantly exhibited than in the first year of the general fighting. His invasion of Bohemia ended in catastrophic failure. He was victorious at Prague, but beaten at Kollin, and compelled to withdraw the remnants of his sorely stricken army north of the Erz Gebirge. As the net of his enemies, French and Imperialists, Austrians,

Russians, and Swedes, closed round him in the late summer of that year, his thoughts turned to a suicide pact with his beloved sister. But with the call to action the black mood of the man of temperament passed away. Hurrying westwards into Saxony to meet the French, he surprised the army of the Prince de Soubise at Rossbach, and there inflicted upon
Nov., 1757 it a crushing defeat, duly celebrated at the Tabernacle in London by that eloquent Methodist preacher Mr. Whitefield as a crowning victory for the Protestant cause. Meanwhile Daun was in Silesia, and here on the hard-fought field of
Dec., 1757 Leuthen, under a bitter December sky, Frederick routed that sound Austrian general, who, a few months earlier, had compelled him to accept defeat.

The energy and skill with which, in this wonderful autumn campaign, Frederick drove the enemy from Saxony and Silesia, with an army shaken and decimated by earlier defeats, have compelled the admiration of soldiers in every subsequent generation. To Napoleon, the greatest of them all, the battle of Leuthen, "a masterpiece of movements, manoeuvres, and resolution," was alone sufficient to rank Frederick with the captains of undying fame.

The essential character of the war problem in the east was not altered by these triumphs. It could never be hoped that Prussia, a country vulnerable to an extreme degree on every frontier, could be effectively guarded against invasion. The only question was whether Frederick, the sovereign of this small, poor, ill-populated state, could keep an army in being against the united powers of two great empires, each able to bring into the field armies numerically superior to his own and infinitely more elastic. That the answer to this question was favourable to Frederick was not only due to the military genius which enabled him again and again, as at Liegnitz (August 14, 1760), at Torgau (November 3, 1760), and at Schweidnitz (August 9, 1762), to attack and defeat the enemy, but also to the defective combination and mutual jealousies of his Russian and Austrian opponents and to certain ingrained defects of temperament of which he was able to take full advantage. If the morale of the Russians had been equal to the scale of their armies, if Fermor had not
1758 turned eastward after the drawn battle of Zorndorf, where he took heavy toll of Prussian manhood, if Soltikov had not

surrendered himself to debauchery after his crushing victory 1759
at Kunersdorf, or if after that great Russian-Austrian
triumph the Austrians under Daun had been prompt to
pursue the advantage, Frederick would have been inevitably
driven to take that fatal potion which was his alternative to a
dishonourable peace. There seems, however, to be an inherent
lack of orderly perseverance in the Russian character. In the
Seven Years' War the Russians advanced again and again
into Prussian territory. They seized Colmar and settled down
in Prussian Pomerania. They penetrated to Frankfort-on-
Oder and even to Berlin. They fought three savage battles
with the Prussians and inflicted on them terrible losses; but
they never clinched their victory. When the Tzarina Elizabeth
died on January 5, 1762, a little, desperate, haggard man, his
face unwashed, his clothes old and much soiled with grease
and Spanish snuff, but with some leisure yet for the flute and
French verses, and capable, as was proved on the field of
Schweidnitz, of dealing a savage blow at his opponent, was
still hanging on among the Silesian hills with a following of
war-battered veterans as ragged and desperate as himself.
Elizabeth's death was his salvation, for it put a friend upon
the Russian throne in place of an enemy. Peter III was the
king's ardent admirer. With the Russians withdrawn and
the Turks menacing her eastern borders, Maria Theresa was
at last compelled to sign the Peace of Hubertsburg (February
15, 1763). The idea that Prussia could be decreed out of
existence by an Aulic Council, even if it were supported by
the armies of the three greatest states in Europe, was shown
to be an idle dream.

In the western and maritime area the sea power of England,
directed by the genius of William Pitt, was destined to secure
for the Protestant combination its greatest triumph. While
the main result of the eastern or continental war was conservative, the consequences of the great conflict between France
and England were revolutionary beyond all expectation.
Frederick, by his great exertions, prevented a violent change
in the balance of German power. He saved Prussia from
destruction and secured his hold on Silesia; but England
gained a new empire in the east and in the west. Here was a
vast alteration in the weights and balances of the world. At

the end of the war the North American continent had been secured for Anglo-Saxon expansion and India for Anglo-Saxon rule. The French, who had threatened to bar the western advance of the English colonists in North America, had been driven from their stations along the Ohio. The British flag flew from the fort of Quebec. The destiny of a huge continent was determined. In India Robert Clive, a young officer of the East India Company, had laid the foundations of that extraordinary polity which combines under the political direction of a northern and Protestant people more than three hundred million Orientals, whose almost infinite diversities of race, language, and religion present to their impartial masters an opportunity and a problem.

At first things went ill with the English. The French in Canada with their Red Indian allies had the advantage of the early exchanges. In the Mediterranean, Minorca was lost, to the rage and shame of a people ill accustomed to marine reverses. Calcutta fell into enemy hands. There was failure before Rochfort, and a British fleet disabled by storm before Louisburg. But then, as so often happens when the English go to war, the reserves of moral and material power began to accumulate, and, under the impulsion of a great leader, to tell on the result.

July., 1756

A vast combination of offensives directed against France in every part of the world began to yield remarkable rewards. Louisburg (the key to Canada), Fort Duquesne (the French outpost on the Ohio, the link between French Canada and French Louisiana, and the kernel of a possible French empire in the middle west of North America) fell into English hands. So, too, did Goree, and with it the French West African slave trade. English subsidies and English soldiers were despatched to the assistance of Duke Ferdinand of Brunswick, who sustained the Protestant cause in the Hanoverian area, and in so doing found his task not a little lightened by the active raids of the English navy upon the French coast. A decisive victory over a more numerous French army at Crevelt (June 23) announced that a new military talent of high quality had been enlisted in the Anglo-Prussian cause.

1758

America was the principal goal of Pitt's effort. It is his supreme merit as a statesman that he divined its importance and regarded all other operations in the war as subsidiary to its conquest. It was the "fountain of our wealth, the nerve of our strength, the nursery and basis of our naval power."

Pitt's great design for the destruction of French power in Canada by a triple attack directed from west, south, and east, though incapable of exact execution, was indicative of a mind equal to the scale of its task, and was, in fact, successful. Wolfe's victory over Montcalm on the heights of Abraham (September 13, 1759) has never been reversed. French Canada, for ever impenetrable to the creed, the language, and the outlook of the islander, passed under English control, a fragment of ancient France embedded in northern ice. The sea power of England guarded the conquest.

Given the balance of naval strength which prevailed at that time, the result of the war, both in the west and the east, could hardly have been otherwise. The population of French Canada, though more effectively organized for war, was greatly outnumbered by the thirteen flourishing English colonies along the Atlantic Ocean. Two million men have an advantage over fifty thousand, which in the end is bound to assert itself. What was lacking to the English colonies was not courage or enterprise, but the power of combination. An English fleet, an English army, and an English plan of campaign mobilized resources which had long been present and enabled them to exert their due effect.

A share of the credit for the great marine and colonial triumphs of this time is due to the English Parliament, which provided a sounding-board for the passions, cupidities, and grievances of the sailors, merchants, and colonists. It was impossible for London, as it was not impossible for Paris, to forget the needs of its nationals beyond the seas.

English constituencies possessed colonial interests and affiliations. The members for Poole were the champions of Newfoundland. Devizes held a watching brief for the Carolinas. For Paris there was nothing of the kind. Wanting such an organ for concentrating the voices from the sea, the French marine administration was at the mercy of court favour. Good ministers like Machault were allowed to fall without a murmur, bad ministers like Moras to rule without a challenge. In the critical year of 1759 the French Mediterranean fleet was crippled by Boscawen at Lagos, and the

French Atlantic fleet in great part destroyed by Hawke in Quiberon Bay. Even if the campaign of Wolfe had miscarried, these two naval actions were sufficient to settle the issue of the American war.

In India, where the dissolution of the Mogul Empire afforded a free field for European ambitions, fortune first favoured, and then for similar reasons deserted, the French. Site for site, England was more advantageously placed than her rival. Bombay was a finer port than Mahé, Madras more central than Pondicherry, Calcutta more convenient for commerce than the French station at Chandernagore. But in the race for political influence and power the French at first drew

1740-8 ahead. During the War of the Austrian Succession, when La Bourdonnais commanded her fleet, and Dupleix from Pondicherry was working for an empire to be won through Indian alliances and a Sepoy army, and Bussy, a brilliant oriental linguist, was weaving diplomatic webs in Hyderabad, the influence of France was predominant in southern India, Madras even, for some years, passed into her hands.

After the Peace of Aix-la-Chapelle the tables were turned. Of the two rival East India Companies the English was incomparably the stronger in commerce and finance. England had the better men on the spot and was prepared to give them more effective support and assistance from home. France withdrew La Bourdonnais and Dupleix, England discovered Robert Clive, Stringer Lawrence, and Eyre Coote. While French ships from their distant base in Mauritius refused to cross the Indian Ocean in the monsoon, there was no season of the year at which naval help was not available for the support of the English interest. The idea that a handful of Frenchmen could aspire to give the law to the Deccan seemed to politicians in Paris to be the wildest folly. A handful of Englishmen, inspired by Robert Clive, succeeded in demonstrating that a plan of political dominion even wider and more foolhardy could in effect be accomplished.

1725-74 The career of Robert Clive, the son of an impoverished squire, who started as a merchant's clerk in the employment of the East India Company and founded an empire, is one of the romances of the world. Clive died by his own hand at the age of forty-nine. His whole period of Indian service, which was broken by two visits to England, did not exceed twelve

years. In his first spell he made England supreme in the
Carnatic; in his second he reconquered Calcutta from
Suraj-ud Dowlah, defeated his army at Plassey, defeated the
Dutch, cleared the French out of Bengal and the northern
Circars, destroyed their influence in Hyderabad, and estab-
lished British power in the valley of the Ganges. In the third
and not the least honourable period of his public service he
organized and purified the civil administration of Bengal.
Extraordinary daring characterized his military enterprises.
At the age of twenty-six he led five hundred men to Arcot,
the capital of the Carnatic, and there held a crumbling
fortress against ten thousand Indians with a stiffening of
French troops for fifty days. On the decisive field of Plassey   1757
he brought three thousand men into action, of whom nine
hundred only were Europeans, against a force of forty
thousand infantry and fifteen thousand cavalry, and with a
loss of less than a hundred men routed his opponents.

   With one exception all the great political secrets of British
rule in India were revealed to him. He saw that a European
leader of Indian troops who was prepared to take extravagant
personal risks could work miracles with his men; he realized
that no great political result could be obtained without Indian
alliances and co-operation; he set his face against corruption
and contended that some day all the scattered possessions of
the East India Company must be brought together under
one political head. The chief blot upon the fame of a bold
but insensitive man is that he perpetrated a fraud upon a
Hindu blackmailer. Omichund was a rascal, but even a
rascal should not have been permitted to provoke a signal
display of British bad faith.

   By April, 1761, the French had nothing left of their Indian
Empire. Their last Governor was an Irishman by descent,
who had fought for the Jacobites in the '45, and had still
an unexpended balance of hatred to discharge against the
English people. Lally Tollendal had the impatient courage
of his race, but, knowing nothing of India or its people, and
being of a vehement and umbrageous temper, he outraged
every susceptibility and committed every mistake. Such an
Irishman was capable of wrecking any cause. The unfortunate
Lally lost India for the French on the hard-fought field of
Wandewash. There is no aspersion on his courage or loyalty;

but in Eyre Coote he met a soldier hardly surpassed by Clive himself. Magnanimity in face of disaster is not one of the special French virtues. Six years after the fall of Pondicherry (1761) a barbarous crowd gathered in the Place de la Grève to enjoy the last agonies of this passionate son of Erin as, under the clumsy axe of the Paris executioner, he expiated a pro-consul's failure. To Clive a grateful but not uncensorious country awarded a medal, a statue, and an Irish peerage.

When the war was at last brought to an end by the Peace of Paris in 1763 the terms, though less favourable than Pitt would have had them, secured acquisitions of territory for England and her colonies on such a scale as to change the current of her history. Save for the few factories which she held in January, 1749, France was evicted from India. Canada and Senegal passed to England. Minorca was restored. Florida was surrendered by Spain. The constellation of the English West Indies was enriched by the addition of St. Vincent, Tobago, Dominica, and the Grenadines. Even though the French were allowed to retain fishing rights off Newfoundland and in the St. Lawrence, and received back some valuable West Indian islands, it was from the English standpoint a great peace. A contemporary not unjustly described it as "the most honourable peace this nation ever saw."

A vast increase of commercial prosperity enabled England to bear without distress the burden of a long and costly war, at the conclusion of which, as Adam Smith afterwards pointed out, "her agriculture was as flourishing, her manufactures as numerous, and her commerce as extensive as they had ever been before." Far otherwise was the position of England's ally on the continent. "Prussia's population," writes Frederick, "had diminished by 500,000 during the Seven Year's War. On a population of 4,500,000 that decrease was considerable. The nobility and the peasants had been pillaged and ransomed by so many armies that they had nothing left except the miserable rags which covered their nudity. They had not credit enough to satisfy their daily needs. The towns possessed no longer a police. The spirit of fairness and order had been replaced by anarchy and self interest. The judges and the revenue authorities had given up their work owing to the frequency of invasions. In the absence of laws a spirit of recklessness and of rapacity arose. The nobility and the merchants, the farmers, the working men and the manufacturers had raised the price of their labour and products to the utmost. All seemed intent upon ruining each other by their exactions. That was the terrible spectacle which the formerly so flourishing provinces offered after the conclusion of the war. The appearance of the provinces resembled that of Brandenburg after the end of the Thirty Years' War." Forged in such a flame of adversity, the Prussian will took on the hardness of steel, and by the gentler courts of Germany, where the arts flourished, was regarded as something minatory and barbaric.

Compared with the terrible cost of Silesia, the English sacrifices in the Seven Years' War seem to Germans to be a supreme illustration of the harsh inequality of fate. Twenty Europeans only fell on the field of Plassey, one hundred and ninety-four at Wandewash. The cost of the conquest of Canada, according to Pitt, did not exceed one thousand five hundred lives. The blood price exacted from England for two great empires was multiplied five times and more in many of the major actions in Frederick's campaign. But if the initial cost, measured in lives, was low, plenty of trouble was yet to come. Before many years had passed there broke out on American soil that formidable conflict between the Mother Country and her colonists which led to the foundation of the United States of America.

BOOKS WHICH MAY BE CONSULTED

T. Carlyle: *Life of Frederick II of Prussia*. 1858-65.

B. Williams: *The Life of William Pitt, Earl of Chatham*. 1914.

J. R. Seely: *The Expansion of England*. 1885.

A. duc de Broglie: *Frédéric II et Marie-Thérèse*. 2 vols. 1883.

A. G. Bradley: *The Fight with France for North America*. 1900.

A. C. Lyall: *Warren Hastings*. 1889.

A. C. Lyall: *The Rise and Expansion of the British Dominion in India*. 1907.

Macaulay's Essays (Clive, Warren Hastings, Chatham). 1852.

L. B. Namier: *The Structure of Politics at the Accession of George III*. 2 vols. 1929.

J. S. Corbett: *England in the Seven Years' War*. 1907.
F. L. Carsten: *The Origins of Prussia*. 1954.
W. L. Dorn: *Competition for Empire, 1740-63*. 1940.
W. C. B. Tunstall: *William Pitt, Earl of Chatham*. 1938.
K. Feiling: *Warren Hastings*. 1954.

CHAPTER LXIII

THE WAR OF AMERICAN INDEPENDENCE

The consequence of the conquest of Canada. The English colonies in North America. Trade restrictions. Direct taxation. The obstinacy of King George. The Boston tea-party and the Philadelphia Congress. The misconduct of the British forces in America. George Washington. The entry of France and Spain. The peril of England. Illusions produced by her defeat.

PROMINENT among the causes of the War of American Independence were those very British victories which had been so lightly purchased. The expulsion of the French from Canada, and of the Spanish from Florida, by relieving the English colonists of two dangerous neighbours, weakened their dependence on the mother country. Having less need of English help, the colonists were the more ready to challenge English pretensions. Many had willingly borne arms in the great French War. Few were willing to take a share in liquidating its financial liabilities. When George Grenville 1765 proposed a stamp tax to defray part of the cost of an army for the protection of the colonies, motives niggardly and narrow were combined with others which belonged to the best political inheritance of the Anglo-Saxon race to frustrate the imposition.

Of all the European settlements in the new world, the thirteen English colonies in North America enjoyed the largest measure of liberty. Though they were subject to the British crown and Parliament, they were in effect allowed to manage their own affairs with little interference from Westminster, save in one particular. Imperial trade was subject to regulation conceived to be in the mutual interest of the mother country and its colonial daughters. "Economic planning" on the grand scale is never likely to be successful over a tract of time, and the old English colonial system furnishes a good example of the friction which may be generated by a well-meant endeavour to regulate the commercial and industrial life of scattered communities from a distant centre. The colonies were forbidden to start factories which might compete with the industries of the mother country. They were compelled to ship their exports in British or colonial vessels manned to the extent of two-thirds by British or colonial crews, and in respect of a long list of enumerated articles, including many of their staple products, were constrained to discharge their cargoes in English ports. On the other hand, Englishmen were forbidden to smoke tobacco grown elsewhere than in America or Bermuda, and bounties were paid to the lumbermen of New England to encourage the industry in naval stores.

At the stage of economic development which had been reached by the English colonies at the beginning of George 1760 III's reign these regulations were not felt to be seriously burdensome. The time was not yet ripe for colonial factory development, and so long as the colonists were prepared to allow the mother country to provide them with manufactured goods it was no hardship to ship raw produce to English ports and to obtain in exchange the products of English factories.

There was, however, one restriction which caused the greatest irritation. If the piety of New England was founded on the Bible, its prosperity was not a little dependent on rum. The Molasses Act of 1733, by virtually prohibiting the importation of French-grown sugar, molasses, and rum, in the interests of the British plantations, struck a blow at the New England distilleries which, but for the enormous success of colonial smuggling, might have been sufficient in itself to produce a rupture. It is a singular reflection that had it not been for the activity of the bootleggers of the eighteenth century the primary impulsion which led to the foundation of the American republic might have been a restriction imposed by the port-drinking legislators at Westminster on the American trade in rum with the native Indians.

The rift came over direct taxation. The English have always quarrelled over money, and the English colonists in America (for the Irish element was then negligible) who resisted Grenville's stamp tax were faithful to the habits of their ancestors. On the old familiar fighting-ground "No taxation without representation" they protested against an impost which, though small in itself, was large in relation to their parsimonious budgets. It was an English issue dividing men of English race on either side of the Atlantic. America had its Tories or loyalists, England its Americans or Whigs. The three greatest British statesmen of the time, Chatham, Burke, and Fox, were opposed to the coercion of the colonies, and in their opinion supported by a substantial section of the British middle class. So domestic was the complexion of the quarrel in its early stages that officers of the king's army and navy could, without social stigma, resign their commissions rather than bear arms against their kith and kin across the ocean.

American historians now recognize that there was more substance in the English case than their predecessors had been generally willing to allow. The future of North America was not yet secure. There was always danger from the Indians. There might, given European complications, be a renewed attack from France and Spain. A colonial defence force, somehow provided, seemed to be a reasonable insurance against incalculable risks. Such a course the colonies out of mutual jealousies had hitherto been unable to finance, and there was no reason to think that an attempt which had failed in 1754, when the French danger was at its height, would succeed ten years later when the French had been decisively driven from the field. Was it, then, outrageous that the British Parliament in the exercise of its sovereign rights should impose a tax upon the colonists to be spent in the colonies upon an army exclusively designed for colonial defence?

The easy-going, pleasure-loving legislators of the British upper class, suddenly confronted with the strange problem of governing distant empires, were ill qualified to understand the rough democracy which across the Atlantic waste still cherished with fervour the ideals of the Cromwellian age. Even more serious, seeing that he had made himself master of Cabinet and Parliament, was the incomprehension of the king. In view of the violent outcry occasioned by Grenville's taxes, the most ordinary prudence counselled their abandonment and the surrender of any prospect of supplies from the colonies other than those which might be freely voted by the colonial assemblies. To George III, however, there was only one way to deal with mutinous colonists, the way of force. He would make no concession on the point of principle. The withdrawal of the stamp tax in 1765 was flanked by a parliamentary declaration that Britain had full right to tax her colonies, and a number of trifling duties on glass, lead, paper, and tea imposed (1767) by Charles Townshend, more for the purpose of illustrating a principle than of bringing in a substantial revenue, fanned the flame of colonial discontent to fever height. Even when it was clearly shown that the new taxes cost far more to collect than they were worth and were fast driving Massachusetts to rebellion, the king declined to surrender the point of dogma. By a majority of one vote the Cabinet of Lord North, while abandoning the other Townshend taxes, decided to retain the duty upon tea. It would be difficult to conceive an act of greater folly. At the utmost the duty was estimated to yield £16,000 a year; and the ministry, in order to conciliate public opinion, had expressly declared (May, 1769) that they did not propose to levy any further taxes upon America for the purpose of raising a revenue. The reply of the Americans was a war signal. On December 16, 1773, a body of men disguised as Mohawk Indians boarded three ships in Boston harbour and threw their whole cargo of tea into the water. The British Cabinet retaliated by closing the port of Boston, by remodelling the Charter of Massachusetts, and by an act enabling prisoners indicted on capital charges in that state to be sent for trial, should it appear that they could not be fairly tried in the province, to some other colony or to Great Britain.

The colonies rallied round Massachusetts in its resistance to these punitive measures. A solemn League and Covenant was formed binding the subscribers to abstain from commercial intercourse with Great Britain until their hated orders had been repealed. On September 5, 1774, delegates of twelve States met in Congress in Philadelphia to concert measures of resistance against the British Crown. Each side speculated upon the weakness and division of the other.

The British conduct of the war was no less unfortunate than the policy which had made war inevitable. There was in the colonies an important body of opinion actively favourable to the maintenance of the British connection, while an even greater number of colonists were indifferent or uncertain. To conciliate these friendly or wavering colonial minds, to respect the property of every friendly American, and wherever possible to enlist the help of American loyalists in the tasks of civil government should have been a prime object of British policy. Nothing of the kind was done. While the Indians, whose support had most unhappily been invoked by the British, alienated every frontiersman with their excesses, the army of Lord Howe, largely composed of Hessians and Hanoverians, pillaged indifferently the houses of friend and foe. It is a sufficient commentary upon their deplorable conduct that during the whole course of the war no more than 2,500 loyalist volunteers were enlisted in the British ranks.

Nevertheless, had not France and Spain entered the lists on the American side, the colonists might have lost the war. Even the genius of George Washington, by far the greatest man on either side, was unable to protect the American revolution from a series of crushing defeats. Long Island, Trenton, Brandywine were black days in the military annals of the "Sons of Liberty." There is nothing wonderful here. The American state was in the making. In Philadelphia, the capital of the young federation, where everything was raw and experimental, and state sense, state loyalty, and state cohesion had still to be created, the civilians could give no lessons to the soldiers. It was Washington, and he alone, who in the camp of Valley Forge, amid the dire hardships of a bitter winter, brought back a severely shaken and ill-provisioned army to a sense of disciplined efficiency and once more made of it an instrument of victory. So little was the revolution the work of a convinced and united people that at no time in the war did the army of Washington exceed twenty thousand men.

On October 17, 1777, an English army under General Burgoyne, advancing southwards on New York, was forced to capitulate at Saratoga. Stirred by this thunderclap, which sounded round the world, monarchical France, in a wild mood of jealousy, revenge, and enthusiasm, entered on a war for the establishment of an American republic.

For Louis XVI and Marie Antoinette no policy could have been more improvident, for not only did the American war give the final push to the tottering edifice of French finance, but the spectacle of republicanism triumphant and monarchy overthrown beyond the Atlantic kindled in every forward-reaching mind in France the vision of a Europe remade after the new American pattern of republican liberty. The fact that the emancipation of the American colonies was effected with the help of France and Spain made an enormous difference to the sentiment with which the struggle was regarded on either side of the Atlantic. The American war ceased to be a domestic and became an international quarrel. The colonists had appealed to the foreign enemies of England and secured their help. The colonial revolt, originally regarded as a small domestic quarrel, had widened out into a formidable coalition which taxed the resources of Great Britain in every quarter of the globe. As if the hostility of the Bourbon monarchies was not enough, the Dutch joined in against their old commercial rivals, and a league of neutral northern powers, headed by Catharine of Russia, menaced interference with the British Navy if it continued to molest neutral trade at sea. Great Britain had never been more isolated or in greater peril. If she was compelled to fight the Dutch on the Coromandel coast, in Ceylon, and in Sumatra, if Hyder Ali deluged the Carnatic in blood, if eight West Indian islands were lost owing to the greatly increased efficiency of the French Navy, if Minorca and Florida were wrested from her, the prime cause was the obstinacy of her own colonial children. Chatham was not the only British friend of the American cause who, when the aid of foreign powers was invoked by the insurgents, felt with a passionate intensity that henceforth there could be no word of surrender.

War is the parent of illusions. The French idealized without understanding the liberty and equality of a slave-owning republic. The Americans regarded the French, from whom they were widely separated in all fundamental points of character and temperament, as paladins of chivalry nearer to them and more congenial than the cross-grained English from whom the colonists had derived their race, their language, their literature, and their constitution. Another illusion was fraught with graver consequences. The defeat of England in the colonial war engendered a general belief that the history of the English was wound up. The Parliament of Westminster was compared to the Diet of Warsaw, the factions of English political life to the ruinous dissensions of the Poles.

That England's sun had set was the firm belief of rulers so powerful and intelligent as Frederick of Prussia, Catharine of Russia, and Joseph of Austria. The prestige of England, which stood so high in 1763, was depressed beyond all due reason by the capitulation of Yorktown eighteen years later. It has always been found difficult to take Britain's measure.

Proceeding upon a gross under-estimate of its adversary's power, revolutionary France, as Imperialist Germany in our own time, was destined to receive a serious shock.

From a purely political point of view there seemed much to justify this unfavourable estimate. There was nothing glorious or even moderately skilful about the English government (1770-1782) which lost the American colonies. Lord North, the Prime Minister, did not believe in the war, but allowed his will to be directed by the king. The Cabinet system was broken down. The Whig party was in decomposition. The fitful star of Chatham finally sank below the waters in 1778; the clear effulgence of his son's cold and powerful intellect had not yet risen above the horizon. The war was ill managed, unpopular, unsuccessful. Only the brilliant opposition speeches of Charles Fox kept alive a flame of political imagination in Westminster. Increasingly the country was becoming restless under a system which permitted so much corruption, so much incompetence, and so many failures. There was a cry for the political emancipation of the industrial towns; alternatively for a restriction of the king's power to corrupt Parliament. But when at last in 1782 the Whigs came into Jan., power once more and in the following year made the Peace of 1783 Versailles with America, recognizing the independence of the American republic, the continent merely saw that an empire had been lost. It did not perceive that a constitution had been saved. Yet such was the case. The failure of the king's

American policy involved the breakdown of the last effectual experiment in personal rule which has been tried in Britain.

A yet greater thing passed unnoticed. The defeated country was fast becoming through a series of unprecedented economic changes the workshop of the world and the principal centre of its finance.

BOOKS WHICH MAY BE CONSULTED

W. E. H. Lecky: *History of England in the Eighteenth Century.* 8 vols. 1878-90.

James Truslow Adams: *The Founding of New England.* 1921.

G. B. Hertz: *The Old Colonial System.* 1905.

G. L. Beer: *Commercial Policy of England towards the American Colonies.* 1893.

J. L. Hammond: *Charles James Fox.* 1903.

Sir George Trevelyan: *The American Revolution.* 1905.

S. E. Morison: *The Oxford History of the United States, 1783-1917.* 2 vols. 1927.

Cambridge Modern History, Vol. VII.

E. B. Greene: *The Revolutionary Generation, 1763-1790.* 1943.

B. Lancaster and J. H. Plumb: *The Revolution.* 1958.

L. H. Gipson: *The Coming of the Revolution, 1763-75.* 1954.

J. C. Miller: *Origins of the American Revolution.* 1945.

CHAPTER LXIV

ENGLAND BECOMES
THE WORKSHOP OF THE WORLD

*The foundation of English commercial credit. The Bank o,
England and the National Debt. Consequences for the Protestant succession and the growth of industry. Sea-borne timber
and sea-borne coal. England becomes the workshop of the
world. The bounty of Nature. The neglect of government.
The Puritan spirit. The inventors. The improvement of communications. The new age of capitalism. The shadow side.
The catastrophe of the French wars. Neglect of home conditions. Adam Smith and Karl Marx.*

1697 AMONG the consequences of the English wars against Louis
XIV were the establishment of the Bank of England and of
the English National Debt, innovations bitterly contested at
the time, but so far-reaching in their civilizing effects that
without them a comparatively poor agricultural island could
never, despite the brilliance of its mechanical inventions or
the wealth of its mineral resources, have developed into the
workshop of Europe and the principal loan market in the
world. The sound system of bank credit laid down in the
reign of William III enabled the economic consequences of
the steam engine and the spinning jenny to be exploited to
the full. Had the mechanism of finance in England been
defective, as it was in France, this could never have happened.
The engines of the Industrial Revolution, which made England so rich and powerful that she was able to stand the
strain of the Napoleonic wars, were moved by the oil of
finance; and at the heart of the English financial system stood
the Bank.

 Europe had long been familiar with banks and bankers.
To change money, to store money, to lend money, are
operations as old as the bazaars of Babylon and Egypt. The
money changers of Greece and Rome, the Jewish usurers, who
emerged after the barbaric invasions, the bank of Genoa,

which financed the Crusades, the Lombards, who have given a name to a famous English street, the Medicis of Florence, who raised revenue for the Papacy, the Fuggers of Augsburg, who sustained the empire of Charles V, the goldsmiths of London, who stored the wealth of its merchants and made advances to Charles II, all these agencies in different degrees performed some of the functions of a modern bank, eased the operations of commerce, and promoted the accumulation of wealth. It was only, however, with the foundation of the Bank of Amsterdam in 1609 that the mechanism of commerce and finance began to assume its modern shape. In this populous and thriving city stocks and shares were bought and sold, "bulled" and "beared," currencies were exchanged, loans were made to governments, and a growing volume of commerce was passed through a machine which enabled it to be conveniently and expeditiously dealt with. Such an example could not fail to impress the people with whom the Dutch were brought into the closest economic relations. London beheld the strange spectacle of a small neighbouring country finding the means of financing navies, armies, and great commercial enterprises out of all proportion to its exiguous area and population. Sir William Temple, one of the wisest statesmen of Charles II's reign, realized the strength which Holland derived from a National Debt and a National Bank, and wished England to follow the Dutch example. The system had merits of incontestable value. It provided a safe investment for the savings of the ordinary citizen, and was therefore an incitement to private thrift. It enabled nations to raise money more easily, and consequently to sustain the burden of large undertakings. It furnished commerce with capital contributed by individuals who were not merchants. For a régime of financial caprice it substituted one of financial regularity. Before the introduction of banking and long term loans to the state, the governments of Europe were in continual default. Elizabeth, indeed, most parsimonious of queens, had furnished a rare and solitary example of solvency to her generation; but the Dutch, though large spenders, were solvent throughout the whole of the seventeenth century, because they had adopted a sound method of financing state expenditure.

The example of the Dutch was reinforced by the pressure of

a disordered currency and an expensive war. The idea of a state bank, which had been pressed upon the government by William Patterson, a brilliant and imaginative Scot who had made his fortune in London, was carried out in 1694 by Charles Montagu, Earl of Halifax. Since a loan was required to finance the war, a corporation known as the Governor and Company of the Bank of England was formed to raise it, and guaranteed upon the security of the taxes an interest at eight per cent. Despite strong opposition, the Whig Bill for a Bank of England received the assent of Parliament; but so little were the doubts of politicians shared by the City of London that within ten days after the books were open, the whole amount of the loan (£1,200,000) was subscribed. Without it the British navy could not have gone to sea.

To the Tory squires the new system of Whig finance appeared to be an odious design levelled against the landed interest and certain to bring ruin on the country. But the Bank was too strong for its enemies. It survived the attacks of the goldsmiths and the competition of a land bank, which had been specially set up to bring it to the ground. It received the privilege of issuing notes (1697) and was then given a monopoly till 1810. Among the causes which promoted the Protestant succession, none was more powerful than the general belief that the Jacobites, were they restored to the throne, would repudiate the National Debt, which had made possible the victories of Marlborough. The first step on the road to the Industrial Revolution, which has spread the factory system over the world, and so multiplied its wealth and population, was taken when English credit was put upon a modern basis.

The forest-haunted music of Germany recalls to us an age when the material civilization of northern and central Europe depended almost entirely upon its woodlands. For more than two thousand years men lived for the most part in wooden houses, sailed in wooden ships, warmed themselves at log fires, and drew from the forest the materials out of which were fashioned the common utensils of domestic use as well as the instruments of agriculture and industry. Long after the Italians had shown the way in stone, brick, and marble, and the art of brickmaking so well known to ancient Rome had been rediscovered by the contemporaries of Caxton, the principal cities of northern Europe continued to be built largely of wood. It was a wooden London which went up in flames when Charles II was king, a wooden Moscow which burned itself to a cinder under the eyes of Napoleon. So persistent was the rural tradition that even the first steam engine was encased in a carriage of wood, as the first power loom was worked by a bull.

The problem of preserving forest timber had ever since the fifteenth century been a matter of intermittent concern, as trees were felled in abnormal numbers to meet some exceptional need, such as the mining of silver, or the manufacture of porcelain or glass. But to the maritime states of the west, as they developed in the seventeenth century, the timber supply was no mere local convenience, but a primary requisite of national power. After a million oaks had been felled to build the navy of the Commonwealth, John Evelyn, the most charming of humanists, asked in his *Sylva*, the most delightful of books, how soon by a scientific system of plantation the marine future of England was to be preserved. It is a tempting conjecture that the navy of Nelson was built out of timber which owed its existence to the providence of this engaging Surrey squire. But England in a matter so vital was not content to rely upon its home supplies. The virgin forests of Massachusetts were called in to save the antique glades of Windsor, of Hatfield, and of Selwood. In this, as in other directions, the new world was called in to supply the deficiencies of the old.

Meanwhile another source of fuel, known far back in the middle ages, had become a commercial proposition. In the seventeenth century, coal shipped from Newcastle came into general use in London. It was important for the new era of European history which was now to develop that the most forward maritime and commercial nation should have recently rebuilt its capital in stone and brick, should have founded a state bank of issue and deposit, and should by its free use of coal have given a far-reaching advertisement to the source of power which was about to transform the economic structure of the world.

Earlier by more than half a century than any other country in Europe, England assumed the character of a modern high farming industrial state. She ceased to be a land of peasant husbandry and small domestic industries, and of roads so bad that even on horseback, the sole sure means of conveyance, the journey from York to London occupied a week. The wasteful system of mediaeval tillage with its scattered holdings in the open fields increasingly gave way to the enclosures of improving landlords, practising with the novel aid of roots and grasses a scientific rotation of crops, which increased the food supply, and consequently the population. First water power, then steam power, transformed the conditions of economic life. The iron industry, which in Queen Anne's reign was faced with the imminent danger of a fuel famine, found in the rich coal measures of the midlands and north an unexpected impetus to vast developments. Wood gave place to steel, charcoal burners to pitmen. The age of fairs and travelling pedlars was succeeded by the development of a busy retail trade carried out all over the country in village and town shops. In half a century (1760 to 1821) the population of England rose from six and three-quarter millions to twelve millions. Such a scene as Britain presented after four generations of invention and activity had never yet been witnessed, a scene of communications rendered swift beyond the wildest dreams, of factories crowded with ingenious labour-saving machinery and polluting the pure air with their smoke, of industries which drew their raw material from one hemisphere and sent their finished goods to another, of huge and hideous towns, hastily constructed, and of a population whose lives from early childhood were ruled by the sound of the factory bell and constrained to a bleak and exhausting discipline of toil.

The causes which made Britain the pioneer of industrial capitalism were in part due to the bounty of nature. The climate was moist and therefore suited to the cotton industry. Of water power there was no lack in the northern and north-western regions of England. Most important of all there was abundance of coal and iron juxtaposed and convenient for transport by water. The coalfields of Britain were larger than any which had been opened out in France and Germany and closer to important harbours. On the basis of iron, coal, and textiles, Britain built up a type of civilization which has been copied all round the world.

That these natural opportunities were so fully utilized was due not to any high standard of popular education, but to an atmosphere peculiarly favourable to industrial invention and to the swift and ready exploitation of its results. The governing aristocracy of England, unlike the French nobility, was interested in commerce. Wanting money for the luxuries which money could command, the Whig lords were not the men to despise a fortune obtained through a factory or a mine or an Indian investment. Moreover, having successfully curbed the powers of the crown, they had no disposition to see an autocratic government revived in another form. The English parliaments of the eighteenth century may be criticized for doing too little; they can hardly be attacked for doing too much. To the self-sufficient, acquisitive spirit of a money-loving population they offered no obstacle which can be accounted serious.

In such an atmosphere of relative freedom—and it may be noted that Britain after the Scottish Union was the largest free trade area in Europe—the descendants of the Puritans came into their own. Excluded from an active concern with politics until 1828 the Nonconformists applied a grave and intrepid energy to the pursuit of opulence. Labour they regarded as a sacrament, pleasure as a sin, the making of wealth a sign that their service was acceptable to the Lord. Entering with a rugged determination into almost every form of industrial and commercial enterprise, but specially attracted to iron, they had a large share in the making of a new England, less tranquil and lovely, but richer, more powerful, and vastly more crowded than the old.

These changes, however, would have been impossible but for the inventions. A small handful of remarkable Scots and Englishmen, fewer than would be required for a football match, succeeded by their ingenuity in transforming the economic life of the country. No doubt they derived support and inspiration from the atmosphere of their age. Science had been spreading its influence ever since Francis Bacon preached the value of the Inductive Method, and some of the inventors, notably James Watt, who first gave a decisive 1736-industrial value to the steam engine, were men of science. 1819 Yet more important probably than actual scientific training was the idea, which the Royal Society had so powerfully helped to spread, that knowledge was a growing thing, and that by observation and experiment new truths could be brought to light. Once aroused, the spirit of curiosity was inevitably turned upon the principal preoccupation of the British people. This was no longer, as in the Puritan age, religion, but the pursuit of wealth through industry and commerce.

Some of the great inventors were poor operatives without science or education, but guided by a mechanical tact in relation to the appliances of their own industry which amounted to genius. Such were Kay of Bury, who in 1733 by his invention of the flying shuttle more than doubled the work which the weaver could perform, besides improving its quality, and James Hargreaves, whose spinning jenny (1754) multiplied eightfold and more the productive power of the weaver. Such, too, was Richard Arkwright of Preston (1732-92), inventor of the spinning frame, founder of the English cotton industry, and parent of the factory system. Few Englishmen have exercised a more profound influence on civilization than this vigorous Lancastrian, who, after being successively a barber's apprentice and a wigmaker, made a series of inventions for carding and spinning cotton which rendered large scale production possible, and in the factories which he set up to exploit his discovery, established that system of massed and disciplined labour which is characteristic of the capitalistic age.

Being dependent on water for their power, the early textile factories were erected by the side of waterfalls, generally on some high desolate moor far from the natural centres of population. In such spots it is still a common experience to come across the ruined shell of a gaunt high-chimneyed building, once the scene of busy activity, but long since deserted. The substitution of steam for water as the motive power in cotton mills rendered it profitable to concentrate factories in towns. Since power could now be generated wherever it was convenient, it was no longer necessary to transport workers to distant water. The village factory followed the cottage industry into the limbo of antiquities; the application of steam to machinery led straight to the factory town.

James Watt, the Greenock engineer, did not discover the

use of steam as a motive force, nor did he create the steam engine. It was in brooding on the defects of an engine already fifty-eight years old that this delicate, fretful, melancholy genius hit upon the secret of the separate condenser (1769), which enabled steam power to revolutionize industry. The Newcomen engine had been employed for pumping in mines; but at deep levels it was useless, and at all levels, through waste of heat and other causes, defective in power and uncertain in operation. Watt cured these defects by his device of a separate condenser. One brilliant thought gave to mankind the empire of the mines with all that followed from such a conquest, more power, more machinery, more light and warmth, a higher standard of comfort for a large population. A subsequent invention of the rotary motion, imitating the movement of the water wheel, brought the steam engine into the cotton factories. This was in 1781, the year of the British capitulation at Yorktown. All unnoticed, a new link more profitable than the broken skeins of imperial monopoly and preference was forged by the shy mechanical inventor between the United States and Britain. American cotton worked up in the mills of Lancashire went in the next century the round of the world.

These mechanical ideas were made effective only through the close association of the inventor with a great man of business, who had a faith in steam which no financial losses or anxieties could defeat. Without the help of Matthew Boulton, a hardware manufacturer of Birmingham, Watt's inventions might have been left to rest unused. Boulton, summoning Watt to his aid (1775), set himself to make steam engines for the market. He raised the capital, gathered the labour, erected the works, and eventually convinced the public. His sanguine energy and indomitable resource combined with the mechanical inventions of his sensitive friend accomplished in the space of a decade a revolution which in other circumstances might have taken a century. The first successful engine was turned out of the Soho works in 1776. Four years later forty engines were despatched to the Cornish mines. By 1789 steam had established itself as a dominating factor in most of the staple industries of England.

In the first half of the eighteenth century the great obstacle to industrial development in Britain was the state of the communications. While France possessed canals and roads which were the admiration of every traveller, the English roads, the supervision of which was confided to unpaid parish officers, were disgraceful, and English canals non-existent. So long as this state of things continued and many roads were impassable save in the summer months, while others, being too bad for carts or coaches, admitted only of packhorse traffic, no great industrial expansion was possible. But at last towards the middle of the century the British public began to take note of an evil which had been too long tolerated with an indulgent eye. Turnpike acts were passed under which improvements, substantial if unsystematic, were made. William Brindley, an illiterate genius, engineered the Bridgwater canal between Liverpool and Manchester; and then under the vigorous impulsion of three great engineers, Metcalfe, Telford, and Macadam, the long accumulated arrears were cleared away and the country was enriched by a system of roads, bridges, and canals, as good as any to be found in Europe. The age of packhorses receded into the past, the short-lived age of stage coaches began. "In the year 1770," writes Joseph Aston in his *History of Manchester* published in 1816, "there was only one stage coach to London and one to Liverpool, which went from Aston into Manchester, and these set out only twice a week. There are now seventy distinct coaches which run from hence, of which fifty-four set out every day, and sixteen others three times in the week, to their different places of destination. In the year 1754 a flying coach was advertised, and boasted that, 'however incredible it may appear, this coach will actually (barring accidents) arrive in London in four days and a half after leaving Manchester.' The mail coaches now constantly travel that distance in thirty hours, and on several occasions when Bonaparte was tottering to his ruin, and on the news of the terminating battle of Waterloo, the Traveller, the Defiance, and the Telegraph coaches came down in eighteen hours." That was the brief but golden age of English travel, immortalized in the pages of Pickwick, when the horse was in his glory and the traveller had time to relish the beauties of the country and the humours of the road. The coming of George Stephenson's railway (1829) closed that chapter in

English history, and opened an era of greater mobility, greater wealth, and greater restlessness for mankind.

By the close of the Napoleonic Wars the character of a capitalist society, such as has since become general, was already discernible in Britain. Capitalism in some form or other has existed since the dawn of history. What was distinctive of the new capitalism was that it was not, as in previous ages, mainly agricultural or mainly commercial, but to a predominant degree industrial. It involved a divorce between capital and labour over a wide sphere of economic work in which capital and labour had been generally combined. In the new factories which blackened the skies the operative had nothing but his labour to sell. The employing class bought labour, the working class sold it. For the old relations based on custom and sweetened by human sentiment there was now substituted the cash nexus between master and man.

1815

The evils proceeding from this rapid and soulless industrialization were not brought home to the conscience of the nation till the forties of the nineteenth century. The problems were new and such as a Parliament dominated by wealthy country squires was ill fitted to appreciate. What was going forward in Lancashire and the Black Country, the sweated labour of women and small children, the shameful housing, the neglect of all amenities, the disparity between wages and profits, the uncertainty and impermanence of employment, failed to attract the interest or to stir the sympathy of the legislators of Westminster. Even Burke, whose flaming imagination embraced the Indian and American scene, and the vast significance of the French revolution, had no eyes for the urgent domestic problems of the Industrial Revolution. As the law forbade trades unions, Labour was unorganized and dumb.

The long war with France, though it had no effect in arresting the expansion of British industry and trade, was from every other point of view an unmixed misfortune for Britain and the world. The problems of the new industrial society, which were sufficiently novel and important to tax the undivided powers of a laborious and intelligent government, were by reason of the war deprived of any examination which was not positively unhelpful. While the government of England was struggling for its life with revolutionary and Napoleonic France, and the governing class were stricken with the fear of revolutionary danger at home, it was vain to expect that the needs of the new unknown, half-barbarous industrial population which had been so swiftly multiplying itself under the strange conditions of the factory in the northern part of the island would be sympathetically considered. Even William Pitt, who at one moment showed a real flash of interest and comprehension, recoiled from the task of alleviating the lot of the wage-earning population. The mentality which in and out of Parliament sustained the existence of the Slave Trade till 1807 was one element in the mental atmosphere of that time. Fear of the revolution was another. Both were unfavourable to a prudent handling of the social problems of the Industrial Revolution.

Adam Smith, saluting the dawn of the new industrial age in the *Wealth of Nations* (1776), exults in the vast accretions of wealth rendered possible under a régime in which trade is free, machinery general, and labour minutely subdivided. In his classic treatise, which is the Bible of Free Trade, the sagacious Glasgow professor discerns the tremendous economic powers latent in the British people which a system of liberty would release. The sober confidence of the Scottish economist was justified in the event. Free Trade paid: industrialism was a source of accumulating material prosperity; by whatever tests national wealth may be measured, its progression all through the nineteenth century was unimpeded. But ninety-one years after the publication of his *Wealth of Nations*, when the British capitalistic system had reached maturity, and was fast spreading through Europe, Karl Marx, a German Jew, resident in London, applied his critical intelligence to the examination of its result. Where Smith had seen only the sunlight, Marx saw only the shadows thrown upon the human scene by the unimpeded exercise of individual liberty, a subdivision of labour so minute as to stunt the intelligence and empty life of the craftsman's joy, an ever-widening gulf between wealth and poverty, a loss of stability and permanence which was characteristic of the older forms of society, and the relentless exploitation of the proletariat by their employers. The picture was overdrawn and in some important respects untrue to fact; but attention

1818-
83

was directed to serious and undoubted blemishes, which,
if they did not justify revolution, called imperiously for
reform.

BOOKS WHICH MAY BE CONSULTED

P. Mantoux: *La Révolution industrielle au XVIIIème Siècle.*
Tr. M. Vernon. 1928. (Excellent bibliography.)

J. Aston: *A Picture of Manchester, 1804.* 1826.

Edward Baines: *History of the Cotton Manufacture in Great
Britain.* 1835.

R. N. Boyd: *Coal Pits and Firemen: A short History of the Coal
Trade and the Legislation affecting it.* 1892.

R. E. Prothero: *The Pioneers and Progress of English Farming.* 1888.

R. H. Thurston: *A Century's Progress of the Steam Engine.* 1901.

S. Smiles: *The Lives of the Engineers.* 5 vols. 1874.

C. Beard: *The Industrial Revolution.* 1901.

J. L. and B. Hammond: *The Town Labourer.* 1917.

J. L. and B. Hammond: *The Skilled Labourer.* 1919.

J. A. Hobson: *The Evolution of Modern Capitalism.* 1894.

A. Toynbee: *Lectures on the Industrial Revolution of the Eighteenth
Century in England.* Ed. Lord Milner. 1908.

T. S. Ashton: *The Industrial Revolution.* 1948.

T. S. Ashton: *An Economic History of England: the 18th Century.*
1955.

CHAPTER LXV

STRANDS OF HISTORY

Liberty. Socialism. Industrialism. Nationalism. Revolution. War.

IT WAS important for the coming age that in an empty continent offering boundless opportunities for innovation and enterprise a new gospel of liberty and equality had been proclaimed as the slogan of a triumphant republic. The American declaration of rights gave the cue to every friend of liberty in the old world. What the Americans had made themselves by revolution the Europeans might become by a similar exercise of daring. The spirit of liberty took many forms, constitutional with Mirabeau, revolutionary with Danton, romantic with Schiller, Shelley, and Lamartine, prophetic with Mazzini, intellectual with Condorcet and J. S. Mill, practical with Cobden and Cavour, militant and adventurous with Cochrane and Garibaldi; but once aroused it embarked upon a contest which is still unconcluded. Surviving the crimes of the French Revolution and the terror of Napoleon, it succeeded by the end of the nineteenth century in founding parliamentary institutions in every important European country with the exception of Russia.

Like the Alexandrian age, the times which have now to be surveyed witnessed an immense increase in the scope, velocity, and complexity of events. In less than a hundred and fifty years the population of Europe grew by more than three hundred and fifty millions, and that of the United States by more than a hundred and thirty millions.[1] Cities became larger, governments became more powerful. Armies and navies, budgets and businesses, public revenues and private fortunes rose to a scale never hitherto imagined. New modes of transport enabled huge bodies of armed men to be con-

---

[1] The population of Europe has been estimated by Dr. R. R. Kurzynski at 100 millions in 1600, at 152½ millions in 1700, at 173 millions in 1789, and at 525 millions in 1934.

veyed hundreds of miles from their homes and to be pro-
visioned with regularity for years together. New methods of
communication annihilated distance, new methods of propaganda schooled opinion. The information at the disposal of
governments was brought to an extraordinary pitch of completeness. In a single day more business would pass through
a Prime Minister's house than would have been concentrated
for his handling during a year in the time of George III.

The immense increase in the population of Europe was due
rather to man's increasing power over nature than to any
surprising advance in the arts of government. Not that the
age which we are about to survey was barren of political
ideas or happy improvements. The definition, elaborated by 1772-
Ricardo, of rent as a surplus due not to labour or capital but 1823
to the original and indestructible powers of the soil directed
attention to unearned increment in all its forms and supplied
to socialism one of its strongest theoretical arguments. The
discovery that trade prospered best when freed from fiscal
fetters, and the complementary principle that in a world
governed by competition labour must be defended against
capitalist exploitation, led by two distinct and differing paths
to a society in which material enjoyments were alike vastly
more numerous and better distributed than ever before. Yet
the problem of poverty was not solved. Every workman had
a pistol pointed at his heart. A change of fashion, the bankruptcy of an employer, the failure of a distant harvest, the
crash of a bank, the fraud or improvidence of a group of
speculators, might throw him out of employment and reduce
his family to want.

The problem of bringing happiness to the swiftly expanding
democracy of hired town workers who begin in this period to
constitute the main part of European society was far too vast
and complex to be solved quietly or by any single body of
statesmen. The alleviations which in course of time were
provided by factory acts and the regulation of mines, by
trades unions and co-operative stores, by state insurance and
state pensions, by the public education of the young and the
public assistance of the old, were only gradually discovered
and partially applied. The "condition of the people question,"
though always of the first importance, was never steadily and
continuously kept in the forefront of political attention.

Other causes or diversions, more melodramatic and attractive, such as the rivalry of nations, the thirst for empire, the appetite for markets, were apt to ensnare the attention of statesmen or inflame the passion of mobs. The history of Europe, then, cannot be narrated strictly as the sequence of those multitudinous and almost insensible changes which transformed a society in which mill-owners and landowners were predominant into one in which a town clerk, a borough engineer, a medical officer of health, or a schoolmaster may make all the difference to the happiness of a community. It would be too great a simplification of issues to regard the European story as nothing but a struggle of classes, a clash of economic interests. That would be to underrate the rich and varied stuff of human nature, the distractions of statesmen and the waywardness of events. In actual life even the most important social problems which press upon a generation are never removed into a laboratory, and after dispassionate examination there and then thoroughly and scientifically solved. The real nature of social ailments may for many years on end be completely ignored. We may search the memoirs of Guizot, one of the greatest Frenchmen of the nineteenth century, without finding evidence that he was aware of the soul of the underworld and of its many troubles.

1787-
1874

Europe then, when confronted with the facts of the industrial revolution in England, did not say to itself, "The strange new things which are happening in England will in due course of time happen on the continent also. Here too factory towns will rise and belch their smoke into the air. Here too the labour of children will be exploited for gain, and nevertheless more and more children will be born into the world to be housed, fed, educated, employed, and governed. Everywhere before many decades are passed English conditions will be repeated. Everywhere society will be transformed by mechanism and capital, and everywhere governments, if they are to survive, will be compelled to make provision for a new population, owning no capital, uprooted from the stable economic conditions and ancient pieties of village life, without standards, without traditions, without loyalties, the flotsam and jetsam of rude and jostling competition. We are entering in fact upon an industrial age. We must forestall its dangers, anticipate its needs, guide its course." Europe said nothing of the kind. So far from attending to the faint signals of the coming industrial democracy which were already visible in the sky, it plunged into the wars of the French Revolution and the Empire.

CHAPTER LXVI

REVOLUTION IN FRANCE

Strength and weakness of France. Privilege. The food supply. The King's opportunity. The Deficit. The Estates General. The aspirations of France in 1789. Versailles and Paris. The first emigration. The fall of the ancien régime. *The Proletariat and the Clubs. Mirabeau. The Constitution of 1791. The revolution and the Church. The revolution and private property. Gains of the peasantry. Varennes. End of the Constituent Assembly.*

VICTORIOUS in America and nearly three times as populous as Great Britain, her vanquished rival, with enormous agricultural resources, a flourishing textile industry, splendid roads and canals, and a foreign trade which had increased five hundred per cent. since the death of Louis XIV, France was nevertheless confronted by grave domestic problems. The evil which was immediately obvious was financial. She was threatened, or believed herself to be threatened, by an appalling bankruptcy. What was more fundamental was that she lacked social equality, equitable taxation, political freedom, and an efficient executive. Privilege, mediæval and unprofitable, pervaded every portion of the body politic, privilege of the church, of the nobility, of the provincial estates or assemblies, of the judicial corporations and trade guilds. Privilege polluted justice, deflected the main burden of taxation on to the shoulders of the poor, and denied the prizes of the army, the navy, the church, and the magistrature to the most intelligent middle class in Europe. Privilege was now indefensible and odious. The higher clergy in France, who paid no taxes, had fallen far in public esteem by reason of their wealth, their worldliness, and their vices. The nobles, who were for the most part non-resident, had ceased to discharge any social function. They took their rents and feudal dues, exacted *corvées* or labour services, and, having no duties to perform, were a burden on the community. Exceptions personal and local were naturally to be found. There were good, improving landlords among the nobility, and in certain districts, notably the Vendée, nobles, living on their estates, after the manner of English squires, retained the devotion of their dependants.

But absenteeism was the rule. Publicists even thought and wrote of the French nobles as descendants of the Franks, as Teutons quartered on an alien soil and exploiting a subject Celtic population.

The revolution came because the monarchy was unable to solve the question of privilege, was not strong enough, in a word, to overthrow the remains of feudalism which, in France as in most other continental countries, cumbered the ground. Another problem of an economic order baffled the governments of the *ancien régime*. The food supply of the people, not yet reinforced by the potato, was insecure. Despite all the agricultural wealth of France, and the brilliant luxury of her upper class, sections of the population were from time to time exposed to the horrors of starvation.

This was not due to forced industrial development. Though in comparison with the Germany of that day France was highly urbanized, and Paris had even as many as 750,000 inhabitants, the methods of industry, as also of agriculture, were still for the most part mediæval. The proletariat of the French Revolution was not composed of nomad and up-rooted factory hands, but of unorganized domestic workers and peasants. Such a society had no grievance against capital as such, or against ownership of land. What they wanted was bread, and bread, partly owing to archaic systems of cultivation and partly owing to internal customs duties, they were not able always to secure. The consequences were grave—chronic bread riots, and, in the large towns and many country regions, a mass of embittered destitution.

When Louis XVI mounted the French throne in 1774, the currents of European favour were running fresh and strong for enlightened despotism. Frederick of Prussia had set a fashion which others sought to follow. Even in Catholic Austria and Spain it was the experience that progress came from above, reaction from below, and that Kings and Queens were as liberal as their Diets were conservative. After the long and inglorious reign of Louis XV France was ready to welcome a new Charlemagne, who out of the plenitude of his wisdom would reform the state.

For such a rôle the young King was entirely unfitted. Louis had every private virtue, honesty, piety, amiability, good sense, but he could not govern. The clearness of mind, the decision of purpose, the sense of opportunity, the gift of steady application, which make the statesman, were denied him. Instead of directing events he drifted with the tide. Marie Antoinette, the Austrian, was of stronger metal, but 1755- to the public the unpopular symbol of an odious alliance, 93 and to statesmen the inspiration of all that was frivolous in the Court and obstructive of their frugal or innovating policies. Her beauty and charm brought no help. An enemy, she was too proud to conciliate or forgive. To the critics of Versailles she appeared to be the siren who was drawing the ship of state on to the rocks.

The best chance of forestalling revolution by reform was lost when the young King, in search of popularity, recalled the Parliaments and so raised up against the march of progress an obstinate barrier. An organized force will always defeat unorganized opinion. The better mind of France was with Turgot, the greatest of Louis' ministers, when he proposed to 1727- abolish the guilds and to free the corn trade: but the Parlia- 81 ment of Paris also was popular as the sole effective check on the Crown, and so when the King let Turgot go after thirteen months with nothing done but the memorable exhibition of frustrated reforms, there was no outcry, but a resigned conviction among thoughtful men that the promised reformation of France would not come from above, but must be sought elsewhere. Later the King summoned to his counsels 1739- the Genevan banker Necker, a Protestant and republican, 94 who hit the humour of the time by financing the American War on loans, but fell under a dark shade of unpopularity as soon as he began to set up provincial assemblies, to relieve the Intendants of their administrative duties. Necker was dismissed in 1781, and thereafter the problem of finance dominated all other domestic issues in France. How was the deficit to be filled? Measured in cash it was not so formidable a task as it appeared to be, for an additional tax of six or seven francs per head could have enabled the country to balance its budget. But in terms of political psychology the balancing of the budget was beset by tremendous difficulties, for it meant the acquiescence of the privileged classes in a proposal that they should pay their proportionate share. Minister after minister failed to secure from the nobles the one concession which could have averted the storm. Calonne, the most daring and intelligent of the series, who had the happy idea of summoning an Assembly of Notables in 1787, failed like all the others, and with the more resounding crash, since he attempted to tell the country something of the real truth. "France," he wrote, "is a kingdom composed of separate states and countries, with mixed administrations, the provinces of which know nothing of each other, where certain districts are completely free from burdens, the whole weight of which is borne by others, where the richest class is the most lightly taxed, where privilege has upset all equilibrium, where it is impossible to have any constant rule or common will; necessarily it is a most imperfect kingdom, very full of abuses, and in its present condition *impossible to govern*." All expedients had now been exhausted save one, which was pressed on the Government from every side. On August 8, 1788, in an atmosphere of extravagant fears, suspicions, and hopes, the King summoned the States-General for the following year, and recalled Necker, the oracle on money, to his old office of managing the finances of France.

No great reform had ever issued from this archaic body, in which clergy, nobles, and third estate had hitherto deliberated and voted apart. None such was now expected by Necker. What that financier hoped of the States-General was money wherewith to balance the budget and close the yawning gulf of the deficit. No plan for constitutional reform had been prepared in advance by the Government, nor any directions for the guidance of an inexperienced assembly of twelve hundred men. Though it had been settled (January 24) that the numbers of the Third Estate were to be equal to the nobles and clergy combined, the Government had not even decided the vital question whether the Orders were to sit together or apart. The immense movement of resolute and excited political opinion which was evoked by the summoning of the Assembly to Versailles was a phenomenon which Louis had not expected, and could not diagnose.

Yet constitutional reform in some shape or other was clearly inscribed in the *cahiers* or instructions which were drawn up in every quarter of France or circulated by eminent men during the critical period. The mind of France as revealed in these documents was not republican; but that taxes should not be levied without popular consent, and that the *taille* should be abolished, was, despite many divergent interests, a common aspiration. One *cahier*, widely circulated, and drafted by a brilliant young ecclesiastic, sketched a constitutional monarchy very much on the lines of that which was established in France after the fall of Napoleon. Its author was Talleyrand, Bishop of Autun, who was destined in 1814, after the turmoil of the revolutionary wars had subsided, to administer to France the very medicine which, wiser than many, he had in vain prescribed in his youth.

Once assembled at Versailles, the members of the Third Estate succumbed to the spell of crowd psychology. They had met together at a moment of vast excitement and measureless hope, and were resolved from the first to give France institutions which would be the envy and model of the world. Everything seemed possible to a generation which had seen in the first balloon an augury of the conquest of the air, and in Mesmerism a new and mysterious power over the operations of the human mind. Imbued with such a spirit, the members of the Third Estate were not disposed to tolerate the opposition of the privileged orders. They declared themselves to be the National Assembly (June 10), and at a famous meeting in the Tennis Court (June 20) swore that they would not separate until they had given a constitution to France.

The task was prodigious. The American Constitution was hammered out behind closed doors by a small body of highly competent men in the tranquil Quaker city of Philadelphia. The more numerous Assembly of Versailles carried on its deliberations in a country seething with anarchy and under the menacing pressure of the Paris mob. It was hard enough in any case wisely to reform the ancient structure of the French monarchy: but the task was rendered yet more formidable by the responsibility of governing France which events thrust upon the Assembly.

There was a camarilla at Court detesting concessions to the people, and passionate to curb the pretensions of the Assembly and the mounting disorders of the capital by a show of force. To them Louis so far yielded as to dismiss Necker, odious on a triple count as protestant, *parvenu*, and reformer, and to order the formation of a camp of regular troops near Versailles under the command of Broglie, a tried and famous veteran. For the moment Louis, who had himself volunteered reforms, was captured for the policy of the strong hand.

July 14, 1789

To this threat of reaction the democracy of Paris made the famous reply which France still celebrates as a national festival on July 14 of every year. The Bastille surrendered to a mob armed with the plunder of the Invalides, and probably financed by capitalists who saw in Necker the sole chance of financial recovery. There was little glory in an attack on a fortress whose guns were useless and obsolete, and much shame in the circumstances which preceded and followed its surrender: in the wild panic of the population of the capital, in the carnival of pillage, in the mutiny of some troops and the rowdiness of others, and in the brutal slaughter of a garrison which had surrendered on terms. But the capture and destruction of this ancient prison on the outskirts of Paris, though soiled by abominable crime, was a political masterpiece. All through Europe the fall of the Bastille was hailed as the end of secretive tyranny and arbitrary imprisonment, and as heralding the dawn of the age of freedom. Henceforward Paris steps into the forefront of history. Her Commune became a powerful government, her National Guard, in which many criminals were enlisted, the germ of a people's army, the grim brutality of her crowds a source of compelling terror in the dark days which were to come. The fall of the Bastille was a sharp advertisement to the Court that Paris did not intend the Constitution to fail, and that what Paris willed, France must accept. "This is a great revolt," said Louis, when he heard the news. "No, sir," replied the Duc de Liancourt, "it is a great revolution."

The eclipse of the monarchy was now complete. It could

neither protect its friends nor overthrow its enemies. The wretched King was compelled to every indignity, to countermand the troops, to dismiss his ministers, to recall Necker, to bless in public the taking of the Bastille, and to accept in public the new tricolor cockade, which had been devised as the flag of the enfranchised nation by Lafayette, the liberator of America and the elected commandant of the National Guard. But still Paris was uncertain of its prey. So long as the King was at large he might be dangerous, resume, it was thought, his old reactionary tricks, collect troops, defeat edicts, plot a flight. The feeling grew that he would be safer in Paris, where he would be watched by the Commune and hedged in by the National Guard. A young woman of great beauty and much eloquence, wife of Roland, a grave inspector of mines, preached this doctrine to a circle of ardent friends.

By this time the machinery of revolutionary agitation was well understood in the capital. There were funds and organizers, simpletons and fanatics, and a plentiful supply of ruffians when rough work had to be done. In the first week of October there was also a pretext for a *coup*. The King had summoned the Flanders regiment to Versailles, had refused a decree, was said to be meditating flight. The Royal Guards had trampled on the tricolor. The spectre of reaction, laid in July, was again rearing its sinister head. Such beliefs, coupled with a shortage of bread (October 5), were sufficient to set in motion the famous march on Versailles, begun by a band of hungry women crying out for bread, but followed by the National Guard under Lafayette, which in the days of October brought the King and Queen back to Paris and to the bleak imprisonment of the Tuileries.

One night in July after the fall of the Bastille, when anarchy was rife, and the houses of the nobles were going up in flames, Talleyrand came secretly to the Comte d'Artois, the King's younger brother, and urged that Louis should dissolve the Assembly and restore order by force of arms. Out of humanity the King declined, and d'Artois, despairing of protection, fled across the border, leading the first of those successive waves of emigration which brought so much harm to France and to Europe. It is difficult to overstate the evils which proceeded from the presence beyond the borders of France of bodies of angry, energetic, empty-minded nobles, in league with the enemies of their country, and conspiring either through foreign war or domestic strife to uproot its new institutions. All the greater calamities which overwhelmed revolutionary France, the execution of the King and Queen, the mania of suspicion, the terror, the atrocities, the proscription of moderate and humane opinions, are not obscurely connected with the fears excited by the implacable hatred of the *émigrés*, by the power of their armed allies within and without the country, and, most disquieting of all, by the suspected presence in every part of France of secret sympathizers with the royalist cause.

Meanwhile the Assembly in a spirit of exulting confidence, as though the known oracles of philosophy would answer every riddle of the practical life, addressed itself to the task of framing a constitution for France. In one respect its work was marvellously simplified, for it had nothing to destroy. Aug., The castle of feudalism offered as little resistance as the 4, Bastille itself. In the course of one feverish August night 1789 nobles and clergy, provinces, municipalities and corporations, abandoned in a paroxysm of fear and generosity their feudal rights and privileges. The old order crumbled away in the shock of a revolutionary emotion, which the Assembly in great part shared, but did nothing to originate or direct. Never has a famous society so violently renounced its historic past. If the monarchy had been vanquished and shamed in a desolating war, its humiliation could not have been more complete. After the fall of the Bastille everything was chaos: the administration, the Army, and with serious results for the future of France upon the seas, the Royal Navy, which had acquitted itself so well in the American War. The peasants fired the muniments of their masters. Nobody obeyed the law or paid taxes. The National Guard, a great militia, devoted to the revolution, sprang up in every quarter of France to defend its cause. One thought flew through the country whispering its siren music in every heart. The people were Sovereign. The cumbrous monarchy of the old *régime* was a vast imposture. Frenchmen were no longer, and had never been, subjects. They were citizens, members of a free and equal confraternity, with the right to make peace and war, to conclude treaties, to administer justice, to regulate Church, Army, and Navy, to draft laws and impose taxes.

No power could obstruct, none defeat the general will expressed through the National Assembly, its lawful organ. The *esprit de corps* of particular groups, whether provinces or municipalities, social classes or professions, trade guilds or Corporations, must give way before the dictates of indivisible France. The charcoal burner at his furnace, the blacksmith at his forge, the farmhand following the plough, awoke to find himself part sovereign of France, as good a man as his lord, and endowed with impregnable rights, the right to be free, the right to own property, the right to speak his mind and to resist oppression. Such was the logic, such the sentiment, which captured France in the summer of 1789, and such the appeal of the new democracy to the subject peoples of Europe. Enshrined in the large, untested phrases of the Declaration of the Rights of Man, which was prefixed to the Constitution of 1791, this philosophy travelled far and wide, lighting lamps of pride and of aspiration in innumerable homes.

Against the seductive force of this democratic logic the voices of moderation and wisdom were of little avail. The belief in the essential goodness of human nature which underlay these theories was the source of most of the terrible disasters which now in swift succession assailed France. It was not a race of political angels, but a people needing, perhaps more than any other for the full development of its great qualities, the firm hand of authority, which was surrendered to its own devices by this sleek and optimistic theory.

Below the level of the bourgeoisie was a proletariat, starved in mind and body, and brutalized by neglect and the operation of unequal laws, a proletariat of smugglers, brigands, desperadoes, criminals. On the night of the taking of the Bastille women and children danced by torchlight round the decapitated heads of three blameless French gentlemen. The grim warning was not taken. The King and his ministers would not direct the Assembly, the Assembly would not govern France or police Paris. When King and Assembly were moved to the capital, the true centre of sovereignty was transferred to the political clubs, of which the most important was that of the Jacobins, soon to become the heart of a wide federation and the real ruler of France. To the operations of these revolutionary bodies, who terrorized the legislature and fostered mutiny in the army, no opposition was ever offered.

1749-91   History will always be interested in Mirabeau, adventurer, statesman, demagogue, publicist, as the man who endeavoured and failed to check the mounting surge of anarchy and to save the crown of France. To him, as to Mounier and other wise men, it was abundantly clear that only a strong executive could preserve France from the abyss. But where was strength to be found? It was not in the King, nor in his elder brother, the Count of Provence, nor in Lafayette, the vain, incapable commandant of the National Guard of Paris.

Every intrigue for the foundation of a powerful royal ministry foundered. All proposals likely to fortify the executive in the new constitution, such as a second chamber, an absolute veto, the right of the King's ministers to sit in the legislature, broke on the same rock of democratic doctrine. Mirabeau could not even count upon a full royalist vote, for many royalists were wreckers, bent upon making the constitution as bad as possible in order to discredit democracy. Concluding that nothing could be done with the Assembly at Versailles, Mirabeau secretly proposed to the court that they should retire publicly to Rouen. Of all his many expedients this perhaps was the least desperate: yet it came too late, for France, though she did not yet know it, was already at heart a republic. The constitution which finally emerged from the cauldron of debate retained that anarchical dispersion of powers which the Assembly found and did nothing to correct. The monarchy survived, but as a shadow only, for the real power belonged to some forty thousand municipalities which paid what taxes they chose to levy, and alone could call out the National Guard. A fatal distrust of executive authority evidenced by an overweening belief in popular election was one of the most serious defects of the first attempt of the revolution to organize France.

Another blemish proceeding from the same democratic logic was the civil constitution of the clergy. It was a cardinal maxim of the revolution that corporate bodies were dangerous to society, and since there was no corporation so wealthy, so influential, or with so long a record of intolerance as the

Church, it was specially marked out for the resentment of an anti-clerical Assembly. Blow followed hard upon blow, first the abolition of tithe without compensation, then a confiscation of all church property, the suppression of the religious orders, the release of monks and nuns from their vows, and a great reduction in the ecclesiastical establishment. Yet since doctrine and worship were left unaffected, these provisions, however drastic, might not have caused an insuperable obstacle. The Church might resent the loss of its wide acres and noble endowments and the arrangement by which the clergy became the salaried dependants of a democratic state; but a state church had long existed in France, and no Christian could condemn a measure which deprived the prelates of their superfluities and added to the scanty pittance of the parish priest. The crowning offence which made the quarrel irreparable was the requirement that the bishop should be chosen by the electors of the department and the *curé* by the administrative Assembly of the district.[1] Catholic bishops and Catholic *curés* might then be chosen by laymen who were Protestants or even atheists. It was reasonable to surmise that a church thus officered and recruited would drift far apart from its ancient moorings, more particularly since at the same time French citizens were forbidden to recognize the authority of any bishop or metropolitan whose see lay outside the kingdom. It was inevitable that the Pope, who had not been consulted at any stage, should condemn the Civil Constitution, and that it should wound the conscience of the Catholic world. No error of the Constituent Assembly was so far-reaching in its consequences as this gratuitous affront to the religious convictions of the people. At the beginning of the revolution the village *curés* had thrown in their lot with the popular cause, and the value of their support had been great. Now the clergy was split in two. The compliant sort took the oath to the Constitution, retained their cures, and drew their salaries; the braver sort rebelled. Rather than accept a schismatic church they went out into the wilderness risking starvation, imprisonment, and death, but carrying with them the loyalty of a faithful flock. The *prêtres insermentés* became from the first a formidable centre

[1] Such were the new administrative areas created to efface the old local loyalties and privileges of France.

of opposition to the revolutionary state. They were to be found in the Vendée and in Brittany, and wherever the white cockade took the field against the tricolor. In defeat and persecution they were yet triumphant, for out of the purification of their sufferings the Church in France renewed its moral life.

In all these provisions there was nothing of socialism. The French Revolution attacked privilege, not property. The members of the Constituent Assembly reposed such belief in the liberty of the individual that they assailed even those forms of economic association such as trades unions which have been found necessary in later times for the protection of the weak against the strong. The peasant was enabled to cultivate and sell as he pleased. Serfdom was abolished where it existed, quit rents disappeared, game laws were mitigated, the lord was deprived of his right over the commons. But if the incidents of the land system were altered, the foundation remained the same. The soil of France was still tilled by peasant holders, farming tenants, or upon that system of metayer or share tenancy under which landlord and tenant shared expenses and profits. A scheme of agricultural communism or state ownership was never even suggested.

A strong material tie, arising out of the very necessities of the state, bound the peasantry to the revolution, and secured that in part at least the work of the Constituent Assembly would not be reversed. To govern France the Assembly required funds; and these it sought to find in the issue of notes or *assignats* secured on the property of the Church, and afterwards on that of the Crown and *émigrés* as well. An original issue of four hundred million francs (December, 1789), which was regarded as an advance on the proceeds of the sale of church property, was soon found to be insufficient. Further needs were met by fresh issues, with the result that inflation set in, that the assignat lost its value, and that land changed hands at a derisory price. The rapid degeneration of a nation's currency, while ruinous to many, always inures to the profit of some. The fall in the value of French assignats impoverished the Treasury, the *rentier*, and the townsman, and contributed to maintain revolutionary excitement in Paris by engendering an atmosphere of speculation and panic. But the peasant who acquired land for a mere song was a gainer, and for this reason, among others, he, together with many a land speculator from the town, had cause to bless the revolution and to dread the reversal of its work.

The prisoners of the Tuileries viewed with a helpless sense of horror and disgust the mounting tide of revolution, the violence of the Jacobin Club, the bloodthirsty incitements of the Press, and the incessant capitulations of the Assembly to the dictation of the mob. Where everything was distasteful, the civil constitution of the clergy appeared to the King as a crowning affront. He felt that he could never reconcile this enactment to his conscience or bear to receive the sacrament from a constitutional priest. On the Monday before Easter 1791 an event occurred from which it appeared that even the promptings of the private conscience were not to be respected. On that day the King and Queen desiring to make their Easter Communion at St. Cloud, were turned back by the mob. The indignity was decisive. The Royal Family resolved to escape to the frontier where Bouillé at the head of a royalist force could afford them protection. Before he left Paris the King drew up a manifesto abrogating the constitutional edicts which he had been compelled to sign, and requiring their amendment.

The fugitives were turned back at Varennes (June 21). From that moment the monarchy was doomed, for the King had come out as the open opponent of the constitution, at heart an *émigré*, a friend of the unsworn priests, a fomenter of civil war, and the ally of foreign counter-revolutionary Powers. For ten weeks he was suspended from his functions and a government, republican in all but name, allayed the fears that the removal of the monarchy would spell the dissolution of France.

When the Constitution was completed (September 14, 1791) the Assembly put an end to its own existence. Already by an act of abnegation, which did little service to France, it had decreed its members to be incapable of election to the new legislature. Lightly sacrificing the experience which had been garnered by two years of intense political application, the framers of the first French constitution were prepared to entrust its working to untried men. Nothing turned out according to plan. It was the fate of the expiring Assembly, which believed in Liberty, Fraternity, and Equality, and had worked for a democratic state safeguarded by a universal and democratic peace, to level the path for a military tyranny, and to sow the seeds of general war.

BOOKS WHICH MAY BE CONSULTED

For surveys covering the whole period the reader is referred to the following:

G. P. Gooch: *Annals of Politics and Culture.*   1901.

The Cambridge Modern History.   1902-10.

The Cambridge History of the British Empire.   1929.

A. J. Grant and H. Temperley: *Europe in the Nineteenth and Twentieth Centuries* (1784-1932).   1932.

Edward Fueter: *World History. Tr.* S. B. Fay.   1923.

C. A. Fyffe: *History of Modern Europe.*   1924.

B. Croce: *History of Europe in the Nineteenth Century. Tr.* H. Furst.   1934.

C. Seignobos: *Political History of Contemporary Europe since* 1814.   1901.

For the most recent books:

The Annual Bulletin of Historical Literature, published by the Historical Association.

For Chapters LXV-LXXII the reader is referred to:

The Cambridge Modern History, Vols. VIII and IX.

L. Madelin: *The French Revolution. Tr.* Curtis.   1930.

Lord Acton: *Lectures on the French Revolution.*   1910.

A. Sorel: *L'Europe et la Révolution française.*   1889.

A. De Tocqueville: *Ancien Régime. Tr.* M. W. Pattersen.   1933.

H. Taine: *Origines de la France contemporaine.*   1876.

Carlyle: *French Revolution. Ed.* C. R. L. Fletcher.   1907.

J. M. Thompson: *French Revolution: Documents.*   1933.

A. Aulard: *Histoire politique de la Révolution française. Tr.* Miall.   1910.

Lecky: *History of England in the Eighteenth Century.*   1892.

Seeley: *Life and Times of Stein.*   1878.

Oman: *Peninsular War.*   1902-30.

H. A. L. Fisher: *Napoleonic Statesmanship: Germany.*   1903.

H. A. L. Fisher: *Bonapartism.*   1909.

E. L. Woodward: *French Revolution.*   1934.

F. Masson: *Napoléon inconnu.*   1895.

Vandal: *L'avènement de Bonaparte.*   1902.

H. Houssaye: 1815.   *Waterloo.*   1900.

L. G. Wickham Legg: *Select Documents.* 1905.

A. T. Mahan: *Influence of Sea Power on the French Revolution.* 1893.

L. Gershoy: *From Despotism to Revolution,* 1763-89. 1944.

G. Lefebvre: *The Coming of the French Revolution,* 1789. *Tr.* R. R. Palmer. 1947.

P. Geyl: *Napoleon, for and against. Tr.* O. Renier. 1949.

J. M. Thompson: *The French Revolution.* 5th Ed. 1955.

BIOGRAPHIES

Mirabeau, by P. F. Willert. 1898.

Robespierre, by A. Matthiez. 1921, 1925.

Danton, by H. Belloc. 1928.

Talleyrand, by Duff Cooper. 1932.

Napoleon, by H. A. L. Fisher (1924), J. Holland Rose (1902), J. B. Fournier (1912), Jacques Bainville (1932).

William Pitt, by Rosebery (1910), J. Holland Rose (1925).

Burke, by John Morley. 1921.

Fox, by J. L. Hammond, 1903; Christopher Hobhouse. 1934.

Wellington (The Duke), by Philip Guedalla. 1931.

The Foreign Policy of Castlereagh, by C. K. Webster. 1934.

IMAGINATIVE LITERATURE

Dickens: *Tale of Two Cities.*

Anatole France: *Les Dieux ont Soif.*

Stendhal: *La Chartreuse de Parme.*

Tolstoi: *War and Peace.*

T. Hardy: *The Dynasts.*

CHAPTER LXVII

WAR AND TERROR

*The Girondins. The outbreak of war. Its effects. Danton.
The quarrel with Britain. William Pitt. The Polish Question.
The influence of minorities. Fall of the Girondins. The Terror.
The year of Robespierre. Thermidor. The persistence of a
regicide government. The Directorate and Bonaparte.*

THE LEADERSHIP of the new Assembly fell to a body of young
and eloquent men of the middle class, who, since they were
drawn from the south-western area of France called the
Gironde, soon became known, and are to this day remembered, as the Girondins. Of the art and science of government
the Girondins knew little; but they possessed, and were able
to communicate to others, a glowing enthusiasm for the
republican idea, and a missionary impulse to spread it
through Europe. Vergniaud and Isnard were the orators,
Brissot the diplomatic adviser, the wife of Roland the Egeria
of the party. The dazzling dreams, the sentimental enthusiasm, and the tragic end of the Girondins have secured them
many friends. Upon them, however, must rest the chief
responsibility for a long and terrible war, which destroyed
the system of Richelieu and left France a permanently
enfeebled member of European society, shielded from imminent danger on the eastern border only by heavy taxes
and a universal and compulsory system of military service.

In the atmosphere of angry suspicion which prevailed in
Paris the chief enemies of the revolution appeared to be the
émigré, the non-juring priest, and the Austrian Emperor.[1]
Upon these accordingly the Girondins concentrated their
animosity, holding that nothing was more likely to make the
position of the King and Queen impossible and to open the
road to a Republic than a policy of sharp decrees against the

[1] Technically until 1804 Archduke of Austria and until 1806 Holy Roman
Emperor.

émigrés and priests followed by a foreign war against the brother of the Queen.

Pretexts for a war were not lacking. Leopold of Austria could complain of French encouragement given to a revolution in Belgium, of German princes dispossessed of feudal rights in Alsace, of Avignon snatched from the Pope and annexed to France, of the novel and disquieting principle that the people of a country have the right to determine their own allegiance, and yet more important than these other occasions of friction, of the dangerous position of his sister the Queen of France. To Marie Antoinette's entreaties that he should summon a European Congress to deal with the French Revolution and concentrate an armed force to give effect to its decisions he could not be altogether indifferent. After Varennes, he issued, in conjunction with the King of Prussia, a declaration from Pilnitz (August, 1791) which seemed to threaten France with the combined action of the European Powers, if Louis were not accorded the treatment which his status deserved. Yet the situation, though grave, was still not beyond repair. A cold, prudent, long-headed man, much occupied with the internal problems of the Austrian empire, Leopold had no desire to embark upon a quixotic crusade against the tumultuous democracy of France. Prompt to threaten, he was reluctant to act, and hoped that when Louis had accepted the Constitution the need for action had passed away. But as autumn melted into winter, and every week brought fresh news of revolutionary violence in Paris, the Emperor's mind turned more and more towards an armed intervention. On all sides he was pressed to stem the tide of militant French democracy; by the *émigrés* who were gathered at Coblentz, by Catharine of Russia, by Gustavus of Sweden, by the King of Spain, and more particularly by Marie Antoinette, who saw in an unsuccessful French defence against foreign invasion the one chance for the salvation of her husband's crown. But then, before his slow resolution ripened to action, Leopold unexpectedly died. His successor Francis, young, vigorous, and care-free, was prompt to take up the Girondin challenge. This took the form of a peremptory demand that the Elector of Trèves should dismiss from his territory the armed force of *émigrés* who were collected at Coblentz. It was a demand intended

1747-92

1792-1835

to precipitate war. Though the French army was disorganized, and Austria and Prussia were leagued against them, Brissot and his followers were confident of victory. At the shock of war the peoples of Europe would rise against their tyrants. Everywhere thrones would fall. The principles of liberty, fraternity, and equality would conquer the world. Robespierre, an oracle of the Jacobin Club, reasoned otherwise, thinking that the war would restore prestige to the French Crown. But Robespierre's hour had not yet struck. A Girondin ministry, with the able Dumouriez at the Foreign Office, swept their country into war (April 20, 1792).

Then it was discovered that, if revolutionary France was to be effectively defended against the monarchies of unreformed Europe, Louis XVI must cease to reign and France submit to a strict form of tyranny very remote from that extreme dispersion of political authority which had found favour at the opening of the revolution. The war led straight to the fall of the Monarchy, the establishment of the Republic, and to the formation of the government of the Terror. It imparted a deeper note of savage apprehension and passion to the anxieties which had been caused by dear bread and soaring prices, by the widespread prevalence of disorder, and by the ceaseless agitation of the bloodthirsty press against counter-revolutionary activities. It was therefore the exciting cause of terrible crimes, and of a shameful fashion of bloodthirstiness which has been surpassed in modern times only by the communists of Russia. But the war had other consequences more profound and enduring. Revolution was identified with patriotism. For the first time the vast latent energies of the French people were deployed in defence of a cause which was regarded as the common concern of every citizen in the land. For the first time France emerged as an organic nation, its institutions based on popular assent, and maintained against a world in arms by a people in revolution, the masters and servants of a revolutionary state.

Another consequence was inevitable. As the military spirit of the French people was aroused, the idyllic professions of pacifism and cosmopolitan brotherhood which had decorated so many revolutionary speeches passed swiftly into the background. Old diplomatic principles, familiar objects of territorial ambition, resumed their empire. The ghost of

Louis XIV returned to direct the counsels of the Jacobins. Fraternity was thrown to the winds. The Girondins were drunk with vainglory and the lust of conquest. They determined to isolate Austria, that they might rob her of Belgium, and bring the French frontier to the Rhine.

For the moment, however, the impolicy of the Girondins had launched France all unprepared (for the royal army was in dissolution) against Prussia and Austria, the two strongest military states on the continent. The result was what might be expected. The first hostile exchanges were sufficient to show that the revolution had no army upon which it could rely for the defence of the country. There was cowardice, indiscipline, failure, and, as invariably happened after every military reverse, the cry of treachery. It was during this period of agonized uncertainty, when the old army had proved itself incompetent, and before the new volunteers of the revolution had proved their worth, that the fate of the monarchy was decided. How, it was asked, could the war be made to succeed, while Louis, the friend of the enemy, reigned in the Tuileries, dismissing his Girondin ministers, refusing a decree for a big military camp near Paris, holding out, so it was believed, secret encouragement to the invader?

At this crisis, when the Prussian army was marching on France, and its chief was threatening Paris with destruction if the royal family was injured, a great, gross revolutionary figure rose above the tumult and took sudden command. The memory of Danton is red with violence. It was he who organized the attack on the Tuileries (August 10, 1792), when the gallant Swiss Guard were hacked to pieces, and the King and Queen were delivered over to captivity, and a Convention was summoned to proclaim a Republic; nor can he be acquitted of condoning the terrible September massacres in the prisons, which were planned to influence the elections to this new Parliament. Nevertheless more than any other revolutionary character of the time Danton was a statesman and a patriot, with an eye for essential needs, a mind clear of illusions, and a rare power for decisive action. He aimed at giving France a convinced republic instead of a disloyal monarchy, a centralized government in place of anarchy, and new armies highly disciplined and permeated by the revolutionary faith in place of the crumbling and doubtful fragments of the army of the Crown. The Girondin idea of a crusade against all the crowned heads of Europe soon struck him as fantastic. The man who pulled down the French monarchy became in diplomacy a pupil of the *ancien régime*.

To Danton as to all statesmen in time of war terror was a necessary instrument of policy. The one intolerable thing, as long as foreign enemies were on French soil, was disunion among Frenchmen. That such disunion existed was a suspicion widely entertained. Every misfortune at home and abroad, the high prices, the bad trade, the foreign war, the disquietude about the king and the priests, was calculated to swell the ranks of the malcontents. A counter-revolution was no impossibility. Such measure of terrorism as was necessary to cow the enemies of the revolutionary state Danton was always prepared to employ.

The birth of the Republic was signalized by a flimsy aureole of lightly purchased victories, which in the course of a few weeks (September 20 to November 7, 1792) placed Savoy and Nice, the Rhenish states, and the Austrian Netherlands, under the heel of the plundering armies of France. Goethe,

Aug., who was present at the cannonade of Valmy, when the Duke
20, of Brunswick's Prussian army, reputed to be the best in
1792 Europe, gave way, after trifling losses, before Kellermann, predicted the advent of a new era in human history. The democratic experiment was something more substantial than mere literature. The Prussian Guard had given ground before it. Better than any monarchy, so it appeared, the ragged distracted democracy of France had captured the real secret of power, which is never a function of mechanism but always an ardour of the soul. Moreover, the Republic was a government of conquest and propaganda. The compulsion of a universal doctrine, the constraint of an empty purse, combined to impel it to a course in which the rôle of the missionary was blended with that of the bandit. France could not afford the expense of peace. It must hold and exploit its victories. More particularly did Austrian Belgium present itself as a desirable acquisition. Here was a gold mine, rich in any case, but capable of yielding its full measure of tribute only were the Scheldt open to navigation and Antwerp revived as London's rival in the markets of the

world. It mattered little to the Convention that this river had been closed by an international agreement to which France herself was a party. Such instruments, violating the law of nature, Republican France was prepared to treat as scraps of paper. So, declaring to the world that the Scheldt was open, and that France would offer assistance to all peoples struggling to be free, the Republic light-heartedly embarked upon the course which brought it up against the tenacious and formidable hostility of Britain.

Here was a nation, proud, compact, and wealthy, which was ruled by a government at once aristocractic and popular. The unity which France had now won through revolution, England had acquired in the twelfth century. Civil liberties intoxicating from their novelty in France were in England matters of long established usage. There was nothing which revolutionary France could teach Britain in the matter of Parliamentary government which was not better understood at Westminster than in Paris. There was no part of Europe in which the gospel of the Revolution was likely to be less attractive than Britain, for the reason that the best part of that which republican France had now to offer this conservative island already possessed.

William Pitt had been Prime Minister since 1783. He was a Whig by origin, a financier by taste, and a consummate master of that art of Parliamentary oratory which had never been more important in the history of Europe. It was his fate, while earnestly working for a long spell of peace and internal reform, to lead his country into the war which ended with Waterloo. Of that war he saw the first twelve dark and desperate years. In some respects he was not a great war minister, frittering away the nation's resources in paltry but very costly West Indian expeditions, and, save that he sent Nelson to the Mediterranean, showing little appreciation of the grand lines of martial strategy. But the French rightly discerned in Pitt their greatest and most persistent enemy. He was the soul of every European coalition against them, and as he rose from the Treasury Bench, night after night, and year after year, to put fresh courage into the gentlemen of England by his grave and lofty eloquence, he stood out as the personification of a collective will which could never accept the thought of defeat.

As in the days of Louis XIV, the long duel between Britain and France arose out of the settled policy of the island kingdom never willingly to acquiesce in the annexation of Belgium and Holland by a great continental power. Such designs revolutionary France had by 1793 clearly revealed. She had conquered Belgium, she was threatening Holland, she had torn up the Treaty of the Scheldt, she was inciting by her decree of November 19 the King's subjects in Ireland and elsewhere to rebellion, and on January 21, 1793, she outraged the feelings of the British people by executing Louis XVI. Without a navy she challenged the first naval power in the world.

The entry of Britain into the war introduced an element of single-minded and concentrated opposition to the revolutionary cause which had hitherto been wanting. The main preoccupation at this time of Russia, Prussia, and Austria was 1772 not France, but Poland. That unfortunate country, already diminished by a first partition, was about to endure at the hands of its acquisitive neighbours a second and yet a third 1793- operation of the same nature. At the time when the French 5 Republic was proclaiming the generous doctrine of self-determination, the military monarchies of the East were busy in procuring the extinction of a nation. The story is one of the most shameful in the annals of the continent. On May 3, 1791, Stanislas Poniatowski, the King of Poland, had accepted a constitution which bade fair to remedy the chief weakness which had hitherto paralysed the Polish state. The *liberum veto* was abolished. The crown was made hereditary; the nobles were subjected to taxation. Varieties of religious belief were permitted. It was reasonable to suppose that, so reformed, Poland might yet play an honourable and useful part in the economy of Europe. But though the constitution was acknowledged by Prussia and Austria, the prospect of a strengthened Poland accorded ill with the voracious appetite of the Tzarina. In 1792 Catharine invaded Poland, and, having beaten down a brave resistance and abolished the Constitution, invited Prussia and Austria to a sharing of the spoils. By every consideration of honour these two Powers should have felt themselves precluded from upsetting a constitution which they had expressly guaranteed, and from attacking a country which they had undertaken to defend.

Under the stress of temptation they were untrue to their engagements. In the partition, repartition, and extinction of Poland, Prussia and Austria, though divided by bitter jealousies, played a dishonourable and collusive rôle. They carried off their booty and smashed the patriotic rising of

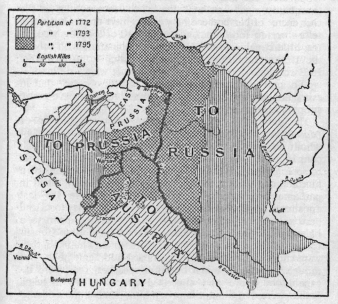

THE PARTITIONS OF POLAND

Kosciuszko. It was not until October 10, 1795, that the third Treaty of Partition blotted Poland from the map. For four critical years the gobbling up and deglutition of this vast territory had absorbed the main part of the attention of Austria and Prussia, had fatally impaired the effectiveness of their co-operation against France, and had enabled the Republic to establish itself firmly in the face of Europe.

The clue to the understanding of revolutions is that they are worked by small fanatical minorities. The French Convention, which proclaimed the Republic, executed the King, sent the Girondins to the scaffold, and established the Terror, was returned by the votes of some six per cent. of the total electorate. The main body of the French people, after the first blaze of enthusiasm had died down, wanted nothing so much as to be allowed to manage their own concerns in tranquillity, and were well content to leave politics to the club men. Either because he was too inert or too busy, too selfish or too indifferent, too frightened or too disgusted, or too little capable of entering into combination with others, the average respectable citizen stood aside from the battle. In Paris, where political interest was most widely diffused, it would appear from the report of a careful observer that in every one hundred and thirty persons only one gave active support to the Terror.

The vast majority of the Convention, known as the Plain or *Marais*, belonged to that moderate, colourless, uncertain, but wholly respectable section of the French middle class, which constituted the·strength of the nation. To such it was natural to seek guidance from the Girondins, who were returned a hundred and twenty strong, and were already established in parliamentary reputation. The Girondins were the last apostles of the liberal idea. They believed in liberty local and personal. They had a vision of France settling down to a blameless and brilliant existence under a Republican Constitution the finest in the world. Being essentially humane, they were shocked by the crimes of August and September. But though they could make beautiful speeches, they were incapable of brave and concerted action. They attacked Robespierre, but did not imprison him; assailed the assassins of September, but did not prosecute them; realized the dangerous opposition of revolutionary Paris, but would neither close the clubs, nor curb the Press, nor provide the Convention with the necessary safeguard of an armed force on which reliance could be placed. One man might have saved them from destruction, and offered to do so; but the Girondins were too respectable to clasp the strong but blood-stained hand of Danton. To the average Frenchman no respectability remained to a party which had given a regicide vote, and when the Girondins through cowardice and ineptitude allowed themselves against their better judgment to

be outmanoeuvred by the Mountain into sending the King to
the guillotine, they had decreed their own extinction. After
that no moderate Frenchman would lift up a finger to help
them.

The spring which followed the execution of Louis was
crowded with disaster for the regicide state. With England,
Spain, and Holland added to the circle of her enemies, with
her armies withdrawn from Belgium, with Dumouriez, her
best general, gone over to the enemy, with insurrection ablaze
in the Vendée and in Lyons, and with Toulon at the mercy
of the British fleet, the Republic was fighting with its back to
the wall. It was the stress of these terrible anxieties which
swept the Girondins clean out of the political scene, and
founded that firm and terrible instrument of autocratic rule
which succeeded amidst much bloodshed and cruelty in
restoring the military situation.

The Jacobin Government consisted of a small secret Cabinet
or Committee of Public Safety for the general direction of
policy, of a somewhat larger Committee of Public Security for
police, of a revolutionary tribunal for the dissemination of
terror, and of a plan for the strict supervision of generals in
the field by civil agents of the purest fanaticism known as
représentants en mission. The Convention, scornfully described by Dumouriez as a body of three hundred scoundrels
and four hundred imbeciles, continued to sit, to debate, to
legislate; but its authority was gone. A *coup d'état* led by
Henriot (June 2) had eliminated those Girondin orators whose
eloquence had so often charmed and delighted the assembly.
The party of these brilliant idealists had not even been able to
defend its leaders from proscription or the scaffold. It could
not police its debating hall. Paralysed by the publicity which
its principles forbade it to renounce, it was overshadowed by
the new Cabinet, by the Commune of Paris, by the Jacobin
and Cordelier Clubs, and by the disciplined and vocal ruffians
who dominated the revolutionary committees in the forty-
eight sections or electoral districts into which the capital was
divided. Other times required other methods. The stress of
war had created an immense acceleration in affairs: swift and
ruthless action in place of the interminable loquacity which
had so long perplexed and arrested the march of government
was the note of men like Carnot at the War Office and Jean

Bon Saint-André at the Marine. The Jacobins, who saved the Republic, were giants of industry. Science came to their aid. On July 27 an order was sent from Paris to the armies on the frontier in a quarter of an hour. The semaphore telegraph, one of the secrets of an impending military Empire, had made its début in the service of France.

1758-   The man of the new era was Robespierre, the lean lawyer
94 from Arras, who entered the Committee of Public Safety on July 28, 1793, and for one amazing year, memorable for its military glories and domestic shame, was the real ruler of France and the master spirit of Europe. What a catalogue of Jacobin triumphs belongs to the reign of Robespierre! The royalist revolution put down in Lyons, Toulon recaptured, the Duke of York beaten at Hondschoote, the Austrians defeated at Wattignies and Fleurus, Belgium reconquered, Holland invaded, French soil everywhere liberated from the invader. It is the year of the first *levée en masse* of the nation in arms, the year, though not the official natal year, of that system of military conscription which still brings a dark shadow into every Frenchman's life, the year in which Carnot began to organize the armies which made for Napoleon his instrument of conquest.

In Paris the year of Robespierre marks the culmination of the Jacobin Terror. The man was of the type of Lenin, a fanatical believer in an inspired text. As Karl Marx was to the Russian, so was Rousseau to the French revolutionary. Part of his power with the Parisians lay in his plain simplicity of purpose, and in a life reputed to be free from the taint of peculation. "You may laugh at him now," said a contemporary, "but that man will go far. He believes every word he says." The ease and malice of his oratory, the violence of his views, coupled with a great dexterity in the arts of political management, made him almost from the first a leader among the Jacobins. He was the master of the Paris revolutionary machine before he became a director of national policy. Scrupulously and elegantly dressed, well-mannered, ostentatious in his professions of republican virtue, he had for every dissenter from his narrow creed the one and simple remedy of the guillotine. In March he sent Hébert and Chaumette to the scaffold for their anarchy and atheism. In April the knife fell upon Danton and Desmoulins, who in the *Vieux*

Cordelier, the one piece of real literature produced in the revolution, had advocated a return to clemency and moderation. At last the man-eating tiger overreached himself by a law (the law of 22 Prairial) which threatened·the life of every member of the Convention, for the legislators were deprived of their immunity, and the last feeble safeguards for the protection of persons accused for political offences were swept away. In self-defence even cowards may pluck up courage. There were men in the Convention led by Barras and Tallien who resolved that the tyrant should perish and saw that with a careful organization of forces outside the assembly the deed could be done. Meeting the Jacobins, not with eloquent speeches, but with their own weapons of calculated force, these capable men achieved a swift and easy victory. On July 28, 1794 (9 Thermidor by the Republican Calendar), the Hôtel de Ville was invested and stormed by a force largely drawn from the Section Lepelletier, a well-to-do quarter of the city. There Robespierre was found, his jaw shattered by a bullet wound, and thence he was hauled, all bleeding, to the scaffold that he might die under the knife, as his many victims had died before him.

June 10, 1794

The long nightmare was over. The hateful epidemic of butchery, which in Paris alone had cost two thousand six hundred victims, came to a sudden end. Moderates and Dantonists seized the wheel of power, abolished the Commune, closed the Jacobin Club, amnestied the Vendéans, and recalled the Girondins. The dark miasma of suspicion which had poisoned the political life of Paris passed away with Robespierre's fall and Jourdan's great victory at Fleurus. In her sudden deliverance from fear and humiliation the country swung back into the sunlight of gaiety and hope. No more fanatical gloom! No more ravings of a bloodthirsty press! No more guillotining of the brave, the good, the beautiful, the innocent! Frivolity resumed its long-interrupted reign. But if France ceased to be Terrorist, she remained revolutionary. The members of the regicide Parliment could make no advances to the party of reaction. For them it was a matter of life and death so to manœuvre that, whatever the future government of France might be, regicides from the Convention should stand at the wheel.

June 25, 1794

How that government should be framed was now a main
1743- pre-occupation. Condorcet, the best of the Girondin thinkers,
94 had devised a constitution, containing, like the German
Constitution of 1918, all the last refinements of democratic
philosophy, but plainly unworkable and never put into
execution. Something was wanted having in it less of a
democracy and more of concentration and force, but at the
same time securing the continued predominance of that
moderate revolutionary element which had triumphed at
Thermidor. There was one serious danger obstructing the
approach to a solution of the problem. The reds of Paris,
who had suffered the defeat at Thermidor, though greatly
weakened by the suppression of the Commune, were still
armed, still formidable, still in full possession of the technique
of a revolutionary *coup d'état*. On May 1 and June 2, 1795,
they attacked the Convention, but were on each occasion
repulsed. Then at last a decision was taken which, had it
been adopted earlier, might have saved the monarchy. The
National Guard was placed under a committee of soldiers.

The answer to the constitutional riddle was found in an
imposture which survived for four years under the name of
the Directory. Since a dictatorship was as yet unthinkable,
executive power was entrusted to a body of five men, elected
for a term of five years. It was thought to avoid mob rule by
the establishment of two chambers, the Ancients and the
Five Hundred, elected upon a limited franchise, and yet to
secure responsibility to public opinion by a requirement that
every year one-fifth of the executive and one-third of the
Legislature should be changed. But behind this pleasurable
façade of moderate liberty there was concealed the awkward
fact that a government of regicides could not afford to trust
the people. The constitution was accompanied by a decree,
providing that two-thirds of the new Parliament should be
drawn from the Convention which had voted the King and
Queen to the guillotine. All the moderates and royalists in
Paris were up in arms against this violent interference with
electoral liberty. They had been happily delivered of the
Terror; they now wished to be quit, once and for all, of the
politicians whose cowardice and fanaticism had made the
Terror possible. A movement was organized by those sections
of the city which represented wealth, respectability, **or**

conservative opinion, to put an end to the regicide body. In the first week of October twenty-six thousand men were said to be mustered for the attack.

The new Directors were a motley body bound to one another by a common complicity in regicide, but otherwise intentionally drawn from different sections of the revolutionary camp. Rewbell was a stiff Jacobin lawyer from Alsace, Carnot and Letourneur were engineers, Lépaux a visionary Girondin. Barras alone, the least estimable of the five, possessed a flair for political action. At two critical junctures the vulgar, theatrical, peculating libertine from Provence showed himself to be a man of the moment. In Thermidor he pulled down Robespierre. In Vendémiaire he descried Napoleon Bonaparte.

This young Corsican general of artillery, who in the autumn of 1793 had distinguished himself at the siege of Toulon, happened to be in Paris without employment in those anxious October days when cries of "Vive le Roi" were again heard with acceptance in the Paris streets, and the last Assembly of the Revolution was trembling before the mutterings of a reactionary storm. There he made the acquaintance of the most powerful of the Directors, who discerned his worth, and entrusted him with the defence of the threatened chamber. The military dispositions of General Bonaparte announced the hand of a master. He sent Murat galloping to Sablons for the guns, and against a tumultuous force devoid of artillery established an immediate and decisive advantage. One brief cannonade efficiently directed cleared the streets, rescued the government, and gave to its saviour an overwhelming claim to military promotion. He was at once made general of the Interior, and in the next year received, again with the favour and support of Barras, the hand of Josephine Beauharnais and the all-important Italian Command.

Oct. 3-5, 1795

CHAPTER LXVIII

THE COMING OF BONAPARTE

France and Europe. The lure of Italy. Bonaparte's Italian victories. Campo Formio. Consequences for Italy. Fructidor. Egypt. The second Coalition. Syria. The effect of the Syrian Campaign on French opinion. Sieyès. Brumaire. Survival of social equality. The Consulate. Marengo and Lunéville. The British attitude. Ireland. The Blockade and the Rights of Neutrals. The Peace of Amiens.

BY THIS time the generals and diplomatists of the Directory had secured for France a position of tremendous ascendancy in western Europe. Holland had been overrun by Pichegru and converted into a client Batavian Republic, Belgium and all Germany to the Rhine frontier were annexed as integral parts of the Republic. Savoy was French. A French army was quartered on the Italian Riviera. Prussia, Spain, and Tuscany had withdrawn from the war. The stage was cleared for a conflict between the revolution and those two Powers in the world which represented in their strongest and most pertinacious form the counter-revolutionary spirit, Protestant Britain and Catholic Austria.

Behind her tutelary waves and winds Britain stood impregnable. Nature was her friend, sending storms to wreck Hoche's expedition to the Irish, and foiling every minor plan for the assistance of those latent rebellious sentiments which were assumed to exist in the English democracy. A direct attack upon this obstinate island could offer only slender encouragement to a brigand state in quest of quick returns. Such an attack must necessarily be naval, and therefore, since the old royal navy had been demoralized by revolution, highly speculative. The outlay would be large, the yield uncertain.

Very different was the prospect offered by Austria. One jewel of the Austrian crown little prized (by reason of its distance from Vienna) by its owner, who had more than once attempted to exchange it for Bavarian territory, had been conquered already. France had Belgium, and proposed to keep that rich coal-bearing and highly urbanized province, which lay adjacent to her frontier and within easy reach of her capital. But richer, more attractive, more romantic than Belgium were those wide provinces of the Italian peninsula, which acknowledged the direct rule of Austria, or were content to follow in her wake. The Milanese with its famous constellation of Lombard cities was a province of the Austrian Empire. Tuscany was a Habsburg Duchy. Naples, though governed by a degenerate Spanish Bourbon King, followed the strong guidance of Marie Caroline, his Habsburg wife, and might on that account, for purposes both of plunder and propaganda, be added to the catalogue of France's enemies. In Italy then everything conspired to invite the military enterprise of the French Republic, old tradition, the charm of the climate, the variety and wealth of the crops, the opulence of the cities, the wonderful treasures of the galleries and museums, the reputed weakness of the enemy, and the assumed readiness of the Italian population to throw off the Austrian yoke.

There was yet a further incitement to an Italian campaign, which weighed heavily in the minds of the anti-clerical government in Paris. The Pope had made himself extremely difficult. He had refused to accept the Civil Constitution of the clergy, and had encouraged the resistance of the non-juror priests. Of all the counter-revolutionary forces in Europe, none had been more troublesome than the Vatican. Its hidden hand was found everywhere, among the *émigrés* of Coblentz, among the rebels of the Vendée and Brittany, and in every parish of France where a non-juror priest was held in honour by his flock. A French Ambassador had even been murdered in Rome. The condign punishment of this troublesome pontiff and the annexation of his backward and ill-governed state were accordingly among the favourite projects of the Directors, as, in plumed hats and gorgeous uniforms, they discussed the regeneration of Europe in the gilded halls of the Luxembourg Palace.

In the French armies, which now contained the flower of the nation, illusions persisted which had long faded away among

Italian, cast in the imperial mould, and recalling by his exploits the glories of ancient Rome. Though he was severe, he seemed to come as a liberator, bringing with him the breath of a new freedom and wide-ranging prospects of Italian power. Much was forgiven to the young general who broke the Austrian strangle-hold on the Italian people, and invited them to work the institutions of a modern state. The Italian *literati* praised him to the skies; the best Lombards crowded to his court; and the Cisalpine Republic, though resting on French bayonets, acted for many years as a seminary of statecraft in a land where the tradition of public duty had long been atrophied by foreign rule.

With Prussia and Austria withdrawn from the war, France and Britain stood face to face. Between them lay two questions, striking deep into the heart of politics, the Rhine frontier which Britain would never concede, the monarchy which the victorious armies of France would never accept. Moderate men there were in France prepared to give a trial to liberalism, and to explore the possibilities of constitutional monarchy and an English peace. Such, when once they were returned in numbers to the Councils, were adjudged by Barras, the Director in Paris, and by Bonaparte, his military friend in Italy, too dangerous to live. "I have come here to kill the royalists," said Augereau, the general's emissary, with characteristic frankness, as he brought his troops into Paris for the *coup d'état* of Fructidor. Suspect deputies were seized in their sleep and shipped off without trial to Cayenne. Military commissions in the provinces dealt freely in sentences of death and deportation. The elections in 49 departments were cancelled. Among the victims of this September violence were some of the noblest names in France: Pichegru, the conqueror of Holland; Barthélemy, the diplomatist who signed the Prussian treaty; and Carnot, the organizer of victory. Barras, however, the ex-terrorist, was secure, and with him a Jacobin government so bad and purposeless that only fatigue and indifference could have preserved it, until Bonaparte was ready to seize command.

While cultivated Germans were delighting in Goethe's *Wilhelm Meister*, or reading a new plan for eternal peace put out from Königsberg by Immanuel Kant, the French Jacobins, relieved of dynastic opposition, had gained another

Sept. 4, 1797

lease of life, and persevered in their lucrative policy of plunder and conquest. They made the best of their opportunity. Revolutions were initiated in Switzerland, Rome, and Naples; 1798- and the Helvetian, the Roman, and the Parthenopean[1] 9 Republics were added to the list of French dependencies. The politic scruples of Bonaparte, who knew the Latin peasant to be religious, and wanted his body for the wars, weighed little with the anti-clerical rulers of France. The Pope of Rome was treated with little more respect than the King of France. His person was seized and transported across the French border to Valence.

The year of Bonaparte's triumphs in Italy contains one of the darkest pages in the British calendar. In April and May the fleet upon which everything depended was paralysed by serious mutinies at Spithead and the Nore. The crisis was overcome by that commixture of firmness and good sense which has often in the annals of England mitigated the penalties of long insensibility. The legitimate grievances of the sailors were redressed, the ringleaders were hanged, discipline was restored, after which with a swift and memorable resilience the navy proceeded to win the two victories of Oct., Camperdown and the Nile, which changed the history of 1797 Europe. In the first of these actions Duncan obliterated the Dutch navy; in the second Nelson destroyed the French Aug., fleet which had conveyed Bonaparte to Egypt, and so, by 1798 a swift cannonade in Aboukir Bay, secured for Britain a naval preponderance in the Mediterranean, which was never lost.

For in 1798 Bonaparte was in Egypt. Invited by the Directory to invade England, he had preferred, after a careful examination, to assail the enemy at that point in her worldwide sphere of influence where he expected that a French success might exercise a most shattering effect on her confidence and stability. Vast chimerical projects floated into a mind which was already fired by the fame and example of Alexander. From Egypt he would create an Eastern Empire, perhaps march on India, perhaps on Constantinople, and bring the shopkeeping island to a beggar's repentance by the destruction of its trade. In this design he was counting on the help of Tippoo and the Mahrattas. "You are," he said

[1] *I.e.*, Neapolitan.

to his army, as he embarked at Toulon, "one of the wings of the army of England."

July,
1798
Modern Egypt, with its superficial glaze of French civilization, dates from the battle of the Pyramids, where Bonaparte destroyed the savage power of the Mamelukes. His expedition restored a long lost province to European civilization and advertised its archaeological interest to the West. From the valley of the Nile and all over the Aegean the Odyssey of the marvellous foreigner continued to inspire hopes of liberty and to furnish a pattern of civilized and ordered rule. It was a force in Greece, and penetrated to Albania, whence a great adventurer, whose Mosque still dominates the citadel of Cairo, came forth to lay in the valley of the Nile the foundations of a modern state. Among the many imitators of Napoleon none was more influential than Mehemet Ali, the ancestor of a line of Pashas, Khedives, and Kings, who, by his fiery and domineering energy, built out of Napoleonic ideas the Egypt which we know.

Nov.,
1798
The news of Nelson's great victory brought into being the Second Coalition. From Naples, where the Queen and her friend Emma Hamilton were thrown into wild paroxysms by the appearance of the conquering hero, the will to war passed swiftly through Vienna to St. Petersburg and to Constantinople, until it was moulded by Pitt's statesmanship and by British subsidies into a large design for driving France behind her ancient frontiers, and for the overthrow of her Jacobin government. The early successes of the allies were astonishing. In one brief summer campaign (1799) all that Napoleon had gained in Italy and all that the Directory had added to his gains was lost to the Republic. Suvoroff, a meteor out of wind-swept steppes, a Tatar peasant general, very old, very small, and very fiery, inspired into his Russian following

Aug.
15,
1799
a spirit as indomitable as his own. He beat Moreau at Cassano, helped to rout Joubert at Novi, and sent the little Franco-Italian republics clattering to the ground like a pack of cards. But the wild soldier of genius could not endure the pretensions of his pedantic and overbearing allies. There was nothing in common between Suvoroff's savage impetuosity and the slow deliberate formalism of Austrian warfare. Fortunately for France, before the next act of the Italian drama was played, the Tzar had broken with the Allies, and

Suvoroff was far away in his native land. Meanwhile victories won by Masséna at Zürich and by Brune in Holland had saved France from complete disaster.

With the entry of Turkey into the war Napoleon's dreams of an Indian expedition were replaced by the narrower objective of a Syrian campaign. With thirteen thousand picked troops he reached Acre, and was there stopped by two resolute men, Sydney Smith and Phélippeaux, his old school-mate. It was a blessing in disguise. What was to be feared from the Syrian campaign was not the quality of the Turkish troops, which was low, but the vast and waterless spaces over which a Turkish army in retreat might succeed under skilful guidance in luring a pursuing foe. Only after the most serious losses was Napoleon able to extricate his army from Syria. That he could without disaster have led it over the highlands of Anatolia, if such was ever his intention, is hardly credible. From these dangerous temptations he was saved by a fortunate and humiliating repulse. Mar., 1799

To the making of his career the Turkish war was of rare and unexpected assistance. If the invasion of Egypt was romantic, still more poetic was the glamour which attached to the Syrian campaign. Home-staying Frenchmen, however much they might mock at the Pope and the priest, read with a thrill the bulletins of the young French general who had taken Palestine, had set up his quarters in the Monastery of Nazareth, and had read the Bible to his officers under a Syrian sky in places sanctified by Christ and His apostles and made glorious in the eyes of Frenchmen by the exploits of the first Crusade. The recovery of Palestine from the Turk, which appealed even to the Baptist chief of a British Cabinet at the end of the Great War, was an idea which exercised a yet more powerful attraction for the countrymen of St. Louis, living under the sordid rule of the Directory. The name of Bonaparte was on everybody's lips. Before he returned to France, leaving his troops to fend as best they might, he was already the hero of a nation, and its uncrowned master. The news of a brilliant action against the Turks at Aboukir balanced the grim fact that a splendid army had been wasted on a profitless expedition. July, 1799

After ten years of war and revolution France desired

nothing so much as peace and ordered self-government. The country was tired of confusion and anarchy, of unrepaired roads and endemic brigandage, of schools without teachers and hospitals without nurses, and of the dragging royalist insurrection, which paralysed the life of fourteen departments. Even in the circle of Paris politicians there were men who saw that only a soldier's sword could cut France free from the entanglements of faction and establish an era of ordered liberty. One of these was a remarkable political figure, who, in the worst months of 1799, was brought into the Directory from the embassy at Berlin, His name was Sieyès.

1748-
1836

No one was more deeply concerned in fixing the shape of the revolution, which he was now determined to transform, than this clear-thinking unfrocked priest, the champion of the Third Estate, the oracle of the Constituent Assembly, the creator of the artificial departments, the hammer of the Church, the adviser of the Girondins. That a thinker of such antecedents and of such authority should, from within the inner circle of the government, now decide to call upon the military arm was a fact of great significance. In the furtherance of his high ambition, Bonaparte, landing at Fréjus on October 9, could have wished for no more dexterous or effectual ally.

Nov.
9,
1799

On a dull November evening the last scene of the French Revolution was enacted in the orangery and park of St. Cloud. Thither on the false pretext of a Jacobin conspiracy the Councils had been transferred, there they were encompassed by armed men, and thence in the gathering gloom, they were ignominiously dispersed at the point of the sword. The critical moment in a day of hazards and uncertainties was when Lucien Bonaparte, the young President of the Five Hundred, left the Assembly, and, on the fictitious plea that daggers had been raised against his brother, called upon the troops, who were mustered on the terrace, in the name of the law to clear the hall. Paris was unmoved by the imposture and violence incidental to the destruction of Parliamentary liberty. No tears fell over the Directory and the Councils. They had talked wildly and governed ill. All through France the *coup d'état* of Brumaire (November 9) was acclaimed as the dawn of a new era. A few weeks later the country by a vast preponderance of votes accepted a new Constitution, which gave to Napoleon as the first of three Consuls plenary authority over its destinies for the next ten years.

The Republic remained and not in outward form only. Bonaparte was a child of the revolution, equally in the sense that like so many other brilliant men he was enabled by reason of that great social convulsion to come into the forefront of affairs, as also because his youthful mind had been formed by the literature of criticism and revolt which had heralded the storm. A free career to talent could never fail to appeal to him. It was the essence of democracy, the mainstay of power, the secret of the military successes, which had made Europe tremble before the Revolution. This side at least of the revolutionary conquest Bonaparte resolved to preserve. Political liberty might go, social equality was vital. The amazing preponderance over Europe which France obtained during the Consulate and the Empire is not only to be explained by the genius of its leader, but is also due to the fact that by the destruction of privilege the best talent of the most populous of the highly civilized countries of the West was available for his service. Talleyrand was at the Foreign Office, Fouché at the Police. Men of science, a thing incredible at Whitehall, were given portfolios. The Council of State was the most efficient body of experts which Europe had yet seen. For the most part the marshals of the victorious armies had risen by merit from the ranks.

To the appeasement of France Bonaparte brought all the gifts of skill, insight, and detachment which the problem demanded. He was neither Jacobin nor royalist, but being raised above the strife of factions could see the needs of the country as a whole. Reasoning that the peasantry were religious, he restored the freedom of Catholic worship and made a Concordat with the Pope. The Vendée was pacified. The tyrannical laws of the Jacobins were repealed. Gaudin, an able financier, was called in to give France, which he succeeded in doing, a system of direct and indirect taxes, at once fairly assessed and not too onerous, changes which, coupled with the foundation of the Bank of France in 1800, inaugurated a condition of financial stability to which the country had long been a stranger. In all these necessary and welcome measures the First Consul marched with his country's mind. For a time the voice of liberal opposition

1802

was heard in a small assembly known as the Tribunate, which the ingenuity of Sieyès had intercalated into the Constitution for the ventilation of grievances. Even this slight concession to freedom was found excessive. The Tribunate, becoming inconvenient, was suppressed in 1807, and perished without a murmur of sympathy or protest.

The task of bringing peace to Europe was far more difficult. Though Paul of Russia had withdrawn from the coalition, and was fast bound in admiration to Bonaparte, Austria and England were still in the field and obdurate to the First Consul's advances. Austria, then, as the more vulnerable of his two opponents, was singled out as the first object of attack, and with an ease which offers a surprising contrast to the campaign of the previous year, Austria was defeated. The single victory of Marengo (June 4, 1800), which threw France into paroxysms of enthusiasm, and gave to the Consulate the necessary baptism of military glory, was sufficient to bring toppling to the ground the ascendancy which the Austrians had built up for themselves with Russian aid during Napoleon's absence in Egypt. In Paris nobody cared to observe that Bonaparte had failed to relieve Masséna in Genoa, and that only by the sudden return of Desaix from the south had he been saved from calamitous defeat at Marengo. It was sufficient that like Hannibal he had crossed the Alps, boldly thrown himself across the enemies' communications, and with fifteen guns against two hundred, won a crushing victory. In the next December the triumph of France was clinched at Hohenlinden. The Austrians had not been fortunate in their commanders. Napoleon had been pitted against the aged Melas, Moreau against an Archduke of eighteen years.

Dec. 3, 1800

Chastised by these two defeats the Emperor sued for peace, and at Lunéville (February, 1801) assented to a map of Europe which brought the French frontier to the Rhine, and recognized the four client republics, Batavian and Helvetian, Cisalpine and Ligurian, which had been set up as outlying spurs of revolutionary propaganda and influence. A Europe so constituted the Cabinet of William Pitt could never accept.

Feb. 9, 1801

The general outlook of Britain towards the French Revolution had been determined at its very outset by a dazzling political pamphlet, which was the more impressive since it

came from the pen of an Irishman and a Whig. Burke's Nov.,
Reflections instilled into the Tory majority who governed the 1790
country a deep horror of the Revolution, which the advent of
Bonaparte to power did nothing to diminish. A small
minority of clear-sighted independent men like Charles Fox
divined the great civil qualities of the First Consul. By the
great mass of the nation they were unperceived. To them he
was the creature of an odious and criminal movement, the
last and most formidable of the revolutionary bandits, who
had deluged Europe with blood, an ogre noted for a long
carnival of Italian rapine, and more recently for alleged
atrocities in Syria, the murder of Turkish prisoners who had
surrendered on parole, and the poisoning of invalids whom
it was cumbersome to save.

It is nevertheless an amazing instance of insolent fatuity
that when in 1799 the First Consul expressed to the British
Government his desire for peace, the reply came that the best
guarantee which France could give of her sincerity would be
the recall of her legitimate sovereign. Such an answer, as
Talleyrand was quick to note, came ill from a German who
sat upon the Stuart throne.

In the long controversy with France, Britain had experienced continual anxiety from the griefs, discontents, and
conspiracies of Ireland. So it was during the war of the
American revolt: so it proved again to be when the ideas of
the French Revolution, alighting first among the educated
Protestants of the north, spread sparks far and wide among
the downtrodden and passive Catholics in the southern and
western part of the island. Of all European peoples, the
ignorant and priest-ridden Irish Catholics were most remote
from the innovating and impious temper of the French
Revolution. But when men are told that they are wronged;
when they realize that they are disfranchised in their own
country; when they are invited in the name of liberty and
equality to throw off an alien yoke, and to take their lawful
share in the ruling of their native land, then, no matter how
conservative they may be, the appeal will go home. This is
what happened in Ireland. The Protestants of the north led by
Wolfe Tone, the founder of the United Irishmen, called upon
their Catholic compatriots to claim the right to sit in the
Parliament of Dublin. The Catholics made their claim and

were refused, rose in rebellion and were crushed. Then Pitt, seeing many difficulties and dangers resulting from the existence of two Parliaments under one crown, carried out the Legislative Union of 1800, under which a hundred seats in the House of Commons and thirty-two in the House of Lords were accorded to Protestant Irishmen. The constitutional change, though violently resisted by the Protestant patriots of the Dublin Parliament, and carried out only by extensive bribery, was for the moment effective. Ireland gave little serious trouble during the Napoleonic wars: but the Irish question, which is proverbially fatal to British statesmen, closed the famous ministry of Pitt. That wise statesman had seen from the first that it was essential for the success of the Union that Catholic Irishmen should be returned to the Parliament of Westminster. He believed that Catholic emancipation was just; he argued that it was politic; he knew that it was safe. The Catholic vote, which might be dangerous in Dublin, would be harmless in the prevailingly Protestant Mar., atmosphere of Westminster. But the King, out of respect to 1801 his coronation oath, opposed an obstinate negative. That Pitt thereupon resigned, and never thereafter presumed to press his policy, is one of the major calamities of Irish history.

In his enterprise of striking England to the ground, Napoleon hit upon the idea of a continental blockade. Starting from the premise that England was a nation of shopkeepers, he concluded that such a country could receive no wound more fatal than the closure of every continental market to its goods. Accordingly Spain was directed to invade Portugal, while a French garrison dragooned the miserable Sovereign of Naples into a commercial policy conformable to the French design. It was plain, however, from the first that a Mediterranean blockade was in itself of little value. If English merchandise could penetrate into Hamburg or Lübeck, or even Stockholm or St. Petersburg, the blockade was broken and the game was up. The policy was not one which could succeed by halves. It must either succeed entirely or not at all, and what was formidable and ultimately ruinous to Napoleon was the fact that, drawn by the mirage of a universal blockade, he was condemned to the pursuit of a universal Empire. There was, however, a moment at the beginning of 1801, when this costly and exorbitant folly was nearer to success than at any subsequent stage of the war. Paul I of Russia was a half-crazy tyrant, whose brutality was partly redeemed by a whimsical enthusiasm for the Knights of Malta, and by a passionate admiration for the genius of Napoleon. In December, 1800, this strange Muscovite savage came forward as the champion of the higher morality in the maritime war. Gathering Denmark, Sweden and Prussia under his wing, Paul formed a League of Armed Neutrality for the protection of neutral rights, and with the special object of injuring Britain. It had been an old point of weakness in the armoury of that country that its navy in searching neutral vessels for enemy goods or contraband of war had often caused loss and inconvenience to their owners. How the right of search should be exercised, with what restraints and safeguards, courtesies and compensations, was and remains a thorny problem of international law. The doctrine of "the Freedom of the Seas," the view that neutral ships plying on their lawful occasions should be free from molestation from belligerent navies, was promulgated by Catharine II of Russia in 1780, was in 1800 revived by Paul, and to this day, though the American navy threw it to the winds in the latest phase of the Great War, remains a live issue which divides opinion. That Paul I should have succeeded in getting the Northern Powers to defend the principles of the Armed Neutrality was for Napoleon an unexpected piece of good fortune, which he was prompt to seize. But just as the combination was assuming a menacing shape, as the Prussians were marching into Hanover and Danish troops were taking station in Hamburg and Lübeck, the whole machine was shattered in pieces. In March, 1801, the Tzar was strangled in a palace revolution. In April the Danish fleet was broken by Nelson's guns at Copenhagen. Under the stress of this double shock the Northern League, which at one time promised to complete the continental blockade, came to a sudden and inglorious end.

These events, the assassination of the Tzar, the battle of Copenhagen, and the retirement of Pitt, prepared the way for the Peace of Amiens (March, 1802). It is the fashion of English writers to say that Addington, the new Prime Minister, who was not made of hard metal, surrendered too much. French writers take the opposite view. England at

least retained her naval supremacy unimpaired, and of her
many overseas conquests held on to Trinidad, which she had
taken from the Spaniards, and Ceylon, which she had
wrested from the Dutch. If it be true that the French could
never have forced her to give up the conquests which she was
prepared to surrender, it is also true that these overseas
territories would easily be recaptured by a superior naval
power on the resumption of war. The worst augury for
future peace was the lack of a commercial pact. So long as
English merchants in France were treated as enemy aliens,
there could be no true understanding between the French
and English peoples.

CHAPTER LXIX

CONSULATE AND EMPIRE

*Napoleon's civil qualities. The Concordat. The Codes. The
University of France. Renewal of war. The Empire. The
new Charlemagne. The camp of Boulogne.*

NAPOLEON RESTORED the respect for authority in France. He
found chaos and left order, inherited mutiny and created
discipline. For ten years the passions which rent the social
fabric had raged unchecked, while those moral forces which
helped to strengthen it had suffered a disastrous eclipse. The
sentiment of reverence had been laughed away. Religion,
antiquity, the long descended traditions of France, even the
common decencies of life, had been made to appear as
absurd and irrational survivals from a tyrannical past.
Napoleon was a Voltairean, without formal religion or established morality, and with social manners of which the best
that can be said is that while they were sometimes gracious,
kindly, and dignified, they were often characterized by un-
feeling brutality. But he was a man born for command, and
quick to discern that union was the secret of national
strength. Every force which tended to assist social cohesion
found in him a champion; religion, because it was "the
mystery of the social order," education, because it could be

moulded to his will, the spirit of precision and science in government, because it ministered to power, outward decorum as a preventive against the biting wit of Paris. It was his task to reconcile the new France with the old, to rally priest and *émigré*, Jew, Protestant, Atheist, and Jacobin to the service of the state, and to compel them to minister to its grandeur. In his search for stability he ended by marrying into the proudest and oldest House in Europe. His government was of a form new to France, a scientific despotism based on the plébiscite. Three times, in 1800, in 1802, and in 1804, he sought and obtained authority from the people. In quick succession the popular voice made him First Consul for ten years, Consul for life, and finally Emperor. No European monarch could claim so good a title.

In according to Napoleon this remarkable and ascending measure of confidence the French people expected him to give them in return the golden blessings of peace. This he did not, perhaps could not, achieve. On the contrary his advent to power led up to a war which, after nearly uniting central Europe under French rule, culminated in a military collapse so complete that, forfeiting even the earliest conquests of the Revolution, France was driven back within the ancient limits of the monarchy. It is one of the ironies of history that a family whose name is synonymous with martial renown actually diminished the area of France. The first Napoleon lost Belgium. His nephew, though he acquired Savoy and Nice by a diplomatic bargain, forfeited Alsace-Lorraine in an unsuccessful appeal to arms. It was given to a bourgeois Republic of black-coated lawyers and doctors to recover for France, with the aid of a wide circle of allies, some of the territory and most of the influence which was lost in the catastrophes of the Napoleonic house.

If the conquests of Napoleon were ephemeral, his civilian work in France was built upon granite. In every quality required for civil administration, in imagination and initiative, in propulsive power and minute attention to detail, in clearness of head and capacity for work he stands supreme. With extraordinary speed the devastation wrought by the revolution was repaired. In the atmosphere of hope and excitement, which prevailed in France during the Consulate, prodigies were performed in every department of administration central and local for the improvement of the material condition of the people. The hampering conditions of the *ancien régime* were no longer present. There were no corporations, Parliaments, or Provincial Estates, no blocks of privileged citizens standing outside the general law. The prefect in his department, the sub-prefect in his arrondissement, the mayor in his commune, operating on a plain, unobstructed surface, executed the commands of the Head of the State.

July, 1801   The Concordat with the Papacy was not the least important part of Napoleon's policy of reconciling the new world with the old. Among the army chiefs who retained the acute atheism of the revolutionary period, as also among the political and intellectual Parisians, the change was distasteful and derided. It seemed to be the surrender of a gain for civilization, a relapse into the darkness of mediaeval night, an invitation to the priest once more to recover his lost empire over the mind of man. But Napoleon looked beyond the army chiefs and the intellectuals of Paris to the vast mass of the peasantry, who formed the manpower of his conscript armies. He had divined the leadership of the priest in the revolt of the Vendée, had seen the Italian peasant kneeling before the little wayside shrine, and knew that religion was a power among simple men. The schism in the Church was an open wound, which, if not promptly healed, would corrupt and endanger the body politic. Napoleon therefore decided to make the plunge. In 1802, after protracted negotiations, conducted on his side with a brilliant mixture of force and fraud, he came to terms with the new Pope Pius VII.

Very different, however, from the Church of the *ancien régime* was the new Roman Catholic establishment which resulted from the Concordat and from the organic articles by which it was accompanied. The broad acres and remunerative tithes, the princely salaries and establishments, the imposing assemblies and vast social influence, which had belonged for many centuries to the prelates of the Gallican Church, were now things of the past. The Napoleonic bishop, an indifferently paid menial of a jealous state, was allowed neither to travel outside his diocese, nor to summon a synod, nor to correspond with Rome without the consent of the civil power. The Church indeed was permitted to live and to function. The Angelus again called the peasant to prayer, the white surplice of the priest again fluttered in the sunlight, the congregation of the faithful again clustered round the altar or kept the Sunday rest without fear of persecution. Once more bishops were nominated and consecrated after the practice of the *ancien régime*. But the Church had lost its independence, and sunk to the position of an impoverished and subservient client of the civil power. It was no longer the sole office of the priest to be the spiritual father of his flock, helping the sick, consoling the dying, instructing the young in the elements of religion. He was expected to read the army bulletins from the pulpit, to urge the laggard to the colours, and to instil into tender minds through the catechism of Napoleon the duty of implicit obedience to the Head of the State.

It may yet be asked whether it was necessary for Napoleon to come to terms with the Pope. A Gallican Church, orthodox in faith, but independent of Rome, was an alternative which in the prostration of religious life then prevailing, and with so many ardent priests killed in the civil wars, might have been accepted by the vast majority of the French clergy. But though Napoleon threatened the negotiating Cardinals with Gallicanism he did not adopt it. He had need of the Papacy. Low as that ancient institution had fallen, so low that in common with William Pitt and Thugut, the Austrian Chancellor, Napoleon believed its days to be numbered, he could not afford to throw away its support. "The old machine, which would crumple up of itself," might yet be of use in assisting him to regiment the Catholics of other lands.

The codification of French law, perhaps the most enduring of Napoleon's achievements, was a dream old as the fifteenth century, and an integral part of the revolutionary creed. But a period of torrential legislation is unpropitious to a task which demands a steady view of the legal landscape. The Revolution decreed that there should be a code, prepared numerous drafts, but in its feverish rush left nothing accomplished. Napoleon took up the suspended work, and by his personal energy and interest swiftly drove it to a triumphant conclusion. The Civil Code did not, of course, spring from the brain of one transcendent legislator. The main legal principles of the *ancien régime*, alike of the Roman Law which prevailed in the South, and of the Frankish *coutumes* which governed the North, together with those parts of the

1804

revolutionary legislation which commended themselves to Napoleon and his advisers, were fused together and distilled into a volume, so beautifully clear that the layman may read it with enjoyment, and so succinct that it may be carried without embarrassment in the pocket of a great-coat. The merit of the Civil Code is not that it is exhaustive, or that it has prevented the growth of case law, or that it is flawless in form and substance; but that in firm intelligible outline it fixes the structure of a civilized lay society, based on social equality and religious toleration, on private property and coherent family life. The moment was opportune. A few years earlier the Code would have glittered with revolutionary extravagance, a few years later it might have been darkened by the shades of despotism. Drafted as it was in the fresh effulgence of the Consulate, when Napoleon was dealing out even-handed justice to all sections of French society, it presented, not only to France but to all Europe, a handy prospectus of a country faithful to a long tradition of family discipline and private ownership, but at the same time tenacious of the best fruits of a lay and liberal revolution. That is the chief European significance of the Civil Code. Through the institution of civil marriage and divorce it spread through Europe the idea of a community capable of dispensing with clerical aid. To the religious confessions marriage must always be a sacrament. In the Code it is a civil contract which may be cheaply made and cheaply revoked in the drab office of an unsanctified layman. For the first time since the acceptance of Christianity by Constantine a settled and ordered European state legalized in a code the thoroughly secular life.

From this it should not be inferred that Napoleon undervalued the forces of religion and family discipline as elements in social hygiene. The exact opposite is the case. The ideas of Napoleon upon family life were of Roman austerity. For him the authority of the father could not be too strong or the subjection of the wife too complete. "Do you not know," he said, "that the Angel told Eve to obey her husband? Morality has written this article in all languages. *A fortiori* should it be written in French in the Code." But the tide of revolutionary secularism was too strong to be resisted. Napoleon curtailed the facilities for divorce, which had been provided by the revolution, but was compelled to accept the institution.

It is a note of Napoleon's greatness that, not content with launching the enterprise of the Civil Code, he took a substantive and often a decisive part in the discussions upon the draft in the legislative Committee of the Council of State. Minute technicalities did not interest him, but he had an eagle eye for any issue which touched upon the broader aspects of sound policy, and whenever these came into the field of vision he was prepared with a clear and forcible view. In general he wanted France to be a land of moderate not too minutely divided properties, of despotic fathers and obedient children, and of a rightless and dependent womankind. In all these particulars he succeeded in stamping the impress of his powerful convictions on the law of France.

More than any other influence the Civil Code spread through Europe the fame of the institutions of the new France. Here was the pith and kernel of the revolutionary philosophy in a shape made practical for the use of men. Here was a combination of fruitful innovation and ancient usage. Here was liberty combined with order. Not since the Institutes of Justinian has any compendium of law been so widely copied.

There were four other Napoleonic Codes. Two of these, since they were drafted under the Empire, and deal with the trial and punishment of crime, are defaced by the imprint of arbitrary power. A long list of savage penalties (including confiscation) shows that the framers of the Penal Code were far from reflecting the best thought of their time in the sphere of criminal legislation. The Code of Criminal Procedure is subject, albeit to a less degree, to the same reproach. Though it gives the accused the benefit of an open trial and a jury, these memorable advantages, the bequest of the revolution, were counterbalanced by other provisions, drawn from the jurisprudence of the *ancien régime* or from the imperial requirements of Napoleon, which were less favourable to the protection of the weak and innocent. Of these it is here sufficient to note the secret preliminary inquisition under the *juge d'instruction*, and the fact that the nomination of the jurors was entrusted to the prefects.

While this legal work was proceeding, a scheme of intellectual discipline for the Empire, rigorous as that of the Jesuit Order, was gradually taking shape in Napoleon's mind. The happy-go-lucky system prevailing in England, where young gentlemen whose real interests were in cricket and fives, battledore and peg top, were flogged into a smattering of Greek and Latin accidence by pedagogues who could not be dismissed from their posts even by King George himself, was wholly foreign to the Emperor's mentality. He would have regarded it as an act of political insanity to leave the education of a people to the chance play of private enterprise and endowment. Private schools must indeed exist, for in the stress of war there could be little public money for education, but private schools must submit to public control. Amusement was no part of education. Life was serious. The young should be educated for the polity and in a military Empire must be taught to serve, to march, and to die.

A University, controlled by the state, co-extensive with the Empire, and charged with the duty of organizing and supervising all branches of public instruction, was set up in 1808 to give effect to these ideas. The strange seed germinated in a soil prepared for centralization, and Napoleon's University of France, divided into local academies, survived with some transformations into the twentieth century. In all this there was little enough of democracy. Nothing was done for the primary schools, which were left to private agencies. Even in the sphere of secondary education the state *lycées* and colleges failed to cover half the ground. If, then, the reign of Napoleon is remarkable in the educational history of France, it is not because the state was generous to education, but because it was hostile to intellectual freedom. On the one side of the Channel was the careless, enjoying Etonian, repeatedly flogged and indifferently taught. On the other side, in a *lycée* which partook of the melancholy of a monastery and the rigour of a barrack, was a cheerless little boy in a tight uniform, drilled, spied upon, crammed with information, and, in the process of his rough adjustment to the Emperor's Spartan purpose, starved of the wholesome pleasures of youth.

It was a blot upon Napoleon's character for prudence that, having everything to gain by a prolonged peace, he should have so ordered his policy as to excite to the utmost degree the apprehensions of his rivals. In London it was noted that while English ships and English goods were rigorously excluded from French ports, the power of France was continually advancing. The English Cabinet was not indifferent to these changes. When it saw a French garrison established in Holland it began to reconsider its undertaking to restore the Cape. When it realized that Piedmont and the Valais were annexed to France, and that the Swiss and Cisalpine Republics had received new Constitutions, which brought them more clearly than before under French influence, it raised the question of compensations. When it learned that a great military expedition, more powerful than the avowed objective seemed to warrant, had sailed for the recovery of the black republic of San Domingo, it suspected, and with reason, that Napoleon was harbouring vast ulterior designs in the western hemisphere. But more sinister even than these disquieting symptoms was the evidence that the recovery of Egypt and the expansion of French territory in India still occupied a place in the schemes of the First Consul. A report from the pen of Colonel Sebastiani published in the *Moniteur* on January 30, 1803, and depicting the popularity of the French in the East, and the ease with which Egypt might be reconquered, confirmed the worst suspicions of the intentions of Napoleon. But if war were again to break out in the East, Malta with its superb harbour and famous fortifications was an essential point in the English defence. Accordingly, despite the terms of the Treaty of Amiens, England declined to evacuate the island. Her decision, to which she was urged by the rulers of Russia and Turkey, each apprehensive of Napoleon's oriental designs, was technically incorrect. Yet in thus forcing a war can she be blamed? Secret instructions issued by Napoleon to General Decaen show that the project for French aggrandizement in India was already fully formed.

May, 1803

Before any serious blow had been struck in the war, a remarkable constitutional revolution took place in France. It was undoubtedly the will of the French people that the *régime* of Napoleon, which had brought France great benefits, should be protected against the opposite dangers of Jacobin violence and royalist reaction. These dangers, which were still acute, had since the general pacification of the Vendée taken the form of plots to assassinate the First Consul either by a bomb attack or by an armed affray. One such attack engineered by royalists missed its aim in 1800. Another, wider and more disjointed, since it included not only royalist fanatics such as Georges Cadoudal, but even famous generals of the Republic like Moreau and Pichegru, was, with the active and shameful connivance of some subordinate English ministers, in course of preparation during the autumn and winter of 1803, and in the spring of the following year. Napoleon was well served by his police and *agents-provocateurs*. He knew that famous Republican soldiers had been artfully entangled in the fringes of a royalist web, woven by the Comte d'Artois from his retreat in England, that Moreau had talked to Pichegru, that Normandy and Brittany were to be stirred to revolt, and that the whole conspiracy was timed to explode on the arrival of a Bourbon Prince.

Who was that prince? It so happened that the Duc d'Enghien, the last descendant of the House of Condé, was in March, 1804, residing at Ettenheim in Baden, close to the French frontier. Napoleon determined to take his life. Though Moreau, Pichegru, and Georges were already under arrest, and all immediate danger had therefore disappeared, this innocent young man—for d'Enghien had, as Napoleon knew before the end, no complicity in the plot—was kidnapped, hauled off to Vincennes, and was there in the early dawn of March 21, 1804, hurriedly and secretly shot.

Carried out with a frigid determination, which shocked the conscience of the civilized world, the Corsican crime produced its designed effects. Never again did the Bourbon Princes meddle with a plot for the destruction of Napoleon, or the republicans suspect him of covert royalism. The blood of the innocent young prince was a pledge that the First Consul had ranged himself with the regicides. Even the most hardened Jacobins felt that hereditary power confided to a House now so irretrievably embroiled with the *ancien régime* could have no consequences likely to endanger the great conquest of equal rights, which it had cost so much bloodshed to secure. On April 23 Curée, a moderate regicide, proposed in the tribunate the adoption of the hereditary principle. The idea took form in a shape which commended itself alike to the ambitions of Napoleon, and to the classical taste of a people still largely revolutionary and dreading nothing so much as the restoration of the Kings. A *Senatus Consultum* of May 18, 1804, conferred upon Napoleon the title of Emperor of the French. The change received every species of confirmation which the constitutional repertory of the time could supply, the voice of the Senate, the vote of the people, the consecration of the Pope. Nobody can doubt but that it was acceptable to the nation, for the red light of the assassination plots was a signal which all could read that, failing heredity, one life alone stood between France and chaos.

Inevitably the name and example of Charlemagne captured the imagination of the new Emperor of the French. He would be the new Charlemagne, gathering the Latin and Teutonic peoples under his imperial crown, allotting client kingdoms and principalities to members of his family, treating the Pope as his chaplain, assembling in a brillant court a new class of hereditary nobles, which, since they owed everything to his favour, would add security to the throne. At St. Helena he said, "I felt my isolation, so I cast anchors of safety all round into deep waters." Yet every anchor was a challenge Mar., to Vienna, the self-promotion of the Corsican to the imperial 1805 dignity, his assumption of the Lombard Crown in Milan, his significant visit to Aachen, the city of Charlemagne, that he might test the submissive loyalty of the Rhineland. It was clear that the Holy Roman Empire was doomed. That superfluous political cobweb was swept off the German ceiling by the strong broom of the new Charlemagne in 1806. Meanwhile a new hereditary Austrian Empire, created two years earlier, and destined to go down in 1918, had experienced a baptism of ruinous defeat.

The War of the Third Coalition was waged between Aug., England, Austria, Russia, Sweden and Naples on the one 1804 hand, and France and her satellite Spain, on the other. It is characteristic of Pitt, who was the chief architect of the Coalition, that he contemplated, when the war was over and victory won, the summoning of a Congress to devise a federal system for the maintenance of a European peace. Napoleon, too, had a scheme for reorganizing Europe as a commonwealth of enlightened but unfree peoples under French hegemony; and there are some friends of European unity who still regret the frustration of his dream.

The campaign was to open with the invasion and conquest of England. In this island, so near, but so mysterious, Napoleon expected to find a down-trodden population, eager, when once a French army of liberation was in its midst, to shake off the tyrannous yoke of George III, as their American colonists had been enabled to do, also with French assistance, not thirty years before. At St. Helena he said that the *canaille* of London would have welcomed him, and that he would have set up with general acclamation republics in England and Ireland. Of the social cohesion of the English people or its new-born industrial strength he divined nothing. Had it been given him to witness the energetic preparations of the British Government, or the patriotic response of the people, he would have known that England would never become "a French island like Oléron or Corsica," and that, grave as were the risks of the Channel crossing, they would be surpassed by the perils awaiting an invader among the downlands or hopfields of Kent.

The narrow seas were never crossed. An army of 210,000 men, gathered in great camps along the North Sea and Channel coast, for two years awaited the order to embark. The signal did not come. Nelson was watching the Toulon fleet, Cornwallis was blockading Brest. Every French or Spanish squadron was under the close observation of an enemy as confident by reason of superior skill and numbers as his rival was dispirited. It followed that the one condition without which the whole enterprise was doomed to failure was never realized. Not for twelve hours was Napoleon able to concentrate in the Channel a fleet sufficiently strong to protect the transport and disembarkation of even a small detachment of his troops. Yet only when the news reached him in August, 1805, that Villeneuve, commanding the French-Spanish fleet, had run back into Cadiz harbour did the Emperor abandon hope. The column at Boulogne, which still commemorates his great ambition, recalls at the same time the heroic vigil of English sailors, living hard on mouldy biscuit or salted pork, and in all weather, fair and foul, keeping the seas in their tossing castles of oak, that the independence of England, and with it the liberty of Europe, might be preserved.

On a grey October day when all danger of invasion was Oct.
passed and Napoleon was far away in the heart of Bavaria, 21,
Nelson won the annihilating victory over Villeneuve which 1805
to the end of the war established beyond challenge the
British mastery of the sea. Attacking in double column with
twenty-seven sail of the line, he destroyed the combined
fleets of France and Spain which had been lured out of Cadiz
harbour to their doom. Yet the victory of Trafalgar, though
it placed the French and Spanish colonies at the mercy of the
British fleet, brought little pleasure to the nation, for Nelson
had fallen in action and a strong Austrian force under Mack, Oct.
a general of whom much was expected, had only a day before 20,
capitulated at Ulm to the encircling army of the French.   1805

CHAPTER LXX

THE CONTINENTAL BLOCKADE

*The French hegemony in central Europe. Napoleon's diplo-
macy. Tilsit. The continental blockade. The problem of Italy.
Quarrel with the Pope. The Spanish intervention. Importance
of the Spanish War. Bayonne. The royalism of Spain. Birth of
Spanish Liberalism. The Constitution of 1812.*

NAPOLEON'S sea plans had failed, but the failure was followed 1805-
by that surprising sequence of victories at Ulm and Austerlitz, 7
at Jena and Friedland, which compelled first Austria and
then Prussia to sign an ignominious peace, and by an arrangement made at Tilsit between Napoleon and Alexander of
Russia, fastened upon Central Europe the hegemony of the
French Empire. Miracles do not happen in history. But the
effect on the political landscape of the campaigns of 1805,
1806, and 1807 has in it the suddenness and completeness
which partake of the miraculous. As on every other occasion,
Napoleon profited by the military mistakes of his opponents,
of which the gravest was the decision of the Austrians and Dec.,
Russians to force a battle at Austerlitz, before the Prussians 1805
had thrown their weight into the war and were in a position
to menace his communications. Besides this astonishing

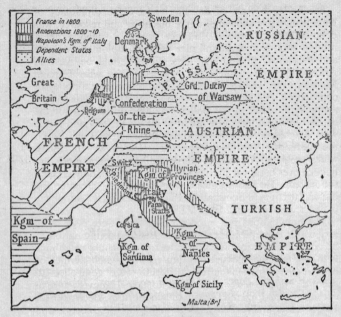

THE CONQUESTS OF NAPOLEON

error of military judgment, there was present in this, as in other coalitions, a fatal weakness arising from a long heritage of political difference between the leading allies. There was little friendship between the Prussians and Austrians. Having withdrawn from the war in 1795, Prussia, under the timid rule of Frederick William III, was in no hurry to endanger the substantial advantages which she had derived from a policy of peaceful neutrality, and only under the special pressure of the Tzar, and as a consequence of the violation of her territory by the army of the Rhine as it marched south-eastwards upon Ulm, was she stirred into offering, under the name of an armed Dec. neutrality, a show of opposition. It was then too late. The 22, Austrians were knocked out of the ring at Austerlitz, before 1805 the Prussian army was ready to strike.

During these years of dazzling victory the diplomacy of Napoleon, while showing infinite ingenuity and resource, was open to serious reproach. France needed a friend. Talleyrand, a good European and nice judge of diplomatic weights and measures, advised that this friend should be Austria. After Ulm, and again after Austerlitz, the wise Foreign Minister urged in vain upon his ambitious master a policy of conciliation, under which Austria might be assisted to aggrandize herself in the Balkans as a compensation for the losses which she would be asked to accept in Italy and in the west. To these counsels Napoleon turned a deaf ear. Even the mutilating Treaty of Pressburg (December 26, 1805), which robbed Austria of three million inhabitants, and handed over her loyal Tyrolese to Bavaria, struck him as being too lenient. He had no measure to mete out to a beaten foe but an extremity of humiliation which left behind it a smouldering passion of revenge.

The humiliations put upon the Prussians were even more serious. It is no pleasant thing for a self-respecting nation to be compelled by an alien power to rob a friendly neighbour with whom it has no quarrel, but to this signal sacrifice of honour the Prussians after Austerlitz were compelled to submit. Napoleon required them to take Hanover, and to declare war on England (Treaty of Schönbrunn, December 15, 1805). Honourable Prussians thought this disgraceful, and when a little later it was learnt in Berlin that Hanover was being secretly offered back to England, even the government Aug., of Frederick William III winced at the treacherous affront. 1806 Prussia declared war and suffered defeat on the fields of Jena and Auerstädt.

At Tilsit (July 8, 1807) the victor, undeterred by the eloquent entreaties of Queen Marie Louise, exacted the uttermost penalty, short of complete annihilation, which it was in his power to inflict. A new Duchy of Warsaw under the King of Saxony in the east, a Kingdom of Westphalia under Jerome Bonaparte in the west, were equipped with stolen Prussian provinces to keep the beaten enemy in check. Crushing indemnities, a burdensome army of occupation, a strict limitation of the native armed forces, completed the subjection of this stout and valiant people. At St. Helena Napoleon regretted his leniency, persisting in the bad delusion of conquerors that a vanquished nation can be permanently destroyed.

Meanwhile Alexander I, the pleasant, enthusiastic, new-found friend of Tilsit, appeared to offer to Napoleon advantages more solid than any which might be derived from the Austrian or Prussian alliance. The Tzar publicly acknowledged Napoleon's conquests, and in secret articles bound himself, should England decline to accept the mediation of Russia, to join in the continental blockade and to force Denmark, Sweden, Portugal and Austria to make war upon English commerce. With such powerful help Napoleon June, expected to rivet his dominion on the west, He stood at the 1807 summit of his fortunes, delivered as by a miracle through the crowning victory of Friedland from a thousand perils. Austria and Prussia were at his feet. Russia was his ally. Pitt was in his grave. Could it be that the islanders under such a man as the Duke of Portland would dare to refuse him peace?

The islanders were most disobliging. Apprised of the secret Sept., articles of Tilsit, George Canning, the young Foreign Minister 1807 in the Portland Cabinet, seized the Danish Fleet at Copenhagen before it fell into the hands of his enemies. By this invidious attack upon a weak and innocent nation Canning completed Nelson's work at Trafalgar and secured for his country the undisputed mastery of the seas.

The continental blockade, which was henceforth Napoleon's only bludgeon against England, involved, if it were to be exactly enforced, the political control of Italy and Spain. Of these two Latin countries Italy offered a problem altogether lighter than that which was presented by the fierce and obstinate nationalism of Spain. That Napoleon was an Italian in blood and speech was in itself a strong letter of commendation to a people which despite its inveterate political divisions yet cherished a sentiment of national pride. Moreover, Italy, unlike Spain, was long habituated to invasions from the north. If the French rule were foreign, it was no more foreign than the Austrian and Spanish domination by which it had been preceded. Rather it was more congenial. In the bustling cities of Lombardy the forward-reaching ideas of the French Revolution had made many converts before the ragged legions of Bonaparte had burst upon the Italian plain. Italy, then, was ill-prepared morally to resist

Napoleon. She had neither a national monarchy, nor a national army, nor a national tradition. When once the spine of Austrian resistance was broken in the north, as it was after the double shock of Marengo and Austerlitz, it was a light operation to evict the weak Bourbon King of Naples, and to establish French governments in Florence and Rome. The exclusion of British wares, therefore, from the ports of Italy was a policy confronted, indeed, by many obstacles, as, for instance, attacks launched from Sicily with British aid, but nevertheless capable of execution with the resources which Napoleon had at his command. The serious difficulty was moral. The exact execution of the Italian blockade involved a breach with the Pope. It was an extraordinary lapse of judgment in a man of genius who was fully alive to the importance of conciliating Catholic sentiment in his wide Empire that, rather than tolerate the neutrality of the Vatican, Napoleon deported and imprisoned the Pope, annexed his May, territories, and incorporated them into the departmental 1809 system of the French Empire. The Italians were probably of all the Mediterranean races the least religious, but the Papacy was one of the historical glories of their country, and they resented its abasement. Among Napoleon's grave errors there was none destined to shake so profoundly the fabric of his power, not in Italy alone, but all over the Catholic world, as this gratuitous affront to the Papal See and to the Roman tradition.

While this sharp quarrel with the Pope was proceeding, Napoleon launched his attack upon Spain, a country the most religious in Europe, the least affected by ecclesiastical innovations, and despite a weak, inglorious, and ill-soldered government, proudly and quixotically patriotic. This he did, although he must have known the general character of the geography and climate of the Iberian peninsula, how the whole mountain and river system of the country lay athwart the path of an invader from the north, and how in that high tableland of central Spain, now parched with torrid heat, now frozen with the blasts of an Arctic wind, no large army could hope to support itself without a commissariat corresponding to its entire needs. But graver even than sun and frost, river, mountain, and waste was the obstacle presented by the psychology of the Spanish people. The Spaniards were withdrawn from the general life of Europe. They had different ideals, different thoughts, different customs. A certain negligence, half pride, half indolence, had impeded the development of the forms of material prosperity which elsewhere are found to be favourable to intellectual curiosity and enterprise. Only a third of the country was cultivated. Despite a vast overseas Empire, there was no Spanish commercial navy. Even the Mediterranean carrying trade was conceded to foreigners. Ignorance was general, poverty without reproach. The emancipating philosophy of the eighteenth century made no appeal to the peasants and monks, the priests and vagabonds, the smugglers and brigands, who constituted the greater part of the Spanish population. An enlightened monarch like Charles III, the best of the Bourbon Kings, who expelled the Jesuits, put down the bull fights, and endeavoured to stimulate the languishing industries of the country, so far from acquiring merit in the eyes of his subjects by reason of his salutary reforms, was on that very ground the object of their hearty dislike. On his death in 1788 the obscurantism which had never really been shaken in the provinces promptly recovered its sway in the court and the government. It may readily therefore be imagined how repugnant to Spain was the notion of a foreign anti-papal philosophy enforced by the bayonets of France. The Spaniards cared nothing for the rights of man, but everything for the Catholic religion and their provincial customs. The weights and measures of Europe meant little to this proud and serious nation of individualists, for whom Church was nearer than town, town than province, province than kingdom, and kingdom than all the rest of the world. So faintly were they impressed by Napoleon's power that a little province like Asturias with an armed force of eighteen thousand men did not hesitate to raise the standard of revolt against the French Empire. The fact that Madrid, which was the centre of the road system, was for many years in French occupation, made no difference to the Andalusians of the south, the Gallegos of the west, or the Catalonians of the eastern littoral. The Spaniards did not fight on a nice calculation of probabilities. Often as they were beaten by French generals, they were never abashed by French prestige. Though their armies were ill-found in guns and cavalry, though their

1759-
88

discipline was ragged and their *morale* uncertain, in the guerilla warfare most suited to their country, and most harassing to their foe, they were past masters. Always the French were in the neighbourhood of a savage, elusive, and persistent antagonist; nor was the long line of their communications from the Pyrenees to Madrid at any time secure from the Spanish sniper, the Spanish cut-throat, and the Spanish ambush.

The Spanish insurrection, which was the first of a series of national risings against the French Empire, was rendered vastly more injurious to Napoleon by reason of the fact that it gave to the small land army of England the theatre in which it could most effectively deploy its resources. Up to the moment when the Cabinet decided to give assistance to Portugal and Spain, the English army had been frittered away upon a number of disjointed enterprises, in the Vendée, in the West Indies, in Holland, in southern Italy, which exercised no sensible influence on the general course of the war. Now that they were confronted with the great task of driving the French north of the Pyrenees with the aid of the national levies of Portugal and Spain, English soldiers were able not only to bring their own weight to bear upon the issue, but also to stiffen the resistance of the Iberian peoples.

That this great opportunity was used to the full, that the small English army in Spain was not rashly squandered, but so husbanded that in unison with its local allies it was able to keep a large French army pinned down in Spain, and ultimately to drive it across the Pyrenees, is due to the prudent genius of a great commander. Arthur Wellesley had already broken the Mahratta power on the field of Assaye. The 1803 Peninsular War gave him the opportunity of showing that singular combination of military and diplomatic prudence without which the available resources of Portugal and Spain could never have been effectively directed against the common enemy. The tactics of his first were those also of his last Aug., European victory. At Vimiero as at Waterloo victory lay 1808 with the thin red line of steady British infantry, well posted and well concealed, who had been taught to reserve their fire until such time as it could be relied on to destroy the heads of the advancing columns of the enemy. That the line could be relied on to beat the column was the core of Wellesley's tactical philosophy, and the chief military lesson of the Peninsular War.

Of the manner of Napoleon's entry into Spain and the nature and consequence of the shock which was thus administered to the Iberian peoples, a few words may fitly be said here.

1806   On the eve of Jena, and counting on a flood tide of Prussian victories, Godoy, the unpopular favourite of the Spanish Queen and the real ruler of the country, ordered the mobilization of the Spanish army. The gross indiscretion, sinking deep in Napoleon's mind, was avenged with the finest
Oct.,   Machiavellian skill. In place of an immediate and expected
1807   penalty Spain was compelled to sign a treaty at Fontainebleau, under which she promised to join in an attack on Portugal, the little country which had filled so many English cellars with its vintage, sheltered so many English fleets, and alone of continental markets was still wide open to English trade. But the conquest of Portugal, which was easily effected, was only a prelude to a larger plan. It was not sufficient that the Portuguese Regent had been driven from his capital and had taken ship for Brazil. Napoleon had determined to evict the Bourbons from Spain. Under the convenient pretext of the Portuguese campaign, French troops poured across the
Feb.,   Pyrenees, seized the frontier fortresses, and advanced to
1808   Madrid. Indignation flamed up against the favourite, who had opened the gates of Spain to an infidel enemy. A riot broke out at Aranjuez, the spring residence of the King and Queen, when it was learned that they were meditating a flight with their favourite to the Indies. The miserable Charles abdicated the throne to save the life of Godoy, and his son Ferdinand was installed in his place. But by this time Murat was in Madrid, and Napoleon was master of the situation. He refused to recognize the new King, and Charles was instructed to withdraw his abdication. Eventually the whole Spanish Royal Family, King, Queen, and heir-apparent, were decoyed to Bayonne, and there compelled to renounce all claim to the monarchy of Spain. The vacant monarchy, after
May,   having been refused by Louis, was accepted by Joseph
1808   Bonaparte, while Murat, given the choice of Portugal and Naples, wisely decided to rule in Naples.

The Spaniards were monarchists and clericals. It is a July, measure of their backwardness that they accepted without a 1808 murmur the incapable autocracy of Charles IV. The Cortes had fallen into desuetude, the age of the newspaper press had not yet begun, and the riots and conspiracies which helped Napoleon to carry out the *coup d'état* of Bayonne were directed not against the principle of monarchy, but against the hated influence of the royal favourite. From this deep devotion to the monarchical principle the Spaniards were detached neither by the ineptitude of Charles, nor by the vulgar vices of Marie Louise, his wife, nor by the cowardice and treachery of Ferdinand, the heir-apparent; nor yet were they attracted by the liberal constitution which had been drawn up at Bayonne, nor by the prospect of a progressive and imperialist Government under Joseph Bonaparte. If Joseph had been an angel from Heaven, and the constitution of Bayonne had been verbally inspired, the Spaniards would still have persisted in their idealization of the despicable Ferdinand. All through the Peninsular War this wretched Prince remained the idol of the Spanish people. That he had cringed to Napoleon, that he had showed abject cowardice, that he had plotted against his father, that he was without a grain of intelligence, that he was treacherous to his friends, all these considerations counted for nothing in comparison with the single fact that he was the rightful heir to the Spanish crown. Accordingly the downfall of the Napoleonic *régime* in Spain was inevitably followed by the restoration of Ferdinand.

Nevertheless, though the old Spain came back with Ferdinand, the struggles and miseries of the Peninsular War had created in the country the elements of a liberal and national party. In the absence of the Crown, the Spaniards had been compelled to fend for themselves. They had set up a central Junta or Council, which had been constrained by the advancing tide of French conquest to retire first to Seville, and afterwards to Cadiz. Here a Cortes had met and a constitution had been drafted, and here for the first time a battle was joined on the fundamental issue of personal liberty which, giving rise to two political parties, known respectively as *Liberales* and *Serviles*, continued to divide the political mind of Spain all through the nineteenth century. The Constitution of 1812, though it accepted the principle of the hereditary monarchy, and confined the suffrage to Roman Catholics, was a document representing the radical opinion of the sea coast towns, and of some of the military leaders, rather than the stiff conservatism of inland Spain. It provided for universal suffrage, for a single Chamber, for Colonial representation, for the abolition of the Inquisition and the confiscation of its property. Its provisions were, therefore too advanced for Spain, and never put into execution. Nevertheless this liberal instrument possesses an enduring importance in Spanish history. If it never became a machine of government, it was a flag of insurrection, standing as it did for the establishment of an all-Spanish Parliament, voting taxes, making laws, and limiting the monarchy and the power of the Church. From Spain, the most reactionary corner of Europe, the term "Liberal" came into English politics.

CHAPTER LXXI

NAPOLEON AND GERMANY

The Napoleonic government. Prussia resurgent. Goethe as a liberator. The German contribution to European letters.

THE NAPOLEONIC government of Germany was a harsh but salutary episode in the history of the German people. Much useless detritus was cleared away. Many helpful ideas were scattered abroad. Both by way of stimulus and by way of reaction communities which had long marked time in torpid self-sufficiency were prompted to undertake serviceable reforms. A great simplification of the complicated political geography of Germany, involving the suppression of a hundred and twenty small states, was carried out in Paris in 1803 as a consequence of the compensations which had to be offered to the German Princes who had been compelled by the French conquest to forfeit their possessions on the left bank of the Rhine.

The Muse of History cannot afford to neglect these sordid transactions. Out of the Act of Mediation, as it was called, there emerged a Germany more manageable and easy to unite, and ultimately therefore, more formidable to her western neighbour.

In broad outline Napoleon's scheme for Germany followed the classic lines of French diplomacy. A confederation of the Rhine under the Presidency of the French Emperor was formed as a makeweight against the two beaten and angry enemies, Austria and Prussia. Of this confederacy some member states were new creations carved out of conquered and enemy territory, while others, like Bavaria and Würtemberg, were ancient members of the *Reich*. Nothing better illustrates the difference which has come over Germany since those times than the ease with which this League was launched upon its course and the large measure of support which Napoleon received from the German Princes in the prosecution of a policy inimical to German nationality. He had indeed bribes to offer to the rulers—monarchies for Bavaria and Würtemberg, a grand duchy for Baden, as well as marriages into the charmed circle of the Imperial family; and after Austerlitz and Jena there was no armed force among the Germans capable of standing up against the Grand Army. But the true explanation of a curious phenomenon is to be found neither in fear nor in corruption. The general play of popular sympathy, both in Bavaria, where the Austrians had long been regarded as a menace, and in the Rhineland, where the Prussian was little loved, was favourable to France until the pressure of Napoleon's blood tax turned favour into bitter hatred. No tears, then, were shed by the princes of this Rhenish Confederation when Austria lost her ancient place of pre-eminence in Germany, and the Holy Roman Empire received its quietus. No sympathy went out to Prussia in the hour of her abasement. Even in the Kingdom of Westphalia, where a strange mixture of Hessians, Hanoverians, and Brunswickers were forcibly combined under King Jerome, Napoleon's engaging but frivolous youngest brother, the best German families came forward to help the alien government.

There are some who think that a Germany so balanced and composed, with Prussia shorn of her Westphalian and Polish Provinces, with Austria extruded, and with a League of German Princes receiving its political direction from France, would have been a factor making for a more stable world.

July, 1806

Aug. 6, 1806

1807

Be this as it may, the experiment was never tried in time of peace. Napoleon's Germany was from first to last an engine of war directed against England. Cut off from colonial trade, and at the same time denied an entry into French markets, held down by foreign armies of occupation who were far gone in the evil habits of pillage and peculation, drained of men and bled white for money, the Germans may be pardoned if, revising their first friendly estimate of the French, they ended by wanting nothing so much as a German nation strong enough to throw off the foreign yoke and ever after to defend the German Rhine. Only the Jews, liberated from the Ghetto and raised to equal citizenship with German Gentiles, continued to regret the downfall of Napoleon, their liberator.

When finally the reaction against alien rule took shape in Germany, the head and heart of the movement was found to be Prussian. In this kingdom, which had long been a magnet to attract able men from every part of the country to its service, the lesson of Jena had sunk deep in the minds of a small group of energetic and thoughtful patriots. It is the glory of Scharnhorst and Clausewitz, of Stein and Hardenberg, that the problem of Prussia was seen in its widest dimensions as one not merely of military reform but of national revival and awakening. Broadly speaking, the result of their work was to give a servile army and a servile nation some of the honourable characteristics of freedom.

Not often have the true lessons of a military *débâcle* been so clearly apprehended as lying in the moral field. Only a real statesman like Stein would have discerned that it was germane to the military resurgence of Prussia to grant a measure of self-government to the Prussian towns and to attend to the social condition of the peasantry. That he was not above taking lessons from the French, who had emancipated the peasantry in Poland and in Westphalia, is no disparagement to his prudence.

It is characteristic of the condition of the German Empire at the end of the eighteenth century that Goethe, who created the newer literature of his country, was neither Christian, hero, nor patriot. His long life, beginning in 1749 and ending in 1832, was contemporaneous with an age of violent and repeated change. He was a boy of seven at the opening of the Seven Years' War. He wrote *Götz von Berlichingen* in the last year of Louis XV, and immediately afterwards stormed the reading public of his own and other countries with *The Sorrows of Werther*. When the French Revolution broke out he was a man of forty, twenty years older than Napoleon, and already the most famous literary figure in Europe. The storms of the Revolution and the Empire swept over Germany without ruffling his marmoreal composure and his indifference to the fortunes of states. Living a sheltered life as an official in the little court of Weimar, he pursued self-culture as an end, deriving his inspiration, in so far as it was drawn from books, not from the tedious and lifeless work of earlier German writers, but from the vast romantic material of Shakespeare, from the dramatists and poets of Italy and Spain, and from the masterpieces of classical and oriental literature. Owing little to the German mind, and holding the Prussians in contempt for their barbarity, Goethe welcomed the genius and saluted the conquests of Napoleon. The defeat of the French Emperor at the battle of Leipzig came to him as a disappointment, and the greatest lyric poet of Germany makes no contribution to the literature of the War of Liberation.

Yet in a profound sense the army of German liberators numbers no figure of equal stature. By his massive achievements in prose and verse Goethe freed the German people from the unintelligent subservience to French models, which, ever since the Thirty Years' War, had been a blight on the national intellect. His lyric poems spring fresh from a lover's passion. His prose, lucid, serious, elegant, is always the vehicle of positive knowledge or ripe meditation, never of obstruse metaphysic, or of ideas imperfectly grasped. To the narrow specialism of the Universities he opposed a vast curiosity embracing great tracts of art, science, and literature. He wrote on optics and botany, studied oriental tongues, and discovered the intermaxillary bone, bringing to science what is rarer and more valuable than the gift of accurate mensuration, the art of divination, so that his work is rich with ideas and suggestions, which in a later age have been found to be of value. The chief vices of German literature had been obscurity, pedantry, and lush sentimentalism. Goethe is often dull, but never obscure; often learned, but never pedantic; often governed by the passions inspired by his innumerable loves, but never to the extent of losing that chastening sense of form which is one of the properties of an accomplished egoist. Had he learned from the French the art of making a brief well-proportioned book, he would have added yet another to the many services which he rendered to the German people.

The idea of the French revolutionary writers that human virtue depends upon the legislator was not shared by Goethe, and is contradicted by the whole tenor of his teaching, which is the creed of a self-sufficient genius, untroubled by the fume and fret of politics and unconstricted by national prepossessions. To the French belief in legislation as the prime condition of human progress Goethe opposed the picture of a man of commanding physical and intellectual endowments, who, through love and letters, art, science, and administration, strenuously endeavoured to cultivate his soul. In the tiny courts and sheltered backwaters of Germany, where the stream of life flowed stilly through narrow channels, the prodigious energy of this multifarious, myriad-minded writer was a revelation of what an artist, under the application of no external stimulus, could from his own intellectual and emotional resources achieve. When all around at Weimar was stationary, Goethe's temperament was ever young and experiencing, his genius was always in movement, pouring out a flood of plays, poems, novels, treatises, and with so little adherence to type, that it turned from the mediaeval romantic drama, which inspired Walter Scott, to the severest Classicism, then plunged into the Orient, and finally survived to welcome the splendours of Byron. Working this perpetual and self-renewing miracle, Goethe the egoist and anti-patriot gave to the German people a new station in the intellectual hierarchy of Europe.

In this work he was not alone. Lessing, Schiller, Herder, and Heine are ranked with justice among the glories of German literature. Of these Heine was a Jew, and imbued even to a lesser degree than Goethe with the quality now so generally and doubtfully prized of hot German nationalism. 1799- Heine, whose childhood was spent in Düsseldorf, when it was 1856 the capital of the Grand Duchy of Berg and part of the

Napoleonic Empire, preferred the French to the Germans, and, like all German Jews, venerated Napoleon, the liberator of the Semite race. Schiller alone cherished political enthusiasms characteristically German; but even Schiller, most eloquent of German apostles, was compelled to seek his 1759 lessons in liberty from the Dutch. 1805

The tumultuous movements of the German mind which belong to this period, and the very considerable achievement of many German authors, were not generally appreciated until Madame de Staël published her brilliant book on 1810 Germany. Then it was discovered that the people who had been overrun by the Napoleonic armies, and treated with the contumely due to an inferior and subject race, were in fact the possessors of a treasure of contemporary poetry and prose, that in the range and depth of its perceptions, and in the richness and originality of its forms, surpassed any recent work which had been put out elsewhere on the continent of Europe. By 1815 Germany had found herself, not indeed as a political unity, but as a power in literature and science. The spiritual summit which she then reached, the range of spiritual influence which she then enjoyed, have never been recaptured. It is a remarkable fact that the zenith of German literature belongs to an age of political impotence and division, when Goethe and Schiller were friends at Weimar, and German patriotism stood at its lowest ebb. The old-fashioned picturesque imperial Constitution is not, then, altogether devoid of merit, or the victorious march of German nationalism immune from reproach. It may be asked whether, in the last analysis, Weimar has not done more for the human spirit than Berlin, and whether the system of small German states has not been more favourable to liberty and to the cultivation and refinement of the emotions than the modern *Reich*, assailed by the tempests of world politics and racked by the passions of internal strife.

CHAPTER LXXII

THE DOWNFALL OF NAPOLEON

*The first cracks. The Russian War. The German War of
Liberation. Reasons for the postponement of German unity.
The campaign of 1813. Napoleon's lost chances. His continuing military skill. Elba. The return of the Bourbons. The
Congress of Vienna. The re-settlement of Europe. The
triumph of legitimacy. Contrast with the Peace Treaties of
1919-20.*

WITH NAPOLEON'S Spanish enterprise the first cracks began to
appear in the fabric of the French Empire. The capitualation
of 23,000 French troops at Baylen (July 19, 1808) was a clear
signal that in Spanish nationalism a new force had emerged
capable of upsetting the French Empire. Taking courage
from Spain, Austria, under the advice of Count Stadion,
determined to renew the struggle, and while Napoleon was
chasing Sir John Moore back to Corunna, the Austrians were
penetrating Bavarian territory. The speed with which
Napoleon, having restored the situation in central Spain,
April, rushed back to repel the Austrian menace, the brilliance of
1809 the movements by which in three fiercely contested battles
(of Abensberg, Eckmühl, and Landshut) he succeeded in
crushing the Austrians on the middle Danube, the check
which he experienced before Vienna, and the hard-won
July, victory at Wagram, while illustrating his undiminished
1809 brilliance as a commander, bring out the increasing measure
of the difficulties by which he was surrounded. The Austrian
army with which he was confronted in these encounters was an
altogether different instrument from the force which he had
vanquished at Marengo and at Austerlitz. It was better
trained, better handled, and in better heart. When soon afterwards Lainé objected to Napoleon that Austria was a spent
power, he replied, "Then it is evident that you were not on the
field of Wagram." Moreover, apart from the renewed
activity of Austria, there were other indications that the

948

Spanish example was infectious. A revolt in the Tyrol against the Bavarians, disjointed Prussian risings, slight in themselves and checked without great difficulty, were sufficient to indicate new strains and stresses in the fabric. In France, too, a certain lassitude was beginning to show itself. At a conference which Napoleon held with Alexander at Erfurt in 1808 Talleyrand had observed that Belgium and the Rhine frontier were the conquests of France, and that the further conquests were those of Napoleon alone.

Meanwhile Napoleon was gradually drawing forward towards that wild Russian adventure which, more than the Peninsular War or the British navy, brought the French Empire in ruins to the ground. The ostensible cause of the rupture was the open refusal of Russia in December, 1810, to close her ports to neutral ships, and her adoption of a tariff favourable to Colonial and adverse to French imports. Napoleon was not prepared to tolerate the defection of his Russian ally from the continental system. He had long been doubtful of that swift friendship which had been formed on the raft of Tilsit in 1807. He distrusted the Tzar, and knew that the distrust was mutual, that Alexander did not easily forgive his encouragement of the Poles or his Austrian marriage, and that the continued blockade, unpopular every-where, was nowhere more irksome than among the merchants and nobles of Russia. He determined, therefore, to force the issue, hoping, perhaps, that, as at Friedland, a decisive victory won upon the border of the Russian Empire might produce a victorious peace, and cherishing also, for he was now ambitious to add to the rôle of Charlemagne the renown of Alexander, the dream of using Russia as a half-way house between Europe and the East. "People will want to know," he said, "where we are going. We are going to make an end of Europe, and then to throw ourselves upon other robbers more daring than ourselves, and to become mistress of India."

There was no second Friedland, and no peace, but by the middle of August, 1812, Napoleon was at Smolensk half way between Niemen and Moscow, without any decisive victory to his credit, and with his great army shaken by the loss of a hundred thousand men. It was then that, abandoning his earlier and more prudent plan for a two years' campaign, he determined to push on into the heart of Russia in quest of the smashing victory which might once again bring the Tzar to his knees; but as in Spain, so in Russia patriotism was a real thing. To make discomfort for the invader there was no sacrifice, even to the burning of Moscow, which the Russians would not endure. Though Napoleon was in the Kremlin, Alexander, with the Prussian Stein at his elbow, refused to listen for a moment to overtures of peace. It was then given to Napoleon to experience the answer which Russia will always make to the enemy who embarks on the unequal contest with a Russian winter. The retreat from Moscow, which began on October 18, finally destroyed the instrument by which Napoleon had fixed his domination on Europe, and gave the signal for that insurrection of the German peoples against his rule which brought in its train after an epical struggle defeat, abdication, and exile.

1813　　The German War of Liberation, while it is memorable as marking the destruction of Napoleon's power in central Europe, sowed the seeds of that strong sentiment of all-German loyalty which has transformed the politics of the modern world. For the first time the German peoples were possessed by a common passion. Every German had suffered from the rigours of Napoleon's blockade and from conscription. To free the Fatherland from the intolerable yoke of an alien tyranny and by some means to prevent the recurrence of the French peril were aspirations common to all, but more particularly strong in northern Germany, where poets, philosophers, and pamphleteers combined to proclaim the gospel of a German nation.

As yet, however, there was no such nation, but only a hot ferment of national feeling by the help of which a nation under strong political direction might ultimately be built. That direction was not forthcoming. No German state was sufficiently powerful by itself to defeat Napoleon, and to rally all Germans under its leadership. In Prussia, where national feeling was strongest and leadership most enlightened, there was as yet no army sufficient for the purpose. The early defeats of the Prussians and Russians at Bautzen and Lützen were a sufficient indication of the fact that Germany could not owe her salvation to Prussia alone, even if she could count upon the support, which had been assured her by the

Treaty of Kalisch, of a Russian army. It followed that the liberation of Germany could not be effected without active help from the Austrian Empire. Now the Austrian Empire was in the main a non-German power, which had steadily reduced its commitments in the west. It had abandoned Belgium and the Rhine frontier, it had given up its old possessions in Swabia, it had seen the disappearance of the Holy Roman Empire, not without a sentiment of relief, and it was more interested in securing a hold on northern and central Italy, and consequently upon the Vatican, than in resuming the dangerous and ungrateful task of sheltering Germany from French aggression in the west.

Austria, then, had no interest in the idea of a united Germany. Prince Metternich, who was now directing Austrian policy, had views as to the future of Germany which were diametrically opposed to those which were entertained by Hardenberg and Stein in Berlin. Whereas the Prussian statesmen wanted to evict Napoleon from Germany by force of arms, and thereafter to create a united German state, Metternich wished to impose his mediation on the contending parties, to negotiate Napoleon out of Germany, if possible, to detach the Rheinbund from their dependence upon France, and thereafter to form a loose German federation of equal states under the presidency of Austria. It was the Austrian view which prevailed, and the postponement of German unity until 1870 is due to the fact that, the military help of Austria being essential to the liberation of Germany in 1813, Austria was accordingly able, with the willing co-operation of the south German states, to frame a Germany according to her mind.

Prussian historians count it as one of the tragedies of German history that the national and liberal sentiments inspired by the War of Liberation were allowed to run to waste like an African river in the sands, and that as the result of the heroic efforts and sufferings of that time Germany emerged with a federal constitution so framed as to paralyse its action and to deprive it of any real power in the counsels of Europe.

The tremendous campaign which Napoleon waged in Germany in 1813 was not, then, fought against a united people, but against governments entering into the war at different

Feb., 1813

1773-1859

stages, and not easily coalescing, despite common sentiments, into a common plan of action. Austria was jealous of Russia. The troops of the *Rheinbund* during the early part of the year still served under Napoleon's banner. Save for a common desire to be rid of the French, there was no ultimate political agreement between the governments of Vienna and Berlin. It was, however, common ground between Russia, Prussia, and Austria that Napoleon must give up his Polish and German conquests. This he declined to do. "What is it you wish of me?" he said to Metternich on June 26, 1813. "That I should dishonour myself? Never. I shall know how to die, but never to yield an inch of territory. Your sovereigns, who were born on the throne, may get beaten twenty times, and yet return to their capitals. I cannot. For I rose to power through the camp."

Oct., 1813   It was this intractable spirit, rather than the military disasters which were soon to ·follow, which compelled Napoleon's abdication. Even after the crushing victory at Leipzig, where the last great Napoleonic army, raised by incredible exertions, was fatally broken, the allies offered to treat (November, 1813), on the basis that France should retain her natural frontiers, the Rhine, the Alps, and the Pyrenees. That offer was rejected. Later when France had been invaded, and one signal defeat had been inflicted on the defending army, the terms were harder, but even then (February 4, 1814), with the sacrifice of Savoy and Belgium, and the acceptance of the old frontiers of the French monarchy as they existed before the revolutionary conquests, Napoleon might have retained his throne. After this last chance had been rejected, there was no other thought in the mind of the allies but that he, like so many of his royal victims, must cease to reign.

That England would never permanently allow Napoleon to retain Belgium, nor France continue to obey him, if he relinquished this cherished prize of the Revolution, are positions which have often been advanced and plausibly defended. But when the history of the Revolution and Empire is presented, as a drama proceeding to an inevitable close by reason of this fatal conquest of Belgium, which Napoleon was inexorably bound to defend, and England determined by considerations equally cogent to contest, then it is pertinent to observe that even after Leipzig the allies were willing to contemplate a treaty in which Belgium was left to France. There can be no more impressive testimony to the respect which the military strength of Napoleon continued to inspire in the breasts of his enemies.

The issue of war depended less on numbers than on will-power. In his last two campaigns, the German and the French, Napoleon was faced with overwhelming numbers. Almost all Europe was leagued against him. Even Bernadotte, one of his old officers, now Crown Prince of Sweden, brought a Swedish army into the field against his former master with a view to securing Norway and possibly also the Crown of France when the spoils came to be divided. While in the German theatre of war Russia, Prussia, Austria, and Sweden were closing round Napoleon, Wellington was driving the French across the Pyrenees. Yet, despite these formidable odds, Napoleon fought these last campaigns with a resilience and skill which have excited the wonder of posterity. Though his troops were for the most part young and untrained, his Marshals weary of war, his cavalry insufficient, his numbers inferior to those of his antagonists, he succeeded in defeating the main allied army under Schwarzenberg in the two days' fighting outside the walls of Dresden on August 26 and 27, 1813 and had he been, after his earlier fashion, prompt and effective in pursuit, might have compelled his adversary to consider terms. Afterwards he allowed himself, through some remissness of will, to be encircled and crushed in the terrible carnage of Leipzig. Yet the operations which he carried out in the following year, with a handful of raw troops, against the armies of Blücher and Schwarzenberg in the valleys of the Seine and the Marne, are accounted among his master-pieces. In these, acting on interior lines and striking now at the Prussians in the north, now at the Austrians in the south, he beat the enemy again and again by the swiftness of his movements and the impetuosity of his attack. It was all in vain. Blücher was an antagonist whose will was as fierce and pertinacious as his own, a general without nerves, indefatigable in anger and unflustered by defeat. Repulsed three times, the old Prussian fell back northwards on reinforcements, and, returning to the fray on the stiffly fought fields of Laon and Craonne, opened for himself and his allies the

road to Paris. Outpaced, Napoleon followed westward, and,
finding that the capital had been surrendered to the enemy,
took station at Fontainebleau. There the Marshals, war-
April, weary themselves and interpreting the lassitude of the
1814 country, exacted abdication; and thence, after a farewell to
the Guard, which made him a figure of sentiment in every
cottage in France, he left for Elba, voyaging southwards
amid the execrations and threats of the people. The making
of history for the next ten months was left to other hands.

1754- It was Talleyrand, a renegade priest and a married bishop,
1838 who persuaded Alexander I that the Bourbon House must be
recalled to rule in France. Improbable as it might seem that
France would willingly accept the government of a fat old
gentleman, who for twenty-five years had lived in exile
estranged from all the stirring events and glories of that time,
there was, in truth, no alternative. Louis XVIII at least
represented a principle, a tradition, a fragment of the political
faith of France. He at least might be thought to promise
repose and the goodwill of Europe to a much tried and
deeply apprehensive people. After the escapade of the
Revolution and the Empire the old monarchy seemed to be
the least unsafe of expedients; but not even the pen of
Chateaubriand, most eloquent of French writers, could make
it glorious; nor the English-looking constitution imposed by
the allies convert it into an instrument of wise and generous
liberty. The white flag, by which the famous tricolor was
replaced, was a fitting emblem of the family which returned
to its home, having learnt nothing and forgotten nothing in
an epoch of tumultuous change.

The terms accorded to the conquered country (Treaty of
Paris, May 30, 1814) were marked by a politic moderation.
No indemnity was asked, no foreign occupation was insisted
on. There was not even a stipulation that the treasures of art
which had been stolen from the galleries of Europe should be
restored to their rightful owners. That the foreign conquests
of Napoleon were surrendered went without saying; but it is
noteworthy that despite the completeness of the allied victory
and the length and bitterness of the war, Louis XVIII was
accorded a territory slightly more extensive than that which
had belonged to his brother before the revolution broke out.
The simplest exercise of common sense was sufficient to show

the allies that Louis, their client, would never keep his doubtful throne under the shadow of a Carthaginian peace.

The detailed settlement of Europe was left to a Congress
summoned for November to Vienna. Here the aristocracy
of the old *régime*, light-hearted in the moment of their great
release, surrendered themselves to an orgy of brilliant
dissipation. As Paris danced after Thermidor, and London
after the 1918 Armistice, so through that autumn and winter
Vienna danced while the Corsican was safe in Elba and the
officials were working out the structure of a new Europe.
In this circle of emperors and kings, princes, nobles, and
diplomats Marie Louise, the faithless wife of Napoleon, was
studious to display her tiny feet.

The new map was shaped by statesmen for whom revolution
emanating from France was the greatest of all dangers to the
well-being of mankind.

The eastern frontier of France was therefore lined by a
series of buffer states or provinces destined to protect the
tender body of central Europe from revolution: in the north
a kingdom of the Netherlands, which lasted till 1830, when
the uneasy union between Calvinist Holland and Catholic
Belgium was dissolved; in the south a Sardinian kingdom,
strengthened by the incorporation of Genoa and Savoy,
while the intermediate region of the Rhineland was entrusted,
mainly at the instigation of the British Government, to the
wardship of Prussia. Nobody then foresaw the union of
Germany under the Prussian crown, or that change in the
balance of European power which still makes Germany
formidable to her neighbours. Far otherwise was the outlook
in 1814. Then France was regarded as the general enemy,
and Prussia as the power best qualified to keep a watch upon
the Rhine.

With the same idea of recalling Europe to conservatism and
sobriety, the Austrians were accorded that dominant position
in northern and central Italy which soon provoked the conspiracies and wars of Italian nationalism. They were given
the kingdom of Lombardy and Venetia, they recovered
Trieste and the Dalmatian littoral, had the satisfaction of
seeing an Austrian archduke reigning in Florence and an
Austrian Archduchess in Parma, and since Ferdinand IV,
with whom they were connected by ties of family, politics,

and creed, was replaced in Naples after the death of Murat in 1815, their influence was spread from one end of the peninsula to the other. Indeed, out of the wars of the Revolution and the Empire, Austria emerged with the greatest share of the spoil, her population increased by some 4½ million, her control of Italy little short of complete, and as the President of a newly established but loosely jointed Germanic Confederation.

These arrangements were reached without great expense of controversy as part of a general design for repelling the influence of France from those countries in which it had been spread by the conquests of Napoleon. The principal difficulty arose in that region of the middle east of Europe where the problem is still most thorny. What was to be done with the Grand Duchy of Warsaw, which Napoleon had carved out of the Polish Provinces of Prussia and handed over to be governed by the Saxon King?

What was to be done with Saxony itself? Russia wanted Poland, Prussia wanted Saxony, and had these two states been left to their own devices, Poland and Saxony would have been wiped off the map. Such a prospect, however, was most unpalatable to Austria and France, the one refusing to see her Prussian rival so aggrandized, the other cherishing strong views upon a liberated Polish state. It was a question which brought the Congress to the brink of war. Eventually a compromise was reached under which Prussia received some two-thirds of Saxony and the Rhine provinces, while Poland was erected into a constitutional kingdom under the Tzar.

Talleyrand's formula of legitimacy summed up the spirit of the settlement. It was legitimacy which restored the Bourbons to France, saved Saxony for the Wettins, and confirmed the power of the royal house of Sardinia. No respect was paid to nationality or to the wishes of the populations concerned. In all essentials, therefore, the statesmen who drew up the settlement at Vienna were sharply opposed in aims and principles to the artificers of the Europe in which we now live. The Peace Treaties of 1920 constituted a democratic settlement made possible only by the downfall of those very monarchies to which the Congress of Vienna had entrusted the policing of Europe. The settlement of 1920 created new Republics, redistributed frontiers, accepted the dissolution

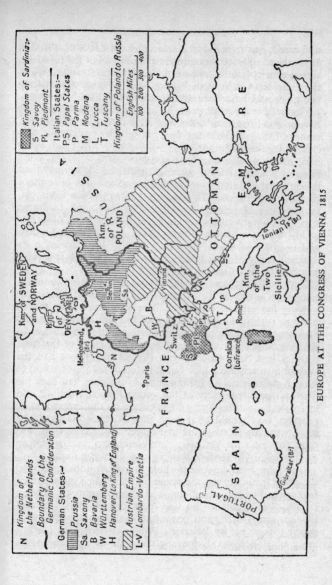

EUROPE AT THE CONGRESS OF VIENNA 1815

of the old Austrian Empire, and built up a Europe on that principle of self-determination which had been preached by the French revolutionaries, but was afterwards long lost to view. To the Congress of Vienna the principles of President Wilson would have been anathema. Guided by Metternich, Talleyrand, and Castlereagh, it held that the well-being of Europe was to be secured not by compliance with the assumed wishes of the peoples concerned, but only by punctual obedience to legitimate authority.

By a stroke of fortune for the conservative cause the allied sovereigns and ministers were still gathered in Vienna when it was learnt (March 7, 1815) that Napoleon was once more on the soil of France. To wind-up the work of the Congress, to proclaim Napoleon suspect and outlaw, and to frame terms of military alliance against him was the work of a fortnight. Before a blow had been struck every diplomatic card had been taken from Napoleon's hands. Had the issue on the field of Waterloo gone otherwise, he would still have succumbed to the united strength of Europe.

Yet of all modes of conducting his desperate adventure a campaign aimed at Brussels offered the fairest chance of rallying the support of France. For centuries, seeing that it brought with it the great estuary of the Rhine, Belgium had possessed a symbolic, almost mysterious, value in the eyes of the French people. Over and over again the soil of this little country had been watered with French blood, nor had the ambition to acquire it ever failed to haunt the imagination of French statesmen. As the conquest of Belgium had been the first and principal glory of the young French Republic and its loss the most damaging commentary on the Empire, so its recovery now would be a prize than which none would be more welcome to the heart of France. Napoleon, then, was June, right to strike for Brussels, and Wellington, taking station 18 on the field of Waterloo, was right to deny the road.

1815 One long June day, memorable in human annals, decided the great duel between the revolution and the dynasts which had opened with the cannonade of Valmy twenty-three years before. Wellington's thin line, part British, part German, Belgian and Dutch, and powerfully aided as the shades of evening drew on by Blücher's Prussians, shattered the last army of Napoleon. Judged by the scale of modern battles the action was trivial.[1] Measured in terms of the spiritual exaltation which it occasioned there have been few greater victories, for Waterloo was the last act of a tragedy, the end of one age and the beginning of another.

It is much to the credit of British statesmanship that when, after the Hundred Days, a new arrangement had to be made with France, the vanquished country was still treated with moderation. If Prussia had had her way, Alsace and Lorraine would have been among the sacrifices required from the restored government of Louis XVIII. Wellington and Castlereagh, however, saw that nothing would be more certainly calculated to undermine the authority of the Bourbons than a crippling loss of territory. It was to the interest of England, as it was to the advantage of Europe, that the old dynasty, despite the tremendous handicap of its estrangement from the military glories of the Napoleonic period, should nevertheless be helped to reconquer and retain the loyalty of the French people. This, it was rightly judged, would have been a hopeless task if the full Prussian programme of spoliation had been sanctioned. France was, indeed, condemned to lose the Duchy of Bouillon and part of the Ardennes to the Netherlands, to hand over the forts of Saarlouis and Landau to Germany, to pay seven hundred million francs as an indemnity, to submit to an army of occupation for a period of five or three years, and to restore the art treasures which she was permitted under the earlier peace to retain. In these stipulations there was nothing intolerable to French pride, but the apprehensions of Alexander I, who doubted the wisdom of restoring the Bourbon House to France, were justified in the event. The plant of legitimacy failed to flourish upon soil still covered by the lava of revolution. The concert of Europe could neither save France from convulsions, nor prevent the return of Bonapartist ideas and the creation of a Second Empire. But with all its shortcomings it gave to Europe forty years of comparative peace.

[1] Wellington's army, "the worst equipped army with the worst staff ever brought together" in the view of its Commander, consisted only of 23,900 British 17,000 Belgian and Dutch, 11,000 Hanoverian, 5,900 Brunswickers, and 2,800 Nassauer troops.

CHAPTER LXXIII

METTERNICH, CASTLEREAGH, AND CANNING

Aims of the Allies. The Concert of Europe. The Holy Alliance. Germany. The system of Metternich. Austria and England. The War of Greek Independence. Mehemet Ali and the Egyptian intervention. George Canning. Rôle of the British Navy in securing the independence of Greece and South America.

THE FRENCH Revolution and Napoleon had caused so much trouble to the governments of Europe that once "the Corsican ogre" had been shipped off to St. Helena and King Louis XVIII had been safely reinstated in Paris, the one idea dominating the sovereigns and ministers of the Great Alliance was that on no account must the French Revolution and Napoleon be allowed to recur. As in 1918 the exhausted peoples of the victorious *Entente* said with one voice "No more Prussian militarism," so in 1815 the conquerors came to a common resolve that there must be no more French revolution and that every germ of liberal opinion must be promptly killed lest it might develop into the malignant revolutionary fever. Behind the grim reaction which is the prevailing note of continental policy during the next twenty-three years was always the memory of what revolution had recently been and the haunting fear of what it might again become.

It was natural that these sentiments of resentment and panic should be most keenly felt by the three autocratic powers whose countries had been invaded and whose pride had been humbled by the armies of Napoleon. The monarchs of Russia, Austria, and Prussia had no difficulty in reaching the conclusion that it was their duty to Europe and to civilization to band themselves together against the spirit of revolution and to strike it down wherever it might show its ugly head. In this enterprise they hoped, but failed, to enlist the continuing sympathy and support of the British government.

Britain had emerged from the Napoleonic wars with a new

industrial system and a new empire. She had obtained Malta, the Cape of Good Hope, Mauritius and Ceylon, and had successfully defended Canada in a war against the United States which had broken out in 1812 over the right of search on the high seas. She was developing a great trade with the Spanish and Portuguese colonies of South America which had taken the occasion of the Peninsular War to revolt against their respective mother countries. She differed from her continental allies by reason of the fact that she had large and expanding non-European interests, and that she had never been invaded by Napoleon. Moreover, even under her most reactionary governments, England maintained her parliamentary system and civil liberties. Castlereagh, the foreign minister who carried the country triumphantly through the concluding stages of the Napoleonic war, was denounced by his compatriots as the incarnation of all that was reactionary and obscurantist. Compared to Alexander of Russia and the Austrian Metternich, the English Tory was an angel of liberal and enlightened good sense.

Yet England, though differing in many respects from the continent, could not, having played so great a part in the war, refuse to take a leading share in the reorganization of Europe. The war had forced the country out of its insularity, had brought English statesmen into a close association with the political chiefs of other countries, and had created in the midst of the Great Alliance a diplomatic *esprit de corps*. A genuine feeling of mutual esteem bound Metternich and Castlereagh. Though Britain would not be a party to the Tzar's mystical Holy Alliance (a declaration of Absolutist and Christian principles which had no legal consequences) she joined a much more practical concert of Europe (November 20, 1815), in virtue of which the participating powers (Russia, Austria, Prussia, and Britain) pledged themselves to maintain the exclusion of the house of Bonaparte from France. A League of Nations was not contemplated by statesmen who repudiated the principle of nationality; but it was provided by the terms of the Quadruple Alliance that the contracting powers should meet together at agreed periods to discuss their common interests and matters affecting the peace and security of Europe.

At the moment nothing better could be devised than this

concert of four great powers pledged to one another to protect the cause of European peace. It soon became evident, however, that the union of the powers was more apparent than real. Whereas Metternich wished the Quadruple Alliance to be an active instrument for the suppression of liberal movements throughout Europe, Castlereagh took the view that it was no part of the duty of the four powers to interfere in the internal government of states. Castlereagh was a Tory, and in the eyes of his Whig opponents the incarnation of Tory tyranny, the tool of the Tzar's Holy Alliance, which he had refused to join, and the enemy of liberalism all over the world. But Castlereagh, while he wanted to strengthen Germany as a barrier against France and Russia, and valued the Austrian alliance as a prop of European conservatism, had no desire to see England drawn into the domestic broils of the continental states. Tory as he was, he knew his countrymen too well to suppose that they would permit themselves to be enrolled in Metternich's repressive police. The difference between the English view of policy, which was essentially liberal, and that of Austria, which was sternly conservative, steadily widened, until, with the death of Castlereagh and the accession of Canning to power, it led to an open rupture.

Aug., 1822

Meanwhile a closer union of the three continental autocracies was formed in 1820 and continued till 1826, to give effect to the policy of resisting liberalism and revolution. It was this so-called Holy Alliance which muzzled intellectual life in Germany, stamped out the constitutional movements of Italy, restored autocracy to Spain, refused to recognize the insurgent democracies of South America and came into stark collision with the more liberal philosophy of England at the Congresses of Troppau, Laibach, and Verona. Goethe said, of this "Holy Alliance," that "nothing greater or more useful for mankind had been invented"; and the opinions of Goethe are entitled to respect. After the horrors and tribulations of the Napoleonic wars the statesmen of the victorious nations owed it to mankind that some method for the better organization of international relations should be essayed. Such had been the view of Pitt; such was the dream of Alexander of Russia, who flashed out now a mystic vision of Christian unity, now a less nebulous plan for a general league of the signatories of the Treaty of Vienna; such, too, was the intention of the cool and businesslike Castlereagh. The Triple Alliance of the autocrats fell far short of the Tzar's primal enthusiasms, of Castlereagh's liberally-minded caution, or of the conditions which should govern an effective organization of Europe. It reposed upon no foundation of public opinion, ran counter to the strongest popular aspirations of the age, and, being championed by the master of the Muscovite army, the most formidable in Europe, aroused suspicion in the western world. Yet as a practical instrument for bringing some measure of peace, order and decency into European society, the Holy Alliance, which was the system of Metternich, appealed to the disinterested intelligence of Goethe.

The idea that Europe could be ruled on principles of negative conservatism was wholly chimerical. The age of Scott and Byron, of Shelley, Coleridge and Wordsworth, of Froebel's experiments in child education, and of Robert Owen's adventure in socialism, was not one of intellectual inertia, but of rare imaginative achievement.

It was idle to suppose that a Europe stirred by so many dreams and thoughts, with its poets and romancers, its ardent university youths, its disbanded soldiers and sailors eating their hearts out for new enterprises, would long accept without a murmur and out of sheer exhaustion the peace settlement of Vienna. The peacemakers after the late war have been violently attacked for having paid too close a regard to the principle of nationality and the supposed wishes of the populations concerned. Still more general, but for the opposite reason, was the restlessness under the peace settlement of Vienna during the age of Metternich. The Italians and Czechs chafed under the Austrians, the Belgians under the Dutch, the Poles under the Russians and Prussians, the Serbs and Greeks under the Turks. The hopes cherished by Germans of the nobler kind that national unity and constitutional government would result from the vast energies of the liberating war were cruelly disappointed. There was no unity, but a Diet of thirty-nine states, each able to conduct its own foreign policy, and to frustrate by its solitary vote every important decision of the Federal *Bund*; no German cohesion, for foreign powers like Denmark and Luxemburg had seats in the Diet; no vigorous parliamentary life save in Bavaria and Baden, but a uniform spectacle of unenlightened, secretive despotism. Despite a formal promise of parliamentary liberty, the feudal nobility of Prussia saw to it that nothing like a parliament met in Berlin. German liberals, always a minority, envied, as they reflected upon the impotence and political sterility of their country, the brilliant debates of Paris and Westminster, and asked themselves whether the fatherland had gained anything of value from the great effusion of its blood and treasures in the Napoleonic wars.

The main root of the trouble was that the Germans themselves were not agreed upon any constructive design for the future of their country, Some wished for a Germany united under Prussia, some for a Germany owing allegiance to the Austrian Crown, others for a federation in which Austria, Prussia, and the lesser states might form mutually co-operating and balancing groups. To the outer world Germany seemed to move in metaphysical mists, and to be, as Michelet afterwards described her, "the Asia of Europe."

It was not only the denial of national rights which was secretly tormenting European peace. There was in the area controlled or influenced by the three autocracies a stern repression of opinions. All the apparatus of Papal control, the Jesuits, the Inquisition, the Index of Prohibited Books, was once more brought into play. In Italy the clericals supported by Austrian bayonets directed the schools, controlled the Press, and prevented any published deviation from the strictest path of Catholic orthodoxy. Under the restored Spanish monarchy, the Church with its vast endowments, its fiscal immunities, with the support of an ignorant and superstitious population, was in a position to direct the policy of the state. In half-Protestant Germany intellectual abasement was happily incomplete. The University of Göttingen, founded by George II and enjoying a relative immunity from government interference owing to its privileged position in the Electorate of Hanover, offered a welcome spectacle of academic liberty. Elsewhere after 1820 academic repression, under directions from Vienna, was the order of the day.

Over against this reactionary and non-national Europe was the spectacle, heartening to liberals in England, of the continent of America, in the north a powerful Republic which had achieved its freedom, in the south and centre a number of communities which under the inspiring leadership of Simon Bolivar of Caracás, and with not a little unofficial help from English seamen and merchants and most notably from the brilliant Lord Cochrane, were struggling to liberate themselves from their European masters. With these two Americas England in virtue of her advanced commercial development was in special contact, taking full advantage of the spread of cotton cultivation under the stimulus of the cotton gin (invented in 1793) in the Carolinas, and capturing all the European trade with the insurgent states of the Latin South. Indeed, as one Creole state after another threw off the yoke of its European master, as Cochrane liberated Peru and then Brazil, as Bolivar declared the independence of Colombia and Iturbide of Mexico, it became plain that a new commercial empire was offering itself to the fortunate adventurers of Britain. An appeal went up from the merchants of the City of London that the British government should regularize an expanding trade by giving official recognition to the rebel states.

The Englishman who had to deal with this South American 1770 question was George Canning, a brilliant orator and wit, who, 1827 though a member of a Tory government and a stout opponent of Parliamentary Reform, was in foreign policy an exponent of that new type of popular and liberal diplomacy, which, since it descended to Palmerston, an adoring disciple, was for nearly half a century a thorn in the flesh of continental autocrats. It was no part of Canning's policy to abet a collective system for enforcing discipline in foreign lands. If Austria with Russian and Prussian assent chose to put down revolution in Naples and Piedmont, that was her affair. If France sent an army into Spain to crush a military revolt which had forced a constitution upon a clerical and autocratic king, that again was no matter calling for English concurrence 1823 and support. On the contrary, the French invasion of Spain was viewed in London with grave anxiety. What if the French army, after crushing the rebellion, were to stay in Spain, what if it were to invade Portugal, England's ally, what again if it were to help the Spaniards to recover the Indies? Such alarming contingencies Canning was determined to prevent.

To the horror and indignation of the autocrats, he recognized the South American rebels.

Great as was the sensation caused by this radical announcement, it would have been greater still if the position of the South American states could have been regularized, as Canning proposed, by a joint declaration from London and Washington. The United States, however, acting on the advice of John Quincy Adams, determined to make her own 1823 pronouncement. In a famous message to Congress President Monroe announced his doctrine of America for the Americans and issued a solemn warning to the old world that no fresh European settlements would be tolerated on American soil. The "Monroe doctrine" anticipated Canning's pronouncement, but what preserved the South American continent through the greater part of the nineteenth century from European attack was not so much the excellent aspiration of the republican President as the efficient fleet of the British King.

The British fleet, which played so large a part in the emancipation of the South American colonies, next contributed to the liberation of Greece.

The struggle of the Greek people to liberate themselves from the Turkish yoke emphasized the two opposing tendencies in international life. To the Jesuit-trained nobles of Austria Greek nationalism was a disease, from the contagion of which, were it to spread into the Danube valley, they rightly augured the ruin of their state. The gentry of England had no such apprehensions. English nationalism they enjoyed, Irish nationalism they had suppressed, Indian nationalism was in a distant future. Education made them Philhellenes, public life made them parliamentarians, their sympathies as sportsmen went out to a small nation struggling to be free. When Byron died at Missolonghi, a martyr to Hellenic liberty, the romantic enthusiasm of the English for April the Greeks spread out far and wide into the streets and 19, taverns. No one stopped to ask how much of that ancient 1824 Hellas, which young men were taught to admire in the halls of Oxford and Cambridge, still survived in the herdsmen, the brigands, and the sea-pirates of Greece and its islands. The name of Greece was a talisman. Though Turkey was still the official friend and make-weight against Russian designs in the east, the mass of England was behind George Canning, when at last he was brought to recognize the Greek insurgents as belligerents, and joined with France and Russia to save them from extinction.

The Greeks who made the war of independence were neither in culture nor in blood (save to an inconsiderable and hypothetical extent) connected with the countrymen of Plato and Aristotle. Descended for the most part from unlettered Slavs and Albanians, they were content that their minds should be in the keeping of the monks and priests of the Byzantine Church. They spoke Romaic, a form of Greek fashioned by the lips of goatherds and seamen, drawing freely from the vocabulary of the Turk, the Latin, and the Slav, and racy with all the mariner's slang of the Aegean. They used the Greek characters; but as an influence on the education of the liberators the poems of Homer and the tragedies of Aeschylus might almost as well have been written in Chinese.

Every national movement of the nineteenth century owes much to the inspiration of antiquity. The Serb went back to Stephen Dushan in the fourteenth century, the Italian to Dante and Virgil, the Bohemian to Czech ballads of reputed antiquity, the Irishman to Erse. Korais, a Corfiote schoolmaster, had the brilliant thought that the literature of ancient Greece might be translated into a tongue intermediate between the august original and the *argot* of the common speech. By creating a new language this industrious scholar helped to call into being a new nation.

The way for the Greek insurrection was prepared by a succession of shocks which in the opening years of the nineteenth century impaired the strength of the Turkish Empire and seemed to portend its approaching dissolution. Serbia rose in 1804, under Kara George, the swineherd, and claimed its independence. Ali of Janina made for himself an independent power on the Adriatic. Mehemet Ali, an Albanian adventurer, 1769-obtained control of Egypt. In these circumstances the wealthy 1849 Greeks of the Dispersion, who had founded (1815) under the name of Philike Hetairia a secret insurrectionary society in Odessa, discerned a new and flattering hope for the future of their race.

A first rising (1821) under Prince Alexander Ypsilanti, an

aide-de-camp to the Tzar, being ill led and ill contrived, and failing to receive the Russian and Roumanian help on which it had counted, was easily crushed by the Turkish armies in Wallachia. The Greeks, however, possessed one advantage not ordinarily enjoyed by rebels against constituted authority. On sea they were superior to their adversaries. So long as the Greek navy had no enemy but the Turk on the water, the fire ships launched by the wealthy Greek islanders were able to keep the enemy at bay, and to land reinforcements where they were wanted on the mainland. For three years the Greeks of the Morea and the islands, aided by volunteers from the west, maintained a not unequal struggle, marked by horrible atrocities on each side, against their formidable antagonist. Then the situation was suddenly transformed by the intervention on the side of the Sultan of the powerful Pasha of Egypt.

Mehemet Ali, the founder of Egyptian independence was an Albanian Moslem from Kavalla, and the exact coeval, since he was born in 1769, of Bonaparte and Wellington. A quick eye for the main chance, and extraordinary tact for circumstance, led him at each step of his energetic career to take the course, however treacherous and violent, which produced a margin of advantage for himself. He did well as a tax-collector, better as a tobacco merchant, best of all as a commander of an Albanian contingent in the Ottoman army. With the aid of this, the only reliable military force in the country, he made himself master of Egypt. The Turks were expelled, the British were beaten, the Mamelukes were slaughtered, the arms of the conqueror were carried victoriously to Mecca and Khartum. With a fleet newly purchased from the west, and an army largely recruited from the Sudan and organized by the experience of a French officer, the Pasha embarked upon a vast and ambitious policy, which, though originally calculated to obtain from the Sultan the island of Crete and the provinces of Palestine and Syria as a reward for the suppression of the Greeks, comprised among its secret and ultimate ends the total overthrow of the Turkish Empire.

At first the Egyptian intervention against the Greeks seemed to be an omen of utter ruin to their cause. The army of Egypt overran the Morea, the navy of Egypt dominated the Aegean. It was soon made known in the west that Greek captives were being sold as slaves in Cairo, and that the whole population of the Greek mainland was in danger of extermination. On that Canning intervened. Though he was a Tory by tradition and the member of a Tory government which viewed all rebels with disfavour, he was not prepared to see the most illustrious corner of Europe and the original home of its civilization settled by a population of fellaheen and negroes. Rather than acquiesce in the extermination of the Greeks he invited the intervention of the powers. Austria and Prussia refused, out of their steady hatred of liberty; Russia, having other subjects of quarrel with the Porte, and France, out of sentiment, accepted.

With Russia and France, then, Canning concluded the Treaty of London (July 6, 1827), which, since it contemplated an autonomous Greek state under Turkish suzerainty, to be obtained by a "pacific" naval blockade, is the real foundation of Greek independence.

Though Canning died in the next month (August 8) and was succeeded by Tory ministers wholly out of sympathy with any policy calculated to weaken the Porte or to strengthen the Tzar, his work was not undone. Out of the pacific blockade sprang the unauthorized naval fight in the bay of Navarino (October 20, 1827) when the Egyptian and Turkish fleets were utterly destroyed by the fleets of the Triple Alliance. After this, no matter what protests were made, the legitimate indignation of the Porte was inevitable. A British fleet appeared before Alexandria, a Russian army marched to Adrianople, a strong French force was thrown into the Morea. When the Tory government fell in England in 1830 and Palmerston, who was a Liberal, came to the Foreign Office, the way was cleared for the recognition of a new Greek state entirely independent of Turkey. Diplomacy, acknowledging perforce the irregular work of the soldiers, sailors, and adventurers who had taken part in the battles and forays of the war, threw a veil of royal respectability over the infant polity. A Bavarian prince was called to rule over a kingdom which, since it lacked Thessaly and Crete, was hardly workable and comprised but a fraction of the Greek-speaking race. Nobody could tremble at Otto's tiny monarchy. Yet the resurrection of Greece, little as it altered the balance of power in Europe, was a most significant fact.

It was here that the first successful blow was administered to the autocratic government of Europe by Congress; here that the Ottoman Empire received its most sensible wound; here that the modern spirit of nationalism, afterwards destined to govern Italy and Poland, Bohemia and Ireland, and to bring the Austrian Empire to the ground, won its first romantic and resounding triumph. In the earliest Greek as in the latest Irish phase of nationalism, the human types recur: Kolokotrones and Michael Collins, Korais and Arthur Griffith, Canning and Lloyd George, the fighting conspirator, the literary dogmatist, the liberal statesman.

When we consider the terrible events by which the Greek wars of independence were marked, the ruthless massacre and mutilation of Turks by Greeks in the Morea, the extermination of the whole Greek population of Chios and of most of the inhabitants of the Greek quarter of Constantinople by their enemies, and further reflect upon the long series of savage encounters by which alone the national principle has, at last in our own days, been established in the Balkans, it is natural to ask whether Balkan nationality has been worth that price. If it be remembered that the position of the Greek population under Turkish rule was in the eighteenth century by no means intolerable, that the Greek Church under its Patriarch was allowed a full measure of liberty, that the commerce of the Levant was in the hands of Greek merchants, that the Greeks monopolized certain branches of trade and industry, and were accorded four of the great offices of state, it is clear that, without the ferment of the national idea, Balkan unity might have taken another turn which would have been entirely compatible with the material comfort of the Christian subjects of the Porte. Yet the price of greater quiet under the capricious and mutable tyranny of the Turk would have been great also, an estrangement from the progressive currents of western thought and a permanent temper of servility, incompatible with self-respect and cutting at the roots of self-improvement.

BOOKS WHICH MAY BE CONSULTED

C. A. Fyffe: *History of Modern Europe*. 1924.
C. K. Webster: *The Foreign Policy of Castlereagh*.
H. Temperley: *George Canning*. 1926.
Algernon Cecil: *British Foreign Secretaries*. 1927.
W. A. Phillips: *The War of Greek Independence*. 1897.
G. Young: *Egypt*. 1927.
W. A. Phillips: *Mahomet Ali*. 1907.
A. Toynbee: *A Study of History*, 3 vols. 1934.
Sir Harold Nicolson: *The Congress of Vienna*. 1946.
E. L. Woodward: *Three Studies in European Conservatism*. 1929.
C. K. Webster: *The Congress of Vienna*. 1937.
R. W. Seton-Watson: *Britain in Europe*. 1937.

CHAPTER LXXIV

THE REVOLUTION OF 1830

Britain and world trade. Spread of mechanical inventions. Relative backwardness of German industry. Survival of democratic society in France. The difficulties of French constitutional monarchy. Louis XVIII. Strife of French parties. Rising tide of liberalism. Charles X. The July revolution. Louis Philippe. Spread of revolutionary ferment. The birth of Belgium. The agony of Poland. Link between Poland and France.

FIVE YEARS after Waterloo, Hegel, eminent among South German philosophers, wrote thus of the English: "The material existence of the English is based on commerce and industry, and the English have undertaken the weight and responsibility of being the missionaries of civilization to the world; for their commercial spirit urges them to traverse every sea and land, to form connexions with barbarous peoples, to create wants and to stimulate enterprise, and first and foremost to establish among them the conditions necessary to commerce—viz., the relinquishment of a life of lawless violence, respect for property, and civility to strangers." It was not, then, as masters of an empire that the English appeared to foreigners, nor so that they considered themselves, but rather as universal traders dispensing the abundance which mechanical improvements and mineral resources had newly created in their own country, and bringing back in return produce from every quarter of the globe. Though Australia had been discovered and claimed, though Canada had been successfully defended in a brief war against the United States, and Ceylon, the Cape and Malta had been added to the overseas possessions of King George, and though the old colonial system of preferential trade between the mother country and its daughter states had survived the successful revolution of the American colonies, nothing would have been more foreign to the English ideas of that time than that trade should be confined to the British possessions. The rich markets of the continent lay close at hand. South America, liberating itself from the yoke of Spain and Portugal, opened out vast possibilities to English trade. The coal, the pig-iron, the textiles of England were essential to the needs of the continent. Out of the exchange of English manufactures with the food and raw materials of distant lands there arose a development of international trade such as had never previously been known in history.

It was the special note of the nineteenth century to spread through Europe and the outer world those mechanical inventions and that type of industrial civilization which were first developed among the Anglo-Saxon peoples. In 1819 the Atlantic was crossed by a steamship. The next decade witnessed the inauguration of the railway systems of Belgium, France, and Germany. In the forties, thanks to the work of Morse, the American inventor, the telegraph spread through Europe. The fifties brought submarine cables, the sixties the transatlantic cables. The seventies witnessed the formation of the international postal union and the development of the transatlantic grain trade, which made the harvest of the new world available for the populations of the old. The concluding decades of the century were remarkable all over western Europe for a growth in the size of towns, and for an alteration in the balance between urban and rural population. More particularly was this noticeable in Germany, a country which as late as 1871, when the Empire was founded, could be described as consisting mainly of free landowning peasants and powerful cultivating squires, with few large towns and no considerable urban population, but which, through the combined influence of railways, overseas expansion, inventions in steel and electricity, and the exhilaration consequent upon the victorious war with France, quadrupled its urban population in the sixty years between 1849 and 1910.

The progress of industrialization, which had been so rapid in Britain, proceeded at a far slower pace on the continent of Europe, saving only in that small area of Belgium which ever since the thirteenth century had been noted for its crowded and busy urban life. The revolutionary movements which broke out in various parts of Europe in 1820, in 1830 and in 1848 were not the product of factory discontent. There were, in truth, few great aggregations of factories, either in France or in Germany, during that period. It is noted by Dr. Clapham that between 1815 and 1848 two towns only in France, St. Etienne and Roubaix, grew rapidly, and that three-fifths of the pig-iron produced in the country came from hundreds of little charcoal furnaces scattered among the woodlands. In Germany the situation was not dissimilar. The Germans had many advantages over their English competitors. Their middle class was better educated, they were superior in the arts of design, they had more chemical knowledge, and could claim that the cutlery of Solingen had a wider market and a higher repute than any cutlery in Europe. Nor was there any country which had a larger heritage of metallurgical experience. Nevertheless the mind of Germany was so little occupied with the newer types and scales of economic development, and its industries, even such as were concerned with the exploitation of the rich mineral resources of the country, were so greatly retarded by lack of science, capital and enterprise, that it was not until about 1840 that the great Silesian coalfield, which has proved to be in recent years an apple of discord between Poland and Germany, began to be worked.

The restoration in France, though providing once more the spectacle of a King and a Court, made little change in the condition of the French people. The *ancien régime* had gone for ever. Society had been too profoundly altered by the vast convulsions of the Revolution and the Empire to recapture the irregularities, anomalies, and confusions which made the government of the old monarchy a mountain of abuses. The nobles never recovered their ancient sway. The episcopal grand seigneur was a distant memory becoming steadily fainter. All the main conquests of the Revolution, equality before the law, the liberty of the subject, the National Guard, the unity of the kingdom, the new judicial system, remained unaffected by the return of the Bourbons. Nobody had the power to repeal the Codes or to abolish the Legion of Honour or to dissolve the Napoleonic University. Even the Concordat, which was so offensive to clerical sentiment, was too strongly rooted to be torn up and cast to the winds. The restored monarchy, with its absolutist and clerical tradition, appeared ill adapted to a society which was now profoundly equalitarian and, in its middle and most influential region, prevailingly secular.

The experiment of a constitutional monarchy was started under every possible disadvantage. Not only was it hated by some and unfamiliar to all, but it implied a whole catalogue of political virtues which thrive only when men are not too bitter and implacable to adjust their differences. The constitution of England could be copied. The good-humour, the moderation, the pleasant give and take, the graded loyalties which made the working of that constitution successful were less easy to emulate. Whereas in England a newspaper of the period was full of sport and advertisements, in France, still trembling with the exasperation caused by the Hundred Days and by the White Terror which followed them, a newspaper was little more than a fierce political diatribe. The French legislator did not hunt the fox. No French Epsom or Newmarket sweetened the severity or abated the logic of his political meditations. He thought with a bitter clearness, spoke with a bitter violence. If he was a diehard royalist, he assailed the Charter and the Concordat, and worked for the restoration of the estates which had been confiscated in the revolution. By the opposition school the noble and priest were hated with a rancour sharpened by apprehension, while the monarchy was denounced for its subservience to foreign powers, for its abandonment of the tricolor, and for its acceptance of a peace derogatory to the pride of a military nation.

The position of Louis XVIII, uneasily poised between two 1814 nations, two philosophies, and two traditions, was one of 24 extreme difficulty. He owed his throne to the national humiliation of Waterloo. He had been brought back in the baggage of the allied armies, an inglorious, unromantic figure, to rule over a people thirsting for glory and romance. The tyranny of circumstances constrained him to drastic and unwelcome economies. He could not go with the ultra-royalists who dominated his First Chamber since they pursued the chimera of a return to the *ancien régime*. Equally he feared the revolutionary possibilities of liberalism. In the blinding violence of opposing factions the middle way was difficult to find and hard to keep. Louis both found and kept it. The electoral law of 1817, limiting the franchise to a narrow circle within the middle class, in its main principle governed France for thirty years.

It is to the credit of this sagacious and witty old gentleman that, after he had rid himself of his first impossible Chamber, which was more royalist than the King, he enlisted ministers by whose advice and support he was enabled to avoid the folly of extremes and to give to France a spell of peace and material prosperity, during which she put her finances in order, paid the war indemnity at a reduced rate, liberated her soil from foreign armies, and took a place once more in the Councils of Europe upon an equal and honourable footing. The names of Richelieu, of De Serre, of Decazes, and in a lesser degree of Villèle, a good financier who disliked adventures, deserve to be honourably mentioned in the roll of French parliamentary statesmen.

Outside a charmed circle of some 80,000 electors two opposing movements proceeded with accelerating velocity: first a renewal of the spirit and energy of the Roman Catholic Church, which set itself by a well-knit series of missions and by a determined onslaught on the universities and schools to reconquer for the Faith great tracts of French life which had lapsed into Paganism; and secondly a militant anti-clericalism, finding a new and secret organ in Carbonarism, a society derived from Naples, and aimed against tyranny in all its shapes. The liberalism of Europe was not, then, as Napoleon maintained, mortally stricken on the field of Waterloo. Not five years had passed before the conservative governments of the west were unpleasantly reminded that the spirit of revolution was still abroad. There was ferment among the university students in Germany, there were riots in Manchester, insurrections in Naples, Piedmont, and Spain, in Sicily a demand for independence, in Portugal the portent of a constitution, in Greece premonitory tremors of nationalism, in France a splutter of little Carbonarist revolutions, and the sensational murder in 1820 of the Duc de Berry, the King's nephew and the next King's eventual heir, by the dagger of Louvet, a fanatic. These movements were unripe, and even when most serious, as in Naples and Spain, easily put down by two obedient instruments of autocracy, the royalist armies of Austria and France. But when passions have once been roused to fever heat, wise government becomes more difficult than ever. After the Duke of Berry's murder, royalist feeling in Paris was too fierce to admit of a liberal ministry. To his keen regret Louis was compelled to dismiss his favourite Decazes, and to transfer his confidence to Villèle, the mainstay of the Right. The Press was muzzled. Heartened by an easy and almost bloodless progress across Spain, a French army, marching under the old royalist colours, put down the Spanish liberals, restored Ferdinand to power and freedom, and by this faint aureole of victory created in the old King's mind the illusion that all would yet be well with the legitimist cause in Europe. But already Canning was guiding British policy on liberal lines; already Brazil, Peru, and Greece had declared their independence, and no shrewd observer could doubt but that the tides of liberalism were fast rising in the world.

Shrewdness and observation were alike denied to the elderly bigot who mounted the French throne in 1824. Charles X, differing from his pleasant, easy-going brother, was ·a man of strict, autocratic, and clerical principle. "I would rather chop wood," he said, "than reign after the fashion of the King of England." He was deaf to all the calls of the future, obedient only to the voice of the past. A lively and sceptical generation, still largely pagan and becoming increasingly liberal and Bonapartist, learned with amused contempt how the new King had got himself crowned after the ancient rites at Rheims, how he had lain prostrate on velvet cushions and allowed his body to be pricked in seven places by a golden bodkin, that it might receive the blessing of the Holy Oil.[1] And when this mediaeval ceremony was followed by a law granting pecuniary compensation to the *émigrés*, by another law enacting stern penalties for sacrilege, and by a royal order dissolving the National Guard, who had demonstrated in favour of constitutional reform, amusement was succeeded by a gathering volume of impatience, irritation, and fear. The idea spread, fomented by the unconcealed desires of the ultra-royalist papers, that the King meditated a *coup d'état* to overturn the constitution and to bring back the *ancien régime*. That this was in effect his design was made plain to all, when, dismissing Martignac, an adroit and moderate statesman, who might have saved the Crown, Charles summoned Jules de Polignac to his side.

Polignac, a visionary professing to receive direct guidance from the Virgin, was reaction personified. He had been one of the original *émigrés*, had been imprisoned under the Empire, and had refused to swear to the Charter in 1815. His very name was a challenge, and when it was known that Bourmont, the General who had betrayed Napoleon before Ligny, was to be Polignac's Minister of War, a mark of ignominy was added to the general distrust inspired by his Cabinet. Yet it is notable that under the last and weakest minister of her last and weakest legitimate King, France captured Algiers, inaugurating by that notable feat of arms the recovery of the north African littoral for the Latin races, and laying the foundation of the wide African Empire which she is now studious to support as a makeweight against the man-power of Germany. Paris, however, was not interested in Algiers, but in the nearer controversy between priest and layman, crown and people, which soon drew to a sharp climax. On July 25, 1830, ordinances were issued from the Royal Palace of St. Cloud, limiting the freedom of the Press, dissolving the Chambers, and altering the electoral law. The King and his favourite had shown their hands. It was plain that they meant not only to refuse the demand for an enlarged franchise, which had been gathering force throughout the

[1] The popular belief that this ceremony took place may have been unfounded. What is certain is that Charles touched for the King's evil after coronation.

year, but to tear up the Constitution itself and to blot out liberty in all its forms. The purport of the royal programme was no sooner apprehended than it was regarded as an intolerable insult. To the royalist *coup d'état* Paris responded by three days of fierce fighting, which drove the King from his throne and sealed the fate of the ancient monarchy of France. The revolution of July is notable as the act of a single city. Paris decided the fate of France. Before the royalists in the provinces had time to open their eyes, the issue was decided against the White Flag at the Paris barricades. Not less surprising to the multitude was the government which emerged from the tempest. A large share of the street fighting had been done by men like Cavaignac, who wanted a republic, or else by the Bonapartist supporters of a Second Empire. Yet the progeny of the revolution was neither a republic nor an empire, but the bourgeois monarchy of Louis Philippe, the head of the House of Orleans and the son of that Philippe Égalité who had embraced the revolutionary cause, given a regicide vote, and perished on the scaffold. It was a good and ingenious notion cherished at that time by many men of liberal temper and notably by Thiers, a young Southerner of genius, then fast rising to the front in the sphere of history, politics, and journalism, that Louis of Orleans, who as a young man had fought in the revolutionary armies, and had afterwards tasted the sorrows and trials of poverty, would give to France the satisfying blessing of a democratic monarchy. None of the disabilities which had made Charles X impossible attached to Louis. He was a man of the new world, simple and homely in his ways, who would accept the tricolor and the lay institutions of a democratic state, and, since the precedent of the English revolution of 1688 was much in the minds of the little knot of politicians who made the July monarchy, he appeared as a French William of Orange fated to heal the disorders of the nation and to inaugurate a long and prosperous period of constitutional rule in a country ill used to tempered freedom. Before the population of Paris realized what was afoot, the Prince had been brought by his adherents to the Hôtel de Ville. There publicly adopting the tricolor, and embracing before the assembled crowd Lafayette, "the hero of two worlds," and the "grand old man of the revolution," Louis Philippe obtained for his new and unsteady government a necessary baptism of popular applause.

Sparks from the Paris furnace flew fast and far among the unsound timbers of "congress Europe." The Belgians rose against the Dutch, the Poles against the Russians, the Carbonari against the priestly governance of the Papal States. A wild clamour for a war of liberation to be undertaken in the grand old revolutionary manner in relief of suffering peoples ran along the Paris pavements. There were serious riots. For more than a year the new French government trembled for its life. Eventually the storm was weathered. Louis Philippe would have nothing to say to the maniacs who would have involved France in a war with England over Belgium, with Russia over Poland, and with the Austrian Empire over Italian nationalism. It is his chief title to statesmanship that, keeping the peace with the great Powers, he 1830 gave to his country eighteen years of prosperous and advanc- 48 ing economic life.

The revolution which broke up the ill-compacted Kingdom of the Netherlands started with a riot in Brussels on August 25, 1830. The Belgians had long chafed under the stiff rule of their Dutch masters. They hated the Protestant religion and the Dutch spirit of religious tolerance and racial monopoly. They knew themselves to be more numerous and eloquent; they believed themselves to be more cultivated and genial. Accordingly they regarded it as intolerable that Dutch should be prescribed as the sole official language, that the Walloon populations should thereby be excluded from public life, and that almost every important civil and military office should be given to a Dutchman. To the countrymen of Rubens these Dutch airs of superiority were intolerable. Inflamed by the example of Paris, they determined to throw off the alien yoke.

A monument in the Place des Martyrs in Brussels marks the burial place of six hundred Belgian volunteers, who died fighting in the streets against the Dutch regulars in September, 1830. Their sacrifice, which struck the imagination at the time, proclaimed but did not secure the cause of Belgian independence. The modern Kingdom of Belgium was made not by the military prowess of the Belgians but by Anglo-

French diplomacy with some little help from the French army. Its architects were Palmerston, the new Liberal Foreign Minister in the Whig administration of Lord Grey, and Talleyrand, ·the well-chosen ambassador of France in London. Palmerston's love of liberty, coupled with Louis Philippe's ·and Talleyrand's resolve never on any account to reopen the old quarrel with England, enabled the issue to be settled on the lines of Belgian independence without a general war. Had Palmerston sided with the Dutch and autocracy, or had Louis Philippe accepted the Belgian crown which was offered to his second son, the old quarrel between France and England would have flamed out anew with consequences which must have been fatal to Belgian freedom. The co-operation of the two countries localized and solved the problem. The Belgian crown was offered to Leopold of Saxe-Coburg, that long-headed, well-informed uncle of Queen Victoria, who, having taken his first wife from the English royal family, was now, as evidence of impartiality, prepared to marry a French Princess. A wiser choice could not have been made. Leopold surmounted all his difficulties, a dangerous Dutch invasion, a hardly less dangerous French rescue, and the deep dissatisfaction of the Belgian people at the loss of Luxemburg and Limburg, which was imposed upon them by the Powers at the Conference of London. The real triumph lay with the policy of Palmerston. Belgium was free from Holland, but equally free from the risk of being incorporated in the military and commercial system of France. A *régime* of perpetual neutrality was imposed on her. Under the famous treaty of 1839, which seventy-five years later was described as "a scrap of paper," Belgian neutrality was guaranteed by five Powers, among which were numbered Prussia and France, in addition to England, who by this expedient of neutrality secured, as she thought, the prime political interest which she had defended through many centuries with the blood of her sons.

Far removed from the protection of the liberal diplomacy of the west the Polish insurrection of 1830 ran a very different course. The Tzar Nicholas, who had viewed with indignation and alarm the July revolution in Paris, was preparing to inflict condign punishment upon the insolent democracy of

France, when he was stopped short by a serious insurrection in Warsaw. Here a body of Polish officers and landowners, ill relishing the prospect of being marched off against their friends the French, and hoping that something good might result for Poland from the spread of the revolutionary flame, captured the government, and, having the treasury and army of a small constitutional state at their disposal, flung a challenge to the might of the Russian Empire. For hard upon a year the Poles fought valiantly against their giant opponent, receiving and inflicting heavy losses, but eventually (September, 1831) succumbing in the unequal contest. An end was then made of the last vestige of Polish liberty. Congress Poland was deleted from the map, and absorbed in the levelling and autocratic system of the Russian Empire, gaining thereby in industrial strength, but losing, as Polish historians assert, the spiritual virtues of ardour and faith which result from freedom.

One consequence of this frustrated movement was an emigration of Polish artists and writers to Paris, which for many generations after 1831 became the intellectual capital of the Polish race. The early dispersion of Polish soldiers of fortune was reinforced by a flight of professors, poets, and musicians who advertised the claims of the Slavonic genius in the most polite capital in Europe.

The Polish revolution, therefore, of 1830, though it appeared to result in calamitous failure, was not altogether in vain. It reminded Europe of the existence of a body of national sentiment, which was still strong, of national wrongs which were still unappeased, and of a national temper which was bold to the point of temerity. The French did not forget that the Polish rebellion was a consequence of their domestic insurrection, that it had been encouraged by prominent Frenchmen, and that at a critical moment it had shielded them from the possibility of a formidable attack. To these considerations they remained sensitive. A bond was formed between Poland and France which is still an appreciable factor in the politics of Europe.

BOOKS WHICH MAY BE CONSULTED

Cambridge Modern History, Vol. X. 1907.

J. H. Clapham: *Economic Development of France and Germany*. 1921.

Lowes Dickinson: *Revolution and Reaction in Modern France*. 1892.

Chateaubriand: *Bonaparte et les Bourbons*. 1814.

P. Thureau Dangin: *Histoire de la Monarchie de Juillet*. 1884-92.

Memoirs of Beugnot, Chateaubriand, Guizot.

E. Faguet: *Politiques et moralistes du XIX siècle*. *Tr*. 1928.

H. Pirenne: *Histoire de Belgique*. 1903-33.

P. Guedalla: *Lord Palmerston*. 1926.

Duff Cooper: *Talleyrand*. 1932.

Roman Dyboski: *Poland*. (Nations of the Modern World Series.) 1933.

J. P. T. Bury: *France 1814-1940*. 1949.

F. B. Artz: *Reaction and Revolution*, 1814-32. 1934.

J. Plamenatz: *The Revolutionary Movement in France*, 1815-71. 1952.

CHAPTER LXXV

THE AGE OF PEEL

The old Parliament and the new Society. Liberty of criticism. Advance of public education. Whigs and Tories. Reform Act of 1832. Sir Robert Peel and the foundation of the Conservative party. Repealers, Socialists, Chartists, Free Traders. Steady growth of the Social Services.

MEANWHILE ENGLAND was slowly rising to a sense of the new and formidable problems presented to her by the development of factory life. It was a great misfortune, the consequences of which are felt to this day, that for twenty precious years when the whole mind of the governing class ought to have been given to providing the new factory population with schools and public hygiene, with good houses and well-planned towns as well as with museums and libraries, parks and playgrounds, the country was engaged in a bitter war with France, and that when the war was finally brought to an end and Napoleon was banished to St. Helena, the war mentality survived for many years, counselling fear, diffusing distrust, and standing in the way of any full and dispassionate consideration of the "condition of the people question." Of that continuing war mentality Lord Sidmouth's "Six Acts" in 1819 may be taken as a last example.

It was a further unhappy circumstance that, under the long Tory administration of William Pitt, the House of Lords assumed that overwhelmingly Tory complexion which it has never since lost. The reform of Parliament was in consequence delayed for many important years and carried only in 1832 under the menace of a special creation of Whig peers and in the midst of a political ferment to which England had been a stranger since the civil wars. The country, then, continued to be governed by the old-fashioned machinery (which answered well enough to the requirements of a small rural population) of landlords at Quarter Sessions and landlords at Westminster. The charmed circle of Parliamentary life was not, indeed, and never had been altogether closed to great fortunes, however made, or to shining talents sponsored by noblemen. An Indian fortune gave the Pitts to Westminster. The father and grandfather of Sir Robert Peel were among the makers of industrial Lancashire. But while Old Sarum returned two members to Parliament, Manchester and Birmingham went unrepresented.

The results were such as might have been expected. An aristocratic debating society was called upon to cope with the problems of an economic *régime* of which no country had any experience. The factory with its discipline, the huge industrial city with its swarms, the swift increase in the population, the spectacular growth of fortunes in the cotton trade, these were in truth portents announcing a new era in the conduct of human affairs, the full measure of which the unreformed Parliament was slow to seize. It was not therefore wonderful that Parliament went astray, that it interfered when it should have allowed things to slide, and that it allowed things to slide when it should have interfered, that it legislated for instance, to prevent cheap corn and did not intervene to prevent cheap slums.

There was a great deal of untended and unnecessary misery in England during the years immediately succeeding the war. A ruined continent was in no condition to purchase the goods which England was anxious to export. While taxes and rates were high, wages were deplorably low, and as always happens after a war or when the march of scientific invention is abnormally swift, there was much unemployment improvidently dealt with. A badly administered Poor Law put a premium on rural idleness by its system of outdoor relief and family allowances. A vexatious system of Protection raised the price of bread to a hungry population and throttled foreign trade with a complicated machinery of duties. That smuggling should grow out of Protection and that a spirit of lawlessness should be bred by smuggling was as natural as that night should follow day. Violent habits may be softened by humane laws, but the state of the penal law, until it was reformed by Romilly and Peel, was exactly calculated to educate the poor in a spirit of reckless and sullen defiance. For a trivial offence, the theft of a cow, the burning of a rick, the snaring of a pheasant, some villager driven desperate by hunger might find himself sentenced to transportation or death.

Even as late as 1834, when Parliament had been reformed and a Whig government was in office, six agricultural labourers of Tolpuddle in Dorset were sentenced to seven years of transportation for administering an illegal oath to a branch of a Friendly Society.

As for the new factory population, it presented problems of such novel complexity that it would be strange if they had been promptly and adequately dealt with by the unreformed Parliament. Vast evil-smelling slums were allowed to grow up in which quick fortunes were made out of an ill-paid, under-nourished mass of immigrants from the villages. A window tax put a premium on dark and ill-ventilated rooms. But of all the deplorable features of English mill-life in the early post-war period, none was so hateful as the ruthless exploitation of little children. Even when at last in 1819 Parliament stepped in and passed a statute, notable as the first of the Factory Acts, for dealing with child labour, it did not do more than limit the hours of labour of children to twelve and a half hours and forbid the employment of children under nine in certain factories. So imperfectly educated was the public conscience that even this utterly insufficient Act was a dead letter for lack of inspectors to enforce it. Six years later, when another bill was introduced to protect the children, it was stated in Parliament that "in the best mills children were compelled to work twelve and a half hours a day and in others for fifteen or sixteen."

Nevertheless, in spite of much unintelligent reaction due to panic and many intolerable industrial conditions due to the cupidity of employers and parents, England enjoyed one precious advantage. The people were free to grumble aloud. Parliaments met. Newspapers criticized the ministers and the monarch. Juries returned verdicts against the Crown. Even in 1819, when reaction was at its height, there was a stiff Parliamentary opposition to Sidmouth's "Six Acts" for curbing the liberties of the people.

By slow degrees a notion began to spread abroad that the education of the masses was a national responsibility and not a matter which could be wholly left to the competing appetites of rival sects. Not that educational competition was valueless. The Church and the sects were first in the field. When no secular agency was available and at a time when it is doubtful whether any motive less powerful than religious zeal could have enlisted the necessary social effort to bring education to the poor, the unsectarian British and Foreign School Society and its rival, the Anglican National Society, 1812 occupied the ground. Their methods were bad, their resources slender, their teachers (for both societies believed in the monitorial system) were for the most part children in their teens. The story of their quarrels and jealousies cannot be read without a sense of shame. But at least they were pioneers in the greatest of the social services. The state has never wished to discard their work. It has never dared to build up in England a complete plan of systematic national education. Rather it has taken the existing elementary schools, Anglican, Free Church, Jewish, Catholic, as it has found them, and gradually, by assisting them with public funds, by inspection, and by the enforcement of higher educational standards and the institution of a regular scheme of training for teachers, brought them to a relative degree of efficiency. The process began in 1833 with a grant of £20,000 to the two societies and was carried to a further stage by the establishment of a committee of the Privy Council for education in 1839. Not till 1846 was there any state provision for the training of teachers.

Three great impediments obstructed a national advance against the fortress of ignorance: the guarded monopoly of the Established Church, the exorbitant claims of the factory, and a low and cheap view of the kind of education that was good enough for the children of the poor. Some of these obstacles had already been attacked before 1848. The University of London, founded in 1825, opened the gateways of the higher learning to non-Anglicans. A series of statutes beginning in 1819 and ending after a great political agitation in the Ten Hours Act in 1847 limited the hours of industrial toil for children and adolescents under eighteen, and established the precious principle that an industrial state must ensure some measure at least of leisure for its members. These were valuable conquests. So too was the foundation of the Mechanics Institutes for the spread of scientific knowledge among intelligent artisans. By the twenties and thirties of the nineteenth century it was beginning to be realized that education was a source of national power and the essential basis of a sound national life.

Much yet remained to be done. England had to wait till 1870 for universal compulsory elementary education, till 1891 for gratuitous education, till 1902 for secondary schools aided from public funds; but at least it is significant that as early as 1825 Henry Brougham, a great law reformer and by reason of his boisterous and innovating temper one of the most widely known and acclaimed of political figures, published his *Observations on the Education of the People*, which at once 1827 went through twenty editions and led to the formation of the Society for the Diffusion of Useful Knowledge.

Jan.- The Whig party indeed suffered a long eclipse. Save for the Sept., brief Grenville-Fox administration, rendered glorious by the 1806 abolition of the Slave Trade, the Tories ruled England from Pitt's accession in 1784 until Lord Grey in his old age came 1784- back to London from his country home in Northumberland 1832 to carry the Reform Bill which had been the dream of his youth. But the English form of Toryism was very different from the Austrian—the kind providence which has presided over English politics furnishing the best Tory leaders with a measure of pliability and good sense, without which the country would hardly have survived the industrial and social changes of the nineteenth century, save at the cost of revolution. William Pitt, whose long administration fixed the Tory tradition during the early part of the nineteenth century, was as far as possible removed from the mentality of Metternich. He was suckled in the Whig religion of constitutional liberty, and though, as we have seen, under the stress of the French war he found himself obliged to postpone the enlargement of the franchise, never became a narrow or selfish Tory. Like Disraeli afterwards, he divined the lamentable condition of the industrial poor. But for the King, he would have had Catholic Irishmen sitting in the Parliament at Westminster, and this fundamental generosity of outlook was shared by the best of his successors, notably by Canning and Robert Peel and Huskisson. Even the Duke of Wellington, the sternest of Tories, was prepared in the end to assent to Parliamentary Reform. The age of Metternich is not then a period of immobility in the domestic history of England. On the contrary, it is one in which great measures were passed, and great changes sanctioned, exhibiting the growing liberality of the English political mind. Trades Unions were legalized in 1824, the tariff simplified in 1826. First the Protestant dissenters were admitted to office, then the Catholics to the vote. Finally, the Reform Act of 1832, passed in response to an overwhelming body of opinion in the country, enfranchised the middle class, liberated the House of Commons from aristocratic control, and led by a natural sequence to the democratization of town government, to the reform of the Poor Law, to the abolition of slavery, and to the removal of tariff restrictions (1846) upon the food of the people. It is notable that if Parliamentary Reform was carried out by a Whig, Catholic Emancipation and Free Trade were brought in by Sir Robert Peel, a great Tory Minister, who was capable of adjusting his principles to the lesson of facts.

The peaceful acceptance by a domineering aristocracy of the democratic claims of an industrial age was largely due to the character of this strong Parliamentary statesman who for more than forty years (1800-50) strove in the forefront of the

Tory battle. Home, school, and university combined to make Peel a Tory and to range him, when he entered Parliament in 1809, behind Liverpool and Wellington, the Tory leaders. But his was a mind powerful, honest, courageous, and "prone to receive the daily deposits of insensibly changing opinions." He moved slowly, for "he was converted with the conversion of the ordinary man," but he moved in the end and just in time, and, having once from conscience changed his convictions, had the nerve to speak his mind and to face what is always difficult for a born parliamentarian, the obloquy of the rank and file of his party. Most of the great measures which he either passed or accepted in middle age he had vehemently contested in his youth. He opposed, but afterwards himself carried, Catholic Emancipation and Free Trade. He opposed, but afterwards loyally accepted, the Reform Bill. In the Tamworth manifesto, which on the advice of Barnes, the editor of *The Times*, he issued to his constituents after the great defeat of his party on Parliamentary Reform, he announced a new life for a party no longer Tory, but Conservative. "My object," he explained in May, 1838, "for some years past has been to lay the foundations of a great party which, existing in the House of Commons and deriving its strength from the popular will, should deaden the shock between the two antagonistic branches of the legislature." This, then, was Peel's final contribution. Coming into office in 1841 at the head of a ministry of unparalleled ability, he made his government the instrument of a series of important social enquiries and reforms. If England during the latter part of the nineteenth century became a cheap place to live in, if her trade was world-wide, and the whole world was her granary, if a deficit had been turned into a surplus by the reduction of import duties, if her banking and currency had been placed on a firm foundation and her legal system relieved from many of the worst defects which had been pointed out by Jeremy Bentham, the great benefactor of legislators all the world over, the result is not a little owing to "the extraordinary abilities and ordinary opinions" of Sir Robert Peel.

It was an unquiet and tumultuous time. In Ireland, always on the fringe of revolution, Daniel O'Connell was pressing the claims first of Catholic Emancipation and afterwards of

Home Rule. In England Robert Owen was demonstrating in 1771-theory and practice the beauties of socialism, to be followed 1858 by the Chartists agitating for the six points of their Charter (universal suffrage, payment of members, the ballot vote, the abolition of property qualifications, annual parliaments, and equal electoral districts) in the hopes that a strict numerical democracy would cure all evils. And finally, more powerful than all, there sprang upon the scene Richard Cobden, the 1804-inspired salesman of calico, whose crusade against the Corn 1865 Laws, preached with incredible vehemence and force, won for England cheap bread and free trade. It was the great service of Peel, that, avoiding the extreme views of the radical doctrinaires on the one hand, and braving the wrath of the squires and the rectors on the other, he steered his country down the middle way of liberal reform.

So, while the continent was shaken by revolution in 1830 and again in 1848, there was in England a smooth and tranquil enlargement of liberty and well-being. The English did not look far ahead. Great risks were run and much suffering was caused through deference to vested interests and unchecked economic appetites. But in the moments of real emergency the right action was taken. When revolution threatened, the middle class was admitted to power. An epidemic of cholera produced the first Public Health Act, a 1846 potato famine in Ireland helped Peel to abolish the Corn Laws. By the time of Metternich's fall England had a re-formed Penal Code, a beginning of state-aided education, statutes to promote hygiene and to limit child labour, and a fiscal system which bore lightly on the poor. Parliamentary statesmanship, though it had failed to provide a standard of education of which an intelligent German, like the Prince Consort, could approve, had nevertheless laid the foundation of that great system of social services which, more than any other force, has preserved the country from revolution.

The triumph of Free Trade in England was a victory of town over country, of the new manufacturing over the old landlord interests, of a middle class which while furthering its own material advantage incidentally promoted the interests of the poor. It was not only the long purse of the millowner which decided the day for Free Trade. If rural England had been united against the fiscal revolution, the result might have been otherwise. But rural England was not united. Landlords were on one side, farm labourers and cottagers were on the other. It was not least among the controversial advantages of the Anti-Corn Law League that in "the hungry forties" Cobden and his followers were able to represent the landlord not as the friend but as the oppressor of the poor.

Inevitably the policy of the cheap loaf postulated a navy which could rule the waves. If it emptied the villages, it crowded the towns and brought in its train a great development of population needing more food and raw materials from overseas, more markets for its exports, and more ships wherewith to supply its wants. A wide Empire, a great mercantile marine, a powerful navy could alone guarantee the food supply of a people so unevenly distributed between agriculture and industry and so numerous that it was idle to suppose that the tilth and pasture of a small island could ever again, save at a cost too ruinous to contemplate, suffice for its support.

Expanding material prosperity spread a strong tide of optimism through the land in the years immediately succeeding the abolition of protection. The profligate George, the 1837- fatuous William no longer shamed the throne. Victoria was 1901 queen, bringing youth, decorum, and good sense to the discharge of her office, and by the happy accident of her sex bringing also the severance of England from the unpopular entanglement of the Hanoverian Electorate. The first international exhibition was held in London in 1851, in an atmosphere of exhilaration and hope. Had not a young poet nine years earlier dreamed of seeing—

the heavens fill with commerce, argosies of magic sails,
Pilots of the purple twilight, dropping down with costly bales;

dreamed also of a time when—

the war-drum throbbed no longer and the battle flags
were furled
In the Parliament of man, the Federation of the World.[1]

Poems by Alfred Tennyson. In two volumes. London, 1842 12 mo.

But Europe was not ready for internationalism. The Free Trade doctrine of Adam Smith was countered by the reasoned Protection of Friedrich List, the German economist. The example of England in opening her doors to the imports of all the world was not followed. On the contrary, the next two decades witnessed an explosion of militarist nationalism on the continent which shattered the work of the Congress of Vienna and killed for the time being all those civilized aspirations for a better and more harmonious international order which free traders and poets were prone to entertain.

BOOKS WHICH MAY BE CONSULTED

G. M. Trevelyan: *British History in the Nineteenth Century.* 1922.

J. L. Hammond: *Age of the Chartists.* 1930.

W. Bagehot: *Sir Robert Peel.* (Biographical Studies.) 1907.

G. M. Trevelyan: *Lord Grey of the Reform Bill.* 1929.

G. M. Trevelyan: *Life of John Bright.* 1925.

George Peel: *Life of Sir Robert Peel.* (Dict. Nat. Biography.)

H. W. C. Davis: *Age of Grey and Peel.* 1929.

E. Halévy: *Histoire du Peuple Anglais au XIX siècle.* Eng. tr., 1926-35.

G. T. Garratt: *Lord Brougham.* 1935.

N. Gash: *Politics in the Age of Peel.* 1953.

A. Briggs: *The Age of Improvement.* 1959.

CHAPTER LXXVI

THE JULY MONARCHY

Strength and weakness of the Monarchy. Revival of Bonapartism. Louis Bonaparte. Socialism. St. Simon, Fourier, Proudhon, Louis Blanc. The revolution of February. The Second Republic. The Days of June. The Coup d'État of December. The age of Nationalities opens.

Feb., THE MONARCHY of Louis Philippe, after a life of eighteen years,
1848 perished as it had been born, in a Paris revolution. It was a government of many virtues, directed by a prudent, experienced, and laborious King, and served by statesmen of talent, integrity, and force. Casimir Périer and Thiers, Molé and Guizot, were Prime Ministers whose patriotism and ability have never been challenged. Though the suffrage was limited to a narrow circle of two hundred and fifty thousand electors, the parliamentary oratory of France was never richer in volume and splendour. Trade prospered, there was a beginning of railway development, the work of consolidating and extending the Algerian conquest continued. The two besetting temptations of the French people, internal revolution and wild foreign military adventure, were successfully repressed. In Guizot France possessed a scholar-statesman who understood the need and prepared the way for a general system of state-aided popular education. Yet, for all its excellent qualities, and real services to France, there was never a government which fell with so little regret.

The death of the Duke of Orleans, the popular heir to the throne, in a carriage accident in 1842 was not in itself sufficient to account for the catastrophe. To a logical people like the French there was a fundamental flaw in a *régime* which was neither true monarchy, nor true republic, nor true Empire, but a hybrid, without the historical glamour of the legitimate crown, or the democratic appeal of the republic, or the military renown of the House of Bonaparte. The very virtues of the government were a cause of offence, its policy of compromise, its desire to keep on good terms with England, its avoidance of flashy foreign risks. Lamartine, the leader of the romantic movement in literature, summed up the verdict of the people in the deadly phrase "La France s'ennuie." The kind bourgeois King with his large "sentimental umbrella" and his obtrusive domestic virtues was condemned by the common citizen as a bore.

Graver and more creditable reasons lay in the background. Alienating the Church by its laicity in education, the government took no pains to conciliate the intellectuals. It would neither enlarge the franchise nor advance proposals for improving the condition of the people. While England under the Reform Act of 1832 made rapid progress along the pathway of liberal legislation, abolishing slavery, reforming town government, and remodelling the Poor Law, Guizot, who directed policy during the last eight years of Louis Philippe's reign, steadily resisted even the most moderate demand for the extensions of the suffrage. In the ferment of opinion which prevailed a policy of flat negation was bound in the end to lead to disaster.

Eventually two currents dashed themselves with fatal force against the fabric of this drab, cautious, and uninventive administration, of which J. S. Mill truly said that it was "wholly without the spirit of improvement and that it wrought almost exclusively through the meaner and more selfish impulses of mankind." The first was Bonapartist. As the years proceeded, what was painful and ruinous in the policy of the great Emperor was forgotten, the grinding tyranny of the conscription, the destruction of the flower of French manhood, the foreign invasions, and the loss of territory, while poets, pamphleteers, and historians combined to decorate the wonderful epic of French victory which was recalled by the very sound of his name. Even the story of the Hundred Days during which Napoleon had appealed to the Jacobin spirit in the provinces and to the liberal intelligence in Paris was counted to him for righteousness. While Béranger sang of his wars, and Victor Hugo celebrated his victories in the *Ode à la Colonne*, the memories and conversations of the exile at St. Helena, being arranged with a view to the future of his dynasty, presented the Empire as a transitional fabric, designed to promote liberalism and nationality, but ruined through the malice of the dynasts before it had been able to display the full measure of its beneficent quality. This view of the Empire, not as a despotic but as a liberal and democratic thing, steadily gained ground. The legend of the little corporal, who, carving his own way to fortune, toppled over throne after throne, and then died a martyr to British tyranny in a wind-swept island in the Atlantic, built itself up with many affecting and pathetic circumstances in the heart of the people. When in 1840 the ashes of Napoleon were brought back to be buried at the Invalides in Paris the second Empire was as good as made.

1808-73 A Pretender was at hand. Louis Bonaparte was the son of the King of Holland and Hortense Beauharnais his wife, the nephew of the Emperor, and since the death of the Duc de Reichstadt in 1832 the head of the Napoleonic House. He was a strange, studious, ruminating young man, full of dreams and expedients, and possessed by a firm conviction that he was destined to revive his uncle's line in France. Twice, first in 1836 and again in 1840, he had made a dash for the French Crown. Twice he had experienced humiliating failure. Ridicule did not abash him or failure divert him from his course. In 1848 he was a needy exile in London, having seen life from many sides—as a *carbonaro* in Italy, as a fugitive in the United States, as a prisoner in Ham, as a journalist and pamphleteer—yet still nursing his imperial dream. In a little volume entitled *Idées Napoléoniennes* he had announced the entire programme of a Liberal Empire.

The second current was Republican and Socialist. The philosophy of 1789 had been egalitarian in its conception of political and personal rights, but had not attempted to abolish private property, nor to protect the artisan's standard of comfort, nor to interfere with the liberty of industrial exploitation. Trades unions were included in the general aversion from corporations as instruments of privilege which characterized the thought of that time, and since all associations were condemned, the artisan was deprived of the benefits which flow from the use of the strike or from the fixed habit of collective bargaining. These individualist ideas were now, however, fast giving way to a new view of society. The Assemblies of the Revolution had freed men from the fetters of privilege, but had left the problem of poverty as formidable and as unresolved as ever. The question was then asked whether poverty was really necessary or whether it was not possible so to reorganize society as to give to all, if not an equal, a reasonable, share of the world's material wealth. A remarkable body of political literature, which exercised a wide influence through Europe, grew up round this eternal problem. The followers of Saint-Simon preached universal peace, the abolition of the hereditary principle, the international organization of labour, and a system of distribution to each according to his capacity. Fourier proposed to abolish the State and to substitute *phalansteries*, or working cells. Louis Blanc advocated national workshops. Proudhon threw into the discussion the famous and dangerous epigram that "Property is theft." The words Socialism (invented by Pierre Lerroux in 1838) and Communism were minted and swiftly passed into the common currency.[1] An idea spread abroad in the lower ranges of Parisian society that a great upheaval was at hand when the valet would drink his master's wine and the lady's maid go in her mistress's finery. Amid much that was fantastic and violent one practical idea of far-reaching value was evolved. It is expressed in the title of a popular treatise written by Louis Blanc in 1837. *The Organization of Industry*: in place of the *laissez-faire* of Liberalism the *savoir-faire* of socialist doctrine.

Socialism, which is as old as poverty itself, takes different forms in different minds. To some it is the suffusion of industrial life by humane and Christian principles, to others the equalization of wealth and opportunity, to others again the public ownership and control of land and the instruments of production, while others—the disciples of Karl Marx—advocate the dictatorship of the proletariat to be won as the prize of a class war. There is guild socialism, municipal socialism, national socialism, in accordance with the view taken of the body most fitted to organize and direct industrial enterprise. To some, most logical of all, national socialism is not enough. These thinkers note the uneven geographical distribution of natural power throughout the world—in Europe, England, Lorraine, the Ruhr, Silesia; in America, Pittsburg. They ask whether it is just, for instance, that the

[1] In England the word Socialist, used to denote a follower of Robert Owen, appears in the Co-operative Magazine for 1827.

raw materials for the equipment of a modern army should be available in Japan and not in China, or that Roumania and not Italy should have oil, and fail to see how world peace can be secured without some planned international distribution of the world's resources. In a word, they are international socialists. Soon after the end of the Great War, when American and English coal was selling at famine prices in Italy, an Italian delegate to the League of Nations advocated the international ownership of coal and other raw materials of industry.

Whatever form of socialism be preferred, the reorganization of industry on humane and scientific principles is obviously a task requiring the protracted and combined labour of many patient and intelligent minds. The French socialist writers threw new ideas into the air and supplied to discontent an intellectual authority. What they did not do, and were not given time to do, was to prepare the minds of an experienced political class to work out concrete proposals. The revolution was upon them before they could school a generation of disciples. Heine has described the fiery atmosphere of Paris in 1842. "Today," he wrote to a German newspaper, "when I visited some of the factories in the Faubourg Saint Marceau and discussed there what kind of reading matter was being spread among the working men, who are the most powerful element among the working classes, I thought of Sancho's proverb, 'Tell me what you have sown today and I will predict to you what you will reap tomorrow.' For here in the workshops I found several new editions of speeches by old Robespierre, Marat's pamphlets at two sous a copy, Cabet's *History of the Revolution*, Cormenin's poisonous little works, and Buonarotti's *Baboeuf's Doctrine and Conspiracy*—all writings which smell of blood. The songs which I heard them singing seem to have been composed in hell and had a chorus of the wildest excitement. Really people in our gentle walk of life can have no idea of the demonic note which runs through these songs. One must hear them with one's own ears—for example, in those enormous workshops where metals are worked and where the half-naked, defiant figures keep time to their songs with the mighty blows which their great iron hammers strike upon the ringing anvil. . . . Sooner or later the harvest which will come

from the sowing in France threatens to be a republican outbreak." It is clear from Heine's words that what was in the
minds of the Paris workers was not a Fabian or scientific
transformation of society, but a violent and bloodthirsty
political revolt.

In the summer holiday of 1847, Odilon Barrot, the liberal
leader, having failed in the Chamber to extract concessions
from the government, counselled a campaign in the country
for Parliamentary reform. Banquets were held, speeches
were delivered, toasts (not always loyal) were drunk. In a
crescendo of defiance the demand was made that Guizot
should be dismissed, that the Parliament should be purged
of placemen, and that the franchise should be extended.
Prominent among the orators was the romantic figure of 1790-
Lamartine, the favourite poet, historian, and orator of 1869
France, the Adonis of every salon, and the prophet of republican idealism. The government resisted the appeal, forbade
a banquet, and suddenly found itself confronted with a
reformist riot in Paris, which by a sharp and unexpected turn
of fortune, hinging perhaps on the chance volley of a frightened patrol, developed into a formidable republican rising.

It was on February 24, 1848, the second day of the street
fighting, when the barricades were up in the workmen's
quarters and *Vive la Réforme* had given place to *Vive la
République*, that the King, very old, tired and humane, finding
that the National Guard was against him and auguring
wrongly that France was behind the National Guard, lost
nerve, abdicated in favour of his grandson, and bolted to the
safe refuge of a Surrey villa. As Louis Philippe faded out of
France, Louis Bonaparte stepped in, a man of forty, at once
mystic and Lothario, looking like an opium eater, and speak-
French like a foreigner. A little later, finding the moment
unpropitious, but having adroitly advertised his existence,
he withdrew to England to await his call.

For the second time a revolution in Paris had determined
the fate of France, but now it was a revolution which liberalism was unable to capture or direct. Under the violent pressure of the mob a Republic was proclaimed, and pending the
summoning of a constituent assembly a provisional government was named in two newspaper offices, one socialist, the
other radical, to administer the affairs of the country. The

difficulties of the situation which confronted this small body of untried and widely differing men were immense. The city was in a state of delirious excitement, vast schemes of social organization being demanded by some, while others with equal fury and insistence called for an instant war against the tyrants of Europe. It is to the credit of Lamartine, the pacific Foreign Minister, that he refused to substitute the red flag for the tricolor and in place of a dangerous military crusade contented himself for the moment with a liberal manifesto. The social revolution was kept at bay by a brave but disastrous promise of employment for all, and by the establishment of national workshops for the relief of the unemployed.

The new Assembly was to be elected by universal suffrage. A truth was then discovered which, had it been divined by Louis Philippe and his ministers, might have saved the monarchy. In a land of peasant proprietors universal suffrage may well yield not a radical but a conservative result. An electorate of two hundred thousand well-to-do bourgeois guaranteed neither loyalty in the Chamber nor confidence in the country, encouraged corruption, aroused jealousies, deadened enthusiasm. But universal suffrage would have been for the monarchy a gilt-edged investment. On its first application after the revolution of February, the poll being the heaviest on record, it returned a Chamber of bourgeois, in which the republicans were only as one to eight. To the members of this Parliament, the first to be elected in France on such a system and therefore the first to reflect in adequate measure the antique pieties of the countryside, it was a matter of life and death to conquer the red peril in Paris. How precarious their position was, despite the tremendous weight and authority of the provincial vote, revealed itself on May 15, when a mob invaded the Chamber, decreed its dissolution, and declared war against the Kings of Europe. A desperate situation was then saved by the timely appearance and correct behaviour of the National Guard; but what if the attack were repeated? It was decided to grapple firmly with the evil at its source and, as a first step, to close the national workshops which had been running at a ruinous loss and had been the means of attracting a vast concourse of unemployed men into Paris. Upon that stern and necessary decision there ensued a struggle in the streets of Paris which suffices to explain, such was the deep horror which it inspired, the surprising political manifestations of the ensuing months. For four torrid June days the regulars and National Guard under General Cavaignac fought an insurrection, so formidable and desperate, though it was conducted without leaders and apparently without premeditation, that ten thousand casualties were the price of victory. The vast majority of the French population, having property in land or in the funds, acclaimed the triumph of the army, noted the scale of the peril and demanded of their future governors so to rule that the red spectre should not again dare to raise its head.

In the midst of these dreadful anxieties the Assembly produced a preposterous constitution, organized for deadlock and manacled against change. The new Republic was equipped with the rival autocracy of a single Chamber and a President, each elected by universal suffrage. The inspiration of America was obvious; but it was forgotten that while the powers of the American President are limited by the rights of the States of the Union, the new President of the French Republic, who was to be chosen for four years and not to be re-eligible, would be master of a bureaucracy which interfered with the life of every town and village in the land.

In the plébiscite which ensued (December 10, 1848) Louis Bonaparte was returned head of the poll, by more than four million votes, above Cavaignac the saviour of society, above Lamartine the orator, and despite his thirty-nine years of shabby inglorious exile. The name of Bonaparte was enough, standing in every cottage of the land for discipline, power, and renown.

Yet he was not a free agent, but confronted by a Chamber, fresh from the polls, conservative in complexion, and prepared, if Legitimists and Orleanists could compose their differences, to restore the monarchy; a Chamber in which he had no personal following and from which he could expect no loyal or enduring support. A liberal and nationalist by temperament he was compelled to trim his sails to clerical and conservative winds, and, abjuring his past as an Italian *Carbonaro*, to send aid to the Pope against the Roman Republic. The *coup d'état* of December 2, 1851, was his stroke for liberty and power. By that contrivance of consummate force and fraud, breaking an oath, violating a constitution, imprisoning many leading soldiers and politicians, and shooting some twelve hundred innocent citizens in the streets of Paris, Louis Bonaparte made himself master of France. The Chamber was dissolved, its members were imprisoned or dispersed, his own lease of power was prolonged; and yet, though the coup was denounced by Victor Hugo and Tennyson, on "the morrow of it," as has been well said, "Louis Napoleon appeared not as a tyrant but as a tyrannicide." As against the Chamber which had voted itself a salary, disfranchised three million electors by an electoral law the full consequences of which were perhaps not perceived, and refused revision, the President appeared well justified. "The people," said Broglie, "has the government it prefers and the bourgeoisie the government it deserves." To the Sardinian Minister the Prince President, who was now Emperor in all but name, observed, "Now I can do what I want. I shall do something for Italy."

A new page of European history was about to unroll itself, marked by the triumph of nationalism, with its brilliant idealism, its disciplined citizenship, its vivid political interests, but also with its blind passions, its great conscript armies, its wars of extermination, its standing threat to international harmony and peace. In the initial stages of that great movement of the human spirit, which has brought new perils into Europe, Louis Bonaparte played a decisive rôle. After attacking European reaction where it was at its worst in Russia, the author of the crime of December more than half achieved the union and the liberty of Italy.

BOOKS WHICH MAY BE CONSULTED

H. A. L. Fisher: *Bonapartism.* 1909.

Guizot: *Mémoires.* 1864.

E. L. Woodward: *Studies in European Conservatism.* 1929.

Lowes Dickinson: *Revolution and Reaction in Modern France.* 1892.

Louis Blanc: *Ateliers Nationaux. Ed.* Marriott. 1913.

H. Heine: *Letters to the Augsburger Allgemeine Zeitung,* 1840-3.

Odilon Barrot: *Mémoires.* 1875-6.

F. A. Simpson: *The Rise of Louis Napoleon.*

P. Guedalla: *The Second Empire.* 1932.

A. de Tocqueville: *Souvenirs*. Tr. 1896.

L. Blanc: *Histoire de Dix Ans*. 1843-5.

P. Thureau Dangin: *Histoire de la Monarchie de Juillet*. 1884-9.

D. W. Brogan: *The French Nation from Napoleon to Pétain*, 1814
1940. 1957.

A. L. Guerard: *Napoleon III*. 1943.

CHAPTER LXXVII

THE RISORGIMENTO

*Italy in ferment. Pio Nono. The Republican tradition. Mazzini.
The Sardinian contribution. The Roman Republic. Venice
and Manin.*

EVEN BEFORE the fall of the French monarchy the fire of
revolution which was destined to make 1848 a memorable
year in Italian history was crackling among the rotten
government timbers in Sicily and Naples. In that spring, as
the flame spread northwards, constitutions came down in
showers from the trembling hands of penitent or dissembling
princes. The revolution touched Rome and Turin, Leghorn
and Pisa, Florence and Milan, and when the news came that
Vienna was in the hands of the mob and that Metternich
himself had at last been chased from power, even unwarlike
Venice took heart under Manin, seized the arsenal, and
proclaimed a Republic.

In this wide revolt against prevailing conditions the
primary and most generally shared emotion was the desire
for those elementary political and civil liberties which belonged to England and had been secured by France, and of
which, under the despotic but yet innovating and enlightened
rule of Napoleon, the whole Italian population had been given
a fleeting glimpse. To be free from police espionage, from
arbitrary imprisonment, from an obscurantist censorship of
newspapers and books, from harassing restrictions on travel,
and, in those regions in which the rule of Austria prevailed,
from a ruthless system of conscription which dragged the
contadino from the village to serve in a foreign army and in

distant lands, these were aspirations which Italians, otherwise differing in their political outlook, might agree to cherish. Italian unity was a different matter, for this involved as a preliminary step the expulsion of the Austrians by force of arms from Lombardy and Venetia, and at once raised the grave question how Italy thus liberated should be organized. It was because no single and certain answer could be given to this question in 1848, because some desired a federation under the Pope, others a unitary republic, and others again a monarchy under the Sardinian house, that the miscarriage of the Italian revolution in this year of turmoil and opportunity is principally to be attributed.

To most Italians the hopes of Italian liberation seemed at first to depend upon the rare and engaging portent of a liberal Pope. After the harsh tyranny of Gregory XVI there succeeded in the summer of 1846 a Pope who, having the heart of an Italian and a reformer, shone out the more brilliantly not only by reason of the contrast which he presented to his predecessor, but also because his spirit was in tune with a widely prevailing and honourable mood of liberal Catholicism at that time. All Italy was soon apprised that Pio Nono (Pius IX) had amnestied patriotic Italians who had been condemned to prison for political offences, that he had protested against the Austrian occupation of Ferrara, a town in his own dominions, that he had set up a civic guard, and that he was taking in hand the reformation of government in the Papal State. To many a devout Italian peasant and landowner the intelligence that the Pope was a reformer was a sufficient warrant that reform was good; and though the reforming zeal of the Pope was wildly exaggerated and was soon effectively checked by the course of events, it is difficult to overrate the advantage which his preliminary association with the reforming movement secured for the Liberal cause. Many conservatives who, had it not been for Pio Nono, would never have been drawn into the national movement at all, remained staunch to the cause of Italy after the Pope had abandoned it. Indeed, it may even be doubted whether the movement of Italian nationalism would ever have assumed such proportions as to make of the Italian problem one of the foremost political questions in Europe, had it not been for the original benediction of the Pope.

The enthusiasts for Italian liberty failed to foresee what was in fact inevitable, that the spiritual head of the Catholic Church could never encourage a war against the chief Catholic Power in Europe. Pio Nono cannot be blamed for declining (Allocution of April, 1848) to make war on Austria. Had he done so, he would have risked the defection of the German Catholics and compromised the unity of the Catholic Church. None the less his refusal to have part or lot in an Austrian war was rightly regarded at the time as a grave blow to the Italian cause, for of all the plans then put forward for Italian liberation a federation under Papal Rome was the least impracticable. Indeed, seeing that the union of Italy could not have been otherwise made in 1848, patriotic Italians and devout Catholics may rejoice together that the plans for making it were then frustrated.

Republicanism was a tradition deeply rooted in Italian soil, but it was a republicanism of the city, not of the nation, and consequently a memory which made for political disharmony rather than for national union. It was the office of Mazzini, the anti-clerical son of a Genoese doctor, to change 1805- the quality and direction of the nation's thought by preaching 72 with rare and single-minded devotion the doctrine of the Republic one and indivisible. Mazzini is the saint of the Italian republican movement. That his country should ever accept the rule of a king, whether Neapolitan or Sardinian, seemed to him impossible, for the Neapolitan he knew to be corrupt and the Sardinian he judged to be retrograde. A republic alone, linked in perpetual and pacific bonds with free republics all over the world, was worthy of Italy. The dream was chimerical; characteristic of a conspirator whose hand was against all governments and who, like most liberals in '48, put his faith not in battlefield decisions but in the power of enthusiasm and reason to bring men to see political perfection. Yet if the Austrian white-coats needed something sharper and more material to expel them from Italy, it must not be concluded that Mazzini's life was a failure. The moral fervour of the nationalist movement was largely due to the teaching of this exalted visionary and of the Association of Italian Youth which he founded in 1831 in a garret in Marseilles to promote his ideas.

Meanwhile the heart of the Italian problem was the

presence of the Austrians in Lombardy and Venetia. It was useless to talk of Italian unity so long as old Marshal Radetzky, with 75,000 white-coats and the strong fortresses of the Quadrilateral, dominated the situation in the north. The idea that such an army led by such a commander could be defeated by the untrained irregulars of the republican faith was shown in the event to be very wide of the truth. There was only one possible nucleus round which an effective and organized resistance to the foreign army of occupation could be organized, and that was the army of the Sardinian Kingdom. Naples and the Pope proved broken reeds. Such potential military resources as might have been latent in the province of Venetia were left undeveloped. Even the Lombards after the famous days of May, when the population rose against their Austrian garrison and expelled it with heavy July, losses, played but a secondary rôle in the military operations 1848 of the campaign. But the army of Charles Albert, slow though it was to enter the fray and slow to grasp its opportunities, offered by so much the most effective challenge to the enemy Mar., that when all was over, after the army had been beaten at 1849 Custozza and Novara and the broken-hearted king had abdicated his throne and fled to a Portuguese exile, no doubt could be entertained by any sensible man that it was from Piedmont if anywhere that the liberation of Italy would proceed. If the army of the little sub-Alpine kingdom had been ill led by its morbid self-tormenting sovereign, at least it had fought to a finish and endured disproportionate sacrifices in a cause which concerned the whole Italian people. This was not all. When Charles Albert abdicated, he left his successor, Victor Emmanuel, to rule in Turin over a country which, though beaten in war, had received in the *Statuto* the blessings of a liberal constitution, so durable that it survived till the days of Mussolini and so well-contrived that it provided a framework within which Piedmont was able to become, under the masterly guidance of Cavour, the most modern and progressive State in Italy.

Meanwhile the Risorgimento pursued a dramatic and memorable course in the famous cities of Rome and Venice. Pio Nono's April Allocution had been an intimation to the world that a Pope could take no further part in the unification of Italy. It followed as a necessary consequence in nationalist logic that the papal territories must be governed by a lay authority as an integral part of the new Italian State. It was hopeless to talk of a United Italy if there intervened between the north and the south the dominion of a temporal sovereign who discountenanced the war of liberation and might feel himself free to support the Austrian enemy. The brutal logic of the new situation was felt by the brutal Roman mob. Rossi, the enlightened minister whom Pio Nono had summoned to his counsels, was murdered in open day (November 5, 1848), and the Pope, fleeing to Gaeta from a situation which he was no longer able to control, left the Roman revolution to run its course.

The events which followed printed a deep mark on the imagination of Italy. A Constituent Assembly was summoned which deposed the Pope from his temporal power, proclaimed a Roman Republic, and set up a triumvirate with Mazzini at its head to govern the Roman State. Such an enterprise conducted in plain defiance of the Catholic Church and of the secular States which might arm in its support was doomed to disaster. A Roman Republic, however brilliantly defended, could not expect to prevail against a French Prince President angling for Catholic votes or an Austrian Emperor bent on recovering his supremacy in Italy. In fact, the Republic was crushed by the French (June 30, 1849). Yet though its life was short, the Roman Republic was for two reasons a memorable episode. "It was essential," wrote Mazzini afterwards, "to redeem Rome; to place her once again at the summit, so that Italians might again learn to regard her as the temple of their common country." Here was a flash of true political discernment. The establishment of the Roman Republic, which was defended with a fine light-hearted Italian gallantry against Oudinot's disciplined French army, awoke in the minds of the Italian people the idea that Rome might again become their political capital, an idea not realized until 1870, but ever since 1848 present to the political consciousness of that part of the population which cherished nationalist ambitions. Another reason has made the Roman Republic memorable in the annals of the Risorgimento. The defence was conducted by Garibaldi. 1807 This great blond leader of irregular troops, who hated priests, 82 worshipped liberty and had returned from a wild life in

South America to help to make his beloved Italy a free republic, now with his following of shaggy red-shirts burst into the very heart and centre of the Italian drama. Of political wisdom Garibaldi was utterly devoid. He was neither a master of Italian letters like Mazzini nor a profound statesman like Cavour, but as a daring captain of irregular troops and as a leader capable of inspiring rough followers with the elements of a simple and passionate political faith he had a certain Homeric grandeur. Four thousand volunteers, rather than capitulate to an enemy on Italian soil, followed Garibaldi out of Rome; and his retreat across Italy, with its many romantic episodes and tragic close, secured for him the confidence and admiration of Italian patriots.

The Venetian Republic, though it held out against its besiegers till October 24, 1849, had no real chance of survival after the Sardinian defeat at Novara (March 23). The lesson of the campaign was not lost upon Manin, the brilliant lawyer of Hebrew extraction who had been the soul of the Venetian defence and the guiding spirit of the Republic. It was clear to him through the failure of the movements in Rome and Venice that Italy was not to ·be unified on the Mazzinian plan, but only by the Sardinian Kingdom with the support of France. Charles Albert's doctrine that Italy could manage for herself had been exploded on two stricken fields. Isolationism was dead; so too was the idea that a strong regular army could be routed by republican guerillas. A new spirit of patriotic opportunism entered into the politics of the national party, replacing the improvident ardours which had led to the fiasco of the '48. Of this effacement of republican enthusiasm during the fifties there is no better illustration than the conversion of Manin, the creator of the Venetian Republic, to the idea of an alliance between Victor Emmanuel and Napoleon III.

1804-57

BOOKS WHICH MAY BE CONSULTED

Bolton King: *A History of Italian Unity.* 1924.
G. M. Trevelyan: *Manin and the Venetian Revolution of* 1848. 1923.
G. M. Trevelyan: *Garibaldi.* 1933.
W. R. Thayer: *The Dawn of Italian Independence.* 1893.

Mazzini: *Essays, translated by T. Okey.* 1894.

E. L. Woodward: *Three Studies in European Conservatism.* 1929.

J. A. Hübner: *Une année de ma vie.* 1848-91.

D. Mack Smith: *Cavour and Garibaldi,* 1860. 1954.

E. E. Hales: *Mazzini and the secret societies.* 1956.

G. Salvemini: *Mazzini. Tr.* I. M. Rawson. 1956.

CHAPTER LXXVIII

AUSTRIA AND GERMANY IN REVOLUTION

Metternich's Austria. Kossuth. Democratic revolution. Slavonic and Magyar aspirations. Reaction in Bohemia and Hungary. Victories of Windischgrätz and Jellaçiá. Statecraft of Schwarzenberg. The German revolution. The catastrophe of Liberalism. The Parliament of Frankfort decides for the exclusion of Austria and the rejection of republicanism. Frederick William IV. Reaction triumphs in Berlin. Rivalry between Prussia and Austria. Austria triumphs at Olmütz. Otto von Bismarck. The Prussian philosophy of the State.

THE GOVERNMENT of the Austrian Empire, though sweetened by negligence and frivolity, was slow, secret, arbitrary, and confused. It was so tightly wrapped in layer upon layer of formalism, and had been so effectively screened from the spirit of improvement, that anomalies and abuses which had long been eradicated in the West here flourished in undiminished vigour. While the nobility of Austria and Hungary enjoyed every form of anti-social privilege, while they were exempt from military service, relieved of taxation, and placed 1835- beyond the reach of the common law courts, the peasantry 48 were hard bound in the fetters of mediaeval subjection. Emperors came and went. The unintelligent Francis was succeeded in 1835 by the imbecile Ferdinand. The peasant question, which involved a radical reconstruction of the local government of the Empire, was left unsolved. *Quieta non movere* was the maxim of Austrian statesmanship under Metternich. A police the most repressive and inquisitorial in Europe spied into everything and endeavoured to defend the lively Viennese from the insidious poisons of Western thought.

A system of this kind cannot last for ever. New formations of opinion, sceptical and derisive, liberal and constructive, racial and combative, began to manifest themselves as early as the thirties. In Vienna it became the intellectual fashion to deride the Government. Racialism rushed in with a sweep from Poland; liberalism like a fine rain filtered through from Paris and London. In Pressburg the Hungarian Diet drove forward with its demand for the use of the Magyar language instead of Latin in debate and for a comprehensive scheme of social reforms; and as the racial temperature rose in Hungary it mounted also in those areas of the Hungarian Kingdom which were inhabited by non-Magyar races, among the Croatians and Serbs of the south, among the Rouman peasants of Transylvania in the east, among the Ruthenes of the north and the Slovaks of the west, and stirred to a new point of impatience and aspiration the literary and antiquarian nationalism which in Bohemia was assuming a political shape among the Czechs. The archpriest of the new crusades was Louis Kosssuth, whose brilliant powers as orator and journalist, first directed towards securing the substitution of Magyar for Latin in the Hungarian Diet and afterwards deployed in a passionate campaign for Hungarian independence, awoke in every part of the Empire the latent flames of a furious and disruptive racialism. By the spring of 1848 this powerful demagogue had been for eight years preaching his radical and nationalist doctrines to assemblies of his haughty and tempestuous fellow-countrymen.

1802-94

Upon a Government thus corroded and assailed the shock of the February revolution in Paris fell with a shattering force. One day's riot (March 13, 1848) led by professors and students and supported by civilians put an end to the rule of Metternich, gave Vienna to the people, and dislocated for the time being the central administrative instrument of imperial rule.

Thereupon the difficulties peculiar to the composite Austrian State began to reveal themselves. Autocracy had capitulated. A Central Committee for the defence of popular rights ruled in Vienna. The old ministers had been cleared away. A parliament elected by universal suffrage for all Austria, Hungary excepted, was engaged on a Constitution.

The main part of the army was busy in Italy. The cleansing tides of liberalism which were sweeping through Germany had touched all the capitals of the Austrian Empire, creating in the minds of educated men a common desire for constitutional or parliamentary government, for civil liberties, for the redress of peasant grievances, and for an end of autocracy. In such circumstances a thorough transformation of the Austrian State upon liberal and constitutional lines seemed to be entirely feasible. The spirit was hopeful, the goodwill abounding, the moment apparently propitious.

In Prague and Pressburg as well as in Vienna there was an eager and confident expectation that in the abeyance of the Imperial power great and salutary reforms could be carried through; nor was that expectation altogether falsified. It is to the credit of the men of '48, acting both in the Austrian and Hungarian legislatures, that they tackled the rural question boldly, that they abolished the peasant servitudes and the legal distinctions between nobles and commons, and that in the course of a single month they did more permanent good to the rural population of the Austrian Empire than had been achieved since the days of Maria Theresa.

But over this fair prospect of constitutional progress there spread swiftly a terrible shadow. It was the special weakness of the Austrian Empire and the strongest argument against innovation that to the grievances of individuals and of classes there was added the factor of racial discord. No sooner, therefore, was the constitutional question raised in Austria than every race began to stake out for itself a position of safety in the new ground plan of the Austrian State. The Court was powerless to resist or even to influence these formidable developments. The control of the army and foreign policy was granted to Hungary; to the Bohemians the promise of an independent legislature and local institutions.

A new series of issues of far-ranging importance was at once raised. There were many Germans in the Austrian Empire who were well content to see power transferred from a secret Committee of Imperial Ministers to a free parliament elected on a wide suffrage, so long as the predominant direction of policy remained in German hands; but there were few who contemplated with equanimity the secession of

Hungary or a constitution under which the Slavs of the Empire would exert an authority corresponding to their numerical preponderance. Bohemian constitutionalism was all very well, but what German could look with favour upon a Pan-Slavic Conference summoned to Prague on June 2 to consider the possibilities of a union of all the Slavonic races? Such a union, could it be effected, would spell the immediate dissolution of the Empire. Ever since the seventeenth century the subjection of the Bohemian Czechs had been a cornerstone of Austrian policy, a prime condition of internal peace. That this peasant race, with its heretic traditions and under the leadership of a few poets, philologists, and romantics should now aspire, not only to enjoy Home Rule, but to become the citadel of Slavonic influences and propaganda throughout the Empire was regarded by German Austrians, who had not lost their old imperial pride, as a pretension at all costs to be abated. Hungarian Home Rule stood upon a somewhat different footing, for the Hungarians had always been a ruling, never a subject, race; but that the Hungarians should be allowed to have an independent army, an independent paper currency, and an independent foreign policy was rightly regarded as a serious blow to the unity of the Empire and a palpable deduction from its strength. The miscarriage of the revolution was due to the fact that it brought such policies as these in its wake.

Reaction set in towards midsummer. On June 17, 1848, Prince Windischgrätz turned his guns upon the city of Prague and with one resolute cannonade, postponing for seventy years the realization of Czech liberties, crushed the Bohemian rebellion. Heartened by this triumph and with good news flowing in from Naples and Rome and from the victorious field of Custozza, the Court addressed itself to the far more serious problem of dealing with the Hungarians. In this enterprise, the natural difficulties of which were aggravated by the anarchical condition of Vienna, the Imperial Government was assisted by the desperate unpopularity of the Magyars among the Slavs and Roumanians, and more particularly in Croatia, the region in the Hungarian Kingdom in which the Slavs were best organized, most advanced in civilization, and most warlike. The feeling between Croat and Magyar had never been cordial; and at the Diet of Agram, which was the Croatian parliament, violent protests were wont to be made against the forcible adoption of the Magyar tongue. To turn the Croat against the Magyar, to invite the Slavonic and Roumanian inhabitants to pay back, with usury, the heavy debt of injuries which they had received from the dominant race, was no doubt a hateful policy; yet it was to this policy that the Austrian Government was driven, and to this policy that it owed its continued existence.

The anti-Magyar spirit of the Croatians was embodied in the person of Josef Jellaçić, a colonel of the Austrian army who wanted nothing so much as to force the Magyars into war, to crush them in the field of battle, and to restore the authority of the Empire. The Imperial Government was sensible of the value of this popular Croatian soldier, whose word alone was sufficient to ensure the loyalty of the Croatian troops serving in Italy and at whose behest the Croatians might be trusted to go forward against their Hungarian foes. Despite the protest of the Magyar leaders, Jellaçić was appointed Ban of Croatia and proceeded to march upon Pesth at the head of forty thousand men. War was now inevitable, and as the war passion mounted, Kossuth with his following of democrats seized the helm of state in Hungary, provoking at once a violent tremor of sympathy among the liberals of Vienna, who, seeing that Hungary was safely placed in the charge of radicals, regarded an active alliance between the two armed democracies as the last chance of saving the cause of liberty. But the forces of Austria were altogether too strong for their opponents. While Windischgrätz easily put down the Viennese, Jellaçić defeated on the plain of Schwechat a Hungarian force which was marching to their relief. Oct. 30, 1848

With that double triumph reaction flowed back with a swelling tide. There was an end of democracy in Vienna, an end of constitutional progress, and with the execution of Robert Blum, a delegate from Frankfort, a sharp reminder to the Germans that Austria was set upon a backward course. The army had saved the Empire from disruption, and from the army there emerged a remarkable statesman by whose vigorous and daring initiative victory was driven home and secured in the constitution of the state; Count Felix Schwarzenberg came upon the scene in 1849 and died in 1852. In those three years this haughty and aspiring aristocrat procured the resignation of the imbecile Ferdinand, called Francis Joseph, his young and vigorous nephew, to the throne, broke with the help of a Russian army the Hungarian revolt, centralized the institutions of the Empire, and braving the risks of a Prussian war restored the old predominance of the Austrian Empire in the German Federation in accordance with the treaty of 1815.

Dec.
2,
1848

The emotions of western Europe were deeply stirred by the tragedy of the Hungarians, who, if they had acted oppressively towards their subject peoples, were yet in their traditional practice of public discussion, as in their passionate and tenacious struggle for personal liberty and responsible government, members of the fellowship of progress and freedom. As the valiant campaigns of Görgei and Bem, and the courageous radicalism of Kossuth, under whose guidance the Hungarians had established a republic, were followed with admiration, so the news of the capitulation of Villagos and of the terrible penalties which were exacted from the defeated army were received with indignation and horror. In the very excess of the Austrian triumph were seeds of future trouble. Not least among the causes which secured popular support in England for the Crimean War was the feeling of resentment against Russia for the sinister part which she had played in stamping out Hungarian liberties and in riveting the old Austrian fetters upon the Italian and German peoples.

Aug.
14,
1849

In Germany, where there was no racial problem and no question of expelling foreign tyrants, the revolutionary impulse, which was as strong here as in Austria and Italy, assumed a unitary and liberal form. Though there were republicans, more especially in the south-west, and these heady and warlike, the party of the republic was in a clear minority. Most Germans were at the beginning of 1848 reformers, most reformers were liberals, and most liberals were believers in German unity. Distrusting the capacity or the willingness of the German Princes to grant constitutional reforms, and despairing of the Diet, they believed that Germany could be unified on liberal lines only through a Parliament of the whole German nation freely elected and entirely independent of the cumbrous and ineffectual assembly of delegates which had been imposed upon the country by the Congress of Vienna. Encouraged by the overthrow of Louis Philippe and without guarantees of support from the Princes, the leaders of German liberalism summoned a preliminary Parliament to meet at Frankfort to prepare for the election of a national assembly out of which it was hoped that a new Germany would arise through the peaceful process of discussion. That Assembly met on May 18, 1848. It contained some of the finest characters and noblest minds in Germany. It was patriotic, ambitious, laborious, quick to resent foreign injuries, solicitous to extend German power, and notable as having created the original nucleus of a German navy. After elaborate discussions characterized by a high seriousness it produced a democratic constitution for united Germany, of which there was no feature more valuable than a long array of scrupulous provisions for the protection of personal liberty. Yet its work was in vain. It is one of the tragedies of modern history that this Assembly, launched on a vast surge of national enthusiasm, was unable to accomplish its self-appointed task, and that the union of Germany was achieved, not by the give and take of Parliamentary argument but by the blood and iron of civil and foreign war.

The causes of this catastrophe to German liberalism have now briefly to be enumerated. The Assembly, though it reflected the best mind of the learned, official and professional classes, failed adequately to represent either the nobles or the wage-earners or the big interests in business or finance. Defective in these respects and lacking tradition and party discipline, the Parliament was at once confronted with two problems of enormous complexity and hardly admitting at that time of a pacific solution. What was to be the shape of the new Germany? Should it include the whole Austrian Empire, or only that part of it which was German, or was even German Austria to be left outside the framework of the German state? The first question was readily answered in the negative. It was no great sacrifice to German legislators to decline to admit into the German family the Czechs, the Magyars, the Croats, and the Roumanians who were subject to the Austrian Crown. But to the proposal that German Austria should be shorn off from Germany there were at once violent and serious objections. How, it was argued,

April,   The offer was refused. The King would accept no crown
1849   which was not tendered by the Princes, no constitution which
the governments of Germany had not confirmed. In the
proposals of the Frankfort Parliament he discerned a concession to the evil principle of democracy, an armed struggle
certainly with Austria, probably with Russia, and many
serious strains within the German Reich itself. Rather than
assume the title of Emperor of Germany at the invitation of
an Assembly which he had come to despise and distrust,
which had enacted universal suffrage and the secret ballot,
he preferred to remain undisputed master of his loyal
Prussians, to shatter the work of the Frankfort Parliament,
and to bring to a sudden end those designs for a liberal and
united Germany which had inspired the aspirations and
energies of so many honourable and patriotic men. The
wheel of fortune had now turned full circle, and the Prussian
army, stamping out revolution in Saxony, Baden, and Hanover, earned the gratitude of every German Prince who was
trembling for his throne.

But now when the storms of revolution were cleared away
the Prussian King found himself confronted by Schwarzenberg, the imperious master of a resurgent Austria. There
ensued a memorable struggle between two contrasted policies
which brought upon Prussia a deep diplomatic humiliation.
Assuming that Austria was now outside the *Reich*, that the
old German Diet was dead and done with, and that it was
open to him to form by the voluntary association of German
Mar   governments a fresh union under Prussian leadership,
20.,   Frederick William had summoned a federal parliament to
1850   Erfurt, propounded a federal constitution, and succeeded in
gathering under his fatherly Prussian wing not, indeed, as he
had hoped, any one of the four kingdoms, but twenty-eight
of the minor German states. To all this policy Schwarzenberg
was violently opposed. He refused for a moment to contemplate the exclusion of Austria from Germany, insisted on
reviving the Diet under Austrian presidency, required at the
point of the sword that Prussia should renounce her new
league of Princes. At one moment in Hesse-Cassel, where
Austria as the agent of the Diet espoused the cause of a
tyrannous Prince, and Prussia was ranged behind his outraged
subjects, the forces of the rival powers barely escaped collision.

War, however, was avoided, since the Prussian army was judged to be unequal to the challenge, and at the price of complete submission at Olmütz Prussia purchased an inglorious peace.

Nov. 29, 1850

Among the spectators of these transactions was a young Pomeranian squire, a member of the Berlin Parliament, whose courage, eloquence, and conviction at this crisis gave him an authority often exceeding that enjoyed by the King's ostensible ministers. This was Otto von Bismarck, destined to be one of the greatest figures in Prussian history. Of vast physical strength, a powerful orator, a gay companion, a brilliant linguist, and born to every subtlety of the diplomatic art, Bismarck united all the qualities of the consummate politician with the breadth and simplicity of purpose which are essential to the highest forms of statesmanship. He, too, wanted German union, but not at the cost of the Prussian monarchy, the Prussian army, or the Prussian tradition. "We all wish," he said, "that the Prussian eagle should spread out its wings as guardian and ruler from Munich to the Donnersberg, but free we will have him, not bound by a new Regensburg Diet. Prussians we are and Prussians we will remain." The strong inherited conservative principles of a Prussian Squire taught him that the future of his country would be moulded, not by the speeches of liberal politicians aping English institutions, but by the hard discipline of the camp. The failure of the Parliament of Frankfort, the frustration of his own King's designs at Erfurt, filled him with a savage joy. He could not tolerate the idea of a Parliament raised above the Prussian King and qualified to move a soldier or a gun in the Prussian army. Against Radowitz, the Prime Minister, he counselled an Austrian peace, which, however ignominious it might be, would come as a welcome release from the insupportable prospect of the Prussian eagle moulting in the cage of a German League.

With the disappearance of Metternich and the emergence of Bismarck the rivalry between Austria and Prussia, which dates back to 1740 when Frederick II seized Silesia from Maria Theresa, was carried by swift and calculated stages to a violent climax. On the field of Sadowa the Austrians were defeated by the Prussians, the old world by the new. With a

1866 violent wrench the German *Reich* was shaken free from the ancient Austrian encumbrance which not even the mighty hammer of Napoleon had been able to crush. More effectually and finally than the Viennese revolution the Prussian needle guns swept the grandmotherly spirit of Metternich out of the German scene.

Yet the system of Metternich, seeing that it brought Europe peace for forty years, has secured for the Austrian statesman the plaudits of a generation which has recent knowledge of the tribulations of war. Metternich had many attributes of a great political leader, a brilliant and engaging presence, a cool head, a vast comprehension of affairs, a firm and patriotic will. His prestige as the liberator of his country and as the principal artificer of the new Europe was immense; the confidence reposed in him throughout the German-speaking world almost unbounded. In the counsels of the autocrats his was the directing mind, so that the period between 1815 and 1848 has not unjustly been called the Age of Metternich. Yet this accomplished aristocrat, whose morals were so loose, whose principles were so strict, and whose influence was so wide, laboured under one of the greatest intellectual disabilities which can vitiate the judgment of a statesman. He saw no mean between revolution and autocracy, and since revolution was odious, he set himself to repress that which is the soul of humane life in society, the very spirit of liberty.

In a second respect the system of Metternich ran counter to a vital and growing tendency of opinion. The Austrian Empire was built on the negation of nationality. Its merit, as some would say, depended on the fact that it held together in the bonds of a political, religious, and fiscal union a number of races whose balancing antipathies were its surest support. The union had never been easy, and with the new spirit of nationality which the French Revolution had let loose in Europe it became more and more uncomfortable. "My nation," said the Emperor Francis II, "is like a worm-eaten house; if one part is moved one cannot tell how much of it will fall." Metternich was determined to take no risks. So long as he was responsible for the conduct of Austrian affairs, nothing essential was changed, neither in Italy, nor in Hungary, nor in Bohemia, nor in the Slavonic and German possessions of the Austrian Crown, nor was any precaution omitted against the invasion of novelty. The Catholic priest formed the conscience and shaped the mind; the Catholic policeman checked the infiltration of political literature from the West; the Catholic soldier was ready to defend with his bayonet a state which had been formed by the marriage of princes, and knew no political principle but obedience to a crown. There was neither a free Parliament, nor a free Press, nor a free University, nor even an enlightened bureaucracy, by whose means the people of the Austrian Empire might receive the rudiments of political education.

By contrast Prussia was more compact, progressive, and efficient. Industry indeed still remained for the most part on the old domestic footing, poor in coal, in capital, in organization, and so backward in its development that as late as 1840 less than 40 per cent. of the cotton looms in Prussia were driven by power. But conditions favourable to industrial and commercial progress had been laid. A Zollverein or customs union founded by Maassen in 1818 for the purpose of drawing together the scattered Prussian dominions behind a low tariff wall proved to be so seductive that, coupled with good Prussian roads and the happy Prussian immunity from obstructive tolls and customs, it succeeded in the course of thirty years in bringing all the German states within its net. By this great business achievement the foundations of a united Germany under Prussian control were securely laid.

Other credentials for the leadership of the German people became more evident as time went on. Austria was an agglomeration of polyglot states occupied with the thorny internal problems which the conciliation of differing races naturally brings in its train. Prussia, on the other hand, was almost entirely German. While Austria was becoming more and more drawn towards the East, the interests of Prussia were concentrated within the German *Reich*. Whereas Austrian policy under Metternich was directed to the simple object of repressing national and liberal tendencies, and to maintaining by a strict system of police repression the traditional ascendancy of an absolute monarchy and an absolute church, the policy of Prussia was inspired by a zeal for knowledge and by a practical and progressive business spirit. Between a Government whose creed was summed up in the precept of obedience, and one which was taking active steps towards the development of the material wealth and intellectual power of the people, there was no even balance. The period which elapses between 1815 and the Revolution of 1848, though it has little lustre, is significant as marking the preparation for the union of Germany under the Prussian crown.

Within that period a theory of the State was developed in Prussia by a great philosopher, which, since it was closely correspondent with the ethics and institutions of the Prussian people, quickly gained an ascendancy among them, and 1821 afterwards spread far and wide as an element in a comprehensive system of philosophical idealism. Hegel expounded with all the weight of his intellectual authority the doctrine that the State was "God walking upon earth," that States were superior to their pledges, that right must have might, and that might was right. Whereas Bentham, the English radical, argued that the object of the State was to procure the greatest happiness of the greatest number, Hegel maintained that individual well-being or happiness was of no account when it conflicted with the greatness of the State. Force, then, was justified, and since states were founded on force, war was a part of political well-being, the world was as it ought to be, and as the spirit rules the world all that succeeds must be good. The object of the State could never be universal philanthropy, but always its own special welfare. The only superior of the State was the world spirit, and the world spirit judged the State by its success.

It is easy to see how sharp a conflict there must always be between this mystical conception of the State as divinity and those theories deriving from Rousseau which regard it as the product of a social contract based on voluntary choice and consent. In Hegel's view God made Himself manifest in a noble or governing class whose authority could only be impaired by popular election.

Whereas French democracy derived from Rousseau, the cult of an omnipotent State which prevailed among the Prussians found full and explicit warrant in the teaching of Hegel. The logic of tyranny was gilded by the ethical beauty of sacrifice. The State was God. In the name of that abstraction millions must be prepared to work, to suffer, and to perish.

Such was the Spartan philosophy of the people for whom fate was preparing the leadership of Germany.

BOOKS WHICH MAY BE CONSULTED

Metternich: *Mémoires*. 1880.
J. Maurice: *The Revolution of* 1848. 1857.
Bismarck: *Thoughts and Recollections*. 1933.
J. W. Headlam-Morley: *Bismarck*. 1899.
H. von Sybel: *Deutsche Geschichte im 19 Jahrhundert*.
Leger: *Histoire de l'Autriche Hongrie*. 1920.
C. G. Macartney: *Hungary*. (Nations of the Modern World Series.) 1934.
F. W. Newman: *Select Speeches of Kossuth*. 1853.
C. Grant Robertson: *Bismarck*. 1918.
Hegel: *Philosophie des Rechts*. 1821. *Tr.* 1896.
Sir Lewis Namier: 1848, *the Revolution of the Intellectuals*. 1946.
A. J. P. Taylor: *The Habsburg Monarchy*, 1809-1918. 1948.
A. J. P. Taylor: *Struggle for Mastery in Europe*, 1848-1918. 1954.
A. J. P. Taylor: *The Course of German History*. 1945.

CHAPTER LXXIX

THE END OF THE IBERIAN EMPIRES

The revolt of the American colonies of Spain and Portugal. Character of Spanish rule in South America. Importance of the Jesuits. The part of England in the Wars of South American Independence. The restored Bourbon Government in Spain. The need of popular education. The Spanish Liberals fail to take account of the spirit of regionalism. Contrasts in Spanish history. Reduction of Spain's general influence.

AN IMPORTANT consequence of the revolutionary and Napoleonic wars was the rupture of the ties which bound Spain and Portugal to their possessions overseas. As the foundation of the United States was one of the greatest political transactions of the eighteenth century, so in the age of Castlereagh and Canning the severance of southern and central America from European control marks the further triumph of colonial liberty. Yet history never repeats itself. The story of the falling away of the Spanish Indies bears little resemblance to the circumstances attending the revolt of Massachusetts and Virginia. While the British colonists rejected the yoke of a country which a few years before had issued victoriously from a great European war, the first blows for South American independence were struck when Spain and Portugal had been sunk to the lowest pit of political degradation by Napoleon. The North Americans pleaded in defence the unjust and unconstitutional taxation of an autocratic King. The Spaniards of the Indies advanced no such apologies. So far from objecting to the autocratic powers of the legitimate sovereign of Spain, it was one of the original pretexts justifying their revolt that Ferdinand VII, who stood for old-fashioned autocracy, had been set aside for the democratic fashions of a 1814- French intruder. The Council of Castile, which ruled over 33 the Spanish Indies, was a meddlesome body. The archives of the Vice-Royalties of Mexico and Peru were piled high with royal edicts testifying to its minute and paternal solicitude. Yet the colonists experienced no galling sense of vexation from an interfering despotism which was softened by distance, diluted by corruption, and evaded from sloth. Theoretically the most over-governed people on the planet, in practice the colonial Spaniards went much as they pleased. Individual governors might be oppressive. Of oppression exercised from Spain itself there was little sense.

The Spanish Empire had its dark spots, the forced labour in the Peruvian mines and on the great public works in Mexico. The liberal looks with disfavour upon a system which drove the Indian to the altar under the compulsion of the lash, and subjected the intellect of the continent to the tyranny of the Church. Yet peace, which is one of the supreme blessings, was preserved by the Spaniards over the whole of their vast dominions. A population part Spanish, part Creole, part Indian, and part Negro, was held together under a common system of policy and belief. South America has often been more disturbed and less content than during the last century of European rule. Indeed, the result of the revolt of the Spanish colonies was to substitute for the long *Pax Hispanica* an epoch of inter-state wars and domestic revolutions, which has not yet reached its term.

The United States was founded by a solid block of English colonists, all nourished in traditions of liberty, and many descended from ancestors who had left their native land in a movement of fierce indignation and despair. There was no such tradition of rebellion, no such inheritance of constitutional liberty, among the Spaniards and Creoles of the southern hemisphere. The Spanish Indies were regarded not as colonies to be peopled by free immigration from the mother country, but as royal domains, and settlement within them as a privilege only to be accorded by the Spanish Crown. The idea of exterminating the Indian population, or of making South America an all-Spanish country inhabited only by "hundred per cent. American-Spaniards" was wholly foreign to the Catholic philosophy of the monarchy. Spaniards were filtered into the Indies as the Jews now into Palestine, only with a laxer hand and a larger tolerance of evasion. It was an assumption of policy that the main part of the population would be Indian or half-caste, schooled in loyalty to the Spanish Crown by the unremitting propaganda of the religious Orders. In this task the Jesuits played a leading part. With their ejection in 1768 the Spanish Indies were deprived of the presence of the one powerful educational agency that steadily inculcated the duty of obedience to the Spanish Crown. This loss was not repaired. As the British conquest of French Canada reduced the power of the motives which bound the American colonies to the mother country, so the abolition of the Jesuit Order four years later sapped the loyalty of the Indies to Spain.

England had her revenge for the assistance which Spain rendered to her revolting American colonists in the eighteenth century, for she played a large part in the liberation of the southern hemisphere from the Iberian kingdoms. An English fleet destroyed the best part of the Spanish navy at Trafalgar, and, when Junot invaded Portugal, conveyed the Portuguese royal family to its place of exile in Brazil. The first impulse to the revolt of Argentina was supplied by the ·landing of a British expedition at Buenos Aires in 1806. It was an English admiral, the brilliant Cochrane, who swept the Spanish fleet from the Pacific, and assisted in the liberation of Chile and Peru; an English force of six thousand adventurers which formed the nucleus of the army with which Bolivar, the liberator, gave life to the Venezuelan and Colombian republics; an English statesman, George Canning, who, to the delight of all the liberal drawing-rooms in London, announced, with his wonted *bravura*, as he gave recognition to the liberated republics, that he "called the new world into existence to redress the balance of the old." When Bolivar died in 1830, the southern part of the American hemisphere was, largely with the aid and connivance of the Anglo-Saxon peoples, broken up into a number of independent republics.

So the old feud between the Anglo-Saxon and Iberian peoples, which had begun under Queen Elizabeth, was continued on new lines. When the English stopped, the citizens of the American Union took up the pursuit. They annexed California and New Mexico in 1848, Cuba and the Philippines fifty years later. Spanish writers complain that of all the enemies of Spain, heretics of the Anglo-Saxon race have been the most redoubtable and fortunate.

The loss of an Empire, though it wounded the pride, did not injure the prosperity of the Spanish nation. Judged by every economic test that can be applied, Spain is richer and 1935 happier now than ever before. Her population has nearly doubled. Her internal resources have been immeasurably increased. The mediaeval Spain of the Peninsular War is fast disappearing from sight.

One consequence of the emancipation of the Indies was, however, of continuing importance. The falling away of the Indian revenue, which had been a substantial element in the old royal budget of Spain, confronted Ferdinand VII and his successors with a choice of evils. If the government were to pay the army, it must tax the Church, if it were to tax the Church it must offend the people. For the Church in Spain was not as in Italy an anti-national force, but on the contrary the very soul of Spanish nationalism. Whereas the Spanish liberals could never free themselves from the imputation of being imitators of the French radicals, atheists in religion and cosmopolitans in politics, the Church was regarded as the chief bulwark of the centralized and autocratic monarchy upon the preservation of which the strength and unity of Spain was thought to depend. Yet though the contending forces were thus unevenly mobilized, the preponderance of the Church was not unbroken. At recurrent intervals the poverty of the crown brought power to the liberals, for the army chiefs would intervene and at the point of the sword demand a livelihood for their soldiers at the expense of the priests.

Thus the political history of Spain after Ferdinand's restoration in 1814 illustrates the difficulty of establishing the principles and practice of free government in a Roman Catholic country. The seeds of liberty had indeed been sown. A Cortes had met at Cadiz in the crisis of the Peninsular War. A constitution had been framed. A certain body of 1812 liberal principles had secured the support of an active-minded minority in the seaport towns and in the army; and there were henceforth never wanting in Spain, even during the darkest days of reaction, men who would take risks for constitutional government, for the freedom of the Press, or for religious toleration. Yet so long as the Church controlled education, and through its vast social and material power dominated opinion, there was no possibility of framing a real political electorate in Spain. The long reign of Isabella II (1833-68), though nominally constitutional, was in reality a sequence of military dictatorships. The first Republic (1873-4), though adorned by the flaming eloquence of Emilio Castelar, broke down for lack of Republicans.

No mere change in political mechanism seemed able to give to the Spanish people that vigorous and sustained interest in national politics without which it is impossible to work free institutions. The Bourbons were recalled in 1874 and duly bitted and bridled by a specious constitution. Universal suffrage was introduced in 1910. Neither of these changes, seeing that sixty per cent. of the population was by reason of the ecclesiastical monopoly of education still illiterate, made a reality of Parliamentary life. In a population of more than twenty million there were, according to the estimate of Alfonso XIII, only some six thousand politicians.

In these circumstances the parliamentary life of Spain was a genteel mockery. Since the government in power "made the elections" it was expected of the sovereign that he should

give to each party in turn the right of dissolving the Cortes
and thus of determining the political character of the ensuing
chamber. Ministry succeeded ministry with bewildering
rapidity. A sterile system of rotation, arranged for the
convenience of the politicians, deprived the government of
any power of framing large and courageous policies for the
benefit of the country and made Parliament impotent in a
period of actual crisis. The real remedy for this evil was not
a dictatorship, such as Alfonso XIII tried between 1923 and
1930, when the constitution was suspended and General
Primo de Rivera was given full power to govern Spain, but
the education in letters and politics of the Spanish people.
This experiment, which the Bourbon monarchy never made,
is now, for the first time essayed, on paper at least (1931-),
under the Second Republic.

The Spanish people has never been easy to conquer or to
govern. Their restless and revolutionary temper, noted by
Livy, has subsisted with little change to the present day. The
parching sun, the dry, bitter, dust-laden winds seem so to
work that afflictions of the soul such as communism and
socialism, clericalism and syndicalism, develop in the Spanish
climate in their most violent forms. And as in the climate, so
in the temperament of the people, there is an absence of
gentle gradation. Nothing is consecutive. Riot follows
siesta, siesta follows riot. Long stretches of political passiveness are broken by sudden spasms of violent disorder. If
thought about the welfare of the nation is under-developed,
the sentiment of personal independence is high and the
attachment to local liberties of an almost savage tenacity.
It was one of the misfortunes of the Spanish liberal movement
of the nineteenth century that, being influenced by French
models, it took no account of that spirit of regionalism which
is one of the strongest facts in Spanish character, strong
particularly among the Basques and the Catalans, the first
clerical, absolutist, mediaeval, the second fiercely radical and
atheist. It was in vain that Ferdinand VII essayed to put
down Catalan autonomy in a series of decrees (1828-33).
The Catalan problem was not so easily disposed of. Again
and again, in 1844, in 1863, in 1870, in 1874, a Catalan rising
reminded the government in Madrid of these stiff, redoubtable opponents who, stationed on their eastern seaboard,

thought so differently about men and things from their Castilian masters. Catalonia was no more to be supressed than Catholic Ireland. The monarchy of Alfonso XIII and the Second Republic have alike been compelled to recognize its claims.

The particularism of the Basques, a smaller and less formidable people stationed on either slope of the Pyrenees, was made redoubtable only by its association with the claim of Don Carlos and his descendants to represent the legitimate branch of the Bourbon house. The two Carlist wars (1834-9, 1872-6) were nourished by the vigorous animosity of the Basque for the Castilian. As the Jacobite cause in England was supported by the Highland clans, so the Carlists, who represented clericalism, autocracy, and reaction, drew the main part of their following from this primitive and valiant people, whose speech is thought by some to represent the original language of the Iberian race.

Ever since the peace of Utrecht Spain has played a secondary and distant rôle in the affairs of Europe. Once she was a central influence, a nursery of imperial statesmen and men of letters, a buttress of orthodoxy, a place of pilgrimage, a conduit of Arab civilization, and later the splendid metropolis of a great and powerful empire. The country which gave Trajan and Hadrian, Marcus Aurelius and Theodosius to the government of the Roman world, Quintilian and Seneca, Martial, Lucan, and Juvenal to the enrichment of Roman letters, was no remote appendage to the Roman polity, but close to the heart of its business and culture. Even greater was the importance of Spain during the age of faith, when the theology of the Latin Church was on the anvil, and the shrine of St. James of Compostella was accounted among the holy places of Christendom, and during that long and fruitful interchange between Latin and Arab civilization which was brought to an end by the Christian conquest of Granada. During all these centuries Spain exercised a wide power, whether as a principal pillar of the Catholic faith or as the medium through which the thought of Aristotle and of the Arabians was diffused through the West. Out of Spain came Dominic, the hammer of the Albigensian heretics, and Averrhoes, the fountain-head of philosophic pantheism, and, when the tides of Protestantism

threatened to submerge the rock of the Catholic Church,
Ignatius Loyola, who bade the waves recede. Of the great
movement which is described as the Counter-Reformation
Spain was the spear-head. No part of Europe was untouched
by its influence. The pen of Cervantes and Calderon, the
brush of Velasquez and Murillo, shed lustre on a nation
which for more than a century was feared and admired for
its wealth, its power, and far-reaching ambition.

All this imperial magnificence is now a thing of the past.
Under the Bourbon house Spain soon became a satellite of
France and its colleague in the long colonial rivalry with
England. Equally with France, Spain paid the penalty,
emerging from the revolutionary wars too weak to reclaim
the American Empire, which was fast slipping from its old
moorings, and too much distracted by the clash of old and
new philosophies to live at peace with itself. A succession of
contemptible sovereigns—Ferdinand, Christina, Isabel—
reduced its influence in Europe to a nullity.

For a long time past Spanish decadence has been a familiar
theme in the pages even of Spanish scholars and historians.
As they contemplate the vast possessions once held under the
Spanish Crown and now lost, whether from indolence or pride
or from incapacity blended with that mood of listless renunciation, as if nothing in this world very much mattered, which
is part of the religious character of the people, and then think
of the new French Empire in Africa or of the wide dominion
of the Anglo-Saxon race, they are tempted to infer some
mysterious decline in native vigour and efficiency. Yet of
this there is, in truth, little evidence. There has been a change
of orientation rather than a decay of the national character.
Those who know Spanish history best find that in every age
the Spaniard is true to type. A modern author reflecting
upon the Spanish American scene, as it unfolds itself today,
finds no grounds for pessimism.

"There has been no decadence," writes Azorin. "A world
is newly discovered. Twenty nations are created. One single
language effaces a multitude of indigenous languages. Vast
works of irrigation are constructed. Roads are planned.
Woods are cleared, land is broken up and cultivated. High
mountains are scaled, rivers of immense breadth are over-
spanned. Multitudes are instructed and trained. Municipal

institutions, all alike, are disseminated over thousands of towns and cities. Industry, commerce, navigation, agriculture, the care of flocks, all spring into life on a new portion of the planet, enriching peoples and nations. And who carried out this gigantic work? France, England, Italy, Germany, Austria, Russia, all united in one supreme and titanic effort? No. One nation alone; alone, with help from nobody: Spain. And how many inhabitants had Spain after founding the greatest of modern countries? We must not limit our view to the area of the peninsula. Spain is the peninsula and the twenty American peoples."[1]

Since the Great War Spain has drawn nearer to her daughter nations. There is no talk of a revival of the empire. The Spanish American peoples will not renounce their independence. Yet when the League of Nations meets every autumn at Geneva there is a renewal of spiritual intimacy between the scattered members of the Spanish dispersion. Confronted with the strange and complicated portent of Europe, Spain and her American daughters stand together.

BOOKS WHICH MAY BE CONSULTED

Cambridge Modern History, Vol. X., chapters 7-10. 1907.

H. V. Temperley: *Canning*. 1926.

W. B. Stevenson: *Twenty Years' Residence in South America*. 1825.

Lord Dundonald: *Narrative of Services in Chile, Peru and Brazil*, 2 vols. 1859.

J. W. Fortescue: *Dundonald*. 1895.

M. A. S. Hume: *Modern Spain*. 1923.

Bertrand and Petrie: *The History of Spain*. 1934.

Butler Clarke: *Modern Spain, 1815-1898*. 1907.

Sir C. R. Markham: *History of Peru*. 1880.

V. Cherbuliez: *L'Espagne politique*, 1865-73. 1874.

Y. Guyot: *L'Évolution politique et sociale de l'Espagne*. 1899.

L. Teste: *L'Espagne contemporaine*. 1872.

A. R. Oliveira: *Politics, economics and men of modern Spain*, 1808-1946. 1946.

J. B. Trend: *Bolivar and the Independence of Spanish America*. 1946.

[1] Azorin: *An Hour of Spain*. Tr. Alice Raleigh. The gifted virtuoso omits to notice English capital and German immigrants.

CHAPTER LXXX

THE CRIMEAN WAR

*English Russophobia. The defeat of Russia prepares the way
for the triumph of Italian nationalism. The affair of the Holy
Places. Lord Stratford de Redcliffe. The outbreak of war.
The policy of Napoleon III. The conduct of the campaign.
The French Emperor decides for peace. The Treaty of Paris.
Cavour and Florence Nightingale.*

BY THE middle of the nineteenth century the cause of nationality, which was destined to win its extreme triumphs in the
peace treaties of 1920, had received a decisive and apparently
irretrievable overthrow. What prophet would then have
foreseen that within two decades the Germany of Thackeray's
Vanity Fair would be united under the Prussian and the Italy
of Pio Nono under the Sardinian Crown, or that Hungary
raised from its bed of deepest humiliation would be accorded
a place equal with the German in the constitution of the
Austrian Empire? Against the possibility of such developments it would have been sufficient to point to the hatreds,
jealousies, fears, and ambitions which had for so many
centuries poisoned the political life of the German and
Italian peoples, to the recent miscarriage of the universal
revolution, and to the nature of the obstacles, now apparently
more formidable than ever, which blocked the paths to the
success of any similar movement in the future. And of these
the greatest was Russia. The vast size of the Russian Empire,
the scale of its armaments, its slow but apparently irresistible
expansion over the Asian plateau, its reputed designs on
Constantinople, created, more particularly in England with
her Oriental interests, a vague but persistent feeling of alarm,
which was combined with a vehement aversion from the whole
political system of which Russia was the principal prop and
pillar in Europe. To the contemporaries of Palmerston and
Thackeray no feelings of admiration or regard mitigated the
sinister impression aroused by the name of Russia. The

genius of the Russian people in literature and art, in science, music, and dancing, had not yet become part of the common stock of European civilization. The engaging quality of the Russian peasant was unsurmised. It was only known that Nicholas I, Tennyson's "icy Muscovite" and "o'ergrown Barbarian of the east," who succeeded in 1825, had none of the liberal sentiments of his predecessor Alexander I; that he held his own subjects under the compression of a secret police, that he had crushed with merciless severity the insurgent Poles, that he had helped Austria first to muzzle the press of Germany, then to subjugate Hungary, and finally at Olmütz to humiliate his Prussian rival; that his government was, as De Tocqueville described it, "the corner-stone of despotism in the world," a fatal bar to the revision of treaties, to the liberation of nations, and to the revival of those generous hopes which had suffered eclipse in 1848. When Turkey, which had carried out some constitutional reforms, declined to hand over Kossuth and other Hungarian fugitives to Russian or Austrian vengeance, the Turkish Minister accredited to the Court of St. James for a time became the idol of the London populace.

Out of this mentality prevailing among the British people arose an unpremeditated war in the east from which Austria, outraging her Russian benefactor by an invidious neutrality, and, in the words of one of her statesmen, "astonishing the world with her ingratitude," emerged in a position of dangerous and friendless isolation. By smashing the strong links which bound Austria to Russia the Crimean War created the conditions which led to the liberation of the German and Italian nations. This is the chief political significance of a contest entered into without necessity, conducted without foresight, and deserving to be reckoned from its archaic arrangements and tragic mismanagement rather among mediaeval than modern campaigns.

The affair arose out of a dispute between Greek and Roman monks as to the custody of certain Christian shrines in Jerusalem, a quarrel paltry in itself, but deriving importance from the fact that the Greek claims were pressed upon the Porte by the Tzar, the Latin by the Emperor of the French. A troublesome, irritating, protracted dispute ended in a decision so hotly resented by Nicholas that he mobilized an army on the Pruth and sent to Constantinople a hectoring mission under Prince Menschikoff with a requirement not only for immediate satisfaction in Jerusalem, but for a treaty, exceeding all previous claims, which would in effect secure for him a protectorate over the orthodox subjects of the Porte. These proposals the Porte, contrary to the advice given by Stratford de Redcliffe, the British Ambassador, decided to reject.

The conditions have now passed away under which it is possible for an ambassador to involve his country in war. Telephone and telegraph make him the submissive instrument of Cabinet policy; but in 1853, the telegraph being imperfectly developed, a strong ambassador in a distant mission with clear views of his own and with a weak Prime Minister and Foreign Minister above him could, especially if he had reason to believe that his own views coincided with popular prejudice at home, take a line of his own and commit his country. Stratford de Redcliffe was believed to be in this position. His view of eastern affairs based on long experience was one of ruthless clarity, He admired the Turk, distrusted the Tzar, and may have thought that the time had come when Russia, whom he regarded as England's most formidable enemy, should be made to experience a great diplomatic or military defeat. Though he knew that Aberdeen his Premier and Clarendon his Foreign Secretary stood for peace, he was aware that Palmerston, the most popular member of the Cabinet, was on the spirited side of politics, and that the man in the street was blindly Russophobe. On these grounds it was long believed that Stratford de Redcliffe was the real author of the Crimean War. The despatches of the famous ambassador do not bear out this contention. Stratford urged moderation. But despatches never tell the whole story. The sagacious Turk knew well that he had a friend in the "great Elchie" and that British battleships were not far off. The mere presence in Constantinople of this able, high-minded, very temperamental diplomat was sufficient, apart from his formal despatches, to frustrate every successive proposal for the accommodation of the dispute. It stiffened the spine of Turkish resistance and wrecked the Vienna note, which could have settled all to the satisfaction of the French and English Governments, though the Tzar and even the Turkish Ambassador to the Austrian Court had expressed themselves satisfied with its terms.

When accordingly war broke out between Turkey and Russia, the Russians opening hostilities by the invasion of the Principalities, the Turks firing the first shots at Oltenitza (in Moldavia) and the Russians replying by sinking the Turkish fleet off Sinope, all Britain was aflame, as at a felon blow struck by a bully. Even to the more prudent section of the British Cabinet the Tzar's policy was deeply suspect since as far back as 1844 he had spoken to Aberdeen of the Turk as "a sick man" and had himself recently propounded to Sir Hamilton Seymour, the British Ambassador at St. Petersburg, the idea that Russia and England should unite in despoiling his estate. So after much hesitation, and with peace-seeking diplomacy still busy in Vienna, England decided to embark on the war (March 27, 1854).

In this enterprise of propping up the Turk, France stood by England's side. It would probably be unfair to suggest that Napoleon III's dominant motive was military glory. His people wanted and had been promised peace. "The Empire is Peace", they had been told. "We have immense waste territories to cultivate, roads to open, harbours to deepen, canals to complete, rivers to render navigable, railways to link up. Opposite Marseilles we have a vast dominion to assimilate to France." All this required peace. But in the foreign policy of Napoleon, which appears so fluid and opalescent, there were always a few fixed points. One was a revision of the treaties of 1815 to be obtained, if possible, from a European Congress; another some assistance to Italy; a third the avoidance of the specific mistakes which had led to the downfall of the first Empire. As the uncle had been overthrown by the sea-power of England, the nephew was resolved upon an English alliance. If that involved a war with Russia, so be it. The Russian was as good an enemy as anyone, unpopular with French clericals as a schismatic, distasteful to French republicans as an autocrat, and to the Emperor personally, by reason of the Tzar's insolence in denying him his proper title, a source of irritation. In the "Four Points" which stated the war aims of England and France there was much for England, since Russia was to be denied influence in the Balkans and warships in the Black

Sea, much for the Austrians, since the Principalities and the Danube were to be freed from the Muscovite, but very little for France, though it was France that would contribute the larger part of the expeditionary force. Still, a joint enterprise with the solid Britons was calculated to give stability to an adventurous, new, and precarious throne.

Sebastopol, the great naval port of the Russian Empire in the Black Sea, was selected as the chief military objective in a campaign which was principally aimed at the marine forces of the enemy, and thither, since the Russians had evacuated the Principalities and there was no fighting to be done in the Danube valley, a motley armada of French, English, and Turks, the English some 26,000 strong, the French slightly more numerous, proceeded from the Bulgarian port of Varna in mid-September of 1854.

It was a mad enterprise. Since the Turks unaided had repulsed the Russians from the valley of the Danube, and since all risk of a Russian advance upon Constantinople was overpast, there was no valid reason why the allies should waste a man or a shilling upon a siege which, even if successful, would make no sensible impression on the huge resources of the enemy. And if the objective was insane, the methods were tragic. The English army, without ambulances or proper transport, marched into action clad in uniforms fitted only for a London parade ground, nor did it even occur to the government of the greatest engineering country in the world to ease the transport of supplies from the port of Balaklava to the camp by laying down the necessary five miles of light railway.

The landing was uncontested, the first battle (at the Alma) was a victory, and had the attack been pushed home, as Lord Raglan, the English commander, advised, there is some reason to think that the northern half of the city at least might possibly have succumbed to the allies. The disastrous decision was, however, taken to march away the troops, to sail round to the south where there was better harbourage, and thence to renew the encounter. The precious element of time squandered by the attacking was used to the full by the defending force. The fortifications were improved out of recognition, and Sebastopol was protected by the genius of Todleben, by the frosts and tempests of a Crimean winter, and, since the city was never completely invested, by the constant accretions of relieving troops. Eventually, but not before cholera and frost-bite had taken a heavy toll of all the armies, the French stormed the Malakoff fort (September, 1855) and the armies entered upon a wilderness of scorching ruins, which had once been and was again to become a thriving city,

Having won the crowning victory, Napoleon was entitled to call for peace, but now the high-spirited Palmerston was English Premier, and the war spirit of his countrymen, being at last thoroughly roused, and being ill satisfied with the meagre glories of Balaklava, Inkerman, and the Redan, called for a resolute prosecution of the war. An adroit shaft from the Emperor's diplomatic quiver pierced this warlike folly and brought peace in view. If the struggle were to continue, Napoleon explained, it must comprise among its larger objects the liberation of the Poles. At that devastating threat, unwelcome in London, abhorrent to Berlin, and full of evil omen in St. Petersburg, Europe was sharply recalled from foolishness to common sense.

The Treaty of Paris (March, 1856) secured for the allies all the objects for which they had professed to contend. The Principalities (Moldavia and Wallachia) were restored to their former position. The Danube was made free to navigation. Warships were forbidden on the Black Sea. The Sultan undertook to confirm the privileges of his Christian subjects, on the understanding that the Powers should not interfere with his domestic government. The Russian protectorate over the eastern Christians was abolished. As a reward for her neutrality the rights and privileges of Serbia, while still remaining as before under Turkish suzerainty, were guaranteed by the Powers. It was a further note of the allied victory that Russia was compelled to return Kars (in Asia), which she had recently wrested from the Turks, and to cede part of Bessarabia to Moldavia.

Such were the provisions, many of them of transitory value, which the allies were able to exact from the government of the new Tzar Alexander II. Though a fresh lease of life had been given to the Porte, the victors were unable to arrest the march of Christian freedom in the Balkans or the revival of Russian navalism in the Black Sea. Indeed, it was

Napoleon who sponsored the new Roumanian kingdom when England, absorbed in the Indian Mutiny, was too busy to protest. As for the Black Sea clauses of the treaty, they were repudiated by Russia in 1870, all Europe acquiescing in a lawless but natural act which it was powerless to obstruct. For the moment, however, and for many years to come Russia was a disabled giant, crippled by the terrible effect of the long, hideous midwinter marches to the relief of Sebastopol, when ox-wagons sank deep in the snowdrifts and hundreds of thousands of honest peasants perished on the way.

Seated at the conference table at Paris was a stout, spectacled, whiskered figure, affable and fluent of speech, and fully primed with technicalities of every sort—the Count Cavour, since 1852 Prime Minister in Piedmont. After the fiercest parliamentary tussle, this far-seeing statesman, gambling as the greatest statesman must often do for the highest stakes, persuaded the Turin Parliament (January, 1855) to send a Sardinian contingent to the Crimea. Fortune favours the brave. At the cost of twenty-eight lives, lost when a division of his countrymen went into action at the Tchernaya, and some thousand casualties from cholera, Cavour earned the right at the end of the war to raise the wrongs of Italy at the council table of Europe.

Equally daring and decisive in another sphere was the action of a gently nurtured English Victorian lady, who, moved by the tales of suffering at the front, went out to nurse the troops at Scutari, and by her personal example and fiery energy then and thereafter raised the whole status of the nursing profession, improved the standard of public hygiene, and, more powerfully perhaps than any other single influence, won for the women of her country the right of entry into serious and useful callings. The extraordinary achievement of Florence Nightingale in defying the conventions of the age in her great work for the relief of human suffering is one of the few compensations for the waste and havoc of the Crimean War.

BOOKS WHICH MAY BE CONSULTED

P. Guedalla: *Palmerston.* 1926.
Sir Edward Hamley: *The War in the Crimea.* 1891.
A. W. Kinglake: *The Invasion of the Crimea.* 1877.

Pierre de la Gorce: *Histoire du Second Empire.* 1908.

Spencer Walpole: *A History of England from the Conclusion of the Great War in* 1815. 1890.

Sir E. T. Cook: *The Life of Florence Nightingale.* 1925.

W. R. Thayer: *The Life and Times of Cavour.* 1915.

F. A. Simpson: *Louis Napoleon and the Recovery of France.* 1923.

P. Guedalla: *The Second Empire.* 1932.

S. Lane Poole: *Life of Stratford Canning.* 1888.

English Historical Review, 1933. 1934.

H. W. V. Temperley: *England and the Near East. The Crimea.* 1936.

Sir John Marriott: *The Eastern Question.* 4th Ed. 1940.

C. Woodham Smith: *Florence Nightingale.* 1951.

CHAPTER LXXXI

THE UNIFICATION OF ITALY

England's miscalculation in the Near East. England and the Risorgimento. Cavour's debt to English Liberalism. The modernization of Piedmont. Austria in Italy. The interview at Plombières. The Italian campaign of 1859. The truce of Villafranca. National movement in central Italy. Ricasoli in Tuscany. The cession of Savoy and Nice to France. Cavour and Mazzini. Garibaldi in Sicily and Naples. Cavour and Victor Emmanuel march south. The retirement of Garibaldi. Concluding stages of the National movement. The Roman question. Italy alienated from France.

ENGLAND'S CRIMEAN enterprise was based upon three mistaken estimates: an undue respect for the striking power of the Tzar in scenes of action far remote from the heart of the Russian Empire, a failure to appreciate the capacity of the rude Christian peoples of the Balkans to maintain a position of sturdy independence, and finally, despite many lessons of the past, a continuing faith in the power of the Turk to give to his Christian subjects, under appropriate western guidance, the benefits of a just and enlightened rule. These doctrines, which continued to inform British policy in the Balkans until they were rejected by the march of events in the eighties and nineties, cost the country twenty-five thousand lives in the Crimea and much subsequent alarm, perturbation, and waste of effort.

In Italy, whose achievement of unity under the House of Savoy is the next great episode of European history, the influence of England was more fortunately and inexpensively exerted. In the happy nick of time, when Italy was at the crisis of her fate, and the cause of Italian nationalism, threatened by internal dissensions and external peril, needed encouragement, every English envoy accredited to an Italian Court was the friend of Italian freedom. Wherever Liberals were gathered together in England, in the Universities, in the clubs, in the country houses, and in Parliament, the prevailing sentiment was one of hope that the cause of clericalism and absolutism, hateful to a Protestant and constitutional people and rendered yet more odious by Gladstone's revelations of the atrocities connected with the administration of justice in Naples, would suffer a complete overthrow. More important still, Palmerston and Russell, each as strongly favourable to Italian liberty as the Queen and Prince Consort were adversely affected towards it, were at the helm of affairs in 1860, when at the least sign of encouragement from London, France or Austria might have intervened to prevent the junction of central and southern Italy with the north. The strong and open declarations of these two statesmen on behalf of Italian freedom and the uncertainty in foreign countries as to how the British Navy would be instructed to act, if any attempt were made from outside to bolster up the satellites of Vienna and Rome, were important contributions to the success of the Italian cause.

There is another respect in which the Italian movement was indebted to England. Cavour was a disciple of English liberalism. It was his ambition to create first in the little Kingdom of Piedmont and ultimately in the larger sphere of a united Italy the kind of polity which he found in England, a constitutional monarchy broad based on the practice of liberty and religious toleration, keeping the Church within its proper sphere, pursuing a policy of free trade, developing railways, and applying to the promotion of industry and agriculture all the scientific and technical knowledge of the time. French abstractions made no appeal to the practical intelligence of a man who had been a banker, a manufacturer, and a farmer before he rose to be a statesman. But if business was an essential part of his training, Parliament was the congenial theatre for the display of his larger powers. He excelled in debate, abounded in persuasion, invited and exulted in controversy. During his long administration (1851-59, 1860-62) the practice of responsible government took root in Italy: and of the foreign conquests of English liberalism, none has been so important as the mind of Cavour.

The state governed by Victor Emmanuel II consisted of four incohesive parts, of which one only (the recently incorporated Republic of Genoa) was in any way identified with the historic glories of Italy. Savoy on the French side of the Alps, albeit the original home of the royal house, was in language and sentiment to be reckoned as a province of France rather than an integral part of Italy. Piedmont was a poor backward sub-alpine region, with no claim on the admiration of Italians for its services in the past and with little prospect, so it must have seemed, of contributing to those particular spheres of literary and artistic excellence in which the Italians take special pride. As for Sardinia, it was a malarious and barbarous island. Genoa was different. Here was a city which had played a great part not only in the history of the Mediterranean, but in the marine enterprises of the world; Genoa, however, was in decrepitude, and being a recent member of the Piedmontese State and still chafing under the unfamiliar yoke, was a cause rather of anxiety than of strength to the government of Turin.

Out of these unpromising and disparate materials Cavour determined to build up a state which, alike for strength and efficiency as for its bold practice of Parliamentary government, should acquire and retain the direction of the Italian movement. In these designs he was assisted by a Parliamentary constitution inherited from the last reign, by a virile people, by a coarse, energetic, but thoroughly patriotic sovereign, and by the best army at the disposal of an Italian government.

The Piedmontese Risorgimento, as it was conceived by Cavour and his like-minded contemporaries, involved reforms which could be accomplished only at the cost of a sharp encounter with the Church. That encounter, despite the troubled conscience of the libertine king, was successfully carried through. The Siccardi law attacked ecclesiastical jurisdiction and the privileged position of the priesthood before the law. The Rattazzi laws curtailed the top-heavy ecclesiastical establishment, cut down the vast incomes of the higher clergy, and closed more than three hundred monasteries.

In the teeth of the most violent opposition from the Vatican civil marriage was enacted. By such enactments Piedmont in a very few years began to rank, not as before among the most retrograde states of Italy, its energies dispersed, its intelligence fettered by tradition and obscured by priestcraft, but as a modern emancipated and practical community. These improvements were confirmed by a balanced budget, by a series of commercial treaties, and by the steady application of the government to the expansion of railways, to the improvement of agriculture and of industry and to the building up of an army strong enough, should occasion arise, to drive the Austrians across the Alps.

Outside Tuscany and Piedmont the least badly governed part of Italy seems to have been those provinces of Lombardy and Venetia which were already administered by Austria. Nothing, however, which the Austrian government did for the improvement of the material condition of its Italian subjects could alter the fact that this alien power was the cornerstone of reaction throughout the peninsula, that it was under Austrian protection that the bad papal government in the Romagna was enabled to flourish and King Bomba to practise his notorious irregularities in Naples. Not for one moment would Mazzini, the arch-contriver of conspiracies, permit it to be forgotten that Austria was an enemy to be overthrown by fair means or foul. Weaving skein after skein of conspiracy, each more desperate than the last, this indomitable fanatic watered the soil of Italy with the blood of martyrs.

For Cavour also, Austria was the enemy, but while Mazzini thought in daggers and conspiracies, it was a primary factor in Cavour's plans that Italy should be liberated in open war by the joint armies of France and Piedmont. In Turin, then, all was martial preparation, while in Paris along the *coulisses* of the Tuileries there was an unceasing hum of expectation and intrigue.

At last in the July of 1858 Napoleon, always at heart a

Carbonaro, but long uncertainly balanced between contending pressures, took a characteristic and decisive step. Secretly and without consulting his ministers, he summoned Cavour to meet him at Plombières in the Vosges, and there in the course of two conversations sketched out his plan for Italy without the Austrians; a north Italian kingdom stretching from the Alps to the Adriatic, a monarchy to be patched up for some-body in the centre, a Papal State (since clerical opinion would require that the Pope should remain in Rome), a reformed Naples, the whole perhaps bound together in some form of confederation with the Pope as President. That there should be a war went without saying, but it must be a war waged upon a pretext which would appeal to the Emperor's subjects, a war in which Austria would be made to figure as the power-ful aggressor, Piedmont as the weak and innocent state battling for its mere existence. In some circumstances and always provided there were compensation for her sacrifice, the aid of France could be counted on. As an honorarium she would ask for Savoy and Nice, Savoy, the original home of the Sardinian dynasty, Nice, as it unfortunately happened, the birthplace of Garibaldi. A marriage would crown the political treaty. The Princess Clothilde, a child of fifteen, would give her hand to the Prince Jerome Napoleon, a libertine of thirty-seven years, who, if he laboured under a reputation of cowardice in the field, was praised for a senti-mental fidelity to his mistresses. Perhaps this ill-assorted couple might reign together some day in Florence. A Bona-parte in Tuscany, a Murat in Naples, these were possibilities flitting in the opaque background of the Emperor's mind. With this bargain, no easy one for his royal master to digest, but with the comfortable knowledge that the French Emperor was henceforth his accomplice, Cavour returned to Turin to work for war.

At his next New Year's reception, Napoleon casually announced that he regretted that his relations with Austria were not so good as they had been. The vague words flew round Europe and were taken as an omen of impending war. Yet such was the balancing temper of the Emperor, such his belief in the method of international conference, that after all war might not come. Then, when things looked black for Cavour, the Austrians, who could always be relied on to play into the hands of an enemy, were so obliging as to issue an ultimatum demanding disarmament from Turin. The *casus belli* required at Plombières had been provided. Austria was the aggressor, and with a light heart and overweening confidence the paladins of France marched again under a Bonaparte into the plains of Italy.

For the student of military history the Italian campaign of 1859 is chiefly to be remembered as a catalogue of mistakes. It might have been thought that with their long warning of impending trouble the Austrians would have ·paid some attention to the development of their railways. The military mind, however, is slow to absorb technical inventions, and Watt and Stephenson might almost have lived in vain, so little were the potentialities of the railway discerned by the rival governments and their commanders in the field. A single line only connected Vienna with Trieste. From Trieste to Venice, a distance of seventy miles, there was no railway at all. To such an extent did the old leisurely fashion of campaigning still prevail, that although the Austrians forced the war and had their army massed on the Piedmontese frontier they made no effort to dispose of the Piedmontese before they had effected their concentration with the French. With a degree of incapacity almost inconceivable Giulay advanced into Piedmont, then retired, and passively conceded the initiative to his antagonist.

Despite the glamour of his name the Emperor of the French was no general. A plan of campaign regardless of railways, for it had been furnished by a veteran of the Napoleonic wars, stood in lieu of the promptings of native wit; and the obedient student of Jomini as he marched his army northwards across the enemy front should have been exposed to many an awkward thrust from a vigilant antagonist. Yet since the Austrians were even less efficient than the French, everything succeeded with the army of invasion, the march to the north, the advance eastward on Milan, the two fierce collisions, in which nothing seems to have worked out according to plan, at Magenta, and again at Solferino. By July, thanks to the courage of the rank and file, the allied sovereigns were masters of Lombardy.

At this point of the campaign (July 11, 1859), with the cries of the wounded of Solferino still echoing in his ears, Napoleon sought out Francis Joseph, the young Austrian Emperor, and made with him a truce at Villafranca. It was an act which then and afterwards laid him open to the charge of the basest treachery to the Italian cause, for without the consent of Victor Emmanuel and on the morrow of a definite military success he suddenly wound up the war, taking Lombardy for Piedmont, but leaving the Austrians established in Venetia. He was content for the moment, seeing that he had not fulfilled his share of the bargain, that the compensations should be waived. "You shall pay me the cost of the war," he said to Victor Emmanuel, "and we will talk no more of Nice and Savoy."

The fury of Cavour when he heard that these terms had been accepted by his King was such that he resigned his office. We can well appreciate the measure of his disappointment. He had been promised an Italy from which the Austrian power would be entirely eliminated, an Italy free from the Alps to the Adriatic, and now when Piedmont had made its war effort, when all Italy had been stirred to the boiling point, when two victories had been already won, when Milan had been recovered, and when a large French army was on Italian soil, a peace was made which left Austria as firmly established as ever in a famous Italian province, and as competent as ever from that point of vantage to maintain the whole fabric of clerical, autocratic and anti-Italian interests against which the policy of Piedmont had been from the first an emphatic protest. From the moment that Napoleon made his peace at Villafranca, the whole sentiment of Italy changed towards him. An aversion from the French, as traitors to the cause of Italian liberty, swiftly replaced the glowing enthusiasm which had greeted the liberators on their triumphal entry into Milan. Yet of all the actions of his career there have been few more judicious than Napoleon's sudden decision to close the Italian campaign after Solferino. His casualties had been heavy and there had been cases of cholera in his camp. In all those details which are essential to the successful conduct of a long campaign, in transport, in supply, in hospital equipment, his army was gravely deficient. His humanity, and humanity is always judicious, had been stirred by the terrible scenes of an actual battlefield.

He reflected that the enemy, though shaken, was still intact, and likely, with the protection of the famous quadrilateral of the Venetian fortresses,[1] to oppose an obstinate and perhaps successful resistance to his advance. Even if there were no risk to be apprehended from Germany, it was still doubtful whether the allies would be able to conquer Venetia; but the German risk was grave. An urgent message came to him from Paris that a Prussian army was mobilized on the Rhine, and, if he did not promptly conclude with the Austrians, would be at the throat of France. Amply, therefore, was he justified, though on grounds obscure to Cavour and his friends, in staying the havoc. A conference at Zürich was to settle the future of Italy.

The episode which ensued was one of those spontaneous ebullitions of popular feeling which defeat all the calculations of statesmen. Central Italy, by the voice of the people, declared for Piedmont. The little Principalities, Modena, Parma, Tuscany, rose against their Princes. In Romagna, in Umbria, in the Marches, there was the same quick spasm of enthusiasm for the new kingdom of Italy which was burning in the north. Here was a situation unforeseen at Plombières, contravening the scheme of the French Emperor for a Tuscan Kingdom to be governed by Prince Napoleon, odious to the Pope, since it entailed the mutilation of his territory, hateful to Austria, whose princely clientèle was ejected from power and liable to be overset, either by the enthusiastic opposition of Italian republicans, to whom the rule of Piedmont was odious in every point, or by the intervention of foreign powers. The situation, however, was saved by three circumstances. Among the central States of Italy by far the most famous and influential was the Grand Duchy of Tuscany, which for a hundred and twenty-one years had been ruled over with mild and distinguished sagacity by Princes of the House of Lorraine. It was here, one would imagine, that particularism would be strongest, and that an easy hearing would be found for arguments based on the long tradition of dignified independence evolved by the Tuscan State, and the loss of prestige attaching to the acceptance of Savoyard rule. By a singular piece of good fortune, it so happened that when, under the strong pressure of national emotion, Leopold II,

Aug., 1859- Mar., 1860

[1] Verona, Mantua, Peschiera, Legnano.

the last of the Lorraine Dukes, was expelled from his throne, the leadership of the Tuscans passed with popular acclamation not to a hotheaded and officious demagogue but to a nobleman of unblemished character, ardent patriotism, and substantial good sense. At the critical moment when everything might have gone wrong in Florence, and if in Florence then in Modena and Parma and other parts of central Italy, 1809-Benito Ricasoli brought the Tuscans firmly and decisively to 80 reject the solution of a separate kingdom and to accept the House of Savoy. Among the architects of Italian unity the name of this steadfast Tuscan baron deserves to be remembered.

All this local movement, however, though ratified by plébiscites, might easily have been brought to nothing by foreign intervention; but here Italy was helped by the warm sympathy of the English government and by the fact that Napoleon was already, through the conversations at Plombières, the accomplice of Cavour. That astute Piedmontese statesman was now again, after a brief retirement, in charge of affairs (January 20, 1860). He knew the thoughts which were flitting in Napoleon's mind, how he would like to see his cousin established in Florence, a Prince Murat reigning in Naples, and the position of the Pope safeguarded, but he remembered also that the Emperor had first suggested, and then after Villafranca waived, a claim for compensation. That claim Cavour was now willing to satisfy, if Napoleon would accept the adhesion of the Italian States to the Kingdom of his royal master. The bargain was struck. The great formulae of democracy were observed and as a plébiscite gave Tuscany and Modena to Italy, so, by the same expedient of a popular vote, Savoy and Nice passed into the possession of France.

The transaction cannot be interpreted in terms of the outcry of patriotic Italians. The new Kingdom of Victor Emmanuel was rid of an obscurantist and priest-ridden province which it would have been difficult to educate and costly and impracticable to defend. But the transfer of Savoy, if for these reasons it involved no real deduction from the strength of the Italian Kingdom and was in any case handsomely paid for by the acquisition of the central provinces, was no unmixed blessing for Napoleon. Here, it was said in London

and other European capitals, was the first modest beginning
of a policy for extending the eastern frontier of France and
for revising the treaties which had been framed by the victors
in the Napoleonic wars to curb the torrents of French ambition. Queen Victoria complained bitterly that England had
been made a dupe; and even his free trade treaty with Cobden,
which cost Napoleon so much in domestic popularity, did
not undo the unfavourable impression which the seizure of
Savoy imprinted on the English mind. From that moment
the capital of goodwill towards the French Empire began
sensibly to decline in Europe, and Napoleon to be regarded
as a disturber of the peace, an enemy of the existing order,
who, even under the veil of a quixotic and sentimental
crusade, worked always for the restoration of the continental
preponderance of France.

Among the difficulties besetting the liberation of Italy none
was greater than the problem of dealing with Mazzini and
his school of republican conspiracy. For a statesman like
Cavour, who believed in the action of regular governments,
regular armies, and established forms of diplomatic pressure
and inducement, nothing would have been more dangerous
than open dealings with avowed conspirators or any apparent
complicity in their designs. Yet it could not be denied on a
cool view of the situation that conspiracy, however hateful,
however criminal, however desperate, had at least the effect
of advertising the discontents of Italy abroad, and of raising
the political temperature at home. To have discouraged
conspiracy altogether would have been tantamount to an
assault upon the chief dynamic influence in the Italian movement. Cavour could not afford to throw away so powerful
a weapon. His object was not to alienate the conspirators by
rigour, but to attract them by seduction, and publicly to disown
any activity likely to be ill viewed in Paris and in London.
Conspiracy was met by conspiracy. In La Farina's National
Society Cavour had under his hand an organization which,
since it accepted power under the monarchy, complied with
his main purpose. Above all he made a convert of Garibaldi,
who, during the campaign of 1859, wore the King of Sardinia's uniform as commander of an irregular force of
Hunters of the Alps, which had been formed for the express
purpose of engaging the great guerilla leader in the work of

the royal army of the north. The importance of this conversion was soon to be demonstrated.

While these great transactions were going forward in the north, Crispi, a hard-headed and subtle republican conspirator, was stirring Sicily to rebel against its Bourbon king. The man was formidable, the conspiracy wide, the temper of the island, being long attuned to rebellion, suggested the possibility of a flaming republican success. Crispi needed a sword. A soldier was required who could fan conspiracy into rebellion, concentrate rebellion into war, and out of war bring victory; and seeing that the sword of Garibaldi, the defender of the Roman Republic, was now idle—to what other quarter could Crispi more naturally turn? Once launched, the idea became everybody's secret; Garibaldi for Sicily and the liberation of the south.

There were many substantial grounds, fully present to the calculating mind of the wise Cavour, for postponing, if possible, the fusion of the south into the kingdom which had been so recently formed and was still so imperfectly compacted. The south was very different from the north, in racial composition, in social texture, in the degree of its education, in its aptitude for modern life. It had been long barbarized by bad government and the baser forms of superstition. Brigandage was endemic—societies secretly formed for crime were a cancer preying on the vitals of the nation; and to this accumulation of moral and political evils there was added the problem of southern destitution, with all its complex antecedents in the laziness of man and the niggardliness of nature. A premature assumption of these unfamiliar southern problems might break the back of the new Italian government with its capital in Turin. Postponement, however, was impossible. The revolutionary movement in Sicily was a thing altogether outside Cavour's capacity to prevent. It might be guided, but it could not be stopped. It might assume a dangerous republican form or be schooled into acceptance of the monarchy. The best hope rested on Garibaldi. On May 5, 1860, with Cavour's secret connivance, that great commander set sail for Sicily. He had with him the uniform of a Piedmontese general and used as his watchword "Italy and Victor Emmanuel."

The story of Garibaldi's amazing Sicilian adventure, how

at the head of a ragged and motley band of volunteers, bare of treasure and with no serious military equipment, he landed at Marsala, stormed Calatafimi, fought his way into Palermo, and at the end of three months cleared the island of royal troops, is, even when full allowance is made for the cowardice and ineptitude of his opponents, and for the general sympathy of the Sicilians, a great example of moral leadership in war. Having won Sicily he crossed the Straits. The great naval Powers who might have obstructed the passage, for one reason or another, let him pass, and then on the Neapolitan mainland among the wrinkled Calabrian hills and on the shining levels of the Campagna the same miraculous story repeated itself, of cowardly enemies, dissolving armies, acclaiming crowds. The King did not even defend the capital, but fled to Gaeta, leaving Naples to the enemy.

The triumph of Garibaldi was almost complete; but it was perhaps fortunate, seeing that he dreamed of a brigand's dash at Rome and Venice, that Bourbon garrisons in Gaeta and Capua forbade a precipitate advance. A sharp fight on the banks of the Volturno showed the Garibaldians that even a Neapolitan force sallying from Capua could sometimes show its ugly teeth.

The magical success of the Redshirts had from the first been watched from Turin with feelings of mingled anxiety and admiration. There was the risk that the whole movement of Sicilian and Neapolitan liberation might break down in sheer anarchy. There was the further danger that Garibaldi, who had already been with difficulty restrained from attacking the Papal States, would now march on Rome and, colliding with the French, provoke a diplomatic difficulty of the gravest kind with Napoleon. In either event the cause of Italian liberation would be seriously compromised. It would be an ill start for the new Kingdom of Italy to be compelled at the very outset to put down a nationalist insurrection in Naples and Sicily. It would be not less disastrous if Napoleon, in order to protect the Pope from a Garibaldian *coup d'état*, should be constrained to embark on a serious campaign in central Italy.

That these dangers were successfully avoided was due not

only to the remarkable qualities shown at a critical juncture by Cavour, Garibaldi, and the King, but also by a surprising demonstration in favour of the Piedmontese monarchy among the population of Naples. With great wisdom Cavour decided that the time had now come for Victor Emmanuel to show himself in central and southern Italy and to settle with Garibaldi before the Redshirts had time to set foot on papal territory and there to make mischief which could not be repaired. The programme, which was laid before Napoleon, was carried out with punctuality and despatch. A motley force of Papalists under the adventurer Lamoricière was dispersed by Cialdini at Castelfidardo (September 18), and with the surrender of this composite and cosmopolitan army the whole resisting power of the one central Italian territory which still stood for the old cause of foreign occupation and clerical control was broken beyond repair. A Parliament was then summoned to Turin to approve the policy of the Government and to press for the speedy adhesion of Naples and Sicily. When the plébiscite was taken, an overwhelming vote (October 21) announced the triumph of Cavour and the defeat of Mazzini. The danger of a southern republic balancing and defying the northern monarchy was overpast. The one man who could have fatally wrecked Italian harmony swallowed, when the great moment came, his personal griefs, prejudices, and vanities. Though at heart a republican, Garibaldi commended and accepted the cause of the King in whose name he had fought and whose uniform he wore. Together they drove in triumph into Naples. Together they had helped to make Italy a nation.

It was then that Garibaldi reached the apex of his renown. He had won and surrendered the south, he had held and resigned a dictatorship. He had been offered and had refused titles, wealth, decorations. Civilized respectabilities meant nothing to this child of the Pampas. He knew that wild fowl languish in the cage. With a sublime simplicity, taking with him some seed-corn, some vegetables, some salt cod, and a little borrowed money, he turned his back upon the plaudits and vanities of Naples and sailed away to a life of hard work and poverty in the island of Caprera. There among shepherds and goat-herds he meditated how best to complete the redemption of Italy.

THE GROWTH OF ITALY

For Venetia and Rome were still wanting to the Italian kingdom, the first to be gained only through the defeat of Austria, the second defended by France and, save in the event of a complete reversal of French policy or of a sudden collapse of French power, unlikely to pass out of papal governance. Accordingly the final stages in the unification of Italy depended less upon the efforts of the Italians themselves than upon changes in the balance of European power greater than any which Italy was able unaided to effect. The acquisition of Venice was no fruit of Italian victory, but of a secret offensive and defensive alliance most prudently concluded with the Prussians in April, 1866. The Italians indeed took part in the war to which that alliance was by intention the prelude, but they gained no victories. Rather they were defeated by land and sea. The prize of Venetia was won on the field of Sadowa by the formidable Prussian army which had been organized by Von Roon, was led by Moltke, and was the instrument of the far-reaching policy of Bismarck.

Four years later the victories of that same Prussian army led to the recall of the French troops from Rome and so opened the way to the establishment of the new royal government of Italy upon the Quirinal, where it has since remained, the embodiment of the very spirit of Italian nationalism, throwing its challenge, now loud, now low, to the priestly court and cosmopolitan rule of the Pope.

That the solution of the Roman question should have been so long delayed is a matter of surprise only if we refuse to recognise the large part played in politics by implacable men holding absolute and rigid opinions. To Antonelli, the adviser of Pius IX, it was as inconceivable that any concession should be voluntarily made to those who sought to abridge by an inch the full extent of the Papal State, as it was intolerable to Garibaldi that a priest should be allowed to subtract for the conduct of his own cosmopolitan and obscurantist policies an inch from the sacred soil of the Italian people. But between these two extremes there were intermediate opinions. Napoleon III, whose merit it was to take a cool and detached view of heat-raising problems, advanced plausible arguments in support of the contention that, while the Papal States, being notoriously mismanaged, should be sensibly reduced, the Pope should retain Rome and the Roman patrimony. To that view, which was equally repugnant to strict clericals and Italian patriots, but was nevertheless grounded on a correct appreciation of the balances of Europe, the Emperor of the French continued to adhere.

Cavour, too, had a solution of the Roman question. In exchange for the Temporal Power he offered to the Church complete spiritual independence, but Cavour died in 1861, and the Roman question continued to torment the government of Italy and the conscience of Europe. Twice the irrepressible

Garibaldi essayed a thrust at his old enemy in Rome. Twice he was foiled. At Aspromonte (August 29, 1862) he was turned back by the Piedmontese, at Mentana (November 3, 1867) he was defeated by the French while the royal army of Italy, which had undertaken to defend the Papal State from every attack, looked on in helpless neutrality.

Little profit was derived by Napoleon from the Italian blood which was shed on this ill-starred field. "Les fusils Chassepot ont fait merveille," wrote General de Failly of the new French rifles—words which were not easily forgiven by a sensitive people condemned to endure with such patience as they could command the defeat of their greatest living national hero under circumstances of peculiar humiliation. Out of regard for the clericals of France the Emperor had thrown away the prospect of a valuable alliance with a kingdom which he had helped to create and which stood deep in his debt. The result was serious, for there came a time in 1870 when, needing Italian help and failing to find it, he was obliged unfriended to face the formidable onset of Germany in arms.

Nearly a century has elapsed since the various peoples of Italy who, though they spoke the same language, inherited the same culture and occupied the same ground, had been wont to view one another with animosity and distrust, were brought together under the rule of the Piedmontese monarchy. The union that in its opening decades had seemed in the highest degree precarious has weathered the storms of time. The special differences between South and North have been reduced, the monarchy has taken root, a strong and even fierce Italian patriotism has burnt away the inveterate local prejudices of earlier times. No Italian would desire to see a return to the days when his country was divided and powerless.

This success of the unification of Italy is the more remarkable seeing that the monarchy was devoid of many of those supports which in other lands have assisted monarchical institutions. No ancient aristocracy surrounded the throne, no long-descended renown enhanced its prestige, no brilliant victories brought elation to its subjects. As the Italian reflected upon the unification of his country, he was forced to admit that but for the help of France and Prussia Italy could not have been made one. The Italian navy had suffered defeat at Lissa, the Italian army at Custozza. The Church, which in other countries was apt to throw the whole weight of its influence into the scale of monarchical authority, was bitterly hostile to the kingdom which had shorn it of its patrimony and deprived the Holy See of its ancient political pre-eminence. By the Bull *Non Expedit* (1874-1903) Catholics were forbidden to take an active part in the politics of the kingdom. In Rome itself the violence of the schism was most keenly apparent. The Pope regarded himself as a prisoner in the Vatican, the two courts were at daggers drawn and the two societies, the Black and the White, albeit living in the same city, might have belonged, so far as friendly intercourse went, to two distant hemispheres.

Nevertheless the monarchy survived. A remarkable body of conscientious statesmen stood round Victor Emmanuel II during the first decade of the kingdom, and working on the high tide of enthusiasm which had been engendered by the movement of the Risorgimento carried on the work of Cavour. Italy remembers with gratitude the names of Ricasoli and La Marmora, of Lanza and Sella, of Minghetti and Spaventa, as those of men who, when the new state was in the making, shouldered the hardest part of the initial toil. When in 1876 power passed from the Right to the Left the foundations of the new Italy had been soundly laid. The English example of Free Trade and the coming of the railways supplied an unassailable economic argument for political union. Even if separatist tendencies had been stronger than they were, steam and water power would have made return to the old customs barriers unthinkable. However much the Tuscan may have differed from the Piedmontese and the Venetian, or the Neapolitan from the men of the north, plain and unmistakable considerations of economic convenience forced them together and bowed them to a common yoke.

BOOKS WHICH MAY BE CONSULTED

Bolton King: *A History of Italian Unity*. 1924.
W. R. Thayer: *The Life and Times of Cavour*. 1915.
F. A. Simpson: *The Rise of Louis Napoleon*. 1925.

Pierre de la Gorce: *Histoire du Second Empire*. 1908.

H. von Treitschke: *Historische und politische Aufsätze*, Vol. II (Cavour.) 1871.

G. M. Trevelyan: *Garibaldi*. 1933.

Bolton King: *Life of Manuel*. 1912.

E. L. Woodward: *Three Studies in European Conservation*. 1929.

D. Mack Smith: *Cavour and Garibaldi*, 1860. 1954.

E. W. Gladstone and others: *The Unification of Italy*. 1955.

CHAPTER LXXXII

TOWARDS GERMAN UNITY

The strongest obstacle to German national unity. Otto von Bismarck. Circumstances of his rise to power. The Prussian army saved from the Prussian Parliament. The defeat of Prussian liberalism. Frustration of the Austrian plan for the reform of the German Empire. The Polish rebellion of 1863. Bismarck obtains the Russian alliance. The Danish Duchies. The War of 1864 and the Treaty of Vienna. The Austro-Prussian condominium in the Duchies breaks down in 1865. Napoleon III. His acquiescence. His Liberalism. His Mexican adventure. The Emperor Maximilian. Decline in French prestige. Bismarck reassures Napoleon at Biarritz. Universal suffrage offered to Germany. The Seven Weeks' War. Bismarck's moderate use of victory. The Treaty of Prague. Anger in France. The new German constitution. Contrast between Italian and German national states.

IT WAS unlikely that the triumph of Italian nationalism should fail to revive the hopes of German union which had been cruelly shattered in the ruin of the liberal revolution. What the little military monarchy of Piedmont had done for Italy the much larger and more powerful Prussian Kingdom might easily achieve for the Germans. That sentiment was widely diffused, and yet, though the Italian and German problems were separated by an important difference, Austria was in either case the enemy. In Italy the Austrian was an alien. Among the Germans he would never be so regarded. Rather he was bone of their bone, flesh of their flesh, an integral part of their corporate historic life, and to many, especially to such as lived in the south, much to be preferred to the Prussians. Many Germans who vaguely wanted German unity shrank with horror before the spectre of an Austrian war, many clamoured to make Germany a nation while averting their eyes from the odious but necessary price. No plébiscite of the German people, if taken at any time in the sixties, would have given a majority in favour of a war with Austria or for a Germany placed under the Prussian heel. Only a Government ruthlessly prepared to defy public opinion, to divide Germany, and to face the horrors of a fratricidal strife, could contemplate the undertaking. Only the most elaborate military and diplomatic preparations could ensure its success.

The titanic figure of Bismarck, who held that no man should die until he had smoked a hundred thousand cigars and drunk five thousand bottles of champagne, was Nature's lavish response to these exacting requirements. It is the special property of this extraordinary man that, while infinitely flexible in detail, he envisaged from the first the large conditions of the German problem and allowed no scruples of conscience to interfere with the execution of his plans. In 1862, a year after Cavour's death, he told Disraeli that he intended at the earliest opportunity to make war on Austria. "Take care of that man," said the wise Jew; "he means what he says." And exactly four years later, with all Germany dubious or hostile and with no following but the soldiers, Bismarck got the war which from the first he had seen to be essential to his political designs.

His wonderful administration, which lasted from September, 1862, to March, 1890, was marked at its outset by one of those rare constitutional struggles which are of enduring importance in the history of nations. William I, who had taken over the management of Prussia as Regent in 1858 on his brother's incapacity, was a plain, dutiful Prussian soldier who from his experience of the revolution had conceived a deep dislike of popular movements. There was nothing of German idealism in this elderly sovereign. It was sufficient for him that Prussia should be strong and never again through military weakness be compelled to swallow humiliation. In

1803-
79

Albert von Roon the King found a War Minister to his heart. Together they worked out a plan for the enlargement and reorganization of the Prussian army. They asked for more regiments, for a three years' instead of a two years' term of service. The Lower House of the Prussian Parliament threw out the Bill. Neither side would give way. The deadlock was protracted, Parliament refusing supplies, Von Roon and his master ultimately raising fresh regiments as if supplies had been voted. A general election only returned a House less conservative and more determined to obtain control of the government than the last. It was now no longer a question of three years' service *versus* two. The claim was made that in Prussia, as in England, Parliament must be supreme, that army, finance, foreign policy should be governed in accordance with the will of the people as expressed through their representatives. If that claim had been conceded, the whole history of Germany and Europe would have taken a different turn.

That it was successfully resisted was due to the dominating intervention of Bismarck. Summoned by Von Roon to save the situation, the new Minister-President put heart into the King, who had actually written out his abdication, faced the blizzard of the politicians, and despite a tempest of obloquy maintained the position that in Prussia the army was a thing too sacred for the Legislature to control. When the war was successfully over in 1866, he obtained a parliamentary indemnity for the expenditure which had been incurred without authority; but there was no element of penitence in the politic gesture. Neither then nor thereafter was Bismarck prepared to accept the English system. The crushing victory in the Austrian war enabled him to defy with impunity counsels founded on the success of insular liberalism, and to grave deep upon the constitutional life of Germany the principle that, although a Parliament may vote new taxes and discuss laws, three things lie outside and beyond it. Neither may it prescribe the army, nor frame policy, nor, as in England, make or unmake governments. To the last days of the Hohenzollern Empire these principles continued to inform constitutional practice in Germany.

It must not be imagined that the championship of responsible government in Prussia went by default. The German

Liberals were for the most part well-educated and patriotic citizens, who, while they valued national strength, were equally concerned for the protection of national liberty. They had the sympathy of the Crown Prince and of his intelligent, enthusiastic, but unwise English wife; they were supported by the learning and authority of the Universities; and there was no argumentative missile drawn from the vast arsenal of English experience which they were not competent to discharge at the head of the opprobrious Junker who single-handed and defiant held the fort for autocracy. But Prussia was not England. It was more feudal, more military, and, since the factory system had hardly begun, much less industrial.

For all these separate reasons liberalism was in Bismarck's eyes an ineffectual force, safe to insult, easy to supplant. Englishmen he liked and respected; but English principles of government, transplanted to Prussia, would work ruin. A necessary prelude, therefore, to the Austrian war was the rout of the Anglophiles and votaries of freedom in Germany. Here Bismarck's triumph was complete and enduring. His success is blazoned across the history of the world. He led Germany into the path of long-range policies of aggrandizement based upon long-range military and naval programmes. The State was Power. War, as Clausewitz taught, was the continuation of policy. End and instrument acted and interacted. As policies became more ambitious, armaments became larger; as armaments grew, policies expanded. The conversion of Europe into an armed camp was an inevitable consequence of the defeat of Prussian Liberalism in 1862. The road was safe so long as Bismarck was in control. Afterwards it became dangerous. The stakes rose, the risks increased, until it was at last possible for an emotional people to believe that by force of an irresistible destiny or mission they were called upon to play for world power or downfall.

At the very outset of his administration an obstacle, the more formidable because it was concealed, threatened to wreck his whole design. Austria invited a Council of Princes to meet at Frankfort to consider a scheme for the reform of the German Federal Constitution. On the face of it no proposal could be more specious. The German Constitution, seeing that it was the worst in the world, badly needed thorough-going repairs. Of that no one was more acutely conscious than Bismarck; but repairs carried out under Austrian direction and with Prussian complicity could have but one result. Austrian authority would be fortified in Germany. It was therefore essential in Bismarck's view that Prussia should not be represented at Frankfort, that the Austrian plan should be frustrated *ab initio*, and that the way should be kept clear for the constitutional reconstruction of Germany under Prussian influence. The old King of Prussia was slow to appreciate these implications. It was only after a protracted struggle that Bismarck extorted his reluctant acquiescence in the view that an invitation, delivered by a King on the instructions of an Emperor for the promotion of an object affecting the general interests of the German people, should be unceremoniously declined.

1863   The year which witnessed this rebuff to Austria was also marked by an insurrection in Russian Poland which was destined to exercise a wide influence on international affairs. So far as the rebellion itself was concerned, it was quickly and cruelly suppressed. The cause of the Poles, however, had never been regarded in western Europe as a matter with respect to which humane and civilized governments could adopt an attitude of frozen indifference. In France and England and even in Austria public opinion was greatly stirred by the spectacle of a gallant people vainly trying to preserve the elements of its national life under an alien and oppressive yoke. The governments of these three countries accordingly agreed to present to Russia a joint note urging an amnesty and the establishment of Polish Home Rule; and in this not too hopeful diplomatic demand Prussia was invited to concur. There could be no doubt in Bismarck's mind that the answer to be returned to this invitation must be an emphatic negative. For the furtherance of his scheme for isolating Austria it was a brilliant stroke of opportunity that Prussia should be able thus sharply to dissociate herself from any plans calculated to embarrass the Tzar in the handling of his Polish problem. At a moment of high tension, when abuse from every quarter was raining down on the Russian Government, one Power extended the hand of friendship, refusing not only to join in the note, but signing a military convention which bore on the face of it the evidence of a common interest in the policing of a troublesome people. From that moment Bismarck had the Russian alliance, which was the cornerstone of his policy and the indispensable condition of its success. From that moment he could feel assured that in the prosecution of the wars with Austria and perhaps with France, which would be necessary for the completion of his great design, Prussia would be secure on her eastern frontier.

It was a further guarantee of the solidity of the friendship that it was based upon a congenial confraternity of repression. Britain had its subject Poles as well as St. Petersburg, and as the Irish problem vexed the conscience of English Liberals, so in western Germany and wherever German Liberals were gathered together there was a disposition to sympathize with Polish grievances and to entertain suggestions for their relief. All this philo-Polish sentiment was abhorrent to the Pomeranian squire whose receipt for the Polish problem was that the Poles should be converted into Prussians with as little delay as possible, that their language should be stamped out, their culture effaced, their traditions forgotten, and that the liberalism which sought to preserve some lineaments of the Polish nation should be countered by a resolute policy of assimilation. In this task Bismarck was as little disposed to tolerate interference as the Russians. "I would rather die," he said to General Fleury in 1863, "than permit our position in Posen to be discussed at a European Congress. I would rather cede our Rhinelands." And indeed so long as Russia and Prussia stood together, though the Liberals of Europe filled the air with their protests and lamentations, there was not and could not be the faintest hope for Polish liberty.

Meanwhile a quarrel was boiling up in the base of the Danish peninsula which was destined to give Bismarck his Austrian war, to enable Prussia to build the Kiel Canal, opening out to United Germany a new destiny upon the ocean. It is unnecessary to burden the memory with the complicated details of the Schleswig-Holstein question. The kernel of the matter is that these two Duchies, Holstein being within and Schleswig without the confines of the German Empire, but both since 1490 continuously governed by the King of Denmark, were now in dispute. They were desired by Denmark. They were desired by the German Federation.

They were desired and, without a jot or tittle of historical or legal claim, taken by Prussia. The process by which this result was achieved was regarded by Bismarck not without justification as his political masterpiece; and indeed there can be no more characteristic example of his craft.

The quarrel was by no means new. All Germany in 1848 had trembled with indignation at the news that the Danes were attempting to incorporate Schleswig, the most northerly of the Scandinavian Duchies, in their monarchy, and to sever its connection, deemed among the legists and historians of the country to be indissoluble, with the more German Duchy of Holstein. In that year of revolution, when every issue in the national life was put in question, there was no matter upon which German opinion was more passionately unanimous than that the Duchies must be subject to a single ruler, and he (after the death of Frederick VII of Denmark, who had no male issue) a German Prince. Such a Prince the German Diet was able to produce. His name was the Duke of Augustenburg. We may here call him the old Pretender.

A period of confused and inconclusive fighting was terminated by the intervention of the Powers. By the Treaty of London in 1852 it was decided that Frederick VII should be succeeded by Christian of Glücksburg, who should rule both in Denmark and in the Duchies. The thorny problem seemed to be happily solved, for since Austria and Prussia concurred in the treaty it was difficult to believe that its provisions would be upset, and as for the old Pretender he accepted a handsome payment in commutation of his claims.

The quarrel however, was not concluded. In Copenhagen there was a strong current of popular feeling in favour of bringing the Danish frontier southward to the Eider, and a disposition, hotly resented by the Germans, to interfere with the local privileges in the Duchies; and it was while German and Dane were snarling at one another, and the old embers which had been thought to be extinguished were sending out little hot jets of flame, that Frederick VII (March 30, 1863) issued a constitution incorporating Schleswig in his monarchy and giving home rule to Holstein. It was a very sensible solution. It was in principle the solution which was ultimately imposed by the Treaty of Versailles. It allotted the Danish-speaking Duchy to the Danes, and gave to the German-speaking Duchy a practical measure of autonomy, but in Germany it was received with shrieks of horror. The Holstein Estates, which had not been consulted, appealed to the Diet, and since the Diet had been no party to the Treaty of London, it deemed itself free to work for the separation of the indissoluble Duchies from the Danish Kingdom and for their creation into a principality for a German Prince. Again a candidate was not wanting. With obliging hardihood, the son of the old Pretender, averring that he was not bound by his father's renunciation, again put forward the claims of his house.

On November 15, 1863, Frederick VII of Denmark died and was duly, and in accordance with the terms of the Treaty of London, succeeded by Christian IX, who under popular pressure brought into execution King Frederick's Constitution.

It is at this point that Bismarck began to inaugurate the series of diplomatic manoeuvres which ultimately gave to Prussia the Danish Duchies. He had no wish to march with the Diet. As a signatory of the London Treaty he was bound in advance to recognize Christian, on risk of giving offence to England and Russia. It was no attraction for him that the young Pretender, a liberal and a friend of the Crown Prince, should rule over a new German State which would certainly act as a check upon Prussia. He wanted the Duchies for his master. He determined therefore to act not with the Diet but with Austria, a co-signatory of the London Treaty, to acknowledge Christian according to the terms of that treaty, but at the same time to present him with an ultimatum demanding the immediate repeal of the November constitution and couched in such a form that by no possibility could it be accepted. Everything went forward according to plan. The Danes, who had been encouraged to hope that the manifest sympathy of England was no idle talk, rejected the ultimatum. Austrian and Prussian troops invaded the Duchies (January, 1864), defeated the Danes and compelled Christian to sue for peace. By the Treaty of Vienna the Danish ruler ceded his rights over Schleswig-Holstein and over the little Duchy of Lauenburg to the two victorious German Powers. Oct., 1864

A situation of great delicacy was now created. A condominium is never a comfortable arrangement, and a condominium between Austria and Prussia could not be expected to work without friction. Sooner or later the two Powers were bound to determine who should be invited to rule the territory of which they might now by right of conquest dispose. Austria, with the sympathy of the great majority of the German people, supported the claims of the young Pretender which Bismarck was prepared to resist to the end, except upon terms which would have made the Duchies all but in name a Prussian province. The injudicious conduct of the young prince, who settled down in Kiel, opened a little Court, and with the obvious sympathy of the Austrian administration promoted his candidature in the locality, increased the irritation of Berlin. In the summer of 1865 the two countries were on the brink of war. Austria, however, was not then ready to take up the Prussian challenge; nor was Prussian diplomatic preparation complete. A Convention was signed at Gastein which plastered over the cracks and provided a breathing space during which the two Powers might organize their forces for a war. It was arranged that the condominium should cease, and that Holstein should be administered by Austria, Schleswig by Prussia, while the Duchy of Lauenburg should be handed over absolutely to the Prussian King.

Aug.,
1865

So far Bismarck had been extraordinarily successful. Against the predominant and even passionate opinion of the German people, and despite the resistance of the Prussian Court and Parliament, he had frustrated the Augustenburg claim. Without interference from France or England he had carried the Danish war to a successful conclusion; and now that victory had crowned the first efforts of the newly organized Prussian army, and that the old King's appetite for conquest had at last been whetted by the acquisition of Lauenburg, he could look with confidence to the future. With the endless possibilities of friction still existing in the Duchies, it would always be possible at a convenient moment to promote a rupture with the Austrians. Meanwhile it was necessary to work for the complete isolation of the enemy. On the eastern front Bismarck was secure. The Russians could be depended on to observe a friendly neutrality, but it was still necessary to secure if possible the neutrality of France and the active co-operation of Italy.

Napoleon III, like Talleyrand and Briand, was a good European. Though he thought it necessary to give satisfaction to the martial spirit of his people, he believed in peace, in nationality, in government by Congress. He inherited the doctrine which his great uncle had preached at St. Helena, that the formation of large national aggregates was in the interest of European stability. There is no reason to doubt that his sympathy with the Italians and the Poles was genuine and disinterested; and that, always provided that the balance of power in Europe was not altered to the disadvantage of his country, he was willing to contemplate and anxious to assist those large changes in the map of Europe which were necessary to bring the political boundaries of states more nearly in accord with national sentiments. The expansion of Prussia caused him no alarm. Not only did he think it reasonable that the Prussians should have the Danish Duchies, but even the prospect of a North German Federation under Prussian leadership gave him no concern. Would not the southern Germans lean on France? Would he not, in a Prussian war against Austria, be able to repeat the brilliant coup which had extracted Savoy and Nice from the necessities of Piedmont? Would not such a war bring Venetia to Italy? The heart of Napoleon, as Bismarck was quick to observe, was better than his head.

The five years which had elapsed since 1860 brought with them a sensible decline in the force and coherence of the French Empire. The head of the state was no longer the man of the *coup d'état* and the Crimean War. Incessant work and anxiety had taken toll of a constitution which had probably been impaired by dissipation. A grave disorder, characterized by recurrent paroxysms of almost unbearable pain, weakened the will and broke down the springs of enterprise.

And meanwhile, partly as a result of this physical deterioration, and partly that he might give effect to his uncle's doctrine that in due time the tension of autocracy should be relaxed and give place to the freer play of parliamentary institutions, he had begun to liberalize the Empire, permitting (November 22, 1860) the Senate and Legislative body to vote and debate an annual address in response to the speech from the throne, providing certain ministers without portfolio to explain and defend the government measures, and giving sanction to the publication of full shorthand reports of parliamentary debates. In the revival of parliamentary life which followed upon this measure the latent antagonisms of the French people burst into flame. The clericals blamed the Emperor because he had helped the Italians, the liberals because he had abandoned them. The manufacturers assailed his free trade, the Orleanists his confiscations, the adherents of the Legitimate branch his acquiescence in the expulsion of the Bourbons from Naples. The Emperor, who, after his Crimean and Italian trophies, had looked forward to a golden spell of honoured leisure during which he might shape an immortal biography of Julius Caesar, and further enrich his country with railways, telegraphs and banks, found himself exposed to competing and uncomfortable pressures, which it was difficult to resist. On the one hand he was pressed to do something for the Pope, on the other hand to redeem his early promise of Venetia to Italy. At last in an evil hour he was persuaded by his clerical advisers to embark on a crusade, part Catholic, part financial, in the distant land of Mexico.

In this country of chronic and passionate dissensions society was divided into two factions, one clerical and conservative led by Miramon, another progressive and anticlerical which had ranged itself under Benito Juarez, an Indian remarkable for the integrity of his character, the clearness of his views, and the decision of his will, but regarded with vehement disapprobation all over the Catholic world for his vigorous and comprehensive measures to curtail the authority and wealth of the Church. Both parties resorted to arms, both parties borrowed money from Europe; and both parties were lavish in promises of repayment when once the fortune of war had declared in its favour. A Swiss banker in Paris named Jekker had lent money to Miramon and promised the Duc de Morny, the Emperor's half-brother, 30 per cent. of the profits. It was not, however, Miramon, but Juarez who won the war (1861).

To the clericals of France and notably to the Empress the overthrow of the sacrilegious Indians and the establishment in Mexico of a Catholic Empire under French tutelage appeared to be objects attractive in themselves and likely to result in financial profit. Mexico was, indeed, a distant country whose climate and geography were ill understood, but it was known to be large, was reputed to be fabulously wealthy, and, having been conquered by the Spaniards, was suspected, despite appearances to the contrary, of cherishing a steadfast affection for the Catholic Church and for monarchical institutions. Religion, finance, politics combined to point to a Mexican enterprise. It would please the Vatican, gratify the Bourse, exalt the Empire. Moreover, the moment was propitious. The United States was torn by the civil war between North and South. While the Anglo-Saxon Protes- 1861- tants were quarrelling over slavery and state rights, Napoleon 5 might hope to establish upon the American Continent a Latin and Catholic state as an outpost of France and a barrier against the expansive movements of Western heresy.

While these large ideas were taking shape in France, the Emperor joined hands with England and Spain in the more limited objective of a debt-collecting expedition. Ships were sent across the Atlantic, contingents were landed on the distant Jan., and malarious coast, and the new republican government of 1862 Juarez was sharply reminded that European creditors were not to be fobbed off by a two years' moratorium on the foreign debt. This proceeding was certainly high-handed; but far less open to objection than the decision of Napoleon, after his allies had withdrawn, to revolutionize the government of Mexico in the wild and erroneous belief that the people of that country, of whom little was known in Paris, were eager to exchange the new modernizing republic of Juarez for a Catholic and clerical monarchy.

In no long time it appeared that the enterprise of forcing a sovereign upon the Mexican people was far more costly in troops and money than had ever been apprehended. To the person of the French nominee who was invited (July 10, 1863) to mount the Mexican throne no objection could be taken. Maximilian was the brother of Francis Joseph, the Emperor of Austria, and the husband of Charlotte, the daughter of the Belgian King. Tall, handsome, benevolent, with an honourable record of liberality as administrator of the Milanese, Maximilian was a ruler whom any people desirous of mild and honourable governance might have been content to obey. Unfortunately the Mexicans did not want him. They

Disraeli, he had a deep conviction that though the middle class may be liberal, democracy is Tory.

Though it was pretended in Berlin that the final provocation came from Austria, there was no real doubt that it was Bismarck's war. Moltke, who was to command the Prussian army, told the bare truth when he said afterwards, "The war of 1866 did not take place because the existence of Prussia was threatened, or in obedience to public opinion or to the will of the people. It was a war which was foreseen long before, which was prepared with deliberation and recognized as necessary by the Cabinet, not in order to obtain territorial aggrandisement, but for power in order to secure the establishment of Prussian hegemony in Germany." This is no pretty story. "It must be confessed," said Bismarck to Treitschke, with engaging frankness, "that our linen was not always of the cleanest."

The war, which lasted seven weeks, was a revelation to Europe of the results which might be attained by the application of Prussian science and Prussian methods to the military art. The swiftness of the Prussian mobilization, the precision of the Prussian movements, the excellence of the Prussian needle gun, the clever use which was now for the first time made of railways, portended the advent of an era in which the great decisions of history would be governed by the relative capacity of states to make use of their technical and scientific resources, and the direction of war would more and more resemble the management of a vast and intricate industrial business. The ultimatum was delivered on June 15, 1866. In the first week of this war north-west Germany was under the Prussian heel; in the third (July 3) the main Austrian army was crushed at Sadowa (or Königgrätz), in Bohemia. The fight was stiff. The issue was long in doubt; and the day was won only when the army of the Crown Prince was in a position to attack the enemy right flank; but in proportion as the Austrian resistance had been obstinate, so was the catastrophe of their army, when that resistance was finally broken down, irretrievably complete. The way was open to Vienna. It was there that the old king, flushed with victory, decreed and determined to make the peace.

There is no more certain test of statesmanship than the capacity to resist the political intoxication of victory. Unlike

Napoleon I, who with every military success raised his diplomatic terms, Bismarck knew what he wanted and what he did not want. It was no part of his plan unnecessarily to abase or humiliate the Austrians, whose alliance or neutrality might hereafter be precious to his king and country. He did not wish for Austrian territory, or for fresh victories, or for a triumphal entry into the capital of the beaten foe. He was content if Austria would withdraw from Germany, acquiesce in Prussia's acquisition of the Danish Duchies, and in the formation of a North German Confederation under Prussian leadership. He would not even, out of consideration to the susceptibility of the South German governments, put any constraint upon them to join the North German Confederation. Rather he was prepared to acquiesce in a separate federation of the south, should this be desired. Though a great body of his compatriots clamoured for a united Germany, he shrank from such ambitious precipitation, calculating that a North German Federation would be as much as Prussia could then hope to digest or France be expected to accept. Before the war he had made up his mind that the Main should be his boundary, and from this prudent decision he refused to retreat. A pan-German movement was a counsel of desperation, a violent and doubtful expedient to be kept in reserve against the possible event of a Franco-Austrian alliance. It was far better not to force the southern issue, but to allow the South Germans to come into the Prussian Federation when and as they chose. He set his course to catch the breeze of their favour. Though they had fought against Prussia he would have no indemnities, and, on this crucial point eventually vanquishing his master, no annexations. His clemency was promptly rewarded, for before August was out Bavaria, Würtemberg, and Baden had signed military conventions with the government of the north.

On such wise and generous terms Austria was prepared to treat, and almost before Europe had recovered from its surprise at the news of Sadowa, it was faced (August 23) with 1866 the accomplished fact of the Treaty of Prague. The extreme expedition with which Bismarck, resolutely overcoming the opposition of the king and the army chiefs, wound up the war and made the peace was grounded upon the apprehension that, were the struggle protracted, he might be called upon to face the armed opposition of France. He had the more reason for anxiety since two days after Sadowa Napoleon made an offer of mediation which he felt himself compelled to accept. What was chiefly to be feared was that while the main body of the Prussian army was in Bohemia Napoleon would mobilize on the Rhine, and, as part of the general treaty settlement, demand compensation for France at the point of the sword.

That Napoleon entirely failed to extract any advantage for France out of the Prussian wars with Denmark and Austria was made a grave matter of reproach in the French Chamber. With sentiments of rage, jealousy, and apprehension France was condemned to witness the sensational victory which had enabled Prussia to swallow Hanover, Hesse Cassel, the Danish Duchies, to dominate all Germany to the Main, to add four and a quarter million inhabitants to her population, and to overturn the whole balance of power in central Europe, while not a gun nor a man had been moved by the Emperor to secure compensating advantages for his country. "It is France who has been defeated at Sadowa," said Marshal Randon bitterly; and it was a defeat which diplomacy was powerless to repair. Bismarck's blow had been too swift. The French search for compensations came too late. In the period which elapsed between the battle of Sadowa and the outbreak of the Franco-Prussian War the Emperor asked for every kind of solatium, for the Rhenish Palatinate and Hesse, for Mainz and the Saar, for Belgium and for Luxemburg. Such requests unsupported by force were rejected with impunity; but the evidence that they were made was carefully preserved and used at the proper moment with decisive effect to make French diplomacy odious to Bavaria and England.

Meanwhile the new North German Confederation received from the hands of its architect a Constitution which, while it contained little of English liberalism, was strong enough to endure the stormy weather of fifty-two years. The Reichstag or Federal Parliament, being elected by universal suffrage, was based upon a larger measure of democratic support than any English Parliament until 1918; but, in accordance with Bismarckian principles, it could neither make nor unmake governments, nor finance policies, nor control by an annual army act the scale of the military establishments. Accordingly it was not in this democratic assembly that the seat of sovereignty was allowed to rest. The real governing organ of the Federation was a Federal Council (Bundesrat) composed of forty-two delegates from the different States of the Union, which deliberated in secret under the presidency of the Chancellor, who was also the Minister-President or Prime Minister of Prussia. Such a council seemed to many critics to be unnecessarily cumbrous. Why, it was asked, should Prussia give to twenty little dynasties a separate representation in the supreme governing organ of the new State? Would not complete centralization be a simpler and more effective plan? Prussia had the power to stamp out these ineffectual relics of the past. It had dethroned the King of Hanover and put an end to his dynasty. Why, then, should it be at pains to keep alive a number of separate centres of political action and possible obstructiveness, and even, in the case of Saxony, to go so far as to permit a member of the northern Confederation to be separately represented by ministers at foreign courts? There can be no question that Bismarck was wise in resisting the temptation to make of modern Germany a unitary State. The dynasties were deep-rooted in the soil of German history and had a contribution to make to the tasks of government. From their wholesale destruction nothing was to be apprehended but needless difficulties in the north, and the development of a violent aversion among the South German peoples from any thought of closer union. Moreover, there was no risk to strong and efficient government in the federal plan. Prussia had an assured majority in the Council and Prussia was Bismarck. Under the original provisions of this unique constitution the German Chancellor, responsible to his king alone and un-trammelled by a German Cabinet, was the working head of the Government in all its branches. Neither Bundesrat, nor Reichstag, nor Prussian Parliament could dismiss him from office or effectually challenge his will. Year after year the vast figure of the Chancellor dominated the scene, filling Europe with the thunder of his powerful oratory and reading to his wondering compatriots fresh lessons in the art of ruling mankind.

Great then was the contrast between the ordering of the two

national states which owe their being respectively to Cavour and Bismarck. In Italy the triumph of nationalism was associated with the establishment of Parliamentary government on the English plan; in Germany with its decisive defeat. Yet the German polity, though so framed as to secure for Prussian autocracy the final word, refused it few of the lessons which are vouchsafed to the statesmen of Parliamentary countries. At regular intervals the cleansing tides of universal suffrage swept through the Reichstag and enabled fresh formations of opinion to make themselves felt in the political life of the country. These were not always favourable to Bismarck. While the national Liberals employed every instrument of popular propaganda to advocate German union and to give support to the new institutions of the state, Catholicism and Socialism bade him defiance.

BOOKS WHICH MAY BE CONSULTED

J. W. Headlam: *Bismarck and the Foundation of the German Empire*. 1899.

C. Grant Robertson: *Life of Bismarck*. 1918.

Bismarck's *Thoughts and Recollections*. 1899.

Pierre de la Gorce: *Histoire du Second Empire*. 1903.

H. A. L. Fisher: *Bonapartism*. 1909.

E. Ollivier: *L'Empire Libéral*. 1911.

F. A. Simpson: *Louis Napoleon and the Recovery of France, 1848-1856*. 1923.

P. Guedalla: *The Second Empire*. 1932.

Lord Edmund Fitzmaurice: *Life of Lord Granville*.

F. Darmstaedter: *Bismarck and the creation of the second Reich*. 1948.

E. Eyck: *Bismarck and the German Empire*. 1950.

A. J. P. Taylor: *Bismarck*. 1955.

CHAPTER LXXXIII

THE FOUNDATION OF THE GERMAN EMPIRE

Prussian war preparations. Uncertain policy of France. The temper of the French clericals. The Liberals, republicans, and socialists. Émile Ollivier. The Hohenzollern candidature. The Ems telegram. The war guilt. German superiority. Inferiority of the French higher command. Absence of trained French reserves. The campaign. The national rising. Léon Gambetta. The siege of Paris. The assembly of Bordeaux. The Peace of Frankfort and the contribution of Thiers. Alsace-Lorraine. The German Empire. Vast ambitions of Prussia.

WE NOW approach the last and greatest of the three wars which forged the unity of the German nation. First Prussia had forced a quarrel on the Danes, then on the Austrians. The final obstacle which appeared to stand between Bismarck and his ambition was France.

  1864 and 1866

It was not to be supposed that Paris, which had been so greatly perturbed by the Prussian victory at Sadowa, would fail to resent, and within the measure of its strength to oppose, the expansion of Prussian power beyond the Main A philosopher might have reflected that since some day or other German unity was bound to come, France would be wise to extend an early and cordial welcome to a change which she could not expect permanently to avert. But the ruler of a high-spirited, vain, and intelligent people cannot afford to be a philosopher. The moods, the fears, the foibles of his countrymen circumscribe his freedom, and when every *boulevardier* in Paris was certain that Prussia was henceforth the enemy it was impossible for Napoleon to behave as if Germany were the friend. The temper of Paris was well known in Berlin. To Bismarck and his military friends it was clear they could not reckon on completing the half-finished fabric of German unity without a violent clash with France. Strenuously, seriously, and methodically they pushed on the work of military preparation.

  July, 1866

No such clarity or fixity of purpose was discernible in the counsels of the French Emperor. Here everything was opaque, genial, uncertain. War was thought of not as an inevitable stage in a national programme, but as an evil which might be circumvented by diplomacy. Alliances were projected with Austria and Italy. Conversations were held, visits exchanged, but nothing clinched. There was a vague expectation that in the event of war, Denmark, Hanover, Bavaria might welcome the chance of chastening Prussian insolence; but here again nothing was done. Important army reforms were projected but permitted to suffer defeat in an economizing Chamber, which, though it agreed that Prussia was the enemy, never for a moment imagined that the Prussians were a match for the famous professional army of France. Perhaps war might never be necessary. The friendship of France was precious, and like all precious things could be had for a price. In the interval which elapsed between Sadowa and the Franco-Prussian War French diplomacy was busy in the search for compensations which might appease public opinion at home and render it more easy to preserve the peace. There was the Rhenish Palatinate, there was Luxemburg, there was Belgium. These were foolish and dangerous quests. Nothing but harm came from them. When the Bavarians learnt through a French newspaper to whom the secret had been communicated by Bismarck that France had asked for a slice of southern Germany, they had no further scruple about joining the Prussians in the war. The scheme for the purchase of Luxemburg was withdrawn under pressure of fierce and open Prussian hostility. But most damaging of all was the claim for Belgium which Benedetti had been instructed to make in 1866; for when Bismarck, at the outbreak of the Franco-Prussian War, published the draft treaty in which this claim was made, British opinion, regarding Belgian neutrality as the Holy of Holies, veered sharply round to the German side.

Although to outward appearances the Court of Napoleon was still as glittering and lavish as ever, a disturbing sense of anxiety ran through the Tuileries. The Emperor was no longer capable of firm decisions. The heir to the throne was a boy. From every quarter the dynasty was assailed by a gathering volume of irritable and sardonic opposition. It was in vain that sacrifice after sacrifice was made to that great body of clerical opinion which had been the original mainstay of the Imperial power, that the Pope had been defended by a French garrison in Rome, that forty thousand good French troops had been sent upon a Catholic crusade in Mexico, and that Duruy, the greatest education minister of the century, had been ejected from power. The clericals were not content. They could never forgive the sovereign by whose initial intervention the sacrilegious Italians had been enabled to eject the ancient and orthodox Houses of Habsburg and Bourbon from Italian soil and to rob the Pope of the greater part of his Principality. The influential Catholic Bishops, the powerful ultramontane press led by Louis Veuillot, a journalist of fiery temper, regarded it as the primary duty of the French Government to support Catholic interests all over the world and visited every backsliding with their steadfast censures. In democratic nationalism they saw the arch-enemy of the Church, and they applauded the syllabus of 1864, in which the Pope condemned, among other features of contemporary civilization, the institution of universal suffrage, and therefore by implication an Empire built on the plébiscite.

If such was the temper of the clericals, it may easily be imagined that the more progressive spirits found even less to applaud in the Napoleonic régime. There was no glamour about Fould, the Jew financier, or the lawyer Rouher, or the able but unpopular Haussmann who drove the Boulevards through Paris and made of it the modern city which we know. There was no glory, but on the contrary a series of humiliating rebuffs in the later foreign policy of the Emperor. The young men thought that new blood was wanted in the government. The Liberals in the Chamber, a growing body led by Émile b. Ollivier, a French Gladstone but without the Englishman's 1825 courage, clerical, high-minded, cultured, eloquent, clamoured for the enlargement of the liberties of 1860 and for the establishment of responsible government. After a long silence Republicanism recovered its voice in Léon Gambetta, a young lawyer from the south who openly preached the overthrow of the Empire. The socialists, deriving prestige from an international institution, the exiles of 1852, released by successive acts of amnesty, added virulence to the attack.

Most alarming was the fact that during the last two years of his reign, the Emperor was the mark not only of odium but of ridicule. It was inconvenient that he should be denounced as an assassin by the man in the street. ·More deadly was the incessant and brilliant raillery of *La Lanterne*, the organ of Rochefort, of all French journalists of ·that time the most gifted in the art of cruel and irresponsible burlesque.

The situation was one of extreme danger. After the elections of 1869 when, despite official pressure upon the electorate, the opposition polled nearly half the votes of France, it seemed to many that there would be a race between internal revolution and foreign war. Either the Empire would perish from the blows of its assailants from within or by a successful vindication of French prestige abroad might secure for itself a fresh lease of life. There was a third way pressed upon the Emperor by Ollivier and ultimately, after many hesitations, adopted. Liberalism, such as had been found compatible with the existence of monarchy in England and Italy, might be applied to France. A homogeneous ministry, responsible to the popular Chamber, might relieve the Emperor of his crushing burden, satisfy artisan opinion, and by robbing revolution of its *raison d'être*, preserve the dynasty. The experiment was tried. On January 3, 1870, Ollivier found himself head of a Liberal administration. The constitution was reformed in a Liberal sense, the reforms were submitted to a plébiscite, and to the immense relief of the Court were accepted by a majority of nearly six million votes. Everything then seemed to point to peace, prosperity, and a fresh lease of power for the Empire. Lord Clarendon at Ollivier's suggestion began to open projects of disarmament with Bismarck. "On whichever side we look" declared the new French Premier, "there is an absence of troublesome questions; at no moment has the maintenance of peace in Europe been better secured." A month later, springing from the unsuspected source of a Spanish revolution and an empty throne in Madrid, the war broke out which swept away Napoleon and Ollivier and the Liberal Empire, and at the same time enabled the dream of German unity to become an established fact.

On July 3, 1870, Paris learned that Prince Leopold of

Hohenzollern Sigmaringen, a distant kinsman of the Prussian king, the son of Prince Anthony who had been Prime Minister of Prussia, and the elder brother of the Prince of Roumania, had accepted, subject to the confirmation of the Cortes, the vacant throne of Spain. At once a situation of the gravest diplomatic tension was created. The Hohenzollern candidature had been discussed confidentially in Berlin in 1869, when the Prussians were apprised of the French objection to a plan which threatened to·recall the Empire of Charles V and to alter the European balance to the detriment of France. How then did it come about that this obnoxious candidature was renewed? The French government flew to the conclusion that Bismarck was at the bottom of yet another plot to humiliate the French people, and that, unless the candidature was withdrawn before the meeting of the Spanish Cortes on July 20, France would be compelled to draw the sword. On July 6 Gramont, the Foreign Minister, told the Chamber that the honour and interest of the country were involved. Even Ollivier, the liberal, the pacifist, the statesman, who had openly declared (in a German print) that he would be no party to resisting by force of arms the willing union of southern and northern Germany, was stirred to a white heat of indignation by this assumed exhibition of Prussian guile and ill-will.

On this feverish disposition of the public mind there suddenly dropped on the evening of July 11, like manna from heaven, unofficial news that Prince Anthony of Hohenzollern had been induced to renounce the Spanish throne in the name of his son. Great was the surprise, greater the relief. It seemed that the danger was overpast and that the representations of France had produced their effect. The Emperor and Ollivier professed themselves satisfied. Surely this was not only peace but peace with honour? The aged Guizot asserted that he could recall no greater diplomatic victory for France.

The prize of peace, no sooner won, was sacrificed by a wanton act of folly. Gramont, a diplomatist by profession and a great deal more warlike than his Prime Minister, was not satisfied with the bare renunciation of "Father Anthony." He must receive a definite assurance from the Prussian King that the withdrawal had his assent and that the candidature would never be renewed. And he even went so far as to suggest to the Prussian ambassador in Paris that his master should express his regret for the occurrence. Unfortunately Gramont was not alone in his unwisdom. In the Chamber, which had been worked up into a mad fit of intractable passion by the events of the last few days, a fool spoke of guarantees, and the cry for guarantees passing from the Chamber to St. Cloud unnerved the Emperor. Behind the back of Ollivier and his Cabinet he associated himself (July 13) with his foreign minister in instructing Benedetti to meet King William at Ems, and there obtain from him an assurance that he associated himself with Prince Anthony's withdrawal, and would not authorize any renewal of the attempt to set a Hohenzollern on the throne of Spain.

Though the Spanish matter had never been brought before the Prussian Cabinet, the French were right in their surmise that Bismarck was at the bottom of the intrigue. He had in fact left no stone unturned to counter the Franco-Austrian conversations by an alliance which should open Spanish markets to Prussian trade and secure for his country in the event of French hostilities a friendly power beyond the Pyrenees. He pressed the Hohenzollerns to accept the offer, pressed the Spaniards to renew it, pressed his royal master to regard it with favour and to treat it as a matter of strictest confidence, and, while carefully denying official cognizance of the affair, saw that it was discussed at a special meeting of the Council attended by the King, the Princes, and the War Lords. The utmost secrecy was observed, for it was hoped that, before the French were even aware that an offer had been made, the German Prince might be formally accepted in Madrid. Two consequences, each of them grateful to Bismarck, might ensue, a war between France and Prussia or, a degree less desirable, a war between France and Spain. It was, therefore, with bitter disappointment that Bismarck learnt (July 12) that "Father Anthony" had after all made the great refusal, that French diplomacy had triumphed, and that the insolence of the Paris Press was to go unchastised. In his *Thoughts and Recollections* he describes it as the greatest humiliation which his country had suffered since Olmütz.

Gramont delivered him from his dejection. When Benedetti

met the King on the Promenade at Ems, the old gentleman was civil but firm. He would give no guarantee, broke off the interview, and, though twice subsequently requested to do so, would give no further audience to the French ambassador; but he sent to say that he had received an official communication from Prince Leopold withdrawing the candidature and that the withdrawal had his assent. That, in his view, concluded the matter. The relations between King and ambassador, both anxious to avoid war, were marked by perfect courtesy and good feeling.

The royal telegram from Ems recounting these proceedings reached Bismarck in Berlin when he was dining with Moltke and Roon. At once the great strategist saw that the enemy was delivered into his hands. With a little judicious alteration a statement could be issued to the Press embodying the substance of the telegram, but making it appear that the French ambassador had put an affront on the Prussian King and that the King had been compelled to administer to him a sharp rebuff. When Bismarck's draft was read out to the famous soldiers, they were delighted. "It is a challenge," said Moltke. "It is good," said von Roon. Bismarck and the soldiers were right, for it was the Ems telegram which set Germany and France ablaze.

On the morning of July 14 Gramont burst into Ollivier's room with a copy of the *North German Gazette* containing the Bismarckian version of the Ems Telegram. "They wish," cried Ollivier, "to force us into war." It was a day of anguished indecision, the needle of debate in the Emperor's Council pointing now to peace then rapidly swinging to war. At 4 p.m. it was decided to call out the reserves; at 6.30 p.m. to appeal to a congress; but after dinner opinion hardened against peace, and at midnight it was decided that war should be declared next morning. The Empress was present, a known but silent adherent of war, at the evening council when the critical decision was taken. The mind of Paris was unmistakable. "Even if we had no motive for war which we could avow," said the Emperor, "we should, nevertheless, be obliged to resolve on it to obey the will of the people." How little the people knew was evidenced by their street cries, "A Berlin!" and "Vive la guerre!"

If the war was popular in Paris, in seventy-one out of

eighty-seven departments it "was accepted rather with hesitation or regret." It was an unnecessary, insensate war, for which the primary responsibility must rest upon Bismarck and Gramont, upon Bismarck for having engineered the secret candidature and for his alteration of the Ems telegram, upon Gramont for the headlong passion with which he deliberately broke the bridge of peace. King William and the Emperor are not absolved from censure. Against his better judgment, the King, who was the soul of honour, allowed himself to be persuaded to sanction the Spanish venture without consulting France, whom he knew to have an interest in the arrangement. Equally was the Emperor to blame for joining Gramont in the fatal demand for guarantees. That his position was made difficult by the intemperate heat of the Conservative orators of the Chamber and by the fiery tone of the Paris press is true enough, but a strong ruler would have kept his head, and it is noticeable that Thiers, the best politician in public life, was not afraid to speak against the war.

Everything happened with extraordinary celerity. Barely a fortnight divided Europe from a state of profound peace and one of open war. In the dead of the summer holiday the electric telegraph and the newspaper press brought a wholly unanticipated quarrel to a climax, and convulsed two of the most civilized peoples of the world with savage hatred before reason or mansuetude could gain a hearing. On both sides the voice of the soldiers was violently given for war.

To the confusion of all the prophets the famous regular army of France, so far from carrying the war into southern Germany, was put out of action in a month. The result was due to no deficiency in the fighting quality of the French soldier, but to the fact that while the French military system was thoroughly inefficient, the German army was the most highly perfected institution in what was even then the best organized community in the world.

Most instructive is the comparison between the rival nations in the all-important point of mobilization. Whereas a German villager on being called to the colours found his arms and uniform at hand, a French soldier might have to travel across France or even to cross the sea to Algiers to join the depôt of his regiment. The result was that, while the transport of the German army to the frontiers proceeded with mechanical smoothness and regularity, the wildest confusion prevailed on the French railways, so that the Germans were on the frontier in superior force before the French were prepared to meet them. Since Napoleon's sole chance of bringing Austria into the war was a striking initial success, the shocking inefficiency of the French mobilization produced far-reaching consequences.

A second advantage belonging to the invaders is that they had studied with elaborate care, and in the light of the latest developments in field telegraphy and gunnery, the particular campaign which they proposed to conduct. While the French had never dreamed of the possibility that they might be called on to defend their own soil, the Prussian plan for the invasion of France was three years old. The roads were mapped, the carrying capacity of the railways was estimated, and few were the details as to the organization, equipment, and distribution of the units of the French army which were unknown to the General Staff in Berlin. To this carefully prepared fabric of knowledge, a moving screen of observant cavalry made, as the three German armies advanced into France, continual and hourly additions.

It might have been expected that the elaboration of the German military system would have stifled individual initiative. This was not so. It was the principle of the German General Staff to encourage the assumption of responsibility by subordinate commanders, and while the movements of the French armies were often hampered by an excessive deference to central control, no German general seems to have scrupled to march to the sound of the guns and to throw his men into the mêlée where the need was sorest. The brilliant initiative shown by subordinate German commanders is one of the most conspicuous features of the campaign.

In war everything depends upon the joint capacity of the civilian and military Higher Command to work together, to inspire confidence, and to give to the nation and the troops a steadfast and animating direction. In all these particulars France was most unfortunately situated in the summer of 1870. Nowhere either in the Higher Military Command or in the civilian control was there magnetism or method.

Napoleon, an invalid racked by excruciating pain, Le Boeuf, his War Minister; Bazaine, his successor in the Supreme Command, were all in the highest degree technically incompetent. Behind them in Paris was a frightened civilian government, headed by the beautiful but ill-liked Empress and faced with the fast-rising floods of a popular revolution. To this spectacle of military mediocrity and civilian confusion Germany opposed a united nation, a deep-rooted dynasty, and the potent trinity of Bismarck, Roon, and Moltke, backed by an army of officers military and civilian who had been trained in the finest school of public service then existing in Europe.

One final comparison may be added. The Germans possessed a short service, the French a long service system. Whereas the Prussian system of two years with the colours, four with the reserves, and five and a half with the militia was calculated to produce a field army of five hundred thousand men and behind them a vast reserve of trained levies, the French plan of five years' service, convenient enough for colonial campaigns overseas, had no such result. The German regular army, if destroyed in the initial stages of a campaign, could be replaced by troops who had undergone the full period of training with the colours. But when the field army of France was destroyed or dispersed, the country was compelled to fall back upon levies who were for the most part raw and untrained. In the later half of the Franco-Prussian War this disability was severely felt.

The story of that late summer was one of unrelieved tragedy for France. The Germans with irresistible momentum carried everything before them. They defeated MacMahon at Wörth, Frossard at Spicheren, and by these two victories, one in Alsace and the other in Lorraine, each gained on August 6, only two days after the invading army had reached the frontier, they sent such a spasm of depression, indignation, and alarm through the country, that the Emperor resigned his command to Bazaine, and that honest, eloquent, timid Ollivier "with his light heart" was driven for ever from the stage of politics, to be replaced by (August 10) an elderly cavalry officer, the Count de Palikao, in whom the last confidence of the distracted Empress was capriciously reposed.

All these changes were unavailing. Bazaine was not the man to stem the onrush. His retreat was slow, so slow that he allowed the Germans to march round him, to hold him up at Mars la Tour, and after a bloody victory at Gravelotte (August 18) to drive him back eastwards to the shelter of the fortifications of Metz. There the commander of 170,000 men, containing the flower of the French army, permitted himself to be invested. There, with little effort to break through, he remained. There finally (October 27) he capitulated, releasing by his act of cowardice and treachery an investing army of 200,000 men to assist in the subjugation of his country. Meanwhile in those early days of August a field army of regular troops was collecting at Châlons under MacMahon, and it became a matter of crucial importance to determine whither this army, the last free and disengaged force of regulars, could most usefully direct its movement. Wisely, as it would appear, MacMahon counselled that the army of Châlons should avoid immediate contact with the enemy, fall backwards, and, rallying round it whatever scattered elements of military power remained, concentrate before the fortifications of Paris. But the Empress and her advisers would not hear of retreat. They urged that Paris required the relief of Bazaine and a victory in the east, and that, were the army of Châlons to yield ground, the people would rise and upset the throne. Reluctantly and against his better judgment the plain soldier complied, marching his army back to Rheims, and then, having heard that Bazaine proposed to break out towards the north, turning north-eastwards towards the Belgian frontier. Moltke was after him. At the little town of Sedan the French army was encircled, broken by shell-fire, and compelled to capitulate. Among the spoils of that supreme German victory was the person of Napoleon. It was September 2; two days later the Republic was proclaimed in Paris, and while Jules Favre announced to the world that France would not surrender a stone of her fortresses or a yard of her territory, the Empress secretly made her way in the carriage of an American dentist towards the classic home of political exiles. It was the end of Bonapartism, the system of monarchy based upon the plébiscite, which, after nearly uniting all Europe under the sceptre of the first Napoleon, ended by leaving France shorn of territory and prestige and faced by a new and formidable rival.

The war against the Imperial army was concluded. The war against the French nation was now to begin. A cool estimate of the situation might have suggested that a good peace was most likely to be obtained while Metz was untaken and the army of Bazaine still unhurt. Passion, however, does not calculate, and there are occasions in the history of every nation when the manifestation, however blind, of the psychic forces of a people is more valuable than a nice appreciation of profit and loss. The national war, though it may have meant a harder peace, did something to restore the self-respect of the French people and to preserve their courage in the depressing years which lay before them. Desperate, indeed, it proved to be, but full of embarrassment for the enemy, of difficulties perhaps greater than those which confronted the invaders in the early and more professional stage of the conflict. The area of operations was wider, the lines of communications were lengthened and were frequently threatened by *franc-tireurs*; the new French armies springing up in all directions were less easy to measure and to locate. If a substantial system of trained reserves had been available, the French might have converted a grave embarrassment into a serious menace.

The soul of this popular prolongation of the war was Léon

1838-82 Gambetta, the great republican orator from the south, who had first sprung into notice in a *cause célèbre* as the bitter assailant of the empire. Obstacles meant nothing to Gambetta. When the Germans encircled Paris he escaped in a balloon to Rouen (October 7), and by his prodigious and animating energy raised in the course of six weeks an army of 180,000 men. At Coulmier, near Orleans, the new army of Gambetta inflicted upon the Germans their first defeat, and had Bazaine still held in Metz it is possible that D'Aurelles, the victor of Coulmier, might have been able with the assistance of the Paris garrison to break the blockade.

Oct. 27, 1870 But the capitulation of Metz exercised a decisive influence on the course of the campaign by making available for the Germans, at the hour of their greatest need, a large and powerful army. At every point the raw half-trained levies of

Gambetta were met by forces superior in numbers, training, and equipment, so that D'Aurelles was thrice defeated near Orleans, Chanzy after a fierce three days' battle finally overwhelmed at Le Mans (January 10, 1871), and Faidherbe, who had won some initial successes in the north, defeated at St. Quentin (January 19). An attempt, too grandiose for success, to animate the south-east against the invader and from that quarter to create a powerful diversion by a raid into Baden, met with even greater calamity, for Bourbaki's army of 85,000 men, wretchedly equipped and defeated at Montbeliard, was pushed back over the frontier into the neutral territory of Switzerland and there ignominiously disarmed (February 1, 1871).

Meanwhile Paris experienced the unexpected hardships of a siege. Rage and humiliation possessed the inhabitants of this mercurial city who had lightly acclaimed the war with cries of "A Berlin!" and were now condemned to experience the bitter taste of defeat. The shortage of food, the frustration of every effort to break through the war circle, the horrors of the regular bombardment which began on December 27, when the Prussian guns were brought up and were directed upon the civilian population as well as upon the forts, contributed to create in the public mind "the siege fever," as the French called it, which passed by an easy transition into the mania of the commune.

At last, but not before the wild remedy of a *sortie en masse* had been tried in vain, Paris was willing to treat with the enemy. An armistice was granted, elections were held, an assembly gathered in Bordeaux elected Thiers head of the executive and empowered him to negotiate with the enemy. On the main points Bismarck was adamant. He demanded Alsace, a great part of Lorraine with Metz, and an indemnity which he consented to reduce to 200 million pounds. The Prussian was in an unassailable position. When Thiers proved obdurate Bismarck threatened to treat with Napoleon. Only on one point of any serious importance did he make a concession to the eloquent entreaties of the Frenchman. If the German army might be accorded the satisfaction of occupying Paris, he was willing that the French should keep Belfort. The Peace of Frankfort (May 10, 1871) which embodied these terms was imposed by the Germans on the French, as

Jan. 1, 1871

Feb., 1871

the Peace of Versailles was later imposed by the Allies on the Germans. The indemnity was a bagatelle soon disposed of, but no Frenchman gave more than a forced and nominal assent to the cession of Strasbourg and Metz.

1797-
1877
Thiers, the fiery and patriotic statesman who negotiated on behalf of his vanquished country the preliminaries of peace, had warned his compatriots against going into the war and was now freshly returned from a fruitless mission to foreign courts in the hopes of obtaining their helpful intercession. The little man, whose impish form, egg-shaped head, and large spectacles were the joy of the caricaturists, is one of the most considerable civilians in the history of France. He made peace with Germany, suppressed the Commune, and more than anyone else, though an Orleanist by conviction, created the Third Republic, which, surviving many perils of infancy, because of all forms of government it divided France the least, was strong enough forty-eight years later to reverse the verdict of the Franco-Prussian War.

In asking for Alsace-Lorraine and for the great fortress of Metz, Bismarck was perpetuating the quarrel between France and Germany and laying the seed of a future war. It was the greatest, the most serious, and the most far-reaching of the errors committed in the course of a triumphant life. Alsace was indeed essentially a German province, Lorraine was chiefly French. The first of these provinces had been wrested from Germany by Mazarin, the second had been acquired as part of a general European settlement by Louis XV. To both provinces, but in fullest measure to Alsace, a German Empire could claim an historical title. But the populations which had profited by the social legislation of the French were given no opportunity of expressing their will. Without the faintest interrogation of local opinion, they were excised from a nation to which they had become accustomed, and placed under the sterner yoke of the conqueror.

Jan.
18,
1871
A few days before the fall of Paris the German Empire was proclaimed in the Hall of Mirrors at Versailles. The far-resounding victory of Wörth had been won by the troops of Bavaria and Würtemberg under the leadership of the Crown Prince of Prussia, and no sooner had Napoleon surrendered at Sedan than overtures were made by the South German

Schleswig
Holstein
Mecklenburg
Hanover
Rhine
Provs.
Hesse
PRUSSIA
RUSSIA
Saxony
FRANCE
AUSTRIA
Alsace
Lorraine
Wurtemburg
BAVARIA

Prussia, 1864
Added 1866
From France 1871
Other German States
Joined Empire 1871

THE GROWTH OF THE GERMAN EMPIRE

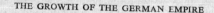

States for admission to the Union. These advances were eagerly welcomed. Though there were many who thought that the moment had now come when it would be possible to establish in Germany a strong centralized State, Bismarck was not of that number. "We do not want an unwilling Bavaria," he said; "we want one which will join freely," and that Bavaria might be a contented member of the *Reich* he was ready to make wide concessions—the control of the army in peace, a voice in foreign policy, a separate Bavarian system of posts and telegraphs. There can be no clearer proof of his wisdom than that the King of Bavaria should have been brought to consent to propose that William of Hohenzollern should take the Imperial Crown.

It is difficult to exaggerate the enthusiasm and self-confidence which these remarkable events created in the German people. Though old-fashioned Prussians, like the King and Von Roon, had little relish for the new Imperial title, the fact that Germany after so many centuries of division and foreign danger had at last been united by a victorious war, that her armies had proved themselves invincible, that she had imposed her will successively on Austria and on France, and that by the recovery of two long-lost provinces she had established a powerful barrier against future danger from the west, filled every German heart with glowing emotions of pride and satisfaction. The Germans had long led Europe in music, in learning, and in the number, influence, and efficiency of their schools and universities. They were now without dispute the strongest military power on the continent. Was it unnatural that Prussian patriots, throwing their minds backward to the obscure origins of their state in a little military outpost of German-speaking men against a wilderness of Slavs, and thence tracing its successive developments, should discern therein the workings of a peculiar and flattering Providence? Was it unnatural that they should believe that the Prussian race, by its frugality, its hardihood, its stern application, its formidable and disciplined violence, was selected to accomplish an historic mission on earth, first as a missionary of German civilization among the Baltic Slavs, then as the protagonist of the Protestant Faith, and afterwards as the Power which delivered the German peoples from their paralysing connection with the Austrian Empire and gave to them an arbitral position on the continent of Europe? These reflections were widely sown from professorial chairs. There were many also, bolder than the vulgar, who cast their minds forward into the future and asked themselves whether an even greater destiny was not reserved for the Hohenzollerns. The world was wide, the salt seas beckoned to new adventures. Nothing was impossible to German heroism, neither marine power, nor colonies, nor the ultimate dominion of the earth. To the State which in an ascending scale of effort had vanquished the Danes, the Austrians, and the French there yet remained another ordeal. The Anglo-Saxon Empire, built up by a nation of civilians, of frivolous amateurs, who had won the palm without the dust, was not immortal. Too long had these spoilt children of fortune been permitted to disport themselves in the sun. The time had come when Providence would reward the industrious apprentice and transfer to solid merit the prizes which had fallen to the favourites of chance. Rome would wrest the trident from Carthage. Such in effect was the teaching of Heinrich von Treitschke, most influential of historical professors and publicists, from his chair in Berlin.

BOOKS WHICH MAY BE CONSULTED

Fyffe: *A History of Modern Europe*. 1924.
E. Ollivier: *L'Empire Libéral*. 1911.
Pierre de la Gorce: *Histoire du Second Empire*. 1908.
G. Rothan: *Souvenirs Diplomatiques*. 1882.
E. Bourgeois: *Manuel Historique de Politique Étrangère*. 1905-6.
E. Bourgeois and E. Clermont: *Rome et Napoleon III*. 1907.
J. Reinach: *G. L. Gambetta*. 1884.
Lowes Dickinson: *Revolution and Reaction in Modern France*. 1892.
F. Darmstaedter: *Bismarck and the creation of the second Reich*. 1948.
E. Eyck: *Bismarck and the German Empire*. 1950.
A. J. P. Taylor: *Bismarck*. 1955.
D. W. Brogan: *The Development of Modern France, 1870-1939*. 1940.

CHAPTER LXXXIV

THE THIRD REPUBLIC

Unpopularity of Republicanism in the provinces. The Paris Commune. The struggle between Paris and Versailles. The foundation of the Third Republic. French Parliamentary Government. France and Germany. Jules Ferry. The problem of Clericalism. Instability of the Republic. Boulanger. The Dreyfus Case. French diplomacy.

DURING THE years which followed the great defeat France gradually built up for herself a new political existence. She was heartily weary of plébiscites, dictatorships, and foreign adventures, and since the idea of Republic had always been associated with war and revolution, the preponderant part of the population dreaded a constitution bearing that name. Out of the six hundred and fifty deputies returned to the Parliament of Bordeaux (February 8, 1871) four hundred prepared to vote for a King.

Nevertheless it was not a King but a Republic which emerged in the end from this strongly monarchical and representative assembly. By slow degrees France came to realize that the monarchy was made impossible by the division between the legitimist and the Orleanist lines, by the obstinate refusal of the Count de Chambord, the head of the older branch, to acknowledge the tricolor, which was the symbol of democratic institutions, and by the manifest and violent aversion of the democracy of Paris from any attempt to bring back the Kings to France.

Paris was Republican and ardent for a revolutionary war against the Germans waged in the grand old manner of Danton and Carnot. It saw that the imperial campaign had been shockingly mismanaged, it believed that under brave leadership the siege might have been broken, and that a pusillanimous assembly of rural conservatives, recently (March 10) moved from Bordeaux to Versailles, had sold the birthright of the country to the enemy and was plotting to restore the evils and inequalities of the *ancien régime*. Rather than submit to the Versaillais, odious on the double count of royalism and pacifism, Paris would fight. The city was hungry, exasperated, wounded by the spectacle of German troops marching in triumph through the Champs Élysées, and charged with revolutionary passions and dreams of every description—Jacobin, federal, socialist, communist, anarchist. The National Guard had been armed for the siege, and when the government of Versailles attempted to withdraw the guns from Montmartre it offered resistance. Baptized by the blood of two murdered generals, the Commune of Paris inaugurated its reckless and ruinous course.

The Paris Commune has passed into legend as the first fiery manifestation of the great revolutionary movement which throws from Russia a challenge to the capitalistic order of society all over the world. This, however, was not its original or dominating character. The genius of the Commune was rather that of Danton than of Lenin, its origin a sudden tempest of Republican patriotism rather than a deep-laid plot to overthrow society. As passion mounted, the movement, originally led by respectable burgesses, took on new colours. The dissolution of France into a Federation of Republics or even the destruction of the capitalistic *régime* throughout the world became for certain sections of the working-class Communards the watchword of the future. But there was no single creed common to the whole complex movement. The Commune of Paris did not even confiscate the gold reserve of the Bank.

Little old Thiers, in his tight frock-coat, was at the head of the government of Versailles, glinting through his large spectacles. Though nothing had yet been settled as to the ultimate constitution of France, for the royalists were in no hurry to take the helm, the provisional government was in fact republican. Yet the gifted, flint-hearted old gentleman showed no weakness. Collecting a strong regular force of 130,000 men, he applied himself with a steady and remorseless persistence to the reconquest of Paris. His severities then and thereafter were tremendous; but there was little compassion for the wild terrorists who had made a shambles of Paris and burned the Tuileries and the Hôtel de Ville. Rather it was counted to the government for righteousness that it had signed preliminaries of peace with the enemy and in "the week of blood" (May 21-8) stamped without mercy on the Paris Commune. A Republic, then, might after all be conservative and free from the terrifying associations of revolution and war, and so it came about that the Paris Commune had a bearing on the political evolution of France, for it showed that while the workers of Paris would always strain against a monarchy, the bourgeois could comfortably accept a Republic.

Thus the Provisional Government, "a republic without republicans," continued in being, gathering strength as it went along, rallying Gambetta, who was a big enough man to learn by experience, and eventually in 1875, when the constitutional statutes were under discussion, giving its sanction by a majority of one vote to the formidable word "Republic." The Royalists had missed the tide. The conservative Republic had triumphed by discharging the task from which through lack of courage and unity the royalists had shrunk. Their failure was merited and could not be retrieved. Two years later (1877), when Marshal MacMahon, the clerical and royalist President, endeavoured to obtain authority for a royalist ministry by dissolving a newly elected Chamber which was too republican for his taste, he received such a lesson from the electors that no subsequent President has ever since dared to exercise his right of dissolution. Not least among the causes of the Conservative *débâcle* that autumn was the belief that the Right under its military and clerical chief would plunge France into war.

The Republican constitution of 1875, which in substance governs France to this day, is inspired by a lively horror of the evils which a despotism founded on a plébiscite had brought on France. There are two Chambers, a Senate and a House of Deputies; and it is by the vote of these two Chambers in joint session and not by a plébiscite of the whole people of France that the President of the Republic is elected. Such a system is well qualified to shelter the country from the dangerous magnetism of sensational adventurers. The Chambers do not elect supermen; their choice falls upon the solid lawyer or man of business whose character and abilities have proved themselves in the Parliamentary arena. They are not in search of a force, but of a figurehead. Ever since MacMahon failed in his attempt to turn the presidential office to the account of the monarchy, nothing has been more injurious to a French President than the suspicion that he is seeking to make a policy of his own or to establish by speech or action a vital and independent contact with the mind of the country.

Parliamentary government, then, on the English model was the gift of the Constitution of 1875 to France. The keys of authority were confided, not to the President, who was elected for seven years, but to a Cabinet responsible to the popular Chamber. France became for the first time what England had been since the glorious Revolution, a strict parliamentary democracy, more parliamentary even, as the French contend, than England itself, since, whereas at Westminster the Cabinet controls the Parliament, in Paris the relations are reversed. In a legislature which may not be dissolved before its natural term party discipline is weak, and small groups, entering now into this combination, now into that, take the place of the great highly organized political combinations which struggle for power across the floor of the

House of Commons. The French Cabinets, then, are short-lived, and since at any moment they may be upset by a new and unforeseen combination, they are compelled to devote to current parliamentary strategy much of the energy which might otherwise be employed upon long-range legislative projects. To these distractions, arising out of the group system, the great burden of patronage incidental to the government of a highly centralized state must be added. The tasks of an English Cabinet Minister are heavy, but at least he is not called upon to fight two hundred votes of censure a session or to canvass the claims of applicants for the village post office.

The French public can hardly expect to follow with reverential absorption a concern at once so kaleidoscopic in its changes and so largely occupied with triviality. The theatres, the salon, the *Académie Française*, the discussion and assessment of current literature, constitute a pleasanter and more absorbing interest. The parliaments of the Third Republic, despite the fire, eloquence, and ability of their debates, have never held a high place in the respect and admiration of the French people. Certain scandals, notably those connected 1888· with the financing of the Panama Canal, have spread an 92 unfortunate impression of corruption. The prestige of antiquity is absent; and the loss has not been replaced by the renown of great ministers achieving with the support of powerful and sustained majorities policies which inflame the imagination of the people.

During all the years between 1870 and 1914 the most profound question for western civilization was the possibility of establishing friendly relations between France and Germany. Alsace-Lorraine stood in the way. So long as the statue of Strasburg in the Place de la Concorde was veiled in crêpe, every Frenchman continued to dream of the recovery of the lost provinces as an end impossible perhaps of achievement— for there was no misjudgment now of the vast strength of Germany—but nevertheless ardently to be desired. It was not a thing to be talked of. "N'en parlez jamais, y pensez toujours," advised Gambetta; but it was a constant element in public feeling, an ever-present obstruction to the friendship of the two countries, a dominant motive in policy, a dark cloud full of menace for the future.

Had the Germans been willing to grant a full measure of autonomy to the provinces, the tension would have been lessened; and there were some French statesmen who hoped that a cordial understanding could be reached by concessions of this nature. It was not so, however, that Bismarck viewed his duty. Alsace-Lorraine constituted in his eyes a necessary curb on the ambitions of a nation who would never forgive the humiliation of defeat. Bismarck had no trust in the pacific intentions of the Third Republic. He was alarmed by the economic resilience of France, by her swift and resolute adoption of a military system based upon Russian principles and calculated to yield a field army of 6,750,000 men and a reserve of half a million, and by the warlike language of some of her statesmen. But for the timely intervention of Queen Victoria and the Tzar, he would, not improbably, have impelled his country into a preventive war in 1875. Afterwards a cheaper way of soothing a restless neighbour occurred to his mind. He suggested that France should annex Tunis. "I have sent," he observed in his racy, idiomatic English, "the fiery steed of French ambition caracoling in the sands of Tunis. They will find it heavy going." It was his hope that, once launched upon a career of colonial conquest, France would brood less upon her lost provinces in Europe.

Among the rare glories of the French parliamentary scene 1832- was an ardent, unconquerable *député* from the Vosges named 93 Jules Ferry, who, though he has left an imperishable mark upon the colonial and educational policy of his country, was pursued throughout his lifetime with the fiercest hatred and detraction. Under the Empire Ferry had been a pacifist and a radical. Afterwards he carved out for himself a course of his own as a colonial imperialist, a conservative republican, and, in the field of education, as a political anti-clerical. Storms of angry controversy gathered round this stout and combative figure, who outraged the cherished maxims of the radicals by his imperialism and of the clericals by his schools. France, it was urged, had no further need for colonies. The monarchy had involved her in the expensive adventure of Algeria, the Empire had committed her to a distant colony in Indo-China. Her birth rate was falling; she had no surplus population to export; all her resources were needed to deal with the one problem which really mattered on her eastern frontier. Was not the lesson of Mexico enough? What was the value of Tunis or Tongking to a country whose prime duty was to the inhabitants of the two lost provinces of Alsace-Lorraine? Such were the views of Georges Clemenceau, the "Tiger," who, having tasted the defeat of 1870, was steadily set on revenge, and by no means anxious to throw Italy into the arms of the Germans for the sake of the cornlands of Tunis.

In such criticism there was a strong pith of good sense. The forward colonial movement led by Ferry contributed, as every such movement must do, to create new stresses and dangers for France. The friendship of Italy was lost over Tunis, peace with England was risked over Fashoda, the relations with Germany and Spain were seriously strained over Morocco. Yet when the struggle came in 1914 the French did not repent of their colonial empire, the second in the world, or of the African man-power which helped them to sustain their European struggle. The ambitious policy which covered "Le Tonquinois," as Ferry was called, with the ridicule of the boulevards was forgiven as the Algerian and Senegalese levies of the Republic took their place in the trenches as citizens of France.

In two other respects Jules Ferry stands out among the French statesmen of the Republic. He legalized trades unions and won the great educational battle which Duruy under the Empire had lost to the clericals. It is to him that France owes the system of universal, free, compulsory education. As Minister of Public Instruction in the de Freycinet Cabinet (1882), he caused the Jesuits to be evicted from their schools, and submitted other teaching congregations to strict regulations. Though out of regard to the colonial interests of France and to the feeling in the army, he was gentle with his antagonist, it was his view that clerical teaching was directed to undermining confidence in the Republic, and that the programmes of the Church schools were not up to the requirements of the age.

There can be little question that in both respects Ferry was right. If the greater part of the French population was illiterate in 1870, if the programmes of study were narrow and obsolete, it was largely by reason of the obstacles which clericalism had placed in the way of expansion of state education. Those

obstacles still existed. The Senate opposed the attack on the
teaching congregations; but the government, proceeding by
decree, circumvented the Senate, dissolved the Jesuits, and so
cleared the ground for the great development of education
in all its branches, which has so far been the most remarkable
domestic achievement of the Third Republic.

In the decades succeeding the Franco-Prussian War, the
struggle of parties in France, though assuming many different
forms as chance accidents, such as the Panama scandal, intervened, was at bottom the old quarrel between clericalism and
the modern world. "Clericalism is the enemy," was Gambetta's war cry (May 4, 1877). The politicians of the Left
feared the priest in politics, in the home, in the school. The
great body of the industrial working class, though they
accepted the rites of the Church in baptism, in marriage, and
in burial, might be trusted always to give an anti-clerical vote.
Tradition had enormous weight with them. In voting against
the priest, they were voting, as they believed, against the
ancien régime, against the return of feudalism, of inequality,
of social oppression, evils which they had learned from their
fathers to hate and to associate with the priests of the Catholic
Church. A hundred years after the revolutionary terror,
constituencies, formerly royalist, voted clerical, while those
which had been Jacobin returned members belonging to one
or other of the parties of the Left.

In the absence of a strong Protestant Church offering an
intermediate body of feeling and opinion, the chasm between
the two halves of France, the one religious, clerical, conservative, and military, the other pagan, anti-clerical, radical, and
friendly to the empire of reason in the affairs of the world,
was very deep and wide; and when the issue was squarely
joined in an atmosphere heated by international tension it
seemed as if France might flame up into civil war. The
opposition until 1892 of the Catholic Church, the presence
of the royalist and imperialist parties, the deep grudges left
by the cruel repression of the Commune, and the steady
growth of Socialist and Syndicalist opinion made the task
of republican defence one of exceptional difficulty. Again
and again the existence of the Republic seemed to be imperilled. Though concessions were showered upon democracy,
though the centre of power in the Chamber moved steadily

towards the Left, the dominant party being first conservative then opportunist, then radical, and finally with Briand's advent to power (1910) socialist, yet always the question remained whether a parliament of bourgeois politicians, predominantly secular in their outlook and divided into bitterly hostile groups, would succeed in governing the mettlesome people of France and securing for it a commanding place in the world.

This inner instability of Republican France received two curious illustrations in the last two decades of the nineteenth century. In 1886, as the Presidency of the dull but respectable Grévy was drawing to a somewhat sordid end, the imagination of the country was caught by the figure of a handsome general riding a fine black horse. It was Boulanger, the late 1837- military governor of Tunis. Men, women, and children were 91 infatuated by the brave spectacle of this plumed soldier from the African wars. Was he not the deliverer, the Mahdi, the chieftain, for whom France had long been waiting, and in any case an electoral asset of the first magnitude? The League of Patriots trumpeted the virtues of the favourite. Naquet, the Jew, organized his elections. In constituency after constituency, for his candidature was advanced wherever a vacancy occurred, the general was returned with handsome majorities. There could be no question that in 1886 and 1887 he was the most popular figure in France, at once Minister of War, mouthpiece of the nationalist or war spirit, and the advocate of a wholesale revision of the constitution.

Thrice, seeing that the voters of Paris were behind him, he might have ridden to the Élysée, dispossessed the President, and seized the wheel of government. But he was a man empty of real conviction and devoid of nerve, and as he allowed one chance after another to slip by, courage returned to the civilian rulers of France. It was resolved to bring him to trial, and the threat was enough. With a charge of high treason suspended over his head, the General fled to Brussels 1891 and there, taking his life, relieved the Republic of a great embarrassment.

Even fiercer were the furies which five years later raged round the name of Captain Dreyfus. It is difficult for those who did not live through the feverish years 1894-1903 to form a conception of the passions which were aroused by the fate of this young Jewish officer who had been condemned to deportation by a military tribunal on the charge of betraying military secrets to the Germans. Half France vehemently held that Dreyfus was guilty, the other half with equal vehemence that he had been cruelly wronged. Lifelong friendships were ruptured, the peace of families was ruined, the conscience of individuals was racked and tortured. A furious anti-Semitic campaign in the Catholic press, fortunately unaccompanied by the acts of terrible violence and injustice which have characterized anti-Semitic outbursts in central and eastern Europe, spread its venom through the land. How, it was asked, could this Jew be innocent? How could the soldiers be wrong? How could it accord with the national interest to impeach the honour of the army, which alone stood between France and the German peril? Of what account was justice to the individual when measured against the safety of the State? Morality eventually prevailed. The testimony of Paul Meyer the palaeographer, the denunciations of Zola the novelist, the confession and suicide of Henri the forger, and the courage of Colonel Picquart, a Protestant who risked his military career for the truth, established the innocence of Dreyfus and routed the military and clerical foes of the Republic. Fortified by this triumph of the civilian conscience, the Cabinet of Waldeck-Rousseau, radical at home and Jingo abroad, gave to Republican France its first long spell of firm and steady government.

Seen through enemy eyes the Third French Republic appeared to be deficient in soundness, stability, and repute. The revelation of incompetence in the Franco-Prussian War, the horrors of the Commune, the swift succession of weak ministries, the violence of party factions, the intermittent financial scandals, contributed to give even to the more experienced observers an unduly low opinion of the aptitude of the French people for the arts of government. The reorganization of the army by Freycinet, the brilliant work of soldiers, administrators, and explorers in Africa, the steady efficient mechanism of the Civil Service at home, the essential justice of the social system, went unperceived. It was felt that Frenchmen were being surpassed by the English, the Germans, the Americans. When Déroulède came to Renan in 1888 and asked him to join the League of Patriots, the old savant replied, "Young man, France is dying, do not trouble her agony." It was a common opinion at the end of the nineteenth century that the Latin races had outlived their glory; but the censure was premature. From the Quai d'Orsay in Paris, a diplomatic service second to none in skill, tenacity, and accomplishments was quickly extending French influence through the world and weaving a network of alliances which recalled the shades of Richelieu and Mazarin.

Based on direct and manhood suffrage the Republic survived all attempts to overthrow it. No disfranchised class battered on the doors of the constitution. No privileged order as under previous *régimes* held the fort of authority against the poor. If the Chamber was not highly regarded, the press was free, the local government democratic, the trades unions ever since 1884 legalized and exempt from government interference. Whereas in Russia and Germany socialism was proscribed and therefore dangerous, the Third Republic could find a place for socialists in the Chamber, in the Cabinet, and even in the Élysée. Millerand, the first socialist to sit in a Cabinet (1899), ended an honourable political career as President of the Republic. Briand, borne to the highest places of the state by the seductions of his Celtic eloquence, showed France how a socialist Prime Minister could break a strike, and later become for many years indispensable at the Foreign Office. The fiery Viviani, one of the greatest orators of his own or any other age, was head of the Cabinet when the war broke out. So far from menacing the stability of the Republic, Socialism, robbed of its power to hurt by manhood suffrage, made a brilliant contribution to the Parliamentary life of France.

The more serious danger came from the Right. From time to time Frenchmen asked themselves whether these middle-class politicians were working for the safety and honour of France. Would they recover the lost provinces? Would they not cut down the army? Was not the whole system of lay, centralized education fatal to the development of those local and provincial pieties which nourish the normal strength of a nation? The sentiment of Catholicism, of royalism, of nationalism ranged itself against the free-thinking and secular atmosphere in which the affairs of the country were conducted. Jews, Protestants, cosmopolitans came under suspicion in accordance with the general law that in times of nationalist hysteria the minority creeds are made to suffer. Yet the Republic triumphed even over the nationalists. It broke Boulanger, defeated the anti-Dreyfusards, established the supremacy of the civil over the military power, and curtailed the influence of the Church in education. When the war broke out France was still a land of civilian freedom.

BOOKS WHICH MAY BE CONSULTED

Bainville: *Histoire de France.* 1924.

Hanotaux: *Histoire de la France contemporaine. Tr.* J. C. Tarver. 1903-8.

J. E. C. Bodley: *France.* 1898.

A. Rambaud: *Jules Ferry.* 1903.

F. C. Conybeare: *The Dreyfus Case.* 1895.

J. Reinach: *Histoire de l'affaire Dreyfus,* 6 vols. 1901-8.

Lowes Dickinson: *Revolution and Reaction in France.* 1892.

H. Poincaré: *Au Service de la France.* 1913-26.

A. Rambaud: *Histoire de la civilisation contemporaine en France.* 1932.

A. Thiers: *Notes et Souvenirs de 1870 à 1873.* 1903.

A. Lavy: *L'Oeuvre de Millerand.* 1902.

J. Bainville: *La Troisième Republique.* 1935.

D. Thomson: *Democracy in France: the Third and Fourth Republics.* 2nd Ed. 1952.

D. W. Brogan: *The Development of Modern France,* 1870-1939. 1940.

J. H. Jackson: *Clemenceau and the Third Republic.* 1946.

CHAPTER LXXXV

INTERNATIONAL CURRENTS

The Vatican and Liberalism. The higher criticism. Lyell and Darwin. Herbert Spencer. Karl Marx. The Fabians.

As THE nineteenth century proceeded, the stock of ideas, beliefs, and habits which European men had inherited from long distant times underwent a profound transformation. History and scholarship, economics and physical science, the zeal of reforming prophets and the profuse ingenuity of mechanical inventors, made of Europe in many important respects a new society. Save for one institution everything appeared to be in a state of flux.

The Vatican, a rock set among the swirling tides of the *Risorgimento*, was immovable. The large and generous outlook, the vast learning, the spirit of accommodation with the march of events which distinguished the leaders of liberal Catholicism in Germany and France were foreign to the Italian prelates who stood round the Papal throne and helped, ·in face of the swift encroachments of the secular power, to shape the policy of the Curia. In a series of pronouncements, the bull *Mirari Vos* of 1832, the Syllabus of 1864, the Infallibility decree of 1870, and the numerous encyclicals (1878, 1881, 1888, etc.) of Leo XIII, the Vatican condemned the fashionable intellectual novelties of the day and those free movements of the human mind which had relaxed fidelity to Roman discipline. Socialism, Liberalism, Communism, Bible societies, freedom of conscience, and freedom of the Press were branded as erroneous. In a sweeping sentence which gave great concern to liberal Catholics the Syllabus of 1864 laid it down as error to hold that "the Roman Pontiff can or ought to come to terms with progress, liberalism, or modern civilization." Assailed in his temporal possessions, the Pope roundly defied the unheeding spirit of the age.

In the Protestant half of Europe religious beliefs were

shaped not so much by the authority of a developing church as by the text of the Jewish and Christian scriptures. That ancient corpus of sacred literature was now subjected to minute examination. The Bible began to be treated not as a thing apart but as any other book; it was submitted to those canons of proof and probability which the scrupulous conscience of the historical scholar applies to a classical text or to a mediaeval chronicle. The idea of biblical criticism was not new. Spinoza, the Jewish philosopher of Amsterdam, had already anticipated in his *Tractatus theologico-politicus* (1670) many principles and conclusions which a hundred and sixty years afterwards found favour with the scholars of Tübingen, but it was not until the later half of the nineteenth century that this new way of treating the Bible began generally to influence the outlook of Protestant theologians, and even to win recruits among the modernizing spirits of the Roman Church. The stir created by *Essays and Reviews* in 1860 and by *Lux Mundi* in 1888 marks the stages by which in England first the Broad Church and then the High Church were brought to accept the conclusions of historical science. In France the most commanding literary figure was a religious historian who had broken away from the Roman Church altogether. In a series of volumes marked by extraordinary learning and insight Ernest Renan told the story of the origins of the Christian Church. An exquisite grace and lucidity of style gave to his work a wide appeal. "Who is this Monsieur Renan of whom everyone is speaking?" asked a young lady of the Parisian ballet (1863). "Is he a member of the Jockey Club?" A negative answer quenched further interest in the sentimental author of the *Vie de Jésus*.

A new sense of reality was imparted to biblical studies by the general adoption of historical methods, and although few scholars went so far as David Strauss (1835) and F. C. Conybeare (1909), who either doubted or whittled away the historicity of Christ, there was a general disposition to observe the valuable distinction drawn by Matthew Arnold, the English poet and critic, between literature and dogma and to find the distinctive character of the Bible not in the theological doctrines which it may be thought to define, but in the power which it shares with all sublime literature of filling and exalting the religious imagination of man.

It is seldom, however, that the work of textual critics attracts the attention of the general public. Mankind was not greatly affected by the discovery of the composite character of the book of Genesis or by the news that the story of the Flood might be traced to a Babylonian fable. The general abandonment of the old notions as to the antiquity of the world and the origins of man was the result, not of textual criticism, but of scientific discovery, and in particular of the work of Charles Lyell, whose *Principles of Geology* was published between 1830 and 1834, and Charles Darwin, whose *Origin of Species by means of Natural Selection* appeared in 1859, and was followed twelve years later by his sensational work on the *Descent of Man*.

In the face of this evidence it was no longer possible to accept the narrative of Genesis as other than a religious and poetical allegory. Geology banished the belief, which lingered for two generations in schoolrooms and rectories, that the world was created in 4004. Adam and Eve retreated before Darwin and the biologists. For the familiar story of the garden of Eden and the tree of knowledge there was substituted a picture of "Nature red in tooth and claw," of an unremitting struggle for survival, of a process continued over millions of years of biological evolution through the elimination of the unfit, and of the final emergence of man from the stock of the anthropoid apes at a late stage in the long chronicle of minute, accidental and insensible variations. As a consequence of these discoveries and theories there was in the sixties and seventies of the nineteenth century a great falling away of intellectual men from the tenets of the churches.

Politics, too, were influenced by Darwinism. If biology was the clue to the understanding of the past, might it not also help to shape the future? Could the statesman afford to neglect the biological factor? Was it not his duty to encourage the stronger and to discourage the weaker breeds? Could a society survive which did not either by legislation or custom co-operate with nature in the elimination of the unfit? Was it not the necessary consequence of Darwinian principles that aristocracy was the only sound principle of government, and competition, economic, political, military, the only certain condition of progress? Many thinkers, oblivious of the fact that brilliant minds are not always united to wholesome bodies, thought that consequences of this nature flowed from the oracles of biological science. Huxley, one of Darwin's greatest disciples, did not thus err, but drew a clear distinction between the ruthlessness of the cosmic process and the essential charities of social life.

The influence of the new biological outlook was the more immediate and pervasive in England because it corresponded with a strong vein of individualism in native speculation and practice which had been evident since William Pitt read and was converted by *The Wealth of Nations*. A series of thinkers, remarkable for force, integrity, and direction, had given to one of the most freedom-loving communities of the world a philosophy corresponding to its needs and qualities. In prosperous times self-help is always a popular gospel, and England in the middle decades of the nineteenth century was a prosperous country, full of new fortunes and new men and ample rewards to ambitious industry. The dominant school of economic and political thinking flattered a society of self-made plutocrats and plutocrats in the making. It believed in freedom of trade, in the greatest happiness of the greatest number as the end of the state, and in the need of confining the interference of government within narrow limits. These were the sentiments of Adam Smith, the patriarch of Free Trade; of Jeremy Bentham, the reformer of English law and the seminal mind of English radicalism; of his disciples, James and John Stuart Mill; as well as of David Ricardo, the leading parliamentary oracle on questions of currency and public finance. Every carpet maker and cotton spinner, every millowner and speculative builder, every merchant and shipper was anxious for nothing so much as to be free of government meddling and to be allowed to get rich in his way. The main weight of nonconformist opinion, always critical of government, was thrown into the same scale.

It was in fact from a scion of stiff English nonconformist stock that much of Europe in the later half of the nineteenth century was content to draw its intellectual guidance. Herbert Spencer, though little esteemed among professional philosophers in his own country, for he was self-taught, self-opinionated, and deficient in subtlety, became in his own lifetime a great European figure. In the eighties and nineties he was supreme in Paris and in most of the academies of the Latin and Slavonic world, nor was there any English philosopher of the century who spoke to so wide an audience. This immense renown was due to no grace of style, for Spencer, though a clear, was a clumsy, undistinguished writer, but to the fact that in a generation which had largely ceased to derive its spiritual guidance from the churches Spencer offered a confident philosophy grounded on natural knowledge. Fastidious people were repelled by this downright mining engineer, this radical agnostic from a middle-class home in Derbyshire, who handled English prose with such hearty indifference to its musical subtleties, who despised Latin and Greek, theology and history, who thought Ruskin barbarous and Dante over-ornamented, and wanted to turn the educational system of the country upside down. But for the ordinary man Spencer was a prophet. He took a naturalistic view of the universe. He propounded a synthetic philosophy which offered "a general theory of evolution as exhibited through all orders of existence." His contempt for received opinions, his vast, rambling miscellaneous curiosity, and his extraordinary talent for generalizing about any fact, however trivial, which came within the range of his experience, made him an impressive figure. He wrote of the evolution of man, of the evolution of the family, of the evolution of social and ceremonial institutions. He offered as a general formula of development homogeneity turning into heterogeneity. He saw society passing from a military and despotic into an industrial and democratic phase. Ethics and politics were part of the science of life, a species of "transcendental physiology." In all this there was a kind of robust optimism, an absence of mystic involutions which flattered the philistine reader. Society, becoming industrial, could condemn the unreason and barbarity of war. Government itself, being a deciduous organ and a remnant of the predatory state, would, as civilization advanced, contract its functions. In time it would be seen that education had been hitherto based upon the most absurd lack of proportion, that "two local groups of facts and figures (i.e., Greek and Roman history), filling a relatively minute space in the genesis of the world, which is in itself but an infinitesimal part of the universe," had been allowed to dominate the field of vision, to the exclusion of the vital truths of physical nature.

People liked to hear all this. They felt that it was new, important, revolutionary. Moreover, they could understand, or believed that they could understand, this plain-spoken philosopher who criticized the accepted views so boldly and offered so large an assortment of confident opinions on every branch of knowledge. The middle class in particular were well disposed to a thinker who, so far from having a good word to say for socialism, was strongly opposed to any form of meddlesome interference by the state.

Yet for all his wide reputation Spencer was a voice crying in the wilderness. Despite his protest, the state interfered with industry, educated children, supported a church, organized public health. If on that side of his philosophy which offered a naturalistic interpretation of the universe he spoke for a large and constantly growing body of opinion, as the prophet of individualism in politics he made no converts. The whole stream of tendency was flowing swift and strong in the opposite direction.

The prophet of the socialist movement was a man as extraordinary for the glow and tenacity of his fanaticism as Mahomet himself. The name of Karl Marx (1818-83) has already been mentioned in these pages. He was the son of a respectable middle-class Jewish family from the Rhineland who sprang into sudden notoriety during the revolutionary troubles of the '48 with an epoch-making communist manifesto.[1] In this flaming document Marx put out a new philosophy of history, a new programme of revolutionary reform, and a new call for international action. He argued that the bourgeoisie had brought into existence its antithesis the proletariat, that the struggle between these two classes was the key to modern history, that the class-conscious section of the proletariat were the communists, and that the communists would be content with nothing less than the "violent overthrow of the whole contemporary social order." Ten immediate reforms, many of them beneficial and since widely adopted by the bourgeois Parliaments whom Marx covered with his hatred and contempt, were then enumerated. But

See Appendix A.

how could a revolutionary admit that desirable changes might be effected by national governments or middle-class legislation? Marx hated nationality with the rancour of an outcast, despised liberty with the arrogance of a despot, and throughout his life lost no opportunity of assailing the class from which he was himself sprung. The vital division of human society was not in the view of this fierce cosmopolitan atheist based on religion or nationality, but upon class. There was no common interest between German employers and German workers, but a common interest among the workers of the world to put an end to the capitalists by whom they were exploited. "Let the governing classes," he concluded, "tremble before the communist revolution. The proletarians have nothing to lose in it but their chains. They have the whole world to gain. Proletarians of all countries, unite."

After the failure of the revolutionary movement on the continent Marx settled in London and there spent the last thirty-four years of his life, always in desperate straits for money, but at every crisis of his pecuniary humiliations helped from the generous purse of Frederick Engels, a German socialist friend and the son of a prosperous cotton spinner with a factory in Manchester. An inspiring presence, a clear, confident, powerful intellect, a fierce domineering temper, a brilliant gift of mordant conversation would have made Marx a distinguished, if disagreeable, figure in any company. "He combined," wrote H. M. Hyndman, "with his commanding forehead and great overhanging brow, his fierce glittering eyes, broad sensitive nose, and mobile mouth, all surrounded by a setting of untrimmed hair and beard, the righteous fury of the great seers of his race with the cold analytical power of Spinoza and the Jewish doctors." Writing in England and nourished by the material relating to English factory life which he procured in the reading room of the British Museum, Marx composed the weighty book on Capital which all the world over has been accepted as the Bible of the Proletariat.

Of the many million Marxists who are now scattered through Europe, few, it may be confidently surmised, have faced the labour of reading through the three long volumes which constitute the sacred text of the Communist religion. The influence of Marx does not depend upon the elaborate

and untenable economic demonstration by which it is sought
to prove that value is congealed labour, or that the surplus
value created by labour over and above the return to fixed
capital is always annexed by the capitalist as profit, or that as
the rich become richer the poor become poorer. Marx,
though a genius, was indifferent as a philosopher and
economist, and as a writer had but an imperfect mastery over
the English tongue. The power of this needy, passionate
exile proceeds from the fact that he was always a prophet of
revolution, attacking with concentrated fury the whole
system of society which offered so sleek a surface to the sky
and demonstrating with an arrogant confidence that throughout history the poor had been despoiled by the rich and were
now by an inexorable law of human progress ordained in
their turn to despoil.

Men are so constituted that they are prone to support a
cause which they believe to be assured of victory. It was
the achievement of this Jewish visionary that he persuaded
the intellectuals of the proletariat in many lands that the
hour of their triumph was at hand. He offered a formula of
human progress suggested by Hegelian philosophy, but in
some important particulars differing from Hegel, which
seemed to set the past, the present, and the future of humanity
in a logical and necessary sequence. Primitive communism
had given way to feudal society, feudal society had been sup-
planted by the capitalistic bourgeoisie, the bourgeoisie were
now to be expropriated by the proletariat. All history was a
struggle of classes for the material goods of life. Class hatred,
class war was the prime law of change. The dictatorship of
the capitalists would be followed by the dictatorship of the
proletariat, and this in turn by a classless society, which
would be the ultimate end of the long and savage scramble
for material things. As for capitalism, it carried within itself
the seeds of its own doom. In a passage which has been often
cited Marx describes the predestined overthrow of the capitalistic system, how as time proceeds businesses become larger,
capitalists become fewer, and the mass of poverty and oppression, of degeneration and exploitation, becomes corres-
pondingly greater. At last the system perishes of its excesses.
The working class, which has grown in number, is developed,
unified, and organized by the very mechanism of capitalistic

production. As they contemplate the growing power of capitalistic monopoly and contrast the opulence of the fortunate with their own ascending scale of misery and want, the wrath of the workers explodes. The inevitable happens. "The centralization of the means of production and the socialization of labour reach a point where they prove incompatible with the capitalistic husk. This bursts asunder. The knell of capitalistic private property sounds. The expropriators are expropriated."

The course of European events was destined to give little comfort to those who placed their faith in a world-wide war of classes. The First International, founded in 1864 to bring the workers of many lands together, was feebly supported, riven with internal discords, and short-lived. Shattered by the Franco-Prussian War, it petered out after an inglorious thirteen years of squalls and squabbles in New York. The Great War was lethal to the Second International, a body rich in political talent,[1] the sinister influence of Moscow to the wider influence of the Third. The hope that internationally organized labour might avert national wars or improve the lot of the workers has been signally falsified in the event. National rivalries have proved stronger than class interests, patriotic and local sentiments than the loyalty to an economic grouping. Forces acting within the boundaries of individual nations, not the resolutions of international labour, have achieved whatever has so far been accomplished in the domain of social reform.

In England, the main scene of his labours, Marx was during his own lifetime almost a cypher. Here socialism did not spring from the brain of a prophet, but was the inevitable result of human compassion working on the circumstances of urban life. Parliament legislated to protect labour, labour organized itself in trades unions or co-operative societies to safeguard its standard of life, and intelligent municipal reformers like Joseph Chamberlain of Birmingham cleared out the slums, reduced the infantile death rate, and brought education and amenities within reach of the poor. While Marx was composing his indictment of English capitalism, measures were passed by Liberals and Conservatives which

[1] It contained Lenin, Mussolini, Briand, Ramsay MacDonald, Liebknecht, Laval, Vandervelde, Pilsudski, Bernard Shaw.

deprived the system of many of its evils. The great voices of Thomas Carlyle and William Morris stirred the social conscience. In the more pedestrian sphere of economics a band of able socialist thinkers, styling themselves Fabians,[1] noted the steady drift towards the collective regulation of industry which was proceeding around them and crowned the process with their applause. In a series of valuable publications the history of the trades union movement was narrated, the anatomy of the new industrial democracy was described, and the development of State and municipal enterprise heartily encouraged. Boldly attacking the Manchester doctrine of *laissez-faire* and the old Treasury tenet that money should be allowed to fructify in the pockets of the taxpayer, the Fabians advocated public expenditure for public ends. The country was told that the worker was entitled to a national minimum of education and health, of leisure and of wages. The *Zeitgeist* smiled on the generous doctrine. While the red star of Marx shone faint and distant through the English mists, the industrious Fabians, living in bourgeois comfort, and preaching "the inevitability of gradualism," stamped their thought again and again upon the pages of the English Statute Book.

Even where the pinch of poverty was most bitterly felt the Marxian doctrine of world-wide class hatred and systematic atheism found little acceptance. Hyndman, the bluff well-to-do Etonian cricketer turned Marxist who founded the Social Democratic Federation, was an inconsiderable figure when compared with John Burns, the un-theoretical leader of the Dockers' strike, or Keir Hardie, the Scottish miner and religious mystic, who, out of the depths of his devout fanaticism, founded the Independent Labour Party. British socialism was a characteristically native product, deeply penetrated by evangelical feeling, and akin to the popular religious movements, Cameronian, Methodist, Revivalist, which from time to time stir the religious consciousness of the British people to new hopes and visions. The element of fierce class hatred which inspired continental movements was absent. "The working man," as Bernard Shaw observed, "respects the bourgeoisie and wants to be a bourgeois: Marx never got hold of him for a moment."

[1] G. Bernard Shaw, Sidney and Beatrice Webb, Graham Wallas, etc.

Meanwhile the gospel of Marx was spreading fast among the workers and intellectuals on the Continent. In Italy, in France, and, above all, in Russia, Marxist doctrines began from the nineties of the last century to captivate the imagination of many of the foremost minds of the younger generation. Poets and professors, teachers and artisans embraced the theory of the class struggle, the iron law of wages, and of the coming triumph of the Proletariat. Ada Negri, an elementary schoolmistress in Lombardy, distilled socialism into her popular lyric verse. Filippo Turati, another Lombard poet, founded a socialist journal. Within the span of a decade Marx had dethroned Herbert Spencer as the leading oracle of political and economic wisdom among the Italians. His fame was bruited in the streets and the factories; the general strike of 1904 attested his posthumous authority. While scholars were finding inspiration in the classical verse of Carducci the Republican, and romantics were entranced by the flowing eloquence of d'Annunzio, the prince of poetical decadents and imperialists, the silk workers of Milan found salvation in Marx. Indeed, the more backward the country, the more likely it was that the influence of that revolutionary thinker would become decisive. In Russia, where the standard of life was unsheltered by trades unions, the teaching of Marx, once introduced into the factories and comprehended in outline, speedily asserted its ascendancy.

BOOKS WHICH MAY BE CONSULTED

Seignobos: *History of Contemporary Europe.* 1909.
Leslie Stephen: *The English Utilitarians.* 1900.
Herbert Spencer: *Social Statics.* 1892.
Herbert Spencer: *The Man versus the State.* 1909.
Herbert Spencer: *Autobiography.* 1904.
E. H. Carr: *Karl Marx.* 1934.
Fabian Essays in Socialism. Ed. G. B. Shaw. 1931.
S. and B. Webb: *History of Trades Unionism.* 1920.
S. and B. Webb: *Industrial Democracy.* 1920.
Charles Darwin: *Origin of Species.* 1859.
Charles Darwin: *Descent of Man.* 1871.
Croce: *History of Italy. Tr.* C. M. Ady. 1929.
Acton: *The History of Freedom and Other Essays.* 1907.

E. L. Woodward: *Three Studies in European Conservatism*. 1929.

F. Nielsen: *The History of the Papacy in the Nineteenth Century*. 1906.

Edmund Wilson: *To the Finland Station*. 1941.

E. H. Carr: *Nationalism and After*. 1945.

E. Halévy: *The Growth of Philosophic Radicalism*. *Tr*. M. Morris. 1952.

CHAPTER LXXXVI

BRITISH RULE IN INDIA

WE HAVE now in the course of our narrative to draw attention to two matters which, though falling outside the scope of a European History, deserve a brief note from the light which they throw upon the character of one of the chief European nations. The first of these is the British conquest and administration of India; the second the stand taken by Great Britain in the campaign against slavery and the slave trade. The conquest of India was never planned, but arose out of the need which English traders in that country experienced of creating the measure of order and settled justice without which commerce cannot flourish. The confusion of India which ensued upon the dissolution of the Mogul Empire gave the English an opportunity for which they had not sought, but were able to improve. As a great American moralist[1] has said, "India fell to British character." The English succeeded in conquering India because they brought with them peace and deliverance from oppression. Their achievement has been remarkable. They have preserved India from foreign attack, and given it the blessing of unbroken internal peace and freedom of trade. There is not an acre of British India the title to which is not inscribed in the books of the British administration and protected by the force of British law. Some forty million acres of desert have been reclaimed for cultivation by the art of British irrigation engineers. Though the number of Englishmen engaged on

1707

---

[1] R. W. Emerson, quoted by the Marquis of Zetland: *Steps towards Indian Home Rule*.

the administration has at no time exceeded five thousand, this alien people has so administered the country that the population has increased by more than 230 millions. Such measure of intellectual and political unity as may now be found in India is due to the English conquest and administration. The one common language which goes from end to end of the sub-continent, the one common medium of higher instruction, necessary, however regrettable, by reason of the great diversity of Indian tongues, is the language of England. At every political gathering of Indians debate is conducted in the idiom of the distant European island. It has sometimes been charged against the British administration of India that ninety per cent. of the population (350 millions in 1921) are still illiterate. It is forgotten by those who launch this accusation that the spread of education is subject to three crippling disadvantages which are not present in any European country. The first and least important of these is an extraordinary diversity of languages and creeds; the second, the prevalence of child marriage, which so decimates the girl population of India that there is a surplus of twelve million males; and the third, the impossibility by reason of the social customs of India of using unmarried women teachers in elementary schools. To anyone who surveys the landscape of elementary education in Europe and America, this last reason alone is sufficient to explain the general illiteracy of the Indian people.

What, however, is most to be remarked as an indication of English character is not the failure of this northern state to give to Indians a complete system of elementary education such as was only with difficulty established in England itself in 1870, but its resolve to impart freely to the natives of India the benefits of Western knowledge. Under the confident guidance of Macaulay, the first legal member of the Council of the Governor-General, it was decided that the peoples of India should be educated in the language, the literature, and the science of their European conquerors. The policy, though founded upon a defective sympathy with the intellectual tradition of the East, and much overdriven, was nevertheless inspired by the generous desire that India should participate in all that was good and precious in the civilization of the conquerors. The results have been surprising. A large class of intelligent lawyers, administrators, officials, teachers, and politicians have absorbed, with uncanny facility, the language and the ideas of Britain. They read English books, pass English examinations, act English plays, cite English law cases, and both as pleaders and Parliamentarians give evidence of 1833 marked dexterity. The fruit of Macaulay's famous minute on Indian education is the development in India not only of an excellent official class, some two million in number, but of a body of educated politicians who, having been taught out of English books to admire liberty, argue that what is good for the English must be good for themselves, and confront the ruling race with a challenge based upon its own doctrines of freedom and progress.

A hundred years lie between the battle of Plassey and the end of the East India Company. The India Act of 1858, which brought the Indian Empire under the direct control of the British Crown, acting through a Secretary of State, marks an end of the period of conquest and inaugurates an era of consolidation and peace. Yet, even during the century when the British were extending their rule by force of arms through central and western India and in the Punjab, their best representatives considered themselves as responsible for the welfare of the native inhabitants. That was the view of Hastings and Wellesley, of Bentinck, Dalhousie, and the Lawrences. The Whigs who passed the Reform Act of 1832 regarded Liberalism not as an article for domestic consumption only, but as a recipe for successful government all over the world. The Indian Charter of 1833 lays down the two great principles that "the interests of the native subjects are to be preferred to those of Europeans wherever the two come into conflict," and that "no native of India or natural born subject of His Majesty shall be disabled from holding any place, office, or 1857 employment by reason of his religion, place of birth, descent or colour." After the Indian Mutiny, when it might perhaps have been expected that the Government would have been swept out of its steady course by the tide of racial passion, the same attitude of paternal tolerance was persevered in. A royal proclamation announced that the rights of the Indian Princes would be respected, that equal protection would be given to all religions, and that all subjects of the Crown without regard to race and creed would be admitted to all offices. Of these important engagements the first two have been scrupulously observed, and the third conceded by slow and guarded stages.

The substantial success of British government in India is attested by the fact that there has been no widespread attempt to overturn it. The Mutiny was not a general rising, but was a military revolt, partial in extent, and quelled with the assistance of Indian levies drawn from the Punjab. Though the outbreak was marked by deplorable atrocities, not on one side only, which left bitter memories, it was succeeded by a period of humane and prudent administration, which, in its endeavour to soothe the religious susceptibilities of the people, erred, if anything, on the side of timidity. In the Great War, when the resources of the Empire were strained to the breaking point, the princes and peoples of India were loyal to the British connexion. Had the British Raj been harsh or oppressive, or adamant against the growing insistence of educated Indians to be admitted to a share in the government, Britain's peril would have been seized as India's opportunity.

Since the Mutiny British India has been ruled by a bureaucracy recruited by open competition. The advantage to India of a government exempt from irregularity, caprice, and corruption, and dealing out even-handed justice irrespective of caste and creed, has been generally acknowledged. The British members of the Indian Public Services have perhaps more nearly than any other ruling class realized the ideal of disinterested government which Plato thought could be secured only if the guardians of the State were shielded from the temptations of ownership and family. Their task has been exacting: to suppress crime, to provide for the needs of a modern state out of the scanty resources of a poor oriental community, to promote the unwelcome novelties of education and hygiene among a backward and superstitious peasantry, and to act as a buffer between hostile creeds and communities.

A political spectacle somewhat analogous to the Indian Empire in the decades before the war would be presented by Europe if we could conceive of it as being inspired for the most part by the mentality of a Tyrolean peasant, disarmed, formed into a single free-trade area, governed by a handful of intelligent and benevolent Chinamen, protected by Chinese junks on sea, and on land by an army mainly stationed on the Urals and consisting of about a hundred and fifty thousand European and seventy-five thousand Chinese troops. That a population of three hundred and fifty millions should be defended by a force not much greater than that which is required for the protection of Belgium is proof that the rule of the British in India commends itself to the great mass of the Indian people.

It has been among the wiser aims of British policy in an increasing measure to associate patriotic and educated Indians in the tasks of government. At first Indians were only admitted to subordinate posts. Before the war they held judgeships in the High Courts and were claiming half the places in the Imperial Civil Service. The seed of parliamentary life, which has now flowered into a mighty tree, was sown as far back as 1861, when a few nominated Indians were summoned to the Legislative Council of the Governor-General.

An all-pervading passion of nationalism, quite foreign to the times of Clive and Warren Hastings, and foreign also to he generation of the Mutiny, has made the task of the Englishman in India more difficult than it was of old. The white skin which in the first century of British rule was a passport to veneration is now, in the eyes of many educated and semi-educated Indians, an affront. Colour feeling is more intense. The removal of the foreign element in the government has become, not indeed an unusual, but an ordinary object of ambition among that small fraction of the population which concerns itself with politics. The students dream of *Swaraj* at the college, and the pressmen and politicians are hot in its pursuit. From the success of the Japanese in
1905 their Russian war it is inferred that the Orient has no further reason to abase itself before the West.

Indian nationalism is a fabric which, with infinite gradations of shade and colour, tends to assume one of two dominant patterns, the first western and constitutional, the second eastern and revolutionary. There is a school of intelligent Indians, who have been soaked in the philosophy of Victorian liberalism and have followed with ardent attention the course of the nationalist and emancipating movements in the West. They have noted the liberation of the American colonies, the grant of responsible government to the British Dominions, the ascending pressure and success of the Irish movement for Home Rule; and they conclude that what has been found good in other parts of the British Empire must be good also for the peoples of India. Their vision of the India of the future is, accordingly, that of a self-governing Dominion of the Crown, like Australia or Canada, equipped with democratic Parliaments and holding its own through the spread of Western enlightenment among the modern nations of the world. These men do not seek revolution. Believing that national independence is on its way, they desire, by the application of steady political pressure within constitutional limits, to accelerate its approach. G. K. Gokhale, the d. founder of the Servants of India and himself an accom- 1914 plished Parliamentarian, was a protagonist, at once subtle and saintly, of this school of thinking.

Others place little value upon Western novelties and maintain that everything precious for Indian life is to be found in the Vedas. They believe in India as a nation but not in India as a Parliamentary democracy. Such was the philosophy of Dayanananda, the founder of the *Arya Samaj*, an association for the revivial of the ancient Hindu spirit, and such essentially was the outlook of P. J. Tilak, the formidable Brahmin who d. organized a violent resistance to the British *Raj* in the Deccan 1919 during the nineties of the last century. It was characteristic of the extreme conservatism of this powerful revolutionary demagogue that he opposed the Age of Consent Bill which was designed to reduce what is generally considered to be the worst blot on the social system of India, the evil of child marriage.

It is possible that British administrators in India have been too stiff in their resistance to these new formations of opinion. Officials crushed by a heavy burden of work in a trying climate cannot be expected to welcome the shock of disturbing ideas such as may impair the efficiency of their smooth and intricate machine. The Indian Civil Service has presented a very cold shoulder to the politicians of the Indian Congress, who, since 1885, have been busy in working up a National Movement, and they have paid little heed to the unceasing attacks of the vernacular press. A certain contemptuous indifference natural to the agents of a benevolent Power which has long usurped the rôle of Providence, has marked the relations of the official world to the effervescent nationalism of the young. Nevertheless, the Service has worked with characteristic loyalty the plans which liberally-minded Cabinets, Secretaries of State, or Viceroys have devised for the contentment of Indian politicians. Lord Ripon's Municipal Councils, the Morley-Minto non-responsible Legislatures of 1909, the dyarchy of the Montagu-Chelmsford Scheme of 1917, under which the nation-building services (local government, education, etc.) were transferred to Indian Cabinets responsible to elected Indian legislatures, while the security services (army, police, etc.) were retained in the hands of the officials, all these successive instalments of political liberty, however unwelcome to the bureaucratic mind, have been recognized as inevitable. That Indian nationalism must colour British policy in India is now a belief common to all sections of British opinion. Already the Parliament in Delhi makes an Indian tariff and checks the imports of British goods in the interests of the Indian producer. Already "dyarchy," introduced as an immense concession in 1917, has failed to satisfy. A self-governing, all-Indian Federation, including the Princes,[1] and with certain safeguards for the maintenance of the Imperial connexion, is now the declared aim of leading statesmen in both countries and embodied in a statute. So far and so fast has Britain been prepared to advance along this perilous road, guided by the two lodestars of the Anglo-Saxon race, of which the first is that all government must rest upon consent, and the second that it is the office of statesmanship to avert revolution by reform.

"East is east and west is west." Indian character and Indian standards present always, in the last analysis, something which baffles the Western observer. In the religious atmosphere of India, where the things of this world are apt to be regarded as dust, the values of life experience an inversion. Otherworldliness ranks before efficiency, learning is in greater esteem than practical vigour. A saint who starves himself in public is widely honoured; a social reformer who clears slums, bridles usurers or battles with the plague is likely to encounter more opposition than applause. Lord Curzon left India an

[1] The Native states, some 700 in number, cover nearly two-fifths of the total area of India.

unpopular figure despite splendid services to agriculture, education, archaeology, and to the general welfare of the Indian people. The hero acclaimed among Indians during the last two decades is a man as different from the dazzling English administrator as it is possible to conceive. Mr. Gandhi has many qualities which, had his lot been cast in a Western land, would have brought him to the front of political life: great personal charm, ardent patriotism, brilliant dialectical ability, a keen eye for publicity, subtlety in attack and defence, a distinguished command of the English language. Such qualities, pertaining as they do to the Western category of political virtues, are easily appreciated by Englishmen. But this little Hindu lawyer who has given so much trouble to the British *Raj* as organizer of a boycott of British goods and as the leader in a campaign of civil disobedience, presents other aspects which perplex and elude. An indubitable saint yet as a member of the money-lending caste a friend to usury, an ardent patriot yet as a politician the beneficiary of the worst slum properties in India, a declared opponent of Western modernism yet not averse from availing himself of the convenience of a Ford car, Mr. Gandhi is an epitome of those picturesque and baffling contrasts which offer so remarkable and exciting a challenge to the patience and prudence of the West.

BOOKS WHICH MAY BE CONSULTED

A. C. Lyall: *The Rise of the British Dominion in India.* 1910.

T. W. Holderness: *Peoples and Problems of India.* (Home University Library.) 1912.

E. Thompson and E. Garratt: *Rise and Fulfilment of British Rule in India.* 1934.

Sir Courtenay Ilbert: *The Government of India.* 1913.

W. W. Hunter: *The Indian Empire.* 1893.

W. W. Hunter: *The Marquis of Dalhousie.* 1890.

T. Rice Holmes: *History of the Indian Mutiny.* 1898.

Marquis of Zetland: *Life of Lord Curzon.* 1928.

R. Temple: *Lord Lawrence.* 1889.

Indian Statutory Commission, 2 vols. Cd. 3568, 3569, XI, 1929-30. (Simon Report.)

Sir Percival Griffiths: *The British Impact on India.* 1952.

P. E. Roberts: *History of British India*. 3rd. Ed. 1952.
P. Woodruff: *The men who ruled India*. 2 vols. 1953-4.
Sir Reginald Coupland: *Britain and India* 1600-1947, rev. ed. 1948.

CHAPTER LXXXVII

EUROPE AND SLAVERY

Slavery in antiquity. Mediaeval serfdom. Plantation slavery in the New World. Relative humanity of Spain. The English slave trade. Movement for abolition. The Emancipators. Importance of Parliament. The Wesleyans. The Economists. The Acts of 1807 and 1833. The fight against the foreign slave trade. Livingstone in Africa. The humanitarian note in modern legislation.

IN THE history of Europe so far as it is known to us there are two chapters marked by a special note of infamy. The first was when the pillagers and pirates of the Roman Republic threw themselves upon the ill-defended opulence of the East, when the Aegean Sea was infested with slavers, and Delos (becoming a free port in 146 B.C.) obtained a hateful renown as the centre of the European slave trade, in which, if we are to believe Strabo, as many as ten thousand slaves would be bought and sold in a single day. But this period of rapine and wreckage, terrible indeed while it lasted, was fortunately short. The good government of the Empire put down slave-raiding; the gentle and humane philosophy of the Stoics softened and elevated the condition of the slave. If there was no movement to abolish slavery, the institution was gradually stripped of its worst evils, passing into predial serfdom and villenage in the fields, and becoming compatible with the exercise of many skilled and refined occupations in the cities. The Roman slave in the later Empire was often a freeman in everything but name. He had been taken into the social fabric of his masters, shared their studies and ideas, contributed to their arts and crafts, and often exercised a positive influence on the direction of affairs. Epictetus, one of the noblest and wisest of Stoic philosophers, endured without repining the status of a slave. The free play of human feeling in private life, the growing sense of responsibility in government, the influence of Christianity, the organization of the Asiatic and African provinces of the Empire, and the absence of those mechanical improvements which inevitably lead to mass production, continued to abridge the number, to improve the lot, and to lessen the industrial importance of the slave population.

Nor was there any serious recrudescence of the evil consequent on the break-up of the Roman Empire. In the middle ages, since agrarian serfdom was widely spread and the demand for urban labour was easily satisfied, the slave trade was a minor evil, flourishing chiefly along the coasts of the Black Sea, but on a scale which bears no comparison either with the slave-raiding operations of the Roman Republic or with the second great spasm of rapine which ensued upon the discovery of the new world.

It is a terrible commentary on Christian civilization that the longest period of slave-raiding known to history was initiated by the action of Spain and Portugal, France, Holland, and Britain after the Christian faith had for more than a thousand years been the established religion of western Europe; and it is the graver since the new slavery was worse and more inhuman than the old. In the ancient world domestic slavery, which was educative and often humane, was more important than the slavery of the mine and the plantation. In the new world this was otherwise. Mass production had come into its own. The demand of Europe for sugar, tobacco, and cotton was fed by the labour of African slaves, herded in barracks, working in gangs, and regimented, as they had been recruited, by soulless and mercenary violence.

Among the slave-raiding countries of the West who opened out this new chapter in human atrocity Spain is distinguished for a relative humanity. In the initial as in the concluding stages of her overseas Empire the cruelty of Spain towards her slave population in the American colonies was as great as that of any other country; but there was a long intermediate period during which the Roman Church honourably endeavoured to improve the lot of the labouring population in the Spanish colonies. The slave was baptized, prepared for the Mass, retained in his family group, and brought through his membership of the Church within the system of Spain. For the British colonies the Church of England made no comparable effort. "It is no more calculated for the negro," said Canning, "than for the brute animal that shares his toil." While the Spanish Church pressed forward on its missionary enterprise, the British planters looked with active disfavour on the attempt to spread among the blacks the disturbing ferment of Christian belief. To this attitude the Anglican Church offered no effective resistance.

The comparative inability of the Protestant religion to moderate the horrors of this infamous traffic is the more serious by reason of the fact that of all European slave traders the British were the most successful and consequently the most guilty. It has been calculated that the total number of slaves imported into the English colonies from Africa between 1680 and 1786 was well over two millions. Statesmen like Chatham supported the trade as a pillar of national strength; to sailors like Nelson it was an essential prop of the mercantile marine. The prosperity of Liverpool and in large part also of Bristol was built on the slave trade. Formidable, therefore, was the task of attacking the immense vested interests bound up in slavery. In the eighteenth century no colonies were so valuable as the sugar islands of the West Indies, and, since these were cultivated by African slave labour, the whole West Indian interest was arrayed against any proposal to abate or destroy the traffic upon which its profits depended. When to this powerful group is added the number of Englishmen who were concerned with the slave-grown crops of the American continent, and the vast body of American opinion which, at any time previous to the severance of the tie between the American colonies and the mother country, could be mobilized in defence of American slavery, the prospect of uprooting the institution may well have seemed desperate.

Yet it was from Britain, the largest slave trader and the greatest offender, that the movement sprang which success-fully abolished slavery in the British isles (1772), then the slave trade (1806), then slavery itself in the British Dominions (1833), and finally so worked upon the conscience of the world as to secure a large and nearly universal concurrence of action for the extirpation of the evil. The credit for securing from Lord Mansfield the famous decision in the case of James Somersett (1772) that the status of slavery was unknown to the common law of England was due to Granville Sharp, a civil servant, inconspicuous in wealth and station, but of a rare warmth of heart and persistence of character, who, once fired by the cruel usage of a negro slave in the streets of London, never rested until he had obtained the verdict which for ever afterwards rid the British islands of the taint of slavery. Thereafter comes a roll of English emancipators whose names even in a general history of Europe are worthy of commemoration: William Wilberforce, Thomas Clarkson, Zachary Macaulay, and James Stephen, whose preparatory labours, sustained over a period of twenty years, enabled Fox to carry the abolition of the slave trade; Thomas Fowell Buxton, the Parliamentary leader of the Abolitionists, who worked up the House of Commons to abolish slavery; and Brougham, who carried the torch through the country; Palmerston, who stopped the slave trade between Portugal and Brazil; and the noble group of missionaries, soldiers, and statesmen, David Livingstone, Charles Gordon, Sir John Kirk, and Lord Lugard, by whose efforts in large measure Africa has been opened up and rid of the curse of the Arab slave-raider. Lecky does no more than justice when he states that the crusade of England against slavery "may probably be regarded as among the three or four perfectly virtuous pages in the history of nations."

The cause of abolition was undoubtedly helped by the successful revolt of the American colonies, which removed a powerful body of pro-slavery opinion from the arena of controversy, and by the Irish Union, which brought into the English House of Commons a body of Irish voters who had no commercial interests to serve and were capable of responding to the abstract call of liberty and justice. These adventitious aids do not, however, explain how it was that a small body of men, none of them in the first rank of politics, were able to master the organized opposition of a lucrative trade which had come to be regarded as essential to national prosperity and naval strength. The fact could not have been accomplished without Parliament. It was because England possessed in the House of Commons an assembly in which hidden things could be brought to light and shameful things exposed in their shamefulness, that it was possible so to indoctrinate the nation with the hatefulness of slavery as to overcome the strong material forces enlisted in its support. It is not without significance that William Wilberforce, the Parliamentary leader of the Abolitionists, was known as the "Nightingale of the House," and that the abolition of the slave trade was carried in 1807 by Charles James Fox, the greatest Parliamentary orator of his time.

Behind this Parliamentary agitation was a movement proceeding from those deep religious and moral impulses which in the later part of the eighteenth century were specially distinctive of the Quaker and Methodist bodies. The committee of six which first (1783) organized a regular anti-slavery campaign in the country was a committee of Quakers. "The Clapham Sect," as the circle of Wilberforce came to be called, was deeply affected by the modes of quickened personal religious experience which John Wesley had preached and by his example recommended. Though other influences co-operated, though Adam Smith contributed his economic good sense, and Jeremy Bentham his rational humanitarianism, the predominant force which made abolition possible was a devout sense of religion and morality informing the lives and so dominating the consciences of a small knot of high-minded and energetic Englishmen that they could not rest until a great wrong had been righted.

The immediate effect of Lord Mansfield's judgment, the first victory in a long campaign, was to liberate some fifteen thousand negroes who had been introduced by their masters into England and were there freely bought and sold. The second stage in the operations was the more difficult and protracted assault upon the slave trade. Again and again, despite the combined influence of Wilberforce and Pitt, motions to abolish the trade were defeated by the slave-owning interest in the Cabinet, in the House, and in the country. Then Pitt died, and Fox, with the aid of the Irish votes, abolished the trade just before slave-grown cotton began to pour into Lancashire, and consequently before Lancashire was supplied with a motive for joining hands with the sugar interest in defence of slavery. The Act was passed in the nick of time, and in 1811 was made truly effective by a law which fixed upon slave trading the guilt of felony and the punishment of deportation.

When it is remembered that the slave trade was put down in the middle of a life-and-death struggle with Napoleon and that every sailor from Nelson downwards declared that its abolition would be the ruin of the British Navy, the courage of Pitt and Fox in utterly disregarding the advice of their naval experts and in steadily pressing even in war-time for the removal of this great outrage on humanity is truly to be admired. Not for the first or last time the wider wisdom of civilian leaders over-ruled the confident counsels of the fighting services.

It was then in her new and striking character of an abolitionist State that England entered the Congress of Vienna and there obtained from the eight leading powers a solemn declaration that the universal abolition of the slave trade was a measure "peculiarly worthy of their attention and conformable to the spirit of the times." To obtain the abolition of the foreign slave trade and of the institution of slavery in the British colonies became henceforth a main object of British policy, steadily and honestly pursued, and engaging the passionate interest of the serious-minded portion of the nation. Eventually Parliament, finding that it was useless to try to persuade colonial assemblies to abolish the institution of slavery, decided to legislate over their heads. In August, 1833, a Bill was passed for the abolition of slavery in all the British Dominions. A sum of twenty millions had already been voted for the compensation of the owners.

The effort to fight the foreign slave trade was, from the nature of things, far more difficult. Only in 1831 did France, only in 1835 did Spain, impose effective penalties against the offence of slave trading, and meanwhile Britain alone took adequate steps to ensure that the law against slave trading was strictly and continuously enforced. Owing to the fact that the United States objected to the exercise of the right of search by British vessels and provided no patrol of her own, most slave traders secured impunity by flying the stars and stripes. More particularly did the slave trade in Cuba flourish until Abraham Lincoln's decree of emancipation (1862).

Much was accomplished by the system of maritime patrols,

though far less than would actually have been achieved had all the maritime Powers contributed their due quota. The destruction of the Portuguese slave trade with the western hemisphere was made possible only by the vigour of the British navy.

There remained the difficult and almost intractable problem of liberating Africa from the Arab slave gangs and the domestic slave trade which was carried on in the heart of the continent. A system of marine patrols, however excellent—and in the forties a sixth of the British navy was employed on African patrol work—was clearly inadequate to cope with so vast an evil. The career of David Livingstone, the Scottish missionary, who, mostly on foot and with few native companions, crossed Africa between 1853 and 1856, opened out a new epoch and pointed to a new way. Livingstone's African journeys brought home to the imagination of the British public the horrors of the Arab slave trade, which had its centre in Zanzibar, and led to a revival of Abolitionist activity, the first-fruit of which was the treaty between Britain and Zanzibar in 1873, which closed the great slave mart in that city. From this time a conviction steadily grew that unless the African continent were opened up, settled with farmers and missionaries, and brought under the control of the European Powers, the poison of slavery would never be fully eliminated. The peaceful partition of Africa among the leading European States, which was perhaps the most striking achievement of European statecraft in the eighties and nineties of the last century, enabled this policy to be carried forward. Other European countries beside Britain were now prepared to take vigorous action for the suppression of slavery and the improvement of social conditions in Africa. The Brussels conference of 1889, convoked by King Leopold of Belgium on the suggestion of the British Government, and attended by the representatives of seventeen states, resulted in an act (ratified in 1892) which has been termed the Magna Carta of the African slave, so complete and far-reaching were the provisions which the participating states, which included Persia, Zanzibar, and the Turkish Empire, bound themselves to adopt. Yet still the evil persists, and still the European crusade proceeds, but now with an ever augmenting promise of success, against the eternal cupidity and cruelty of man.

The long battle against slavery and the slave trade is part of the general spread of humanitarian policy which has given rise to religious missions, expensive social services, and to the formation of societies for the protection of children and animals. Of all the features distinguishing modern from ancient society, this is the most encouraging, and to those who are rendered melancholy by the continuing spectacle of the crimes, the vices, and follies of mankind, the least dubious ground for solace and for hope. The democratic civilization of modern Europe has many flaws, but in the humanity with which it endeavours to shelter the weaker members of the community from the harsh effects of economic competition it offers a plea in arrest of adverse judgment, challenges the splendours of its scientific achievement, and outshines its advance in material wealth.

BOOKS WHICH MAY BE CONSULTED

W. E. H. Lecky: *History of England.*
Sir Reginald Coupland: *Wilberforce.* 1922.
Sir Reginald Coupland: *The British Anti-Slavery Movement.* 1933
Sir Reginald Coupland: *Kirk in the Zambesi.* 1928.
Livingstone: *Narrative of an Expedition to the Zambesi.*
Lugard: *The Dual Mandate in British Tropical Africa.* 1922.
P. M. Allen: *Gordon and the Sudan.* 1931.
H. Wallon: *Histoire de l'esclavage dans l'antiquité.* 1879.
M. Rostovtzeff: *The Social and Economic History of the Roman Empire.* 1926.
Sir Reginald Coupland: *The Exploitation of East Africa.* 1856-1890. 1939.

WAR AND PEACE IN THE BALKANS

Despite the Dreikaiserbund Bismarck is nervous. The Austrian problem and the Dual Monarchy. The Pan-Slavonic movement. Its influence on Russian policy. The reforms of Alexander II. Bulgaria. The Balkan revolt, 1875. The Bulgarian massacres. The Russian invasion and the Treaty of San Stefano. Lord Beaconsfield and the Congress of Berlin, 1878. The breach in the Dreikaiserbund. Gladstone and Disraeli.

EVERYTHING IN the years immediately succeeding the Franco-Prussian War announced the permanence and splendour of the German *Reich*. Its one serious enemy was shattered. It had no rivals within sight. A great population elated with victory supported the authority of the Imperial Crown and paid to the officer corps of the strongest army in the world a willing tribute of subservient admiration and respect. Nothing was to be feared from Russia and Austria, whose rulers were bound to the German Kaiser by cordial relations of personal friendship. When in 1872 the three Emperors met in Berlin and there agreed to defend the *status quo* in Europe, to work together amicably on Balkan questions, to chastise socialism, and to promote reform, the imposing edifice of the new German Empire appeared unassailable. What enemy would be so presumptuous as to flout the *Dreikaiserbund*? Yet Bismarck still shuddered at the spectre of French revenge, and it is interesting to note that before the decade was out Gambetta had descried in Serbia the Achilles heel which would bring the *Reich* to the ground. So early was it apparent that racial movements among the Slavs might threaten the principle of Teutonic authority and deliver a smashing blow at the conservative foundations of Europe.

The internal situation of the Austrian Empire, always difficult by reason of racial friction, had undergone many vicissitudes since the suppression of the Bohemian and

Hungarian revolts in 1848 and 1849. There was first a decade of stern autocratic centralization with Germans everywhere, manning the Hungarian administration, officering the Hungarian army, controlling the Hungarian police, and with the whole intellect and education of the country confided (under the terms of a Concordat with the Pope, August 13, 1855) to the tutelage of the Catholic Church. It was, however, idle to suppose that the Slavonic and Magyar races would permanently accept as the beneficent ordinance of providence the hegemony of the German race. The system of centralized government devised and administered by Alexander Bach, a clever politician of Hebrew extraction, though not lacking in good will, efficiency, or the spirit of improvement, was regarded as an intolerable incubus by races to whom the German tradition, the German mode of life, and the German spirit of ascendancy were fiercely distasteful. It needed but the shock of a public calamity to show how slender was the basis of public confidence upon which the Government reposed and how widely spread was the spirit of disloyalty. When Austria went into the Italian War, the whole fabric of the Empire quaked as if it were built upon shifting sands. The Magyars and Czechs openly rejoiced at Austria's defeats at Magenta and Solferino. The war loan was a disastrous failure. Something, it was felt, must be done to check the mounting tide of racial discontent and to clamp the Empire together, before it was too late. Thereupon opened a period of constitutional experimentation (1860-67) which served only to show how difficult was the problem of combining in any stable form of political union the miscellaneous races of the Austrian Empire.

A half-hearted Federalism was a failure, a system of Parliamentary centralization was no greater success. The Magyars would no more come into a Parliament at Vienna to be voted down by Germans than Ulstermen would sit in a nationalist Parliament in Dublin. At last in 1865 Francis Joseph went to Pesth and invited the Magyars and Croats to table their proposals.

It so happened that at this crisis Hungary possessed in Deák a patriotic statesman of commanding abilities and moderate views, who, while holding that his country had much to gain from its association with Austria and sharply opposing

the advocates of secession, was determined to secure for the
Magyar races the essentials of political liberty and self-
respect. That his task was sensibly lightened by the misfortunes
of Austria in the Prussian War cannot be denied. Dejection
at Vienna was opportunity at Pesth; but it is the task of
statesmen to catch the flying skirts of opportunity, and it
is to the credit of Deák that, profiting by the Austrian defeat
at Sadowa, he made with Beust, the Austrian Chancellor,
the Dual Monarchy of 1867.

Feb.,   The relative permanence of this curious constitution is due
1867   to the fact that it accorded to the two strongest races of the
Empire, the Germans and the Magyars, a parity of power.
In Cisleithania, containing the seventeen provinces of Austria,
the Germans were predominant, in Transleithania (Hungary,
Croatia, Slavonia, Transylvania, and certain frontier districts) the Magyars. "You look after your barbarians," said
Andrassy, the Hungarian, to Beust, the German, "and we
will look after ours." Each part of the Empire had its own
Parliament and local Assemblies, each its own official
language. Though there were imperial ministries for war,
finance, and foreign affairs, there was no imperial Parliament.
Affairs of common interest to Hungary and Austria, such as
the decennial commercial treaty, were discussed in two
Delegations of sixty members each, meeting alternately at
Pesth and Vienna, but deliberating and voting apart, and,
by a precaution which is eloquent of the mistrust and alienation which prevailed, communicating with one another only
through the exchange of written documents. That the sovereign independence of Austria and Hungary might be even
more clearly marked, the *Ausgleich* or settlement was not
an agreement between two peoples and governments, one
with another, but a contract made by Austria and Hungary
separately with the sovereign House of Habsburg.

Thus linked together in an uneasy compromise these two
autonomous Powers faced the hard weather of fifty years,
looking south-eastwards for their future, since the Prussian
guns had driven them from Germany and Venetia, and
therefore plunging more and more deeply into the Balkan
vortex, while they accepted as an earnest of increased efficiency
those principles of parliamentary government, religious
toleration, and secular education, which had now become

fashionable in western Europe. What vast changes had been accelerated by the Prussian victory! In 1867 Austria-Hungary became a constitutional monarchy, and a year later broke the educational monopoly of the Church.

One grave problem remained unsettled. Under the heel of the two dominant races was a restless underworld of Slavs. The Czechs of Bohemia, the Slovaks, Croats, and Serbs of Hungary, could not be expected to welcome the beautiful arrangement which had confided the destinies of the Austrian Empire to the proud Magyar aristocracy and to the German-speaking nobles and burghers of Austria. It is true that the Slavonic population of the Dual Monarchy was divided by geographical situation, by differences of dialect and custom, and in some cases by the deeper chasm of religion, that Czech was sundered from Slovak, Slovak from Serb, and all from Croat and Slovene, and that for many centuries these poor and scattered branches of the great Slavonic family had been conscious of no common ethnic personality. That state of things, however, was now passing away. A Pan-Slavonic movement had begun to stir the imagination of these rude and backward peoples, a feeling that, although they had been ground down under the wheels of history, some by the Turks, others by the Germans and Magyars, they were nevertheless members of a mighty society spread out from the Arctic Ocean to the Euxine, and from the Baltic to the Behring Straits. The movement started with Kollar, the Slovak poet, in 1824, and swiftly spread to Bohemia, where it was taken up by the Czech philologists and men of letters; at first out of a feeling for the common inheritance of Slavonic culture and a desire to explore and command the treasures of thought and emotion which belonged to Slavs all over the world, so that even the humblest peasant, as he toiled for an alien master, might feel himself to belong to a great common brotherhood with a distinctive and honourable contribution to make to the civilization of mankind. But then, as so often happens, the ideas liberated by poets and scholars passed into the domain of controversial policy. Pan-Slavism played a part in the Bohemian revolution of 1848; but Bohemia was a small stage, and the Bohemian revolution was soon over and done with. A larger theatre and a greater fortune were reserved for the movement. Some twenty years later, while Alexander II was Tzar of Russia, Pan-Slavic ideas entered as a directing influence into Muscovite policy. Then this new racial philosophy became a force of the first magnitude, challenging the whole authority of the Porte in the Balkans, and spreading a new restlessness among the many million Slavs who were living, in varying degrees of subjection, within the frontiers of the Dual Monarchy.

1855-81   While Miss Florence Nightingale was blazing new paths to freedom for Victorian womankind, the Tzar Alexander, equally as a result of the Crimean War, was carrying out with the assistance of a handful of enlightened noblemen and officials a great programme of domestic reform. Within the space of a decade he liberated the serfs, remodelled the judicial system, introduced local government, permitted a free press in St. Petersburg and Moscow, and accorded to the Universities a measure of academic freedom. Long afterwards the great work accomplished in the sixties by the reforming Tzar and his associates was looked back upon as the inspiring achievement of an heroic age. Much indeed was done to break the frost of tradition, and to lay the foundations of a sounder social and political system. But Russia is a land in which great ideas are more easily conceived than accurately executed. The measures were great, the men who were called upon to carry them out were not great enough. What was actually achieved fell far short of what was expected. There was an insufficiency of faith, skill, and integrity in the officials, a general aversion from steady political work, and an absence of support from the liberal members of the middle class, who, having been accustomed to tell themselves that no Tzarist government could do anything right, refused, even when great civilizing reforms were offered them, to vary their fixed attitude of opposition.

That would, however, be a very imperfect picture of Russia under Alexander II, in which the Tzar's great programme of reform was the only aspect visible to the eye. It was a reign of stern domestic tyranny, especially after the crushing of the Polish rebellion in 1863 and of protesting nihilism, a reign in which no suspect was safe from the secret police, in which houses were suddenly broken into and men and women transported to distant exile in Siberia, while conversely every member of the government from the Tzar downward was the mark for the dagger or the bomb. This was the time when the young intellectuals of Russia, impatient of the tardiness of reform and intoxicated with the new wine of physical science, began to assail the whole fabric of society with a savage reck-lessness, and, having nothing to suggest in place of all that they were resolved to destroy, earned for themselves the name of nihilist; the time depicted in Turgenev's *Fathers and Sons* and Tolstoi's *Anna Karenina*, when all the values of the old order were sharply challenged by the rising generation, and family harmony was often broken beyond repair as the traditional pieties of the old were confronted with the insolent atheism of the young. With all these revolutionary tenden-cies the Tzarist Government could have no truce. But with this spirit of domestic repression there were combined three other ideas: the unification of the unassimilated peoples of the empire, the conquest of central Asia, and the liberation of the Slavonic nations of the Balkans from the Turkish yoke. Of these policies the first was futile, the second trium-phant (for it was in 1868 that the Russians conquered Samar-cand), while the third, which was the creed of Pan-Slavism, was big with disaster to Russia, Europe, and the world.

The Pan-Slavic idea would have been well enough, had the Slavs of the Balkans been a united family, or the Powers willing to accept the hegemony of the Tzar in European Turkey. Neither of these conditions was realized. When the long Turkish tyranny was finally broken, it became apparent that there was no hate in the Balkans comparable to the animosity of Bulgar and Slav. Then to everyone's surprise it was learned that the people whom Russia had selected as being the leading Slavonic race in Turkey, and upon whom she had lavished years of propaganda and individual education, was, in fact, regarded by the south-western Slavs as an alien and an enemy, and that the establishment by Russian arms of a powerful Bulgaria, so far from putting heart into Pan-Slavism or contributing to the expansion of Russian influence, had the very reverse effect. The newly liberated Bulgaria created a counterpoise to the Muscovites and furnished the Serb with cause for bitter jealousy and offence. Of all this, however, there was no suspicion in the later seventies, when a crisis in the Near East threw Russia into a quasi-isolation and weakened the impregnable *Dreikaiserbund*, upon which the fabric of European stability had hitherto reposed.

In 1875 a revolt against Turkish misrule broke out in Bosnia and Herzegovina, a revolt of misery and irritation, springing straight from the heart of the peasantry. The storm spread apace to Montenegro, to Serbia, to Bulgaria. There was never so comprehensive a manifestation of Slavonic nationalism in the Balkans, so large and resounding an advertisement of their wrongs. But the Turks were too strong. The army of Serbia and Montenegro withered under their attack, and the murder of some 12,000 Christians in Bulgaria by irregular Turkish troops (May, 1876) attested with characteristic emphasis the restoration of Turkish authority over the mutinous peasantry of the Bulgarian nation.

Russia was in no mood to acquiesce in the ruin of the Slavonic cause in the Balkans. She declared war (April, 1877), attacked the Turks alike in Asia and Europe, and after a temporary check before Kars and Plevna carried everything before her. On March 3, 1878, with Russian armies encamped before their capital, the Turks were compelled to sign a treaty at San Stefano, the main feature of which was the creation of a vast autonomous Bulgaria, to be administered under Russian tutelage, and to be garrisoned for two years by Russian troops.

In England, where the old Crimean spirit was much alive among the Tories, the Russian victories were received with a frenzy of indignant alarm. That Turkey should become a satellite of Russia seemed to imperil the whole position of Britain in the East. The Queen, the Metropolitan Press, the "upper ten thousand" were warlike. A silly song—

> "We don't want to fight, but by jingo if we do,
>   We've got the ships, we've got the men, we've got the
>   money too!"

—captured the music-halls. Never was Europe closer to a great conflagration than in the early spring of 1878, when Lord Beaconsfield's cabinet came to Parliament for six millions, ordered the fleet to pass the Dardanelles, called out the reserves, and shed Derby and Carnarvon, the two ministers who stood for peace. Even Lord Salisbury, who had a few months earlier sensibly realized that Russia, with no fleet, no marine population, and a corrupt civil service, could never seriously menace Britain's position in the Mediterranean, was now willing to go to war, unless the Tzar were prepared to submit the whole treaty of San Stefano to the Powers and to vary its terms.

That the peace of Europe was happily saved was due to the good offices of Bismarck, to the brilliant dexterity of Salisbury, and to the readiness of Austria to follow the British lead.

Sensible of her isolation, Russia was persuaded to submit her treaty to the Powers, and to accept proposals which she might otherwise have regarded as wounding to her pride. At the Congress of Berlin (June, 1878) the whole question of the Near East was settled upon lines which safeguarded British interests, extended Austrian influence, and administered a severe check to the Pan-Slavist ambitions of the Tzar. While eleven million Christians were liberated from the Turkish yoke, and Bosnia and Herzegovina were handed to Austria to administer, the vast and sprawling Bulgarian state, the creation of which under the Treaty of San Stefano had been at once the chief fruit of Russian endeavour and the principal cause of British alarm, was reduced to more modest dimensions. For these enormous concessions Russia was compensated by the gift of Bessarabia and by the recognition of Asiatic conquests which the western Powers were in no position to contest.

Measured against Russia's great expectations, these were pitiful emoluments, and when it was learned that England, the principal rival, had secretly obtained Cyprus from the Turks on the pretext that with such a base she would be in a better position to defend the Asiatic possessions of the Porte, the whole mass of transactions could not appear to a Russian in any other light than as a decisive diplomatic defeat. Disguise it as they might, Beaconsfield and Salisbury had triumphed over Gortschakoff. They had given the Balkans a map devised on Anglo-Austrian not on Russian principles. They had confirmed their authority with the Turks, and throughout their enterprise they had received encouragement from Vienna and Berlin. When London acclaimed the two British statesmen who returned with "Peace with Honour," the Tzar could not but reflect how different the result would have been if his friends the Emperors of Germany and Austria had given him a full measure of diplomatic support. From that moment the *Dreikaiserbund* began to totter. A train had been fired in this Balkan crisis which was destined to split the union of the three Emperors and to throw Tzarist Russia into the arms of the French Republic. Of all the results of the Slav rebellion against Turkish misrule this was the most far-reaching in its effects.

Meanwhile England was convulsed by a domestic struggle of extraordinary and memorable intensity. It had been the tradition and pride of the Liberal party to espouse the cause of liberty and justice all over the world. Liberals had supported Italy against Austria, Denmark against Germany, and at the opening of the Franco-Prussian War had championed the treaty for the defence and neutrality of Belgium. To a party cherishing such traditions no European government was more odious than that of the Sultan, nor any people more cruelly wronged than the Christian subjects of the Porte. At the news of the Bulgarian atrocities the greatest of Liberal statesmen, suddenly emerging from his retirement, led a passionate opposition to the Turk-preserving policy of the Tory government. Gladstone was now nearing his seventieth year. He remembered Canning. He had served under Wellington. He had been a member of the first Reformed Parliament. He had fought ten General Elections. At forty-five he had been the author of a famous budget. At fifty-nine he became the head of a great administration (1868-74) which gave England universal education and the ballot, freed the Universities from religious tests, reformed the army, and levelled the first courageous blows at the injustices and anomalies inherent in English and Protestant ascendancy in Ireland. Though a strong Anglican, he had not scrupled to disestablish the Anglican Church in Ireland. Though a large landlord, he had passed the Irish Land Act against the interests of his class and for the relief of an impoverished and embittered agricultural democracy in the sister island. After a long course of unexampled Parliamentary activity he had retired to the noble woodlands of Hawarden, to fell trees, to re-read Homer, and to extend his favourite studies in theology. From these congenial occupations he was sharply summoned by the bitter cry of Bulgarian distress.

The campaign which he then conducted in and out of Parliament is one of the outstanding physical and oratorical achievements in English history. The Court, the aristocracy, the main part of the Press, the overwhelming majority in both houses of Parliament, the unthinking and shallow multitude who live for sensations, were passionately opposed to him. A fierce hatred of Russia, a traditional sentiment of friendship for the Turk, an enthusiasm for spirited and martial gestures, such as the summoning of Indian troops to Malta or the despatch of the fleet to the Dardanelles, obstructed his approach to the ear of the nation. Yet such was the splendour and force of his appeal to the moral sentiments of his countrymen that before three years were out he had talked down the reputation of Beaconsfield and Salisbury, talked the Tories out of office, and talked himself back to the leadership of his party and to the premier place in the counsels of the Crown. That English voters could not be indifferent to the general welfare of mankind was the main burden of his argument. "Remember," he said to the electors of Midlothian in a characteristic flight, "that the sanctity of life in the hill villages of Afghanistan among the winter snows is as inviolable in the eyes of Almighty God as can be your own." He had no fear of the big Bulgaria. With a sound instinct he declared that there could be no greater barrier against the advance of Russian influence in the Balkans than a nation of free men. Not many years afterwards his estimate of the situation proved to be correct. The two halves of Bulgaria, the separation of which had been the main object of British diplomacy in 1878, came together under the stress of national sentiment with the entire good will of Great Britain and to the intense chagrin of the Russian government.

1885

The long duel between Disraeli and Gladstone (1852-80) is the central fact in the Parliamentary life of the mid-Victorian age. It was characteristic of England that the Tory party should accept the leadership of a Hebrew adventurer of genius, who chose the novel as his principal medium for the propagation of political ideas, while the Liberal leader was a High Church English squire, the fine flower of

Far other were the inspirations of Gladstone's wonderful and tempestuous old age. The sentiments evoked by the words Empire, prestige, war, domination, had little seduction for the religious leader of the Liberal party. So far from desiring to extend the British Empire, Gladstone was anxious wherever possible to limit his country's responsibilities. The satisfaction of national aspirations in the Balkans, in South Africa, in Ireland, were objects, quixotic as they appeared to many, for which he was fully prepared to stake his own and his party's fortunes. As a young man he had advised the restora-

Aug., 1881 tion of the Ionian isles to Greece; as an old man he thought it just to return the Transvaal to the Boers.

His second administration (1880-85), though marked by the emancipation of the rural labourers and by an Irish Land Act which granted fair rents and fixity of tenure to the peasants, was clouded by failures in Egypt and the Sudan.   Nor in the last and most desperate of his adventures was he more successful. Braving the Irish Protestant interest and the sentiment of the possessioned class in Britain, "the grand old man" proposed Home Rule for Ireland (1886); Chamberlain, Hartington, Goschen, the strongest of his lieutenants, refused to follow; but the loss of these powerful men and the knowledge that he had broken the splendid party instrument of his earlier triumphs did not weaken his purpose. At the

1893 age of eighty-three, after six years of opposition, the indomitable veteran returned to the charge and, by an extraordinary effort of physical and intellectual power, passed his Bill through the Commons. But the Lords refused to give way, and again the Irish Parliamentary party was disappointed of its hopes. Meanwhile the problem of Ireland had been attacked from a new angle under Salisbury's Unionist administration. A bold and original scheme of state socialism, suggested by Joseph Chamberlain and carried out with courage and intelligence by A. J. Balfour, showered material benefits on the country. But the nation of dreamers refused to surrender its dreams. Good government was not enough. The Catholic Irish wanted, as Gladstone saw, to govern themselves. As time went on they raised their demands. At last in 1921 a measure of independence was conceded to a party of violence greatly exceeding in many respects those Gladstonian Bills

which in the eighties and nineties had convulsed politics and
society in England.

The bitterness and intensity of the passion which the struggle
over Irish Home Rule infused into English politics at this time
can be understood only if we remember the manner in which
the Irish campaign was waged and the alarming perspectives
which it was thought to disclose. The Irish Home Rule
League which had been started in 1870 by Isaac Butt with a
view to obtaining by legitimate parliamentary pressure the
concession of Home Rule for Ireland was only part of a
larger movement. Fourteen years earlier a secret society
known as the Irish Republican Brotherhood had been founded
to sever Ireland once and for all from Britain by force of
arms. The constitutional action of Irishmen at Westminster
was flanked by revolutionary movements outside, by the
I.R.B. in Europe, by the Clan na Gael in America, sworn
and secret fraternities for whom the true method of suasion
was not talk but dynamite; and in the lurid light thrown
upon this darker side of the Irish movement by Fenian outrages many an Englishman who would have voted for a
Parliament in Dublin if Ireland had presented herself in a
gentler guise recoiled from concessions. Moreover in Ireland
itself an agrarian agitation patronized by the political leaders
was prolific in the meaner sort of crime. It was in vain that Oct.,
the Government essayed to suppress Michael Davitt's Land 1881
League. A Ladies' Land League continued the work.

Save for a handful of Protestants the Irish parliamentary
representatives were solid for Home Rule, and by a policy of
systematic obstruction set themselves to make Parliament
inoperative until such time as their policy was accepted.
Fatigued and exasperated by all-night sittings, assailed in
their complacency by gibes and insults, outraged by Fenian
crimes, alarmed by the spectre of republicanism and perplexed by the fact that the good intentions towards Ireland
which they were conscious of entertaining were met by an
ingrained temper of hostility and distrust, the average English
parliamentarians offered an energetic resistance to Home
Rule.

It was, therefore, sanguine of Gladstone to hope, as in
1886 he seems to have done, that the Conservative party,

realizing that there was now in consequence of a recent Redistribution Act a solid block of eighty-six Home Rule votes at Westminster, would take up the cause of Irish self-government. For a moment, indeed, Conservatives glanced that way, for there was a parley between Carnarvon and June, Parnell, the Nationalist leader, but nothing came of it. A 1886 problem which should have been dealt with by a coalition was left to the patronage of a depleted and mutilated fragment of the Liberal party.

Their task was not rendered easier by the character of the
1846- Irish chieftain. All the rebel traditions of Erin were em-
91 bodied in the person of Charles Stewart Parnell. He was in touch with the secret societies of Ireland, England, and America, President of the Land League, Chairman of the Irish party in the House of Commons, the uncrowned sovereign of the Irish race. Every agency obnoxious to England recognized the mastery of this strange and mysterious being of ice and flame. In the House of Commons, the proud, handsome, unsociable Irish landlord with his swarthy beard and dark flashing eyes, sitting still and saturnine among his obedient following, was regarded with a kind of awe. Descended though he was from an old and respected Anglo-Irish county family, he was known to be the foe of Britain. People thought him inhuman and none too scrupulous.
Oct. Indeed before ever Gladstone launched his first Home Rule
12, Bill he had been compelled to put Parnell under lock and
1881 key.

From time to time phrases dropped from the formidable Irishman which disconcerted his Liberal supporters. "No one can set bounds to the march of a nation," he said once, and again, addressing an American audience (February 20, 1880): "None of us, whether we are in America or Ireland or wherever we are, will be satisfied until we have destroyed the last link which keeps Ireland bound to England." Faced with these declarations, Liberals could only hope that conciliation would kill conspiracy, that reform would avert revolution, and that the poison of violence would be strained away from the Irish system by the remedial action of a subordinate Parliament.

Yet Parnell survived the effect of his American speeches, survived also the formidable attacks of *The Times* newspaper associating Parnellism with crime. At last he was broken upon 1889 a point of domestic morals which offended the nonconformist conscience of Gladstone's following. The greatest of Irish statesmen was ruined by the love of a woman. Yet the disruption of the Irish party in the last years of his tragic life, though it temporarily retarded the advance of Irish Nationalism, made no difference to the ultimate fortunes of the movement. The desire of Catholic Ireland to be permitted to manage her own affairs and to lead her own life in her own way was too deep to be destroyed by the humiliation and death of a leader, by the schisms of party, or by vicissitudes in the game of parliamentary debate.

BOOKS WHICH MAY BE CONSULTED

Fyffe: *History of Modern Europe*. 1924.

Wickham Steed: *The Hapsburg Monarchy*. 1919.

C. G. Macartney: *Hungary*. (Nations of the Modern World Series.) 1934.

Seignobos: *History of Contemporary Europe*. 1909.

A. Rambaud: *History of Russia*. 1900.

Isenmann: *Le Compromis Austro-Hongrois de* 1867. 1904.

R. W. Seton Watson: *Disraeli, Gladstone, and the Eastern Question*. 1935.

John Morley: *Life of Gladstone*. 1908.

Monypenny and G. E. Buckle: *Life of Disraeli*. 1929.

E. Denis: *La Bohème depuis la montagne blanche*. 1930.

St. John Ervine: *Parnell*. 1927.

B. H. Sumner: *Russia and the Balkans*, 1870-80. 1937.

W. N. Medlicott: *The Congress of Berlin and After*. 1938.

Sir Philip Magnus: *Gladstone*. 1954.

CHAPTER LXXXIX

BISMARCK AND THE GERMAN REICH

Bismarck, 1870-9. Economic development of Germany. Bismarck adopts Protection. The German Insurance Acts. The policy of repression. The diplomatic revolution. The Dual Alliance of 1879. The Balkan crisis of 1885. Bismarck's relations with England. Bismarck's fear. Achievements of the German people after the Franco-Prussian War.

FOR NINETEEN years after the foundation of the German Empire Bismarck continued to direct the affairs of his country and to influence the fortunes of the world. After the great things which had been accomplished he was well content that Germany should be shielded from domestic change and foreign war. He had no wish for a colonial empire or for aggrandizement in the East, and it was among the cardinal maxims of his policy that the friendship of England should not be imperilled by a challenge on the sea. He was too much alive to the dangers of the situation on the continent to court new adventures. He saw France unappeased, Russia uncertain, Austria still harbouring griefs against Berlin. How to be friends with the Russians without alienating England, with the Austrians without estranging Russia—these continental problems kept his diplomatic powers on the stretch. The isolation of France, the domination of Europe by a powerful German army, and the maintenance of his own autocratic régime, were the guiding principles of his policy. Accidents of longevity amazingly contributed to his success. The Emperor William I, dying a nonagenarian in 1888, lived so long that when at last the Crown Prince Frederick ascended the throne he was an invalid stricken with cancer, and in his short reign of ninety days powerless to affect the course of events. With the tragic death of this liberally-minded sovereign the most formidable of all the obstacles to the general trend of Bismarck's policy was removed.

Meanwhile a change was coming over the economic life of

Germany, similar, save for its greater velocity, to that which England had experienced in her industrial revolution. The decades which succeeded the Franco-Prussian War were marked by an astonishing expansion of German industry and commerce. The country which had been poor became suddenly rich. The population which had been predominantly rural rushed in increasing numbers to the towns, and there multiplied until the balance between urban and rural Germany was decisively reversed. Leadership in two new and most important branches of industry, the chemical and the electrical, fell as a natural prize to the superior education of the German people. The output of coal went up by leaps and bounds, growing from thirty million tons in 1871 to a hundred and ninety million tons in 1913. A process invented in England and associated with the names of Thomas and Gilchrist, which enabled the basic ore of Luxemburg and Lorraine to be put to economic use, led to vast industrial developments and converted the Westphalian coalfield into a region comparable in the activity and concentration of its factory life to the English Black Country. In a single decade (the eighties) the German Empire doubled its output of steel and nearly doubled that of iron. And while industry was thus advancing and transforming the character and occupations of the German people a great impetus was given to marine enterprise. German ships began in swiftly increasing numbers to cross the Atlantic, to touch at African ports, to trade with the Levant and the further East. The old Hanseatic spirit was revived. In the twenty years between 1870 and 1890 the steam tonnage of the Empire multiplied sevenfold. The cry went up for colonies, for protection against American wheat and English manufactureres, and for a spirited policy in every part of the globe. The pressure was such that no statesman, whatever his prestige, could have long held out against it. Bismarck was compelled to concede. In 1879 he adopted Protection as his fiscal policy, and three years later, making a virtue of necessity, started Germany on her colonial career. It may be noticed as an interesting coincidence that the formation of a colonial group in the *Reichstag* belongs to the same year (1883) which witnessed the birth of the A.E.G. (*Allgemeine Elektrizitäts Gesellschaft*), the huge electrical combine which established upon an impregnable foundation the greatest of German scientific industries.

In common with every other European country which experienced the effects of industrialism, the Germany of the seventies and eighties was confronted by the dark shadows of undeserved poverty and made anxious by the spectacle of a restless, miserable, and exploited proletariat. While Wagner was delighting the fashionable music lovers of Europe by the operatic festivals of Bayreuth, the workers in the German mines and factories were exposed to hardships and uncertainties comparable with those which afflicted the industrial population of England before the passage of the Factory Acts. Bismarck was far too great a man to be blind to the importance of the social problem. He saw that if the edifice of his constitution was to stand it must content the workers. He did not trust the unbridled play of private appetites to work out the greatest happiness of the greatest number. Paternalism, which was in the old Prussian tradition, received a new justification and demanded a wider scope in the altered circumstances created by the industrial revolution. The old must be protected against want, the worker must be insured against sickness and accident. Bismarck was no Shaftesbury. He passed no Factory Acts, but in his great scheme for compulsory insurance against sickness (1883), accidents (1884), and old age (1889) he was a pioneer, anticipating, save that he provided no insurance against unemployment, the measures subsequently carried out in England by Mr. Lloyd George as a member of the Asquith Cabinet.

The German Insurance Acts constitute a landmark. Of all the political inventions of the nineteenth century none was so valuable a preservative of society as the discovery of a system of insurance, dependent on the contribution of the state, the employer, and the worker, and protecting the mass of the labouring population against the worst hazards of industrial life. That revolution was so long staved off in Germany was partly due to these valuable measures, by which Bismarck robbed the Social Democratic party, despite its steady growth under persecution, of a compelling and irresistible appeal to the poor.

As the Iron Chancellor advanced in years he became more

fiercely intolerant of opposition. Taking advantage of two attempts on the Emperor's life, he passed, and on three subsequent occasions renewed, a law against the Socialists so sharp that it placed the liberties of the subject under the heel of the police. Only a country seized by a violent spasm of alarm, or altogether lost to the virtue of political courage, could have tamely submitted to the unjust and tyrannical acts of oppression which were thus made possible. By consenting to this harsh legislation the National Liberal party, which had been the mainstay of the German Empire in its early days, and the support of the government in its struggle with the Clericals, declared itself bankrupt of true Liberalism. It was a nation far gone in the practice of passive obedience which entered into the next great European war.

The feeling of Bismarck with regard to France explains the whole of his foreign policy. He conceived of France as the irreconcilable and dangerous enemy of his country, always to be suspected, always to be weakened, always to be estranged from its European neighbours. The north African littoral, fast becoming an object of general ambition, served the turn of his anti-Gallican diplomacy. He encouraged France to take Tunis that she might quarrel with Italy, England to take Egypt that she might quarrel with France. The Anglo-Italian naval understandings which Lord Salisbury concluded in 1887 were fruits of the same long-sighted machinations with the object of leaving France without a friend in Europe. Nor was Bismarck indifferent to the play of political forces in Paris. A monarchist for Germany, he was a republican for France, a republic being, in his opinion, of all forms of government the weakest and the most discreditable.

In the east of Europe, the main diplomatic defence of Germany against a possible coalition fomented by the inveterate hostility of France was that alliance of the three Emperors which, as we have seen, was formed in June, 1873, and was still operative in 1878 when the Congress of Berlin, described by the Tzar as "a coalition of Europe against Russia under the leadership of Prince Bismarck," subjected it to serious strain. The *Dreikaiserbund* survived the crisis. The friendship was patched up. The alliance was renewed again and again; and every three years Europe was publicly informed that the rulers of the three great military monarchies of the east were bound together by fresh ties of comradeship and association. Manifest, however, as were the advantages of a good understanding with Russia, Bismarck never really trusted the Muscovites. He thought their friendship uncertain, their diplomacy tricky. From Gortschakoff, their foreign minister, he was divided by sentiments of fierce personal disesteem. If he were forced to choose between Russia and Austria, it would always be Austria that he would prefer, partly from the call of blood, partly because, were Austria for any reason to resume her old quarrel with the Prussians, she would advance historic claims upon Silesia, upon Alsace, upon the Danish Duchies, upon the very constitution of the *Reich* itself, which would put in dispute all the hard-won triumphs of the Hohenzollern house since the accession of Frederick the Great. And so, when the Balkan troubles of 1878 had been composed, Bismarck determined to make a secret treaty with Austria behind the back of his Russian ally What he did then has been decisive for history. In the impending struggle against Pan-Slavism Bismarck ranged his country secretly and treacherously on the Austrian side.

May,
1882
The Dual Alliance of 1879 became, by the junction of Italy in 1882, the Triple Alliance which lasted to the outbreak of the Great War. To the student of the diplomatic antecedents of that great event, as he works his way backward up the stream of history, the alliance which Bismarck and Andrassy negotiated between Germany and Austria-Hungary in 1879, against Russia and behind her back, presents itself as the original spring. From that moment it was fated that, should Austria and Russia come to blows in a Balkan trouble, the German army would stand side by side with its Austrian ally. "Should, contrary to their hopes and against their loyal desire, one of the High Contracting Parties," runs the principal clause of this momentous treaty of 1879, "be attacked by Russia, the High Contracting Parties are bound to come to the assistance one of the other with the whole strength of their Empires, and accordingly only to conclude peace together and upon mutual agreement." That the treaty was inconsistent with Germany's public undertakings to Russia was a sufficient ground for the special care which was taken to conceal it.

Bismarck did not want a war between Russia and Austria. It was his great ambition that such a war might be avoided. That there could be no greater peril for Germany, or for Europe, was a fact vividly present to his powerful imagination. Yet how easily might a spark be thrown among the inflammable timber of the Balkan States, which would set all Europe ablaze from the Neva to the Aegean! When Eastern Rumelia joined itself to Bulgaria in 1885, and the Serbs, greatly envying the sudden aggrandizement of their hated neighbour, rushed to arms and were defeated by King Alexander of Bulgaria on the field of Slivitzna, Europe was on the edge of war. Everybody knew, or, if they did not know, suspected, that the Serbs were acting on the impulsion of the Austrians. Everybody was aware that, however distasteful the person of Alexander (a Prince of Battenberg by birth) might be to the Tzar, the Bulgarians were the special clients of the Russian Empire. Out of a quarrel between Bulgaria and Serbia, should it be allowed to drag to any length, it was easy to see that friction would arise between their respective patrons, that such contrariety might be succeeded by hostilities, and that with the first shots exchanged between Austrians and Russians all Germany would be involved. Such a war Bismarck strained every nerve to avoid. Such a war, since it was still his opinion that the Balkans were not worth the bones of a single Pomeranian grenadier, he in fact succeeded in avoiding. His word went to Vienna. While he soothed the ruffled feathers of the Russians, he did not allow the Austrians to get out of hand. Thanks to his skill, the Bulgarian crisis passed away without a general convulsion. An awkward little campaign was speedily brought to an end; a contentious vacancy in the Bulgarian throne was happily filled. From the inexhaustible resources of princely Germany there was drawn a sovereign who, while acceptable to Vienna, was not patently abhorrent to St. Petersburg. He was that long-nosed, long-headed, bird-loving Ferdinand of Coburg, "the fox of the Balkans," who eventually, despite all his craft and finesse, brought the Bulgarian people into the Great War on the losing side.

From the web of the anti-Gallican alliances England stood free "in splendid isolation." No government, liberal or conservative, dared to pledge the English people to continental entanglements. The island remained aloof, incalculable, and to continental people provoking and enigmatic. Its ambitions were pursued in regions far distant from the main centres of European life. A handful of Englishmen were ruling in India. A slight sprinkling were scattered over Australasia and the Cape. How solid such a fabric might be no German could readily tell. Trade, navy, empire he was bound to concede, but how accidentally had they been won, how cheaply were they kept by this race of happy, easy-going pirates! One thing only seemed certain to Germans: that English friendship meant Russian enmity. A secret treaty with England, sufficient to detach her from France without frightening Russia, was an idea attractive to some political Germans. Bismarck fished for it, first with Disraeli, then with Salisbury. But the English professed themselves opposed to secret treaties. They maintained that everything must be communicated to Parliament and to Queen Victoria. Moreover, what faith could be placed in English governments, here today, gone tomorrow, and always the sport of electoral caprice? Could a Tory government answer for the actions of its Liberal successor? Salisbury was diplomatically doubtful, and Bismarck was willing to believe that democracies were unable to "deliver the goods."

No treaty then was made between Germany and England during Bismarck's lifetime. The great Chancellor, though he valued English friendship and desired, without too much advertisement of the fact, to draw England into the circle of his associates, was never able to obtain even from a Tory government the firm and secret pledges which alone could satisfy his need. Moreover, as Germany entered the colonial field, occasions for friction with England multiplied. There was friction over Fiji and New Guinea, over south-west and central Africa, over Jamaica and Zanzibar. Whenever German relations with Russia were good Bismarck could afford to bully England. That the islanders should be roughly handled gave general pleasure to the Tzarist government and the German people. But the game of baiting England was safe only when Russia was cordial. At the first touch of frost in Russo-German relations, England was restored to Bismarck's favour.

Still he felt insecure. Despite the *Dreikaiserbund* and the Triple Alliance, and the understanding between Italy and England, and further alliances of Austria-Hungary with the Serbs and the Roumans, and a secret reinsurance treaty concluded with Russia in 1887, Bismarck was afraid. The spectre of a war on two fronts haunted his mind. It is a melancholy commentary on the politics of power that in 1887, after twenty-five years of autocratic rule, Bismarck should have felt himself compelled to come to the *Reichstag* for an army of some seven hundred thousand men.

It is difficult to overestimate the achievements of the German people during the twenty years of Bismarckian peace, which followed the convulsion of the Franco-Prussian War. Great as had been the pace of economic progress, it had not outstripped the organizing power of the German mind. The foundations of public education had been wisely and truly laid. The schools were good, the Universities were numerous, and inspired with a zeal for the advancement of knowledge. Nowhere were the advantages to be derived from the marriage of science and industry more quickly, more generally, or more intelligently perceived. In the field of business the organizing instinct of the German people had led to the foundation of *Kartells* or combines for the maintenance of prices and the limitation of output. Scientific and learned treatises issued every year in prodigal abundance from the printing presses. No people in Europe read more widely or seriously. Music was everywhere—cheaper than in France, more universal than in England, and the best (save for Vienna) to be found in any quarter of the globe.

Almost equally impressive was the stamp of forethought in the handling of the grave social problems which the industrial revolution brought in its train. In town-planning, as in the chemical and electrical industries, the Germans were pioneers. While the creators of industrial England were permitted to toil and die in a sprawling and disorderly congeries of ignoble hovels, the Germans thought and planned beforehand. Their towns and suburbs were for the most part built to an intelligent design, and adjusted to the requirements of convenience and hygiene. The new urban generations were born into a world which had been prepared to receive them.

Darkening all this vigorous and manifold civilization was the thought of war, terrible to some, welcome to others, a preoccupation for all. Germany was at peace, but heavily armed, obsessed with internal suspicions and anxieties, fearing her neighbours and by her neighbours feared. The diplomacy of Bismarck had not tended to lessen the apprehensions of Europe. Too often had he used hectoring language and shown the glint of Prussian steel. Too often had he launched his reptile press against the English and the French, too often reminded the world that the *Pax Germanica* rested upon the bayonets of the German army. It was a serious blot upon his statesmanship that he believed in bad manners and double-dealing. But at least it must be accounted to his credit that he kept his country out of war, avoiding the three dangers which, under less skilful management, brought the Hohenzollern Empire to the ground; an alliance between the Tzar and the French Republic, a naval rivalry with England, and the outbreak of a quarrel in the Balkans so serious as to threaten the continued existence of the Austro-Hungarian Empire, and to precipitate a clash between the Slavonic and Teuton races.

BOOKS WHICH MAY BE CONSULTED

C. A. Fyffe: *History of Modern Europe*. 1924.

J. A. Spender: *Fifty Years of Europe*. 1933.

Lives of Bismarck, by J. W. Headlam-Morley (1894) and C. Grant Robertson. 1918.

E. Brandenburg: *From Bismarck to the World War*. 1927.

G. P. Gooch: *Germany*. (Nations of the Modern World Series.) 1925.

Bismarck: *Thoughts and Recollections*. 1899.

A. J. P. Taylor: *Bismarck*. 1955.

A. J. P. Taylor: *Struggle for Mastery in Europe*. 1848-1918. 1954.

E. Eyck: *Bismarck and the German Empire*. 1950.

W. L. Langer: *European Alliances and Alignments*, 1871-90. 1931.

THE END OF BRITAIN'S ISOLATION

Germany at the accession of William II. Character of the Kaiser. The Franco-Russian alliance. The continental balance. England. The Anglo-Japanese Treaty. Question of an Anglo-German entente. German hostility to England. British Imperialism. The South African question. The discovery of the mines. Majuba. Kruger and Cecil Rhodes. The Raid and the South African War. The Boers and the Kaiser. The construction of the German High Seas Fleet. Egypt—England takes responsibility. Charles Gordon. The reconquest of the Sudan. Omdurman. Fashoda. Death of Queen Victoria. The Victorian age. Edward VII. The Anglo-French Entente.

A STATE composed of soldiers and officials, a society dominated by the military caste, a people still drunken with the wine of victory, an imperial Parliament, elected indeed by universal suffrage, but schooled to vote the military budget at septennial intervals, and save for an insignificant and much persecuted body of socialists submissive to a government which it was unable to change, a Prussian Parliament elected on a narrow oligarchic franchise, and as obscurantist as when it was put forward in the reactionary crisis of 1850, and over all the towering, dominating figure of Bismarck. Such was the German scene in June, 1888, when William II, a young man of thirty-one, succeeded to his father's throne. "There is only one master in this country, and I am he," observed the new Kaiser. Rather than share his power with a Bismarckian dynasty William was prepared to break with the founder of the Empire. In March, 1890, the year in which David Lloyd George, an obscure Welsh Baptist, first stepped into the arena at Westminster, Bismarck was dismissed. Dropping the pilot who for twenty-eight years had steered the ship of state through the tempests, the impulsive Kaiser seized the helm, and found himself in control of the most powerful military engine in the world.

1888 1918

1153

The new autocrat became at once a vital and disquieting force in European society. That he had some admirable and even brilliant qualities was at once apparent. His outlook on affairs was bold and spacious, his curiosity eager and comprehensive, his industry vast, his memory for detail powerful and exact. He was pious, dutiful, patriotic, and sometimes, especially when he spoke of the sea, would rise to the heights of moving eloquence. But with these shining qualities were mingled others of a baser alloy, an egregious vanity, an ungovernable temper, a love of theatrical ostentation which exposed him to ridicule, and a vein of malevolence which merited contempt. There was no flattery so base that he would not accept it, no barbarity so extreme that he would not in a spasm of fury invest it with imperial authority. A nervous excitability and impulsiveness, while it gave a certain zest and charm to his companionship, always made him dangerous as a ruler, so that, after experience of many alarums and excursions, his ministers began to ask themselves in trepidation whether the headstrong and loquacious master of Germany was not in fact deranged in mind.

It would be unfair to class him among the war-mongers. William kept his nation at peace for twenty-six years. There is no reason to doubt the sincerity of the pacifist declarations which at the beginning of every year he addressed to the Prussian *Landtag*. Yet the atmosphere of his court was steeped in militarism. The Kaiser never could forget that he was the supreme war lord, and in his innumerable orations to gatherings of soldiers and sailors made it a duty to inflame the martial ardour of the nation. The intemperance of his language, the unaccountability of his actions, and the numerous indications which he betrayed of a rash and unmeasured ambition, helped to raise the temperature of Europe and to create a climate unfavourable to the smooth and easy transaction of international affairs.

Not long after the fall of Bismarck a treaty was signed, the prevention of which was a principal object of the old Chancellor's diplomacy. Emerging at last from her long isolation, France found an ally in Russia. Here was a country needing armaments which France was willing to supply, railways which Paris (but not Berlin) was prepared to finance, and in view of eventualities in the Balkans (for the Tzar had been apprised in 1888 of the secret German-Austrian Treaty of nine years earlier) looking about for a friend who might serve as a makeweight to the Central Powers. Though there was no quarter of Europe in which the principles of 1789 were so little regarded as the Empire of the Tzar, the French could not afford to refuse the embrace of the Russian bear. The outlines of an agreement were signed in 1891, and on January 4, 1894, were completed by a secret military convention which bound both parties in the event of a German attack upon either to come to one another's assistance with a large army. The document, which provided for the consultation of the two general staffs in time of peace and for instant mobilization on the first news of the mobilization of the forces of any one of the Powers comprising the Triple Alliance, was of an extremely practical character. It was a soldier's document. "The available forces to be employed against Germany shall be, on the part of France, 1,300,000 men; on the part of Russia, 700,000 or 800,000. These forces shall engage to the full with all speed, in order that Germany may have to fight at the same time on the east and on the west."

The Triple Alliance of Germany, Italy, and Austria was now confronted by the dual alliance of Russia and France. Each combination was heavily armed, each ready to spring on the other at the first sign of hostile intentions, but which of the two in the event of a clash might prove to be the stronger no one at that time could confidently predict. It is possible that if the balance of power had so been left the peace of Europe might have been preserved. Meanwhile the secret of the Franco-Russian alliance was carefully kept.

England was an enigma. Her accession to either party might tip the balance. An equilibrium which was relatively stable while the two continental groups were thus massed the one against the other might, by the intrusion of this great naval power into the arena, be violently disturbed. Confidence would be heightened on the one side, apprehension on the other. In Germany the junction of England with the dual alliance might produce a nervous tension akin to claustrophobia, in Russia a mood of heedless and insolent temerity.

The Kaiser was the grandson of Queen Victoria. To that

venerable lady he was always ready to pay the tribute of a grandson's respect; from that uncompromising pen, as from no other, he would accept a sharp but affectionate reproof. Having an easy command of the English language, and a large circle of English relations and friends, he would resort to his grandmother's island as to a favourite playground. To be received at Windsor, to sail his yacht at the Cowes Regatta, to wear the blue and gold of an English Admiral, to taste the plaudits of a London crowd, or to relax in the luxurious ease of an English nobleman's country house gave him great satisfaction. With part of his nature he admired England and its inhabitants, with another part he regarded them with envy and dislike.

In view of the division of the European continent into two rival combinations, a brisk competition between France and Germany for the favours of the island Empire might naturally have been expected. There was nothing of the kind. So far from being courted on the continent during the first fourteen years of the Kaiser's reign, Britain was regarded with a bitter, and sometimes perilous disfavour in France and Germany and Russia. Such was her isolation, and so dangerous did it appear, that in 1902, boldly departing from the tradition of Canning, Palmerston, Gladstone, and Salisbury, the Balfour Government took the momentous step of negotiating in secret and publicly concluding an alliance with Japan.

The swift and momentous assimilation of European knowledge by this distant Asiatic island is one of the miracles of recent history. Before the American Commodore Perry brought home to the Japanese (1854) the strength of Western armaments and the advantages of foreign trade, Japan was sunk in mediaeval ignorance. Two hundred and sixty-eight Daimios, or feudal lords, with their armed retainers or Samurai, ruled the country. There was no navy, no artillery or firearms, no merchant class, no public system of education or general code of law. The ethics of the people were those of a Highland clan in the days of Macbeth. Who then of Commodore Perry's crew would have dreamed that before the end of the century Japan would have abolished her feudal system (1871-3), centralized her government, provided herself with a modern navy and army, a modern code of laws, and a modern system of education, and would in all ways be prepared to play the rôle of a modern state? Yet under the long and memorable rule of the Mikado Mutzu Hito (1867-1912) these extraordinary things were accomplished with a swift and finished dexterity. Accordingly, when in 1902 England sought the alliance of the Mikado's Government, Japan was already the strongest naval Power in the Pacific. With a marine based on British and and an army fashioned on German models, she had overwhelmed the Chinese in one brief campaign. So strong had she become by land and sea, so formidable was the combination of Western mechanism and feudal courage, that three years after the English treaty she emerged victorious from a war with Russia, whereat the whole Orient trembled with delight and the Occident began to talk of the Yellow Peril and to wonder whether the day of the Yellow Man might not be near at hand.

The rivalry of Britain and Russia was an old story. Fears for the safety of India, fears for Constantinople, fears lest a Russian navy might make its entry into the Mediterranean, were quite sufficient, apart from the rooted aversion of English democracy from Russian despotism, to estrange the two countries. An Anglo-German *entente* or even alliance was more easily to be conceived of.

Here there were no ancient deep-rooted causes of repugnance. English and Germans belonged to the same Teutonic family, spoke a language derived from a common foundation, and on many a stricken field had fought shoulder to shoulder. Rather than submit to a Catholic ruler the English had called in a German dynasty to rule over them. They had accepted the ugly German mistresses of George I, the frequent absences of George II, the plain German wife of George III, and the handsome German husband of Victoria. As the reign of the great Queen proceeded, the threads of intercourse, economic, social, intellectual, multiplied between the two countries. Germany became the best foreign customer for English goods, England the most enthusiastic foreign customer for German ideas. Large bodies of intelligent Germans, some of them rebuffed by Prussian militarism, drifted into England, settled there in happiness and content, and contributed to build up the prosperity of Manchester in cottons, of Bradford in cloth, and of Sheffield in steel. The same phenomenon of easy and fruitful intercourse was repeated in the sphere of culture. While Oxford and Cambridge, once liberated (1871) from the thraldom of religious tests, reverberated with the echoes of Teutonic learning, the more eminent professors of Berlin or Göttingen could count upon a band of young English admirers, who, returning to their more civilized but less erudite compatriots, preached the majesty of German knowledge.

In view of such circumstances it is not surprising that some British statesmen, impressed by the dangers of "splendid isolation," should have turned their thoughts towards German friendship. "The most natural alliance," said Joseph Chamberlain (November 29, 1899), the powerful Colonial Secretary in Salisbury's administration, "is that between us and the German Empire." The Germans thought otherwise. To them the alliance which the British statesman described as most natural appeared an unholy and contaminating bond. A general howl of execration greeted the well-meaning overture and announced its inevitable doom.

It is not difficult to trace the history of the sentiments which produced this extraordinary explosion. The Prussians had thoroughly absorbed the lesson which the scribes of Bismarck had been sedulous to inculcate. They believed that liberalism, an English poison, after corrupting the aristocratic virtues of the island race, was now doing its devil's work upon the robust constitution of Prussia. From the momentous struggles which made Germany a united nation they noted that the English had stood aside in unhelpful neutrality, sympathizing hotly with the Danes, appreciably with the Austrians, and at last, when the guns of Moltke were playing on the streets and squares of Paris, openly and sentimentally with the French. The sentiments thus occasioned received yet further aggravation under William II. The new Emperor did not share the Bismarckian view that Germany was a sated power. Still less did his subjects. While the Pan-German League, founded in 1893, proposed that Austria, German Switzerland, and the Netherlands should be incorporated in the *Reich*, the Emperor was content to mark out for himself three new spheres of German influence in each of which he might expect to encounter the diplomatic opposi-

tion of England. The first was the Turkish Empire, the
second the colonies, the third and most important the sea.
Ships were the favourite toy of his boyhood. It was a misfortune for the German people that the construction of a
battle fleet second to none was the ruling passion of the
Kaiser's riper years.

The same lack of self-sufficiency was apparent in England.
Here, too, Imperialism was running its burning course, with
Rudyard Kipling for its prophet and Joseph Chamberlain
for its advocate, and Africa following hard on the heels of
India with dazzling invitations to dominion and trade. The
English were established in Egypt, in Uganda, and in Nigeria.
As usual they had secured the best places: far better than the
Germans, better even than the French, who had Tunis, Algeria,
and Senegal, or than the Belgians, who had been allotted the
vast territory of the Congo. Yet the English were not content.
Steadily during the sixties, seventies, and eighties they
kept extending their tentacles, eastwards, westwards, and
northwards from Cape Colony, until the two Boer Republics,
which retained the quintessential spirit of the older Dutch
colonial civilization, were ringed round, save for an outlet
to Delagoa Bay, by a band of territory owing allegiance to
the British Crown. The climax of British imperialism in this
region was reached in 1889-91 when Cecil Rhodes, fortune-
hunter and empire-builder, snatched Rhodesia. By no German were these developments viewed with a benevolent
eye.

Yet the British Empire in South Africa had its Achilles'
heel in the obstinate fact of Dutch nationalism. The Dutch
settlers in Cape Colony were not imperialists, still less were
the Dutch dispersion in the interior. The Cape Dutch, though
they had learnt to live on amicable terms with the British,
were at heart Republicans, looking forward to the time when,
without any violent rupture, the tie with Britain might be
severed, and a Federal State comparable to the American
started on a course of splendid independence under the
Southern Cross. What gave to this academic sentiment a
point of danger was the attitude of the Dutch Republics
north of the Colony.

In 1836 a body of Dutch farmers, having grievances against

the British Government, which had abolished slavery with indifferent compensation to the slave owners, trekked away from the Cape Colony, and eventually founded two republics north and south of the Vaal River. On these sunny and exhilarating highlands the Boers hunted and farmed, flogged their Kaffirs and read their Bible, a rugged, patriarchal community belonging rather to the seventeenth than to the nineteenth century, and prizing the solitude of their vast airwashed spaces far above the rewards which a town could offer or the pleasures which townsmen may enjoy. Then a serious complication was introduced into the simple structure of South African society. First diamonds were discovered (1869-70), afterwards (1885) gold, the diamonds in unheardof profusion at the place which came to be known as Kimberley, the gold within the territory of the Transvaal on that bleak range of the Witwatersrand where now stands the wide and wealthy city of Johannesburg. Into the solemn tranquillity of the veldt, where life had been wont to move at the pace of an ox-waggon, there suddenly burst a cataract of cosmopolitan town-dwelling fortune-hunters, bringing in their train the turmoil, the luxury, and the mechanism of urban Europe. It may be readily imagined that for the peasant rulers of the Transvaal the discovery of the greatest gold-field of the world created problems in government of unsuspected difficulty.

Meanwhile, before the gold rush to the Rand, the tension between the two white races had been increased by a singularly unlucky incident. Annexed in 1877 under a misapprehension by Disraeli, the Transvaal was restored to the Boers by Gladstone (1881) on the morrow of a serious reverse to British arms on Majuba Hill. It is wise to be generous after victory, but risky to be indulgent in the hour of defeat. By the ignorant Boer an act of magnanimity proceeding from the consciousness of strength was interpreted as a sign of cowardice and debility. Henceforward the Boers despised the Britons, and the Britons, galled by contempt and chafing under defeat, found less reason than ever to admire the spirit of the Boers.

Two remarkable men, one standing for the Dutch, the other for the British cause, dominated the South African scene: Kruger, the Boer Republican; Rhodes, the British

Imperialist. As a boy Kruger had shared in the great trek. 1825-
His skill in marksmanship, his accomplished handling of 1904
horses and oxen, his great ability and physical strength,
gave him a natural pre-eminence in youth. In riper age his
ascendancy was confirmed by toughness, violence, piety, and
craft. A rich gift of peasant humour, a capacity for homiletic
eloquence, and a profound belief in the Divine guidance of
his race added attraction to his rugged character. As he
smoked his pipe in the stoep of his modest dwelling in
Pretoria, chatting with back-veldt Boers, he seemed to be
the embodiment of Republican simplicity. Yet the treasures
of the Rand did not leave him unmoved. He was quick
to discern the value of gold for his young Republic,
how with the tribute levied from the mines it might
dominate the railways, equip an army, and perhaps ultimately,
as many young Boers desired, drive the British into the sea.
For the moment he was on the defensive. The loud-spoken
grievances of the Uitlanders, the foreign community in
Johannesburg, convinced him that these wealthy and powerful men were plotting with the assistance of the British
Government to overthrow his state.

Cecil Rhodes, with all the advantages of England and
Oxford, was built on wider and more generous lines. Of 1853-
sound country stock, he, like the Boers, loved the land. If 1902
he bent the main part of his energies to the making of money,
it was not so much for its own sake as for the opportunities
of power and influence which money would buy. As a
young man he had dreamed of securing the permanent
peace of the world by means of a great scheme of scholar-
ships, which would bring Englishmen and Americans together
in Oxford during an impressionable period of their lives; and
this dream, modified, expanded, articulated, pursued him
through life and fructified in a noble educational endowment.
Unlike the typical Uitlander, he was no bird of passage. He
lived and worked for South Africa, and for the harmonious
co-operation of the two white races. The Dutch he held in
deep and unaffected esteem. There was in them a slow
simplicity which matched his own. But heart trouble made
him impatient. The persistent clamour of the Uitlanders, the
obstinate resistance of the President to reasonable reforms,
affected the soundness of his judgment. In a disastrous mo-

ment he sanctioned a raid into the Transvaal, under his friend Jameson, to put down the Republic and to place the country under the Union Jack. It was in vain that the British Government disowned and denounced the Raid. The harm was done. A flame of racial passion enveloped the country, which under Kruger's fiery and obstinate leadership drifted steadily towards war. Sir Alfred Milner, the new High Commissioner, pressed for reforms. They were not conceded. Recent revelations of the bellicose temper of the young Boers at that time show how difficult it would have been to preserve the peace.

The grievances of the Uitlanders, though widely proclaimed in the London Press, were not in themselves calculated to stir the heart of the British democracy. Nobody had compelled these adventurers to settle in Johannesburg. Nobody proposed to obstruct their withdrawal. They had gone to the Transvaal to make money, and, notwithstanding the vices of the Republican *régime*, had made it, often on a lavish and spectacular scale.

A purely local quarrel in a South African mining city would have left the British public cold. But the quarrel was not local. It was suspected that President Kruger was using the wealth of the Rand to finance a wide-ranging anti-British conspiracy, and that in this enterprise he possessed the sympathy and counted on the support of the German *Reich*. Accordingly, when on the morrow of Jameson's defeat the Kaiser telegraphed his congratulations to Kruger, all England burst into a flame of indignation. The intervention was regarded as unwarrantable and sinister, bad for what it was, worse for what it portended. Fortunately it was not known in London that the Kaiser in his temerity had drafted an ultimatum which a wise ambassador declined to deliver, or that soon afterwards his government was at work plotting a continental alliance against England which broke upon the rock of French reluctance.

1899-1902   Three years passed. The South African quarrel grew into a serious war, which, while it brought volunteers from every part of the Empire to the assistance of the mother country, seriously strained its resources and exhibited to the military critics of the continent the numerous shortcomings of the British Army. Though it was the Boers and not the British who had declared war, the sympathy of the Continent was solid for the Republican armies. The skill, the tenacity, and the courage with which the Boer farmers resisted the professional forces of a great Empire were universally admired. To distant observers it seemed to be a contest between simplicity and luxury, liberty and despotism, God and Mammon. Every victory of the Boers was received with delirious enthusiasm, every setback to their cause by a corresponding measure of disappointment and gloom. In Germany and France the waves of anti-English indignation rose mountains high. Even the Tzar of Russia, whose domestic government was no model of freedom, proposed a general alliance of the continental powers against the unpopular and arrogant island.

Nevertheless Europe was powerless to intervene. With a stock of ill-will against England sufficient to launch a dozen wars, it was compelled to look on while Roberts and Kitchener retrieved the early reverses to British arms and wore down the Boer resistance. No continental power, no combination of continental powers, was in a position to challenge the British Navy. Supremacy at sea dominated the situation. Never so clearly as now had the Continent realized the inconvenience which ensued from Britannia ruling the waves. The lesson sank deep into the mind of the Kaiser and his advisers, impressing more particularly a vigorous young officer of the German Navy by name Tirpitz, who, coming forward about the time of the Jameson Raid, advocated the construction of a High Sea fleet. Accordingly two important consequences followed from the passions excited in Germany by the South African War. First, the road to an Anglo-German alliance, which had been opened by Chamberlain, was for the moment decisively obstructed; second, an argument, which no German could fail to understand, was now supplied for the construction of a fleet which even the strongest naval power in the world would be compelled to respect. Aided by the lessons of the Boer War, the Kaiser pursued with headlong zeal his darling project. It does not seem to have occurred to him that England, whose very existence depended on sea-borne supplies, would feel herself endangered by the presence in the North Sea of a fleet as powerful as her own. Holding that any interference with his favourite plaything was an intolerable personal insult, and that no diplomatic weapon was more suitable for the English than the big stick, he pressed forward with a series of naval bills, for the passage of which it was essential to foment anti-British feeling in the country. That in view of the continental balance of Powers such a course was beset with peculiar dangers for Germany was a reflection which does not appear to have struck his vigorous but volatile mind.

Dividing France and England from 1882-1904 was the complex problem of Egypt. The English had by a fate which seemed to all Frenchmen to be singularly perverse and vexatious stumbled into the inheritance which France had marked out for her own. It was Napoleon who had recovered Egypt for Europe; it was Mehemet Ali, Napoleon's admirer and pupil, who had made of Egypt a modern state; it was de Lesseps, a French engineer of genius, who had in 1869 pierced the Suez Canal. All three were opposed by England. Yet it was England and not France who secured a dominating control of the canal by the purchase of the Khedive's foundation shares in 1875, and England, again, who from 1882 onwards directed Egyptian policy from Cairo. For all this France had only herself to thank. At Bismarck's instigation she had taken up in conjunction with England the cause of the Egyptian bond holders. The two powers had deposed Ismail, the extravagant Khedive, and entered into a *condominium* with the object of restoring the shattered finances of the country. From the exercise of that joint responsibility France deliberately withdrew, leaving England to quell the revolt of Arabi, a malcontent colonel of the Egyptian army, and to straighten out the financial and administrative tangle which the deposed Khedive had left behind him. It was a curious situation. The Liberal Government of Gladstone, hating Imperial commitments, anxious to be rid of Egypt at the first convenient opportunity, found itself compelled to plunge deeper and deeper into the Nile mud, while France, which had no compunction about Imperialism, and would have given her eyes for Egypt, had, in a sudden paroxysm of timidity, left the palm and the dust to her rival.

If the idea of a permanent occupation of Egypt was distasteful to English Liberals, still more abhorrent was the suggestion that any attempt should be made to conquer the

1881

Sudan. The Liberals stood for peace, retrenchment, and reform, aspirations difficult to reconcile with the despatch of a military expedition into a scorching wilderness against a wild horde of fanatical dervishes. Yet the new rulers of Egypt could hardly be indifferent to the fate of a territory which was subject to the Egyptian flag, garrisoned by Egyptian troops, and now menaced by one of those fierce movements of religious fanaticism which from time to time convulse the Moslem world. Of this strange and formidable insurrection the leader was one Mohammed Ahmed, nephew of a boat builder in Dongola, who in 1881 proclaimed himself the Mahdi or Messiah and announced as his object the conquest of the world.

A weak Egyptian army, straying into the wilds of Kordofan and there experiencing an annihilating defeat, gave to the prophet a baptism of victory, and since the commander of the defeated force was Hicks Pasha, an Englishman, created a perplexing situation for the British Government. That the province should be promptly evacuated was a counsel of prudence, that the Egyptian garrisons should be safely withdrawn was an obligation of honour. The first operation was easy, but how to evacuate the scattered Egyptian garrisons without a costly and dangerous expedition was a problem calculated to tax the wisest head.

In an unfortunate hour the Government listened to the *Pall Mall Gazette*. This journal suggested that there was one man who by his extraordinary magnetism and unique gift in the handling of Oriental peoples could rally the Sudanese against the Mahdi, deliver the garrisons, put down the slave trade, and, without the movement of a man or a gun from England, relieve the Cabinet of its anxieties. The man was "Chinese" Gordon, a visionary hero, who in the civil wars of China had borne a charmed life, leading armies, composing differences, and exercising by virtue of a certain spiritual intensity an irresistible spell over the wildest and most savage natures, and who had been since noted for a period of striking personal ascendancy in the Sudan. In a very few days Gordon became the popular favourite, "one of our national treasures," the man of destiny appointed to work the miracle. Nobody stopped to consider whether this brave and mystical figure possessed the steadiness and sobriety of judgment necessary for the accomplishment of so great a task. It was sufficient that he accepted the perilous mission. By February, 1884, Gordon was in Khartum, where from there proceeded a continuous stream of telegrams, impulsive, inconsistent, confusing, and revealing the measure of the Cabinet's mistake in its choice of a Governor-General of the Sudan. A yet greater error was to follow. A year later (January 26, 1885) Gordon was allowed to perish under the spears of the Dervishes. A British army of relief, through the culpable delay of the Government, had arrived just too late to save the emaciated garrison of the beleaguered city and its indomitable commander.

The least important result of this tragedy was to sweep out of office the Government which was thought to have sent a brave man on an impossible errand and to have allowed him to perish at his post through remissness and delay. The wider and more enduring consequence was to inject into English policy a firm resolve to reconquer the Sudan. To the protection of the Suez Canal which was a serious British interest there were now added other reasons founded upon deep popular emotion against the evacuation of Egypt: retribution for Gordon, the liberation of the Sudan from barbaric tyranny, the restoration of military prestige. English ministers might declare that the official policy of the country was evacuation at the earliest moment, but the moment never came. Notable work awaited Englishmen in the Nile Valley. It was now that Evelyn Baring, later Lord Cromer, hiding dictatorial powers under the modest title of Consul-General, embarked upon the great course of administrative reform which made Egypt a solvent and prosperous country.

1885-96 Eleven years passed. The Mahdi died, the Khalifa Abdulla el Taashi succeeded to his power: but change of rulers made no difference to the Sudan. The same fierce fanaticism, the same barbarity, continued to distinguish the tribesmen who dominated this vast province. An Egyptian army officered from England was strong enough to defend the frontiers and to inflict a series of defeats upon the Khalifa and his lieutenants, but a greater and more systematic effort was required if the Sudan was to be delivered from the tyranny of the Dervishes. That effort was at least forthcoming, thanks to the careful preparations of Baring and Kitchener, the Sirdar or Commander of the Egyptian army. In 1896 Kitchener advanced to Dongola. Two years later, vanquishing distance by the railway and numbers by the machine gun, he annihilated his enemy on the field of Omdurman, entered Khartum, and there set up a joint government under the British and Egyptian flags. The victory of Kitchener was a triumph of order and method. For no less than the cost of one of Ismail's more expensive entertainments this energetic and methodical engineer reconquered the Sudan.

Hardly had this feat been accomplished when an unsuspected event threatened to undermine the whole British position in Egypt. A small body of French explorers under Captain Marchand had for three years been marching eastward through darkest Africa, and at last in the late summer of 1898, reached Fashoda, a village on the Upper Nile, and there planted the French flag. The British government instructed Kitchener to meet Marchand and to demand his withdrawal.

Relations between the two countries became at once seriously strained. After the sacrifices involved in the Sudanese campaign England was not disposed to cede the upper valley of the Nile to France on the strength of the presence in Fashoda of a French exploring party from the west. On the other hand, French public opinion could be brought with difficulty to admit that France was not humiliated by the requirement that a brilliant French officer, after a remarkable voyage of exploration, should surrender a territory which he had been the first to reach. Fortunately Delcassé, the French foreign minister, was a statesman who declined to involve his country in a war because of a miserable little hamlet on the Upper Nile of which ninety-nine out of every hundred of his compatriots had never heard. Wisely he foresaw that France might before long be glad of the friendship of England. He determined to order the withdrawal. War was averted: but the fleets had been mobilized and war had come uncomfortably near.

Delcassé, who saved the peace in 1898, stood so clear of popular prejudice that, despite the furious Anglophobia which was occasioned in France by Fashoda and the Boer War, he dared to believe that an understanding between France and England was desirable and might be obtained.

Happy always in his choice of instruments, he sent Paul Cambon to London to work for an *Entente*. On February 28, 1902, Joseph Chamberlain and Cambon were overheard at a party at Marlborough House talking of Egypt and Morocco. Having failed in his negotiations with Germany, the powerful English Colonial Secretary was turning his thoughts to an accord with France.

Jan.
22,
1901
Queen Victoria's long reign had come to an end. The monarchy which she had found weak and discredited she left firmly rooted in the affections of the country. Indefatigable industry and weight of experience had given something of that unique authority to her judgment which belonged to Elizabeth in her later years. It was not, however, her ability in the despatch of affairs, with respect to which the nation knew little, and still less her cast of mind, which evoked the glow of a people's loyalty, but her Teutonic simplicity and warmth of heart, her ready and gushing sympathy, and her capacity for entering into the common griefs and joys of ordinary people, to whom more than to the intellectuals and aristocrats she was temperamentally related. That her court was clean of profligacy and scandal commended it to the esteem of her subjects, who had been outraged by the private life of George IV. In those days, much, even dullness, was forgiven to virtue.

This little old lady, who was so proud and imperious and yet so close to the ways and thoughts of middle-class house-wives, ruled England during a period, extending over sixty-three years, which witnessed an extraordinary effulgence of the nation's genius. Thackeray and Dickens were writing in her youth, Meredith, Kipling, Hardy, and R. L. Stevenson in her riper years. She might have invited to her table, had it ever occurred to her to do so, such a galaxy of historians, beginning with Macaulay and ending with Maitland, as have never laboured under one reign. Among the major prophets the Victorian age may reckon Carlyle, Mill, and Ruskin; among the poets Tennyson and Browning, Swinburne and Matthew Arnold. In divinity Newman, in scientific discovery Darwin and Wallace, in exploration Livingstone, in medicine Lister, in romance Thackeray and Dickens, Anthony Trollope, Charlotte Brontë, George Eliot, and

R. L. Stevenson, in the popularization of science and the rationalistic interpretation of experience T. H. Huxley and Herbert Spencer, in comparative law Henry Maine, stand out among many figures of commanding accomplishments in every category. But the Queen was not an intellectual. Vainly was the superb panorama woven by the imaginative genius of her subjects unrolled before her royal eyes, idle the appeal of their innovating enthusiasms. The Oxford movement, the socialist movement, the rationalist movement, the feminist movement, were all alike abhorrent to her plain and steadfast conservatism. A fiery English patriot and in English politics a fierce partisan, she retained to the end, despite shattering toil and responsibility, the sentimental heart of a German girl.

Delcassé was in wait for Edward, her successor. The new 1901-King of England was made up of amiability. He had no 10 enmities or grudges, other than a personal distaste for his bumptious German nephew, but a genuine desire that England should be in good relations with all the world—with Germany, with France, with Russia. France in particular, where Anglophobia was still so strong, he desired to soften and secure. As Prince of Wales he had amused himself in Paris and made many French friends. In its dealings with France the British Government could wish for no better emissary of good will than the King.

Yet it would be wrong to ascribe to Edward VII a diplo- 1902-matic revolution which was the work of the Balfour Cabinet. 4 The King assisted but did not originate the *Entente Cordiale* with France. His official visit to Paris dispelled hostility and generated enthusiasm, but the *Entente* was due to the fact that the French and English governments had discovered that they were in a position to make a colonial bargain profitable to each. The essence of the transaction was that France recognized the special rights acquired by England in Egypt, while England acknowledged the special position of France in Morocco. The agreement was accompanied by a secret convention, which fixed the limits of the zone of French influence in Morocco in case of an understanding with Spain. At the same time the outstanding differences of the two countries in Newfoundland, Siam, Madagascar, and the New Hebrides were regulated. On the face of it nothing seemed happier or more reasonable than this mutual liquidation of vexatious colonial grievances. Cambon was jubilant over Morocco. The House of Commons was delighted with an arrangement which secured the position of England in Egypt, but Lord Rosebery, who noted that Germany, the strongest military power in Europe, had not been consulted over Morocco, was critical, saying in private that the *Entente Cordiale* with France would eventually lead England into a German war.

BOOKS WHICH MAY BE CONSULTED

J. A. Spender: *Fifty Years of Europe*. 1933.

J. L. Garvin: *The Life of Joseph Chamberlain*. 1932.

Lady Gwendolen Cecil: *The Life of Robert, Marquis of Salisbury*. 1921.

E. Brandenburg: *From Bismarck to the World War, German Foreign Policy*, 1870-1914. 1927.

H. N. Brailsford: *The War of Steel and Gold*. 1915.

J. Bryce: *Impressions of South Africa*. 1897.

Basil Williams: *Cecil Rhodes*. 1921.

D. Reitz: *Commando*. 1929.

S. G. Millin: *Rhodes*. 1933.

Sir Philip Magnus: *Kitchener*. 1958.

A. J. P. Taylor: *Struggle for Mastery in Europe*. 1954.

W. L. Langer: *Diplomacy of Imperialism*, 1890-1902. 2 vols. 1935

LIBERAL REFORMS AND
CLOUDS OF WAR

Peace of Vereeniging. English domestic politics. The Education Act. Liberal opposition. Temperance. Chinese Labour. Tariff Reform. The Liberal decade of 1905-15. Growing power of Germany. Morocco. The Anglo-French Entente. Anglo-German naval competition. Failure of the Hague Conferences. Anglo-Russian Entente, 1907. The Austrian coup d'état of 1908. Danger of war.

IT WAS difficult for the English, an insular and civilian people, fully to apprehend the significance of the diplomatic revolution which had brought to an end the long period of "splendid isolation." The Japanese Treaty, prepared in secret, made little stir; the *Entente* with France was regarded as a happy colonial deal, making for general harmony. The thought of a European war was far from men's minds. So rooted was the insular objection to a conscript army that there were Frenchmen like Clemenceau who regarded the *Entente* as a positive danger to France.

Moreover, England was absorbed in her own affairs. The beginning of the twentieth century found the country still grappling with the resistance of the Boers, who, despite the fact that Pretoria and Bloemfontein, the capitals respectively of the Transvaal and the Orange Free State, were in English occupation, persisted in keeping the field. Their mode of warfare, elusive, mobile, with every farmhouse in the country supplying food and shelter to the little groups of mounted riflemen who harassed an army altogether too small for effective operations over so vast a field, led to severities which attracted public censure. It was thought necessary to build blockhouses, to burn farmhouses, and to gather the evacuated women and children into concentration camps. Such expedients, however inevitable from the point of view of the soldier, were abhorrent to a good-natured population, and though the language of Campbell-Bannerman, the Liberal leader, who spoke of "methods of barbarism," was resented, the fact that such measures were thought to be required constituted an additional argument for the prompt termination of the war. The Government supported Kitchener in his desire for a negotiated peace as opposed to the requirement for unconditional surrender, which was favoured by Milner. The Treaty of Vereeniging was a real effort at reconciliation. Though the Boers were required to come within the Empire, so far from being asked to pay an indemnity they were given three million pounds for the reconstruction of their farms. Soon afterwards General Botha, coming to London, found himself, not a little to his amazement, a popular hero. With cries of "Good old Botha" the sporting population of the metropolis of the Empire welcomed the most formidable of their recent enemies as a good sportsman, a good loser, and a friend.

May 1902

An incident of the war which stirred English crowds to humiliating transports of jollity was the relief of an inconsiderable town on the western borders of the Transvaal. Little, perhaps, would have been made of the siege of Mafeking if it had not been defended by a man of genius whose happy resource and light-hearted sallies, telegraphed home while the siege was proceeding, made him a popular favourite with his countrymen. The name of Baden-Powell, which became known throughout the Empire for a feat of arms, was later celebrated for a civilian triumph. Out of his experience of the veldt the defender of Mafeking made a new and original contribution to the education of the young. The Boy Scouts have now become a world-wide institution and a welcome addition to the character-building forces in society. So from two English wars, the Crimean and the South African, something unexpected has emerged for the relief of man's estate. The Crimea gave Florence Nightingale to the nursing profession. South Africa suggested to Baden-Powell a form of moral training, well suited to the nature of average boys and calculated to correct the monotony of the urban classroom by the open-air freedom and discipline of the wilds.

The Tory party, which was governing England at the Peace of Vereeniging, had been returned to power in overwhelming numbers in the "Khaki Election" of 1900. The Prime Minister was Lord Salisbury, his principal lieutenants A. J. Balfour and Joseph Chamberlain, the one an accomplished humanist and philosopher with a special gift for parliamentary dialectics, the other a Unitarian from Birmingham, who, after a strenuous and successful career in business and in the municipal politics of his native city, had entered Parliament and, exchanging the radicalism of his early youth for an eager and constructive imperialism, was now the most commanding figure in the Unionist ranks. A poll taken in the heat and passion of a war is never indicative of the true balance of political forces, and when the Conservative Government, which had been returned with a mandate to finish with the Boers, proceeded to touch domestic questions, its strength swiftly and sensibly ebbed away. Nonconformity was alienated by its treatment of education and temperance, Labour by the introduction of Chinese labour into the South African mines, and commerce and industry by the initiation of a powerful attack upon the hallowed system of Free Trade.

The real author of the Education Act of 1902 was Sir Robert Morant, one of those powerful civil servants who often, more than their official chiefs, help to mould the policy of their country. It was a big, revolutionary, beneficent measure, transferring the local administration of education from school boards to special committees of the counties and boroughs—that is, to bodies elected by the ratepayers and possessing the powers and responsibilities in finance which such election confers. It was argued that a body which could levy a rate could do more and dare more for education than one which could merely advise. The Act in effect was a challenge to every borough and county to take pride in its schools and to develop them to the best of its ability. Nor was its operation confined to elementary schools. By a bold but necessary departure from existing practice it sanctioned the provision of public aid for secondary education.

Nevertheless, bitter offence was given to the Nonconformists, and therefore to the bulk of the Liberal party, by the fact that denominational schools were taken into the public system and made eligible for aid from the rates. "Rome on the rates," became a popular cry. How, it was argued, was it just, how was it compatible with the religious conscience, that a Baptist should pay rates for the support of a school pervaded by an Anglican or Roman atmosphere? Still more acute was the complaint that in single-school areas, some eight thousand in number, Nonconformists were compelled to send their children to church schools. The debate, which raged furiously through the country, brought out all the latent jealousy of Romanism, Anglicanism, and the domination of the squires. So keen was the feeling that many a pious dissenter "passively" resisted and would go to prison rather than pay his rate.

Temperance was another question much agitated wherever Liberals were gathered together. The evil of drunkenness was widely acknowledged; its connection with crime and social misery established. Every social worker regarded drink as the most potent obstacle to social reform. Many remedies were proposed: total abstinence, local option, the cutting down under a strict licensing system of redundant public houses. It was therefore regarded as a distinctly retrograde step when an Act was passed in 1904 which treated the publican's licence as a property from which he could not be dispossessed without compensation (save in case of abuse) by the licensing justices. To the opposition which was gathering against the Conservative Government on the score of its education policy there was now added the indignation of all the temperance workers in the country.

All this, however, was nothing compared to the emotion excited by Chinese labour and the menace of a fiscal revolution. The English trades unions, which had built up for themselves a position of authority unequalled by any similar organization on the continent, saw in the proposal to import Chinese labour into the South African mines a menace to the standard of life which had been so painfully built up by the persevering effort of three generations. If a block of cheap labour could be transported from China to Johannesburg, would it not be equally open to capitalists to fill the mills of Lancashire and Yorkshire with inexpensive and submissive orientals? If that were done, what would be the position of British workers? The whole trades union movement would be ruined. Wages would fall, standards of life would decline, the gulf between employer and employed would be immeasurably widened. Though the danger that oriental labour would ever be introduced into England was remote and wildly enlarged by party passion, there can be little question but that "Chinese slavery" was an important ingredient in the great revulsion of feeling which returned the Liberals to power in 1906.

A larger and graver issue was raised by Joseph Chamberlain's campaign for Tariff Reform. During a visit to South Africa in 1903 the Colonial Secretary elaborated a policy which might distract the minds of his fellow-countrymen from sordid and trifling squabbles over church schools and public-houses and refresh the waning authority of the Unionist party by identifying it with the majestic theme of imperial consolidation. The votes which the Tories had lost over education, the publicans, and the Chinese might be recaptured by a bold policy of Imperial Preference. Chamberlain returned to England resolved upon an onslaught on English Free Trade, and, resigning his place in the Cabinet, opened "a raging and tearing campaign" in the country. Meanwhile the Conservative Cabinet held the fort, the Prime Minister, Balfour, delicately balancing the pros and cons of the tariff question until such time as, the arrangements with France having been concluded, he felt himself at liberty to face the electorate.

The system of Free Trade had governed England for sixty years, during which time the country had experienced an astonishing expansion of national prosperity. While great industries had been developed and great fortunes had been made, the dietary of the people had been diversified, enriched, and cheapened by grains and fruits drawn from every quarter of the globe. The prosperity of the Lancashire cotton trade, depending as it did upon oriental markets sensitively contracting at the smallest rise of price, was thought to be endangered by any tax, however slight, which might tend to raise the cost of production. Again, shipping and shipbuilding, banking and coal-mining were staple industries which profited by freedom and could only be injured by the imposition of tariffs. That iron and steel should be as cheap as possible was regarded as axiomatic in a country where the uses of steel were so numerous and the application of machinery so widely diffused. The position of London as the monetary centre of the world, the strength of the mercantile marine, the livelihood of the mill hands in the cotton and cloth industries, were all believed to depend upon fiscal freedom. Though it was true that other countries had not followed England in her Free Trade policy and that two countries in particular, the United States and Germany, had notably prospered under protection, English goods still went all over the world. Despite high duties abroad, the old Free Trade maxim that foreign markets could be conquered by cheapness was still valued. The sacrifice of such indubitable advantages seemed to be a gamble, for it was only by a prosperous export trade, based on cheaper products, that Britain could rely upon being able to purchase the food which was required to support her population. When Chamberlain first opened his campaign the memory of the "hungry forties" was still a living thing in the country, nor was there any part of his policy which was more vulnerable to attack than the necessity which it involved, if a valuable preference was to be given to the dominions and colonies, of placing a tax on food.

Against such objections, based on the structure and conduct of British business, Chamberlain unfolded the vision of a great Empire bound together by fiscal ties. The home country was asked to place protective duties on imports, including food and raw materials, primarily in order that it might accord to the dominions and colonies a preference against the foreigner, but also as a shield against foreign competition at home. As the prophet of Tariff Reform, trim, beautifully dressed, an orchid in his buttonhole and a monocle in his eye, toured round the country expounding these views with incomparable vigour, now appealing to imperial sentiment, now pointing to the increasing severity of foreign competition, and in particular to the advance of German industry, he was followed by Asquith, the brilliant spokesman of the Free Trade Liberals. The debate, which raised the most wide-reaching issues, proceeded in every household. Its first political effect was to split the Unionist party, which was weakened by the secession of the Duke of Devonshire and Goschen; its second to contribute to the great Liberal victory of 1906. For the moment Tariff Reform was repulsed.

Prosperity rather than dialect had fought the winning battle for Free Trade.

The Liberal party thus returned to power governed the country for ten years. It stood for peace and Free Trade. 1905- It regarded commerce not as a conflict of rivals but as a 15 system of exchanges made for the mutual convenience of friends. It wanted to reduce expenditure on armaments and to promote the social services, Such grievances as the nonconformists cherished with respect to church schools and temperance, it was concerned to remedy. Colonial preference it rejected. The kind of imperialism which this party favoured was illustrated when Campbell-Bannerman, the new Prime Minister, gave responsible government to the Transvaal and the Orange Free State. There have been few more courageous acts in modern history than the decision to hand over the government of South Africa soon after a bitter contest to the defeated enemy. That "C. B.'s" confidence was not misplaced was shown eight years afterwards when General Botha, bravely suppressing a rebellion stirred up by a few old comrades in arms, led his people into the Great War on the British side.

By the irony of fate this peace-loving, peace-pursuing government fell straight into a European crisis. For the past two years the position of Germany in Europe had been strengthened by a series of events contributing to impair the value of the Russian alliance to France. The first of these was the outbreak of a war between Russia and Japan, the second a series of amazing Japanese victories, and the third a revolutionary convulsion in Russia, closely following upon the military collapse of the Imperial armies in the field. In 1905, while these troubles were proceeding, the moment seemed opportune for Count Schlieffen, the German chief of the staff, to propose that a war should be forced on France. The inhuman idea did not seem criminal or even indecent to the two sinister figures who now directed German foreign policy. It was common ground between Count Bülow, the plausible Chancellor, and Baron Holstein, the grim power behind the throne, that the time was ripe, even at the risk of war, for testing the strength of the Anglo-French *Entente* by a strong diplomatic offensive. Morocco was selected as the point of attack, for it was by permitting France a free hand in Morocco that England had purchased immunity from French molestation in Egypt, and it was rightly conjectured that unless the English were prepared to back the French in Morocco up to the point of war, English friendship would for ever lose its value in the eyes of France.

June, 1905   So the great offensive was opened. The Kaiser was sent on a mission to Tangier to assure the Sultan of his goodwill and support, and soon after the French were compelled to accept, Jan., 1906   under threat of war, the resignation of Delcassé and the summoning of a Conference to Algeciras. Little, however, did the Germans gain from the humiliations put upon their enemy by this clumsy and hectoring diplomacy. Sir Edward Grey, the new Liberal Foreign Minister, rightly judging that the honour of his country was concerned, gave to the French a full measure of diplomatic support at Algeciras, and, being impressed by the risks of a German attack upon France, authorized secret military conversations between officers of the French and English staffs.

The immediate result of the German pressure upon France in the matter of Morocco was to tighten rather than to loosen the Anglo-French *Entente*.

Though nothing was publicly known at the time, and most members of the British Cabinet shared the general ignorance of the public, a decisive step was taken when French and British officers were authorized to construct plans in view Jan., 1906   of an eventual war between Germany and France. Though it was carefully explained that such conversations could not pledge the government, which must always in the last resort be guided by the moral sentiment of Parliament and of the country, a presumption was created in the minds of soldiers on either side of the Channel that, in the event of European trouble, they would fight shoulder to shoulder. Mutual confidences had been exchanged, secret plans had been discussed. The initiation of these military conversations meant that the Anglo-French *Entente* was not merely an adjustment of colonial differences, but an understanding which, on sufficient cause and Parliament being willing, might lead to the participation of England in a European war.

Meanwhile the growth of the German navy had been long watched with anxious eyes by the English Admiralty. The Navy was not in England a party question. It was common knowledge that the protection of the country's food supplies in time of war was dependent on the possession of sea power, and that the coherence of the British Empire itself rested in the last resort on the ability of the British Fleet to keep the seas against its enemies. As a rough guide to Admiralty practice, it was part of the national policy to aim at a two-power standard, a navy capable of dealing effectively with the important navies of the two next strongest naval Powers in the world. But the rise of German navalism at once changed the outlook. No English sailor was disposed to undervalue the seagoing qualities of the German battleship, the skill of German gunnery, or the courage and sea-craft of German crews. Because the English sailor respected the German sailor, he was the more insistent upon the danger proceeding from German naval policy. What sailors thought, the Government and the country thought also. At whatever sacrifice, England must outbuild Germany. In 1906 two steps were taken which showed that the new Liberal government was alive to the danger. The first Dreadnought was launched, and the British Home Fleet was concentrated in the North Sea. The Germans responded by a new Navy Law. The race of naval armaments was now open and unconcealed. Nor did it escape the notice of the British Admiralty that the heavily armour-plated High Sea Fleet was constructed not for distant voyages, but for a conflict with a strong opponent in the North Sea.

The responsibility for this calamitous competition is not a little to be attributed to the fallacious view held by the Kaiser and Tirpitz that there would be a period of time while the German navy was still relatively weak, when the English might be tempted to destroy it, but that once "the danger zone" was passed, all would be well. From this premiss it followed that the more ships Germany laid down, the more swiftly would she pass through the danger zone, and the more certainly conquer the respect and acquiescence of her naval rival. From this ground of psychology and logic the Kaiser was not to be moved.

Any suggestion coming from the British side that there should be an agreed limitation, which would still leave England with more ships than Germany, was resented as an affront in Berlin. When Sir Charles Hardinge ventured

(August 11, 1908) to broach the question of naval limitation at Cronborg, the Kaiser roundly told him that he would rather go to war.

May, 1899 and July, 1907   The international atmosphere of Europe during these years was heavily laden with suspicion and fear of war. Two conferences summoned to The Hague on the initiative of the Tzar to promote peace and disarmament, so far from relieving, contributed to aggravate the situation. The Germans, who were firm set against military or naval reductions, noted with suspicion that while the Tzar proposed to limit effectives, in which Russia could always claim an overwhelming superiority, the development of Russian railways, which was greatly in arrears, was to be subject to no such curb. Britain, too, appeared in an equivocal rôle, on the one hand pressing earnestly for military reductions, on the other hand resisting the proposal upon which Germany and America were united, for according immunity to private property at sea. It was open, therefore, for Germany to say that, while the English were anxious that the continent should disarm, the strongest navy in the world still proposed to exercise its belligerent rights at the expense of neutral commerce in time of war. From these well-meant discussions little that was good resulted.

Meanwhile (1907) a combination thought in Berlin to be utterly impossible was translated into fact. England and Russia, the two rival oriental empires, adjusted their respective spheres of interest in the Middle East. The Anglo-French *Entente* on colonial questions was followed up by an Anglo-Russian *Entente* on Asiatic questions. Nothing could be more reasonable than that two countries should endeavour to eliminate occasions of diplomatic friction, and the Anglo-Russian *Entente*, though criticized by some as unfair to Persia, was generally applauded in England as an important further step towards the peaceful ordering of the world. Very different, however, were the views of this transaction entertained in Berlin. There the Anglo-Russian understanding was regarded as an additional indication of the Machiavellian design attributed to King Edward and Sir Edward Grey of encircling Germany by a ring of enemies.

Germany did not intend to be encircled. More particularly

she was resolved to keep open for herself the Balkan route to the Near East and to the Persian Gulf. Since Austria, her friend and ally, held the gates, it was a cardinal axiom of German policy that nothing must be allowed to impair the close junction between Vienna and Berlin.

The strength of this necessary bond was soon to receive a striking illustration. The political map of the Balkans had, as we have seen, been arranged with infinite difficulty by a concert of the Powers in 1878. The Congress of Berlin had fixed the size of Bulgaria, returned Macedonia to the Turks, and invited the Austrians to administer under Turkish suzerainty the provinces of Bosnia and Herzegovina, whose populations were Serb in origin and in speech. The Treaty of Berlin was not ideal, for Macedonia under Turkish rule proved to be a chronic centre of oppression and disturbance, but at least it possessed the merit of being a settlement which had been agreed to by the Great Powers and could not safely or properly be varied without their consent. How great then was the consternation when it was learned that Austria, without even the knowledge of her German ally, had resolved to annex Bosnia and Herzegovina, and that the Bulgarians Oct., with Austrian encouragement had declared themselves to be 1908 a monarchy independent of the Porte! There was much to be said for these changes. Austria had borne the burden of administering the two Slavonic provinces for thirty years and her work had been good. Bulgaria was permeated by a strong spirit of national pride and independence. But if the objects were desirable, the manner in which it was sought to achieve them was a challenge to the public law of Europe, and a definite threat to peace. How could it be expected that the Serbs could view with equanimity the sudden incorporation of the Bosnians and Herzegovinians, peoples whom they regarded as bone of their bone and flesh of their flesh, in the Habsburg Empire? The annexation sent a flame of indignation through Serbia which was the more dangerous since behind the Serb stood the formidable might of the Russian Empire.

Again war seemed very near. Moltke and Conrad von Hötzendorf, the chiefs respectively of the German and Austrian staffs, urged that the time had now come to try conclusions with Russia and France. Passions were high in

St. Petersburg; Isvolsky, who had been tricked by Aehrenthal, the Austrian Foreign Minister, abounding in fiery denunciations of Austrian duplicity, and every Russian feeling that by this sudden and violent Austrian act the balance of power in the Balkans had been decisively turned against the Slavs. But at this moment, which might so easily have been critical for the fate of the Habsburg Empire, William of Hohenzollern stood by the side of Francis Joseph. The Tzar was given to understand (March 23, 1909) that if he were to draw the sword in this Balkan quarrel he must reckon on the opposition of the German Empire. The threat was sufficient, the sense of humiliation remained. Next year in Vienna the Kaiser boasted that in the Bosnian crisis he had stood by his Austrian friend and ally "in shining armour." It was unwise to flaunt before the world that only so had peace been kept. There were those in St. Petersburg who vowed that never again, were a similar crisis in the Balkans to arise, would the Kaiser find a Russia so submissive to his will.

It is eloquent of the international neurosis of these times that two second-rate men, Aehrenthal, the half-Semitic Austrian Foreign Minister, and Isvolsky, a vain, empty, fire-eating Russian diplomat, were able not only to bring Europe to the edge of a general war, but by their furious personal hatred to infect the relations between their respective Empires with a dangerous measure of animosity. Meeting together at a country house in Bohemia these two ambitious politicians had hatched a plot which was to give Austria her two Balkan provinces and to open for Russia the sea passage to the Mediterranean. The plot was secret and, since it involved a double breach of the Treaty of Berlin, deep-dyed with illegality. Moreover, even if Austria and Russia had held together, the plan for opening the straits would have been regarded by England as a challenge. But Aehrenthal betrayed Isvolsky. Before any steps had been taken to secure the Russian objective, the Austrian conspirator published the news of the Austrian annexations. The Russian was deeply mortified. The clever scheme which was to have earned him the eternal gratitude of his country had turned to dust and ashes, for Russia had lost the straits and Austria had won the provinces. Stung by wounded pride and frustrated ambition, Isvolsky was determined that the Austrians should pay heavily for their Aehrenthal. Among the war-mongers of the period this Russian diplomat ranks high, almost as high as the most fiery and persistent warmonger in Europe, Conrad von Hötzendorf, the fanatical chief of the Austrian General Staff.

Meanwhile, far away in London, Sir Edward Grey, much shocked by these lawless proceedings, proposed the summoning of a European Conference to regulate the situation. What England might do, were France to be drawn into war over the Balkan crisis, was a matter with respect to which neither Cabinet nor Parliament had come to a clear resolve.

BOOKS WHICH MAY BE CONSULTED

J. A. Spender: *Fifty Years of Europe.* 1933.

J. A. Spender: *Life of Sir Henry Campbell-Bannerman.* 1923.

Earl Buxton: *General Botha.* 1924.

G. B. Allen: *Sir Robert Morant.* 1934.

J. L. Garvin: *Life of Joseph Chamberlain.* 1932.

Von Bülow: *Memoirs.* 1931-2.

Grey of Fallodon: *Twenty-five Years.* 1928.

R. Blake: *The Unknown Prime Minister: the Life and Times of Andrew Bonar Law:* 1858-1923. 1955.

F. Owen: *Tempestuous Journey: Lloyd George, his Life and Times.* 1954.

SERBIA AND THE DUAL MONARCHY

Francis Joseph. Racialism in the Dual Monarchy. Croatia feels the call of the blood. The Serbian menace. Exasperation in Vienna. The Turkish revolution of 1908. Its real character. Turkish tyranny unites the Christian States in the Balkans. Agadir and Tripoli. The Balkan League of 1912. Its astonishing triumphs. A European War averted by the Conference of London. The second Balkan War. The defeat of Bulgaria. The Serbs become the leading people in the Balkans. Vienna apprehensive.

1848-
1917
MEANWHILE Francis Joseph, the old Austrian Emperor, lived on in Vienna diligently toiling at his desk, signing and reading, reading and signing, from early morn to night, a tragic figure, could he have felt tragedy, for his wife had fallen by an assassin's hand, his only son had committed suicide, and his nephew and heir-in-law had disgraced himself by a love-match, never forgiven, with a lady below his princely rank. But whether it was because all capacity for emotion had been drained out of him, or from an over-mastering sense of the majesty of his public function, or simply because his nature was shallow and conventional, the old man went on his way unmoved, an ascetic, an automaton, yet acclaimed as the first horseman in his realm, and the first gentleman in Europe. A stiff ceremonial shielded him from the tumultuous world outside. A martial aristocracy defended his throne. An imperial bureaucracy supplied him with the ministers, fleeting and embarrassed, who endeavoured to cope with the anxious tasks of government. Under his long rule, the Austrian Empire had sustained so many shattering blows, the loss of Lombardy and Venetia, the rape of the Danish duchies, the exclusion from the German *Reich*, that it seemed to bear a charmed life, even when it was, in fact, fast moving to its dissolution.

Of all European States the Dual Monarchy had most to

fear from the development of the racial and nationalist passions which were now sweeping through the world, potent in Japan, menacing in India, firing enthusiasm in the British Dominions, and finally transforming political life in the Balkans. For this composite State was based upon the entire negation of racialism. It proceeded on the assumption that eight and a half million Czechs, five million Poles, four million Ruthenes, five million seven hundred thousand Serbs and Croats, three million three hundred thousand Roumanians, and one million three hundred thousand Slovenes would rest content with a system under which the deciding influence was exercised in one half of the Empire by ten million Magyars, and in the other half by twelve million Germans. For many centuries that supposition had been justified. The Austrian Empire had held together under a common creed, a common army, a common crown, until men had come to regard it as an international necessity, a polity, which, however anomalous and difficult to work, served so useful a purpose that, were it abolished, the nature of things would abhor the vacuum. But now the survival of the monarchy was jeopardized from within. Even between the two dominant races, the German and the Magyar, there was harassing friction, the Magyars seeking at every decennial revision of the *Ausgleich* to strip away everything which was substantial in the bond uniting Austria and Hungary, until only a bare personal union between the crowns was left. Still worse were the relations between the Magyars and the many non-Magyar peoples comprised within the Hungarian Kingdom.

All the bitterness which the Irish peasantry felt towards their English masters was experienced by the Slovaks, the Ruthenes, the Roumans, and the Serbs, toward the proud and privileged aristocracy which violently attempted to Magyarize the country, imposing its alien language, its alien schools, and so working the electoral system as to defraud the weaker peoples of their due share of representation in the national Diet.

The growing importance of social and democratic problems, the rise of international labour, the adoption in 1907 of universal suffrage, failed to soften the sharp divisions between the races of the Austro-Hungarian monarchy. When it came to the point, racialism was always the strongest factor in public emotion—stronger than creed, stronger than class, stronger than ties of professional or economic association. Every Parliament and provincial Diet tended to become a racial pandemonium. As an Austrian writer has put it, "the racial shirt was closer to the heart than the Imperial uniform."

Arising out of these serious discords was the prospect that the Empire would be shattered by secessions. The Slovenes of Styria, and the Italians of South Tyrol, worked for severance. The Ruthenes of East Galicia strained against the ties which united them to the Poles in the western section of the Province. The peasants of Transylvania (a province of Hungary) were Rouman not in blood only, but in political sympathy. In Croatia, smarting under the enforced use of the Magyar language on the railway lines, a party was fast growing in numbers and influence which favoured a severance of the land from Hungary and its incorporation in a federation of southern Slavs, which should include Bosnia, Herzegovina, and Cisleithanian Dalmatia, and even, as some forward spirits dared to dream, the Serbian Kingdom. Such inspirations could not be lightly dismissed by the statesmen of the Ballplatz. Rightly the government of Vienna regarded the spectre of a Yugo-Slav or South Slav state with suspicion and alarm. The malady of Slavonic nationalism was not such as to admit of isolation. The Croatians were not merely a body of disappointed Austrian subjects who could be handled as a problem of domestic police. Though belonging to the Roman Church, they were Serb in speech and Serb in race. Loyally as they had served the Habsburg House, when Serbia was a downtrodden province of the Turkish Empire, they could not entirely resist the call of the blood. While Belgrade was Turkish, the devotion of Croatia went out to Vienna; but when Serbia became a free self-governing kingdom, able to hold its own against the Turk and the Bulgar, and standing out as the protagonist of the Slavonic race in the Balkans, the allegiance of the Croats flickered in division and uncertainty. On the one hand was a long and honourable tradition of service in the imperial army, of blood poured out on many a stricken field, of honours toilsomely deserved and generously accorded; on the other was the appeal which came from the presence just beyond their borders of a rugged, valiant, romantic people of their own blood and speech, who, albeit in a lower and more primitive stage of development, had won their way to political emancipation by the sword. It was an appeal which was strengthened by a common hate. To Croat and Serb the Magyar was odious. A wretched tariff war between Serbia and Hungary was the symptom of angry feelings, which winds sweeping across the wide horizon of international policy might blow into a formidable flame.

It is not then to be wondered that the Austrian Government regarded Serbia as an enemy. Here on the southern frontier of the realm was a state, small indeed in population and area, but armed, warlike, and enterprising, with racial affiliations spreading far and wide through Austria and Hungary, a standing centre of Slavonic propaganda, a possible spearpoint of Slavonic attack. It was no idle or extravagant hypothesis to imagine that a movement spreading outward from the Serbs to their kinsfolk in the Empire might produce a complete landslide of its southern provinces, with sympathetic reactions impossible to measure among the malcontent and emotional peoples of the centre and the north.

These Austrian suspicions and animosities were deepened by a terrible crime. There was in the Serbian army (1903) a secret society known as the Black Hand, at once revolutionary and nationalist, which had conceived a fierce abhorrence of the reigning Obrenovitch dynasty, not only in virtue of that old and bloody feud between the rival Houses of Obrenovitch and Karageorgevitch, which had for three generations divided the country, but also because Alexander, the reigning monarch, suffered from the reproach of being at once conservative and pro-Austrian. The officers of the Black Hand did nothing by halves. They entered the royal palace (1903), butchered the King and Queen, and ordered the Parliament to summon Peter Karageorgevitch, a mild and elderly exile, to ascend the vacant throne. It was little consolation to the Austrians to know that the new King of Serbia was an amiable gentleman, who had translated Mill *On Liberty*. They believed that he and his country were in the bloodstained grip of the Black Hand, and that this society, which was developing the idea of a union of all the southern

Slavs under the Serbian Crown, would stop at no crime to effect its purpose.

Statesmen are human. There is a point at which, through the accumulation of worries, the nerve gives way. To that point in the early years of the twentieth century the statesmen of Vienna were steadily moving. Nothing went smoothly. On every side there were obstacles which no industry could overcome, discords which no art could appease, perils which no eye could measure. The atmosphere became charged with exasperation and impatience. To be quit of the Serbs, to read this upstart race of assassins and conspirators a sharp lesson, and to put every wretched Slav in his proper place became an obsession. Again and again the soldiers pressed for a preventive war. But for German discouragement it is probable, if not certain, that the civilians in Vienna would have hearkened to their advice.

In the spring of the year (1908) in which Aehrenthal made his successful but unfortunate coup, an astonishing revolution occurred among the Turks. That barbarous Asiatic people had not been altogether unaffected by their long association with the culture of the West. The American missionary, the French novelist, the Universities of Paris and Berlin, were combining to give to the wealthier sections of Turkish society a new outlook upon the world. A ferment of patriotic nationalism began to make itself felt in the corrupt and decadent society which had so long languished under the enervating and capricious rule of Abdul Hamid. By degrees patriotism took a practical shape. An association, styling itself the Committee of Union and Progress, was secretly formed for terminating the inglorious subservience of the Ottoman race to the western powers and for the creation of a modernized and efficient Ottoman state. It met first at Geneva (1891), flitted to Paris, and finally settled at Salonika (1908). Many of its members were lawyers and doctors, some were Jews, others soldiers. General enlightenment was the professed note of a body which represented, not the rough upland Turks of Anatolia, but the educated class which had been formed in the seaport towns by western culture. Among its members were Enver, a young officer who had learned soldiering in Berlin; Tálaat, a telegraph clerk from Salonika;

and Djavid, a Jew financier. When the third army corps stationed in Macedonia had been secured for the cause, the Committee threw aside its disguises, proclaimed the Turkish constitution of 1876, and prepared to march on the capital.

To the amazement of Europe the revolution of the Young Turks met with instantaneous success. Startled into false professions of sympathy the Sultan accepted the constitution, summoned a parliament, disbanded his spies, and proclaimed the principles of liberty and equality. Soon afterwards (April 27, 1909) he recanted and was deposed. The Young Turks were masters of the state. The long Hamidian rule, founded on tyranny and espionage, was brought to an end. As Mohammed V, the new Sultan, mounted the throne, he was inspired to observe that the safety and happiness of Turkey depended on the "steady and serious application of the constitutional régime."

For a few weeks it seemed to western observers that all the popular notions about the Turks would need to be revised. Here apparently was a Moslem government prepared to repudiate every principle which had governed Turkey in the past, a government of liberals and democrats, of parliamentarians and humanitarians, of statesmen who were pledged to admit the Christian populations of the Balkans into a just and equal fellowship of privilege and power, and to give to the Turkish state all the benefits which modern civilization could confer. In England the Young Turks were acclaimed as idealists anxious to graduate in the school of liberty, and to found a Turkish Westminster on the Bosphorus.

All this was the wildest error. The Young Turks were very far from being liberals. The governing force in their movement was a hot and intemperate nationalism. Nothing was more foreign to their notions or to their practice than an attempt to conciliate the Christian peoples. A methodical and centralized tyranny was substituted for the slatternly extortions and numerous massacres of the Hamidian régime. Disorders grew, outrages multiplied. The state of Macedonia with its mixed populations of Bulgars, Greeks, and Serbs went from bad to worse. New taxes inflamed the Albanians. The union of Crete with Greece was forbidden. In less than two years the harsh government of these Turkish nationalists had achieved a miracle, such as no statesman could have foreseen. A vigorous and formidable Moslem tyranny, led by men who were determined upon one last desperate fling for Empire in an adverse world, suddenly healed the feuds of the Balkans and united the Christian populations into a military league.

The Balkan drama which had begun with the Turkish revolution in Salonika now entered its most critical phase. The scene for a moment must be shifted to Agadir, an obscure port on the Atlantic coast of Morocco. Thither the German Government, annoyed by the despatch of a French military expedition to Fez, despatched with great unwisdom the gunboat *Panther*. The demonstration provoked immediate reactions in Paris, in London, and in Rome. Mr. Lloyd George, the Chancellor of the Exchequer, in his Mansion House speech, went out of his way to warn the German Government that, were war to be forced upon France over such an issue, England would not be unmoved. In Rome the despatch of the German gunboat to the shores of Morocco acted as a spur to Imperial adventure, for Italy had caught the prevailing fever, and not content with nursing claims upon the Italian territory which was still subject to the Austrian yoke, dreamed of an African Empire. Her eye was on Tripoli, and she felt that if the Germans had designs on the North African coast, she had no time to lose. Even Giolitti, the finished Parliamentary artist, to whom adventures of all kinds were unwelcome, but who kept his ear close to the ground, realized the need for speedy action. With hardly a shadow of a pretext, he declared war on Turkey, and sent the Italian army into Libya.

July, 1911

It was clear that if ever the Christian population of the Balkans were to attack the Turks no moment could be more opportune than one in which the main strength of the Turkish army was locked up in Africa and engaged in a losing struggle with the Italians.

Mar., 1912

Nevertheless, the formation of the Balkan League was a surprising achievment, rendered possible by the violent maladministration of the Young Turks, but also by the emergence of a few men of outstanding political stature, of whom one was J. D. Bourchier, *The Times* correspondent in Bulgaria, while another was M. Venizelos, a Cretan hardened in the civil wars of his own island, and, as an islander, possessing a larger and more detached outlook on affairs than most of the politicians of continental Greece.

If the fact of the League was remarkable, its success was still more surprising. At every point the Turk was out-generalled and outfought. The Greek Navy denied him the sea. The Bulgarians defeated the main Ottoman armies in Thrace, first at Kirk-Kilisse, October 23, 1912, and after-wards at Lule Burgas, driving the enemy in utter disorder behind the lines at Chataldja; and while the Bulgarians were achieving these astonishing results in the east, astonishing by reason of their completeness and their speed, the Greeks fought their way into Salonika, and the Serbs had the satis- Oct. faction on the hard-fought field of Kumanovo of wiping 23, out the ancient memories of the great defeat of Kossovo, 1912 which had ruined the Serbian Empire in the fourteenth century. Such a victory, little as its implications were realized at the time, had a vital bearing on the difficult problem of maintaining European peace. It was one of those complete and unexpected triumphs which exalt the spirit of a nation, and was the more inspiring since it led on to the recovery of Uskub, the ancient capital of Serbia, and of Monastir, the key to central Macedonia. In a campaign of six weeks the Balkan League, which had put into the field more than 600,000 men, had practically destroyed all Euro-pean Turkey outside Constantinople.

It may readily be imagined how disconcerting to Austria were these extraordinary events. Serbia, the chief source of Austrian apprehension, came out of this Balkan struggle Dec., with her reputation greatly increased, her territories enlarged, 1912 her aspirations inflamed. In the Conference summoned to London to settle a new map of the Balkans, it was Austria's Aug., prime object to deny to Serbia direct access to the Adriatic. 1913 The little mountain territory of Albania accordingly became a centre of intense diplomatic conflict. The resolution of Austria to keep Serbia out of Albania was matched by the determination of Russia that the Serbs should be given this access to the sea. Europe was brought to the brink of war, but war was averted. The Germans exercised a moderating influence over the Austrians, the English over the Russians, and the difficulty was solved by the erection of Albania into an independent state to be governed by a German Prince.

While the Conference was proceeding in London, the Young Turks, led by Enver, carried through a revolution in Constantinople and reopened the war. The campaign which ensued was marked by two triumphs and one disaster. The Greeks took Yanina, the Serbs and the Bulgarians compelled the capitulation of Adrianople. But the hand of an assassin struck down King George of Greece, a wise ruler, who might, had he survived, have exercised a wholesome influence on his people. The Treaty of London (May 30, 1913) restricted Turkey in Europe to a small area covered by Constantinople and Gallipoli.

Hardly was the ink dry upon this instrument than an internecine quarrel broke out among the victors. Of the three allies who had beaten the Turk to his knees, the Bulgarians had contributed the largest contingent, had faced the most formidable opposition, and had incurred the most considerable sacrifices. It was the impetuosity of their attack which had broken the strength of the Turkish resistance, and had wrested eastern Thrace from the enemy. That Bulgaria was likely to become the predominant power in the Balkans seemed to most observers to be the likely consequence of the Balkan War.

There was a certain solidity in the Bulgarian character, which attracted travellers from the west and inspired confidence. They appeared to be less headstrong than the Serbs, less flighty than the Greeks, less ignorant and stupid than the Turks. In Ferdinand of Coburg they possessed an unpopular, but crafty and ambitious leader, who was known to be favoured in Vienna. Moreover, they were landhungry and ill satisfied with the plunder accruing from their two campaigns. Not only had they failed to win Constantinople, but they knew well that, however weak the Turks might be, Russia would deny them access to the city on the Bosphorus. The great prizes of the war had been seized by their allies, by the Greeks who were in possession of Salonika, by the Serbs whose army was in central Macedonia, and they doubtless suspected, what was indeed the fact, that the Serbs and the Greeks were resolved to maintain their gains at all costs. Since there was a large Bulgarian element in the Macedonian population, the Bulgarians determined, in a moment of wild folly, to attack their recent allies. The Serbs Aug., and the Greeks were prepared for the onset, and, with the 1913 Roumans also invading from the north, the Bulgars experienced a crushing defeat, and were compelled to submit to a humiliating peace.

The course of these tragical happenings in the Balkans had been watched with febrile anxiety and grave disappointment by statesmen in Vienna. The result of the Balkan Wars had been to shatter Bulgaria, the friend of Vienna, to weaken Turkey, in whom the Kaiser had found his most recent ally, and greatly to increase the power of the Serbs. The military triumphs won by this little people had been truly remarkable. They had defeated the Turks, they had helped to take Adrianople. They had materially assisted in procuring the humiliation of Bulgaria. Incontestably now they were the first people in the Balkans, heartened by triumphs, confident of Russian help, dreaming of the incorporation of their kinsfolk in Bosnia and Herzegovina and of a kingdom stretching along the Adriatic coast. Again and again the Austrian General Staff had urged on the Government that this dangerous little nation of peasant soldiers should be taught a sharp lesson before it became too powerful. Despite strong temptation, for Vienna was chauvinist, the soldiers' way had been rejected. What were the alternatives? A patient defence or a radical reconstruction of the Imperial constitution to meet the aspirations of the Slavs? There were wise heads who believed that a solution might be found by giving to the southern Slavs a fuller measure of autonomy and a larger share of influence in the affairs of the Empire. Would it not be possible, it was argued, to substitute for the dual monarchy, resting on the dominion of the Magyars and the Germans, a trialist state founded on the equal fellowship of Slav, Magyar, and German? It was rumoured that Prince Franz Ferdinand, heir to the throne, entertained some such ideas and that his policy ran sharply counter to the dreams entertained in Belgrade and Agram by fervent nationalists of the Serbian race.

BOOKS WHICH MAY BE CONSULTED

J. A. Spender: *Fifty Years of Europe.* 1933.
J. A. R. Marriott: *The Eastern Question.* 1924.
Lord Grey of Fallodon: *Twenty-Five Years.* 1928.
H. Temperley: *History of Serbia.* 1917.

CHAPTER XCIII

BRITISH AND IRISH DISCORDS

The House of Lords question in England. Increasing social friction. Growth of the social services. The English Labour movement. The Irish question. Nationalism and Ulster. The Irish Parliamentary Party and Sinn Fein. The spectre of Civil War. The Irish Americans. Party passion in England. War preparations. The psychology of peace persists.

THE LIBERAL party, which was returned from the polls in January, 1906, with a sweeping majority over Conservatives, Nationalists, and Labour men alike, soon found itself confronted with a serious obstacle. All the principal measures on the party programme, for temperance, for the spread of undenominational education, for Welsh disestablishment, for Irish Home Rule, were either thrown out or appeared likely to be fatally blocked, by the House of Lords. It seemed that, under a Constitution which was nominally democratic, no party, however numerous its majority, however fresh its mandate from the constituencies, could pass a Bill against the wishes of the hereditary Chamber. Liberals argued that in a democratic civilization such a veto exercised by such a body was an indefensible anomaly. In the last resort they held that the popular Chamber should decide. When the Lords took the unprecedented step of rejecting the Budget in 1909, Asquith, who had become Prime Minister in the previous year, determined to go to the country and to ask for a mandate to curtail the powers of the Second Chamber. Should the Lords prove obstinate, he was prepared to recommend the Crown to create four hundred peers. It was in the midst of this grave constitutional struggle, and after a vain attempt to bring the parties to accord, that Edward May, VII died and was succeeded by George V, his second and 1910 only surviving son.

The extraordinary vehemence of the passions aroused by the Second Chamber question may seem strange to a generation which has grown accustomed to the Parliament Act of 1911, under the provisions of which the life of a Parliament is cut down to five years and the Lords are deprived of the power of throwing out a Finance Bill or of rejecting any other public Bill thrice passed in the Lower House in the course of two successive sessions. It was not, however, then realized that a government of red revolutionaries would be unlikely to submit to the two years' delay required under the statute, since it could more speedily execute its purpose of ruining the rich by debasing the currency and of undermining order by corrupting the soldiers and police. The Conservatives believed that the Liberal plan of overpowering the resistance of the Second Chamber would open the floodgates to the tides of revolution which they saw surging through the world. They had been thoroughly alarmed by the Budget of 1909 with its plan for taxing the unearned increment from land, and they saw no limit to the fiscal spoliation of future Parliaments. More bitter still was the reflection that with the disappearance of the absolute veto of the Lords the last obstacle to the passage of Irish Home Rule would crumble. That changes of this magnitude should be forced by a Liberal Government which, having lost its majority of 1906 in two successive elections, was now so reduced as to be dependent on Irish and Labour votes, was regarded by the Conservative party as an aggravation of the offence.

There was some excuse for viewing the prospect with alarm. A movement of revolt against the social conditions in which the great mass of mankind was compelled to live was almost everywhere evident. It had led to the establishment of Labour governments in Australia and to a great spread of socialist and syndicalist movements on the continent in Europe. The workers were demanding a better wage and a better life, with more leisure, more amusement, more opportunity. In

England class feeling was perhaps less violent than in Germany and in France, but it was growing in intensity as Marxist doctrines penetrated to the young men and with every successive demonstration of the fact that wage advances had to be wrung from the employing class by organized agitation. It is a measure of the economic friction in England between 1906 and 1914 that eleven million working days in a year were lost through industrial unrest.

How to build up a civilization in which want of money should not cut the people off from the amenities and refinements of life was a problem to which every progressive government in western Europe was then addressing itself with varying measures of success. Perhaps nowhere were the means of rational enjoyment so widely diffused as in Germany. Here town planning was a long-established institution. Parks and gardens, cheap theatres and concert rooms, bowling alleys and playgrounds ministered to the enjoyment of the shop assistant, the domestic servant, and the factory worker. In the provision of inexpensive, accessible, and innocent recreations the Germans were at least a generation ahead of England. But soul-destroying and terrible as had been the results of the industrial revolution in the British factory towns, the latter half of the nineteenth century had witnessed a stirring of the social conscience, which had made a sensible impression on the life of the people. The Ten Hours Act, passed in 1847 under the influence of Lord Shaftesbury in the teeth of the fierce opposition of good men, was a recognition of the fact that human beings had a right to leisure, the Education Acts of 1870 and 1891 that they could claim of the State to be enabled to put that leisure to liberal uses. Yet despite the social legislation of the Victorian period, there were still great arrears to be overtaken. The British workman still passed his life "under a shadow," liable for no fault of his own, such as the failure of some crop in a distant quarter of the world, to be thrown upon the streets. Outside the operation of the Poor Law the State did nothing for the sick, nothing for the old, nothing for the relief of women in labour, nothing for the maintenance of a good standard of health in the child population. The individual exploitation of children, though greatly mitigated by the Factory Acts, was still a serious impediment to the growth of a happy and healthy community. The English country house was famous for its beauty, its comfort, and its elegance. But the great manufacturing towns had been allowed to grow up anyhow and were as desolate and forbidding as the peculiar combination of rapacious money-making and grim Puritanism was able to make them.

During the eight years before the war a valiant effort was made to lessen these social evils by two able Liberal Administrations. Workmen were insured against sickness, accident, and in some cases also against unemployment. Pensions were given to the old. Three important statutes were passed to shelter the health and promote the welfare of children. By the Sweated Industries Act of 1909 Trade Boards were set up to fix a minimum wage in industries where wages were exceptionally low. The over-long hours of the shop assistant and the coal miner were shortened by Act of Parliament, and a Housing and Town Planning Act was passed. In the hope of increasing the agricultural population, the county councils were empowered to acquire land by compulsory purchase for small holdings and allotments. The Asquith government was not afraid to take lessons in Bismarckian socialism or to import into the statute book the revolutionary principle of the minimum wage.

To the Gladstonian Liberal, nurtured in the Gladstonian *laissez-faire* tradition, no less than to the Conservative, this great expansion of public benevolence and state interference seemed to strike at the roots of moral independence and to menace the financial strength of the country. Far greater was the storm of protest aroused by two other branches of Liberal policy, dealing with organized labour and Irish Home Rule.

While the Socialist parties on the continent came into being before the workers had received any industrial organization, in Britain the process was reversed. Here the trades unions had established themselves as a recognized and, indeed, necessary part of economic machinery long before an active Socialist party had entered the field of politics. In contrast to the French and Italian Syndicalists, who worked for the overthrow of the whole capitalist system by a revolutionary strike, the English Labour movement was a pattern of practical sobriety, preferring near realities to distant dreams, and far more concerned to obtain a minimum wage and an eight-hour day than to embark on violent plans for a wholesale change of society. Thus the Miners' Federation of Great Britain was formed in 1888 to protest against a particular method (the sliding scale) of remunerating labour in mines; while the object of the great dock strike of the following year, led by John Burns and Tom Mann, was to obtain an extra penny an hour for the London dock labourer. Even among those Labour leaders who, like Keir Hardie, had embraced the full socialist programme for the collective ownership of the means of production, distribution and exchange, it was common ground that the revolution could be accomplished by constitutional means. Parliament was not an enemy to be destroyed, but an ally to be won. In 1888 Keir Hardie stood as Independent Labour candidate for Mid-Lanark, and five years later founded the Independent Labour Party. From that day forward the workers of Britain laid siege to the House of Commons, and the success which attended their campaign was one of the powerful barriers against revolution. A party of Labour men nearly fifty strong, from 1906 onwards, was sufficient to secure from the Liberal Government of the day a large measure of attention to social needs.

It was certainly prudent to make it easy for working men to enter Parliament. Indeed, it was a condition of orderly and constitutional progress that every legitimate grievance should be explored and debated, and that every legitimate political ambition should receive its satisfaction on the floor of the House of Commons. The Liberal Cabinets before the war realized this. They introduced payment of members, and strengthened the trades unions by exempting their funds from liability for torts or civil wrongs, and by empowering them to raise a levy for political purposes from the contributions of their members. These measures were passed only after bitter controversy. It was urged that the trades unions were now to be placed in a position of invidious privilege, which would enable them to exercise undue tyranny. That a new class should be helped to gain power for possibly sub-versive ends was thought to be a rash and wicked departure from the tried and ancient ways of English parliamentary life.

The schism in Ireland continued fatally and angrily to divide the leading political parties in the English Parliament. The Liberals were spurred on by the Catholic nationalists of the South, the Tories by the fierce Protestants of Ulster. The remedy of the one party was Home Rule, which meant a popish parliament in Dublin; of the other the maintenance of the Union, sweetened by light railways, land purchase, and general social amelioration. Since each Irish faction was implacable, neither consenting to give ground to the other, the good-humoured give and take of British politics was brought up against an abrupt and baffling obstacle. Home Rule refused to be killed by kindness. Nationalism rejected with scorn the idea of partition. Rather than come under a Dublin Parliament the Ulster Protestants, led by Sir Edward Carson, raised volunteers and prepared to fight. Each party had a case which it believed to be founded on the impregnable rock of justice. In Catholic and Celtic Ireland the bitter memory of ancient wrongs was combined with large aspirations for nationality, freedom, and self-determination. It meant nothing to the leaders of the nationalist movement that the practical grievances of the Irish people had been wholly or largely removed, that as far back as 1829 Catholics had been freed from civil and political disabilities, that the Protestant Church had been disestablished, that the peasantry had been given the land, that special measures had been taken to relieve poverty in the congested districts of the west, that eighty-five Irish members, a full complement, sat in Westminster, or that a career was open to talent for Irishmen in every part of Great Britain or the Empire. The pride of the Irishman was revolted by an administration centred within the grim walls of Dublin Castle, guided by an English Lord-Lieutenant and an English Secretary, and protected by the English army at the Curragh. Denouncing these emblems of foreign servitude, the Irish claimed as of right to be governed by an Irish parliament responsible to an Irish electorate. John Redmond and his following at Westminster were prepared to accept a jealously guarded measure for Home Rule within the Empire such as the English liberals were able to commend. Others went further and were not content with an Anglo-Irish parliament acknowledging the suzerainty of the British Crown and fettered by the terms of a British statute. The Gaelic League founded in 1892 made an appeal to the Ireland which lay beyond the British conquest, in mediaeval mists, and while Arthur Griffiths, an insurgent remarkable for steadiness and integrity, stood for "Dominion status," a new party, styling itself *Sinn Fein*, dreamed of an Ireland violently severed from its British moorings and recapturing its native soul by the revived use of the Erse language and by a renewed familiarity with the ancient literature of the race. A brilliant constellation of scholars and poets threw a shimmer of aristocratic idealism over a movement which in its lower ranges enlisted the lout, the ruffian, and the gunman.

To all these movements the Ulstermen were inexorably opposed. In their eyes the three great causes, of Protestant education in the schools, of free trade with Britain, and of temperance, would be jeopardized by the legislation of a Dublin parliament. In Home Rule they discerned the first step towards secession, and to the establishment in Ireland of a government permanently hostile to the British connection and anxious to damage British interests in every quarter of the globe. As the fatal hour approached when, under the operation of the Parliament Act, it seemed inevitable that a Home Rule Bill would be placed on the Statute Book, arms were smuggled into Ulster. Then while the dark clouds of civil war were gathering in the sky the King summoned a conference to Buckingham Palace, but the quarrel refused to be resolved. Seldom has the public mind been racked by graver anxieties. Would the government have the nerve to use force against the Ulster volunteers? How could the Irish quarrel fail to divide England? Could England rely upon the support of the army? In July, 1914, it seemed as if the stout fabric of the British Isles was to be rent, as never since the seventeenth century, by civil strife.

It promised to be more than a local and insular quarrel. The Catholic Irish in Ireland were but a small fragment of an Irish population dispersed throughout the world. In every British colony and dominion Irishmen were to be found drinking happiness and freedom to the emerald island,

and confusion to its oppressors. In every Australian parliament resolutions were passed in favour of Irish Home Rule. In America the Irish, whose forbears had for the most part emigrated in the middle of the nineteenth century when Irish misery and starvation were at their worst and before any remedial legislation had been applied, were numerous and powerful. They controlled Tammany, a great political machine in New York. They had captured Puritan Boston. They helped to create a strong anti-British opinion in the Middle West. In Chicago alone they numbered more than a hundred dollar-millionaires. It was to conciliate Irish opinion that the Hearst Press, a powerful syndicate of newspapers, consistently blackened British motives and British policy, and that American politicians, seeking for votes in constituencies where the Irish element was strong, were impelled to adopt the popular course of "twisting the British lion's tail." The vigour of the anti-British agitation among the American Irish was not affected by the fact that conditions in Ireland had been vastly improved since "the hungry forties." The memory of those terrible years still dominated the imagination and wrung from the poor Irish serving girls in Boston or New York their hard-won dollars for the Irish cause. It was to America that Parnell applied for financial help against England. It was from America that the Irish nationalists continued to draw their supplies. And as no motive was more powerful with the English Liberals than the desire to remove the Irish obstacle to Anglo-American friendship, so among the consequences to be expected from the frustration of their design none seemed more formidable than the sharp and certain alienation of the American Republic.

An extraordinary political effervescence prevailed in England during the period which lay between the Boer War and the fateful opening years of Armageddon. A spirit of fanaticism invaded a luxurious world which no longer felt itself secure. Pious dissenters broke the law rather than pay the education rate. Well-bred and delicate women smashed windows, scuffled with the police, and by one means and another got themselves sent to prison as a protest against a government which refused them votes. Party spirit ran so high in London over the House of Lords and Ireland that social relations were ruptured. To some Imperialism and tariff

1902-14

reform constituted a religious faith, pressed with sectarian fervour. By others these causes were denounced as synonmous with the exploitation of oppressed peoples by unscrupulous profiteers and the corruption of legislatures by sinister vested interests. The country was full of industrial unrest, the striking habit extending from the mines, the railways, and the factories to the schools. There was even, in the summer of 1914, a mutinous spirit among the officers of the Curragh, who feared that they might be required to march against Ulster. Was the British Empire touching the moment of its decline? Were the Spartan virtues preached by Kipling and derided by Shaw sinking into obsolescence? Indian students in Delhi gleefully noted the successful organization of the Ulster rebellion. To Germans Britain appeared to be a powerful and prosperous country in the throes of a disabling convulsion.

Yet the country had never been better equipped for war. Haldane, a lawyer and a philosopher, who had studied in Göttingen and translated Schopenhauer, had reorganized the army on principles which, while they owed much to German example, were yet adapted to an insular power which might be obliged to take part in continental warfare. To his administrative genius Britain owed the creation of a general staff, of an expeditionary force, complete in all its details, of a Territorial army, and of an Officers' Training Corps. The Navy had similarly been prepared by Sir John Fisher for an eventual conflict with the Germans at sea. Such was its concentration in northern waters that eighty per cent. of its guns were trained upon the German shores. Army, Navy, and the nucleus of a new force in the air, had been brought into correlation by a Committee for Imperial Defence. A war book of secret instructions to be issued on mobilization prefigured with remarkable accuracy the initial needs of the country in the event of a continental war.

Of these studied preparations little or nothing was known by the man in the street. Mr. Lloyd George, "teasing the goldfish" from his station at the Treasury, Sir Edward Carson defying John Redmond, Mrs. Pankhurst and her turbulent train of suffragettes, Bob Smillie and his obstinate miners, seemed to be the most disturbing figures on the public stage. Otherwise all in the midsummer of 1914 was peace. The technical preparations of the war machine had no counterpart in the psychological education of the public mind. Though some journalists rang the alarm bell in London, the warning notes were but faintly audible in the industrial north. Here nothing was nearer to the thoughts of the average civilian than the summer holiday, and few things more remote than the prospect of foreign war.

BOOKS WHICH MAY BE CONSULTED

D. C. Somervell: *The Reign of King George V*. 1925.

J. A. Spender and C. Asquith: *The Life of Lord Oxford*. 1932.

J. A. Spender: *Fifty Years of Europe*. 1933.

L. T. Hobhouse: *The Labour Movement*. 1893.

S. Gwynn: *John Redmond's Last Years*. 1919.

E. Marjoribanks and Ian Colvin: *The Life of Lord Carson*. 1932, 1934.

Richard Burdon Haldane: *An Autobiography*. 1929.

J. Ramsay MacDonald: *The Socialist Movement*. (Home University Library.) 1911.

G. Elton: *England Arise!* 1931.

Sir Harold Nicolson: *King George the Fifth*. 1952.

F. Owen: *Tempestuous Journey: Lloyd George, his Life and Times*. 1954.

H. M. Pelling: *The Origins of the Labour Party*. 1954.

R. T. McKenzie: *British Political Parties*. 1955.

CHAPTER XCIV

MENACING TENDENCIES IN GERMANY AND RUSSIA

The predominance of Germany in Europe. German militarism. Hatred of England. The unwisdom of the Kaiser. The British public and the British Cabinet. Efforts to improve relations with Germany. Closer relations with the Dual Alliance. Russia menaced with revolution. The experiment of Russian constitutional government. The weakness of Nicholas. The race between war and revolution.

AT THE opening of the twentieth century Germany, by reason of the fixity of her purpose, the concentration of her means, the discipline of her people, and the power of her army, was the central figure in the European drama. Austria and Italy were her satellites. Sweden was an admiring friend. Turkey presented a sphere of growing political and economic influence. A worldwide trade, swiftly increasing in volume and importance and assisted by the Government as if it were an offensive operation of war, carried the German flag into every port. Nothing was left to chance. The state ran the railways, protected the home market, subsidized the exports and the ships which carried them. In military and economic strength no continental state compared with the German Empire. The keys of war and peace were in Berlin. The German Emperor could, in the course of a single morning, upset the delicate equilibrium of Europe.

In this remarkable predominance there were three points of danger. Every valid German male had been, was, or would be a soldier. The presence in the country of a large officer caste and of an immense body of men trained to arms diffused a wide professional interest in the art and technicalities of war. All young Germans expected, many young Germans hoped, that among the experiences which life would offer them would be a war for the Fatherland. Such a war they had been taught to regard not as a crime against civilization, but as a good and necessary medicine in the moral history of states. Accordingly they did not, as did so many English, dread, detest, and despise war as a relic of barbarism dishonouring to human nature. Rather they were disposed to welcome it as offering a supreme test of manhood, and the more readily since, judging from recent enterprises, they believed that the next war would be brief, exhilarating, and triumphant. If such were the feelings of the German general public, it may be imagined with what intensity the officer caste, grown restive under the retarded military promotion of a long peace, and its central organ, the General Staff, pressed for the adoption of spirited and provocative policies.

There was a second point of danger. Of all luxuries of the heart the most perilous is international hatred. The Germans, a naive and emotional people, were successfully encouraged to abound in this sentiment. Many years before the Boer War the popular hatred of England prevailing in Germany was so great as to wreck any prospect of a firm political understanding between the two peoples. Later on German statesmen, like Von Bülow, recognised this with regret, but it was then too late to reverse the engines. The anti-English propaganda had been running for half a century, and since it received a fresh stimulus with every Navy Bill, its work was not easily undone. In Britain, anti-German feeling, though vigorously expressed in certain anti-German organs, was, as well-informed Germans admitted, less general and deep-seated. In wide circles of society it was non-existent.

The character of the Kaiser was a further misfortune. His restless vanity, his political infidelities, his love of melodramatic display, and bursts of hysterical violence, maintained Europe in a high state of tension. The extraordinary series of letters which he exchanged with the Tzar Nicholas (the Willy-Nicky correspondence) shows that he was perfectly capable, while professing a warm friendship with England, of intriguing for a combination of continental powers against her. His public utterances were sometimes those of a madman. When some marines started for China in 1900 he adjured them as follows in terms which rang round the world: "You are about to meet a crafty, well-armed, cruel foe; meet him and beat him! Give no quarter! Take no prisoners! Kill

him when he falls into your hands! Even as a thousand
years ago the Huns under their King Attila made such a
name for themselves as still resounds in terror in legend and
fable, so make the name of German resound through Chinese
history a thousand years from now." In private conversation
he was equally dangerous to his country and to the world. It
has been seen how vital it was for the preservation of the
general peace that Austria should refrain from provoking
Russia to a war over a Balkan difference, and accordingly,
how important it was for Germany as Austria's ally to keep
a restraining hand on Austrian foreign policy. Yet despite
the most plain warning of the aggressive temper which prevailed in Vienna, and the fact that on two separate occasions,
in 1908, and again in 1912, Austria had nearly involved
Germany in a war, the Kaiser encouraged his ally to believe
"that whatever came from the Vienna Foreign Office was a
command for him." The record which Count Berchtold,
the Austrian Foreign Minister, made of an interview with the
Kaiser at the Foreign Office in Vienna on October 26, 1913,
brings out in a truly appalling way the reckless unwisdom
of this temperamental sovereign. He tells Austria that war
between the east and the west is inevitable, that the Slavs were
born to serve and not to rule, that the Serbs should be bribed
or forced to place their army at the disposal of Austria, that
alternatively their capital should be occupied and bombarded.
He assures his ally that the Russians are not to be feared,
since a German from the Baltic provinces had reported to
him an observation of the Tzar to the effect that for the next
six years war was impossible for Russia. "As often," says
Count Berchtold, "as opportunity offered during our one
and a half hours' talk to touch upon our relations as allies,
His Majesty ostentatiously used the occasion to assure me
that we could count absolutely and completely upon him."
How calamitous these counsels and assurances were to
Austria, to Germany, and to the world was very shortly
to be made apparent.

It is a deep political instinct of the British people to range
itself against the strongest European power. But at the opening of 1914 the ordinary Englishman expected nothing so
little as that he might be called on to fight in a continental
war. Though he had given a general assent to the under-

standing with France and Russia as likely to promote the cause of peace, and to improve the balance of power in Europe, he knew nothing of the military conventions, or of the international obligations to which his country might in honour be committed. The idea that England would ever be drawn into a general war by reason of a Balkan quarrel would have struck him as wildly fantastic, but the growth of the German navy, with the navy scares which it had from time to time occasioned in his own country, made him uneasy, and he would have felt it to be hardly decent or safe to look on with folded arms while Germany overran Belgium, destroyed France, and occupied the Channel ports. What he had learnt from the newspapers with regard to the German people's ambitions had not encouraged him to hope that, after such triumphs as these, the Germans would be tender to the British Empire. When France and Russia had been prostrated, would it be credible that the victors should refrain from settling their accounts with England? That the mind of the country, as yet innocent and unsuspicious, would thus react to the logic of facts was the calculation of Asquith, Grey, and Haldane, the three men who at this time were most concerned with the shaping of English policy.

It is perhaps a weakness of British Cabinets that they shrink from facing distant and hypothetical questions. What Great Britain would do in the event of a violation of Belgian neutrality, or a German attack on Morocco, or a general war rising out of the Serbian question, was at no time closely examined or narrowly defined in Downing Street. The theory was that the ultimate decision would lie with Parliament, and that Parliament would act according to its understanding of the moral issues, when the occasion arose. The Germans were, however, warned by Haldane in Berlin 1912 that a violation of Belgian neutrality would be gravely viewed in England, and Metternich, the capable German Ambassador in London, was given to understand by the same statesman that British public opinion would not permit the destruction of France. It has sometimes been contended that bolder and more emphatic declarations from the British Cabinet would have averted war. There can be no certainty on such a point. From 1912 onwards the real power in Berlin had not rested with the Emperor alone, but in an increasing

measure with the General Staff. These able soldiers rated
the possible war effort of England on the continent very low.
That the English would be troublesome at sea was conceded.
But Berlin was of opinion that, were war to break out, the
campaign on the western front would be decided in a very
few weeks. The presence of a British Expeditionary Force
on the soil of France, though it would increase the casualty
list, would hardly affect the time table.

Grey did not believe in the inevitable war. His hope was
that while remaining faithful to her engagements to Russia
and France, England might notwithstanding succeed in
improving her relations with Germany. More than once,
but always with unfortunate results, the suggestion was conveyed to the German government that it should enter into a
plan for the reduction of naval armaments. On this line no
progress was possible. Offers made from London in the
honest intention of creating a more friendly feeling between
the two peoples were regarded in Berlin as parts of a Machiavellian design for perpetuating the supremacy of the British
fleet. The pacific overture of Campbell-Bannerman was viewed
in the red light of Admiral Fisher's Jingoism almost "as a
threatening ultimatum." The Naval Holiday, or year's truce
from shipbuilding, proposed by Mr. Winston Churchill, was
stigmatized by the Emperor as "mere humbug." Equally
fruitless was the Haldane mission to Berlin in 1912. The
Germans were not content with an assurance that England
would neither make nor join in an unprovoked attack.
They demanded what the British government could not give,
a specific pledge of neutrality in the event of war. Nevertheless the British Foreign Secretary persevered in his search for
peace. In an atmosphere which had been greatly improved
by the success of the Balkan Conference, an agreement between England and Germany with reference to the Baghdad
Railway and the eventual distribution of the Portuguese
Colonies was nearly completed in the early months of 1914.
By that time, however, two steps had been taken, which
made it almost inevitable that, were an attack to be made on
France, England would be drawn into the war. By an
agreement with the British Cabinet (1912) the French had
concentrated their fleet in the Mediterranean, a redistribution of forces implying nothing less than the assumption by

Great Britain of the naval defence of the Channel coast of France in the event of the outbreak of war. The second step was the authorization two years later of naval conversations with Russia.

Of the future course of that vast military Empire nothing could with certainty be predicted. The Empire of the Tzar was still standing. It had survived the students' riots of 1899, the peasants' revolt of 1902, the calamitous defeat of Russian arms in the Japanese War, and the rebellion of 1905, formidable among other circumstances for a general strike, the most complete so far achieved, and the first experiment in proletarian dictatorship to be tried on European soil. But could it long continue without the tonic of a successful war? Tumultuous forces from within were straining and tearing at the fabric. The student body at the Universities was honeycombed with disaffection. Middle-class liberalism nourished on western culture clamoured for far-reaching constitutional changes. The land hunger of an impoverished peasantry, the heady ferment of Marxist doctrines among the factory workers, the upward thrust of the oppressed nationalities, the bitter cry going up from Siberian exiles and other victims of arbitrary injustice, constituted a menacing body of opposition to the established order.

Assailed from every quarter and deeply discredited by its failure in the Japanese War, Russian autocracy made a pact with revolution. First, it summoned to the capital a central committee of the county councils; then, advancing further on the constitutional path, an elected Parliament or Duma. The news that Russia, the standing 1905 model of an unenlightened despotism, had borrowed the parliamentary system of the west caused a thrill of exhilaration among English liberals. There was scant cause for rejoicing. These Russian assemblies, which followed one another in quick succession, did little to mitigate the unpopularity of the Tzar or to assuage the violent clash of contending spirits. Indeed, since the government did not trust the Duma, or the Duma the government, the community failed to receive the benefits to be expected from the confluence of so many able and patriotic men in a legislative assembly. Nicholas was not the man to ride the storm. Like Louis XVI, he was made for private rather than for public life. A feeble though slightly obstinate disposition, a weak intelligence, an incapacity for grasping the size of events or the character of men, were combined in him with a vein of abject superstition, which was more than once harmful to the interests of the state. It was a misfortune for Germany that the Kaiser's personality was so strong; it was equally disastrous to Russia that the last of the Tzars was so weak, and that, though he was possessed of every private virtue, though he was a perfect gentleman, a loyal husband, and an affectionate father, he was incapable either of a firm comprehension of affairs or of a resolute course of action, but disposed to refer to an ignorant religious quack questions which demanded the balanced consideration of a statesman. In the choice of these blind and desperate expedients he was influenced by his tragic and melancholy wife, whose infatuation for Rasputin, monk, rogue, libertine, and impostor, forms a curious chapter of psychology.

The circle of soldiers and diplomatists who stood round the Russian throne were not pacifists. They wished to see Russia, since she had been forced to retreat in the Far East, established one day, as the result of a victorious war, in the great warm-water port of the Bosphorus. The foreign policy of the Tzardom had been aggressive in the past. It was aggressive still. For the moment, however, there was no urgent desire for war. The railways awaited development. If no intolerable affront were put upon the Serbs, the Russian government would maintain the peace. A serious strike in the St. Petersburg factories which broke out on July 8, 1914, and led to barricades and fighting in the streets, seemed to show that in the race between war and revolution it was revolution which would outstrip its rival and just pass the post.

BOOKS WHICH MAY BE CONSULTED

G. P. Gooch: *Germany*. (Nations of the Modern World Series.) 1925.

Von Bülow: *Memoirs*. 1931-2.

J. A. Spender: *The Last Fifty Years*.

D. Lloyd George: *War Memoirs*. 1933.

Lord Grey of Fallodon: *Twenty-Five Years*. 1928.

Lord Oxford and Asquith: *Memories and Reflections*. 1928.

Winston Churchill: *The World Crisis.* 1923.

Paléologue: *L' Empire des Tsars.*

A. J. P. Taylor: *Struggle for Mastery in Europe.* 1954.

L. Albertini: *Origins of the War of 1914. Tr.* I. M. Massey. 3 vols. 1952-7.

S. B. Fay: *The Origins of the World War.* 2 vols. 1929.

N. Mansergh: *The Coming of the First World War.* 1949.

CHAPTER XCV

THE OUTBREAK OF WAR

Development of a high common civilization in Europe. The murder of the Archduke. The Austrian ultimatum. Austria declares war on Serbia. Sazonov. The war responsibilities of Germany, Austria, and Russia. English feeling. The violation of Belgian neutrality. The responsibilities of Capitalism. General lack of Pacifism. Austria alone, supported by the German General Staff, wants war in 1914. The surprises of the Great War.

BY THE beginning of the twentieth century the peoples of Europe, save for a savage patch in the Balkans, had reached an unprecedented level of comfort and civilization. Representative institutions, though in many parts of the continent ill rooted, ill practised, and ill understood, were universal. The belief that the world was moving towards unity seemed to be growing in strength, despite the militant and nationalist movements of the time. By a unique exertion of provident diplomacy the concert of Europe had divided the African continent without a conflict between the imperial and colonizing powers. Recourse to arbitration for the settlement of international questions was becoming more frequent. The foundation of an International Postal Union (1875), of a common system of copyright, and of an International Office of Public Health (1907) are but examples of the manner in which governments were tending increasingly to co-operate in the management of their common affairs. It seemed as if statesmen had now at last learned the lesson that politics is the art of human happiness. Laws for the protection of the weaker members of the community had been passed in all legislatures. Unjust privileges had been eliminated from the budgets, mediaeval barbarity from the penal codes. In most parts of Europe education was general and progessive. Preventive medicine had greatly prolonged the duration of human life. In all the more advanced countries death from starvation had disappeared from the catalogue of social evils.

From one evil European society seemed to be effectively delivered. Though the physical force at the disposal of governments had been vastly increased by the march of science, there was a refreshing absence of intellectual coma. The Continent was awake from end to end. No writers had a greater vogue than those who assailed the existing order of society and essayed a revaluation of accepted values. In the Victorian age Matthew Arnold had employed his delicate and fastidious gift of ridicule upon the middle-class Philistine. Critics more powerful than Matthew Arnold occupied the stage at the turn of the century. Ibsen and Tolstoi, Nietzsche and Anatole France, Bernard Shaw and Wells spoke to wider audiences upon bolder themes. There was never a time when Europe was made more alive to its deficiencies or was more variously and brilliantly advised as to the means for their removal.

Electrical science had showered gifts upon mankind: light, heat, traction, the telegraph, the telephone, the cinema. The railway had been supplemented by the bicycle, the motor-car, and the aeroplane. Access to literature good and bad had been improved by the growth of public libraries, by the competitive enterprise of publishers, and by the advance in the mechanics of printing. A cheap newspaper press satiated the curiosity of a public whose intellectual discipline had ended with the primary school. But what, perhaps, was a more striking feature of the age immediately preceding the Great War was the growth of a belief that poor working men and women had the right to have enjoyments placed within their reach by contributions from the public purse. Never since the fall of the Roman Empire had public authority been so careful to provide for the common amusements of the people. Never had the human appetite for pleasure received such general satisfaction. Never before were the intellectual contributions of one country so quickly communicated to others. The music of Brahms, the plays of Ibsen, the novels of Tolstoi and Anatole France, the light operas of Gilbert and Sullivan, the popular songs of the English music hall, were part of a general European stock. The obstacle of language was serious. Otherwise there was reason to hope that, given a century of peace, Europe, like the Aristotelian city, might be made one through the forces of culture and education.

This ascending process of civilized well-being was suddenly fractured by a crime. On June 28, 1914, Archduke Franz Ferdinand, heir to the Austrian throne, was shot by Gavrilo Princip, a young Bosnian fanatic, at Sarajevo. It was as if, at a moment of acute political tension, the Prince of Wales had been murdered in Ireland. A storm of indignation swept through Austria-Hungary, where it was believed by many, and thought politic to assume by others, that the crime, though committed on Bosnian soil, was the work of the Black Hand and prompted or connived at by officials of the Serbian Government.[1]

Though a local enquiry conducted by Austrian agents found no direct proofs of the complicity of the Serbian Government, the Austrians were undoubtedly entitled to require a full and comprehensive enquiry into a conspiracy which certainly had roots in the Serbian kingdom as well as in Bosnia. Such an enquiry the Serbs would have been wise in their own interests to have instituted, but, whether by reason of the general election then proceeding, or because the Serbian Cabinet appears to have had information that some attempt was likely to be made upon the Archduke and to have failed to transmit the rumour to Vienna, nothing of the kind was done, and while the press on both sides of the Danube exchanged violent hostilities, opinion in Vienna, fortified by assurance of German support, moved rapidly to the need of war. On July 23 an ultimatum was sent to Serbia, of which Sir Edward Grey said that he "had never seen one state address to another independent state a document of so formidable a character." It was an ultimatum which, since it involved the abdication of Serbian independence, was

---

[1] There is reason for thinking that the murder of King Alexander and Queen Draga in 1903 and the murder of the Archduke in 1914 were both the work of "Avis," the leader of the Black Hand.

intended to be declined and to lead to war, and it was issued at a moment when Poincaré, the President of the French Republic, and Viviani, the Prime Minister, were on the sea returning from a visit to the Tzar. Berlin stood behind Vienna. The German steamship lines were warned, and St. Petersburg, Paris, and London were notified that any interference between Austria and Serbia would be followed by "incalculable consequences."

It may be imagined what consternation this intelligence produced in the Chancelleries of Europe. At once the impression was created that this murder in the Bosnian capital was being seized as a pretext by the Austrian and German governments to deprive Serbia of its independence and perhaps to force on a general war with Russia and France before the Russian railways were ready. The impression was deepened when, after Serbia had accepted seven out of the ten points of the Austrian ultimatum, Francis Joseph was nevertheless, on the advice of Count Berchtold, his Foreign Minister, persuaded to sign the declaration of war against the Serbs. The Austrian army, which had long been thirsting for war against the "nation of assassins," did not intend to be balked of its prey.

July 30, 1914

It was not to be expected that Russia would look on unmoved while the Serbs were wiped off the Balkan map. Sazonov, the Foreign Minister, a man of too excitable a temperament for so grave a post, had conceived great alarm at the designs of the two central powers in the Near East. A German prince had been sent to rule in Albania, a German general to organize the Turkish army in Constantinople. If the Serbs were laid prostrate, what was to prevent the establishment of a German Caliphate running from Hamburg to Baghdad? Sazonov had little love for the Austrians. In spite of the fact that Russian arms had helped to establish Francis Joseph on the throne of Hungary in 1849, the Austro-Hungarian monarchy had crossed the Russian path again and again. While, therefore, he was anxious to find some means of preserving the peace, he was accessible to gusts of warlike temper and far too weak a man to resent the pressure of the soldiers, who, after the news of the bombardment of Belgrade came to Russia, forced a partial and then a general mobilization.

July, 1914

The Kaiser had been naturally fired with indignation at the crime at Sarajevo. The Archduke was his personal friend. The assassination was a hideous, inexcusable crime. It was, nevertheless, most unfortunate that in his early communications with Vienna the Kaiser abounded without reserve in denunciations of Serbia and in protestations of his desire for her punishment.

The *Nibelung* loyalty to his ally on which he prided himself was the worst of counsellors at a crisis when the quality needed was not romance but cool common sense. In view of the character of the Austrian ultimatum, which involved the obliteration of a state previously independent, it could not be contended that here was a quarrel which could be isolated and in which no other country was concerned. The best service which the German Government could have rendered to Europe would have been to exercise a moderating influence on Austria. It is the gravamen against them that they did not begin to exercise any influence of the kind until it was too late and the Austrian military machine was in full motion. They neither supported Sir Edward Grey in his July suggestion that the time limit to Serbia should be extended, 31, nor did they accept his proposal that the question might be 1914 considered by a conference in London. Throughout its intemperate proceedings the Austro-Hungarian government was given to understand that it could count upon the support of the German army. The one power in Europe which could have ensured peace refused its co-operation in the endeavours which were made to obtain it. The German government, which might have prevented the war, took the responsibility of declaring it. As for the German people, they had been so long taught that they were encircled by the Machiavellian concert of their enemies that they found no difficulty in believing that they were now called upon to defend the Fatherland from a wicked attempt to destroy it. More particularly were they apprehensive of the vast Russian armies on their eastern frontier. It was idle to suppose that in the fierce excitement of the moment they would recall the many occasions in recent history when their own government had sought to obtain its diplomatic ends by threat of war or the apprehensions which had been excited in foreign lands by its imperialism.

A yet greater responsibility rests upon Count Berchtold, the Austrian Foreign Minister. Although it was known in Vienna by July 13 that complicity in the crime of Sarajevo could not be brought home to the Serbian Government, he persisted in his policy of a punitive campaign, even in spite of the Serbian concessions, and even when it was clear beyond doubt that Russia would support the Serbian cause. That Austria had much to fear from Serbian revolutionary propaganda within the Empire may be admitted. It is difficult, however, to believe that she had anything to apprehend from the military power of a small country already shaken by two severe wars and faced with the troublesome problem of assimilating her new subjects in the south. Reckless of consequences, she chose the occasion of the odium excited by the Sarajevo crime to settle once and for all with this small but highly annoying neighbour state.

Had a strong and wise sovereign been seated on the Russian throne, it is possible that he might, at the risk of forfeiting the sympathies of the Balkan Slavs, have faced the unpopularity of deserting Serbia in her hour of need. He might have argued that Russia had as much territory on her hands as she knew how to govern; that foreign conquest could bring her nothing which would add to her strength; and that to waste blood and treasure for the sake of Serbia was a piece of idle quixotry likely to bring the fabric of the Empire to the ground. Nicholas, however, was not a strong man. A spirit of mystic resignation replaced in him, as in so many Russians, a capacity for sustained and energetic thought. Ingeminating peace and invoking the Hague Tribunal, he nevertheless permitted the General Staff, always eager for action, to extract from him the permission to order a general mobilization of the Russian army before Germany had taken the step of declaring war. In justification it may be said that his government had urged the Serbs to make those very concessions to Austria which the Kaiser, on first reading them, declared to be sufficient to avoid war.

England had striven consistently for peace during these fateful eleven days when the fortunes of Europe were at stake. The charge of war guilt certainly cannot be brought home to her. It was, however, inevitable, though the country did not realize it at the time, that on the outbreak of a war forced upon France, England, rather than witness the destruction of her ally, would be drawn into the struggle. Yet so little were the English people attuned to the idea of war, that, but for the German invasion of Belgium, cabinet, parliament, and country would have been divided. The unprovoked violation of an innocent country whose neutrality Prussia had solemnly guaranteed settled the mind of the Asquith Cabinet, dispersed the doubts of the Labour party in parliament, and satisfied the people that the war was justly undertaken. The Irish parliamentary party, led by John Redmond, was inspired by the affront put upon a small Catholic people by a powerful neighbour to offer its services in the German war.

The idea that the Great War was caused by the capitalists is a baseless fable. Everywhere, save perhaps in some armament centres, the leading business men were aghast at the prospect of a rupture of the peace. Yet neither they nor the socialist parties were strong enough to arrest the march of the great military machines. When the crisis came, international capital was as powerless as international labour. The socialists, forgetting their views of universal peace, voted the war credits in Berlin and Paris. A fierce and passionate nationalism over-mastered all other forces.

In no European country had policy been conceived on pacifist lines. Every Foreign Office cherished dreams which might be realized in war. France wanted Alsace-Lorraine. Germany wanted more colonies, a larger navy, and hegemony in the Near East. Austria wanted the subjection of Serbia and a port at Salonika. Russia wanted the Bosphorus and Dardanelles. Serbia had designs on Bosnia and Herzegovina, Italy on Trieste and the Trentino, Roumania on Transylvania, to be obtained from Hungary, or Bessarabia, to be wrested from the Russians. Given a general war, all these ambitions would burst out in flame; but war was not inevitable or by any means generally desired. Neither France, nor Russia, nor England, nor Serbia desired war in 1914. There was, indeed, only one government which was wholly and entirely bent on breaking the peace in that year. This was Austria, encouraged and supported by the sinister and overmastering force of the general staff in Berlin, which for months before the murder of the Archduke had been pressing upon the German Government the desirability of precipitating war without delay.

The stunning news that Europe was at war produced in the first instance an extraordinary quickening in the wheels of life. Everyone was busy, excited, exhilarated, hungry for new forms of energy and usefulness. The internal quarrels which had seemed so important a few days earlier suddenly died down before the grave danger to the national life. The strikers returned to their work in St. Petersburg, the suffragettes ceased to annoy in London. In Italy Benito Mussolini, who had just led a formidable revolutionary strike, urged intervention. Every nation believed that its cause was just, that it was oppressed by a malignant enemy bent on its destruction, and that the survival of a moral order in the world was dependent on the victory of its own side. The Germans, who regarded themselves as the exponents of the highest form of civilization as yet attained upon the planet, appeared to their antagonists to have exchanged the humane ideals of an earlier German generation for the Prussian doctrine of naked and unscrupulous force. The flames of the burning library at Louvain cast a lurid light upon the pretensions of the missionary of culture.

To few was it given to forecast the character or duration of the struggle which was opening in that golden August weather. The general impression was that it would be short and sharp and concluded by the clash of the forces by land and sea which had been carefully prepared.

None of the governing factors of the war had been foreseen. Nobody anticipated that nearly all the world would be drawn in, or that it would be a war of peoples waged to the point of extermination, or again the degree to which science, mechanism, and industrial power would shape its character and determine its result. A Polish writer of the last century came nearest to the truth when he pictured the war of the future as a stationary process of deadly attrition in which that people would survive which could longest provide itself with food.[1]

The politicans were no more prescient than the peoples. The passiveness of Belgium, the neutrality of England, Italy,

---

[1] Jean de Bloch. *La Guerre. Traduction de l'ouvrage russe "La Guerre future aux points de vue technique, économique et politique."* Paris, Guillaumin, 1898-1900. 6 vols.

and Roumania had been confidently assumed in the German war plans. It was calculated in Berlin that the German armies would be in Paris in a fortnight and back on the eastern front in six weeks. In London the general staff made provision for four battles of three days each. Well-informed English politicians in the first winter of the war were inclined to the opinion that peace could hardly be delayed beyond the ensuing August for lack of finance. Alone among prominent men, Kitchener, the new Secretary of State for War, took a true measure of the difficulties, prophesying that his country must be prepared for a war of three years. An early estimate that Great Britain would be presented with a bill for a thousand million sterling seemed staggering, but the figure named was but one-tenth of the ultimate total.

It followed that the essential and distinguishing character of this new type of war was not at once apprehended. In England at the outset the popular cry was "Business as usual," the idea being that by carrying on its ordinary avocations as if nothing particular was happening the country could best help to finance the war effort of its allies. By degrees, however, it became apparent that in this clash of peoples the distinction between combatant and non-combatant disappeared, and that only from the fullest possible utilization of the human and material resources of a country was success to be expected. The moral results were truly astonishing. Never have armies suffered such terrific losses without yielding ground. Never have civilian populations thrown themselves with greater ardour and devotion into work for their country. Women showed themselves as heroic as men, in the munition factories, in the clearing stations and hospitals, or carrying their lives in their hands in the service of information. The idle notion that education and urban life were inimical to courage was shown to be ill-founded. Every record for valour previously established was here surpassed. Nor was anything more impressive than the superb social discipline which enabled the Germans so long to defy the depressing effects of the naval blockade and to present a solid military front to the enemy.

BOOKS WHICH MAY BE CONSULTED

Lord Grey of Fallodon: *Twenty-Five Years*. 1928.
Lord Oxford and Asquith: *Memories and Reflections*. 1928.
J. A. Spender: *Fifty Years of Europe*. 1933.
J. W. Headlam-Morley: *The History of Twelve Days*. 1915.
A. J. P. Taylor: *Rumours of Wars*. 1952.

CHAPTER XCVI

THE WAR: FIRST PHASE

*The German war plan. Early German successes. Joffre.
Tannenberg and the Masurian Lakes. The allied victory on the
Marne. The race for the Channel Ports. The defence of the
Ypres salient. Trench warfare. Britain's expanding war
effort. The British Navy. Easterners and Westerners. The
Dardanelles. Italy joins the Allies. The Italian constitution.
The Falkenhayn plan. Spectacular German triumphs in the
East. Repulse of Allied attacks on the German front, in the
West. Verdun and the Somme, 1916. The tanks. The success
of Brussilov. Roumania enters the war. German conquest
of Roumania. Economic hardships of the Central Powers and
the naval blockade.*

To MOLTKE, Chief of the German Staff and the mediocre
inheritor of a great name, belonged the military initiative.
His plan, which was founded on a design elaborated by
Count Schlieffen, the Chief of the Staff in 1905, was, while
guarding the eastern frontier with a few divisions, to put
France out of action by a wide turning movement through
Belgium and Luxemburg, and, when this had been done,
to throw the full force of the German army against the
Russians. It was confidently expected in Berlin that the
French, even if stiffened by a British contingent of a hundred
thousand men, as allowed for under the Schlieffen plan,
could offer no effectual resistance to the impact of so great a

force as four-fifths of the army of the German *Reich*. "Remember," said the Kaiser on two separate occasions to Sir Edward Grey, "we can be in Paris in a fortnight."

Nor was this a vain and idle boast. In every particular of discipline, equipment, and skill the German army of 1914 was the most formidable instrument of war which the world has ever seen. It numbered four million three hundred thousand fully trained and one million partially trained men. Its heavy artillery was overwhelming. The mobilization was a work of art. Thousands of trains, running to time, deposited their human burden on the long railway sidings which had been specially constructed on the Belgian and French frontier in anticipation of "the day." Though the resistance of Liège was an unexpected obstacle costing perhaps 40,000 casualties to the attackers, it did not seriously derange the time-table. The great army of field greys flowed on, reaching Brussels on August 20, demolishing with heavy howitzers fortresses such as Namur and Maubeuge from which a long resistance had been expected, masking Antwerp, into which the Belgian army had retreated, by two army corps, and pushing before it the French and English forces, who in all too insufficient numbers and with an all too insufficient equipment of machine guns, had endeavoured at Charleroi, at Mons, and at Le Cateau (August 26) to offer an opposition to its advance. On September 2 the army of Von Kluck, on the extreme right of the German turning movement, was approaching Paris. The government of France had fled to Bordeaux. The English expeditionary force under Sir John French was pursuing its retreat. It seemed as if the fall of the French capital and the successful conclusion according to plan of the first part of the German military programme could only be a matter of days.

The French army was commanded by Joffre, a stout, good-humoured man of inelastic mind, deliberate habits, imperturbable optimism, and steadfast will. The higher command had committed every possible mistake. It had made no adequate provision for the defence of the north-east. It had expected that the Germans would come through the Ardennes. It had grossly under-estimated their numbers through failing to anticipate that reserve divisions would march with the field army, and, despite the changes which had come over

not vainly made, the Germans had squandered a reserve of
potential officers who could not be replaced, and in the last
year of the war were greatly missed.

On the left of the British trenches the army of Belgium,
under the command of King Albert, lined the Yser, and,

THE WESTERN FRONT 1914-18

partly protected by inundation, withheld until the end of the
war a narrow strip of Belgian territory from the invaders.
The Belgian army, albeit small and severely depleted by
casualties, rendered an essential service. A little English force
thrown into Antwerp in the nick of time had enabled it to
withdraw from the beleaguered city and freed it to take its
share in the defence of the ports.

By the winter it was clear that a profound change had come
over the situation on the western front. A war of movement

had given place to a war of attrition, a thrust at the vitals of France to a slow and exhausting siege of Germany. In long lines of trenches defended by wire entanglements and extending from the Channel to the Vosges the rival armies watched and fought, unable, despite prodigies of courage, to make more than the slightest dint in the rigid contours of the front. In this terrible and exacting duel the Germans possessed great initial advantages. They were more numerous and better trained; they had more machine guns and howitzers, more aeroplanes and flares, and they held the higher ground. They controlled the economic resources of Belgium and the rich industrial region of north-eastern France, containing 80 per cent. of its coal and nearly all its iron. Their flanks, resting on the sea and the Alps, could not be turned.

To the French and British governments it at once became apparent that only if a British land army far larger than the six divisions which had originally been thought sufficient could be raised and thrown into the battle would the balance be restored. Kitchener, the Secretary of State for War, called upon the country for volunteer armies. He contemplated seventy divisions to be formed within three years. His commanding figure and unique prestige secured for his message a special authority. From the first volunteers flocked to the colours, until the Kitchener armies, as they were sometimes called, reached a total of three million men. Even this figure proved to be insufficient. Conscription was resorted to in 1916, but it is doubtful whether any other country could have raised by volunteer effort so large a body of young men for service beyond the sea in a dull and murderous war. While these new armies were receiving their training and awaiting their equipment the chief burden of maintaining the western front lay upon the *poilus* of France.

Though she had been wholly unprepared for any such great military effort on land as was now demanded, Britain was mistress of the sea. Her fleet, which had been collected for manoeuvres in July, and by the wise prevision of Mr. Winston Churchill kept together when the manoeuvres were over, had taken up its war stations at Scapa Flow and Rosyth, and was supported in its operations by a large commercial navy most gallantly and skilfully manned. The tasks laid upon the Fleet were fully comprehended by the British Admiralty and by Jellicoe, the naval commander-in-chief. They were, in brief, the safe convoy of troops to any quarter of the world in which they might be required, the destruction of German ocean-going cruisers and overseas trade, the seizure of the German colonies, and the interception of food and munitions of war destined for the enemy countries. All these functions the British navy unobtrusively accomplished, with some assistance in Pacific, Indian and Mediterranean waters from Japan and France, and in the last stages of the war from the well-trained fleet of the United States.

The consideration of British strategy on land was necessarily affected by naval predominance. Alone among the combatant powers Britain was free to employ her armies in any quarter of the globe. No sooner, therefore, did it appear that there was likely to be a military deadlock in the west than a party grew up in the Cabinet which advocated the employment of British forces in the eastern theatre of the war. It was the argument of the easterners that the German lines in the west were almost impregnable, that in the endeavour to pierce them the attacking force always suffered far more heavily than the defenders, and that the true strategy of the *Entente* Powers was to remain on the defensive in the west, where a large application of men and munitions was comparatively ineffective, allowing the Germans to attack there if they thought it worth while to do so, and to seek a decision in the east, where the appearance of a comparatively small Anglo-French force might rally the Balkan peoples to an effective onslaught on the Austrian Empire or establish a safe channel for the munitioning of Russia. Of this eastern school of opinion Mr. Lloyd George and Mr. Churchill were powerful advocates.

The whole force of the French high command was naturally thrown into the opposite scale. To a Frenchman no object was more imperative than the liberation of the national soil from the invader. The more guns and men England could pour into France, the lighter would be the French burden, and the speedier, so it seemed, the French release. Sir John French and Sir Douglas Haig, the steadfast Scottish cavalry officer who succeeded him in the English command, shared these opinions, and deprecated the dispersion of English war effort. In common with Joffre, they entertained the dazzling hope that a break through, with a great cavalry charge to thrust home the victory, was always possible and sometimes imminent. With the exception of Kitchener, most highly placed soldiers at home were of the same opinion, and pinned their faith to the western front.

Yet in the east an extraordinary event called for the attention of the *Entente* Powers. Russia was the secular foe of Turkey, yet in a war in which Russia, the enemy of the Porte, was co-operating with France and England, its immemorial friends, the Sultan would have been well advised to persevere in a neutral course. From such counsels he was eventually driven by the prestige and pressure of Enver Pasha, by the appearance before the walls of Constantinople of two German cruisers, the *Goeben* and the *Breslau*, by German largesse widely distributed, and by the vexation occasioned by the detention in British docks of two unfinished Turkish ships of war, the cost of which had been defrayed by public subscription. The final hesitations of a tremulous court were overcome by a masterpiece of craft and audacity. The great Russian port of Odessa was bombarded (October 28, 1914) by the *Goeben* and the *Breslau*, which had been fictitiously sold to the Turkish government, the more swiftly and surely to involve it in war. In mid-November, 1914, the Ottoman Empire had entered the struggle on the German side.

The consequences were momentous and far-reaching. Russia, though almost inexhaustable in manpower, was deficient in the industrial mechanism necessary for the nourishment of a modern war. By the autumn of 1914 she had already exhausted her reserves of ammunition and was only able to supply from her own resources one-third of the daily allowance required for the troops.

And now she was faced with the burden of a new campaign against the Turks in the Caucasus. On January 2, 1915, Kitchener received an appeal from the Grand Duke Nicholas for assistance to relieve the pressure on the Caucasus front. It was decided to send an expedition to the Dardanelles. With the Dardanelles blocked, Russia might be forced to fade out of the war for lack of supplies; with the Dardanelles opened, not only could shells and guns be poured into the country at every season of the year, but its discouragement might be arrested, its purpose confirmed, and the tactics of its armies perchance improved by the military lessons of the western war. Other considerations, hardly less attractive, pointed in the same direction. A British fleet before Constantinople would cut the Turkish army in two, open a way to the Danube, and make the lavish harvests of southern Russia available for the allies. The first and most striking diversion of military and naval effort was accordingly an expedition to the Dardanelles. In the background vast political and military issues began to take shape: the winning of all the Christian Balkan Powers to the allied cause, the possible emancipation of the Arab world from the Turks, the possible insurgence of the Moslem world against Britain, the destruction of British power in India and Egypt, or the end of the long Ottoman rule over the non-Ottoman peoples in Europe and Asia. The campaign in the Gallipoli peninsula was more than an expedient for putting new heart into Russia. It was the first strong blow struck in an eastern campaign, which, while failing of its primary object, so developed as to bring the Ottoman Empire to the ground.

Mar. 18, 1915   In the execution of this hazardous enterprise there were many flaws. An attempt to force the straits by the fleet alone was foiled by an undetected minefield and unwisely, as some good sailors think, not renewed. The enemy were therefore fully warned and prepared when, after prolonged and avoidable delays, Sir Ian Hamilton was in a position to effect a landing on the peninsula. Thereupon the immense difficulties of the British undertaking declared themselves to every eye. The peninsula, which is bare of trees, slopes gradually downwards to the coast, providing almost everywhere a perfect field of fire for the defenders. The attacking force, which was too small, and entirely dependent for its supplies upon the fleet, was confronted with every obstacle which German science and Turkish diligence could supply. Nevertheless, not only were landings effected under withering fire at five points on the southern tip of the peninsula, but for many months the best part of the Turkish army was put to serious strain in defending its positions. There was even a moment when, after a substantial reinforcement, success seemed to be within reach of the British. On August 6 a new landing was made at Suvla Bay, which found the Turk wholly unprepared. Then a swift and vigorous advance might have given to Stopford's troops the Anafarta ridge, which was the key to the position. But the opportunity was missed. While forty-eight precious hours were lost by his assailants, Mustapha Kemal Bey, a young Turkish officer, collected a sufficiency of troops and, rushing to the vital point, saved the situation.

The withdrawal of the British forces from the peninsula effected, contrary to every prognostication, without the loss of a man (December 18, 1915–January 8, 1916) was a brilliant example of the naval efficiency which throughout had distinguished the course of the campaign. The enterprise, which had cost 120,000 British casualties, had failed of its main object. The attempt to open the southern waterway to Russia had been blocked by the stubborn resistance of the Germans and the Turks. Nevertheless, it would be rash to assume that the great sacrifice of British life and treasure on that wind-swept peninsula had no compensations for the allied cause. So long as the British, with the aid of magnificent contingents from Australia and New Zealand, were battering at the Turkish gateway, Russia had the strongest of all motives for prosecuting the war. The allies had promised her Constantinople, and by a miraculous twist of fortune Britain was engaged in a campaign which, if successful, would put the prize in her hands. Compared with such a gift no other gain to be expected from successful war counted with the Russian people. They cared little for Serbia; they had no appetite for western conquests, and were soon disabused of the belief that they could beat the Germans. But if Great Britain could have taken Tzarigrad, their huge losses in the Masurian Lakes, in Poland, and in Galicia were made good. So, though the Dardanelles expedition may be defended as having occupied and wasted the best divisions of the Turkish army, its most important military consequence was to keep Russia in the war.

Soon after the Gallipoli landing (May 24), Italy, having long balanced the issue, finally obeyed the call of ancient policies and came into the war against Austria, a much divided and unprepared nation. The lawless invasion of Belgium, though it made a sensible impression upon the generous Italian temperament, was less efficacious than the

for Riga in the hopes of getting astride the military communications from Petrograd, for so St. Petersburg was now called, to the Russian front. So swift and irresistible was the German advance that by the beginning of September it seemed as if the field armies of the Tzar might be cut off from their base and broken, and that the ensuing year might find the Germans established in Petrograd. Such a triumph was denied them. Russky in the north and Ivanov in the south achieved during that month successes which put a term on the German advance and shot a new flame of hope into the government of the Tzar. But if the momentum of the great German drive had exhausted itself, the results of the campaign were sufficiently impressive. The Russians had lost 325,000 prisoners and 3,000 guns, a blow from which the Tzarist army was never able wholly to recover.

The subjection of the Balkans followed. The Turk was assisted to repel the British attack in the Dardanelles; the Bulgars were won over (September 6); the Serbian army, whose campaigning in the previous autumn had been covered with glory, was driven headlong and with devastating losses into the snowclad mountains of Albania, before a small allied force which had been landed at Salonika had time to render assistance. Whenever a German general appeared, he seemed to bring victory, Hindenburg in East Prussia and Poland, Mackensen in Galicia and Serbia, Liman von Sanders in the Gallipoli peninsula. And while these spectacular victories were being won in the eastern theatre of the war, the German front held its ground against the attacks of the French and British armies in the west. Here with an optimism ill-justified by the facts the allied command planned a series of offensives in Flanders, in Artois, and in Champagne, which, save perhaps in the successful surprise action at Neuve Chapelle (March 10-13), were vastly more costly to the attacking than to the defending force. The French command, proceeding on a false arithmetical theory, argued that in a war of attrition the advantages would be with the allies. The Germans knew better. Though they had gained nothing by their lawless employment of poison gas (April 22) after the first surprise at Ypres, on both fronts they had come out victorious in the fighting of that year.

The terrific losses endured by the allies both on the western and the eastern front in 1915 precipitated, as was only to be expected, changes in the higher direction of the war. English public opinion was so far disturbed by the lack of munitions and the evidence of failure at the front as to call for the formation of a Coalition government and for the substitution of Haig for French in the military command. Far graver in its consequences was the change in Russia. The Grand Duke Nicholas was relegated to the Caucasus and the Tzar with Alexeieff as Chief of his Staff assumed the supreme command. Great as were the military talents of Alexeieff, these changes were widely regarded in Russia as signifying the triumph of all those influences in the government of the country which were considered to be most corrupt and most hostile to the effective conduct of the war. The Tzar was the creature of the Tzarina. The Tzarina was under the spell of Rasputin, and Rasputin, an unclean profligate monk, whose combined powers as visionary, healer, and voluptuary gave him a magnetic influence over high-born Russian women, was understood to favour a German peace. Since the Grand Duke was the most formidable of this creature's enemies, his disgrace was widely regarded as a triumph for the monk, a victory for the Germans, and a blot of shame upon the scutcheon of the Tzar. From this time forward the prestige of Nicholas, the Little Father of his people, suffered a swift and uninterrupted decline.

The next year (1916) is specially memorable in the western fighting for two battles on French soil, one extending over seven and the other four months. The attack and defence of Verdun and the battle of the Somme rank among the greatest achievements of human endurance and the saddest tragedies of human waste. At the end of the year little seemed to have been accomplished. The French had repelled their enemy and recaptured almost all the positions which they had held in the earliest phases of the attack. The British, who had lost 60,000 men in the first day's fighting on the Somme, had failed to break the studied and intricate defences of the German line. Yet in reality the two appalling butcheries had altered the balances of fortune. When the French had repelled the invader from Verdun in July and the sustained and heroic effort of the new British levies on the Somme had died down in October, the old German army, the best trained and most highly skilled body of fighting men which the world has ever seen, was no more.[1] Hereafter the Germans were compelled for the most part to depend upon youthful levies whose military qualities were no greater than those of their French or British adversaries. Another fact, calculated to arouse deep anxiety at the German headquarters, was the appearance in the field of a numerous British army able to take over a large part of the line and capable at last of replying to the enemy with a bombardment as violent, as protracted, and as deadly as his own. It was at the Somme, too, that the tank, an armoured car on caterpillar wheels, which could push through wire, trenches, and other impediments, first made its appearance on the battlefield. It was a British invention, long obstructed by military obstinacy, and the key which was ultimately destined to unlock the riddle of the western front. At the Somme, however, this brilliant device made little difference, for it was employed in a manner which was partial, unintelligent, and premature. In 1918 it won the western campaign.

While German arms were encountering these serious obstacles in the west, fortune spun round and round on the eastern front. A brilliant westward thrust by Brussilov, probably the ablest of the Russian generals, demonstrated once more that, when reasonably well equipped and competently led, a Russian army was more than a match for the composite and disaffected levies of the Austro-Hungarian empire. In a campaign of ten weeks, Brussilov took four hundred and fifty thousand prisoners. His success, which shone out the more brightly by reason of the disasters of the preceding campaign, and seemed to remind Europe that a nation which could muster fifteen million men of fighting age was never at the end of its resources, encouraged Roumania to come into the war against the central powers. The adhesion of an ally, so rich in corn, oil, and other forms of natural wealth, was welcomed with acclamation by the peoples of the *Entente* states. But what appeared to be a blessing turned out in the event to be a disaster. The Russo-Roumanian generals were no match for Falkenhayn and Mackensen,

---

[1] The German losses at the Somme have been returned at 500,000, the British losses at 410,000, and the French losses at 190,000.

who, sweeping all opposition before them, entered Bucharest on December 6. The swiftness and brilliance of the German campaign, the skill with which the two great soldiers, the one marching through the Carpathians, the other through the Dobrudja, combined their movements and ultimately converged upon the capital, gained the admiration of military observers. Henceforward the opulence of Roumania, save for the fact that the surface workings of the oil mines had been prudently destroyed by an Englishman, lay at the disposal of the German allies. By this means their power of endurance was notably enhanced.

The Germans had been quick to realize that one of their hardest problems would be to replace the raw materials and foodstuffs from which they were now debarred by the vigilance of the British navy. Walter Rathenau, a Jew eminent in science, business and letters, had undertaken the organization, on a methodical and ingenious plan, of the economic resources of the country. Substitutes were discovered for many popular articles of diet and many necessary raw materials, but despite all that science and organization could do the blockade told upon the nourishment and health of the people. There were signs of scarcity in 1915; more signs of scarcity in 1916, and, despite the welcome help of Roumanian supplies, the pressure became steadily more grievous. The population bore their hardships with an heroic stoicism, buoyed up by the continual noise of triumphs and the confident expectation of victory. When, after the failure at Verdun, Hindenburg and Ludendorff, the twin giants, were Aug. placed in supreme control, the whole nation, imbibing fresh 28, hope, braced itself to a supreme effort. By a long reach of 1916 public authority, the services of every citizen from fifteen to sixty were commandeered by the State.

From the beginning of the war the British navy had controlled the seas. The transport first of the expeditionary force and then of the new armies had been effected without the loss of a man. British troops had travelled to the Dardanelles to Alexandria, to Salonika without let or hindrance. The German cruisers had been swept off the ocean, the German overseas trade stopped, the German colonies cut off from the fatherland, and exposed to inevitable conquest at the first convenient opportunity. Through the British navy the food, the raw materials, the munitions of war of the United States were made available to the allies, but not to their enemies. The task of this maritime police, however tactfully executed, was distasteful to neutral traders carrying wares destined for the continent of Europe. Whenever an American merchant-man was stopped in mid-ocean by an English warship that her cargo might be examined, there was a fierce feeling in the American business community at the high-handed inter-ference of a belligerent Power with the innocent rights of neutrals. The mutual esteem which united Sir E. Grey and Walter Page, the American Ambassador in London, did much to mitigate asperities which under less delicate handling might have resulted in serious trouble. But though it was a fair answer to American objections that, since the Germans were endeavouring to blockade the British coast with their submarines, Britain was entitled to retaliate, it was not to be expected that neutral traders would accept it as convincing. Not until America herself entered the war was the freedom of the seas consigned to oblivion, and the blockade, which had been tempered to American susceptibilities, exercised in its fullest rigour. Then the United States discarded its legal scruples with lightning speed. "Mr. Balfour," said Mr. Polk of the State Department, "it took Britain three years to reach a point where it was prepared to violate all the laws of blockade. You will find that it will take us only two months to become as great criminals as you are."

The traditions of the British navy had been dominated by the ghost of Nelson. "The Nelson touch," a brilliant and dashing sense of opportunity, a swift and certain tact in the manoeuvring of a fleet into battle, was supposed to be the special property of the great British seaman. The nation expected violent clashes in the North Sea, cutting-out expeditions, and a rapid and emphatic assertion of the naval superiority which Englishmen believed to belong to their fleet. Nothing of the kind occurred. The great fleet vanished into the mists of Scotland. Seven British cruisers were sunk by submarines. Months passed, the German battleships remaining safe behind their minefields, while the main British fleet appeared to show no anxiety to emerge from their lair and to engage the enemy. The new developments in naval war-

fare—the mine, the torpedo, the submarine, the smoke screen— Dec.
created new perils and prescribed new cautions. A distant 8,
battle off the Falkland islands, in which von Spee's cruisers, 1914
fresh from a victory off the Pacific coast, were sunk by
Admiral Sturdee, gave encouragement not only because it
finally cleared the enemy from the southern seas, but because
it appeared to prove alike the good intelligence of the British
Admiralty, the capacity of the admiral, and the accuracy of
the gunners. It was not until May, 1916, that anything in
the nature of a general action was fought. That, too, was a
great and bitter disappointment to the British people. They
had expected a decisive victory. They learnt of an encounter
in which the Grand Fleet, though deprived owing to defective
visibility of what should otherwise have been a triumphant
advantage, had nevertheless lost twice as many men and
twice as many ships as their opponents. The first news May
of the battle of Jutland, being received in London, created a 31,
sensation of unforgettable gloom. Was it true that the naval 1916
supremacy of the country now effectually challenged by the
Germans was a thing of the past? Or was Jellicoe right in
husbanding his resources and avoiding unnecessary risks?
The answer came in the sequel. The High Sea fleet never
again steamed out to join issue with the British Navy. If
Jutland was a German victory, it had many consequences
which in other naval campaigns proceed from a final defeat.

While the personnel of both fleets was, then, admirable in
discipline and courage, the Germans were superior in technical
preparations. Tirpitz had envisaged, as the British Admiralty
had not, the exact nature of the problem presented by a naval
action in the low visibility conditions of the North Sea.
Unlike their adversaries, the German ships were designed
neither for speed nor for long-range action nor for distant
voyages, but for the limited objective of a clash in the home
waters. They carried little coal; they provided only the most
exiguous accommodation for seamen. But their shells were
penetrating, their gunnery in the early stages of an action
exact, and their steel protection so heavy that they were
nearly unsinkable. While the inefficient British shells made
little impression upon the thick steel plating of the High Sea
fleet, the Germans were able, when a lightly protected British
cruiser imprudently steamed within range, to pierce her

insufficient armour and to send her with her splendid crew to the bottom of the waves.

One disadvantage, which later developed into a deadly malady, offset these superiorities. While the British sailor was always at sea, the German crews for the most part and save for short excursions were, for lack of accommodation on board, housed in barracks ashore. The effect of this arrangement was ultimately unfavourable to discipline. The sailor ashore catches every germ in the air. In the last months of the struggle a serious naval mutiny at Kiel paralysed the German fleet and precipitated a general falling away from the further prosecution of the imperial war.

BOOKS WHICH MAY BE CONSULTED

The best short histories of the war are:
C. R. Cruttwell: *A History of the Great War*. 1934.
B. H. Liddell Hart: *The Real War*. 1930.
Sir James Edmonds: *A Short History of World War I*. 1951.

For longer histories the reader is referred to:
John Buchan: *The History of the Great War*. 1921-2.
Winston Churchill: *The World Crisis*. 1923-1931.

Most of the prominent actors have written memoirs. Of these the most important are:
D. Lloyd George: *War Memoirs*. 1933.
Concise Ludendorff Memoirs, 1914-1918. 1933.
Von Hindenburg: *Out of My Life*. Tr. F. A. Holt. 1920.
The Memoirs of Marshal Joffre. Tr. T. B. Mott. 1932.
Foch Mémoires. 1931.
Jellicoe: *Crisis of the Naval War*. 1920.
R. Poincaré: *Au Service de la France*. 1913-26.
Sir Ian Hamilton: *Gallipoli Diary*. 1920.
Sir W. Robertson: *Soldiers and Statesmen*. 1920.
Admiral W. S. Sims and B. J. Kendrick: *The Victory at Sea*. 1920.
J. J. Pershing: *My Experiences in the World War*. 1931.
O. Czernin: *In the World War*. 1919.
A. Brussilov: *A Soldier's Notebook*. 1930.
Prince Rupprecht: *Mein Kriegstagebuch*. 1929.
Von Kluck: *The March on Paris and the Battle of the Marne*, 1914. 1920.
Huguet: *Britain and the War*. Engl. Tr. 1928.

Huguet: *Memoirs of Falkenhayn*. Berlin, 1920.
Huguet: *Memoirs of Hoffmann*. Berlin, 1920.
Huguet: *Memoirs of Conrad von Hötzendorf*. Vienna, 1925.

The official English military histories are: Brigadier-General
J. E. Edmonds (France), Brigadier-General C. F. Aspinall-Oglander
(Gallipoli), Cyril Falls (Palestine and Macedonia), Brigadier-
General F. J. Moberly (Mesopotamia); the official history of naval
operations by Sir Julian Corbett and Sir Henry Newbolt; the
official history of aviation in the war by Sir Walter Raleigh and
H. A. Jones. A brilliant light is thrown on the campaign of 1914
by General E. L. Spears (*Liasion* 1930), on the Italian fighting
by G. M. Trevelyan (*Scenes from Italy's War*, 1919), and on the
English attack on Zeebrugge by Sir E. Hilton Young (*By Sea and
Land*, 1924). For the Arabian War see T. E. Lawrence, *Revolt
in the Desert* (1927), *The Seven Pillars of Wisdom* (1935). See also:
A. Moorehead: *Gallipoli*. 1956.
Lord Wavell: *The Palestine Campaigns*. 1951.
Lord Beaverbrook: *Men and Power*, 1917-18. 1956.

CHAPTER XCVII

THE WAR—LAST PHASE

*The U-boat campaigns and the entry of America into the war.
The Russian revolution. The interlude of Kerensky. The
Bolshevik triumph. Lenin takes Russia out of the war. Britain
masters the U-boats. The defeat of Nivelle and the slaughter
at Passchendaele. British conquest of Baghdad and Jerusalem.
Obstacles to peace. The campaign of 1918. Victories of Foch
and Haig. The German revolution. The Armistice. Consequences of the Great War for the world and the British Empire.*

THE NEXT year (1917) was big with two events each destined
to exercise a far-reaching influence on the history of the
world: the entry of the United States into the war, and the
Russian revolution.

The German naval and military chiefs must accept the
blame of provoking the hostility of the United States. With
their eyes open, and discounting the risk, they dragooned

Feb. Bethmann-Hollweg and the Kaiser into the adoption of
1   "unrestricted U-boat warfare," which meant that the submarines would herafter sink merchantmen at sight. They
knew that they would by this open declaration of piracy
bring down upon themselves the enmity of the United States,
for a submarine not two years before had sunk the passenger
ship *Lusitania* off the Irish coast, and nearly provoked a
declaration of war from Washington; but they calculated
that, before American soldiers could effectively appear on
the battlefields of France, the U-boats would have starved
England to submission. It was a great gamble, coming near
to success, but in the end frustrated by the anti-submarine
measures of the British Admiralty, and in its failure bringing
utter ruin on the German cause. So reckless was the German
Government in the opening of 1917 that it tried to tempt the
Mexicans to attack their neighbours by the promise of Texas,
New Mexico, and Arizona, three States of the American
Union. The intelligence of this offer, which was intercepted
by the British Admiralty and communicated to Washington,
finally drove America into the war.

April   On a bright April morning of that year Londoners beheld
2,   with deep emotion the stars and stripes floating in the air from
1917 the Victoria Tower at Westminster, side by side with the
Union Jack. President Wilson had been deliberate, far too
deliberate for the leading Republicans of the eastern coast,
who would have come into the war as a protest against the
violation of Belgian neutrality. But the President, besides
being a man of peace, and compelled to pay regard to the
strong feeling against England which prevailed in many
sections of the American community, had a vision of exhausted combatants invoking his aid and calling upon him
to propose some healing and beneficent arbitrament. For
such an arbitral rôle, as he projected himself into the future,
he believed that Providence had designed him: that was the
rôle he proposed to fill. Nothing short of the blind stupidity
of Ludendorff and Tirpitz could have moved him from his
position of cool and benevolent aloofness.

In the great stirring of American emotion which ensued,
a keen French observer has noted that a real, though unac-
knowledged, factor was a latent sympathy for the parent stock
whence the larger portion of the American race derives its

origin.[1] Rather than allow England to go down, America would give up her long cherished aversion from foreign entanglements.[2] The sympathy for France, based on the memory of Lafayette, though often more obviously displayed, was by comparison superficial.

Ultimately the consequences of America's entry into the war proved to be decisive. The blockade was made more effective by the assistance of the American fleet. The financial burden of the alliance which had hitherto been mainly borne by Great Britain was now not a moment too soon shared with the wealthiest community in the world. And as American loans relieved the financial anxieties of the *Entente*, so the appearance on the western front of a great and well-equipped American army in the last year of the war deprived the central powers of their last chance of making a favourable peace. Armies, however, are not improvised in the twinkling of an eye. The Americans, like the British before them, were slow in imparting to their war effort an adequate momentum, and during the months while their armies were in process of formation the *Entente* experienced the gravest anxieties of the war.

For on March 15, a fortnight before Congress voted America into the war, the Tzar of Russia had been compelled to abdicate. The revolution, which had been long impending, burst out, not, as might have been expected, with a violent and organized upheaval, but in a series of apparently casual and unpremeditated protests, accumulating in volume and significance until it was clear that the whole country, nobles as well as bourgeois, the soldiers as well as the liberals and socialists, had fallen away from their allegiance to the Tzar. First there was a general riot in Petrograd (March 8), coupled with a general disinclination to work, then a cessation of newspapers; on the 10th a tram strike, on the 11th the mutiny of a regiment, on the 12th the defection of the household troops. The movement spread like a prairie fire. It was a revolution of hunger, misery, and fatigue, dashed with feelings of wild resentment as men called to mind the recent

[1] André Siegfried.
[2] In 1910 Admiral Sims of the U.S. Navy, speaking in the Guildhall, said: "If the time should ever come when the British Empire is menaced by a European coalition Great Britain can rely upon the last ship, the last dollar, the last man, and the last drop of blood of her kindred overseas." (Sims, *The Victory at Sea*, p. 65.)

ruin of Russian armies, the long tale of military disasters, the four million Russian casualties, the malversation of supplies, the strong suspicion that the Tzarina under the influence of the profligate Rasputin had been playing into German hands, and finally the reactionary and oppressive methods of Protopopoff, the last and least intelligent of the Tzar's advisers. A Committee of the Duma headed by Prince Lvov endeavoured to govern the country and to conduct the war.

The Russian people were in no mood for such a government. The integrity of Lvov, the ability of Miliukoff and Guchkoff, the fiery eloquence of the social revolutionary Kerensky were of no avail against the Soviets, or workmen's and soldiers' councils, which formed themselves all over the country and were by the month of April gathered together in a central congress in Petrograd. A universal mood of mutinous inertia paralysed government. Telephone and telegraph operators, typists and messenger boys, the props of sovereign power in a modern state, refused their services. In the Soviets themselves the clear-cut logic of the Bolsheviks, who were the extremists, swiftly mastered the tumultuous passions and confused thoughts of simple and hungry men. The plan of this party was large and seductive: bread for all, an immediate peace, the land for the peasants, and a dictatorship of the proletariat. So while Kerensky endeavoured to stir the army to renewed activities, the Bolsheviks set to work to corrupt discipline. Their success was complete and almost immediate. By the end of July, 1917, the Russian front had crumbled in face of the enemy. "No annexations, no indemnities," was the slogan of the new revolution.

Eloquence, and Kerensky had nothing better to offer, could not restore a situation so gravely compromised. The Bolshevik movement, despite a mistimed outbreak in July, steadily gathered strength through the weakness of the provisional government, the victories of the Germans, and the growing misery of the people. How could Kerensky, who could not save Riga and lacked the courage to execute revolutionaries when he caught them red-handed, hope to survive in such a storm? On November 7 (October 25 old style) the Bolsheviks struck their blow, which had been long prepared, and as the Red revolutionaries surged round the

Winter Palace his provisional government fell like a pack of cards.

The organizers of the October revolution were two obscure exiles recently returned to Russia: Ulianoff, who called himself Lenin, and the Jew Braunstein, who had taken the name of Trotsky. Two more formidable or resolute adventurers have never seized the reins of power in a great state. Before three months were over they had taken Russia out of the war, ruined the rich and middle classes, and dispersed a representative assembly which had been convoked to frame a parliamentary constitution for a Russian Republic. Patriotism was as little to Lenin's heart as parliaments. At the Treaty of Brest-Litovsk (March 3, 1918) with the Germans he surrendered vast tracts of Russian territory[1] to the enemy without a twinge of shame or of regret.

It was no part of Ludendorff's plan for 1917 to renew the offensive on the western front. Withdrawing some miles to a position which had been fortified with elaborate care, and was known by the Germans as the Siegfried and by the English as the Hindenburg line, he proposed to allow his opponents to continue the costly assaults to which they were so strongly and religiously addicted. He was less disposed to waste men on aggressive tactics since he was confident that in six or, at the most, twelve months the war would be over on the sea. The U-boats would starve England to submission before the Americans could be convoyed to the shores of France.

The form of warfare to which the German nation, despite the protest of many good citizens, was now committed, will for ever be condemned by the conscience of humanity. A merchantman or passenger vessel torpedoed by a submarine sinks with all hands. There is no means of rescue. Upon the brave U-boat commanders was laid the injunction, the most repellent to a naval officer which can be imagined, to discard the immemorial courtesies of the sea. Yet it cannot be denied that this new and lawless method of warfare contained the promise of success. At the end of April, 1917, there was only six weeks' supply of corn in Britain, and it became clear to the British Government that unless the rate of submarine

---

[1] Finland, Esthonia, Livonia, Courland, Lithuania, Russian Poland.

sinking were promptly reduced the food supply of the island could not be guaranteed. The riddle was solved. Partly by the adoption (forced upon the Admiralty by Mr. Lloyd George) of the convoy system, partly by depth charges and improved hydrophones, and by other expedients too numerous to mention, the U-boat was subdued. A time came when very few of these submarines returned to their base, so completely had the British Admiralty mastered its problem. The courage of the German crews was great. Equally high was the spirit of the officers and seamen of the British commercial marine, whom no dangers, however certain, could frighten from the seas.

Ludendorff's hopes were frustrated on the water. The fighting on land, though nowhere decisive, clearly pointed to an ascending scale of German predominance. An attack Oct., on the Aisne, prepared with the utmost elaboration by Nivelle, 1917 an attractive and much acclaimed officer, who had been called to succeed Joffre in the French command, broke down with heavy losses so murderous as to occasion a mutiny in part of the French army and a sudden lack of confidence among civilians and soldiers alike, which for a time threatened seriously to impair the military efficiency of the French nation. The situation was restored. Pétain, the hero of Verdun, stopped the rot in the French army. Clemenceau, the Tiger, coming to the head of affairs, put an end to defeatist intrigues in Paris. Yet the position remained one of great anxiety to the allied commanders. Fearing lest the shaken army of France might fail under a sudden strain, Haig was confirmed in the resolve for the remainder of the year to concentrate the attention of the enemy on the British front.

All that summer and autumn the rain fell pitilessly on the low-lying ground round the battered Cloth Hall of Ypres, where the British Army with a tremendous concentration of guns was endeavouring to force its way to the Belgian coast. Never were the penalties of bad weather more unevenly distributed. While the Germans, having the higher ground, were relatively comfortable, the British trenches were often waist deep in water. To the ordinary horrors of an intense and continuous bombardment, there was added the danger that men once wounded might drown in the water or suffo-

cate in mud. Nevertheless, the battle of Passchendaele was
continued with a dogged persistence, the Germans yielding
little ground and suffering little by comparison, while the
British casualties mounted up to the huge total of three
hundred thousand. The dull thunder of the guns of Passchendaele heard in many a quiet Surrey village announced one
of those national tragedies, which are all the more terrible
because their necessity is questioned. It is pertinent to ask
whether the French were only to be saved from destruction
by so terrible a wastage of British life, or whether, seeing that
an American army was expected in the following year, it was
not an obvious counsel of prudence for Britain to husband
her man power? Mr. Lloyd George advised strongly against
the battle, but ceded his judgment to the earnest representations of the soldiers. The cost of Passchendaele was evidenced
in Byng's November fighting round Cambrai, when a brilliant
surprise attack launched with the aid of tanks failed to
consolidate its swift and remarkable advance for lack of
reserves.

The catalogue of allied reverses in this troubled year was
completed at Caporetto (October 24), when the Italian army
which had been destined for the capture of Trieste was driven
back to the Piave with huge losses and in unexampled confusion. The catastrophe was the more alarming since it
revealed the extent to which demoralization and war-weariness
had gained ground among troops who were naturally intrepid
and courageous. In truth the Italian Higher Command had
paid little attention to the expedients by which an army
submitted to the terrible nervous trials of modern warfare
may nevertheless be kept in good heart. The Commissariat
was irregular, the guns deficient in number and weight, and
the facilities for amusement and education behind the lines
which were so lavishly provided on other fronts were not
available. In his rare intervals of leave the Italian soldier
would return from the scorching limestone plateau of the
Carso to find his family starving on a maintenance allowance
from the state which was wholly insufficient for its needs. In
such circumstances it is not surprising that his will to victory
faltered, that he listened to the priests if he were a Catholic or
to the Soviets if he were a socialist, and from each of these

very different sources learnt that the war should be promptly stopped.

That after so great a deliquescence of military *morale* the Italian front should have been firmly re-established is a tribute to Cadorna's skill and to Italian resilience. The Piave was held and Venice saved. But when winter came it was still uncertain whether the Italian army, albeit under their new commander Diaz, and reinforced by French and British divisions, would repel with success a renewed assault.

While these disasters were sustained by the Allies upon the Russian, French, and the Italian fronts, a wide-sweeping British movement against the Turks in the East brought the famous cities of Baghdad and Jerusalem under British control. By these military exploits the Arab world was loosened from its Turkish moorings and the prestige of Great Britain in the East was restored. The conquest of Palestine was destined to have further consequences, the fruits of which were amply reaped before the close of the war. By proclaiming its intention to establish in Palestine a national home for the Jews, Great Britain rallied to the allied cause, at a time when money was urgently needed, the powerful and cosmopolitan community which, not from New York only, controls the loan markets of the world.[1]

The time had long passed since Germans were gaily speculating on vast annexations to be obtained at the expense of their rivals. But their arms had been so successful, their domestic war propaganda so encouraging and delusive, that they could not afford to offer a peace which the allies would accept. It was an axiom with the British Cabinet that Belgium should be evacuated, Alsace-Lorraine returned to France, and indemnities or reparations paid to the Allies. These terms the General Staff would not permit to be discussed. Holding that Bethmann-Hollweg, the Chancellor, was veering towards concessions, Ludendorff secured his dismissal (July, 1917) and became till the end of the war the real master of Germany. It was not the first injury the German people had sustained from their leading soldiers. It was the General Staff whose requirements had brought England and America into the war, and it was the General Staff who obstructed

---

[1] That Palestine should neither fall to others nor yet cost money to Britain were also motives of the Cabinet.

the fairway to a peace which would have left the Hohen-zollerns and Habsburgs on their thrones. To the German navy in particular, which had been taught that "a second Punic war" against England was inevitable, it was specially repugnant to abandon the convenient bases of the Belgian ports.

With forty divisions drawn from the Russian front Luden-dorff was entitled to hope that a last bid for victory might yet succeed even in the West. The strategy of his campaign in 1918 was to deliver a blow at the point of junction of the French and English lines so crushing as to drive the two armies asunder and to enable each to be separately overcome. His tactics, which had been carefully rehearsed before Riga, were novel and brilliant. A creeping barrage of unexampled intensity sustained over a front of forty-three miles would blast a hole through which bomb-throwers, flame-throwers, and machine-gunners, specially picked and trained for the work, and rushed to the front in lorries, would stream forward without pause or intermission. Powerful trench mortars and enormous reserves were necessary for the success of the manoeuvre. These Ludendorff possessed.

The hammer blow fell on March 21. On that day a terrific avalanche of shells from 4,000 guns, the first salvo in a battle lasting over seven months, fell upon the Fifth British Army under Gough, which had just taken over part of the French line. Save at Arras on the extreme British left, the attackers, who were favoured by mist and hard ground, carried every-thing before them. The Fifth Army broke. In a few days German guns were playing on the railway line south of Amiens and it seemed as if Ludendorff's plan of severing the two armies was to be achieved. It was not to be. The Germans, who in the speed of their advance appear to have exhausted their original momentum, were held up before Amiens. The fatal thrust was not persisted in. It was decided by what appears to have been a departure from the original plan to make thrusts at other parts of the allied line. First the British were attacked on the Ypres sector (April 9-29) and pushed back twelve miles. Then (May 27) the French were heavily defeated on the Chemin des Dames. But these assaults, though formidable and destructive, were eventually stemmed. Strategists doubt their wisdom, for by the end of June the German line in France showed three great bulges, each offering to an active opponent a convenient target for attack.

In this menacing advance the Germans had sustained enormous losses such as are incidental to the free movement of massed troops under heavy bombardment from the air and fire from enemy batteries, gallantly and skilfully worked. Another consequence might less easily have been foreseen. Whereas the British army was the best-fed army in the war, their opponents had long been on short commons. Accordingly, when the Germans overran the British lines and found them littered with provisions of every sort, they were seized with a sudden feeling of hopelessnes. Then, and only then, they perceived that the real truth about the war had been withheld from them, and that the enemy, who had been represented as being in the last stage of want and inanition, was rioting in luxuries to which Germans had long been strangers. By many channels this sudden awareness of deception spread backward from the front and contributed to make the German revolution.

It was against an army already suffering from an infection of hopelessness that the Allies began on July 18 the great series of offensive movements which, to their surprise (for they had made their plans for another year of fighting), brought the war to a close on November 11. Everything now pointed to success. The losses of the campaign had been more than replaced by the influx of some six hundred thousand fresh troops from America, and though it was not until September that the American army under General Pershing was able to take the field, individual American divisions had fought with the French and English, and at one action at Château-Thierry had greatly distinguished themselves. In every particular of equipment, save trench mortars, the Allies were now superior to their opponents. In the air they had acquired a marked ascendancy. Hundreds of light mobile tanks furnished them with an incomparable instrument for piercing the defences of the enemy. Moreover, the most serious defect which had marred their previous operations was now remedied. Taught at last by the March disaster, the British public acquiesced in the decision to submit its forces on the western front to the supreme direction of a French commander. The man chosen was Foch, an instructed soldier of great authority, keen insight, and irrepressible dash, and the close friend of Wilson, the chief of the British staff; but Foch did not stand alone. With him stood the modest long-headed Weygand, as chief of staff, a living storehouse of facts and figures. The choice was justified. From July 18, when Mangin made a surprise attack upon the southern German bulge with three hundred light tanks and captured thirty thousand prisoners, till the last day of fighting in November, there was no moment of doubt that the power of offensive lay with the allies. But if any day in that long-sustained struggle deserves to be singled out it is that which Ludendorff has described as the "black day of the German army." It was August 8, the days of Haig's surprise attack near Amiens, and it was black not so much because the Germans lost twenty thousand prisoners to the enemy, as because though in sufficient force they were evicted from positions which were held to be secure. From these premises Ludendorff drew the conclusion that demoralization had set in among his troops, and Haig that victory might be obtained by a concerted and violent offensive over the whole front. When the British army stormed the Siegfried line (September 29) the spine of the German resistance was broken.

On the next day Ludendorff asked his government to sue for peace. A month before the revolution broke out in Germany, the chief of the General Staff had thrown up the struggle.

An astonishing succession of allied victories, crowded into a few weeks, brought the long and courageous resistance of the central Powers to an end. First Bulgaria, then Turkey, then Austria were so defeated as to sue for peace. Germany still remained, her army gravely shaken and depleted, yet in the gathering shades of autumn fighting a rearguard action on enemy soil with dogged tenacity. But the German people, who were hungry, miserable, and now plunged in depair, wanted peace, and peace at once; and since President Wilson, in whom Europe descried the arbiter of its fate, boggled at dealing even with a Parliamentary government in Berlin so long as the Kaiser was on the throne, they were well content that the Kaiser should go. It was understood that the allies would have no truck with German militarism. So when the fleet was ordered out to sea there was a mutiny of the Navy at Kiel, and soon afterwards (November 9) the Kaiser and the Crown Prince fled to Holland, and on the same day a republic was proclaimed at Berlin. Brave are the men who in the darkest days are willing to take responsibility for the government of their country. The middle-class German Socialists who now succeeded to the proudest monarchy in Europe were brave and patriotic. Yet it was a serious misfortune for the democratic cause in Germany that the first inevitable act of the new Government was to accept an armistice under which the Germans were compelled not only to evacuate their conquered territory, but to surrender their aeroplanes, their guns, their rolling stock, and the best part of their fleet.[1] All this is brought up against German democracy now. But at the moment there was only one sentiment all over Europe when at 11 o'clock on the morning of November 11 the firing suddenly ceased, a sentiment of overwhelming thankfulness that the long and hideous nightmare was at last at an end.

The war had been won by the democracies of the west. At the end of it the three great military monarchies of eastern and central Europe had disappeared. Though in the stress of the conflict parliamentary debates were little considered, the leading men had been fashioned in the parliamentary arena: Asquith, Lloyd George, Churchill, Balfour, Bonar Law in England, Poincaré, Painlevé, Briand and Clemenceau in France. Again and again it was made evident in Briand's witty words that "war is too serious a thing to be left to the soldiers." The downfall of Germany is not a little to be ascribed to the fact that she had permitted the soldiers too great a place in the national life.

The temporary eclipse of personal liberty, coupled with a vast increase in state control are necessary consequences of modern war. Both evils were cheerfully endured. The English people, less patient of regimentation than other nations, were nevertheless induced to accept conscription and the rationing of food, and a measure of drink control which would have been thought impracticable in time of peace. In every country it was considered necessary to secure

[1] Appendix B.

national solidarity by elaborate propaganda, holding up the enemy to scorn and hatred. To the cruelty and carnage of war there was added the evil of subsidized prejudice and mendacity. In this respect no belligerent country can claim to be exempt from guilt. As the anxieties and perplexities of the war thickened, the men of violent and commanding will came to the front and took control; Lloyd George in England, Clemenceau in France, Ludendorff in Germany, Lenin in Russia. The Cabinet convulsion in Britain in the winter of 1916 was characteristic of the growing concentration of authority which the stern circumstances of the time demanded. A small war committee sitting *de die in diem* under a dynamic chairman was substituted for a coalition Cabinet, very able but much divided in opinion, in which, in the words of Mr. Winston Churchill, one of its members, "every military decision had to be carried by the same sort of process of tact, temporizing, and exhaustion which occurs over a clause in a violently contested bill in the House of Commons in time of peace." It was this government which, under the direction of Mr. Lloyd George and with the occasional assistance of distinguished statesmen from the Dominions, ruled England and the Empire during the last two years of the war.

It might perhaps have been imagined that war, which is essentially inimical to liberty and justice, would have tended to arrest the progress of democracy in the belligerent countries. The bullet, however, is a great leveller. In England, where for many reasons, the absence of conscription being one of them, the equalitarian spirit was less developed than in France and Italy, class consciousness was shamed by the extremity of the peril voluntarily encountered for the general good by plain citizens. The stay-at-home landlord felt humble in the presence of his wounded gardener. The railway porter who had risked his life took on a dignity never to be obtained by the secure plutocrat. What, statesmen asked themselves, can be good enough for a population which is willing to stake its all for the country's safety? Even during the war the British Cabinet passed bills to extend education, to give votes to women, and turned its thoughts to providing "homes for heroes." The condition of the common man and woman was always present to their minds. It was not so with the British Cabinet during the Napoleonic wars.

With a surprising and instantaneous unanimity the British Dominions and colonies rallied round the mother country. Spurts of rebellion, soon suppressed, in South Africa and Ireland, indicated the presence of refractory elements, which were not, however, sufficiently strong to prevail against the momentum of a brotherhood in arms. India, its princes and peoples alike, stood by the Empire, and contributed to its war effort in France, in Gallipoli, and in Mesopotamia. New Zealand lost more men than Belgium. The conquest of German West Africa was effected by General Botha, of German East Africa by General Smuts, of German New Guinea by an expedition fitted out from Australia. The French Canadians, who in another species of quarrel might have proved refractory, were content to serve in a war for the rescue of France. Yet the consequences of this widely spread enthusiasm were not exactly what might have been predicted. So far from leading up to a closer union of the Empire, the war had the effect of loosening the constitutional ties by which that great Commonwealth had previously been united.

Before the war men had talked of a Federal Parliament in London. Afterwards that solution of the imperial problem was so clearly unacceptable that it was never propounded. An exaltation of national sentiment, bred in some Dominions by the achievements and sacrifices of the war, and in others quickened by a spice of Irish or Dutch hostility, forbade the faintest suspicion of subservience.

The Dominions had made good as separate nations. As nations they signed the peace treaties and were admitted to the League of Nations, and as such they claimed equality with the mother country under the common Crown. As the Sovereign acted on the advice of British Ministers in Britain, so, it was contended, should the Governor-General, his Viceregent, act on the advice of South African ministries in Cape Town and Pretoria, of Canadian ministries in Ottawa, of Australian ministries at Canberra, and of New Zealand ministries at Wellington. The claim was conceded. A new picture of the Commonwealth, corresponding with the new aspirations, was enclosed within the framework of the Statute of Westminster (1931), and the war which had furnished to the world the most amazing example of imperial solidarity was at the same time admitted to have dissolved the Empire (India and the Crown Colonies for the moment excepted) into a free association of equal states.[1]

To an extent never previously realized the war was one of extermination. Whole populations were engaged in the combat and were regarded as legitimate objects of destruction. Though aerial warfare was in its infancy, it had so far advanced before the Armistice as to engender a hateful competition in the bombing of cities and the destruction of civilian life. A bomb might fall anywhere, upon little children as they sat at their lessons, upon worshippers kneeling in church, or even upon nurses as they tended the sick. The rights of neutrals were little regarded. The German invasion of Belgium, the unrestricted U-boat warfare, the use of asphyxiating gas were all cruel acts of international lawlessness which may be charged to the German account. On the other side the interference of the British Navy with neutral trade, the appropriation of Corfu as an allied sanatorium, and the blockade of Greece by the French Navy, when it was feared that King Constantine might join the enemy, were in varying degrees actions for which no legal purist can find a defence. How little the humane counsels of international law influenced the conduct of belligerent nations was clearly, as we have already noted, illustrated by the case of the United States. Before she entered the war no country had more steadily or loudly proclaimed her devotion to the doctrine of the freedom of the seas. But once embarked on hostilities, once the rôle of the neutral was exchanged for that of the belligerent, the whole attitude of America changed. The blockade of Germany which a week before had been an international crime henceforward became an American virtue. The freedom of the seas was thrown to the winds, and the energetic American Navy addressed itself to the task of blockading the enemy with a completeness to which the British Admiralty had never ventured to aspire.

No words can paint the pangs and sufferings of this long-drawn agony of the European nations. Some men lost their

[1] The position of the Dominions was thus defined by the Imperial Conference of 1926: "Equal in status, in no way subordinate one to another in any respect of their domestic or external affairs, though united by a common allegiance to the Crown and freely associated as members of the British Commonwealth of Nations.'

reason, others were blinded, others were asphyxiated with gas or had their bodies torn and mutilated with explosions. Many came out of the war nervous wrecks for life. What is surprising and creditable to human nature was that the almost universal reaction to terror was not panic-stricken compliance, but indignant resolve. Every air attack upon England made recruits for the war, every bad week at the front redoubled the energies of the munition workers, every German severity in Belgium made an eventual German success less probable. One of the lessons of the war, if posterity cares to heed it, is the bankruptcy of terrorism as a policy directed against the wills of the progressive and civilized peoples of Europe. The population of Dunkirk, though the town was almost continuously attacked from the air, went about their ordinary occasions almost as in times of peace.

In those belligerent countries which were relatively civilized so long and cruel a war could be maintained only by an immense effort of massed propaganda. Recruiting was nourished by war speeches and war speeches by war fables. Even in England the gravest acts of injustice were committed against enemy aliens who were interned, deprived of their property, and in the concluding stages of the war deported to Germany. To weaken the *morale* of the army by distributing leaflets from the air became during the concluding stages of the struggle a feature of increasing importance. Germans endeavoured to inject mutiny into Russians; English propaganda led many Germans to doubt the justice of their cause and to impugn the veracity of their leaders. The dissolution of the ill-compacted army of the Austrian Empire was accelerated by skilfully devised appeals, prepared in London and distributed by air, to the subject races who had long chafed under Austrian rule.

Perhaps the most striking monument of the success of war-time propaganda is the sudden emergence from the wreck of the Austrian Empire of the Republic of Czecho-Slovakia. Most states have been fashioned by the sword or have grown out of colonization. Czecho-Slovakia is the child of propaganda. How two able exiles, Masaryk, the son of a Slovak coachman, and Beneš, the son of a Czech peasant-farmer, set alight an agitation for the liberation of the Czechs and the Slovaks, with what wholesale desertions from the Austrian army their efforts were rewarded, how French and English brains were enlisted in their cause, with what enthusiasm the evangel of Czech liberation was received in Chicago (the second largest Czech city in the world) and with what sympathy by President Wilson, how 45,000 Czech war-captives in Russia formed themselves into an army, marched across Siberia, and were thence transported to their native country— the narrative of these events constitutes one of the most surprising chapters in modern history. It is not wonderful that the railway station in Prague is called, not after the name of any Czech general or victory, for there were no such names to be inscribed on the humble annals of this peasant and subject race, but after the American President who, impressed by the skilful propaganda of the two illustrious exiles, proclaimed that the establishment of a Czecho-Slovak republic was among the war aims of the Allied Powers.

CHAPTER XCVIII

TREATIES OF PEACE

The Legacy of War. Conditions which shaped the Peace. President Wilson. His great influence. The doctrine of self-determination. The Covenant of the League. Georges Clemenceau. David Lloyd George. The reparations problem, and the English elections. The Italian standpoint. Flaws in the Treaty of Versailles. The dismemberment of Austria-Hungary. The triumph of the Wilsonian doctrine. America withdraws. France allies herself to the Petite Entente. *Organization of the League of Nations. Ideas embodied in the Covenant. Persistence of international rivalries. The war cloud of 1935.*

THE SITUATION of Europe at the time of the Armistice was one of unexampled misery and confusion. The vanquished Empires had crumbled to pieces and the new Republics had yet to acquire authority and confidence. And meanwhile, with government all over central and eastern Europe at its lowest point of experience and efficiency, with loyalties uncertain and divided, with frontiers fluctuating and unsettled, and with exhaustion as the last surviving ally of social order, a task was imposed upon philanthropists and statesmen calculated to strain and indeed to overpower the remedial resources of mankind. Eight million young men, the best and most vigorous of their generation, had been killed in the war. A greater number had been permanently disabled. Equally, if not more, serious, were the losses consequent upon starvation, malnutrition, and disease.[1] Particularly were these evils terrible in Russia, where the horrors of cholera, typhus, and food shortage were aggravated by revolution and continuing war: but they were great all through central and eastern Europe, in war-scourged Poland, where the peasantry were living on roots, grass, acorns, and heather; in Germany, where by reason of underfeeding the number of births in 1918 was actually below the number of deaths; in Austria, where, since the factories were devoid of coal and raw material, every poor home was menaced by the spectre of famine; and in Serbia, where half the male population had been killed, and 35 per cent. were suffering from recognizable tuberculosis. It is difficult to bring before the imagination the hopelessness and dejection which were produced by these dreadful conditions, or to estimate the consequences for the quality of the population of Europe of four years of nervous overstrain and malnutrition. The destruction of fixed capital through high explosives, save in so far as it was the occasion of want and exposure, was by comparison a negligible calamity.

These evils, though specially evident in Russia and the defeated countries, were by no means confined to them. Victors and neutrals also suffered. The losses of France calculated in dead and wounded, in farms ravaged, in factories, mines, and machinery destroyed were enormous. The privations of Italy through lack of fuel were great. Indeed, the ill consequences of the war were felt throughout the world, and nowhere more seriously than in those regions where a slight rise in food prices drives a whole population into want. Such was the case of India, where an epidemic of influenza which might otherwise have been relatively harmless carried off the enormous total of six million lives.

[1] The total number of deaths attributable to the war has been estimated at 25 millions (Gilbert Murray: *Then and Now*).

The extremity of these and other sufferings had produced in the public mind a pining for a world organized on a new and better plan, and, as often arises when desires are strong, a belief that such a world could be brought into being. The aspirations of Russia were centred round the person of Lenin. Western Europe looked for its salvation to President Wilson.

The Treaties of Peace were made under the direction of three democratic statesmen, each possessing astonishing prestige—Wilson, Clemenceau, Lloyd George. Yet while each of these remarkable men exercised his specific influence on the Treaties, so that we may say here is the trace of Wilson, here of Lloyd George, here of Clemenceau, the substance of the settlement was dictated by inexorable facts, which these men were compelled to accept, and which no other set of statesmen, however enlightened, would have been strong enough to vary or disregard had the big three been suddenly assassinated.

First of these shaping conditions was the fact that under the impact of war the old governments of Russia, Germany, and Austria-Hungary had disappeared and that the Poles, the Czechs, the Roumans, and the Serbs were setting up new national governments in their place. If the allied statesmen in Paris had desired to check these nationalist movements, they could have enforced their will only by armed force. And where could they have found that force? The French, the British, and the Italians were weary of war. There was but one fresh army available, and this had already accomplished its mission. Not for a moment would the United States have assented to the employment of even a single American division in a campaign to thwart the national aspirations of the Poles or the Czechs.

A second circumstance was the temper which then prevailed in the European belligerent countries, which had only by the nearest margin, and at the eleventh hour, been preserved from destruction. They held Germany responsible for the war. They observed that it was not the Serbs who had invaded Austria, nor the Belgians who had attacked the Germans, and that it was the government of the Kaiser which had declared war on Russia, Belgium, and France. They were angry, vindictive, unquiet. They wanted redress and safety. No statesman in a democratic age, however independent, can prevail against the clear and passionate wishes of his countrymen. Clemenceau would have ceased to represent France, Orlando would have ceased to represent Italy, if they had not worked for the weakening of the enemy powers, and for the better protection of their respective states. Lloyd George had received an emphatic mandate from his constituencies that the enemy must be made to pay, and if he had not already obtained the internment of the German Fleet at the Armistice would have been asked the reason why by the British people. Of all these statesmen, the one most naturally prone to take a liberal view of the situation, the British Prime Minister, was the most clearly committed to a course of retribution.

Thirdly, it was unfortunate that the Conference should have been held in a capital which was still reeling under the tragedies of the war and the shock of bombardment. In the inflamed atmosphere of Paris the ideals of appeasement fought an unequal battle with those of retribution. The cooler air of a Swiss city, as recommended by the British, would have been more conducive to a happy end.

To Paris, however, the Conference was summoned on January 18, 1919. It was a gathering unique in history, for the war, which had disturbed everyone everywhere, had quickened every resentment, revived every claim, fostered every vision, and sharpened every appetite, and with all these appetites, claims, visions, and resentments a handful of war-weary statesmen, each responsible to an exacting democracy in his own country and pestered by the ravings of a debased press, was expected to cope as best it might. The scene has been well described by a brilliant eye-witness. "The Paris of the Conference," writes Dr. Dillon, "ceased to be the capital of France. It became a vast cosmopolitan caravanserai teeming with unwanted aspects of life and turmoil, filled with curious samples of the races, tribes, and tongues of four continents who came to watch and wait for the mysterious to-morrow.

"An Arabian Nights touch was imparted to the dissolving panorama by strange visitants from Tartary and Kurdistan, Corea and Azerbeijan, Armenia, Persia, and the Hedjaz—

men with patriarchal beards and scimitar-shaped noses, and others from desert and oasis, from Samarkand and Bokhara. Turbans and fezes, sugar-loaf hats and headgear resembling episcopal mitres, old military uniforms devised for the embryonic armies of new states on the eve of perpetual peace, snowy-white burnouses, flowing mantles, and graceful garments like the Roman toga, contributed to create an atmosphere of dreamy unreality in the city where the grimmest of realities were being faced and coped with.

"Then came the men of wealth, of intellect, of industrial enterprise, and the seed-bearers of the ethical new ordering, members of economic committees from the United States, Britain, Italy, Poland, Russia, India, and Japan, representatives of naphtha industries and far-off coal mines, pilgrims, fanatics and charlatans from all climes, priests of all religions, preachers of every doctrine, who mingled with princes, field-marshals, statesmen, anarchists, builders-up, and pullers-down. All of them burned with desire to be near to the crucible in which the political and social systems of the world were to be melted and re-cast."

In this scene of confusion the American President shone at the opening of the Conference with the lustre of a Messiah. At one time he had been violently unpopular with the belligerent nations. He had recommended the "neutral mind" as though ethical differences did not exist, and "peace without victory" as though war held no resentments. But now all this was forgotten. The Princetown professor had brought America into the war. In a series of lofty and eloquent speeches he had defined the aims of the allies and indicated the new political formations in Europe. He had noted that the enemy was "Prussian militarism," that the aim was "to make the world safe for democracy." It was from him that the allies learnt that they were fighting not only to restore Alsace-Lorraine to France, but for a revived Poland with an access to the sea, and for a new republic of Czecho-Slovakia. It was he who had formulated "the fourteen points,"[1] who had negotiated with the German Government, who had insisted on the military armistice. His country wanted no territory and no indemnities. Even in Germany he was widely regarded as an oracle of disinterested morality and

[1] Append.x C.

wisdom, as a prophet sent by the New World to cleanse the impurities of the Old. But whereas other prophets had been voices crying in the wilderness, Wilson was the master of a powerful state. The Allies were dependent on America for their food supplies and finances. While the young manhood of France and England were lying beneath the sod, two million fresh American troops were encamped upon the soil of France.

One weakness in the President's position, obvious to Americans, was not appreciated at the time in Europe. He did not represent his countrymen. He was a Democrat and an idealist. The people who mattered most in the United States at that time were neither the one nor the other. The Republicans had a majority in the Senate, and the Senate in the last resort controlled American foreign policy. It would have seemed, therefore, an obvious counsel of prudence for the President, when once he had decided to go to Paris in person, to have invited the assistance of certain eminent Republican statesmen. But the President was in temper an autocrat and in home politics a bitter partisan. He went to Paris without the Republicans, and the Republicans in revenge upset his plans.

For the Peace Treaties bear Wilson's mark. The new map of Europe was drawn according to that principle of self-determination (a phrase borrowed from the Bolsheviks) which the President had proclaimed as the clue leading through a labyrinth of evils to justice and peace. Over the Poles and their Corridor, as over the Czechs and the Slovaks, he cast his peculiar benediction, perhaps desiring to right the errors of history, but perhaps also recalling how useful was the Polish vote at home, and how numerous and weighty were the Czechs in the city of Chicago. Americans have no right to argue, as some do, that in this fundamental aspect of the peace-making, American idealism was upset by the wickedness of Europe. The new political frontiers of Europe are Wilsonian, and so drawn that three per cent. only of the total population of the continent live under alien rule. Judged by the test of self-determination, no previous European frontiers have been so satisfactory.

In another important respect the treaties are Wilsonian. But for the American President the Covenant of the League would not have been drafted then, and placed within the framework of the Treaties. The idea of a League of Nations was not original with Wilson, but was an Anglo-Saxon conception, foreign to the Latins, which had germinated during the course of the war in many peace-loving minds both in England and America, and had led to the formulation of definite proposals, the most important of which were drafted by Lord Phillimore and General Smuts. But it is one thing to draft proposals and quite another thing in a vast press of competing claims to carry them into execution. Wilson took the Phillimore-Smuts drafts, insisted on placing the problem of the League in the forefront of the Peace discussions, himself presided over the commission which drew up the Covenant, and with his great authority pushed the work to a conclusion. So resolved was the President to force the Covenant on his Senate by making it an integral part of all the Peace Treaties that two precious months went by before the Conference addressed itself to the real work of peace-making.

It is not, therefore, true to say that the Peace Treaties are lacking in idealism, or that they are destitute of principle. They contain an ideal in the Covenant. They follow a principle in self-determination. But the ideal was not one generally shared on the continent: and the principle, albeit just, was full of danger and innovation, for it led to the erection of five new states all of questionable stability, and to large transfers of territory and population at the expense of the Teutonic and Magyar races.

The war against the German Empire ended in a radical and revolutionary peace drawn up by democratic politicans. It recognized the liberation of nations, canonized new republics, provided for the protection of minorities. The general trend of Europe towards nationalism and democracy, which had made itself felt ever since 1848 with steadily increasing emphasis, seems to culminate naturally in Mr. Wilson's peace.

The French Prime Minister was Clemenceau, a rude, sensible, witty octogenarian, utterly empty of illusions, but faithful throughout his violent Parliamentary and journalistic career to three affections, science, France, and liberty. Save that he liked and understood the Anglo-Saxon race, and realized more perfectly than his fellow-countrymen the value of Anglo-Saxon friendship, Clemenceau was the mirror of logical and realist France. The ghosts of immemorial policies, of Richelieu, of Mazarin, of Louis XIV and of Danton, lived again in this brilliant and fiery republican. He had seen his country twice invaded, and now saved from utter destruction only by alliances never likely to be repeated; and knowing that by 1940 Germany would have twice as many men of military age to put into the field as France, he doubted whether any league would avail to protect her. Is it wonderful that his mind should have been filled with two things only, reparations for the past, security for the future, or that when Marshal Foch, with the aureole of victory on his brow, asked in effect for the bridgeheads of the Rhine, Clemenceau, who put no faith in Germans, should have vehemently supported the claim? But here France was countered by the two Anglo-Saxon statesmen, who argued that to detach the Rhineland from the *Reich* was to create another Alsace-Lorraine and to lay the seeds of a future war.

On this Mr. Lloyd George was adamant. What was offered to France in exchange for the Rhineland was the abolition of conscription in Germany and the fixed reduction of the German army to a hundred thousand men, a demilitarized zone on the right bank, and a treaty of guarantee signed by Wilson and Lloyd George pledging their respective countries to defend the soil of France against aggression. Clemenceau bowed to the Anglo-Saxons. But when the American Congress refused to ratify the treaty of guarantee, France felt that she had been induced to part with the Rhineland for a scrap of paper. The French army, it was said, had won the war, but Clemenceau had sold the peace.

As for the English Prime Minister, he brought back trophies for his country such as even Chatham might have envied; the bulk of the German Fleet (surrendered at the Armistice and afterwards sunk in Scapa Flow), and of the German commercial navy, a sphere of influence in Mesopotamia, Palestine, Tanganyika, the most valuable of the German colonies (while other less important colonies were secured for the South African Union, the Commonwealth of Australia, and the Dominion of New Zealand), a share in German reparation payments, and the recognition of the Dominions as qualified to take part in the treaty making and to be separately represented in the League of Nations. Every point in the negotiations which could be won for the British Empire Mr. Lloyd George was successful in gaining.

Judged by the conventional standard of power-politics no triumph could have been more complete. Yet despite his brilliant war-leadership, and all the lustre of his country's achievements by sea and land, Mr. Lloyd George went into the Conference under a handicap. There had been in England the unescapable calamity of a General Election. A rare mood of vindictive passion, strengthened rather than assuaged by the new women voters, had convulsed the electorate. The cry went up that Germany should pay the whole cost of the war, that the Kaiser should be hanged, and that all Germans who had violated the laws of war should be brought to trial and punished. The doctrine had been so assiduously preached that war was a crime, the sinking of passenger ships by submarines was so fresh a memory, that the rank and file of the British electorate may be excused for thinking that the authors of such a war should suffer the fate of criminals. Politicians, of course, knew better, and to statesmen this intense manifestation of national fury came as an embarrassing surprise. Speakers at the election were thrown off their balance. The Prime Minister was no exception. By sheer pressure of popular sentiment he was driven from the noble appeal for national reconstruction with which he had launched his electoral campaign. "Homes for heroes" failed to interest. His audiences were set on the punishment of the enemy. An orator is sensitive to an audience. The Prime Minister's tone hardened. He enlarged on penalties. Though he was careful to make some wise reservations and to disclaim responsibility for the astonishing figures which were recommended by an expert committee, he propounded the legal view that the beaten party pays the costs, and certainly led the country to believe that a very considerable sum could be and should be extracted from the enemy. Afterwards he discovered the truth that Germany's capacity to pay might be more nearly assessed at 2,000 millions than at the fantastic figure of 24,000 millions, at which one British committee of experts had put it. But in the atmosphere of chimerical hopes which then prevailed, the announcement of so low a figure would have been received as an outrage. No figure, then, was put into the treaties. By a wise and statesmanlike provision it was left to a Reparations Commission, on which the United States was invited to serve, to decide what the reasonable figure should be.

The unsettled condition of the Reparations question caused great bitterness of feeling and undoubtedly helped to weaken the German Republic and to retard the economic convalescence of Europe. But it was a transitory evil. Sooner or later, as the British Prime Minister foresaw, business men would meet together and, with or without American help, fix a scale of payments which it was possible for the debtor country to make and profitable for her creditors to receive. The event proved this to be the case. Frontiers are seldom altered without force, but money payments are susceptible of infinite adjustments. By degrees, though not before they had been the cause of much heartburning and confusion, Germany's reparation payments were scaled down until eventually at Lausanne (1932) they were reduced to negligible proportions.

While England agreed with France in thinking that German militarism was the danger, and was willing that Germany and Austria should be stripped of non-German territory, in two vital particulars she parted company with France. Her trade interests demanded a convalescent, a prosperous Germany. Her political interests required that Germany should be peaceful and content. The influence, therefore, of Mr. Lloyd George was cast in the scale of mitigation. He was opposed to the suggestion that the Rhineland should be severed from the *Reich*, or that the whole of the rich industrial district of Upper Silesia should be handed over to the Poles, or that the Allies should be entitled, under the Treaty, to occupy German territory for fifteen years. Collecting the Imperial Cabinet around him in Paris, he secured that the destination of Upper Silesia should be determined by a plébiscite of its inhabitants.

The attitude of Italy was strictly national. No wide philanthropic ideas obscured the vision or warmed the heart of the realist politicians of the Monte Citorio. The League of Nations, which almost consoled many Anglo-Saxons for the war, excited little interest in Milan or Rome. Did it not even, thought the *papalini*, invade the immemorial prerogatives of the Vatican to impose its mediation on conflicting nations? A frontier running up to the crests of the Alps and a line of ports on the Adriatic were more to be valued than a Parliament in Geneva. Italy said to herself: "France is getting Alsace-Lorraine, England is getting the bulk of the German colonies, what do we get?" In the end she was allotted the Trentino, Trieste, and Zara, and helped herself to Fiume, the Hungarian port at the head of the Adriatic sea, by the *coup de main* of d'Annunzio the poet. But even so, she was bitterly chagrined: the Dalmatians, who had been evangelized by Italian missionaries and civilized by Italian artists, were allotted to Yugo-Slavia.

When the terms of the draft treaty were made known to the Germans, they were regarded as staggering in their severity and impossible of fulfilment. The whole scheme seemed designed to keep the country in perpetual subjection. While Germany was to be stripped of her armaments and left naked before her enemy, the allies were entitled to ask for impossible sums, and to occupy German territory as a gage of payment. Loud complaint went up that the instrument differed widely from President Wilson's fourteen points and subsequent speeches, upon the faith of which Germany had, as it was contended, laid down her arms. The prospect of a crushing tribute spread over two generations, and of a long military occupation, the forced destruction, under the eyes of an allied commission, of the mechanism and equipment of the German national army, and the abolition of conscription, were humiliations difficult to bear. Most obnoxious too were the arrangements for the eastern frontiers, the revival of Poland, the Polish corridor to the sea severing East Prussia from Brandenburg (though these were among the fourteen points) and the cession to Poland of a large slice of the industrial area of Silesia which, but for German brains and German capital, would never have attained to its swift and imposing development. That the conquests of the Great Frederick should be thus abandoned through compulsion was of all the conditions of the Treaty that which German pride found it least easy to accept. The loss of Alsace-Lorraine, always a troublesome problem, was comparatively light to bear, and the temporary relinquishment of the Saar valley as a compensation for the injury done by the German army to the French mines a *bagatelle.*

EUROPE REMODELLED BY THE PEACE TREATIES

It is for the Republic of Poland to justify, by its prudence, justice, and toleration, the confidence which was reposed in the Polish nation by the signatories of the Treaty of Versailles.

On its economic side the Treaty was much too harsh, and prejudicial to the stability of the Republican *régime* in Germany, which it should have been the aim of the Allies to assist. But while Englishmen blamed the pact of Versailles for its severity, the prevalent view in France was that Clemenceau, in his endeavour to meet the Anglo-Saxons, had still left the enemy too strong for the peace of Europe and the world.

The Treaty of Versailles has often been condemned as having been imposed and not negotiated. All treaties struck between conqueror and conquered are made under constraint. The Treaty of Bucharest, which the Germans imposed on Roumania, and the treaty of Brest-Litovsk, which they dictated to Russia, are savage exemplifications of that genus. When it is remembered how vast and complex was the ground covered by the treaties, how essential was despatch, how impatient were the war-weary armies for the hour of demobilization, and how easily protracted discussions might have jeopardized a settlement, the desire of the Allied and Associated Powers to proceed as they did becomes intelligible. To the written German criticism of the draft treaty, an allied reply containing some concessions was delivered in writing. For a more generous, open, and elastic proceeding, no allied statesman in that tense and passionate Parisian atmosphere was prepared.[1]

Austria, the prime mover in the war, was the greatest sufferer through its miscarriage. Dynasty, army, empire disappeared in the whirlwind. The Hungarians declared themselves independent and were invaded by the Roumans. The Czechs and Slovaks broke away. The Serbs exploited their victory in the south. In the end a small republic of six million souls, specifically forbidden under the terms of the Treaty of St. Germain to join itself with Germany, save with the consent, only to be obtained by a unanimous vote, of the League of Nations, was all that remained of the famous polity which had ruled over fifteen races and given the law to central

[1] In the freely negotiated Treaty signed with the U.S.A. in 1921, Germany accepted many provisions, including the "War Guilt" clause to which she now objects.

Europe. With a capital city many times too great for its contracted needs, with a Civil Service framed for a wide Empire, with enemy neighbours killing its trade with their tariffs, with a city population bitten with Bolshevism, and a peasantry as mediaeval and superstitious as any in Europe, Austria was plunged into the pit of despair. In the face of the fierce nationalism of the new states a Danubian Zollverein was impossible to impose or to sustain. In the dark landscape there were only two gleams of light, the opera in Vienna and the remedial action of the League of Nations, which at the crisis of its fortune (October, 1922) saved the new Republic from bankruptcy.

The treatment of Hungary under the Treaty of Trianon is of all parts of the peace settlement that which has aroused most misgiving. The Hungarians were stripped of Slovakia, which was transferred to the Czechs, of Transylvania, which was conquered by the Roumans, and of Croatia, which now became part of Yugo-Slavia in the Serbo-Croat-Slovene Kingdom. Some six hundred thousand men and women of Magyar race, some four and a half million of former subjects of the Hungarian crown, passed under alien domination.[1] To the proud Magyar aristocracy the spoliation of their ancient kingdom by peasant democracies without lineage or distinction seemed an intolerable affront. Lost, too, was the lovely mountain region of Transylvania, where the Magyar noble was wont to take his pleasure in sport. His sentiments may be imagined. As easily would the owner of a Scottish deer forest welcome the news of its forced partition among the Irish immigrants in Lanark.

The treaty, then, has left sore places. There is the little republic of Austria, too weak to live comfortably by herself, yet debarred by the peace treaties from joining Germany without the consent of the League. There are the transferred Magyars, there is President Wilson's Poland with its special points of irritation in the Corridor and Silesia, there is the subjection of some 230,000 German Tyrolese and 1,300,000 Yugo-Slavs to Italian rule. To a smaller yet sensible degree the Germans resented the cession of the little woodland districts of Eupen and Malmédy to Belgium, and the tempor-

[1] These figures are probably too favourable to Hungarian claims. According to the official Hungarian census figures of 1910, the number of Magyars incorporated in the new states was 2,945,273.

AUSTRIA AFTER THE PEACE TREATIES

ary submission of the Saar district to the League of Nations. Yet viewed in proper perspective and despite these defects, the political map of Europe is drawn more closely than ever before in accordance with the views of the populations concerned.

Nevertheless, when the Treaty of Versailles was finally signed in the *Galerie des Glaces*, where half a century earlier the Hohenzollern Empire had been proclaimed, everybody felt that a great opportunity had been missed. The statesmen had not been equal to the grandeur of events. They had made a peace which was no peace. American idealists, who were well content that the doctrine of self-determination should be violated in respect to their Red Indians and Africans, joined with English idealists, who were not proposing to march out of India or Egypt, in denouncing the lapses from the high doctrine of self-determination which were noted in the treaties. Human nature, it was widely felt, had failed.

June 28, 1919

Novgorod

Moscowo

Riga

Vilna

Posen

Warsaw

Brest
Litovsk

Oder

Cracow

Dnieper

Kiev

Danube

Bug

Dniester

Danube

~~~~~ Poland and Lithuania
        in 1569
░░░░░ Grand Duchy of Warsaw, 1810
▬▬▬ Boundary of Poland after
        the Peace Treaties, 1919
        English Miles
  0   100   200   300

POLAND

Europe had not been made safe for democracy. The bright
exhilaration of victory was soon blotted by the fog of disillusion, resentment, and despair.

It is too soon to pass a final verdict on the work of the
treaty-makers. They will be judged by the success of the
states which they brought into being or greatly augmented, by the
new Poland, the new Czecho-Slovakia, the new Roumania,
the new Yugo-Slavia, and the new Greece. A hundred years
hence the historian will know. We who are passing through

the zone of maximum friction and uneasiness, when the war passions are still alive and the minorities are wincing under new masters, and before the oil of habit has begun to smooth the springs of the newly-made chariots of state, can hardly with any show of confidence formulate a guess.

It was a common hope and expectation among the Allies not only that America would sign the Treaty, which had been so largely shaped by the President's ideas, but that she would join the League of Nations, which was perhaps the most characteristic and remarkable contribution made by that great American statesman to the problem of international order. In both these respects the United States falsified the expectations of Europe. America neither signed the Treaty nor joined the League. All the hopes, therefore, which had been founded upon American co-operation in scaling down reparations, upon an Anglo-American guarantee to France, upon the assistance which America might render as a member of the League in bringing economic pressure to bear on a peace-breaker were suddenly dissipated. The disappointment was extreme. Yet a close knowledge of American history and the American outlook might have warned Europeans that it was as natural for America to withdraw from Europe, as for England to require the Germans to evacuate Belgium, or for France to demand the restoration of Alsace-Lorraine. The Americans did not come into the war when the neutrality of Belgium was violated, nor when the *Lusitania* was sunk. They decided to fight only when their merchantmen were sunk by German submarines. That outrage they were determined to punish. When the punishment was inflicted they reverted to that policy of withdrawal from European entanglements which they had inherited from George Washington. President Wilson indeed was an idealist: but in his own country he was almost alone.

There the Republican reaction was in full spate. With a sharp swing away from Europe and its miseries "the hundred per cent. American he-man" now coming into fashion was content with the glories of his own nation, enriched beyond the dreams of avarice, and towering above an exhausted and impoverished world.

A terrific problem then disclosed itself. The Central Powers had been beaten by a combination, such as was never afterwards likely to occur, of twenty-seven states, including the United States and the British Empire, two civilian nations who had by superhuman efforts improvised vast armies while the war was in progress. That combined military effort, and nothing less than that effort, had for the moment destroyed the German military machine and made it powerless to alarm the peoples of the continent. But now America had withdrawn, England with a rare unanimity of sentiment had abandoned conscription and curtailed her army and navy, and Italy was racked with civil trouble. France felt herself deserted; faced with a Germany disarmed indeed, but angry, defiant, and full of immense possibilities of mischief, she regarded herself as the gendarme of Europe, the maintainer of the public order established by the Peace Treaties. At Geneva she found friends. These were Belgium and Poland, and the three states which had benefited by the fall of the Austrian Empire, and now were leagued together in the *Petite Entente*. With these states France entered into close political relations. Together they formed a combination to replace Russia as an eastern counterweight to the central races of Germanism.

It was not so, however, that the English and Scandinavian advocates of the League of Nations regarded the future of Europe. The peril which they were anxious to avoid was the division of Europe once more into two rival groups of powers, each arming and plotting against the other. That the small powers of the east, so new, so unstable, and so close to the incalculable forces of Republican Russia, should provide themselves with armaments seemed natural enough. But it was unsatisfactory that this necessity should exist. Under a rational organization armaments would be subject to collective control and disputes would be settled by resort to arbitration or conciliation.

While all countries stand to lose by war, to no country is war more injurious than to Britain, which can feed its population only by the profits of international trading. Here, more even than in France, was the doctrine preached and believed that this was a war to end war. The dream so often entertained, so often frustrated, of a world organized not for war but for peace, once more became alive in the thoughts of men. After the torments of the war the Covenant of the

League of Nations furnished to most Englishmen a gleam of consolation and of hope.

The importance of the League of Nations is that it offers to the world as much world-government as the world can stand. The framers of the Covenant saw that it would be idle to create a super-state to override the national governments. Accordingly they rejected the idea much favoured in France of a League army, or of a League police, or of any other predetermined mode of coercion by which a member state might be compelled to bow to the will of an external authority. Rather than violate by one jot or tittle the sovereign rights of the nation states, the founders were prepared that their League should be an association of national states, each, however insignificant, entitled to equal justice and consideration, and protected from invasion of its domestic prerogatives by the requirement that any decisions of the League should receive a unanimous assent.

How often in the past had men of good will met in conference to promote the cause of peace, and after much eloquent talk and virtuous resolve separated with nothing done! The League of Nations was to be altogether different from these ephemeral and ineffective manifestations. It was to be a permanent organ, supported by national governments, for the transaction of international affairs, with an Assembly of delegates from all the member states, meeting once a year for a month in Geneva, and a Council, originally of nine delegates (five from the larger states), meeting more frequently, while the business of Assembly and Council alike was prepared and executed by an international Civil Service or Secretariat. Other organs were subsequently added, an International Labour Office, for the levelling up of Labour conditions throughout the world, and a Court of International Justice at The Hague. Of this carefully planned machinery for world government the nations were free to make as much or as little as they chose.

The pith of the Covenant consists in the obligation assumed by every member-state to submit his quarrel to the League before resorting to arms. The Covenant does not exclude the possibility of war, but provides tribunals (the Council and the Court) before which member-states undertake in advance to lay their disputes, and prescribes a period during which, should the decision of the League prove to be unacceptable, the aggrieved party undertakes to preserve the peace. Were the League universal, and were its members prepared to obey the Covenant in letter and in spirit, these provisions for conciliation, arbitration, and delay would be sufficient to rid the world of the spectre of war.

Another function entrusted to the League was to obtain, if possible, from its member-states an agreed and progressive reduction of armaments. The evil of competitive armaments was generally admitted; their burden universally deplored; the theory that no state should arm in excess of its strict needs for home defence and the discharge of its international obligations was conceded by all reasonable men. The difficulty was to translate these principles into action, with Germany chafing under her compulsory disarmament, and with France nervously feeling that perhaps after all she was not sufficiently secure from a German attack. It is a measure of the strength and vitality of international fears and animosities that, despite the steady efforts of the League, the load of armaments pressing on Europe in 1935 was actually heavier than it was on the eve of the war.

Among other fruitful ideas embodied in the Covenant is the need for fostering international co-operation of all kinds in time of peace. It was not sufficient that the member-states should abjure war, practise open diplomacy, or reduce their armaments. They must learn to work together through the League not only in the great tasks of humanity, but in all matters of common interest, such as the protection of the standard of life among the workers, or the campaign against the traffic in women and children, or the regulation of the opium trade, or the framing of measures of international hygiene. Perhaps it is in this humanitarian sphere that the League is destined to achieve its most certain triumphs.

At the end of the Napoleonic wars the Congress of Vienna had taken up the question of the abolition of the Slave Trade. In a like spirit the framers of the Covenant took note of the fact that European states had obligations not only to the racial and religious minorities in their midst, but also to the weak and backward peoples in other continents who had come under their control. The principle of trusteeship, the idea that the power of the governor should be exercised for the benefit of the governed, had long been familiar to the British Empire. This principle (under a term borrowed from Roman law) it was now decided to affirm in connection with the territories taken by the allies from the Germans and the Turks. The crudity of conquest was draped in the veil of morality. The annexed territories (with some exceptions) were regarded as mandated by the Allied and Associated Powers, and the annexing States as mandatories obliged at fixed intervals to give an account of their stewardship to a League Commission. That such a requirement was made and assented to was a clear advance in international morality.

A league of peace, comprising ultimately all the nations of the world, and having the Anglo-Saxon race as its solid nucleus and the governments of the British Empire and the United States as the principal instruments of its activity and influence, such was the vision which filled the minds of President Wilson and his English associates, as they sat down in Paris to work at the framework of a new international order. These large hopes were swiftly killed. When the first Assembly of the League met in the autumn of 1920 in Geneva forty-four states only were represented. Russia stood aloof. Germany, Turkey, and other ex-enemy states were not yet deemed ripe for admission: but the gravest blow of all was the absence of the power whose concurrence was essential to the enforcement of economic sanctions against offending members, and upon whose impartiality great reliance had been placed. The work of President Wilson had been repudiated in his own country. America had refused to join the League.

The League of Nations can be no better than the member states of which it is composed. If they wish for peace, the League provides machinery by which peace may be the better secured and maintained, but League or no League, a state which is resolved on war can always have it. Not till the mind of man is filled with the conviction that modern war offers a peril for civilization so great that it is a crime, certain to be visited by condign punishment, for any state acting in pursuance of its own national interest to initiate it, will mankind be effectually rid of this menace. At present the world neither entertains nor is prepared to act upon these salutary and intelligent beliefs.

Meanwhile the League transacts so much international business for which there is no alternative machinery that if it did not exist it would be necessary to invent it. Statesmen have become acclimatized to the strange atmosphere of cosmopolitan consultation which prevails at Geneva. The secretariat has been so composed as to inspire confidence. The work grows, the area of international co-operation extends. For the first few important years the ideals of the League were expounded to the Assembly with authority and conviction by Robert Cecil, one of the framers of the Covenant. At the annual meetings at Geneva the leading statesmen of the smaller nations can make their contributions to international wisdom. Here Hymans of Belgium, Branting of Sweden, Nansen of Norway, Motta of Switzerland, Beneš of Czecho-Slovakia, and Politis of Greece have rendered service to the Commonwealth of Europe. More important still is the opportunity which the League meetings afford for the formation of friendships, the comparison of ideas, the enlargement of knowledge, and the adjustment of differing points of view. Amid the rough jolts and jars of international life the annual month of cool conciliation at Geneva, though little respected by the warlike idealists of Japan, is like Christmas Day and our nearest approach to the mediaeval truce of God.

Yet many as have been the services of the League during the first fifteen years of its existence, it has brought, as we have seen, no moral or material disarmament to Europe. Though much labour has been expended on the problem of how best to reconcile the French demand for military security with the German claim for equality of treatment, the problem has in fact, given the greater population and higher birthrate of Germany, resisted solution. Save in Great Britain, there has been no serious effort to reduce land armaments. British pacifism has not been shared by the governments of Paris or Berlin, of Rome or Moscow, of Tokio or Prague. The Fascist master of Italy has never scrupled to express his belief in force. The Soviet Republic, though lately reconciled to the League, keeps on foot an army nine hundred and forty thousand strong. Japan and Germany have marched 1931, out of Geneva. In 1935 the Third German *Reich*, after more 1933 than a decade of secret and illegal arming, openly reverted to conscription and came before the world once more as a military power of the first class.

A general agreement as to political objectives is the only sure basis for a policy of disarmament. Such an agreement was reached with regard to the problems of the Pacific in 1921 by the United States, Great Britain, France and Japan, and furnished the groundwork for the only substantial measure of disarmament which was reached by diplomatic methods during this period, When the four great naval Powers discovered that they were at one in desiring the policy of the open door in China and the preservation of the territorial integrity of the Chinese republic, naval disarmament became a relatively easy problem. Foreseeing no occasion of political variance, the four Pacific Powers found it easy to agree upon naval ratios, to curtail the size of capital ships, and to provide against the fortification of new naval bases in the Pacific. But when in 1933 Japan broke away from her allies, and by unilateral action seized a province of China, the whole plan for naval disarmament contained in the Treaty of Washington was placed n peril. In point of fact, Japan lost no time in announcing that she did not propose after 1936 to renew the treaty. She was developing a bigger and very controversial policy in China and was resolved upon a bigger navy with which to support it.

As yet there is no agreement as to political objectives in Europe. Germany wishes to absorb Austria. Italy and France are resolved that Austria should maintain her independence. A deep chasm of sentiment and policy sunders Nazi (National Socialist) Germany and the Communist rule of the Soviets. The year which witnessed the return of the Saar to Germany, **1935** so far from ushering in a happier period of international relations, has seen darker storm clouds over Europe than any period since the guns stopped firing in the Great War.

BOOKS WHICH MAY BE CONSULTED

Winston Churchill: *The World Crisis*. 1923.
Harold Nicolson: *Peace Making*. 1919.
F. H. Simonds: *How Europe made Peace without America*. 1923.
J. M. Keynes: *The Economic Consequences of the Peace*. 1919.
H. Wilson Harris: *The League of Nations*. 1929.

A. Toynbee: *Survey of International Affairs*, 1920-23.

H. Temperley: *History of the Peace Conference at Paris.* 1921.

E. M. House and C. Seymour: *What really happened at Paris.* 1921.

E. J. Dillon: *The Peace Conference.* 1919.

Colonel E. M. House: *Intimate Papers.* 1926.

Prince Max of Baden: *War Memoirs. Eng. tr.* 1928.

Ten Years of World Co-operation. (Issued by the Secretariat of the League of Nations, 1930.)

F. J. Berber: *Locarno. A Collection of Documents.* 1936.

E. H. Carr: *The Twenty Years' Crisis.* 2nd Ed. 1946.

E. H. Carr: *International Relations between the Two World Wars.* 2nd Ed. 1947.

CHAPTER XCIX

THE TRANSFORMATION OF TURKEY

Venizelos. The Greek landing in Smyrna. Mustapha Kemal. The pact of Sivas and the Greco-Turkish War. The Greek disaster in Asia Minor. New aspect of the Near Eastern question. Fall of the Lloyd George Government. The Treaty of Lausanne. The New Turkey.

AMONG THE brilliant figures who were drawn to Paris for the peace-making was Venizelos, the Cretan. Few statesmen of that age had surmounted greater difficulties, whether as a leader of irregular troops among his native hills, or as the main artificer of the Balkan League, or as the advocate of an alliance with the *Entente* Powers in the Great War, when the whole influence of the Athenian Court, of the Peloponnese, and of the Ionian islands was thrown in the opposite scale. His horizon was wide, his eloquence and charm were compelling, audacity and finesse were at the service of his ambition. From the first he was certain that the Allies would win the war and that the true interest of Greece was to espouse their cause. It was not his fault if Greek divisions did not fight side by side with the British at the Dardanelles or later come to the rescue of the Serbian army before it was driven to its final disaster in the Albanian hills. And if in the end, after King Constantine had been expelled by the

French fleet, a quarter of a million Greek troops took a share in the final allied victory against the Bulgars, the credit belongs to Venizelos, who of his own initiative settled down upon Salonika and there created a pro-Ally Greek Government and pro-Ally Greek army while Court and Cabinet in Athens were still obstinate in their adhesion to the German cause. For such services Venizelos, coming to the peace-making in Paris, was entitled to expect a high reward.

It was an axiom of Allied policy that whatever could colourably be regarded as of Greek speech and race in European Turkey should be assigned to the Greeks. Thessaly, Macedonia, eastern Thrace presented no difficulties. The crux lay in Asia Minor. Here, widely dispersed in the coast towns and over the upland country were some million merchants and bankers, seamen and shopkeepers, tobacco growers, vine growers, rice growers, and carpet makers of the Greek race, whose situation gave cause for great anxiety. The Turkish power in Anatolia was still alive. Though Syria, Palestine, and Mesopotamia had been wrested from the Turks by British arms, and Allied forces controlled Constantinople and the Straits, in Asia Minor, which was the real Turkey, the hatred of the Christian races was awake and armed. A million Armenian lives had been sacrificed to the Crescent since the inception of the war. And as it was to be expected that the Greeks would be the next victims, Venizelos obtained from the Prime Ministers of Britain and France leave to land forces at Smyrna, suspecting that otherwise the city might fall to the Italians, and hoping that if the worst came to the worst a refuge might here be provided for the Asiatic members of his race. It was an ill judgment. Italians might perhaps have been tolerated in Smyrna, but that the despised flag of Greece should wave over any part of Asia Minor was regarded by every patriot Turk as an intolerable affront. The Greek landing (April 15, 1919), disgraced by crime, roused all that was fiercest and most determined in the Turkish temper and offered to Mustapha Kemal, "the Saviour of the Dardanelles" and the most brilliant officer in the Turkish army, the chance of creating out of the shattered fragments of the vanquished empire a new and independent Turkish State.

Mustapha was now thirty-eight years of age, a fierce,

disagreeable, quarrelsome figure, with a frame of iron (for though born at Salonika he came of stout Anatolian peasant stock), and a will of steel. If his debaucheries, which were sordid, callous, and violent, belonged to the tradition of his race, his clearness of head, his independence of judgment, his gift of military and political leadership were all his own. Turkey for the Turks was his motto through life. As a youth he had joined in the plot to overthrow Abdul Hamid, not out of love for constitutional liberty, but because he saw that under the Red Sultan his country was decrepit, spy-haunted, and the prey of foreigners, and that only by the destruction of that paralysing *régime* could it hope to become strong and free. Fighting in many fields—in the Lebanon, in Tripoli, in the Balkans, on the Syrian front—gave him a wide experience of men and things. He was jealous of Enver, the brilliant pro-German, and shrewdly critical of the policy which had made of Turkey a German tool and involved it in the German ruin. So intelligent a man could not be blind to the larger significance of contemporary events. The moral which Mustapha drew from the Great War was that Turkey had been defeated because she had permitted herself to be entangled and bullied by the Western Powers, because she had remained unprogressive and barbaric and had overtaxed her strength in endeavouring to control non-Turkish races. The cure was emancipation from the foreigner, internal reform, and the education of a self-centred Turkish nationalism in the original Turkish homelands. The old ambitious imperialism of Enver and his gang had broken down in irretrievable ruin. The Turks had been driven from the Canal, from Mesopotamia, from Palestine and Syria, The British fleet was in the Dardanelles. The Sultan was a puppet in British hands. There remained only Asia Minor, and here, too, the west had made a lodgment. Four days after the Greek landing in Smyrna, Mustapha set foot on Asiatic soil, holding a military commission from the Sultan. His mind was made up. "I will stay in Anatolia," he said, "until the nation has won its independence." On September 13, 1919, a representative assembly of Turks, meeting at Sivas, signed a pact to continue the war until the soil of Asia was free of the invader. All that was most virile in the Turkish race rallied round Mustapha Kemal and the National Pact.

He set up a Government (April 24, 1920) at Angora, snapped his fingers at the Sultan in Constantinople, and resolved to build up a new life for his people in the bracing uplands of Anatolia, where the ancestors of the Turkish race, far from the miasmal breezes of the west, had first displayed their steadfast valour to the world.

In the war which ensued everything after some preliminary successes went awry with the Greek cause. At home there was a series of misfortunes and convulsions, abroad a notable breach in the allied front against the Turks. Who could have predicted that young King Alexander of Greece would die suddenly of a monkey's bite or that in the plébiscite which ensued a wave of royalist feeling would sweep Venizelos from power (November 14, 1920) and bring Constantine back with his pro-German following? These events were not without their repercussions on the Asiatic front. The Greek army, spurred by the old king to a rash advance on Angora, suffered a heavy defeat on the river Sakaria (August 23—September 13, 1921) and, being further weakened by the dismissal of many tried Venizelist officers, was in no fit state to offer an effective resistance to the Turks. Little help was to be expected from the Allies. While the Italians hated the Greeks, the French made a separate peace with the Turks (October 20, 1921). The proposal of the Athenian Cabinet that the army of Thrace should be permitted to occupy Constantinople (June, 1922) was negatived by the Powers. Indeed, of all the prominent Allied statesmen, Mr. Lloyd George alone was conscious of responsibilities to the Greek people and eager that the task of finally crushing the Turk, which had been so brilliantly initiated by Maude and Allenby, should be completed by the levies of Hellas and her islands.

The Greeks, then, were left alone to weather the storm. They were unequal to the test. Shaken by defeat, paralysed by schism, and distrustful of their higher command, they crumbled under the next hard blow delivered by the enemy (August 26, 1922) and streamed back, a disorderly rout, to the coast. Stern was the vengeance of their enemies. Entering Smyrna on the heels of the fugitives, the Turks fired the city and massacred all whom they could find of the Greek tongue and blood. More than a million Christians, fleeing that terrible wrath, were rescued from Asia Minor in Allied ships and by a great feat of benevolent organization distributed through Greece and its islands.

Out of the burning wreck of Smyrna there arose an unfamiliar and more hopeful East. Two monarchies disappeared, the Greek and the Turkish, the one an alien institution of some ninety years, the other rooted in the immemorial traditions of the race of Othman. Greece became, by reason of its industrious Asiatic immigrants, richer, stronger, more populous than before. A like concentration of national power marked the new Turkish republic of Mustapha Kemal. Accordingly, the problem of Christian minorities, which had so long vexed the conscience and shaped the policies of the western world, ceased to haunt the chanceries. The minorities had been massacred or driven away, and by the very extremity of that calamity the chief occasion of Greco-Turkish hostility was paradoxically removed. Wise arrangements for the exchange of populations on European soil further assisted the establishment of friendly relations between the governments of Angora and Athens. Thus did the principle of self-determination work itself out through fire and sword in the half-savage East.

Lloyd George, the Gladstonian Philhellene, went down with his Hellenic friends. The rank and file of the Tory party were restive under a leader who so far carried his radicalism into foreign policy as to treat with rebel Ireland, to encourage the Greeks, and to propose the defence of the Dardanelles against the exultant Turks. Alarmed by the spectre of a new war, the Tories gathered in the Carlton Club and dismissed the Prime Minister, "a daring pilot in extremity," who for six years had exercised in peace and war a greater influence on public affairs than any subject of the British Crown since the Duke of Wellington. The fall of the Coalition in Britain set the seal on the triumph of the Turk. Providentially delivered from the ghost of Mr. Gladstone and the aeroplanes of Mr. Lloyd George, Mustapha Kemal, beneficiary of the Carlton Club, quietly crossed the Dardanelles.

At Lausanne in 1923 the Allies were compelled to ratify the political results of the Turkish victory. Everything which symbolized the old *régime* of Western supervision was swept away—the capitulations giving special privileges in justice and finance to the Western merchant, the right so often conceded to the Powers to protect the Christian subjects of the Porte. The Turk was resolved to be master in his own house. The last effulgence of Lord Curzon's eloquence could not undo the effects of Mustapha's victories. The Crescent still flies at Chanak and Stamboul.

The field was now cleared for the series of audacious reforms which, though long debated in the private counsels of the Young Turks, have given to Mustapha the name of a genius and to Turkey the aspect of a modern state. The Caliphate was abolished, the women were compelled to abandon the veil, the schools were laicized, the Koran was ordered to be rendered into Turkish. By an astounding breach with tradition it was decreed (1928) that the Moslem faith should no longer be the official religion of the Turkish Republic. Small things as well as large attracted the innovating zeal of the Ghazi, or "Raider of the Christians," and, lest the devout should persevere in the practice of touching the ground with their foreheads in the course of their devotions, they were compelled to substitute the rimmed hat of the European for the traditional fez. These and other modernizing changes, such as the abolition of polygamy, the introduction of the Latin script, and the adoption of Western codes of law, were accepted without a murmur. The dervish, the chiromancer, the magician, the dice thrower and amulet seller were decreed out of existence. It was sufficient that such changes were recommended by the Ghazi. When a doubt was expressed in the Grand National Assembly at the breach of tradition involved by the abolition of the Sultanate and the Caliphate, Mustapha argued that the last of the true Caliphs had been murdered in A.D. 924, and thus proceeded: "Sovereignty is acquired by force, by power, by violence. It was by violence that the sons of Othman acquired the power to rule over the Turkish nation and to maintain their rule for more than six centuries. It is now the nation that revolts against these usurpers, puts them in their right place, and carries on their sovereignty."[1] At the end of his speech there were shouts of, "Vote, vote!" One single voice was heard declaring. "I am against it," but this was drowned by cries

[1] A speech delivered by Ghazi Mustapha Kemal (October 15 to 20, 1927 Koehler, Leipzig, 1929.

of "Silence!" Stupefied with admiration, the Turks, a nation
of private soldiers, wheeled to the word of their general's
command.

BOOKS WHICH MAY BE CONSULTED

A. Toynbee: *Survey of International Affairs for 1925.*
K. Krüger: *Kemalist Turkey and the Middle East.* 1932.
H. C. Armstrong: *Grey Wolf,* 1932.
Mustapha Kemal: *Speech delivered from October* 15 *to* 20, 1927.
    Koehler, Leipzig. 1929.
W. Miller: *Greece.* (Nations of the Modern World Series.) 1928.
A. Toynbee and M. P. Kirkwood: *Turkey.* (Nations of the Modern
    World Series.) 1926.
H. Nicolson: *Curzon: The Last Phase.* 1934.

CHAPTER C

NEW DICTATORSHIPS AND OLD DEMOCRACIES

*New dictatorships and old democracies. Declining belief in
Liberty. The challenge to Capitalism. The Bolshevik religion.
Lenin. The War of the Reds and the Whites. Russia and
Poland. The battle of Warsaw. Communism in Italy. Benito
Mussolini. The Fascist revolution. Adolf Hitler. The Weimar
revolution. The French in the Ruhr. Stresemann and the
policy of fulfilment. Delays in disarmament. The crash of
1929. Racial philosophy of the Nazis. Victory of Hitlerism.
Post-war Britain. Foundations of British policy. The scare
of Europe. The Refugees. Stalin. Peace and Freedom.*

WITH THE passing of Europe under the harrow of war there
passed also by insensible degrees out of the average thinking
of average men that strong belief in civil liberty and peaceful
persuasion which had been a distinctive feature of the nineteenth century. Before the war there were good reasons for
believing that parliamentary institutions would supply the

sovereign formula for the coming age. No country in the world claiming to be civilized—not even Russia—had been able altogether to withstand the public pressure in favour of responsible cabinets, representative assemblies, and democratic electorates. The Austrian Empire possessed a parliament elected by universal suffrage. The Congress party in India were clamouring for parliaments. It was a general assumption that the path of political progress lay along the line of extending the franchise, educating the voters, and improving the machinery of parliamentary government. This at least was the Liberal faith which Conservatives were compelled with varying degrees of readiness to accept. That every citizen should be able to think as he liked, to speak as he liked, and to vote as he liked was widely regarded as the mark of a civilized polity. Some dangers there might be in the practice of liberty, but they were nothing to the risk of allowing discontents to fester under a system of repression.

A doctrine of *laissez-faire* in the sphere of economics was often, and most strongly in England, allied to this widespread faith in political freedom. The peacetime structure of European society had not been shaped by governments. It was no government which had made the prosperity of Lancashire or the Ruhr, no government which had built up the financial wealth of the Rothschilds, nor any assemblage of governments which had enabled the population of Europe to increase by more than three hundred and fifty millions in a hundred and thirty years.

The capitalistic structure of European society had been due to individual invention and individual enterprise, to a liquid fund of cosmopolitan capital accumulated from individual savings and flowing freely from country to country in obedience to the magnet of private gain. The richest country in Europe was that in which government interference in trade and industry had been confined within the narrowest limits, and the best advertisement for the value of economic liberty was supplied by the trade returns of the British people.

On the other side of the Atlantic was a society of European stock which in the course of the nineteenth century had experienced a fantastic accretion of numbers and prosperity. The social and economic history of the United States of America from the declaration of independence in 1776 to the great slump in 1929 was one of unexampled and continuously ascending prosperity; but, swift as had been the growth of the population, the resources of the continent had been equal to the expanding demand. The vast fortunes accumulated by a Vanderbilt, a Rockefeller, and a Ford were compatible with the enjoyment by the whole American people of the highest general standard of comfort ever reached in the history of mankind.

Apart from the favours of nature this staggering prosperity had been due to a long tradition of individual enterprise. From the earliest colonial days, when every constitution wore "the engaging air of a prospectus," private enterprise in money-making was the note of American society. Everything was made easy for the immigrant, the settler, the pioneer. He was invited to come "right in," could purchase public land in small lots at low prices, was offered free education for his children, and knew that wherever he might settle all the private rights and constitutional privileges belonging to the oldest state in the Union would in due course be his. America was "the land of the dollar." No American citizen was debarred by law or public sentiment from amassing dollars. In the absence of an hereditary aristocracy or any widely respected political class, and since any American citizen might aspire to opulence, inequality was robbed of half its bitterness. Wealth was the prime object of national veneration, not least because it was easily come by and easily lost. The astonishing spectacle of this material paradise was not lost upon Europe. If amid the rush and fever of the American scene voices were sometimes heard denouncing the financiers of Wall Street or the magnates of oil and steel, nobody before the great slump doubted that it was in America, where the acquisitive faculties of man were least impeded by law, that the problem of poverty had been most successfully solved.

Meanwhile in Europe, as the tides of political liberty surged forward, the tides of economic liberty tended to recede. It was reasonable for James Mill in 1820 to think and write of government as a bad thing, because English government at that time was controlled by a small and privileged class and open to the charge of corruption and jobbery. But it was less reasonable to take this disparaging view of government when the whole people had been admitted within the pale of the constitution. A democratic government might not always be wise; but at least it might be expected to protect the interest of the public as a whole. The interference of such a government might be positively conducive to human happiness.

Such a government in particular might be expected to arrest the evils of the capitalistic system. These evils were patent, the wastefulness of competition, the soullessness of limited liability companies, the pressure of sinister influences on legislation, the exploitation of the weak, the great disparities of wealth between man and man. In the years after the war the world was faced with the strange phenomenon of dire poverty existing in the midst of unexampled plenty. While millions went short of food and clothing, crops were actually destroyed as being in excess of remunerative demand. What was the world coming to? It was freely contended that parliaments were bankrupt, that democratic civilization had reached its term, and that *laissez-faire* must give place to "planned economy" all along the line. Even in England a complete reconstruction of the fabric of society was demanded (1919) by the voice of organized labour.

One major evil resulting from the war was the collapse over a great part of Europe of social discipline. The trust in authority was undermined, the fabric of custom broken, and while everywhere the defeated peoples, loosened from their old moorings, watched for new leadership over uncharted seas, this was specially true of Russia. There government was found at its worst and weakest. There the soil of revolution had been most fully prepared, and there too, more swiftly and decisively than in any other region in Europe, emerged at the crisis of disorder a man, a doctrine, and a faith.

The doctrine, derived from Marx, was the substitution, deemed to be the inevitable climax of a long historic process, of communism for the accepted order of capitalist society. It challenged property, the belief in God, the social hierarchy, the middle class, and all the ideas of art, morals, and philosophy on which that class had been nurtured. The deep evangelical piety of the Russian went out to meet a new religion, which, apart from its offers of peace, bread, and the land, proceeded on the maxim that the last should be first and the first last. For though Russian communism denounced religion as "the opium of the people," it bore, like Islam, the marks of a religious faith. It was cosmopolitan, militant, propagandist. Lenin was its prophet, and the Communist Party its Church.

Lenin was a fanatical visionary whose effective power was multiplied threefold by an inner conviction that he was designed by fate to be the commander of a victorious Russian Revolution. Without wealth or station, this obscure conspirator, who had spent much of his life in Siberian prisons, or in cheap lodgings in London or Switzerland, was confident that it would one day be given to him to overturn the old *régime* in Russia, to "liquidate" the bourgeoisie, and to establish the dictatorship of the proletariat. Great animal vigour, a powerful and saturnine mind, a gift rare and precious among Russians for succinct speech, clear-cut views, and despatch in business, coupled with an almost unequalled capacity for making himself disagreeable, secured for him an ascendancy among his revolutionary following, comparable in character to that exercised by Charles Parnell over the Irish Parliamentary Party. The German General Staff, with an intelligent appreciation of his uncanny gift, arranged that he should be conveyed to Russia from Switzerland (1917) in order to poison the *morale* of the Russian army. The poison worked, but before the year was out the poisoner was a Tzar more formidable, more destructive, and more creative even than Peter the Great.

Lenin had no scruples or inhibitions. He was a humanitarian on so large and comprehensive a scale that he could look with composure upon the wholesale destruction which was demanded by the establishment of his system. Famine and war appeared to him not as enemies but as friends, famine because it enraged the peasants against the Tzar, war because the armed conflict of capitalist nations would merge into the yet more terrible civil war between classes through which alone the world could be brought to the Communists' peace. Communism for Russia first, and then for the rest of the world, was his programme. The writings of Marx constituted his Koran. But though he was a doctrinaire and man of the book, he was not without the grain of statesmanship.

In defiance of theory he permitted private trading in 1921, when he saw that unqualified communism was leading to disaster. Nor was he insensible of the value of foreign capital for the support of Russian industries. The wild scheme of Trotsky and Zinovieff for an intensive campaign of revolutionary propaganda in foreign countries did not win his approval. It was better, he thought, first to consolidate the system in Russia itself with such aid as the capitalist countries could afford. In 1921 a commercial agreement was made with England, in 1922 with Germany. He dreamed of a Russia in which every peasant could read and write, and had his cottage heated and lit by electricity.

The instruments of his power were, firstly a highly organized communist party, second a secret police inherited from the Tzarist régime, and thirdly the Red army. If there was terrorism there was no peculation. Lenin and his commissars or ministers drew small salaries and practised the rigid and laborious asceticism which they preached to others. The country honoured their loyalty to the people's cause.

To Lenin, in particular, who ruled Russia for six critical years, and in that time transformed the life and institutions for the people, semi-divine honours were readily paid. Everything was forgiven to the Liberator, the dull and angry pedantry of his voluminous writings, the pitiless rigour of his system, the inhuman glee whic he derived from the sufferings of rich or comfortable men. Devout pilgrims to Moscow even yet defile in an unending cortège before the embalmed corpse of the great revolutionary figure, once so violent and rugged, who lies there in the peace of death, while his will and mind continue to fashion the ideals of the Russian state.

On the threshold of its career Russian Communism was confronted by the great evil of a civil war supported by the allied and associated powers. The motive of the Allies was to keep Russia in the war against Germany by giving assistance to those elements in the Russian population who were still willing to honour their engagements entered into by the Tzarist government. From every quarter of the compass, from Siberia, from the Black Sea, from Archangel and Murmansk, from Estonia, the Bolshevik Government was placed on the defensive. In the east, Kolchak overran Siberia. In the south, Denikin marched upon Moscow. But as formerly

in the Vendée, so now in Russia, the mere fact of foreign interference consolidated loyalty to the revolutionary *régime* and
made the reputation of its defenders. The White armies were
everywhere repulsed, as much by their own disorders,
tyrannies, and follies as by the merits of their opponents. A
brilliant Jew who had graduated in petty crime gained renown
as the organizer of victory, and Trotsky was hailed as the
Russian Carnot.

The Bolshevik Revolution was a portent transcending in
magnitude any movement of the kind of which Europe had
experience. Its efficacy, its ruthlessness, the wide span of its
ambition gave it a strange fascination. Even in conservative
England, the Labour leaders talked of workers' councils, of
the supersession of Parliamentary government by direct
action, and of the General Strike.

All over western Europe statesmen asked themselves how
far this conflagration would spread. In Finland the Reds
were ruthlessly suppressed by the Germans, in Hungary by
the Roumans. But who could forecast the effect of Bolshevik
propaganda in the cordon of new states, some of them very
small, others still unsettled and confused, which had been
set up by the Peace Treaties? In 1920 there was a moment of
extreme danger for Poland, upon which even in a general
history we may be permitted to pause.

Few people had suffered so grievously during the war as
the Poles. Their country had been the principal battlefield of
the eastern campaigns. It had been drenched in blood and
blasted by explosives. It had been the scene of butcheries
such as no pen can describe, of butcheries inflicted and endured by subject peoples. Some Poles had fought in the
Russian, others in the Austrian, and others again in the Prussian armies. All had fought under compulsion. Then by an
extraordinary turn of chance the partitioning Empires were
simultaneously overthrown, and the Poles, war-wracked and
impoverished, found themselves, after more than a century
of subjection, masterless and free.

It is little wonder that the champagne of liberty went to
their heads. At Paris they were like children asking for the
moon. In the east they were like visionaries in search of the
Holy Grail. Under the leadership of Joseph Pilsudski, an

austere socialist conspirator, and one of the great war figures of his age—for ever since the Russian Revolution of 1905 he had been secretly composing the elements of the national Polish army—they resolved to renew the ancient glories of the seventeenth century and to water their horses in the Dnieper. But low as Russian pride had sunk, it had not sunk so far as to tolerate a Polish government in Kiev. The rash invaders were driven back, and Poland in turn was over-run by a Bolshevik army. The roar of the Communist artillery was heard in the streets of Warsaw, and in every capital in Europe it was assumed that nothing was left for this rash and unfortunate people but to make the best terms possible with a powerful enemy. But the history of Poland is a series of surprises. Aided by General Weygand and a staff of French officers, a Polish army under the command of Pilsudski won a victory of amazing completeness. With few casualties on either side, the Russians were pushed back across the frontier and driven to negotiate a peace. By his decisive manoeuvre in the bloodless battle of Warsaw, Pilsudski earned the gratitude of Europe. He had saved Poland from Bolshevism. How far, but for the miracle which he wrought on the Vistula, that contagion would have spread no man can say.

Two other services Pilsudski has rendered to his country. The Poles had no experience in the art of self-government. Suddenly emerging from their long servitude into the full sunlight of liberty they equipped themselves, as was perhaps natural, with a Parliamentary constitution of the most modern and extreme democratic type. They adopted pro-portional representation and universal suffrage for both their Houses, and as they had no less than fourteen parties, none of them closely adjusted to the needs of the novel situation which had arisen from the war, efficiency in govern-ment was made almost impossible. Ministry followed ministry with bewildering speed. There was neither continuity in policy nor coherence in thought, nor guarantee of technical ability. At a critical moment a peasant prime minister might be away on his farm carrying hay, and the ship of state, which had narrowly escaped disaster from the Bolsheviks, might very easily founder on the rock of Parliamentary confusion.

So things continued in Poland going from bad to worse

until Pilsudski, emerging from retirement, rode into Warsaw
on May 4, 1926, and stopped the fooling. What he then did
is proof of a sagacity and moderation rare in the politics of
central Europe. He refused to be President of the Republic,
but promoted a much respected professor to the place of
power. He neither abolished the Diet, nor endeavoured to
form a Fascist party. The veteran soldier of Polish liberty,
the honourable inmate of Siberian and German prisons, did
not propose to turn dictator in his old age. The Diet should
continue to meet, to discuss, to educate itself and the people;
but it should not be allowed to turn out the Government.
Pilsudski held that the business of Parliament was not to
break Cabinets, but to learn from them. Accordingly a
council of proved technicians was chosen to direct the wheel
of state. Their permanence was guaranteed. It was enough
that they were known to have the support of Pilsudski, who
held the portfolio of war, commanded the devotion of the
troops, and still retained the gratitude of the Polish people.

A second benefit conferred upon Poland by this remarkable
man is a good foreign policy. Non-aggression pacts signed
1933, with Russia and Germany have brought a sense of security
1934 to a nation which dreads nothing so much as a renewal of
war in Polish territory. Wider commitments are feared.
Poland is heavily armed, but for defence only. After an initial
burst of disconcerting temerity the Republic of Pilsudski has
learnt to put safety first.

That Bolshevik propaganda made so little progress in the
new states which were created by the treaty is undoubtedly
due to the fact that almost everywhere the peasantry were
enriched by agrarian legislation of a most far-reaching kind.
In Poland, in Czecho-Slovakia and in Roumania, as also in
the little Baltic states, larger properties were divided up for
the benefit of the peasants. There were many who lamented
the disappearance of the great country houses, which had
played their part in the art, letters, and politics of the middle
east for so many centuries. But one of the results of this wide
agrarian revolution was that a strong cordon of peasant
owners was drawn between Russian communism and central
Europe.

The effect of so great a convulsion as the Russian Revolution could not, however, be wholly circumscribed. The period in which we are now living is still dominated by the shade of Lenin. It is not in Russia only that Europe beholds the spectacle of an armed doctrine enthroned in the seat of power, of a totalitarian state ruthlessly repressive of liberty and set upon the creation by a system of increasing pressure of a new type of human being and a new type of society. The grim logic of the Russian Communist has been accepted elsewhere. The maxims of despotism have been imposed by violence and propaganda on the submissive populations of Italy and Germany, at a moment when their will-power was at its lowest. Though Leninism is cosmopolitan, while Fascism, both in its Italian and its German garb, is fiercely nationalist, all these governments are united in their opposition to human liberty. Communists and Fascists alike have given up the idea that political problems should be settled by discussion, that the rights of minorities should be considered, or that an appeal to reason is always preferable to a recourse to violence. The new dictators are as absolute as any Tzar or Pope. The new slavery is penetrating to a degree never previously experienced. Inhumanity, bred of war and revolution, is a feature common to totalitarian tyranny in all three forms.

The fear of the Russian infection played an important part in the politics of Italy. Here, too, the end of the war produced a general feeling of lassitude and disillusion. Italy, it was felt, had suffered so much and gained so little. Revolutionary propaganda had been strong in Italy before the war and had played its part in procuring the *débâcle* of Caporetto; and when victory at last came, and was found to bring nothing but high taxes, dear food, and scanty fuel, Italian working men asked themselves what they had gained from the exertions of the country. A mood of sharp revulsion against existing governments seized the factory hands of the north. The name of Lenin was popular. The portrait of the Russian prophet was circulated. Strike followed upon strike. Old soldiers of the war were mocked in the streets. Since Parliament was elected by proportional representation, the groups were many and the Cabinets weak. Speech was free, debates open; but there was nothing in the government of the country to rally opinion, to strike the imagination, or to prevent the degeneracy of the patriotic spirit. Many of the parliamentary statesmen were able and single-minded, but much of the energy which should have been devoted to the consideration of great national problems was wasted in the barren dialectic of debate or the ceaseless manoeuvring for position.

b.July 29, 1883 This apparent dispersion and paralysis of national forces explains the meteoric rise of Benito Mussolini. He came from outside the parliamentary class, for he was the son of a blacksmith at Forli. Before the war he had edited a Socialist paper. His opinions were too violent for Switzerland; nor could anybody in Italy have been more justly considered a standing menace to the social order. But then war broke out between Germany and Russia. The German Socialists, despite their loudly advertised pacifism, voted the war credits. Mussolini recognized, as in a flash, what this meant. He saw that at the real pinch country comes before everything. The Socialists had not even protested against the violation of Belgium. It was not for him to be more Socialist than his German leaders. With a sharp swing he urged Italy's entry into the war, took arms himself, endured wounds, and "came out at the end burning with patriotism and bursting with ambition, a *condottiere* of fortune, prompt, fiery, clearheaded, shrinking from no violence or brutality, a born master of conspiracy." His first step was to form a party of action. He called it the Fascisti, having in mind the Roman rods, or *fasces*, which were carried by the lictors before the chief magistrate of the State as emblems of authority. It was to be a party of discipline, strict, Spartan, virile, and it was to rule the state. His organization, founded in a Milanese newspaper office (March 23, 1919), grew. It controlled the streets. Sometimes the Fascisti, wearing the black shirt of the *arditi*, or storm troopers, killed their opponents; at other times beat them or degraded them through the forced administration of castor oil. Sometimes in the old-fashioned manner of Italy they sacked the house of a liberal politician from floor to rafter. In the old soldiers of the war, chafing under neglect, the party found material for its militia. On October 30, 1922, Mussolini marched on Rome and, preserving the nominal primacy of the King, took on the conduct of the state.

The development which followed was extraordinary. The Fascisti grew till they absorbed the whole people. No other opinion was tolerated. The Press, the professors, the *litterati* were compelled to conform to the new doctrine. The phial of castor oil, the dungeon, or exile to an island were the penalties of disobedience. The convenient assassination of Matteotti, the leader of the parliamentary opposition, was an advertisement that the old liberalism of Italy was at an end.

In violent reaction against proportional representation, the "Duce" divided Italy into fifteen constituencies (November, 1923) and decreed that the party which obtained the majority should be awarded two-thirds of the seats. That party was his own.

Catholic, anti-feminist, national, authoritarian, the Fascist party was opposed at every point of prejudice to the liberalism which, during the long abstention of the Papalists from active policy, had become the guiding spirit of Italian parliamentary life. By a bold rupture with his past, Mussolini, who had organized a general strike in 1914, declared that strikes and lock-outs were forbidden. Under his Law of Corporations every industry in the country became part of a great public scheme directed with an eye to the protection of the interest of the worker on the one hand and to the prosperity and solvency of the businesses on the other. In the Liberal countries of the west the high-minded persecutions of the Italian dictator were received with sentiments of hostility and alarm. The silencing of the universities, the schooled obsequiousness of the Press, the destruction of parliamentary life, the substitution of brute force for persuasion in every department of national life, seemed to run counter to all those tendencies which had been judged to be most promising in human affairs. Yet humane Italians were found, even from the first, to applaud a movement which, despite the ferocity of its repression, brought into the political life of Italy a sentiment of grandeur recalling the Imperial age. The glowing genius and devouring energy of the "Duce" communicated itself to every part of the body politic. An entirely new standard of efficiency was required of every branch of the Public Service. The trains ran to time. The peculation of officials was severely punished. Great public works were undertaken. A new momentum was given to archaeological exploration, to the rebuilding of Rome, and to the reclamation of malarial regions of the south. By

degrees Fascism, which had at first been viewed as the
violent dream of a lunatic, was received with respect and
admiration. It was not only a policy, but a creed. It opposed
to the militant faith of international communism a faith not
less combative and persecuting, a fervent national socialism,
interpreted, preached, and imposed by an organized political
party. Every force which tended to unite the nation it
respected; every influence which tended to divide or perplex or to illumine it was brutally suppressed. The crucifix
was restored to the schools, the State reconciled to the
Church (February 11, 1929). All antagonism—local, provincial, religious, sectarian—disappeared in a common worship
of the "Duce," recalling in its lavish and unbroken expressions
of homage the cult of Alexander or of Augustus. If the price
was the loss of liberty, it was a price which the Italian was
prepared to pay. Again Italy had produced a man of the
Caesarean mould, a tyrant with the *bravura* of an orator and
the broad sympathies of a man of the people, but a tyrant who
was content to give strength and unity to his own nation
and did not, so it was long supposed, seek, like Napoleon,
to impose his will upon foreign lands.

The remarkable character of the Italian leader, the way in
which he succeeded in correcting the fatigue and despondency
of the Italian people and in harnessing to the use of the State
all the military virtues which had been educated by the war,
his skill in striking the popular imagination, in generating
enthusiasm and confidence, and his success in overcoming
industrial unrest, attracted sympathies in other countries
and led to the formation of Fascist groups or parties.

There was a certain lance-corporal of the sixteenth Bavarian
Infantry reserve division lying blinded with gas in a German
hospital on Armistice Day, who, when he had recovered from
his war disabilities, felt that the German answer to the Communists and the Allies must take some such shape as that
which the "Duce" had ordained for Italy. He was the son
of a small Austrian customs official, and a house painter by
b. calling. His name was Adolf Hitler. Waking up after the
April victorious *camaraderie* of the front line to find the Fatherland
20, brought low, the army broken, the spirit of revolution abroad,
1889 and the social democrats installed in power, this obscure

young man set himself to found a German party on the Italian model. He was a tough, resentful, visionary figure, half crazy with anti-Semitism, as an orator violent, abounding, and hysterical, but disinterested, patriotic, and charged with Teutonic pride. Knowing how great Germany had been, he felt that she had but to will to be great once more. As a middle-class front-line man and a fanatical racialist, he had no use for social democrats, communists, Jews, or liberals. The classic German doctrine of the State as power, the doctrine of Hegel, of Bismarck, of Treitschke, was fixed in the very marrow of his being.

His friends, some of whom were selfless idealists, while others were ruffians of the lowest character, called themselves National Socialists, and were known for short as Nazis (about 1920). They demanded the union of all Germans in a centralized German State, the abrogation of the peace treaties, the return of the German colonies, the disfranchisement of the Jews, the foundation of a national army, and the communalization of the large shops. They attacked pacifism, cosmopolitanism, capitalism, A fanatical German patriotism, which refused to abandon the will to power, marked them out for eventual success. In *Mein Kampf*, a spiritual autobiography mainly written in 1923-4, Hitler sounded his very German defiance of the Jewish race and the Christian virtues: "The great revolutions of this world would have been inconceivable if their driving force had been the respectable bourgeois virtues of peace and order instead of the fanatical—nay, the hysterical—passions which they in fact displayed. And yet our world is moving towards a great revolution, and there is only one question at issue: Will that revolution be the salvation of Aryan humanity, or will it be merely another source of profit for the eternal Jew? The true National State must make it its duty to develop a suitable system of education for its youth so that it may maintain a race of men prepared for the last and greatest decisions of this globe. The first nation to take this road will be the conqueror. The whole character and education of the true National State must find its apex in its racial instruction. It must brand the sense of race and the feeling of race in the instincts and the understanding of the hearts and brains of the youth entrusted to it. No boy and no girl shall be permitted to leave school until he or she has been initiated into the deepest knowledge about the inner necessity and essence of blood purity."

The German Republic had been founded in the dark hour of frustration and defeat. Republicans had set their signature to the Armistice, and Republicans again had signed the Treaty of Versailles. Though the Weimar Assembly, which met on February 6, 1919, to draft a constitution, was elected by so great a preponderance of the German nation that it is idle to contend that the Republic was not the deliberate act of a free people, the sufferings which accompanied its birth and the hardships and humiliations which attended its early course were things not to be forgotten and by some Germans difficult to forgive.

High gales burst upon the Republic from the first. On the one side the Communists and Spartacists, on the other the Reactionaries and Royalists worked for its overthrow. Nor was either opposition a force to be despised. All over Central Europe, and nowhere more than in Germany, the story of the Russian revolution had made a deep impression on the manual worker. The brutalities and miseries which had been associated with the rise of the Bolsheviks to power could not counteract the prodigious fact that in Russia, of all countries in the world, the people had overthrown their masters and were governing a vast empire in the interests of the poor. Spartacism, then, was widely diffused among the industrial workers. It possessed a sacred creed in Marxism and a literature of revolt in the burning pamphlets of Rosa Luxembourg. But Spartacism, though full of sound and fury, lacked military leadership, discipline, organization. Against it was ranged a government which, albeit shaken by the events of the war, could yet command the service of officials and officers of the regular army. More fortunate than the broken Kerensky, President Ebert found to his hand strong and capable instruments. Of these one stood out above the rest—Noske, the Commandant of the National Guard. By stern and timely measures Noske suppressed the Spartacists and enabled the Republic to survive.

There was little sympathy for the Kaiser. To a nation of soldiers it was a sufficient condemnation that in the hour of defeat he had deserted the army. Yet there was enough of military, aristocratic, and imperial sentiment in Germany to embarrass a raw Socialist government which had accepted a peace of compulsory disarmament. Dr. Kapp's "Putsch" in 1920 was an illustration of the ease with which in the uncertain youth of the Weimar Republic a bold *coup de main* might capture the citadel. Kapp, a royalist of no account, seized Berlin with his naval brigade, and frightened the Government away to Stuttgart. Yet the wounds of the imperial war were too fresh to admit the restoration of royalism in any form. The German people stood behind their saddler President, and Kapp was defeated, not by a clash of arms, but by the democratic and effectual weapon of a general strike.

There remained an even greater danger. The deepest feud in Europe was deep as ever. Over against the German people, hungry, exhausted, abased, disarmed, yet still conscious despite the sharp deception of its hopes of great achievements and a shining destiny, stood France at the head of the victorious alliance, brandishing the Treaty of Versailles and demanding the exact fulfilment of its terms. The representative of the retributive spirit in France was Poincaré, a blunt solid, very able and industrious lawyer, and of all the political figures on the French stage during the crisis of the war and afterwards the most commanding. The idea that the exchange of a militarist empire for a Socialist republic denoted an improvement of the German heart, or the British argument that the whole continent would suffer from the ruin of Germany, did not impress this stern lawyer from Lorraine. He wanted reparations and security—reparations at once, security always—and since he did not believe in the German protestations of poverty, but thought that the Germans were fraudulent debtors, seeking by every dishonest ruse to evade their liabilities, he was resolved that they should feel the full weight of a military occupation. So, to the burning indignation of the Germans, black colonial troops were quartered in the Rhineland towns, and, when even thus deliveries were backward, Poincaré marched an army into the Ruhr.

The occupation of the Ruhr, against which every British party protested, was one of those extreme historical misfortunes which, when suffering has reached an intolerable point, supply their own correction. In 1921 the Reparations Committee under French and Belgian influence fixed Germany's reparation debt at 6,600 millions. As one means of evading a fantastic and impossible obligation, the Germans decided to depreciate the mark. But inflation is a tricky sprite, which, once invoked, is apt to evade control. By January, 1923, when the French first entered the Ruhr, 80,000 marks were necessary to purchase a sovereign; by October the sum

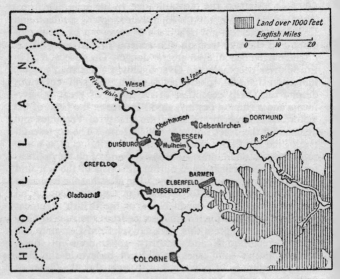

THE RUHR

had mounted to the astronomical figure of 112,000 millions. Great fortunes shrank to a pittance. The whole upper and middle class, and all wage-earners whose livelihood depended on fixed money payments, were plunged in destitution. And while the scale and character of this monetary tragedy were such as to attract the attention of the world, the general economic situation became increasingly difficult both for France and Germany. On the one hand, the French army in the Ruhr strangled German industry; on the other hand, the passive resistance of the German miners and mine-owners, which was financed from Berlin, obstructed the exaction of those "productive pledges" which it had been the prime object of the French invasion to secure. The bitter struggle could not proceed indefinitely. In the autumn the Germans gave way over passive resistance and suddenly in the early summer of 1924 reformed their currency. The French, sobered by a fifty per cent. fall of the franc, threw out Poincaré and called Herriot, the radical leader, to the helm. The stage was then set for the three acts which, taken in combination, improved for a time the political atmosphere of Europe: the Dawes Settlement of 1924, the Locarno agreement of 1925, and the entry of Germany into the League of Nations in 1926.

The war had brought about a complete revolution in the economic relations of America and Europe. Before the war America was Europe's debtor; afterwards she was a creditor upon an undreamed-of scale. At the close of 1923 (the year of the Ruhr) the United States Treasury held obligations of foreign governments alone amounting to the huge total of 2,360 millions, principal and accrued interest, of which sum no less than 920 millions were owed by Great Britain. How could the Government in Washington fail to be interested in the solvency of debtor countries from whom such payments were due? "There ought," said Mr. Hughes, the United States Secretary of State, as far back as December 29, 1922, "to be a way for statesmen to be agreed upon what Germany can pay." Mr. Hughes spoke sense; in any case, if statesmen failed, financial experts under impartial guidance might succeed. That was the importance of the Dawes Committee, which met under an American chairman, and at the happy initiative of the American Government, on June 14, 1924, to find out what Germany could pay. It was a committee of experts working in a cool business atmosphere. Its prime recommendations, the moratorium, the foreign loan, the central bank and the like, seeing that they were subsequently modified, are comparatively immaterial. The true significance of the Dawes report was that the barren folly of attempting to dig reparations out of Germany with the bayonet was finally abandoned for a scheme based on the collaboration, and compatible with the recovery, of the debtor country. Later, at a Conference in London (August, 1924), Herriot accepted the plan and agreed to the evacuation of the Ruhr and the Rhineland towns which had been seized as pledges for payment.

The second stage in the path of European appeasement was 1925 marked by the Pact of Locarno. The idea of a pact of peace guaranteeing the frontiers both of France and Germany was one so violently opposed to the military prejudices of the hour that it seemed hardly possible that it should ever be embodied in a Treaty. In 1922 it had been roundly rejected by the French, and in 1925 it was carried through only by the happy coincidence that in Stresemann, Briand, and Austen Chamberlain the three nations principally concerned were represented by statesmen who were prepared to take risks for the furtherance of European peace. It needed some courage on the part of Stresemann (a dissembling imperialist) to put his hand to a treaty which renounced Alsace-Lorraine; some courage on the part of Chamberlain to pledge his country to oppose France, if she invaded Germany, and Germany, if she invaded France; nor was it entirely easy for Briand, in view of Paris opinion, to renounce the cherished dream of a permanent offensive and defensive alliance with Britain against the ancient enemy across the Rhine. The risks were faced. The Treaties were signed. The war frontier between France and Germany was placed under the guarantee of Britain, Italy, and Belgium. A pledge was given by Stresemann that, while Germany was not content with the eastern frontiers, which had been assigned to her by the Peace of Versailles, she would not endeavour to change them by force of arms. "*À Locarno*," said Briand, "*nous avons parlé européen. C'est une langue nouvelle qu'il faudra bien que l'on apprenne.*"[1]

After Locarno the way seemed clear for Germany's entry into the League. She had undertaken to pay reparations, she had accepted her new frontier on the west, and had pledged herself against warlike adventures in the east. That she should take her seat as a permanent member of the Council on an equality with the victors was a stipulation of the Treaty and regarded by all good Europeans as a matter of course. Yet at the last moment the entry of Germany into the League was obstructed by a series of humiliating and discreditable intrigues. The prospect of the admission of a new Great

[1] "At Locarno we spoke European, a new language which we ought certainly to learn."

Power to a permanent place at the Council table aroused the jealous susceptibilities of the secondary states. The claims of Poland, of Spain, and even of Brazil, were hotly urged, and the admission of Germany having been once vetoed, to the exasperation of Europe, by the Brazilian vote, was at last secured only by an enlargement of the Council, which abridged its authority and influence.

What Geneva might do for Germany remained to be seen. A revision of the war frontiers was not to be expected from an assembly governed by the rule of unanimity: but the grievance of unequal armaments was one which fell directly within the province of the League to adjust. Despite its great economic advantages, the disarmament imposed on Germany by the Treaty of Versailles had never willingly been accepted by a nation of soldiers; and the Germans were entitled to claim, either that they should be allowed to rearm, or that a reduction of armaments should be seriously undertaken by their neighbours. With a rare unanimity of passionate emotion, the youth of Germany claimed equality of treatment, and protested against the continuance of a system which left them helpless before the aeroplanes, the tanks, and the heavy artillery of Poles, Czechs, and Frenchmen. A problem was raised of the greatest delicacy and complexity, the solution of which was not rendered easier by the militant propaganda of the German Press, and by the general and well-founded belief that Germany was secretly supplying herself with forbidden instruments of war. The League's progress towards and agreed all-round system of disarmament was necessarily so slow and so steadily obstructed by the grave apprehensions of the heavily armed Powers, as to suggest the suspicion that nothing serious was intended. Years passed, Stresemann died in 1929, an irreparable loss to the Republic. Still there was no disarmament. The long delays of the League militated against the authority of the Social Democrats who stood for fulfilment of the treaties, and had been prepared to make sacrifices for European peace. For seven years Germany had wooed Geneva, and wooed in vain.

All this time a menacing civil war feeling had been steadily growing in intensity within the limits of the German *Reich*. The revolution of 1919, while it had put an end to the rule of the Court and the aristocracy, had done nothing to impair the position of the great magnates of industry and finance. The chasm between wealth and poverty was never so painfully evident as during the period of the catastrophe of the mark, when vast fortunes were made by fortunate speculators in a time of general misery. It is not, therefore, surprising that communism, which is the fruit of envy and despair, made rapid strides among the German workers.

Meanwhile an economic calamity, the sharper since it supervened upon a series of shattering experiences, brought the Republic to the ground. The miseries of the inflation of 1923 had been succeeded by five years of ostentatious prosperity, when under the stimulus of some seven hundred and fifty million of foreign loans, industries were extended, banks and factories were built, and a wild orgy of extravagant spending announced the advent of a new race of profiteers. There followed in 1929 a great financial crash in New York. At once American money was recalled from Germany with results which were calamitous to German business. Banks closed, factories turned off their hands, revenue diminished. The enormous problem of finding work for the six million unemployed, and of endeavouring to balance the budget, confronted the unfortunate Cabinet of Social Democrats, which had just lost in Stresemann its outstanding statesman.

At the crisis, when the bitter cry of the workless was in every ear, and the red flag of Communism waved freely in the streets, the country was swept by a brilliant propaganda which expressed all the resentments and voiced all the hopes of a leaderless people. Adolf Hitler has already appeared in these pages as a front-line soldier, the apocalyptic organizer of the Nazi party. His object was to clear Germany of the Jews, to stamp out Communism, and to revive the military renown of the German people. Having failed to win power by a military "Putsch" in 1923, he applied himself with conspicuous ability to a constitutional campaign. He was a great orator who could voice in short, vibrating, intelligible phrases the passions good and bad of his countrymen. No arts of the modern impresario were lacking to the conduct of his propaganda. At the end of fourteen years' campaigning this little Austrian Messiah had infused so strong a blast of courage and confidence into a dejected and distracted people, had organized terrorism with so high a hand, and had obtained so complete a mastery of the streets by his brown-shirted storm troops of ruffianly bullies,[1] that he became Chancellor of the *Reich* and master of the German state. The Government had been too weak to suppress the private armies wearing shirts of different colours who paraded the country and menaced the peace. Not least among their sources of weakness was the fact that von Papen, a rich Catholic Westphalian nobleman and royalist, hoping to bring monarchy back on the crest of the movement, had captured the President of the Republic, the old and illustrious von Hindenburg, for the Nazi cause.

The Weimar Republic, which had long laboured under heavy seas, foundered in the great Nazi storm of 1933. Little indulgence was felt for the parliamentary institutions which had failed to bring hope and prosperity to the country. The Reichstag, an assembly of inflamed, bewildered and inexperienced men, was too bitterly divided in opinion and too barren of teachable conservatives to constitute an effective instrument of government. Even Brüning, the last true republican chancellor and a Catholic socialist, had been driven to govern by emergency decrees.

Yet the Weimar Republic had rendered services to Germany which it was convenient to forget. In a dark hour it had restored the currency, liberated the Fatherland from the occupation of foreign troops, brought Germany into the League of Nations as a first-class power and obtained from the Allies a reduction of the reparation debt to a nominal figure. The first difficult steps towards the restoration of Germany to her place in European society had been taken under the Republican government before Adolf Hitler, aided by Goering the airman and Goebbels the propagandist, stormed his way to power and threw an audacious challenge to the four greatest forces in modern civilization, the Catholics, the Protestants, the capitalists and the Jews.

The philosophy of the naive and reckless Nazi ruler is based on the view countenanced by Wagner and Nietzsche and preached before the war by Houston Chamberlain that race is everything and that all the great achievements of the world have been accomplished by the Nordics. It is argued that Christ, Dante, Thomas Aquinas were certainly Nordic,

[1] Known as the S.A. (Schutz Abteilung).

and that the Goths, who were of the same Teuton stock, did more for civilization than the Romans. Adolf Hitler, then, is a racialist. No Jew can be a German citizen. The Old Testament and the Crucifix are suspect; the one is a Jewish publication, the other a Jewish symbol. It is, indeed, as the more constructive thinkers of the movement have already discovered, difficult to harmonize the Christian gospel with a philosophy of the state which derides the brotherhood of man, expels professors of liberal or cosmopolitan principles from the Universities, and deliberately extirpates the spirit of liberty and charity from the educational system of the country.

Wotan, not Christ, is, as many of them proclaim, the real God of the Nazi religion.[1] Fortunately, as by the method of terrorism the party has now been made coterminous with the state, there are many who wear the colours without adopting the creed. Nor is German Christianity utterly effaced. Alike in the Protestant and Catholic Churches brave men have protested in public against the humiliations put upon their faith.

The internal revolution in Germany accomplished by Hitler and his national socialist party is an extraordinary psychological phenomenon. The dread of communism, the hatred of Jews and profiteers, the desire once again to be feared abroad, the need of a government stronger, more progressive, and more sanguine than the Republic, which would repudiate the Peace Treaties and once more launch Germany on the course of ambition and honour, all contributed to make Hitlerism possible. As in Italy with Fascism, so in Germany with Hitlerism, the old soldiers, who had served their country in the trenches and felt themselves miserably needy, and often despised by Jewish profiteers, joined the movement in great numbers. The Germans are always thorough. The significance of Hitlerism is that of all forms of nationalism yet invented or devised it is the most thorough-going. There are to be no classes, no parties, no trades unions, semi-autonomous states, or relics of the old German Federal system, but one centralized corporate state made up from top to bottom of Nazis, wearing shirts of the

[1] "At the moment we Germans are the people which has freed itself furthest from the teachings of Christianity." (Ludendorff on his 70th birthday. *Times* April 9, 1935.)

same colour, giving the same salutes, repeating the same catchwords, holding the same faith. And this uniform, standardized Germany, taking its orders from a single chief, is to regard itself as self-sufficient. One of the first acts of the new chief, when his storm troops had made themselves masters of the streets, was to march his country out of the League and the Disarmament Conference (1933).

In this violent affirmation of Germanism there is much that is familiar. The foreign policy of the Nazis is broadly that of the Pan-German League. They wish to see all European Germans united under the German flag, and to win fresh areas for the German people. The militarism of the Nazis is no new thing in Germany, nor their worship of force, nor their desire for expansion. Nor does it surprise the student of German history to learn of the ease with which German Liberalism was overthrown by Hitler, for since Schiller the Germans have had no great teacher of Liberalism, and since 1848 German Liberalism has been a weak, unprosperous plant. What is new in the National Socialist movement is that centralization replaces the ancient federation, that the old civil service which had weathered the storm of the first revolution is broken down, and that militarism is no longer associated with an Empire or with an aristocratic caste, but becomes enforced as the creed of an equalitarian democracy. The kind of revolution which made France formidable as a military state in 1792 makes Germany a nation in arms (so far as the will to arm is concerned) in 1935. This is the new fact of which Europe and the world must take account.

The Hitler dictatorship, though it favours social equality, is the inverse of democracy. It makes of the citizen not only the servant but the slave of the state. The great democratic maxim that the state should aim at securing the greatest happiness of the greatest number is replaced in the Nazi philosophy by the theory that the end of the individual is to maximize the material power of the nation. The prime function of women is to breed for the state, of men to fight for it. The supreme death is death in battle, the supreme virtue the heroism which faces the enemy and the torments of war. That a population of over sixty-five million Germans should even nominally accept such a philosophy of life is a note of that lack of balance and moderation which goes with the character of this remarkable people, at once the most virile and enthusiastic, the most industrious and submissive, the most methodical and sentimental in the world.

President von Hindenburg died in August, 1934. By an overwhelming majority of votes the German people, acting under strong governmental pressure, accorded to Adolf Hitler, "the Leader," that full supremacy over the totalitarian state which was the goal of his ambitions. His past was not counted against him, neither the early years of ruthless terrorism, nor the suspicion, which a public trial has done nothing to abate, that he had secretly caused the burning of the Reichstag (February 27, 1933), in order to spread fear of the Communists, nor "the blood-bath" of June 30, 1934, when the leading gangsters of his party (including Captain Roehm, one of his earliest allies) were suddenly butchered and their bodies burned,[1] nor the murder of Dr. Dollfuss, the Chancellor of the Austrian Republic, which was engineered by Nazi bands from Munich. These atrocities, reminiscent of the Roman Empire in the third century, were condoned. It was sufficient that Hitler, the wild hero of a Wagnerian opera, stood for a Germany proud, united, and defiant. When in the spring of 1935 he suddenly restored conscription in breach of the Versailles Treaty, an hysterical paroxysm of delight shook the country.

A prophet, but not an administrator. Unlike Napoleon and Mussolini, Hitler is devoid of the specific administrative gift. Behind his mesmeric speeches and the Nazi propaganda so debasing in method, so effective in rule, quiet soldiers, bureaucrats. and captains of industry are reassembling their forces. When the leader goes the old hands will be found placed on the levers of policy, but the policy will not be altogether old. Some items, such as the Second Punic War with England and the war of revenge on France, are no longer regarded as likely to be remunerative. Far more promising as a means of augmenting the territory of the Third *Reich* is the expedient of the plébiscite, inaugurated by the French in 1799 and lately in 1935 exercised with fortunate results in the Saar. What might not be expected from plébiscites in Austria, in German Switzerland, in Schleswig,

---

[1] The official number of butcheries is 77. It seems probable that some 1,200 perished.

in Silesia? It is natural that the Nazi should cherish such hopes. The Germans of the dispersion are his natural associates. The enemy is red Russia. The spectre of that vast, populous, highly-armed, propagandist state, which holds, it is said, the secret spiritual allegiance of seven million German hearts, haunts the directors of German policy, and more than any other single cause ensures the solidity of the Third German *Reich*.

It will be seen then that three forms of government, new in the twentieth century, Russian Communism, Italian Fascism, German Hitlerism, confront the Parliamentary democracies which have their roots either in the English Revolution of 1688 or in the French Revolution of 1789. The doctrines of Hegel and Marx oppose the philosophies of Locke and Rousseau.

These Parliamentary governments are not perfect. In France the executive is too weak, the legislature too strong. The average duration of a French ministry between 1918 and 1934 has been eight months and twenty-five days. Such discontinuity is inconsistent with firm and consecutive government, and though the remedies are well known, and by no means revolutionary (the abolition of the standing committees which usurp the functions and impair the authority of responsible ministers and the right of the Prime Minister to call for a dissolution of the Chamber without the consent of the Senate being the most important), it does not follow that they will be easy to secure. Lesser men may not succeed where the venerable and respected Doumergue, an ex-President of the Republic, taking office amidst unusual applause at a crisis when the prestige of the Chamber was 1934 gravely shaken by the Stavisky frauds, was miserably frustrated. Reforms, however beneficial to the public, are difficult to carry, if they require the assent of bodies who imagine that they will be injuriously affected by their passage. In this respect the amendment of the French legislative system is in the same category as the reform of the English House of Lords.

While on the continent of Europe one throne has fallen after another, the British monarchy has advanced in strength and popularity. The unaffected simplicity and strong sense of public service exhibited by King George V and Queen Mary, and noticeable also in the wide circle of their family, have made a deep impression on the minds of the nation. The rising generation are not growing up republican. The remarkable manifestations of loyal enthusiasm on the occasion of the King's Silver Jubilee in 1935 made it plain to any intelligent observer that a constitutional monarchy had a place to fill in a democratic and equalitarian society.

Parliamentary government holds its ground. The attempts to disparage its value or to demand its supersession have brought discredit upon those who have made them. There is no sign of any desire to depart from the salutary British principle that the Cabinet is responsible for the government of the country to the House of Commons and through the House of Commons to the electorate. It is true that in the growing complexity of affairs Parliament delegates work to the administrative departments or to newly formed statutory bodies like the Port of London Authority or the British Broadcasting Corporation, and there are signs that this process may be carried further; but there is always a Minister of the Crown responsible to Parliament for these agencies. The delegation of functions is not permitted to impair concentration of responsibility. Meanwhile it is before the legislature of Westminster that the great panorama of imperial business is annually unrolled, and there that the largest issues of policy are discussed. Never has there been a measure so long and intricate nor one affecting so many million human beings as the Government of India Bill which was introduced by Sir Samuel Hoare in 1934. The debates upon this unusual and difficult theme have been worthy of the best traditions of English Parliamentary life.

The rise of the Labour party, though it has accelerated the eclipse of the Liberals, already divided among themselves by the unhappy cleavage of 1916, when some Liberals supported the coalition under Mr. Lloyd George while others went into opposition with Mr. Asquith, has agreeably disappointed the alarmists. The leaders of British labour, Mr. Ramsay MacDonald, Mr. (afterwards Lord) Snowden, Mr. Arthur Henderson, Mr. Thomas, Mr. Clynes, were as far as possible from being revolutionaries. Mr. Ramsay MacDonald, though a pacifist, was by temperament a poetical Highland Tory,

Mr. Snowden a robust Yorkshire Radical, Mr. Thomas a full-blown Imperialist. To no one of these men did the example of Russia offer any encouragement. In 1931, when the over-lavish expenditure of the Labour Cabinet had brought the country within sight of a commercial crash, these three men joined with the Conservatives and Liberals in a National Government to balance the budget and to restore the credit of the country.

Contrary to general expectation, an apprenticeship in the Trades Union movement proved to be an excellent prepara-tion for the assumption of high political responsibilities. The labour leaders had much experience in the art of handling troublesome and disagreeable men. They had negotiated with employers, mingled with foreigners at international confer-ences, and they knew, as most members of the House of Commons did not, how the vast majority of men and women in the country really lived. The party, then, despite great deficiencies of knowledge, contained men of ripe human experience and ability. Mr. Ramsay MacDonald and Mr. Henderson made good at the Foreign Office. Mr. Snowden won golden opinions at the Treasury. Elsewhere the faults of inexperience were largely corrected by the loyal help of the Civil Service. Though Labour in its two brief administrations has achieved little in the field of legislation it has taught the country that political capacity is no longer the monopoly of the upper or middle class.

The Hitler revolution is a sufficient guarantee that Russian Communism will not spread westward. The solid German bourgeois holds the central fortress of Europe. But there may be secrets in Fascism or Hitlerism which the democracies of the West will desire, without abandoning their fundamental character, to adopt. That the peoples of England and France will ever, save under the actual spell of war, surrender liberty is difficult to believe.

Ever since "the glorious revolution" Britain has been the most wisely governed of the European states. Cabinets have made mistakes, but never of such a character as to provoke a serious protest under arms or to compromise the future. The nation of civilians stood the shock of war, financed its allies, and accepted without a murmur, and in defiance of a long tradition, the odious burden of military conscription.

The troubles of the peace, graver in most respects than those which assailed France, were surmounted by patience and skill.

Five million men trained to arms found their way back into civilian employment without a shot fired. A police strike, a railway strike, and a coal strike successively disturbed Mr. Lloyd George's coalition government and were each in turn overcome. A nine days' general strike in 1926, at once firmly and generously handled by Mr. Baldwin's government, was no more successful. The great mass of the people of the country sided with the government, which was aided in its struggle by the petrol engine and the novel invention of broadcasting. Workers' insurance, too often miscalled "the dole," was, since it kept starvation at bay, the great safeguard against social despair.

The relative peace of the country was the more remarkable, since, partly owing to the normal increase of population, and partly owing to the stoppage of emigration in the war, Britain had three million more mouths to feed. With less capital for the support of labour, there was more labour to support. A chronic burden of unemployment, far in excess of the normal rate, strained the resources of the Insurance Fund, and strengthened the case of those who wished to revise the Free Trade system, which had carried the country through the war. It was given to Mr. Ramsay MacDonald, the leader of the Labour party, to discard, as head of a National Government in 1931, the policy of fiscal liberty introduced in 1846 by Sir Robert Peel, under which Britain had enjoyed a spell of national prosperity which up to that moment had no parallel in the world.

At this time the British people bore without repining a burden of taxation heavier than that of any European country. The annual service of the debt charge alone amounted to more than 300 million sterling. Fifteen years after the end of the war the state levied 4s. 6d. in the pound on the income of the taxpayer irrespective of the super-tax on incomes exceeding £2,000 a year. Yet it is characteristic of the democratic spirit which prevailed in the country that, despite bad trade and crushing taxation, the level of the social services, higher than that which prevailed in any other country and more expensive, was not seriously lowered. That the health, the education, and the housing of the people should be well cared for was common ground with all parties in the state. No class in Britain at any time since the war experienced the terrible collapse of fortune which came to the Germans through the catastrophe of the mark, or to the French *rentier* through the sudden collapse of the franc. In the areas of unemployment there was great depression and hopelessness. Otherwise, taken by whatever test may be applied, the returns of savings banks, the expenditure on films, holidays, and travel, the boots of school-children, there was evidence of a community not too ill provided with those little superfluities which sweeten the grim monotony of the worker's life.

The old economic ascendancy which was enjoyed by the inhabitants of Britain during the first three-quarters of the nineteenth century was no longer theirs. Other countries had learned to manufacture for themselves and behind the shelter of protective tariffs were supplying their own needs. The trend towards economic self-sufficiency was greatly increased by the war, and by the six thousand additional miles of tariff frontier which were imposed upon the map of Europe, as a consequence of the peace. Over-production, unemployment, and a great falling off in the volume of international trade, were the consequences of this unwholesome development of economic nationalism. To no country was it so injurious as to Great Britain, a third of whose population is concentrated in seaport towns.

It was natural that in these altered circumstances the thoughts of many Englishmen should revert to the possibility of developing, apart from the continent of Europe, and in a happy indifference to its perils and complications, a life of economic and political self-sufficiency in conjunction with the Dominions and colonies of the Empire. The policy of colonial preference was put into action at Ottawa in 1932. The further and more attractive scheme of a Free Trade Empire has failed to evoke a response from the highly protected Dominions of the Crown. But strong as is the sentiment which unites the various portions of the British Empire, it is no longer possible for Great Britain to disengage herself from the politics of the continent, or to confine her trading interests within the borders of her colonies and Dominions. Were there no other arguments against a revival of Lord Salisbury's "splendid isolation" the development of aviation would be sufficient. Britain is no longer an island. If it was a British interest before the war that Germany should not overrun Belgium, or take the Channel ports, or dominate France, it is even more important for national security that these changes in the European balance should not happen now.

As a member of the League of Nations, as a guarantor of the Pact of Locarno, as a Power vitally interested in the preservation of European peace, Britain is compelled to make her contribution to the welfare and tranquillity of the continent. That, despite Ottawa, her commerce will continue to be world-wide, and that her traders will make money out of Argentine and Brazil, out of China and the United States, is one of the few prophecies to which the student of markets may safely subscribe.

Wise men on the continent everywhere agree that it would be a calamity were Britain to withdraw from Europe. It is not that the British are popular. Their superficial defects of manner and bearing are far too obvious to the foreigner, but at least Englishmen are not so unpopular in France as the Germans, not so unpopular in Germany as the French. It is recognized that these eccentric, incoherent, apparently stupid people desire peace, support the League of Nations, and that they are able to exercise a mediatorial office which no other first-class European power can well fulfil.

If the greatest of all present political problems, that of disarmament, should ever be happily solved the result will be largely due to the consistent efforts of British Cabinets, and of statesmen drawn to Geneva from every part of the British Empire, to bring about a better international order, and to prevent a recurrence of the fatal competition in armaments, which led, and could only lead, to an explosion.

For a commercial island peace is a prime necessity. With few exceptions British statesmen have recognized this fundamental axiom of policy. It may also be claimed for British foreign policy that a vein of humanitarian sentiment, sometimes quixotic, sometimes capricious, but always genuine, and deriving through Wesley and Wilberforce from the

Puritan tradition of the seventeenth century, mingles with the coarser stuff of economic or political calculation. No other country in Europe so swiftly or lightly conceives a passion for the oppressed in other lands. Pro-Vaudois, Pro-Catalan, Pro-Émigré, Pro-Slave, Pro-Hellenic, Pro-Italian Pro-Bulgar, Pro-Armenian, Pro-Serb, Pro-Boer, Pro-Belgian, the English idealist, recking little of material profit and loss, helps in shaping the policy of his country and can never be wholly neglected. Across the waters of the Atlantic, another branch of the Anglo-Saxon race exhibits in its public dealing the same concern, not always logically blended, for great humanitarian causes and closely calculated economic gains: an identity of outlook not without consequence for the world. Hence it is that in the hour of her greatest naval triumph, Great Britain was prepared without a murmur to accept the claim of American naval parity, a claim which for centuries past she would have denied with all her might and main to another power. Whatever may be the fate of the European continent, it will at least be the aim of British policy to uphold the Anglo-Saxon peace.

It is reasonable to hope that one ancient cause of friction between the American and British peoples has since 1921 been sensibly diminished if not entirely removed. The subjection of Ireland to the British yoke can no longer be an occasion of offence to the citizens of the United States. Save for the six mainly Protestant counties of the north-east which desired to retain the British connection, Ireland is as free as Canada. The Lord Lieutenant has vanished from Dublin Castle, the Chief Secretary from the lodge in Phoenix Park, the troops from the Curragh and the Royal Irish Constabulary from the streets. The Irish Parliament in Dublin passes laws and the Irish executive endeavours to carry them into effect. The Irish *Seorstat* or Free State flies its own flag, sends its envoys to foreign courts, its delegates to Geneva, its representatives to the Imperial Conference. The new Dominion imposes duties on British goods and may, since the Statute of Westminster, pass laws which are inconsistent with the statutes of the Imperial Parliament. From a recent decision of the Privy Council (1935) it is plain that the Dail, as this Dublin Parliament is called, may even legislate away the provisions of the treaty of 1921 which called the Irish Free State into existence.

If Mr. De Valera, the Republican leader of today, quarrels with the present position of his country under the treaty, it is not because a republic would bring to Ireland a larger measure of liberty or well-being than that which it is now open to her to enjoy, but because for ideal reasons he wishes to see a united Ireland standing altogether outside the British Empire. Having fought for a republic in 1916 and again in 1921, he does not lightly abandon his dream of a republic of saints, nourished on the Erse language, spurning material things and living withdrawn from the world in mysterious isolation and self-sufficiency. The Cabinet of Mr. Lloyd George which made the Irish treaty did not exclude from its consideration the possibility of granting to the republicans of Catholic Ireland the full measure of their demand. It would have been in accordance with the principles of self-determination which governed the continental settlement if the Catholic counties of Ireland which demanded a republic had been encouraged to secede from the Empire, while the Protestant counties continued to remain an integral part of the British state. But quite apart from the military and naval dangers to be apprehended from secession (and the objections which appealed to Abraham Lincoln in America carried equal weight with the British Cabinet in London), the injuries to Ireland resulting from such a severance were not easy to contemplate. How could a policy converting Irishmen into aliens fail to press hardly upon the numerous Irish residents in Britain or on Irishmen desiring to make their careers in the Empire? As a British subject the Irishman is at any time free to better his fortunes in Liverpool or Glasgow; as an alien he might easily find himself excluded. The idea of making foreigners of a people who had played so large a part in the building up of the British Empire, who had given and continued to give so much to English letters and who were bound by so many ties of family connection to the British people, was deeply repugnant. The decision which was then taken may have been erroneous, but it was founded upon an honest belief that the position of complete freedom under the British Crown and within the British Empire offered to Catholic Ireland the best prospect of well-being and was of all

1921

courses that which was most likely in the end to bring about the reconciliation of the Irish and English races throughout the world.

Europe still bears her scars. The rulers of Germany and Russia, Italy and Turkey have won their own way to power through blood. With every roar of the Nazi tiger, the small powers tremble for their lives. Greece is cleft by the deadly feud between the Venizelists and their largely monarchical adversaries. The new republican government of Spain treads uneasily on burning lava. Refugees from tyranny flock into the free countries, Greeks in flight from Asia Minor, Jews in flight from Nazi Germany, Russians who crowd into Prague and Constantinople, Paris and London, rather than endure the rigour of the Soviet rule. Venizelos, the liberator, is a fugitive in Italy. The voyager in the Tyrrhenian sea as he views the low line of the Lipari islands, etched against the flames of the setting sun, may reflect that on those barren strips of rock sprinkled in a waste of waters are immured the last champions of Italian freedom, the last inheritors of the great liberal tradition which made Italy one.[1]

Still the revolutionary governments hold their ground, even the government of the Soviets whose speedy end in the early days of Lenin was so often and so confidently predicted in the west. There is no reason here for surprise.

The durability of the Bolshevik régime in Russia is due as much to its conservative as to its innovating character. The Russian people have long been inured to tyranny. The stern repression of the Soviets, which so deeply offends the liberal susceptibilities of the west, does not shock the notions of this half-Asiatic country. The government of Stalin, the rude son of a Georgian cobbler who graduated in revolutionary politics as a train bandit and a homicide, is not more ruthless, not more savage than the rule of Ivan the Terrible or Peter the Great. The real novelty in Russia would have been not a communist tyranny, but a Parliamentary Republic working in an atmosphere of liberty and conducting affairs by free untrammelled discussion. When Lenin destroyed the Constituent Assembly he decreed that Russia should turn her

---

[1] Since these words were written George of Greece, recalled to the throne by a *Coup d'État*, endeavours to appease the strife of factions.

back on the political innovations of the west and revert to the well-tried technique of the Tzars.

Yet there is this of novelty in the Soviet system. A living religion is enforced by the massed large-scale propaganda of a scientific age, by machine guns and aeroplanes, telephone and telegraph, printing press and film, broadcasting and the regimentation of all the arts. A hundred and sixty million human souls are by a gigantic system of governmental pressure hermetically sealed against the invasion of unwelcome truth. All previous experiments in tyranny recorded in human annals pale beside this colossal achievement.

A planned economy, seeing that in some shape or other it is implied in any scheme of socialism, is not an idea peculiar to Russia. What is impressive here is the scale upon which this grandiose project is now being carried into effect by the Soviet government, the risks which have been run, the opposition which has been overborne, and the sufferings which have been ruthlessly imposed and patiently endured. To predict in any year the varying economic needs of a vast and expanding population is a task calculated to strain to the utmost the abilities of the most experienced government in the world. To adjust economic production and distribution to meet these demands is still more difficult. Yet both these gigantic operations are attempted by the Communist rulers of Russia over the immense territory stretching from the Polish frontier to the Pacific Ocean which is submitted to their sway.

The spectacle of a great people working out a new way of life for itself and boldly defying the accumulated prejudices and traditions of the past is one which cannot fail to arouse interest and curiosity. The core of the new Russian state is a political party of two or three million men and women selected by co-option upon definite qualifications of political belief and rigorously purged from time to time of those members who seem to fall short of the prescribed requirements of knowledge, zeal and fidelity. It is this Communist party, a body dedicated to poverty and obedience and organized in a hierarchy of committees of Soviets, which controls the beliefs and persecutes the vagaries of the Russian people. It is by service to the Communist party that the ambitious man may rise to the forefront of affairs, become a people's Commissar, or Cabinet Minister, or, holding the modest title of Secretary-General to the party, exercise supreme control over the policy of the state. A wide franchise offers to every Russian citizen from eighteen years upwards many fields of public activity. The citizen may speak and vote as a politician in one committee, as a producer in another, as a consumer in a third. One thing is refused him, the liberty to deviate from the Communist faith.

No fair observer will deny certain merits to the Soviet experiment. Education is now general and since 1928 divested of its wilder eccentricities and normally planned. Intelligent concern has been shown for public health and public recreation. Though it has been found necessary to devise special rates of pay for skilled labour, the wounding sense of social inequality which prevails in the industrial towns of the west is removed from the Russian body politic. The natural development of a backward country has been greatly assisted by the continuance of that vigorous programme of mechanization which had been initiated in the later years of the Tzarist régime. New towns have sprung up, new industries have been introduced, a systematic attempt has been made to Americanize, without enlisting the motive of private profit, the industrial system of the country. Seeing that everywhere labour is in the last resort compulsory, there is no unavoidable unemployment. At the cost of its civil liberties a vast population is enabled to enjoy a prison ration of the goods of life.

Two questions, then, inevitably suggest themselves to the observer of contemporary Europe: Will the peace be preserved? Can liberty survive? These questions have often been asked before, but never with the implications which they must now carry, for to each question there is today attached an aspect which is entirely novel and unprecedented. Aviation has come into war. A new scientific technique and apparatus for propaganda has come into politics. Antiquity has never beheld despotisms so penetrating and all-perverse as those which with the help of modern mechanism it has been so easy to set up in Russia, in Italy, and in Germany. It is a light matter now for any government with the tremendous means at its disposal to decree and to enforce the spiritual servitude of the totalitarian State. Equally, it will be a light matter on the outbreak of hostilities for any

Power well served in the air to lay whole cities in ruins almost before the enemy population has woken up to the fact that it is at war. Yet the Europeans, in respect of whom these two questions are necessarily asked, may recall before it is too late that they are trustees for the civilization of the world. For centuries the nations of this continent have lived together in a loose kind of society, often quarrelling fiercely and ignorantly, but always, in the fields of religion and philosophy, science and literature, art and music, giving and taking, lending and borrowing the one from the other. The common heritage of European civilization is the most splendid possession of man. No issue now dividing the nations of Europe is so great as to warrant its destruction.

BOOKS WHICH MAY BE CONSULTED

Arnold Toynbee: *Survey of International Affairs.*

W. H. Chamberlin: *Russia's Iron Age.* 1933.

Lord D'Abernon: *The Eighteenth Decisive Battle of the World.* 1931.

Luigi Villari: *Italy.* (Nations of the Modern World Series.) 1929.

Lord D'Abernon: *An Ambassador of Peace.* 1929.

D. C. Somervell: *Reign of George V.* 1935.

J. S. Barnes: *Fascism.* 1931.

H. J. Laski: *Communism.* 1927.

H. J. Laski: *Liberty in the Modern State.* 1930.

Rudolf Oeden: *Stresemann.* Tr. R. T. Clark. 1930.

Vernon Bartlett: *Nazi Germany Explained.* 1933.

H. F. Armstrong: *Hitler's Reich.* 1933.

F. H. Simonds: *How Europe made Peace without America.* 1927.

Hitler: *Mein Kampf.* 1932.

Sidney and Beatrice Webb: *Soviet Communism.* 2 vols. 1935.

Sir Lewis Namier: *Europe in Decay.* 1950.

D. C. Somervell: *Between the Wars.* 1948.

I. Deutscher: *Stalin.* 1949.

Edmund Wilson: *To the Finland Station.* 1941.

F. Owen: *The Three Dictators: Mussolini, Stalin, Hitler.* 1940

J. W. Wheeler Bennett: *The Nemesis of Power.* 1953.

Sir Harold Nicolson: *King George the Fifth.* 1952.

G. Pini: *The Official Life of Benito Mussolini.* Tr. L. Villari. 1939.

A. Bullock: *Hitler: A Study in Tyranny.* 1952.

Lord Keynes: *Essays in Biography.* 1933.

CHAPTER CI

EPILOGUE

AFTER SOME twenty million years of life upon this planet the lot of the major part of humanity is still, as Hobbes once described it, "nasty, brutish, and short." Of its two thousand million inhabitants some hundred and fifty million are still living very close to the hunger limit. But with all that human misery which prevails in the vast spaces of Asia, Africa, and South America, where thousands of millions of men and women have lived, worked, and died, leaving no memorial, contributing nothing to the future, these volumes are not concerned. Here I have only attempted to convey in the briefest outline a general idea of the story of that section of the human race which, being favoured by the temperate climate of Europe, has so prospered that not only has it peopled new continents with its offspring, but that out of its exertions and conflicts, its dreams and aspirations, standards of well-being hitherto unconjectured have been reached and maintained and widely communicated through the globe.

Only once in this long period did civilized Europe enjoy the blessings of a single government. The Roman Empire, and the Roman Empire alone, held for three critical centuries all that was precious in European life within its clasp. But then the greatest of all calamities happened. The political framework of this majestic polity was broken by the mighty hammer of the Teutonic world. The Empire perished, leaving behind it as legacies of its greatness the voices of Virgil and of Cicero and of Horace and Augustine, the institution of the Roman Church, and the imposing fabric of the Roman law. But the prize of unity, the secret of discipline, the freedom and humanity of the ancient world were lost. Civilization had to be built up again almost from its foundation in a scene of predominating barbarism. East was severed from west, the Greek Church from the Latin. The Papacy, strongest of the institutional forces bequeathed by the Empire, was unable to keep the peace among the combative and passionate peoples who had made the new chaos. Society splintered into minute particles, fief warring upon fief, town upon town. Gradually out of this welter of lawlessness nations emerged centred round the hereditary dynasties of kings.

Within each nation there grew up by degrees a rude system of justice and police; but between nation and nation there was no common ground of law, save in so far as the Roman Church was able to supply it. But even that agency, which had been all through the middle ages the helpless spectator of the crimes, the vices, and the quarrels of men, was weakened at the Reformation. To the ecclesiastical rupture between Greece and Rome there was henceforward added the division between Protestant and Catholic. The wars of religion in the west were succeeded by the dynastic wars of the seventeenth and the colonial wars of the eighteenth century. But from these came no better chance of European cohesion, rather a deepening of the cleft which divided the continent. Yet never was the human mind so widely or sensibly affected by large humanitarian ideas or by the thought of man as a citizen of the world as in the half-century which preceded the French Revolution. Could there once again be upon the continent of Europe a common political framework for a common Latin civilization? The rise and fall of Napoleon provided the answer. Since the break-up of the Roman Empire so much of Europe had never been brought together under a single sceptre, But it was too late; the nations of Europe were too strong. There was to be no *Pax Napoleonica*. A coalition of powers, of which Great Britain was the spear-head, shattered the dream of French hegemony. The revolutionary and Napoleonic wars left Europe exhausted, but were distinguished from other European struggles by the birth of an idea—a permanent Concert of Powers against a permanent revolutionary danger. A long peace of exhaustion rather than of good will was followed by those exciting nationalist wars which made Italy a kingdom and Germany an empire. But still Europe was not at rest. Germany was ambitious of world power, France studied revenge; the partition of Africa and the decay of Turkey illumined ambitions. And all the time in the heart of Europe there was fermenting the poison of suppressed nationalism. It threw fever among the Irish and the Poles, among the Czechs and the Roumans, among the Croats and the Serbs. An atmosphere was produced in which the least spark might fire an explosion.

The tragedy of the Great War was that it was fought between the most highly civilized peoples in Europe on an issue which a few level-headed men could easily have composed, and with respect to which ninety-nine per cent. of the population were wholly indifferent. The main problem of statesmanship is to avert the recurrence of so great a catastrophe: the more so since the place of Europe in the world is no longer what it was in the seventies of the nineteenth century. Then the civilization of this continent seemed to repose upon a basis of unassailable security. The products of European skill found their way with ease into the markets of the East and the West, and purchased in return cargoes of food and raw materials produced under the law of increasing returns. Then there seemed little reason to doubt that despite a staggering birthrate the standard of the wage-earners would be maintained and improved. Real wages were rising, and countries like Germany, where life had been hard and frugal, were swiftly advancing in affluence and luxury. Then the United States was open to European immigrants and provided a market, remunerative and almost illimitable, for European capital. Taking from Europe her surplus men and sending to Europe her surplus supplies, America was an integral factor in the prosperity of the Old World.

Now things are otherwise. The Latin nations of the Western Hemisphere no longer dispense their hospitality to needy fortune-seekers from the Apennines. The doors of the United States since 1924 have been more than half closed to European immigrants. The law of diminishing returns has begun to operate in the farmlands of the West. The secret of the machine is no longer a European monopoly, for India and Japan import machinery from Europe or make it themselves. Mass production in the United States, cheap labour in the Orient, menace from opposite quarters of the globe the standard of the European wage-earner. Even the original home of British industrial strength is invaded. The Lancashire mill hand walks in stockings which are made in Japan.

The fact that Europe is entering into a period when competition may be expected to be sterner than in the past should be taken, not as a discouragement, but as a challenge. The old world, though handicapped by wars and rumours of wars, by tariffs and quotas, by class struggles and strikes, and by every folly which the demon of economic nationalism can contrive, is charged with industrial excellence. It must take its stand on quality. It must live on its taste, its ingenuity, its good sense. Then, with a better spirit at home and abroad, with less bitterness or unrest, and with a shedding of the encumbrances which now manacle progress, European quality will tell in every market. Not otherwise can we expect to safeguard the workers' standard of life, which, though far lower than we would wish it to be, is still the foundation upon which our hopes of a higher civilization must depend.

Europe, then, has now reached a point at which it would seem, as never so clearly in past history, that two alternative and sharply contrasted destinies await her. She may travel down the road to a new war or, overcoming passion, prejudice, and hysteria, work for a permanent organization of peace. In either case the human spirit is armed with material power. The developing miracle of science is at our disposal to use or abuse, to make or to mar. With science we may lay civilization in ruins or enter into a period of plenty and well-being the like of which has never been experienced by mankind.

In the meantime the war has left us an evil legacy. The moral unity of Europe is for the time being broken. Nordic paganism assails Christianity. An insane racialism threatens to rupture the seamless garment of civilization. May future generations close the rents, heal the wounds, and replace our squandered treasure of humanity, toleration, and good sense.

A. PRESIDENTS OF THE FRENCH REPUBLIC

Date of Election

August, 1871.	Marie-Joseph-Louis-Adolphe Thiers.
May, 1873.	Marie-Edmé-Patrice-Maurice de Macmahon, D of Magenta, Marshal of France.
January, 1879.	François-Paul-Jules Grévy. Re-elected 1886. Resigned 1887.
December, 1887.	Marie-François-Sadi Carnot. Murdered 1894.
June, 1894.	Jean-Paul-Pierre Casimir-Périer. Resigned 1895.
January, 1895.	François-Félix Faure. Died 1899.
February, 1899.	Emile Loubet.
January, 1906.	Armand Fallières.
1913.	Raymond Poincaré.
1920.	Paul Deschanel.
1920.	Alexandre Millerand.
1924.	Gaston Doumergue.
1931.	Paul Doumer.
1932.	Albert Lebrun.

B. PRIME MINISTERS OF ENGLAND

GEORGE III, 1760-1820

John Stewart, Earl of Bute, First Lord of the Treasury, 1762-3.

George Grenville, First Lord and Chancellor of the Exchequer, 1763-5.

Charles Wentworth-Watson, M. of Rockingham, 1766.

Augustus Fitzroy, D. of Grafton, 1766-9.

Frederick, Lord North, 1770-82.

Marquis of Rockingham, 1782.

William Petty, Earl of Shelburne, 1782-3.

William Bentinck, Duke of Portland, 1783.

William Pitt, 1783-1801.

Henry Addington (Viscount Sidmouth), 1801-4.

William Pitt, 1804-6.

William, Lord Grenville, 1806-7.

Duke of Portland, 1807-9.

Spencer Perceval, 1809-12.

GEORGE IV, 1820-30

Earl of Liverpool, 1812-20, 1820-7.

George Canning, 1827.

Viscount Goderich, 1827.

Duke of Wellington, 1827-30.

WILLIAM IV, 1830-7

Charles Grey, 1830-4.

Viscount Melbourne, 1834.

Sir Robert Peel, 1834-5.

Viscount Melbourne, 1835-7.

VICTORIA, 1837-1901

Viscount Melbourne, 1837-41.

Sir Robert Peel, 1841-6.

Lord John Russell, 1846-52.

Earl of Derby, 1852.

Earl of Aberdeen, 1852-5.

Viscount Palmerston, 1855-8.

Earl of Derby, 1858-9.

Viscount Palmerston, 1859-65.

Earl Russell, 1865-6.

Earl of Derby, 1866-8.

Benjamin Disraeli, 1868.

W. E. Gladstone, 1868-74.

B. Disraeli, 1874-80.

W. E. Gladstone, 1880-5.

Marquis of Salisbury, 1885-6.

W. E. Gladstone, 1886.

Marquis of Salisbury, 1886-92.

W. E. Gladstone, 1892-4.

Earl of Rosebery, 1894-5.

Marquis of Salisbury, 1895-1901.

EDWARD VII, 1901-10

Marquis of Salisbury, 1901-2.

A. J. Balfour, 1902-5.

Sir Henry Campbell-Bannerman, 1905-8.

H. H. Asquith, 1908-10.

GEORGE V, 1910

H. H. Asquith, 1910.

D. Lloyd George, 1916.

A. Bonar Law, 1922.

S. Baldwin, 1923.

Ramsay MacDonald, January 22, 1924.

S. Baldwin, November 4, 1924.

Ramsay MacDonald, June 8, 1929 (National Labour, August 25, 1931).

S. Baldwin, June, 1935.

C. CHANCELLORS
OF THE GERMAN EMPIRE

WILLIAM I
P. Otto von Bismarck, 1871-88.

FREDERICK III
P. Otto von Bismarck, 1888.

WILLIAM II
P. Otto von Bismarck, 1888-90.
C. George Leo von Caprivi, 1890-4.
P. Chlodwig von Hohenlohe-Schillingsfúrst, 1897-1900
Count and Prince von Bülow, 1900-8.
Theobald von Bethmann-Hollweg, 1908.
F. von Michaelis, 1917.
Count Hertling, 1917.
Prince Max von Baden, 1918.

D. KINGS OF ITALY

Victor Emmanuel II, 1862 (1849)-78.
Humbert I, 1878-1900.
Victor Emmanuel III, 1900

A. HOUSE OF ROMANOFF

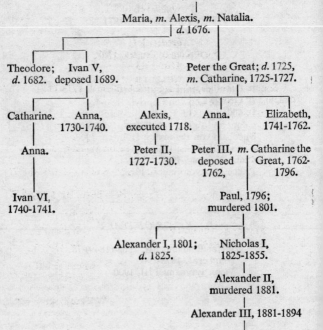

Michael Romanoff, elected Tzar 1613; *d.* 1645.

Maria, *m.* Alexis, *m.* Natalia.
d. 1676.

Theodore;   Ivan V,
d. 1682.   deposed 1689.

Peter the Great; *d.* 1725,
m. Catharine, 1725-1727.

Catharine.   Anna,
          1730-1740.

Alexis,   Anna.   Elizabeth,
executed 1718.   1741-1762.

Anna.

Peter II,   Peter III,   *m.* Catharine the
1727-1730.   deposed   Great, 1762-
         1762,   1796.

Ivan VI,
1740-1741.

Paul, 1796;
murdered 1801.

Alexander I, 1801;   Nicholas I,
d. 1825.   1825-1855.

Alexander II,
murdered 1881.

Alexander III, 1881-1894

Nicholas II, 1894-1917

B. *HOUSE OF HOHENZOLLERN*

Frederick William,
the Great Elector;
d. 1688.

Frederick I,
First King of Prussia, 1701,
1688-1713.

Sophia Dorothea, *m.* Frederick William I, 1713-1740.
daughter of George I
of England,

Frederick II the Great,   Augustus William; *d.* 1758.
1740-1786.

Frederick William II, 1786-1797.

Frederick William III, 1797-1840.

Frederick William IV   William I,
1840-1861.   1861-1888.

Frederick III,
1888.

William II, 1888-1918.

C. BELGIUM—HOUSE OF COBURG

Francis Frederick, Duke of Coburg.

Victoria, *m.* (1) Charles, Prince   Leopold I, *m.* Louise, daughter of
     of Leiningen.   of Belgium,   Louis Philippe of
     (2) Edward, Duke 1831-1865.   France.
     of Kent.

Queen Victoria.   Leopold II, *m.* Archduchess   Philip, Charlotte,
               d. 1909. Henrietta of   Count *m.* Maxi-
                    Tuscany.   of   milian,
                                Flanders; Emperor
                             d. 1905. of Mexico.

                               Albert, *m.* Elizabeth
                        1909-1934. of Bavaria.

                               Leopold, *m.* Astrid of
                        1934-.   Sweden.

D.   *THE BRITISH ROYAL FAMILY*
SINCE GEORGE I

George I, *m.* Sophia Dorothea of Brunswick-Lüneburg.
1714-1727.

George II, *m.* Caroline of Brandenburg-Ansbach.
d. 1760.

Frederick Lewis, Prince of Wales; *d.* 1751.

George III, *m.* Charlotte of Mecklenburg-Strelitz.
d. 1820.

George IV; *d.* 1830.	William IV; *d.* 1837.	Edward, Duke of Kent, 1767-1820; *m.* Victoria, daughter of Duke of Saxe-Saalfeld-Botha and widow of Charles, Prince of Leiningen.	Ernest, Duke of Cumberland King of Hanover, 1837-1851.

Victoria, *m.* Albert of Saxe-Coburg-Gotha;
d. 1901.   *d.* 1861.

Victoria, *m.* Fred- erick III.	Edward VII, *m.* Alexandra *d.* 1920. of Denmark.	Alice, *m.* Louis IV of Hesse.

William II of Germany.

Alix, *m.* Nicholas II of Russia

Albert, Duke of Clarence; *d.* 1892.	George V. *m.* Victoria Mary of Teck. *d.* 1936.

Edward VIII.	Albert, Duke of York	Mary, Princess Royal.	Henry, Duke of Gloucester.	George, Duke of Kent	John. *d.* 1919,

APPENDIX A

THE IMMEDIATE reforms advocated in the Communist manifesto are:

1. The expropriation of landed property and the use of rent from land to cover state expenditure.

2. A high and progressively graded income tax.

3. The abolition of the right of inheritance.

4. The confiscation of the property of all emigrants and rebels.

5. The centralization of credit for the needs of the state by the establishment of a state bank with state capital and an exclusive monopoly.

6. The centralization of transport in the hands of the state.

7. An increase in the state ownership of factories and instruments of production and the redistribution and amelioration of agricultural land on a general plan.

8. Universal obligation to work and the creation of labour armies especially for agriculture.

9. The unification of agriculture with industrial labour and the gradual abolition of the difference between town and country.

10. The public education of all children. Abolition of factory labour for children in its present form. Unification of education with economic production.

Then after detailed criticism of contemporary socialist movements, which now possesses only an historical interest, the Manifesto proceeds to its famous peroration, ending with the slogan which had already figured on the title page of the *Kommunistiche Zeitschrift*:

"The communists consider it superfluous to conceal their opinions and their intentions. They openly declare that their aims can only be achieved by the violent overthrow of the whole contemporary social order.

"Let the governing classes tremble before the communist revolution. The proletarians have nothing to lose in it but their chains. They have the whole world to gain.

"Proletarians of all countries, unite!"

(E. H. Carr, *Karl Marx*, pp.52.3.)

APPENDIX B

THE TERMS of the Armistice which had been drafted by the soldiers and sailors were discussed at great length by the Supreme War Council in Paris as early as October 5-7 and the conditions finally approved by the Council on November 4. Mr. Lloyd George communicated the terms to the War Cabinet in London on November 5, mentioning that Foch thought that the Germans would decline them but was confident that in any case the enemy would be overpowered by Christmas. The terms were drawn upon the principle that the enemy should not be in a better position to resume the combat, if peace negotiations broke down. Thus the naval demands (6 battle cruisers, 10 battleships, 8 light cruisers, 50 destroyers of the most modern type and 160 submarines) were based upon the fact that if no demands were made on Germany she would end the war with 25 battleships "of which twelve would be the most modern and powerful in the world" (Admiral Hope) and would be a source of constant anxiety to the Grand Fleet. The arrangement finally agreed to was that the ships to be surrendered should be interned preferably in some neutral port under Allied supervision. The battleships were eventually brought to Scapa Flow (November 21) and sunk by the Germans. The naval authorities had pressed for surrender, not internment. The civilians, considering that the military and naval terms were very stiff and that it would be difficult for the German Government to accept them, decided for the milder alternative.

APPENDIX C

THE FOURTEEN POINTS were, in brief:

1. Open covenants and no secret diplomacy in the future.

2. Absolute freedom of navigation in peace and war outside territorial waters, except when seas may be closed by international action.

3. Removal as far as possible of all economic barriers.

4. Adequate guarantees for the reduction of national armaments.

5. An absolutely impartial adjustment of colonial claims, the interests of the peoples concerned having equal weight with the claims of the Government whose title is to be determined.

6. All Russian territory to be evacuated, and Russia given full opportunity for self-development, the Powers aiding.

7. Complete restoration of Belgium in full and free sovereignty.

8. All French territory to be freed and the wrong done by Prussia in 1871 to be righted.

9. The readjustment of Italian frontiers on the lines of nationality.

10. The peoples of Austria-Hungary to be accorded an opportunity of autonomous development.

11. Roumania, Serbia and Montenegro to be evacuated; Serbia to be given access to the sea, and the relations of the Balkan States to be settled on the lines of allegiance and nationality.

12. The non-Turkish nationalities in the Ottoman Empire to be assured of autonomous development and the Dardanelles to be permanently free to all ships.

13. Poland to be an independent State with access to the sea.

14. A general association of nations to be formed under specific covenants for the purpose of affording mutual guarantees of political independence and territorial integrity to great and small States alike.

When the Fourteen Points came to be considered at the

Supreme War Council (Nov. 3, 1918), Mr. Lloyd George protested against Art. 2, M. Hymans (Belgium) against Art. 3, and Signor Orlando (Italy) made reserves as to Art. 9. Mr. Lloyd George was emphatic in his opposition to the American doctrine of the Freedom of the Seas, saying, "The English people will not look at it. On this point the nation is absolutely solid." He also laid stress on the importance of demanding reparations for injuries done. Accordingly the following message was sent to President Wilson:

"The Allied Governments have given careful consideration to the correspondence which has passed between the President of the United States and the German Government. Subject to the qualifications which follow, they declare their willingness to make peace with the Government of Germany on the terms of peace laid down in the President's address to Congress on January 8, 1918, and the principles of settlement enunciated in his subsequent addresses. They must point out, however, that Clause 2 relating to what is usually described as freedom of the seas is open to various interpretations, some of which they could not accept. They must therefore preserve to themselves complete freedom on this subject when they enter the Peace Conference. Further, in the conditions of peace laid down in his address to Congress of January 8, 1918, the President declared that the invaded territories must be restored as well as evacuated and freed. The Allied Governments feel that no doubt ought to exist as to what this provision implies. By it they understand that compensation will be made by Germany for all damages done to the civilian population of the Allies and their property by the invasion by Germany of Allied territory by land, by sea, and from the air."

November 3, 1918

APPENDIX D

DANZIG AND THE POLISH CORRIDOR

THE SILESIAN TRIANGLE

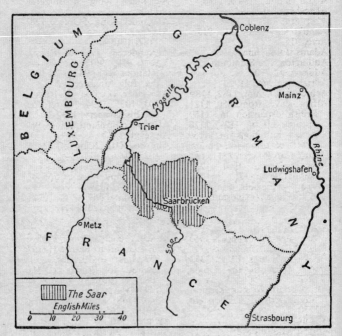

THE SAAR